Curating the Image
Notebook for a Visual Journey

Alfredo Cramerotti

DISTANZ

The images in this book originate from an ever-growing personal archive that dates back more than twenty years. The collection consists of prints of various kinds, including newspaper cuttings, pages from magazines, exhibition invitation cards, email printouts, commercial leaflets, information brochures, organizations' dossiers, family and friends' pictures, drawings and sketches, diaries and journals – a total of almost 2,000 individual images. A sort of contemporary Bilderatlas of Warburghian memory (from the historian of art and culture Aby Warburg, 1866–1929), but double in size. All this imagery was arriving for different reasons, electronically or by snail mail, handed over, given as part of a purchase or exchange. Three years ago, I realized that what I was keeping in the wooden boxes (where they still are, after being scanned) was a 'performative accumulation' that could noticeably be allocated to one of five main visual categories.

I have come to recognize that these categories are the silent visual feed for my curatorial practice and interests. At first, I had assumed that I gathered (more than collected) such an enormous number of visuals for no apparent reason, other than the fact that I liked them – or disliked them – particularly. What I have come to recognize, almost twenty years on, is that these are the codes that structure my visual thinking, with all their limits and potential, their focus and their broadness. In other words, I can see that reflecting on these images has influenced my professional and personal choices.

First and foremost, I have asked myself how I have selected these images over the years. Selection after all lies at the core of a curator's work. In this context, does it simply translate into what hits the optical nerve and what does not. One can safely argue that selecting is somehow central to all that is production, communication and organization of knowledge to build a narrative, a situation, an episode of culture however temporary or brief. Curating, however, implies a much broader range of intellectual and practical activities, and personal and professional skills.

I argue that these practices, that include comparing, distinguishing, choosing and synthesizing, are gaining increased importance in our contemporary lives. We all know how central it is to be able to filter, assess, retain the useful (or helpful) and discard or ignore the useless (or noise) in order to shape an informed opinion or deliver a meaningful deed. Among the manifold increased possibilities presented to us daily, we progressively adjust the criteria for selection to suit our worldview, ambitions, or necessities. In the timeframe vaguely corresponding to my gathering of images, you and I have had to learn how to relate to our respective living contexts in what can be called, 'a mode of selection'. Could this be described as curation?

And what of aesthetics? In certain circumstances they are dismissed as, if not non-essential, at least secondary to a functional society and individual existence. I argue instead that aesthetics is of crucial importance. This has always been evident in certain areas of human culture – obviously art itself – but also in religious movements, sporting events, or cooking. But we also see that, historically, aesthetics has played a major, if not the role, in sectors of the economy like industrial design, publishing, media and communication, wellbeing, and even the medical and pharmaceutical sectors. The aestheticization of life is all-encompassing. In parallel to the above mode of selection, what we now choose, act upon and give form to in our day-to-day living is no longer rooted in a purpose-oriented mode, but relates primarily to the realm of aesthetics.

This is not to claim that art has taken over the world; far from it. But, rather interestingly, images have. We are mainly preoccupied with the business of interpretation. Long ago we abandoned any idea of unequivocal truth, for better or worse. We must now interpret every image. This is not merely welcomed but actively encouraged, taught (mainly through peer pressure) and sustained. It is our most tangible form of freedom. As a curator, I can only relish such a development. When large swathes of the population cannot only consume or absorb images, but proactively put them in motion, creating new systems of relationships between disparate elements (visual or otherwise), casting them in a new light, and helping shift perspective every time something is put in circulation, it means a more mature disposition towards visual language. That is why I think that curating is not just a technical term within the world of art. And a curator's book like this no longer pertains to the theory and practice of exhibition making. The bird has left the nest, and it may not return to it, just make quick visits in passing.

There is no consensus, indeed sometimes conflict, about what a 'curatorial native' approach to life might mean. Is it, ultimately, about problem-solving? Or is it an implicit attempt to mark our territory, so that we can navigate contemporary life with some parameters in mind? Does it indicate a generational shift in knowledge organization that by-passes specialist expertise? Well, this is for another time, another book. Which I am writing. With no images. For now, I want to focus on my personal, noiseless, curatorial visual feed that kept me going, nurtured and sustained over the last two decades. I sketch here below the five categories of images and my thoughts about why these had particular appeal for me. It's about sharing a slice of personal history rather than making a statement of intent. I am exploring how these images became a sort of device for the crystallization of ideas, drives, moments, encounters and situations that helped to form what is me, now.

What I call alpine aesthetics is anything that suggests, or defines, an idea of mountain or an actual alpine scenario with meadows, trees, peaks, snowcaps, skies – either populated or empty of humans and/or other animals. I know where this comes from. I was born in the Alps of Northern Italy, and although I never considered myself a mountaineer or an alpine freak, in time I have had to admit that I have embodied the latter. I just cannot let go an alpine scene, whether on paper or screen or IRL, without getting lost in it for a moment. Back in 2009/10, I even started to put online some findings, posting them on a Tumblr feed. It is still going, a sort of online sketchpad for what ended up in this book (though the images are not the same).

The visage is probably the most instantly recognizable as a visual interest. As it is for many others – I am in good company here – the attraction to faces, eyes, looks, close-ups, portraits and 'seeing ourselves in others' features is undoubtedly rooted in our, and other animals', genetic make-up, let alone being one of the cultural drives par excellence. The major appeal for me is when the facial expression is not related to anything artistic, but it casually comes across for some other reason. I enjoy immensely decoding the lure and magnetism of a look which is subtly (or not) meant to induce some thought or action. Every time I spot one, it reminds me why I work in the arts.

Which brings me to the houseplants section of the book. Now, we know why we like houseplants, we care and tend to them, we grow them like immovable but sensitive children, part and parcel of our household and lives, complete with joy, disaster, tantrum, satisfaction, pride and desperation. I don't have to tell you how much I love plants and greenery, because I know you do too, deep inside. Even if you don't have any in your life. But it is simply impossible to be immune to their tenacity to strive and 'make it', to grow no matter what environment we put them in, to try hard adapting – resiliently adapting – to change, ineptitude, disturbance and turbulence. Sometimes they can't survive. But not without a tremendous, good fight.

The leadership section is mainly populated by a combination of financial and management cutouts with my personal notes and plans, some of them very revealing; it is, in hindsight, a form of outing which I did not think I was capable of pulling off, until I did. This is serious matter, bear in mind. Leadership is not merely about work and colleagues and career progression; it is about how we tackle our problems and difficulties in life, how we communicate to our loved ones and how we inspire our little ones, how we make sure we enjoy what we do and what we are before realizing it is too late. Thought-out articles and quirky ideas, personal coaching and professional development, or vice versa – images that tell a life, actual, anticipated or assumed.

Last but not least, the design approach section. It comprises visuals that suggest, advise or present a certain design-led attitude in whatever discipline or activity. It is interesting to see how something not commonly associated with design, actually uses it as part of its communication codes. Examples are things such as a landscape, a driving lesson, a cooking recipe, a printed office memo or a shopping list, or the packaging of a household item. I figured out that all the above signposts for activities or environments stem from a society in which design holds a central tenet: architecture (both urban and rural), mobility, culture, work protocols, commerce, education and so on.

I would say that roughly fifty percent of the images in the book came across with no clearly identifying reference to author or source. Things like place, date, purpose or details about what, how and why those visuals were made, escaped me. “Cultures” – Kenan Malik writes in the ArtReview magazine in December 2017 – “work not through appropriation but through messy interaction. Writers and artists, indeed all human beings, necessarily engage with the experiences of others. Nobody owns a culture, but everyone inhabits one (or several).” I recognize that, in this book, I took a step in formulating a personal response to the idea of a shared culture. It reminds me that the distinction between seeing and recognizing is traditionally centered on the possibility of the direct personal experience, the first-time encounter, the added value of witnessing. Seeing, art history tells us, trumps recognizing. It is the difference between an artwork on a wall or on the floor in front of us, and the reproduction of that work in a book or website. It is obviously another thing altogether.

However, I argue that human knowledge is in a state of flux and therefore un-attributable. This has resulted in our being able over time to ‘grow’ an experience, and indeed nurture it until it evolves on its own. So now we cannot only perceive something in the flesh or for the first time, but also when our perception of what we already know is increased, and elevated through new relationships and links. This is the logic of the network, as opposed to that of the hierarchical structure. There is a bit of Deleuze-Guattari in this, as well as the online / digital revolution. It is a known path for sure. But I still argue that recognizing is more than refreshing one’s memory because it offers new flights towards destinations often unforeseen. As a matter of fact, it can happen before, during or after an actual encounter with an image or an idea. As it was in my case, elucidated here through almost two thousand individual visuals. If images are affecting our behavior and mediating it, and this, in turn, re-mediates their meaning, realizing this book gave me an understanding of how this is happening. It is a living proof of how much my life is deeply and often unconsciously invested in images. And, dare I suggest, how yours may be too.

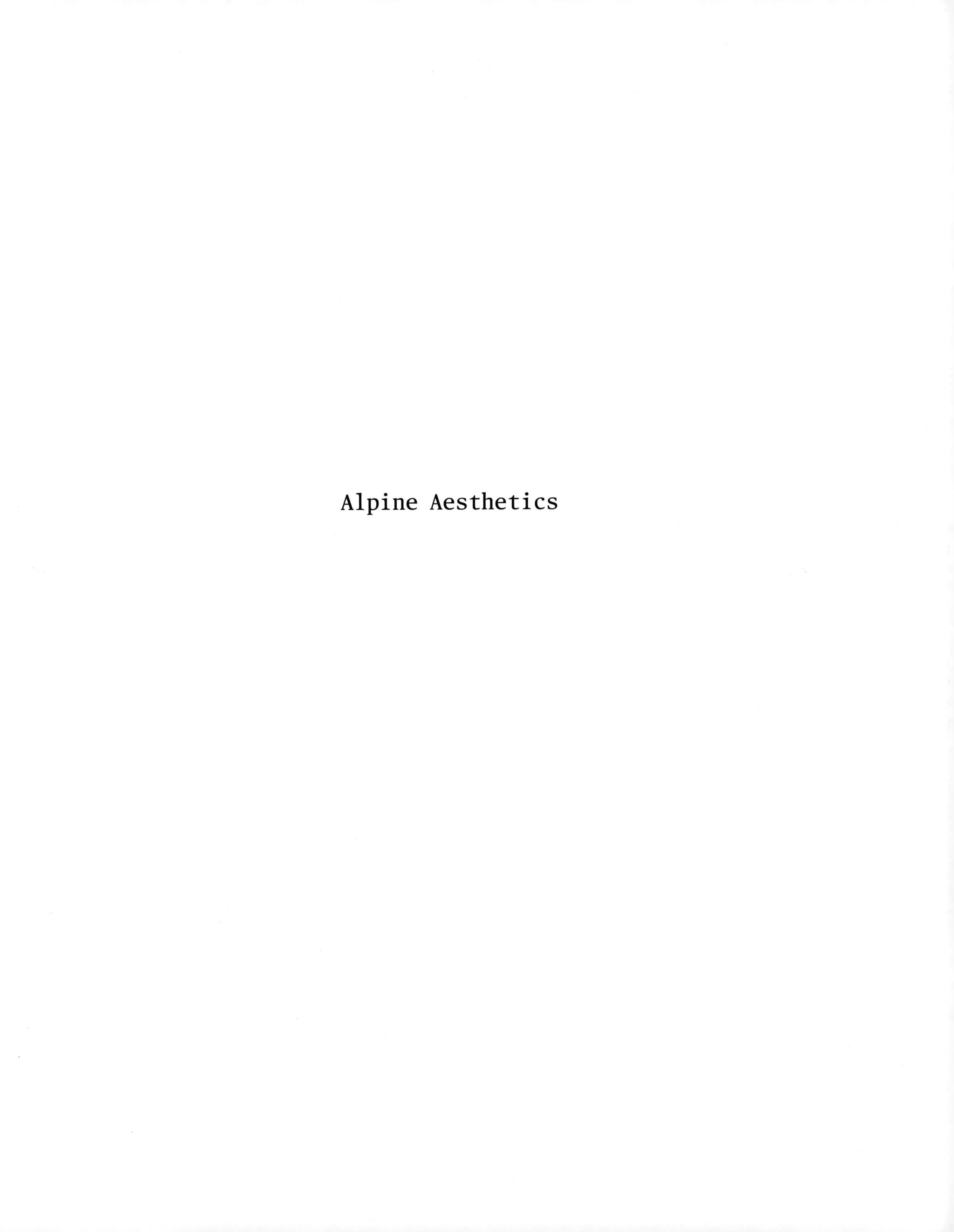

Alpine Aesthetics

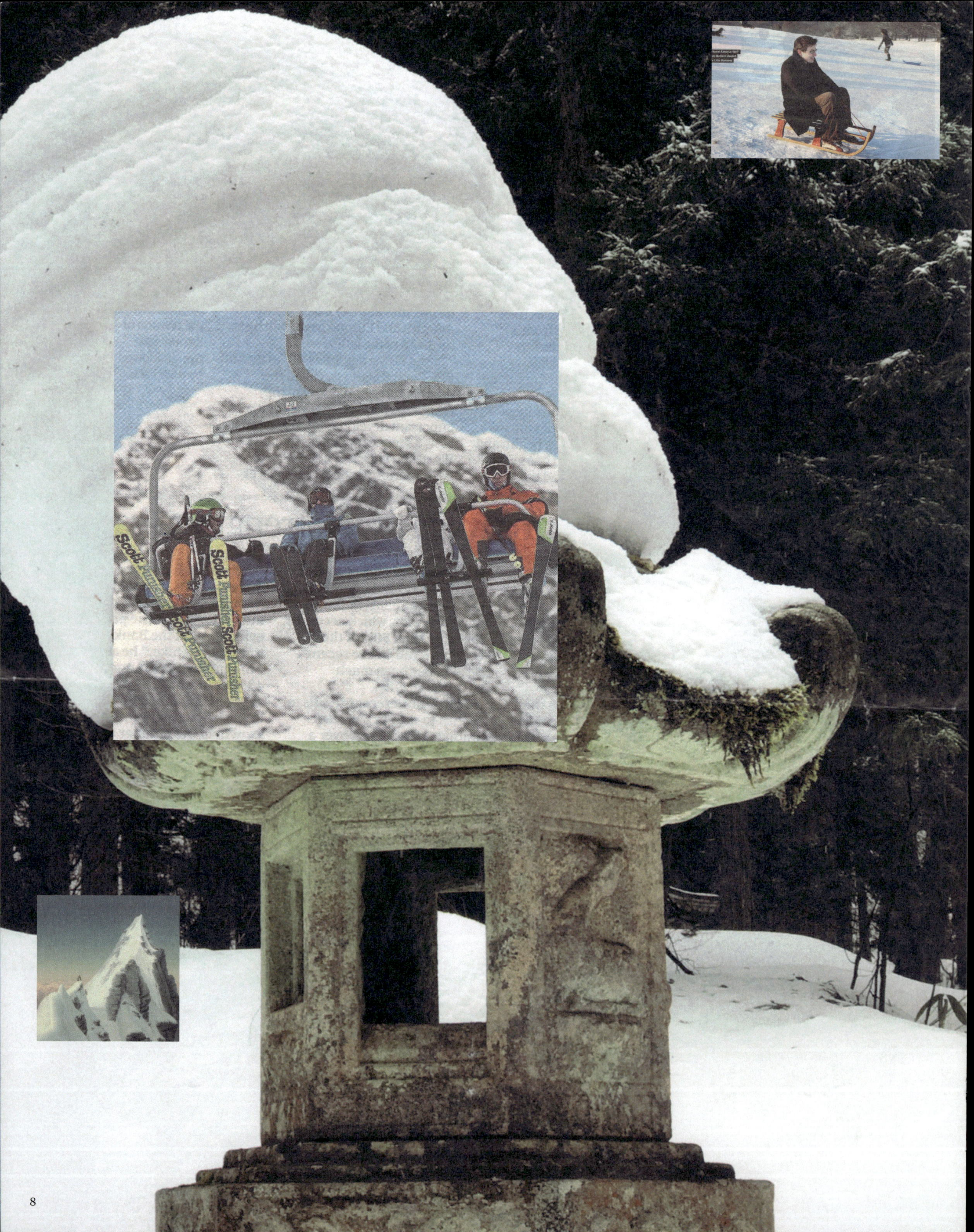
Scott Punisher
Scott Punisher

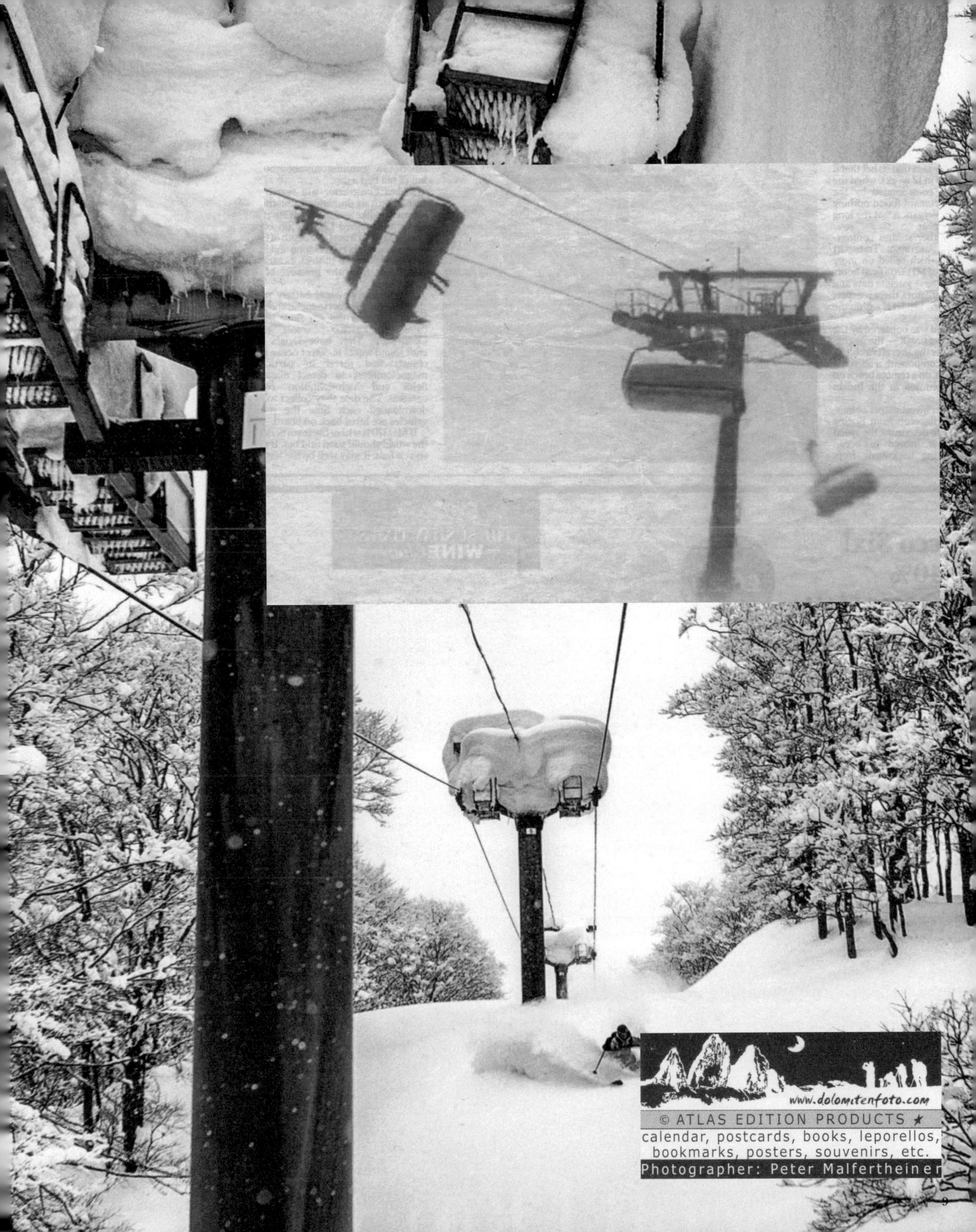
www.dolomitenfoto.com
© ATLAS EDITION PRODUCTS ★
calendar, postcards, books, leporellos,
bookmarks, posters, souvenirs, etc.
Photographer: Peter Malfertheiner

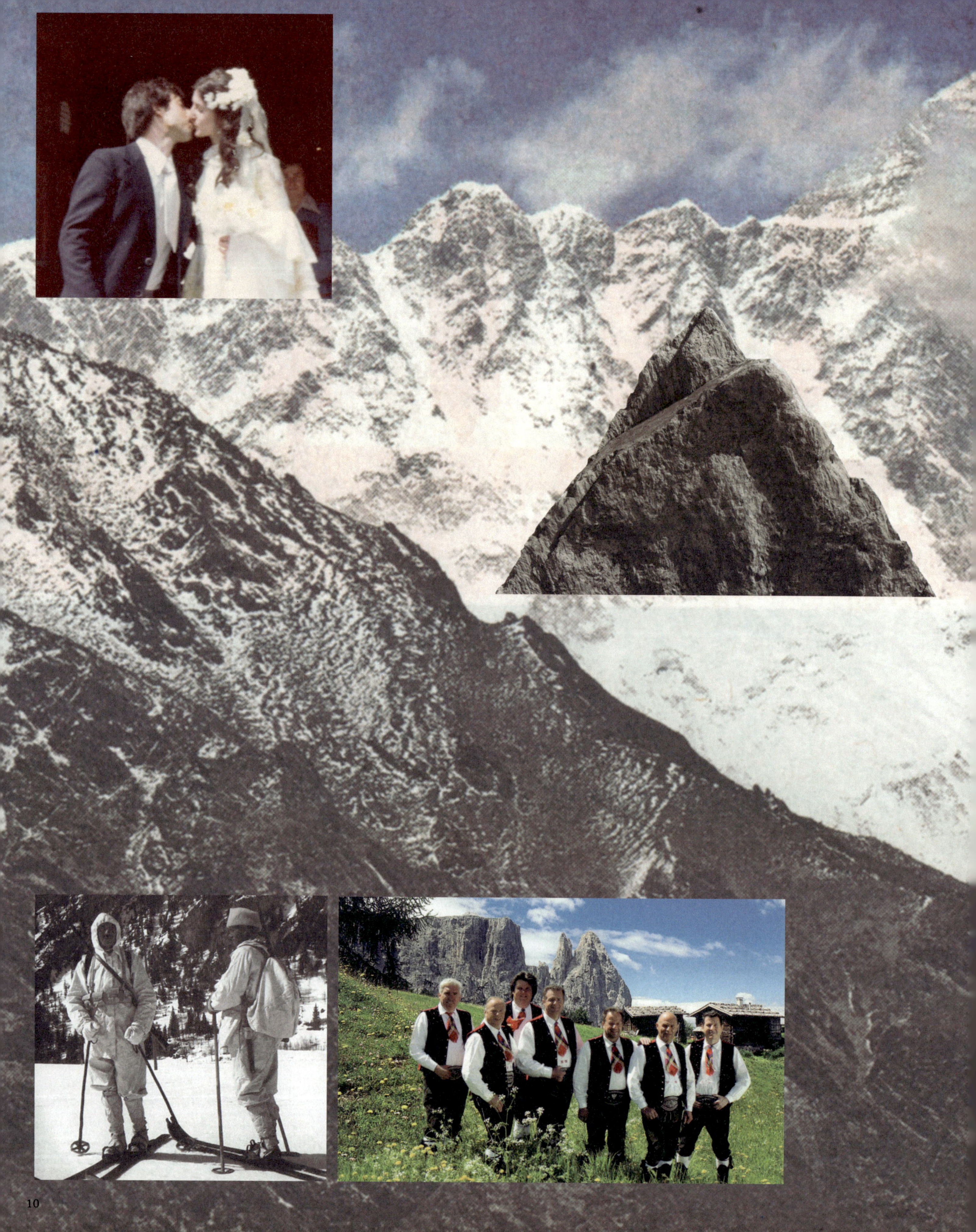

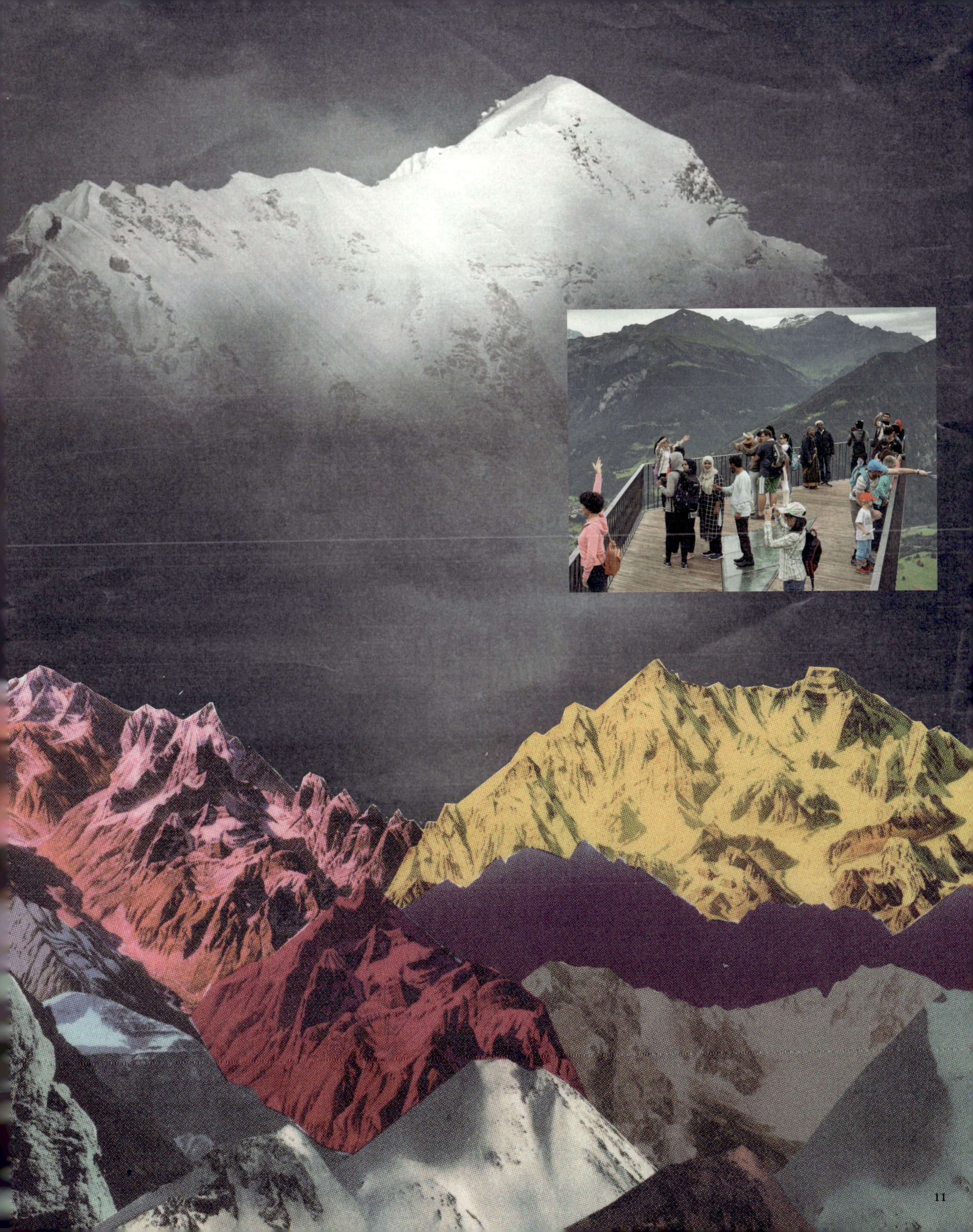

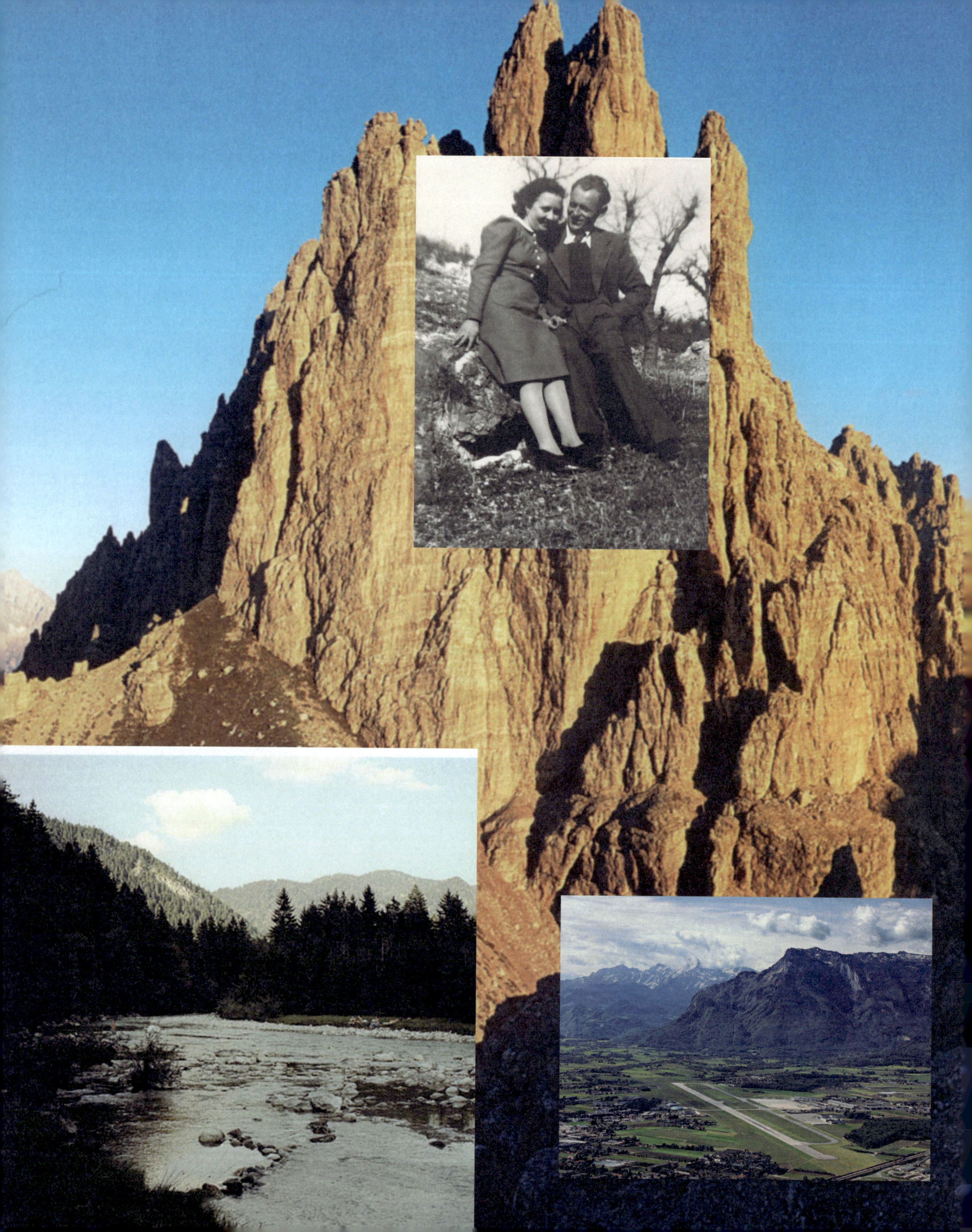

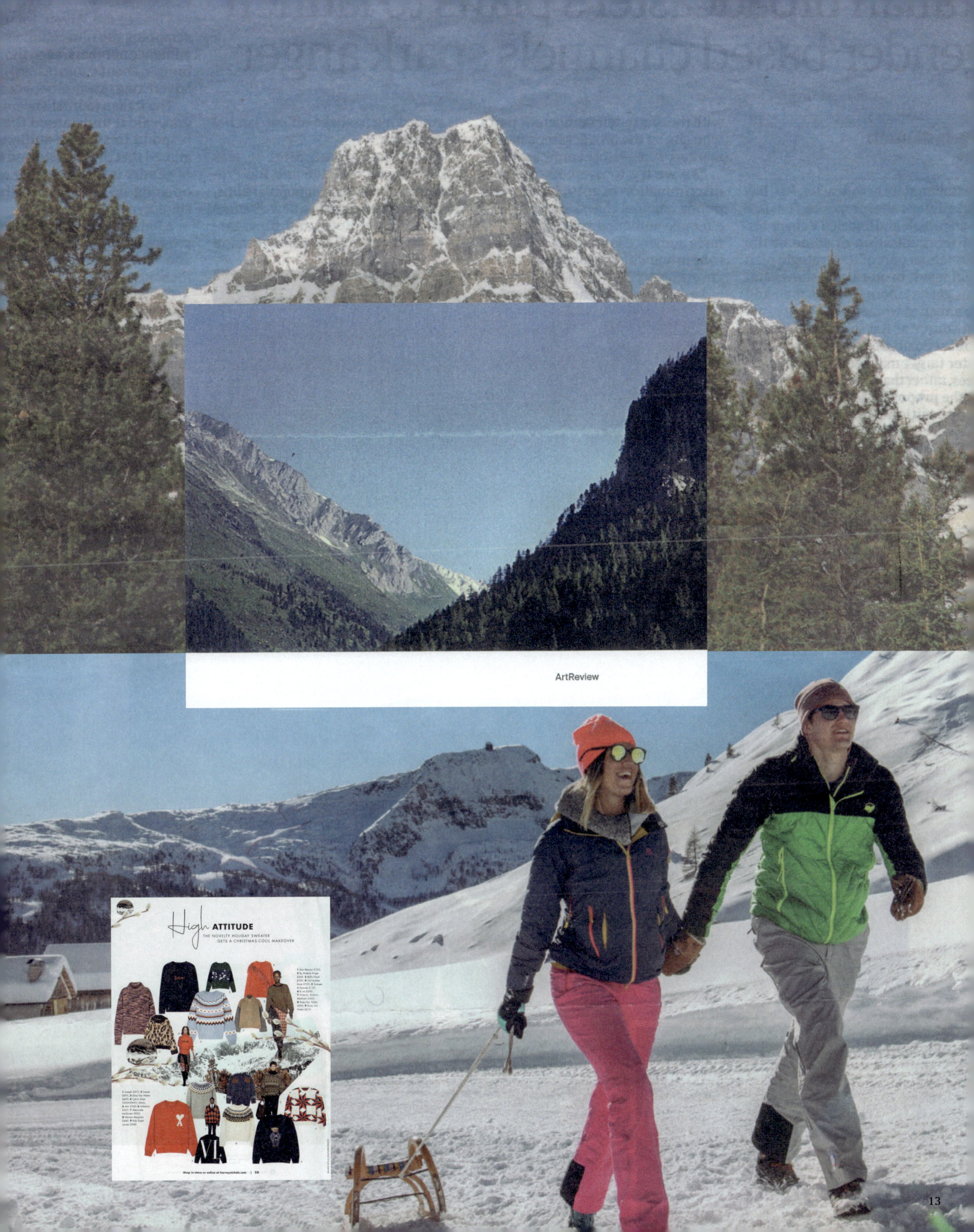
ArtReview
High ATTITUDE
THE NOVELTY HOLIDAY SWEATER GETS A CHRISTMAS-COOL MAKEOVER

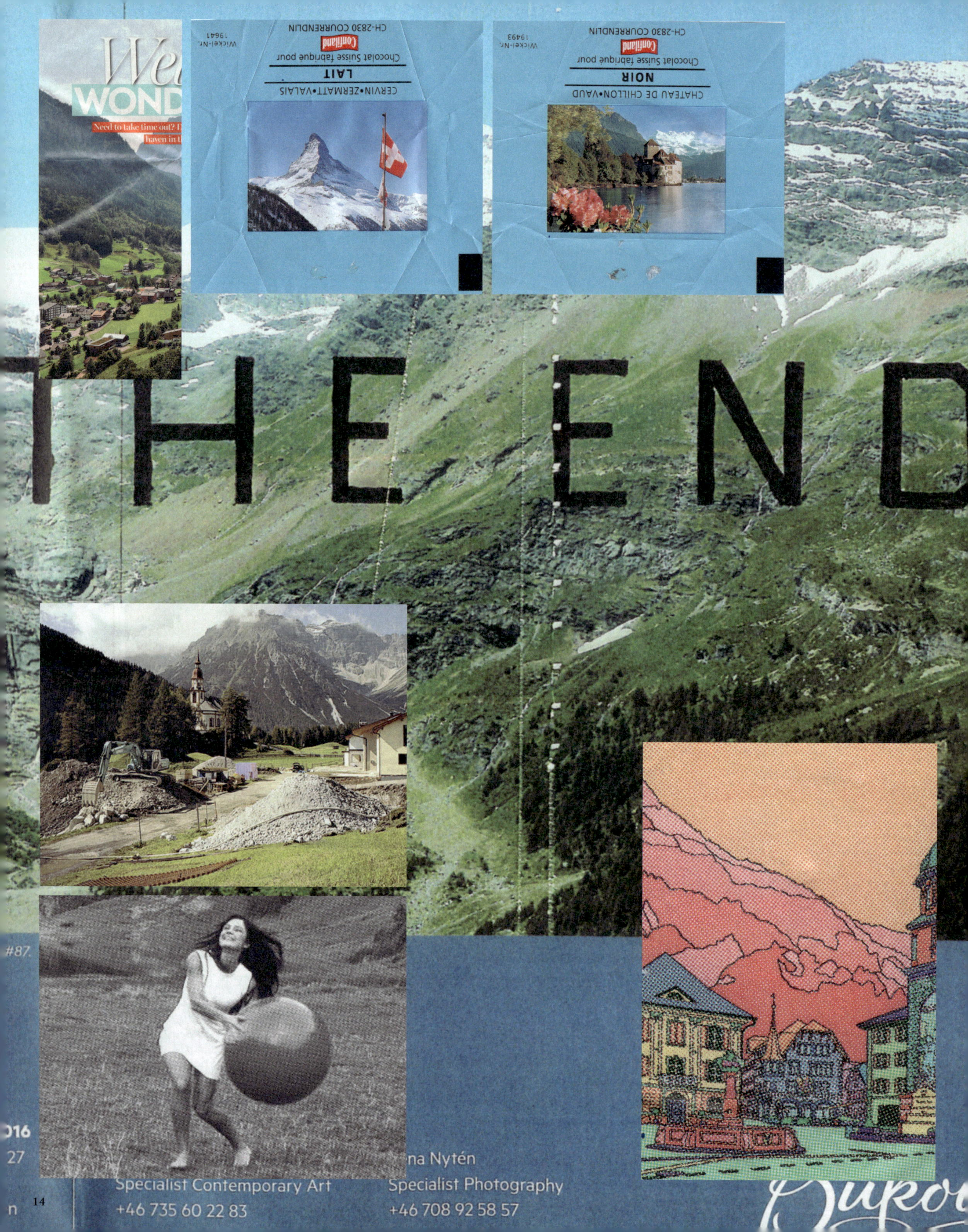

WONDE
CERVIN•ZERMATT•VALAIS
LAIT
Chocolat Suisse fabriqué pour
Confiland
CH-2830 COURRENDLIN
CHATEAU DE CHILLON•VAUD
NOIR
Chocolat Suisse fabriqué pour
Confiland
CH-2830 COURRENDLIN
THE END
#87.
016
27
na Nytén
Specialist Contemporary Art
Specialist Photography
+46 735 60 22 83
+46 708 92 58 57

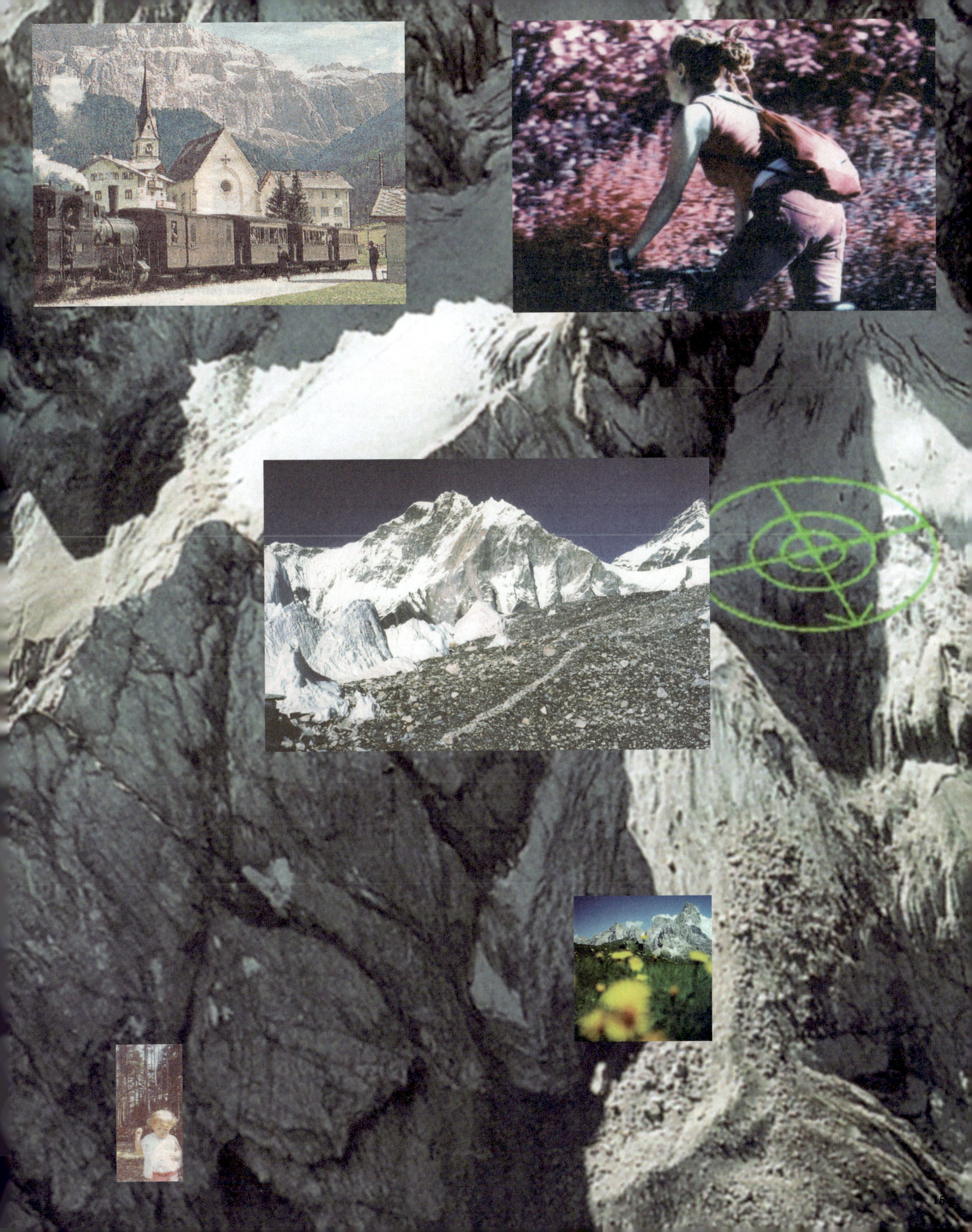

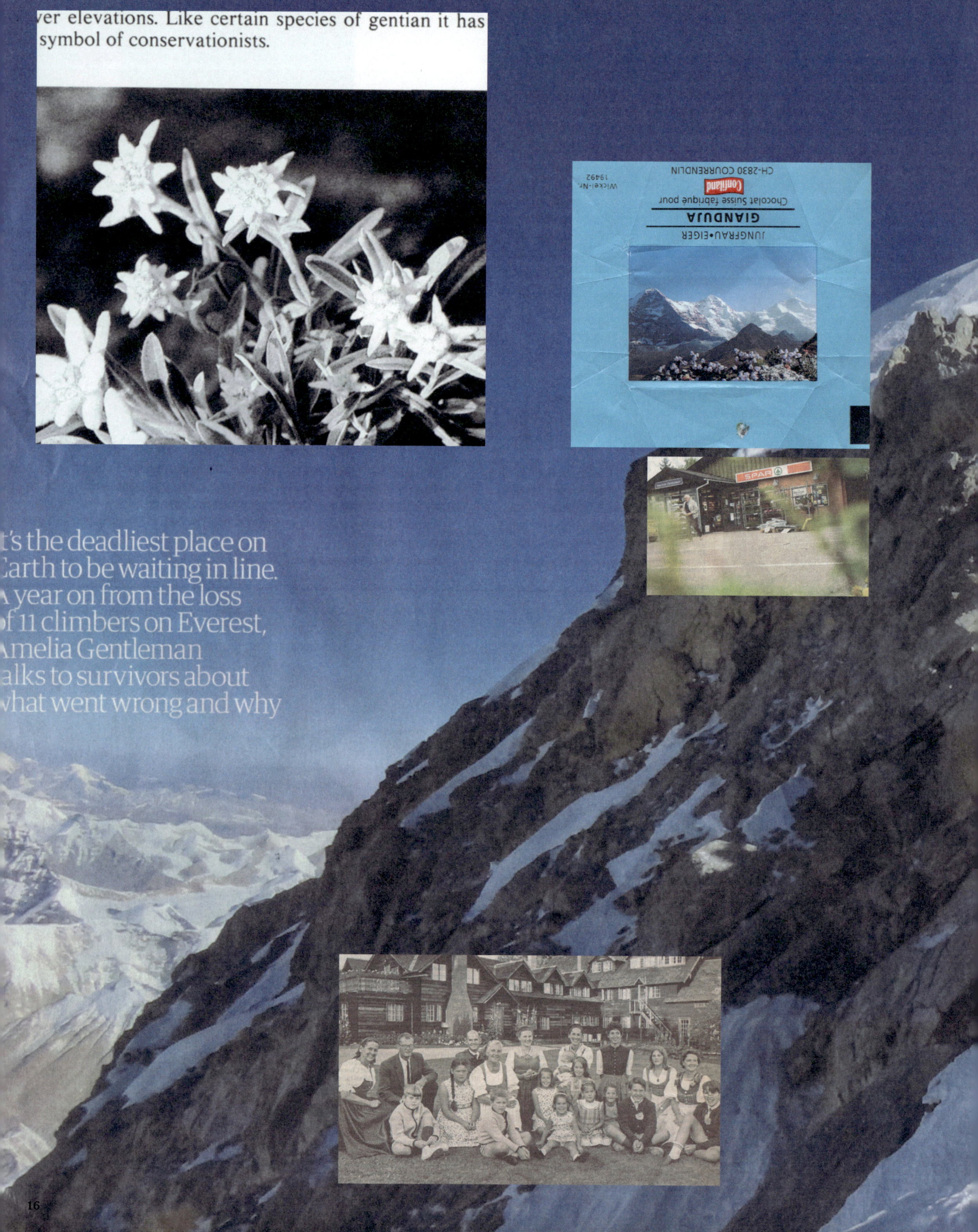
ver elevations. Like certain species of gentian it has
symbol of conservationists.
t's the deadliest place on
arth to be waiting in line.
year on from the loss
f 11 climbers on Everest,
melia Gentleman
alks to survivors about
hat went wrong and why
SPAR

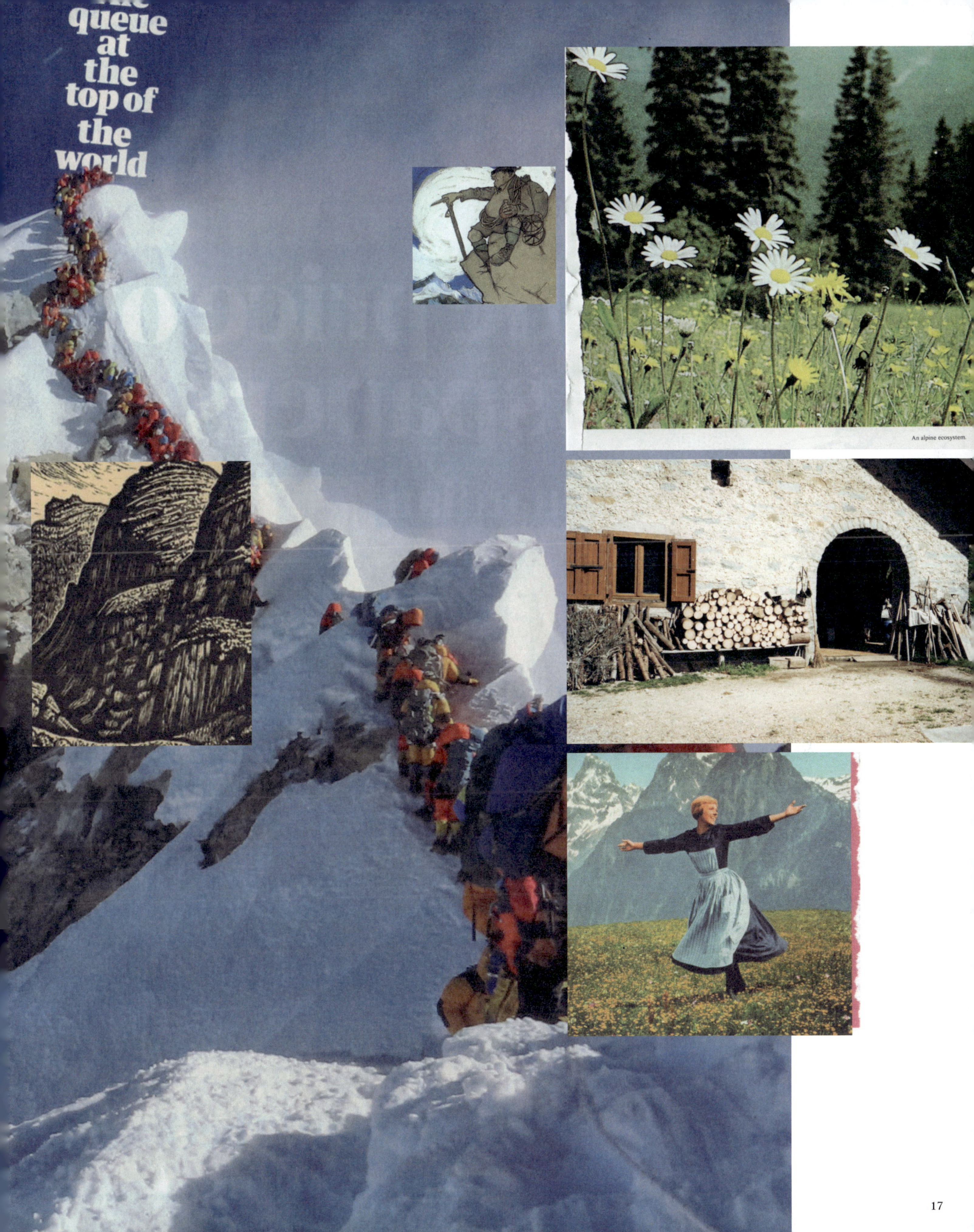
queue
at
the
top of
the
world
An alpine ecosystem.

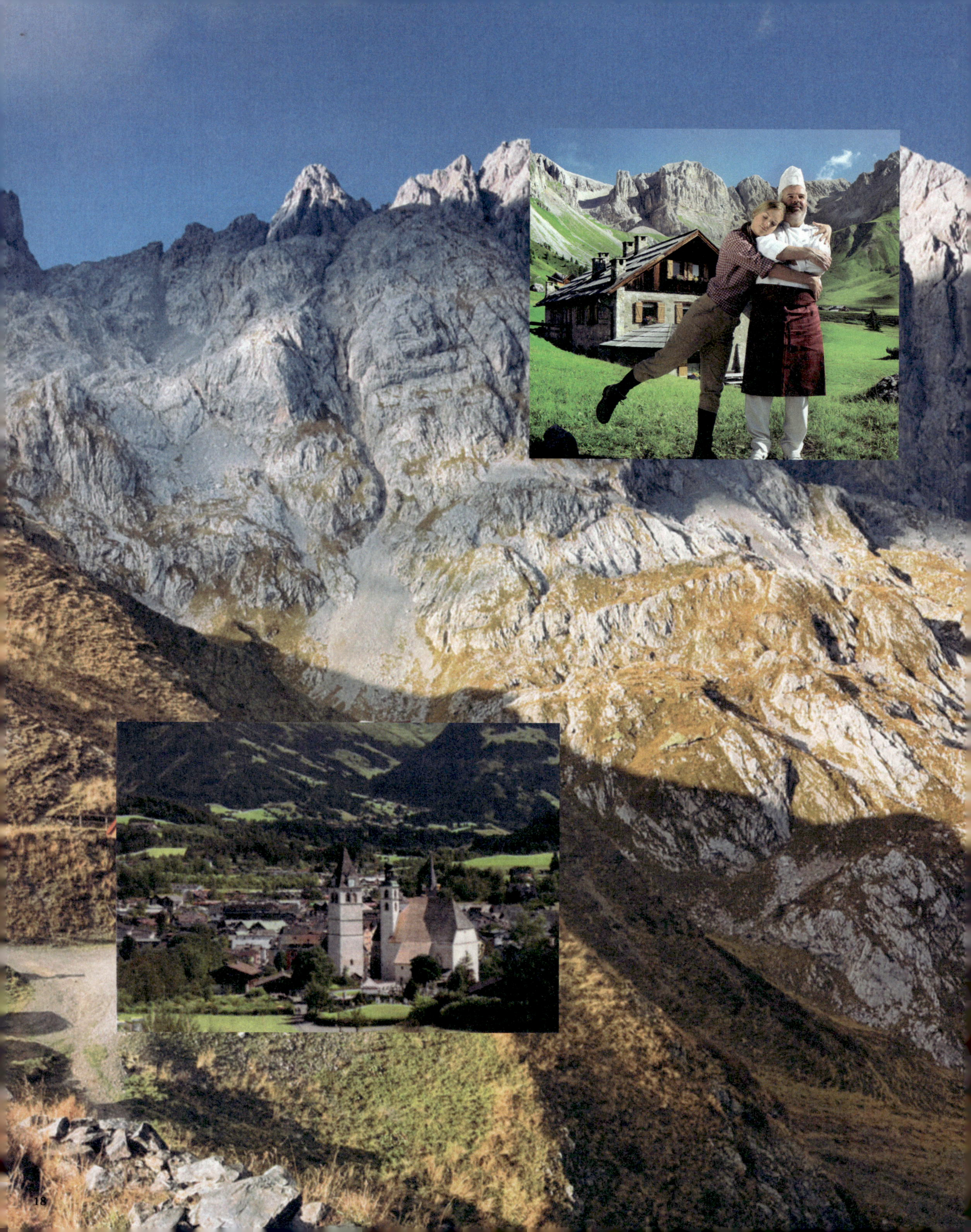

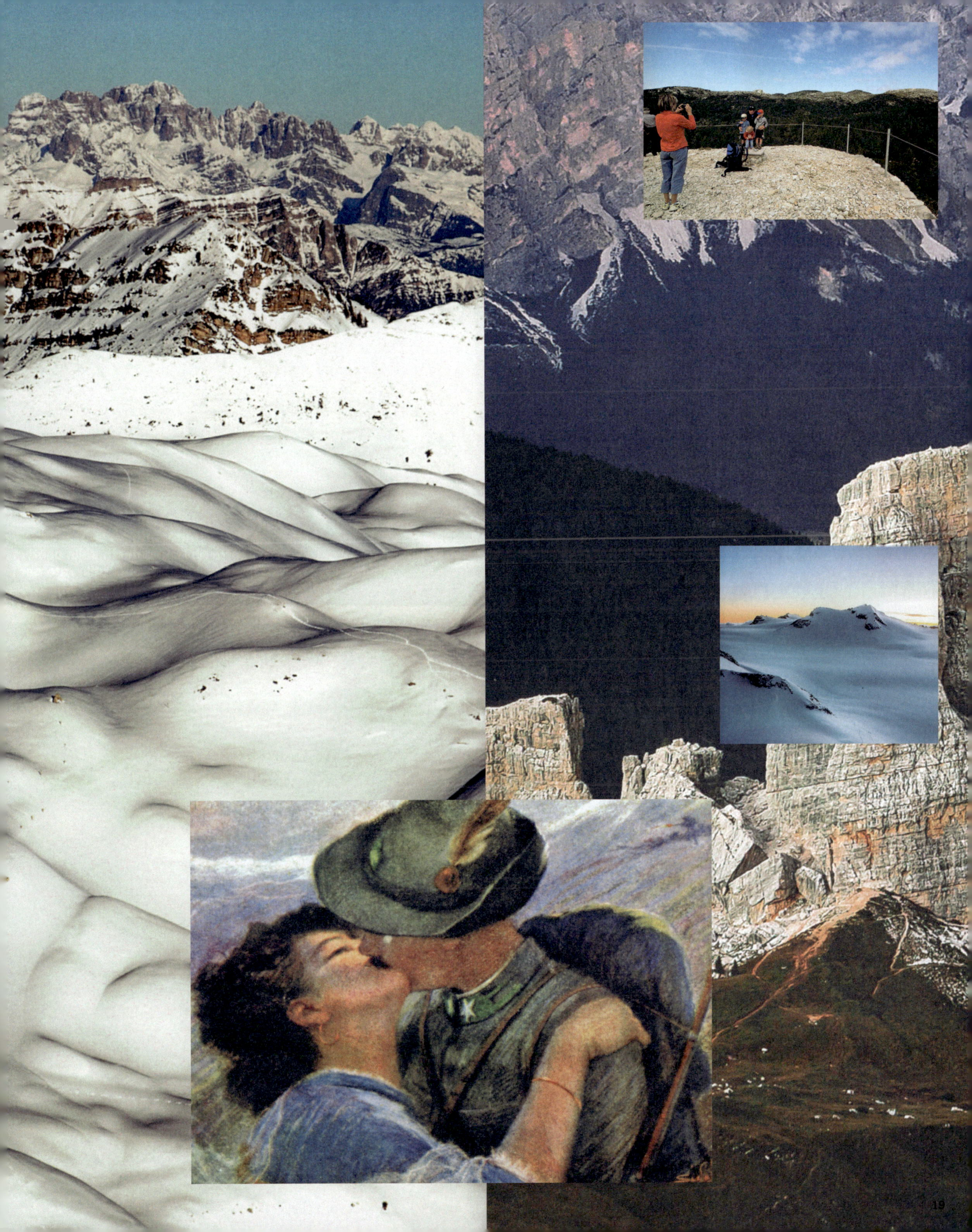

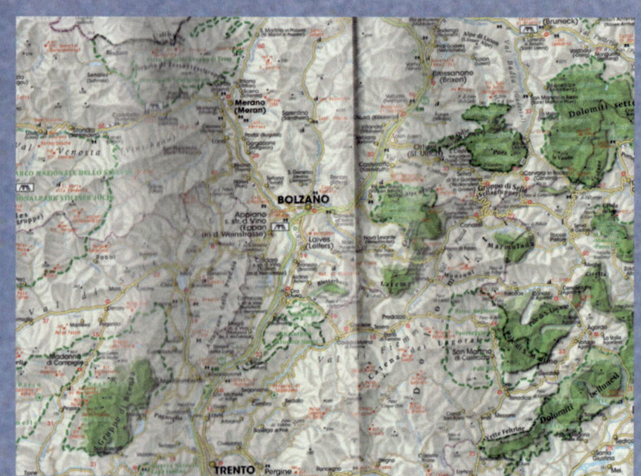
Merano
(Meran)
BOLZANO
TRENTO
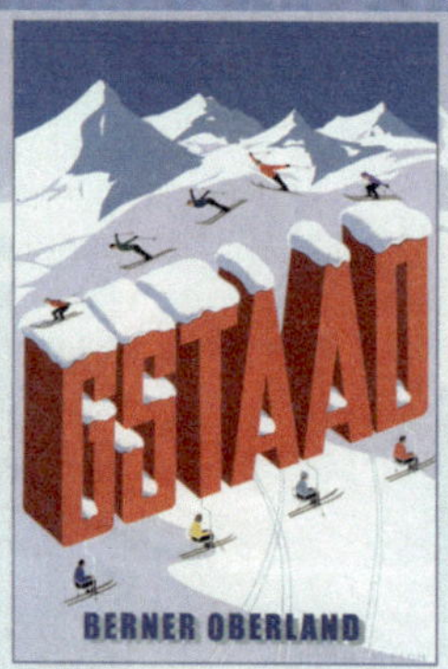
GSTAAD
BERNER OBERLAND
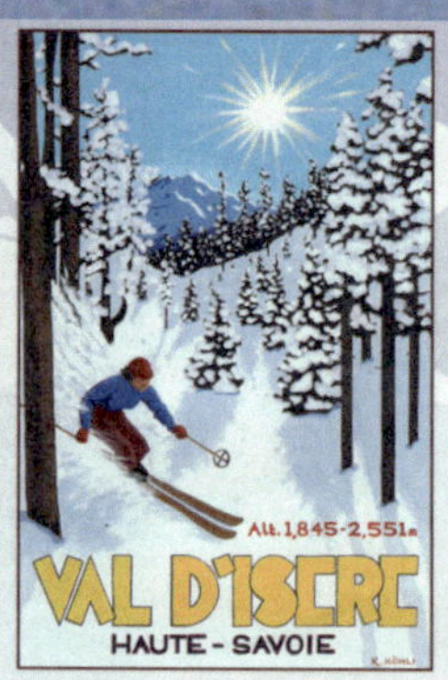
VAL D'ISERE
HAUTE - SAVOIE
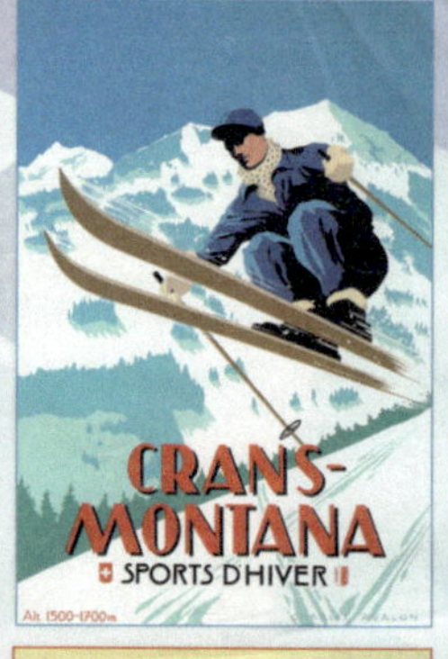
CRANS-
MONTANA
SPORTS D'HIVER
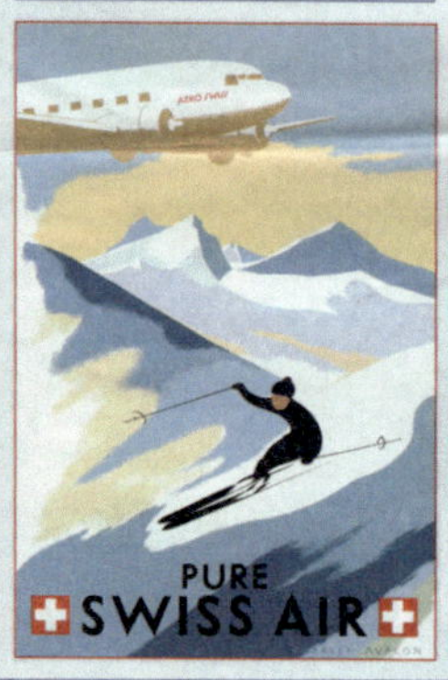
PURE
SWISS AIR
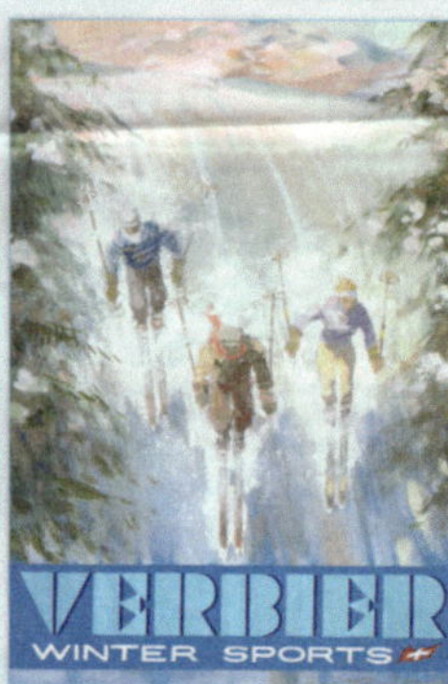
VERBIER
WINTER SPORTS
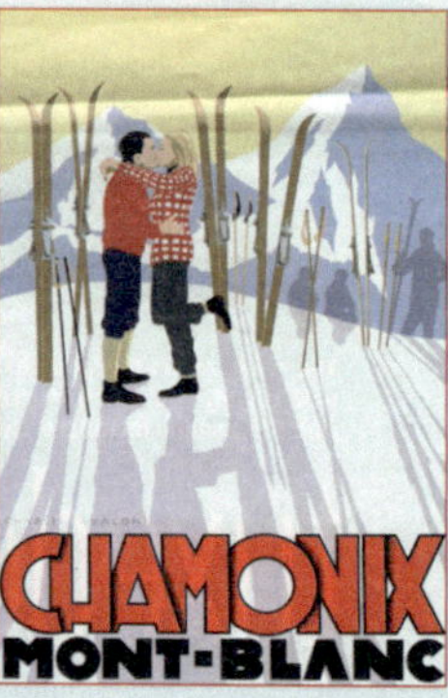
CHAMONIX
MONT-BLANC
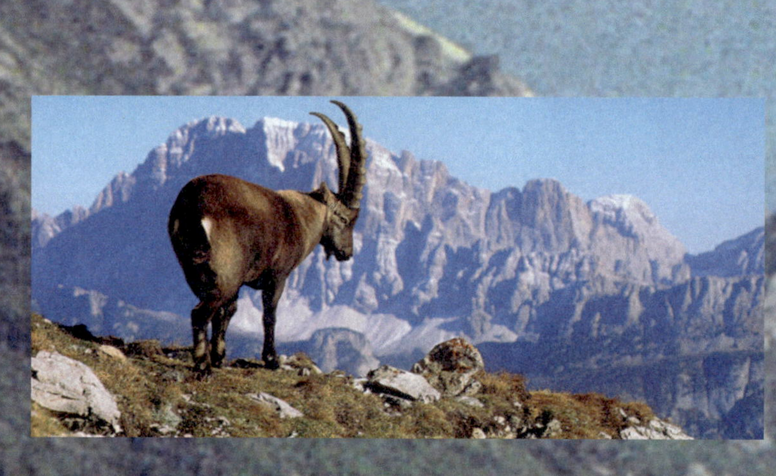

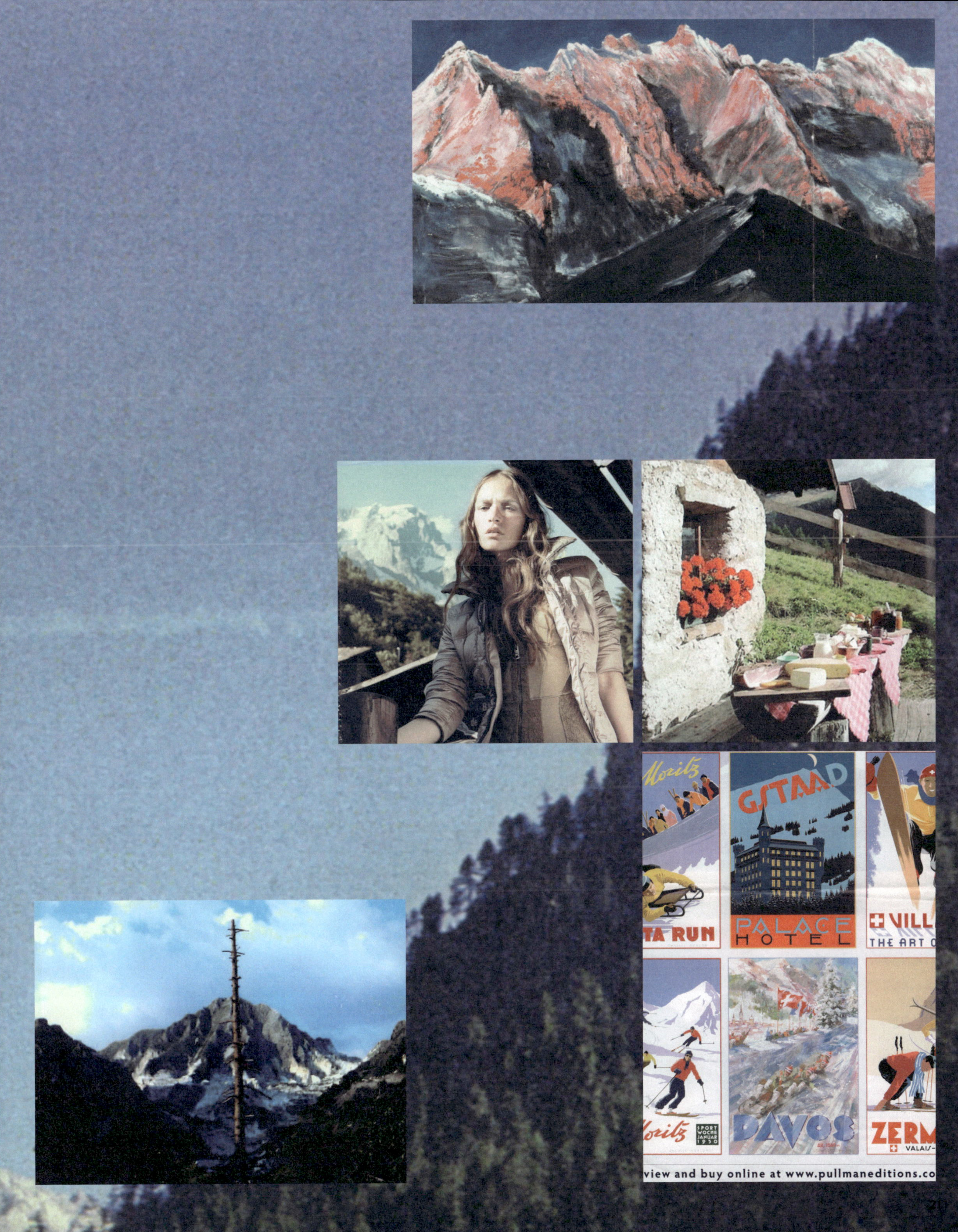

GSTAAD
PALACE
HOTEL
TA RUN
THE ART O
SPORT
WOCHE
JANUAR
1930
DAVOS
ZERM
VALAIS
view and buy online at www.pullmaneditions.co

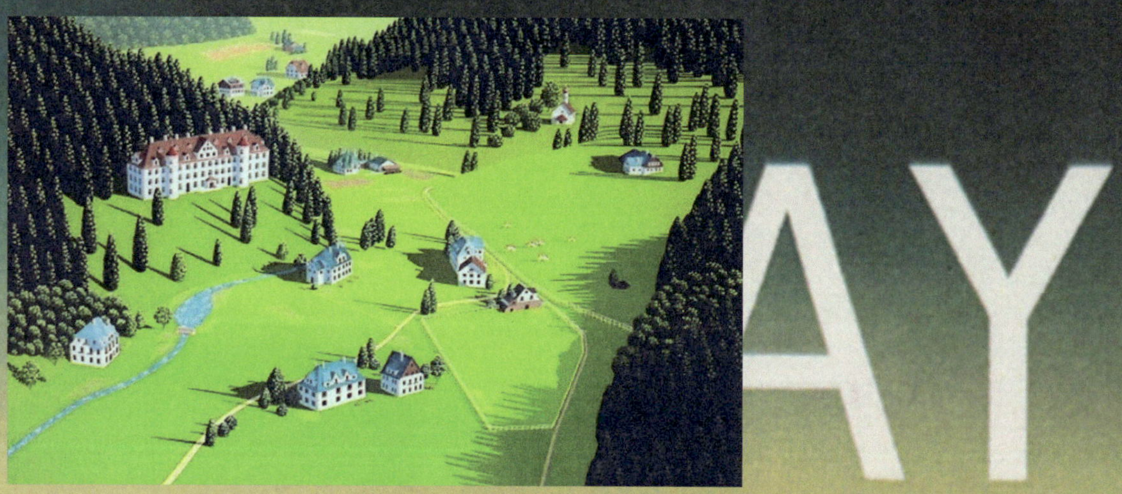

AY

NOTHIN

L

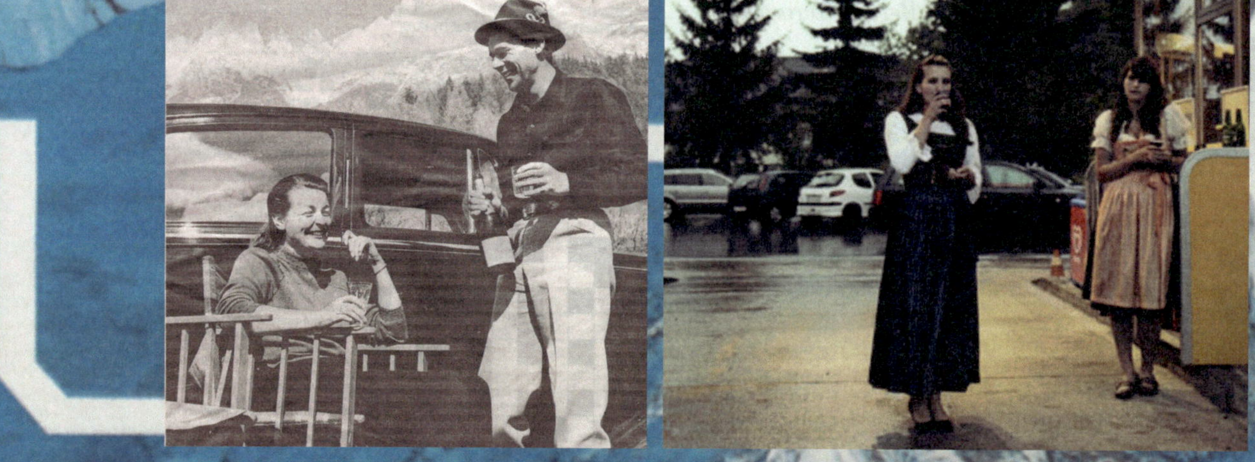

PRIL

Laugen bread with cream cheese

Allergy-related information: contains gluten, milk, mustard. May contain traces of eggs, lupins, nuts, peanuts, sesame seeds, soya.

Use by: 22.12.09 B12352
store at max 5°C
packed under modified atmosphere conditions
BELL AG,4002 BASEL,TEL. +41 (0)800 326 326 100 g
86907

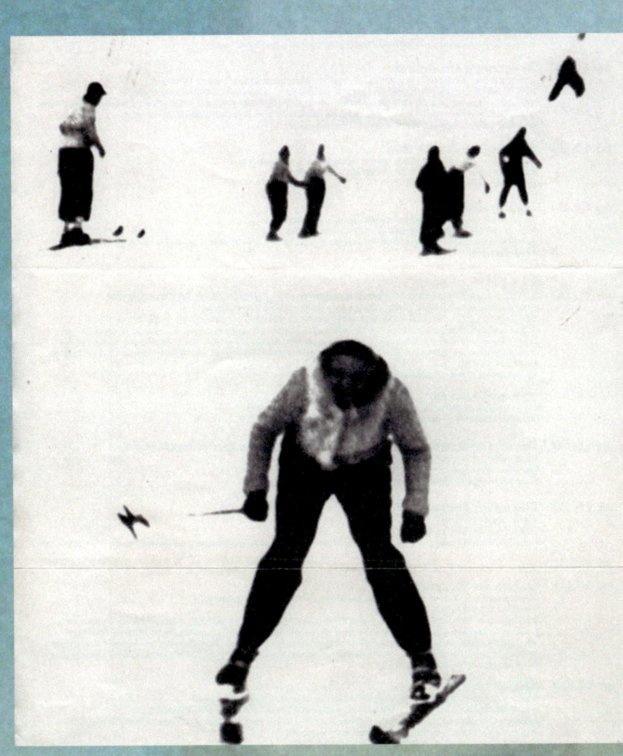

13

March

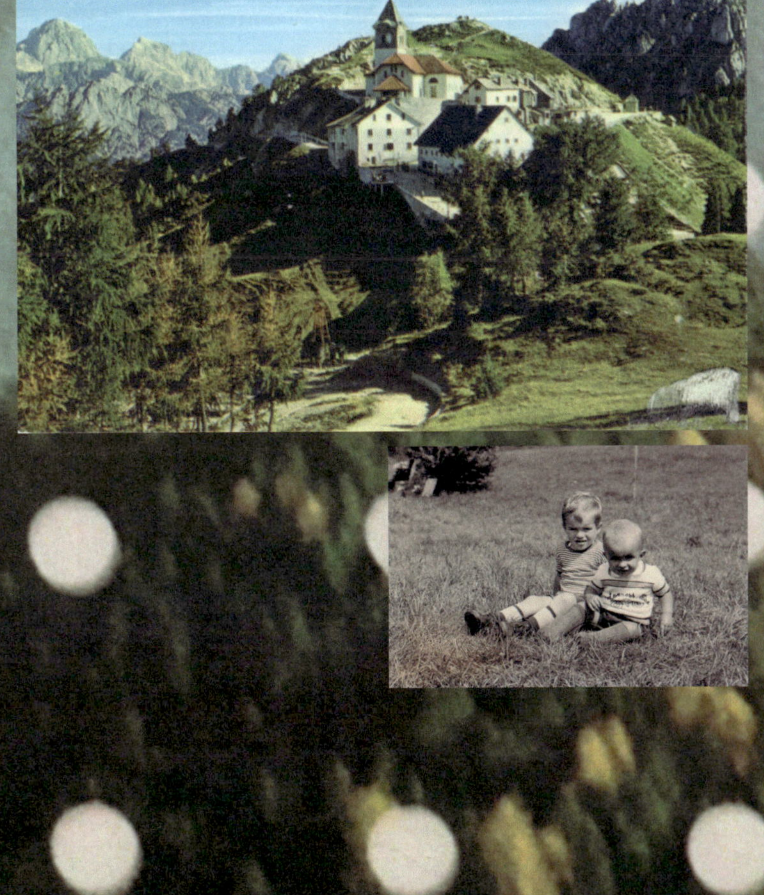

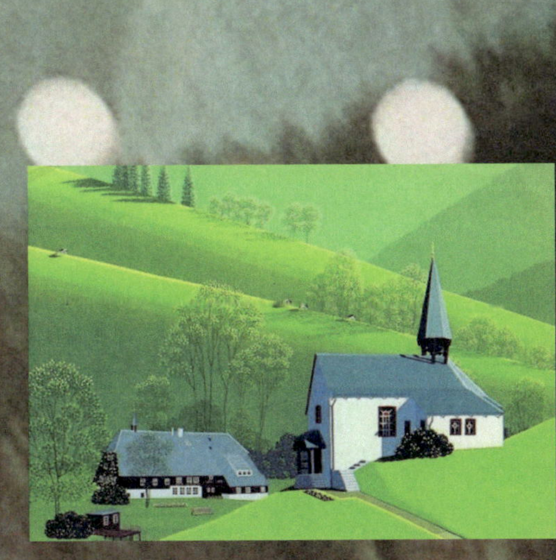

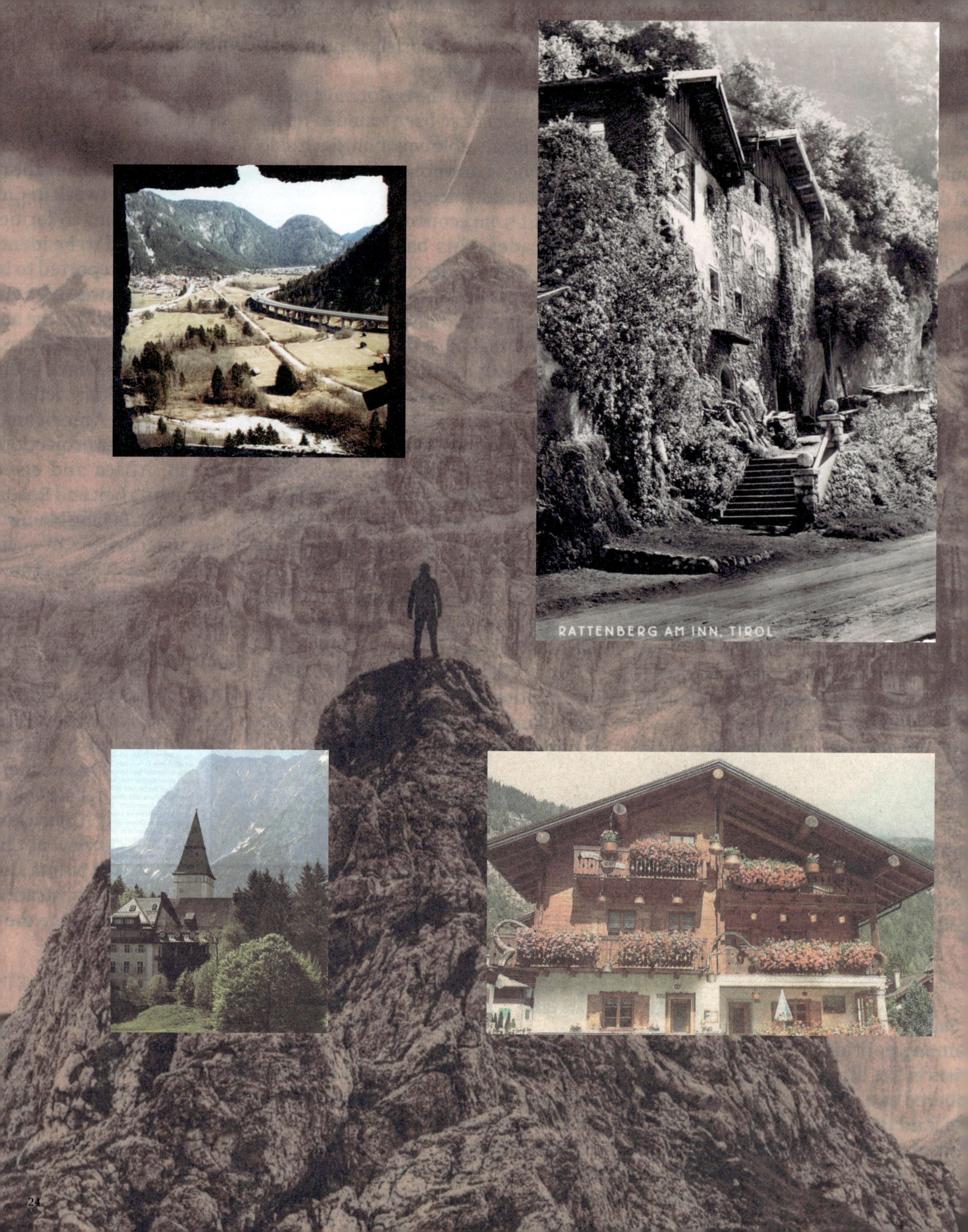
RATTENBERG AM INN, TIROL

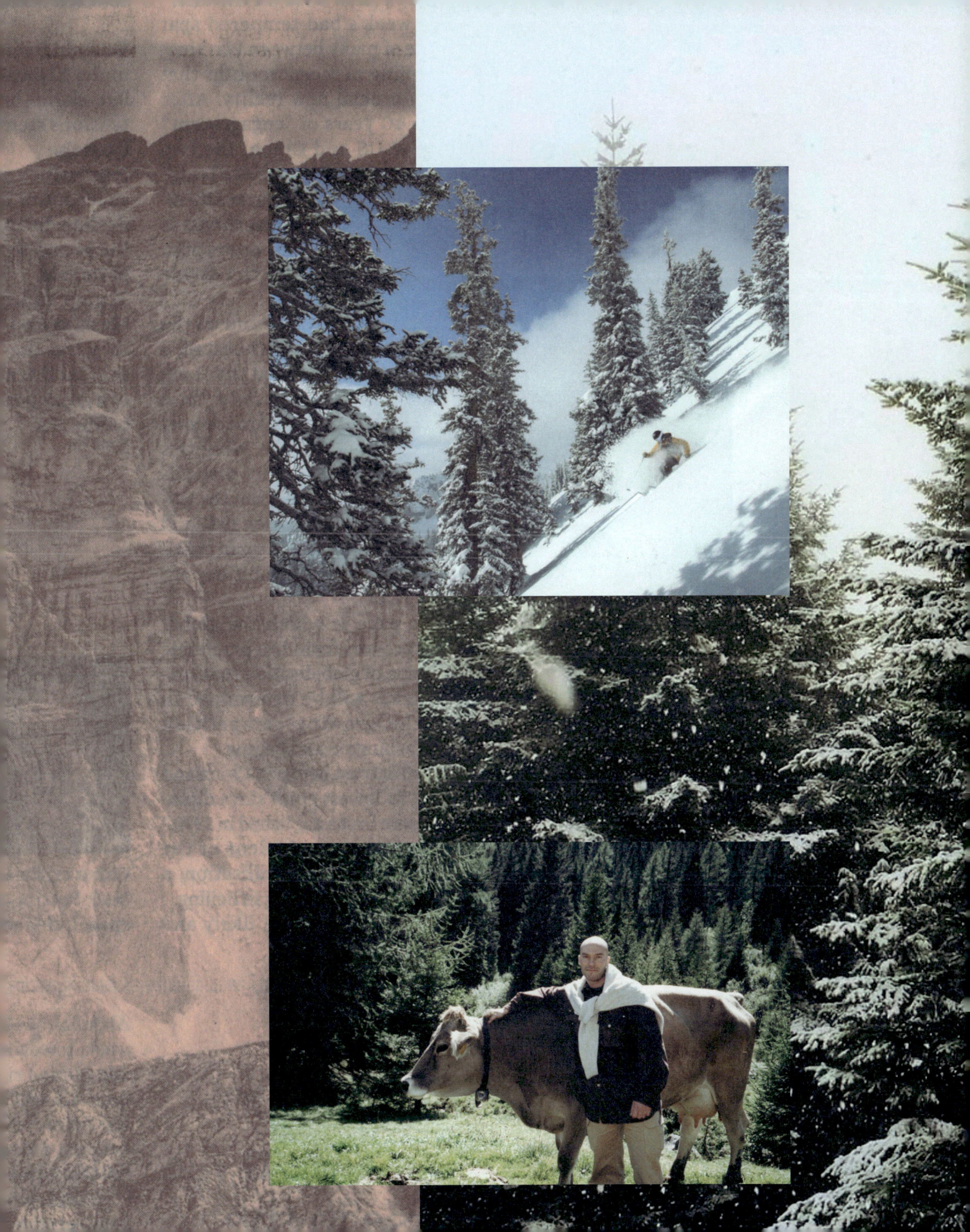

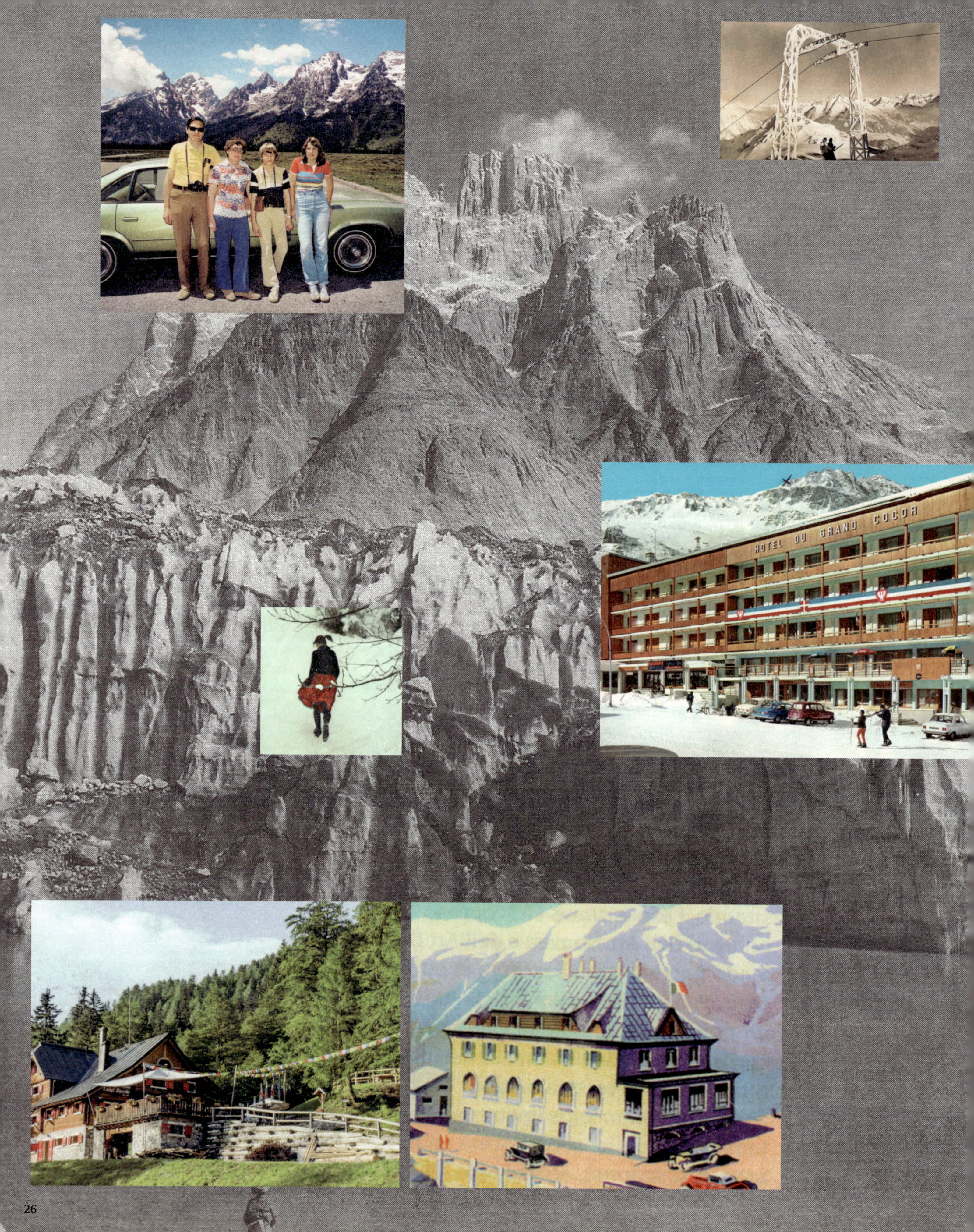
HOTEL DU GRAND COCOR

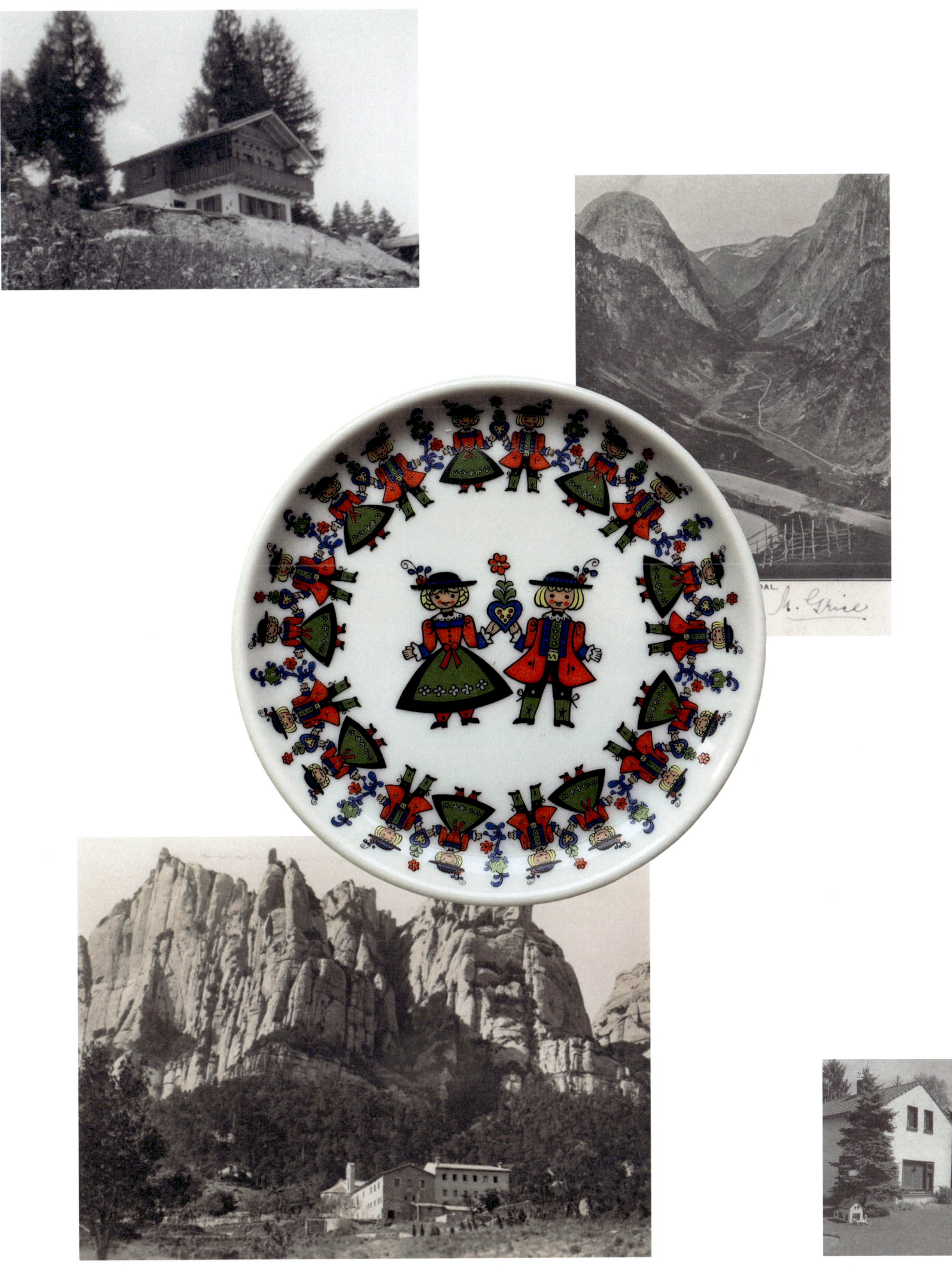
DAL.

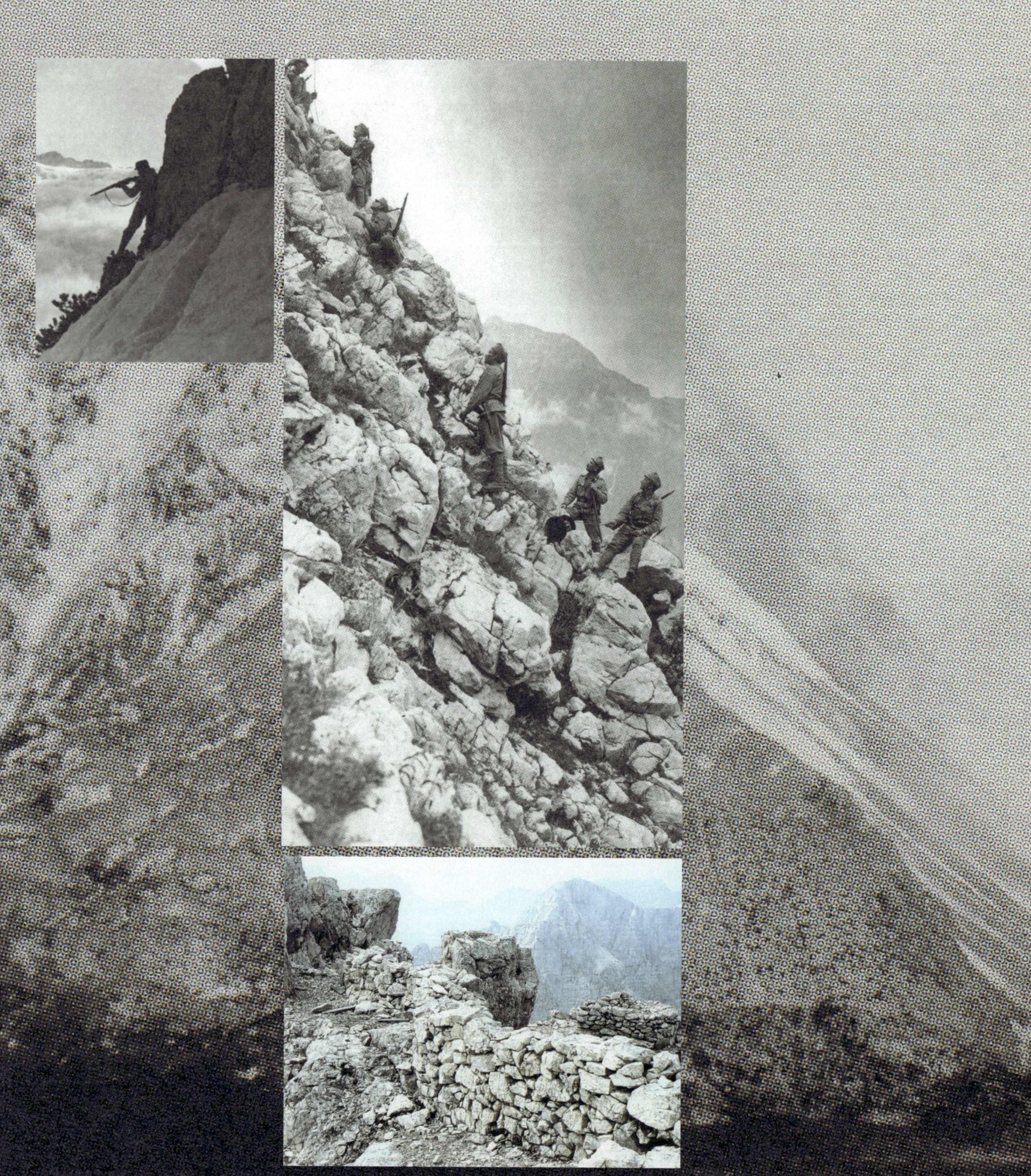

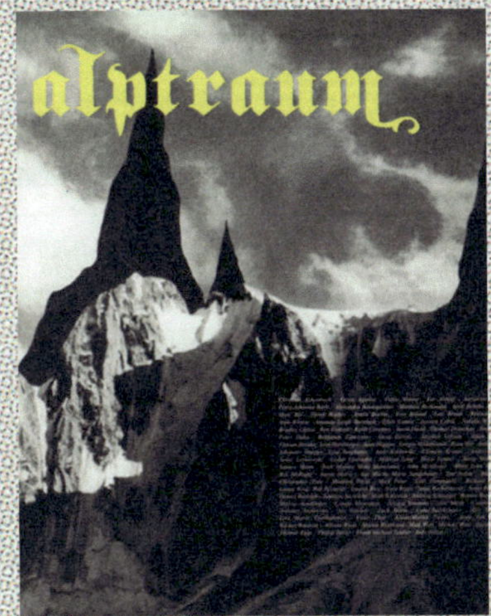
alptraum

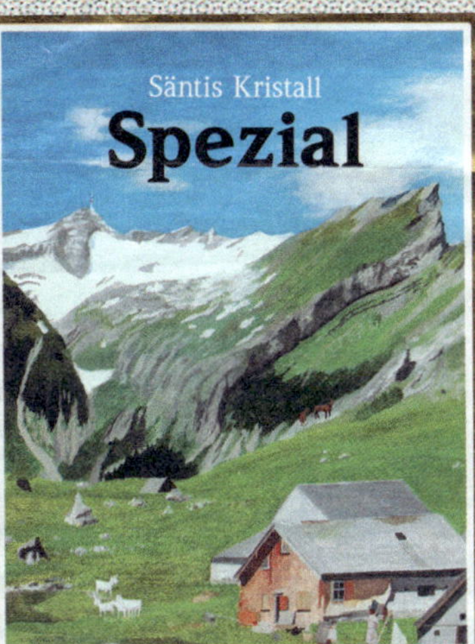
Säntis Kristall
Spezial

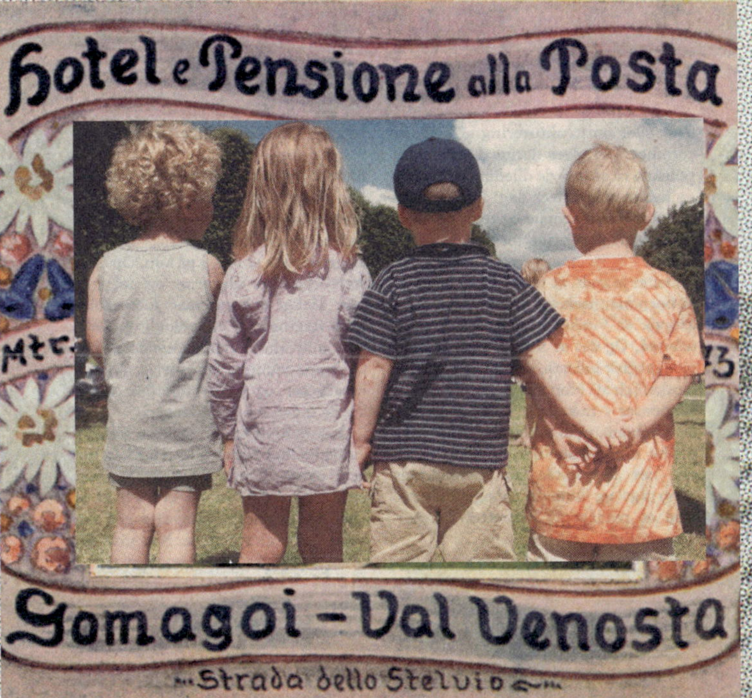
Hotel e Pensione alla Posta
Gomagoi - Val Venosta
Strada dello Stelvio

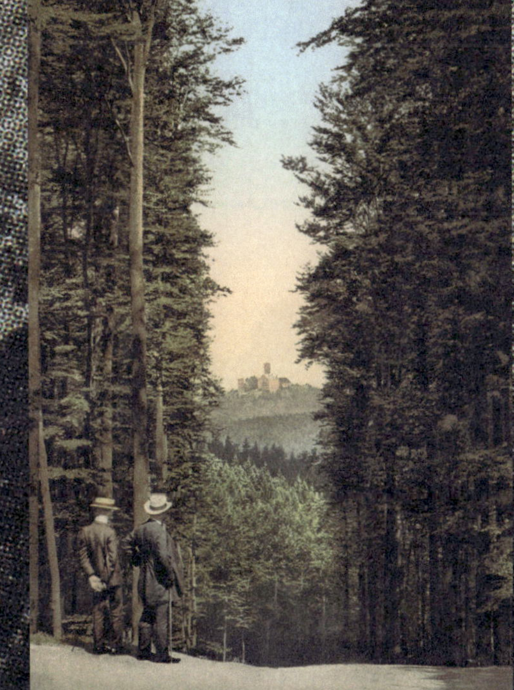

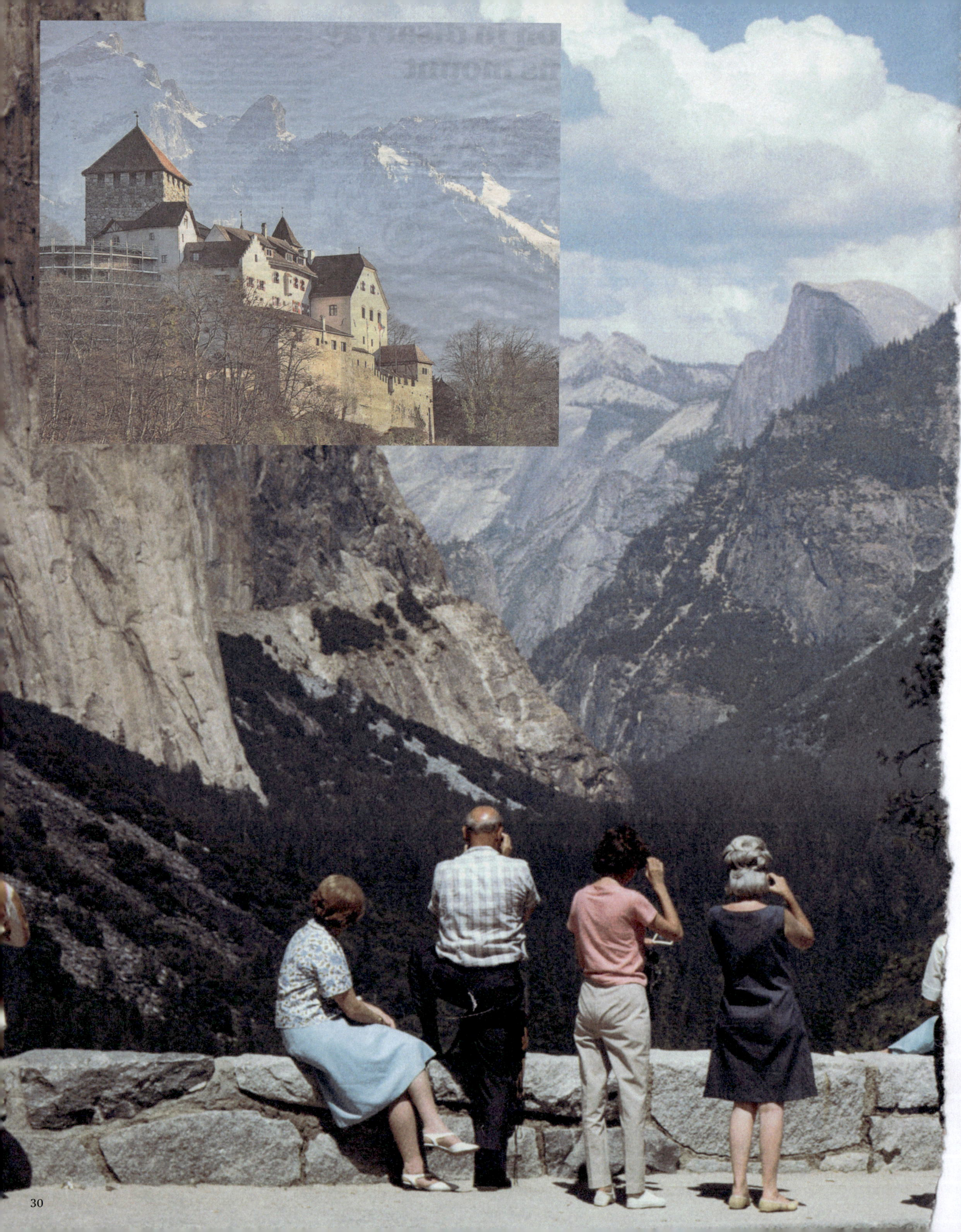

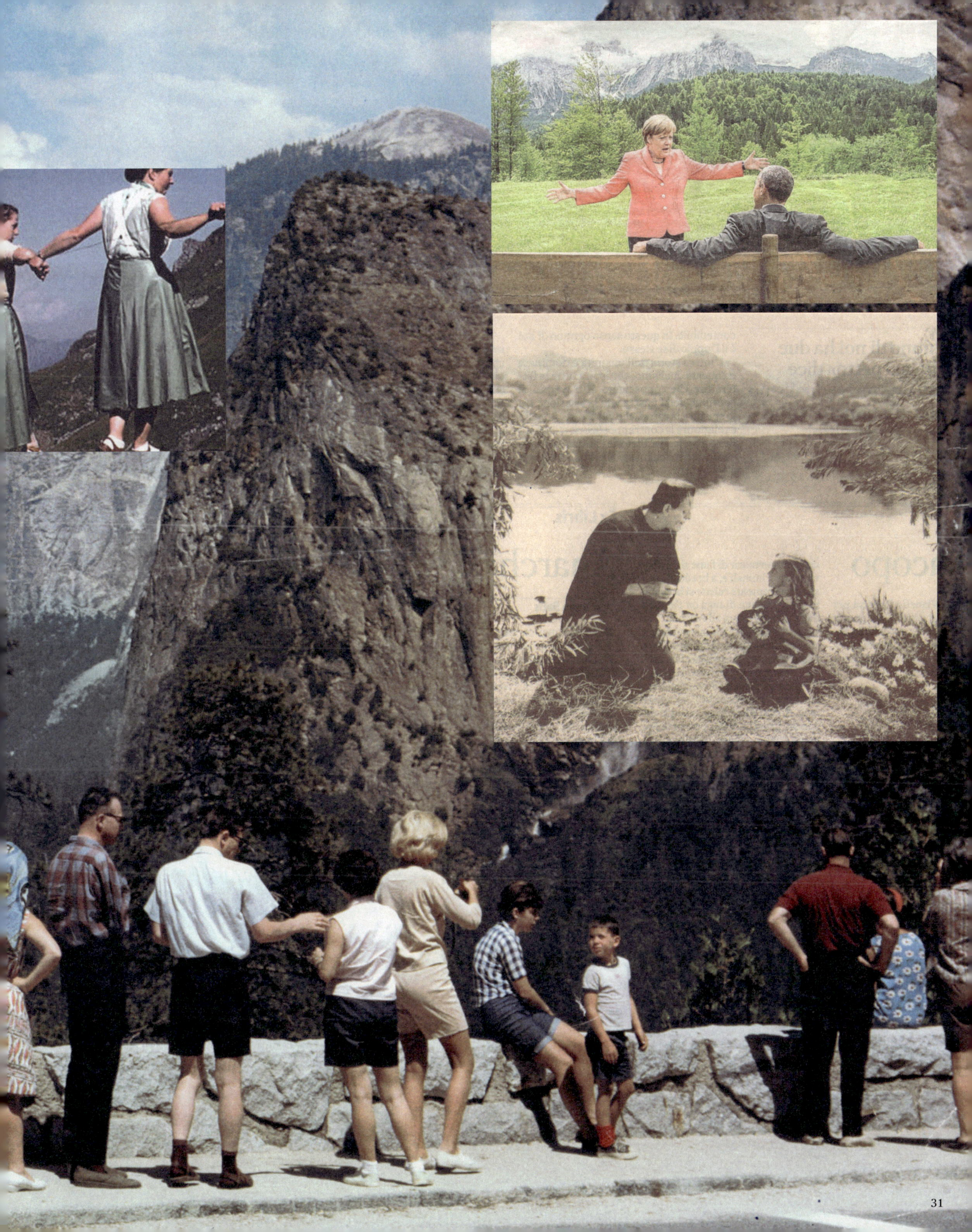

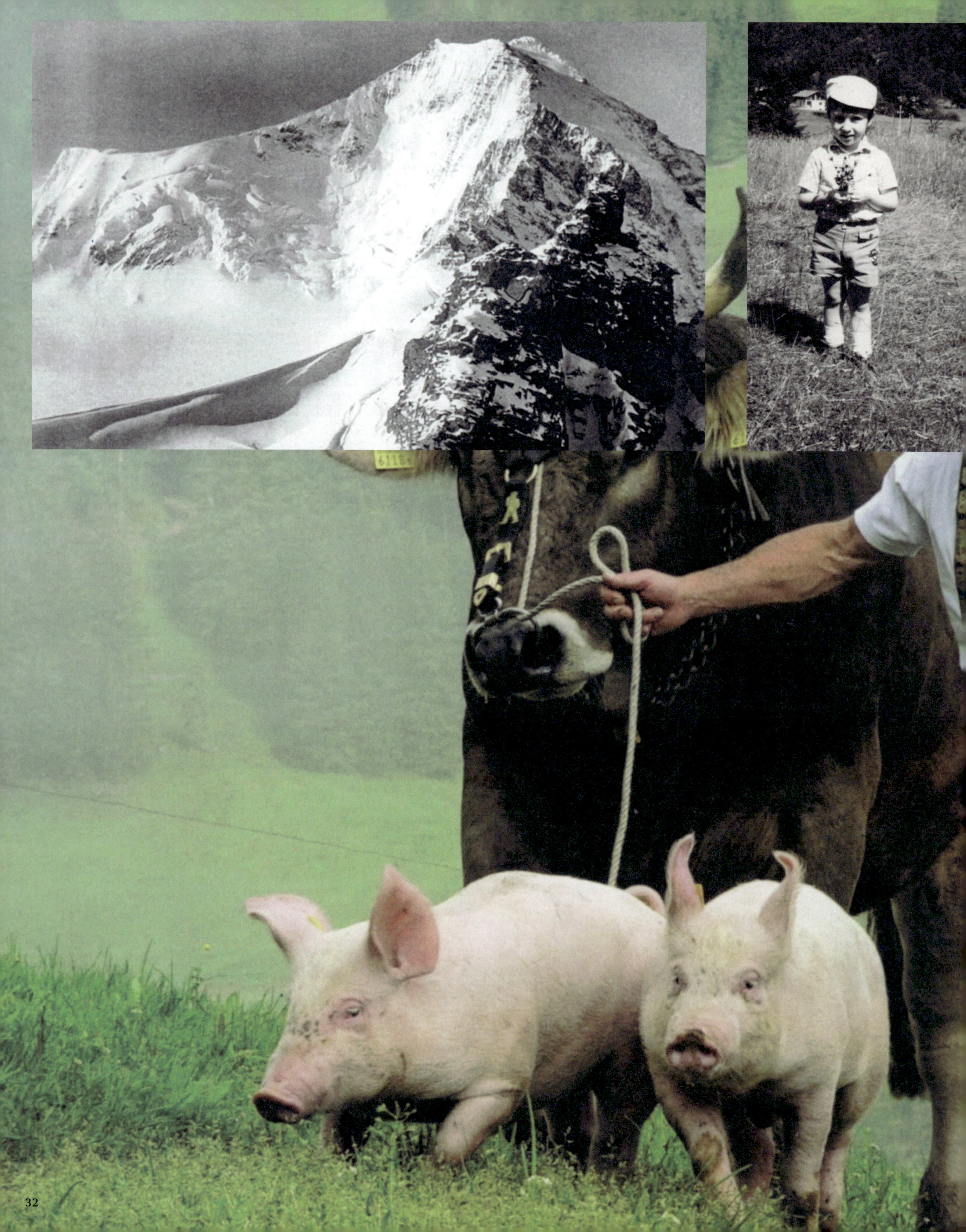

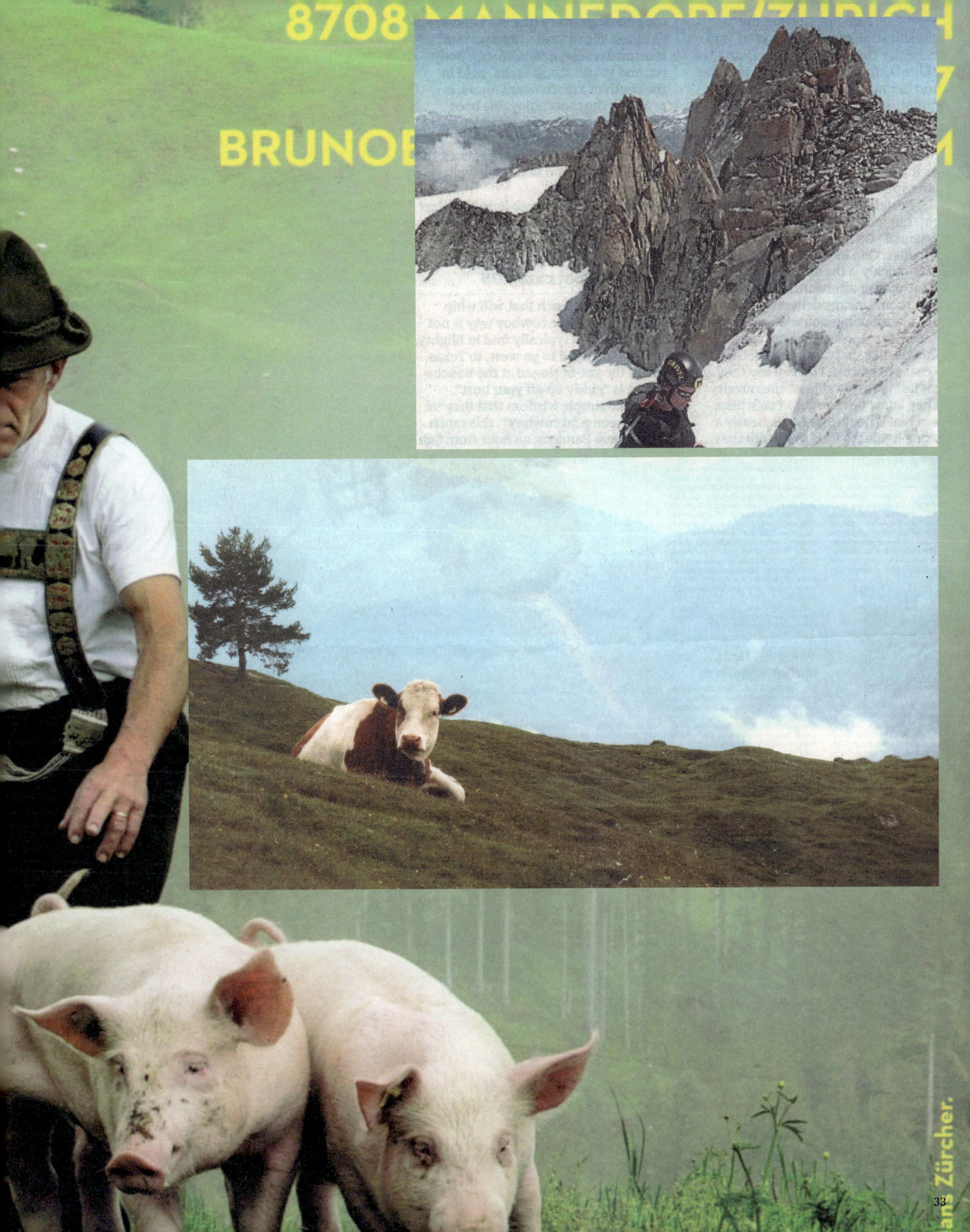

ans Zürcher.

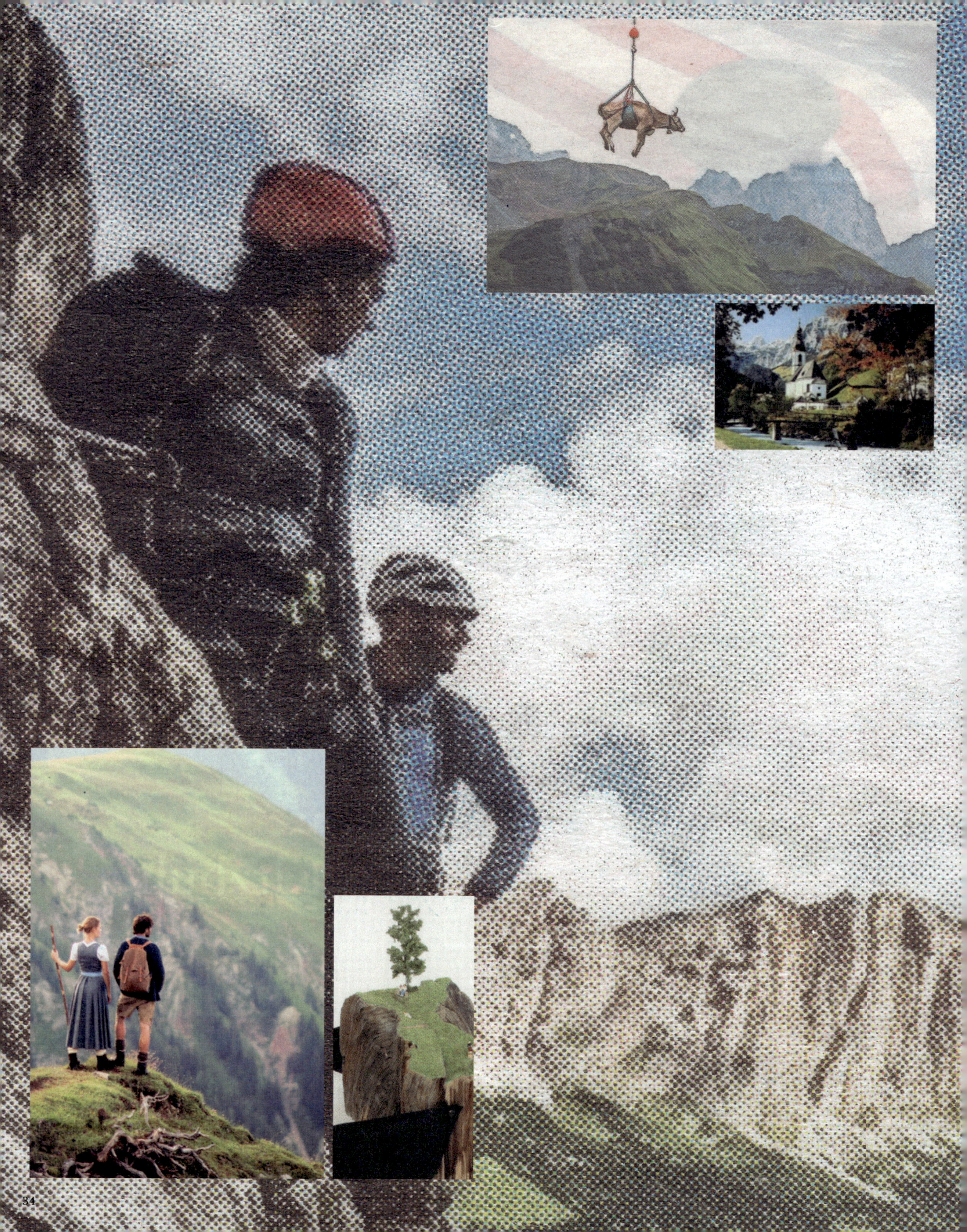

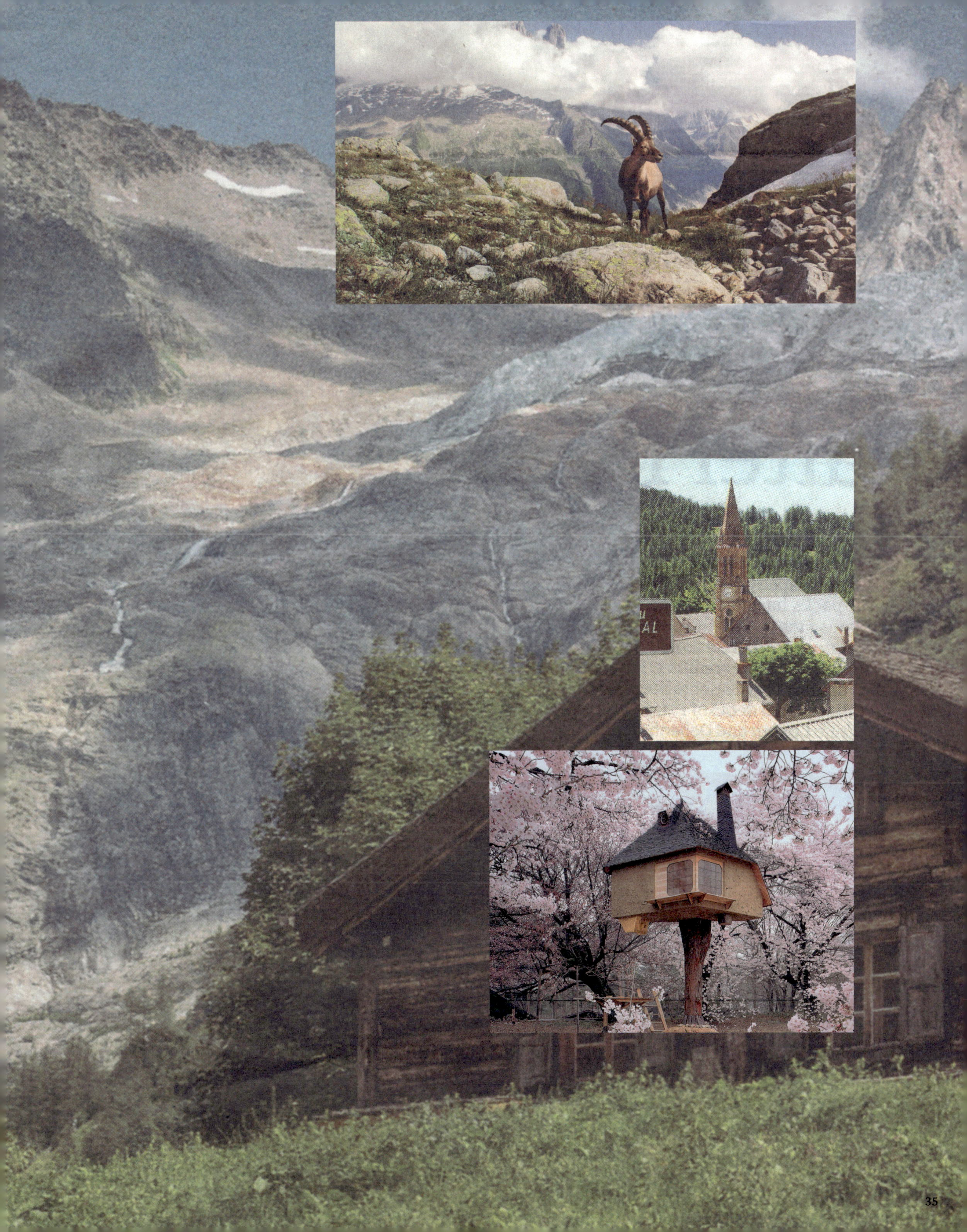

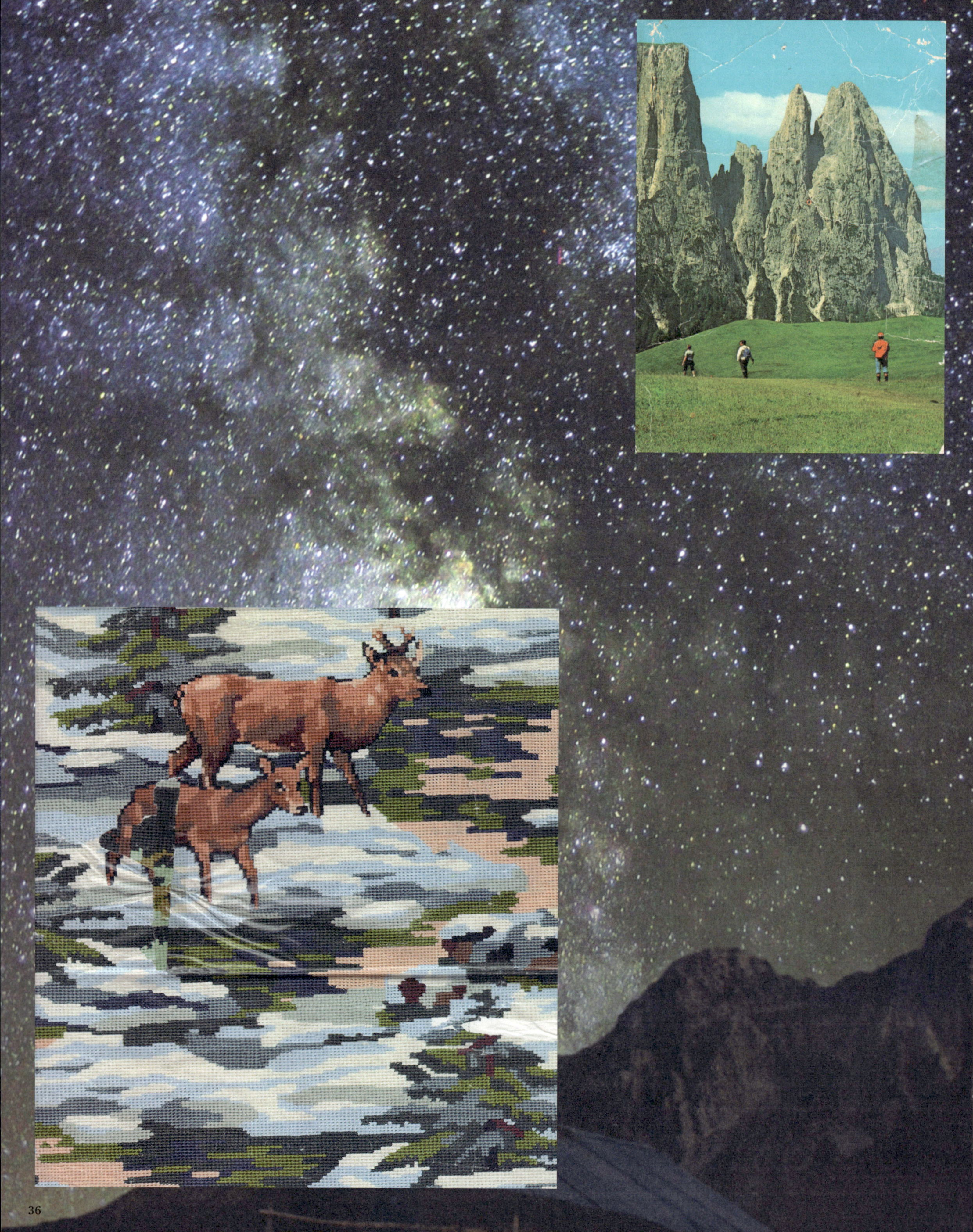

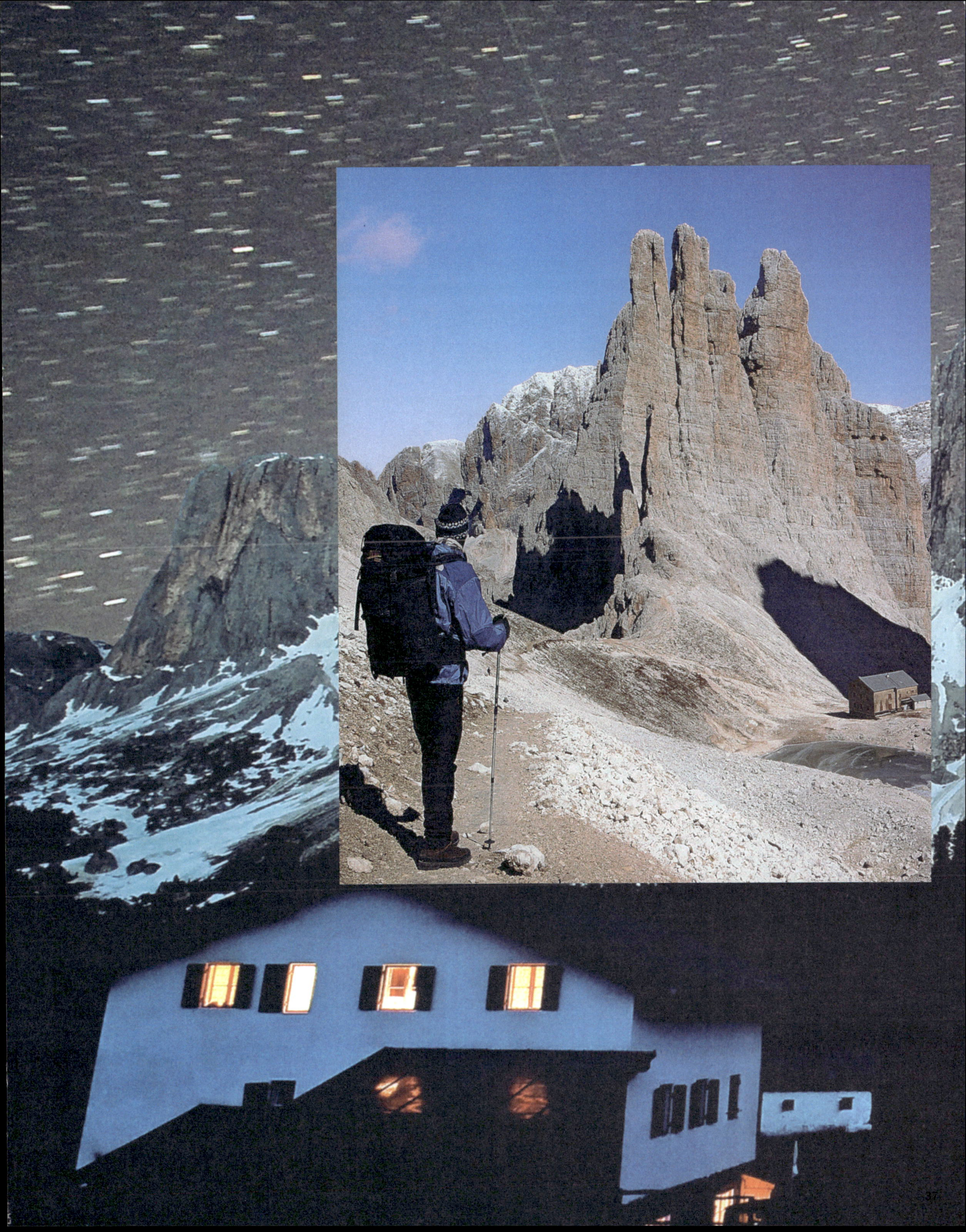

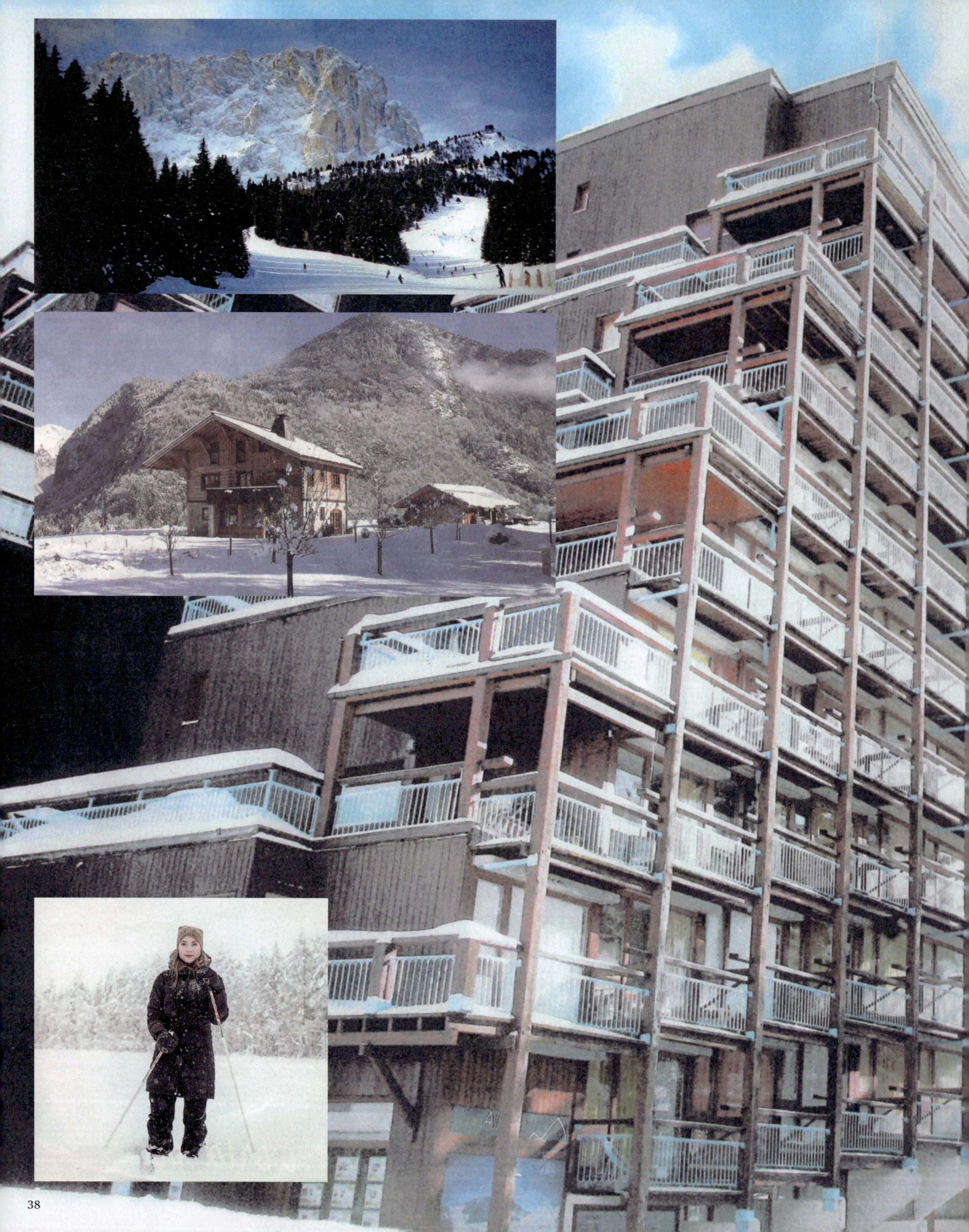

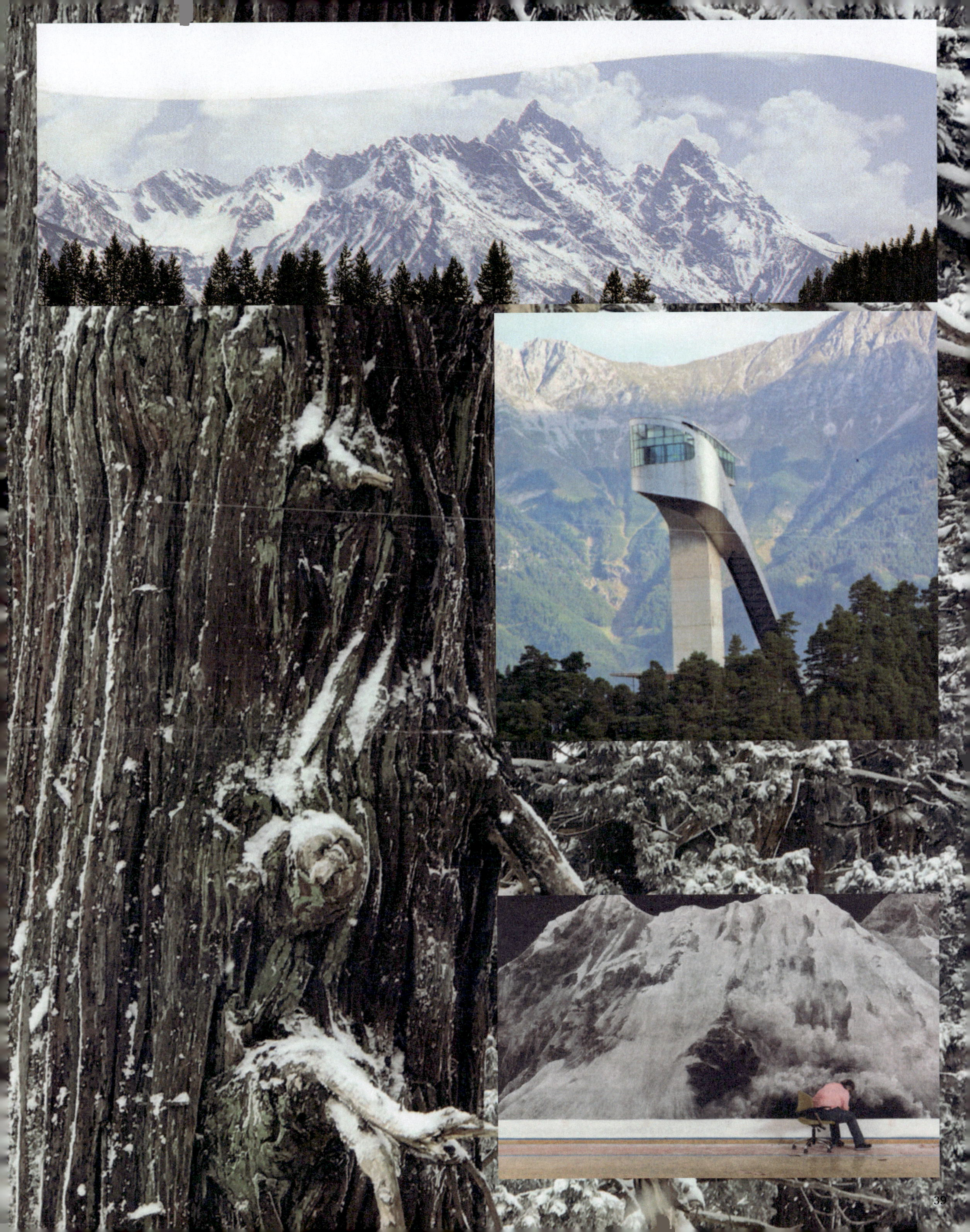

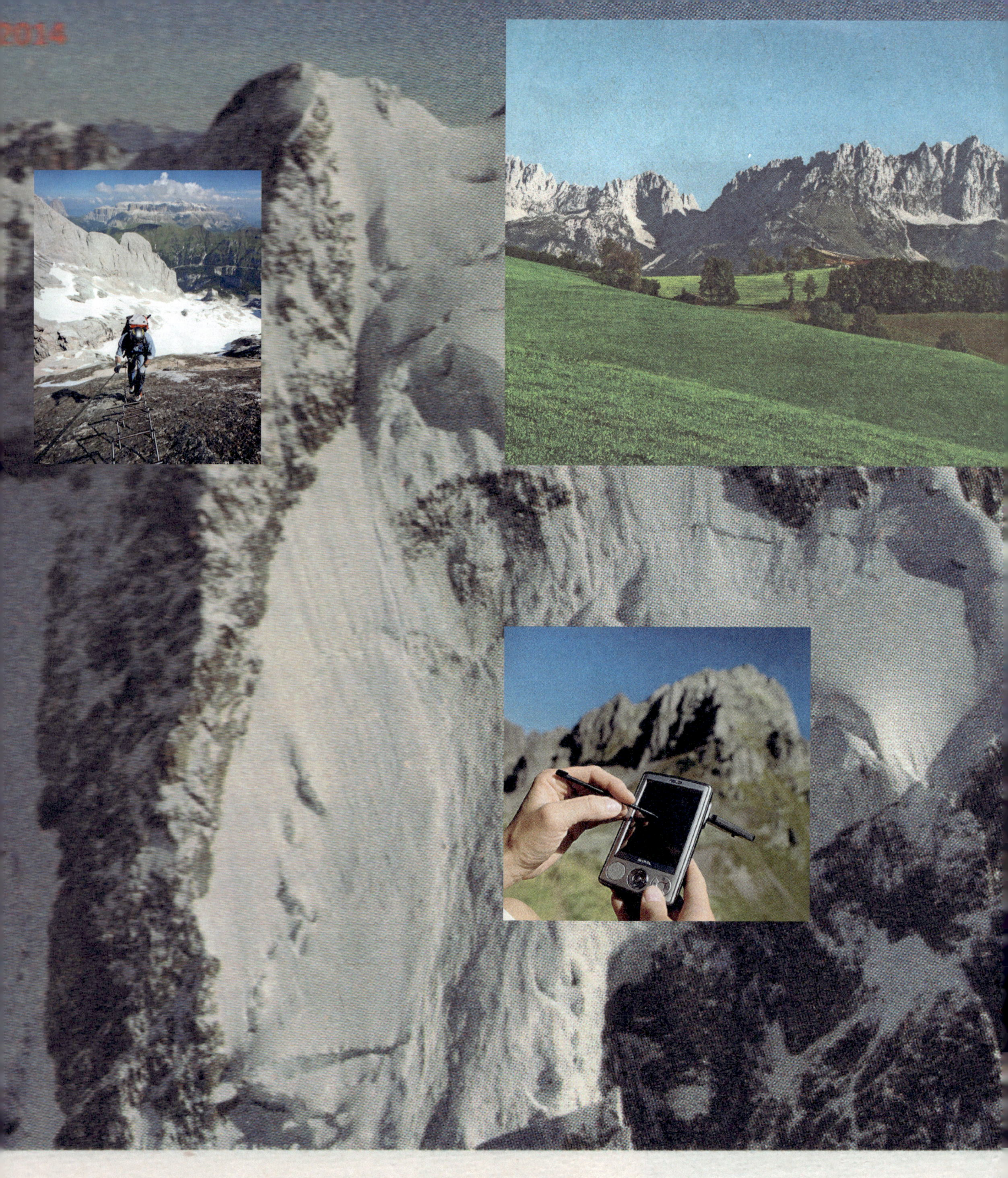

opra due immagini delle Grandes Jorasses ri

di crolli. *In alto* al rifugio Boccalatte-Piolti, ri

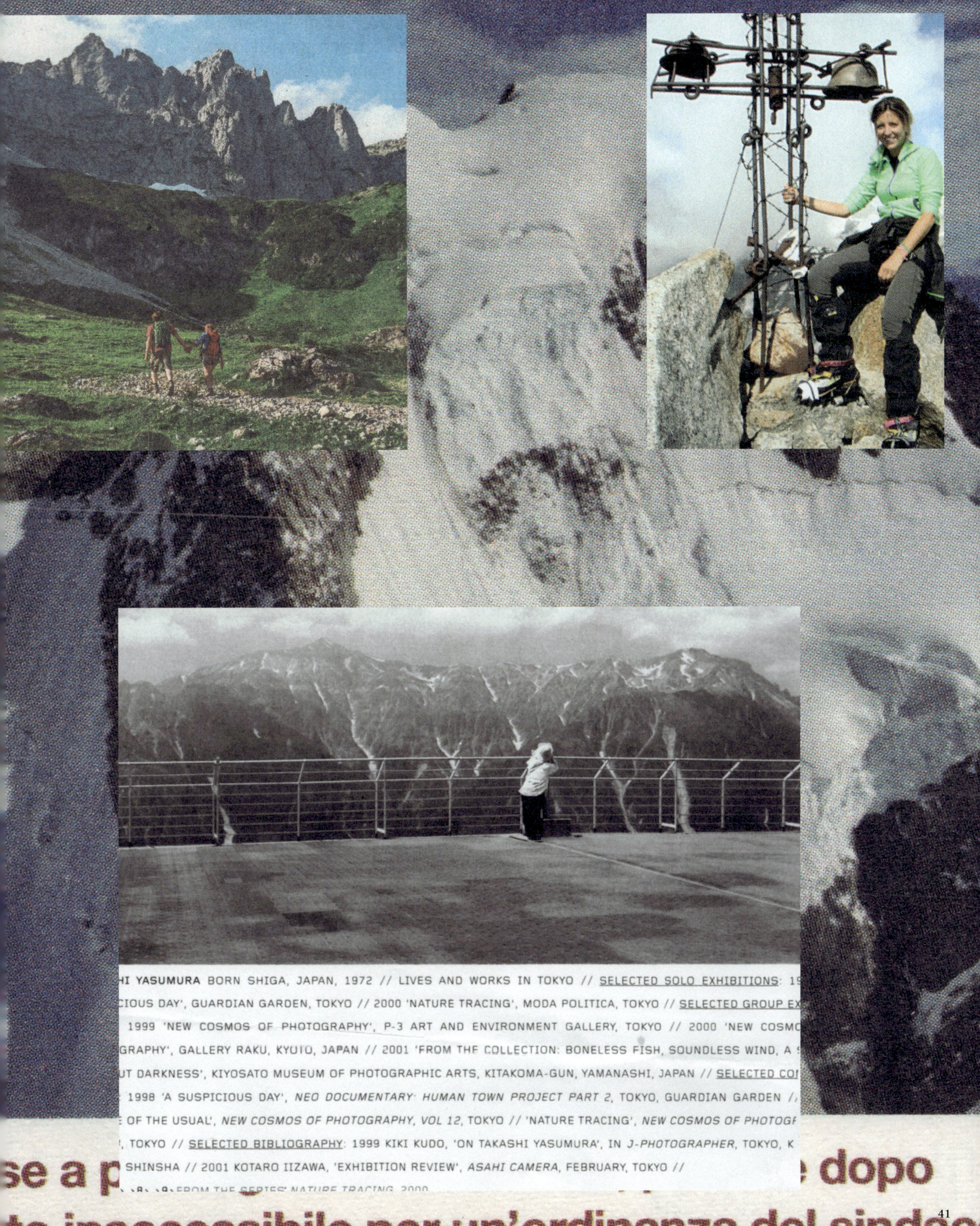
HI YASUMURA BORN SHIGA, JAPAN, 1972 // LIVES AND WORKS IN TOKYO // SELECTED SOLO EXHIBITIONS: 1
CIOUS DAY', GUARDIAN GARDEN, TOKYO // 2000 'NATURE TRACING', MODA POLITICA, TOKYO // SELECTED GROUP EX
1999 'NEW COSMOS OF PHOTOGRAPHY', P-3 ART AND ENVIRONMENT GALLERY, TOKYO // 2000 'NEW COSMO
GRAPHY', GALLERY RAKU, KYOTO, JAPAN // 2001 'FROM THE COLLECTION: BONELESS FISH, SOUNDLESS WIND, A
UT DARKNESS', KIYOSATO MUSEUM OF PHOTOGRAPHIC ARTS, KITAKOMA-GUN, YAMANASHI, JAPAN // SELECTED CO
1998 'A SUSPICIOUS DAY', NEO DOCUMENTARY: HUMAN TOWN PROJECT PART 2, TOKYO, GUARDIAN GARDEN //
OF THE USUAL', NEW COSMOS OF PHOTOGRAPHY, VOL 12, TOKYO // 'NATURE TRACING', NEW COSMOS OF PHOTOG
, TOKYO // SELECTED BIBLIOGRAPHY: 1999 KIKI KUDO, 'ON TAKASHI YASUMURA', IN J-PHOTOGRAPHER, TOKYO, K
SHINSHA // 2001 KOTARO IIZAWA, 'EXHIBITION REVIEW', ASAHI CAMERA, FEBRUARY, TOKYO //
se a p
dopo
to inaccessibile per un'ordinanza del sindac

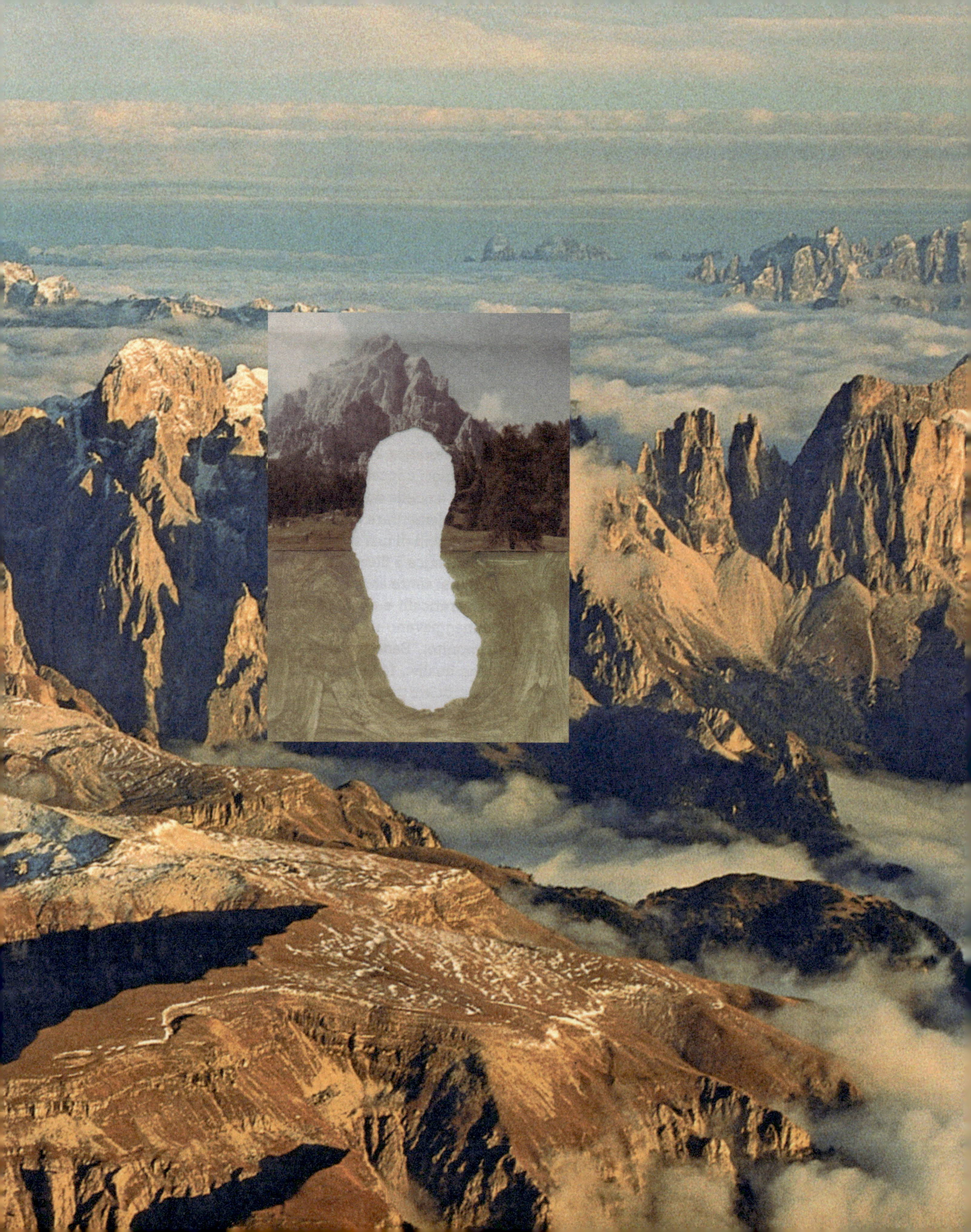

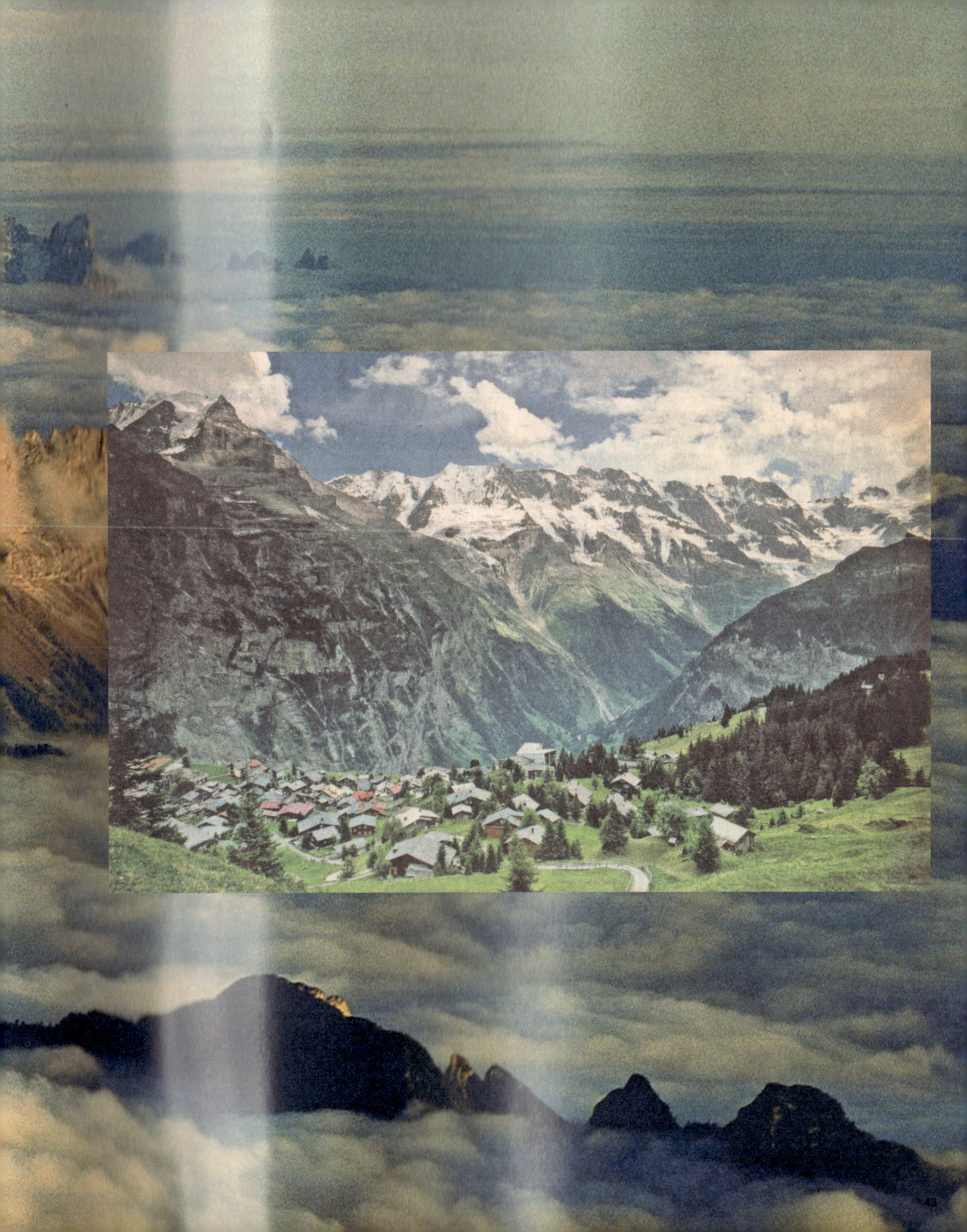

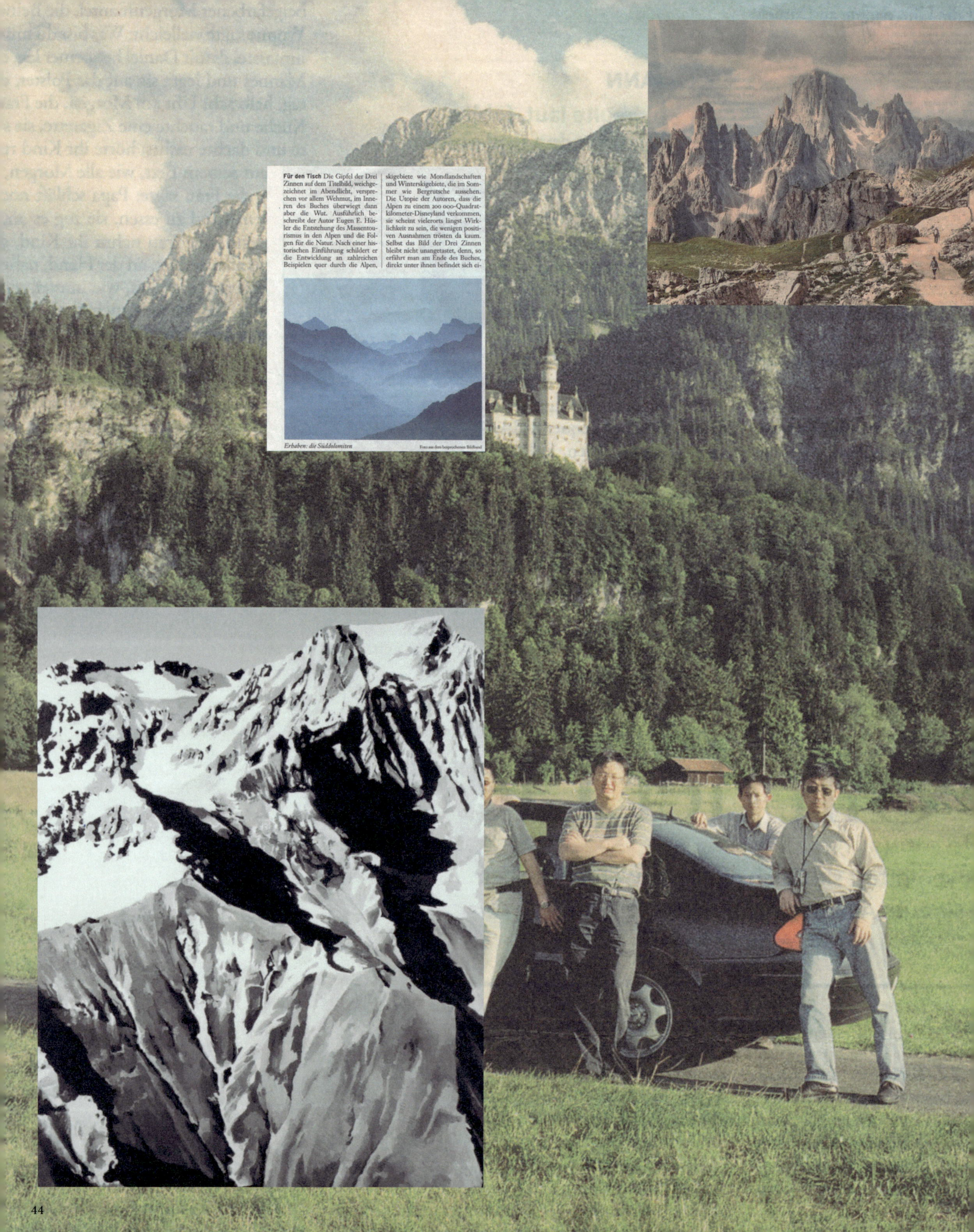

Für den Tisch Die Gipfel der Drei Zinnen auf dem Titelbild, weichgezeichnet im Abendlicht, versprechen vor allem Wehmut, im Inneren des Buches überwiegt dann aber die Wut. Ausführlich beschreibt der Autor Eugen E. Hüsler die Entstehung des Massentourismus in den Alpen und die Folgen für die Natur. Nach einer historischen Einführung schildert er die Entwicklung an zahlreichen Beispielen quer durch die Alpen, skigebiete wie Mondlandschaften und Winterskigebiete, die im Sommer wie Bergrutsche aussehen. Die Utopie der Autoren, dass die Alpen zu einem 200 000-Quadratkilometer-Disneyland verkommen, sie scheint vielerorts längst Wirklichkeit zu sein, die wenigen positiven Ausnahmen trösten da kaum. Selbst das Bild der Drei Zinnen bleibt nicht unangetastet, denn, so erfährt man am Ende des Buches, direkt unter ihnen befindet sich ei-

Erbaben: die Süddolomiten

Foto aus dem besprochenen Bildband

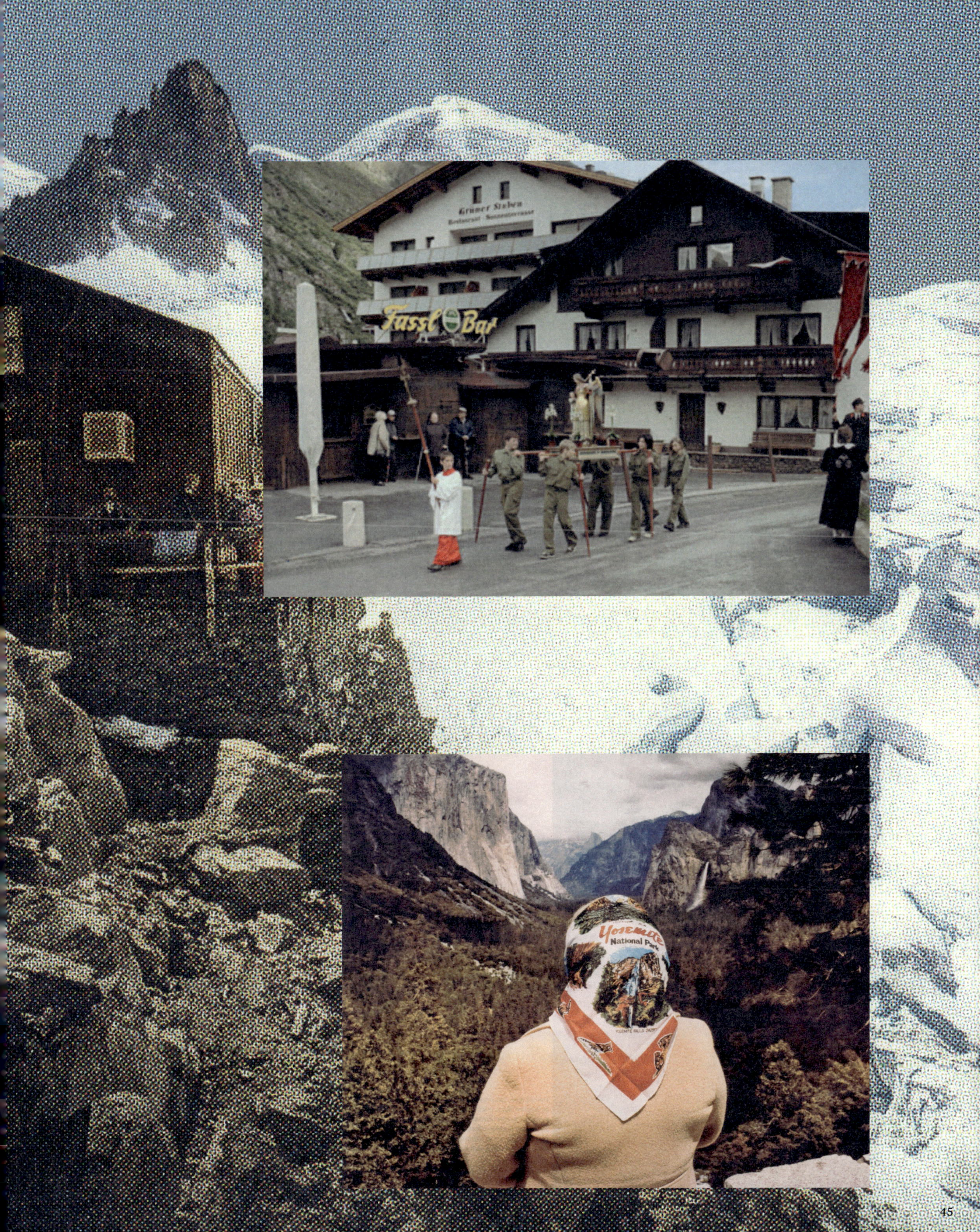
Fassl
Yosemite
National Park

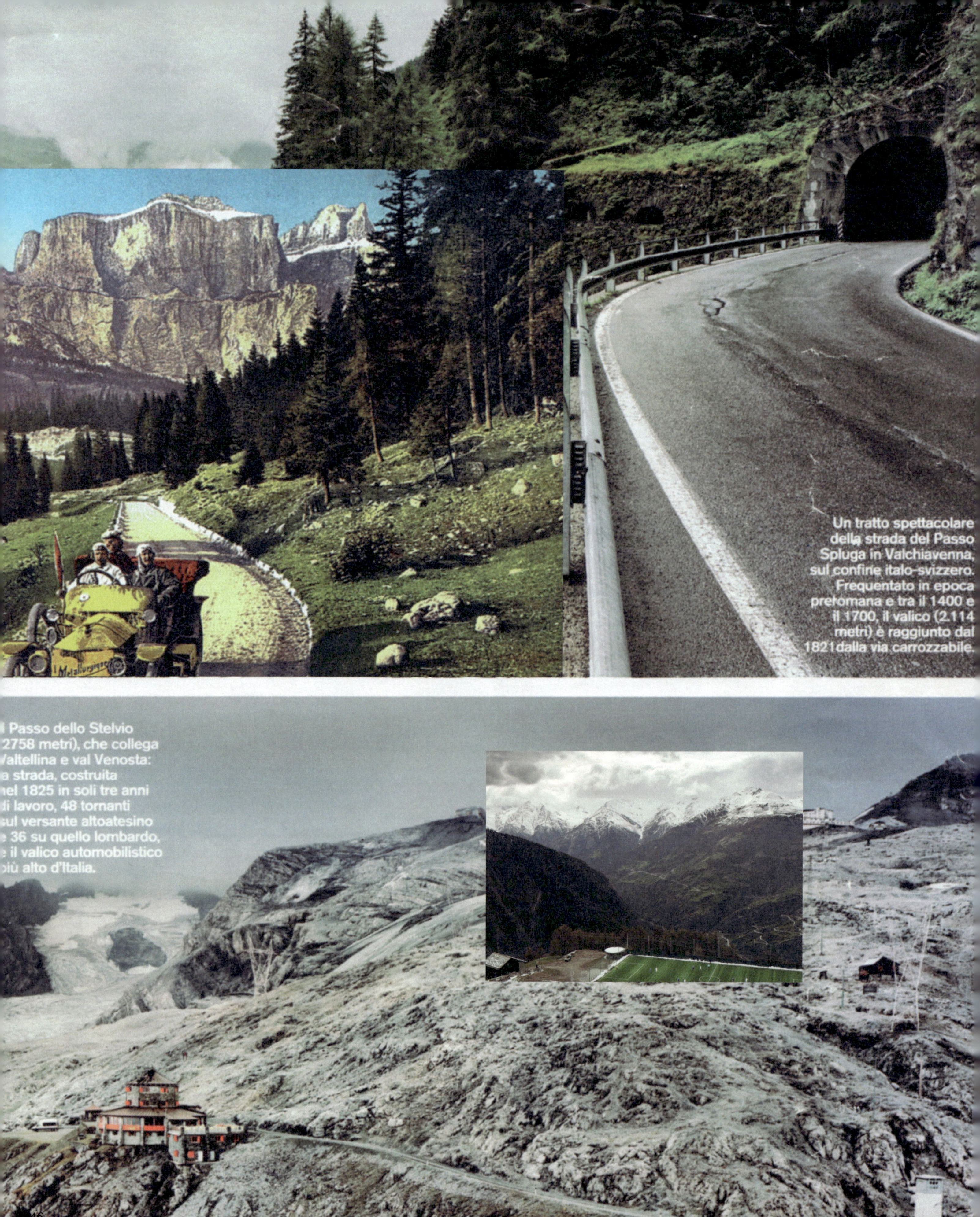

Un tratto spettacolare della strada del Passo Spluga in Valchiavenna, sul confine italo-svizzero. Frequentato in epoca preromana e tra il 1400 e il 1700, il valico (2.114 metri) è raggiunto dal 1821dalla via carrozzabile.

Il Passo dello Stelvio (2758 metri), che collega Valtellina e val Venosta: la strada, costruita nel 1825 in soli tre anni di lavoro, 48 tornanti sul versante altoatesino e 36 su quello lombardo, è il valico automobilistico più alto d'Italia.

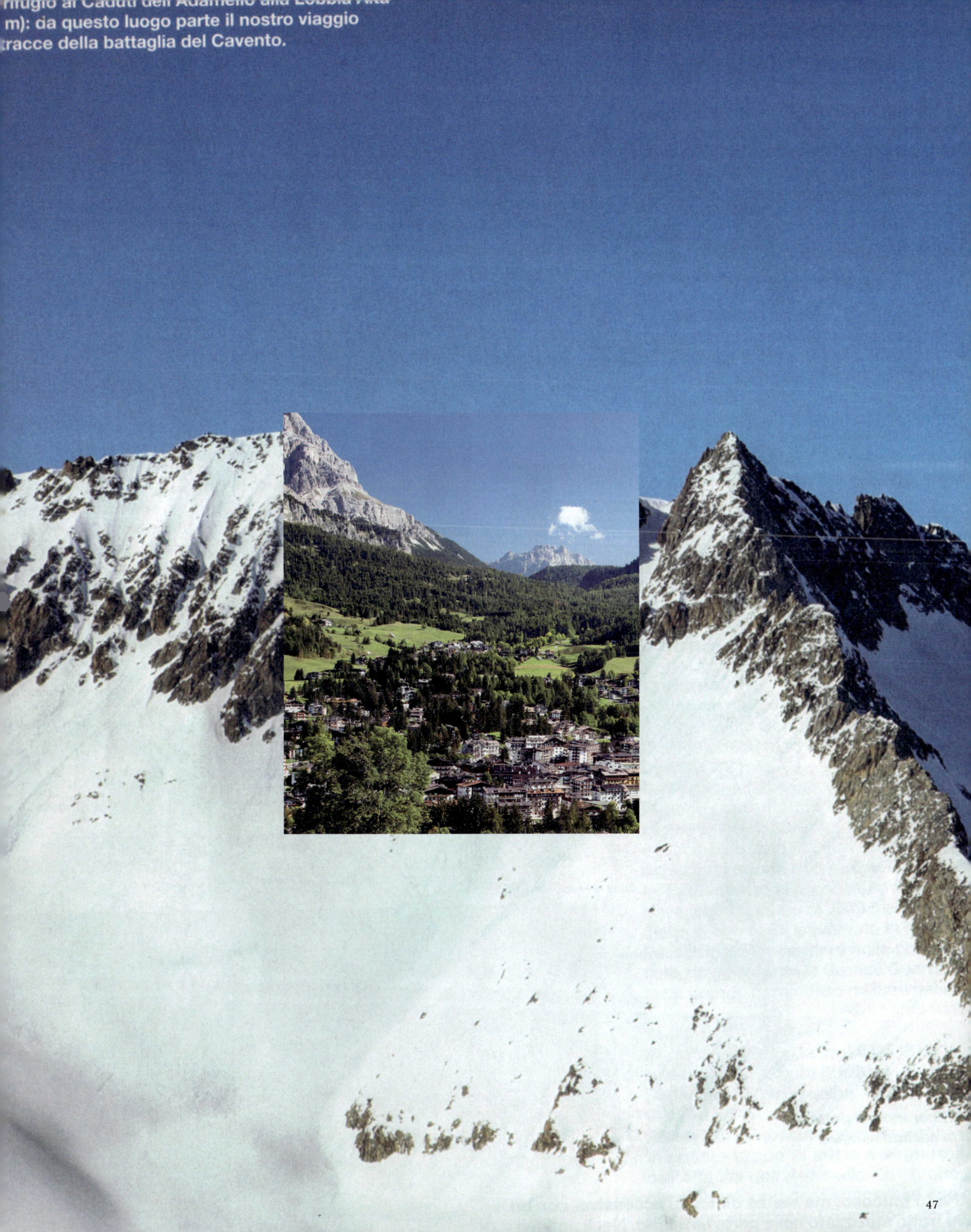

rifugio ai Caduti dell'Adamello alla Lobbia Alta
m): da questo luogo parte il nostro viaggio
tracce della battaglia del Cavento.

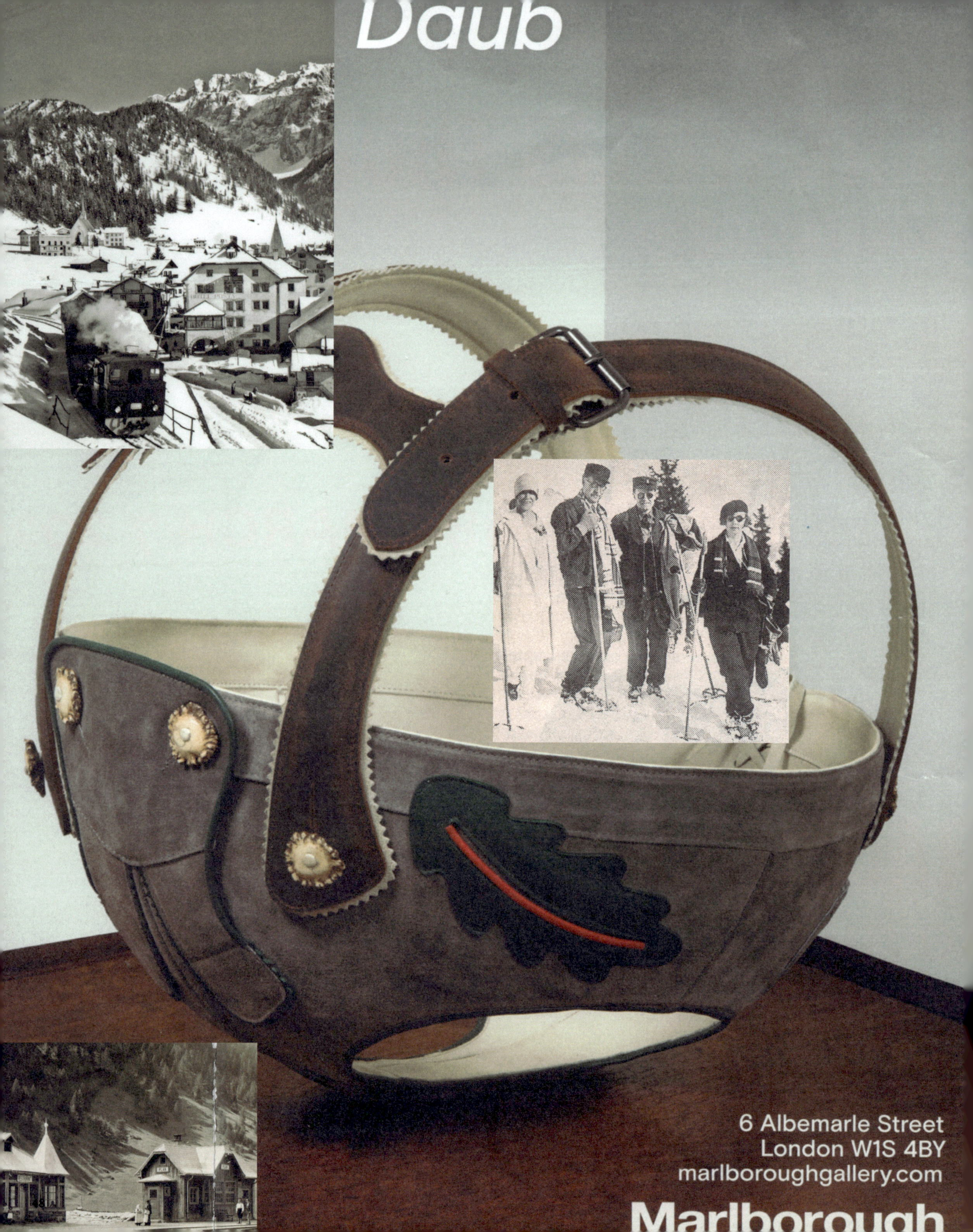
Daub
6 Albemarle Street
London W1S 4BY
marlboroughgallery.com
Marlborough

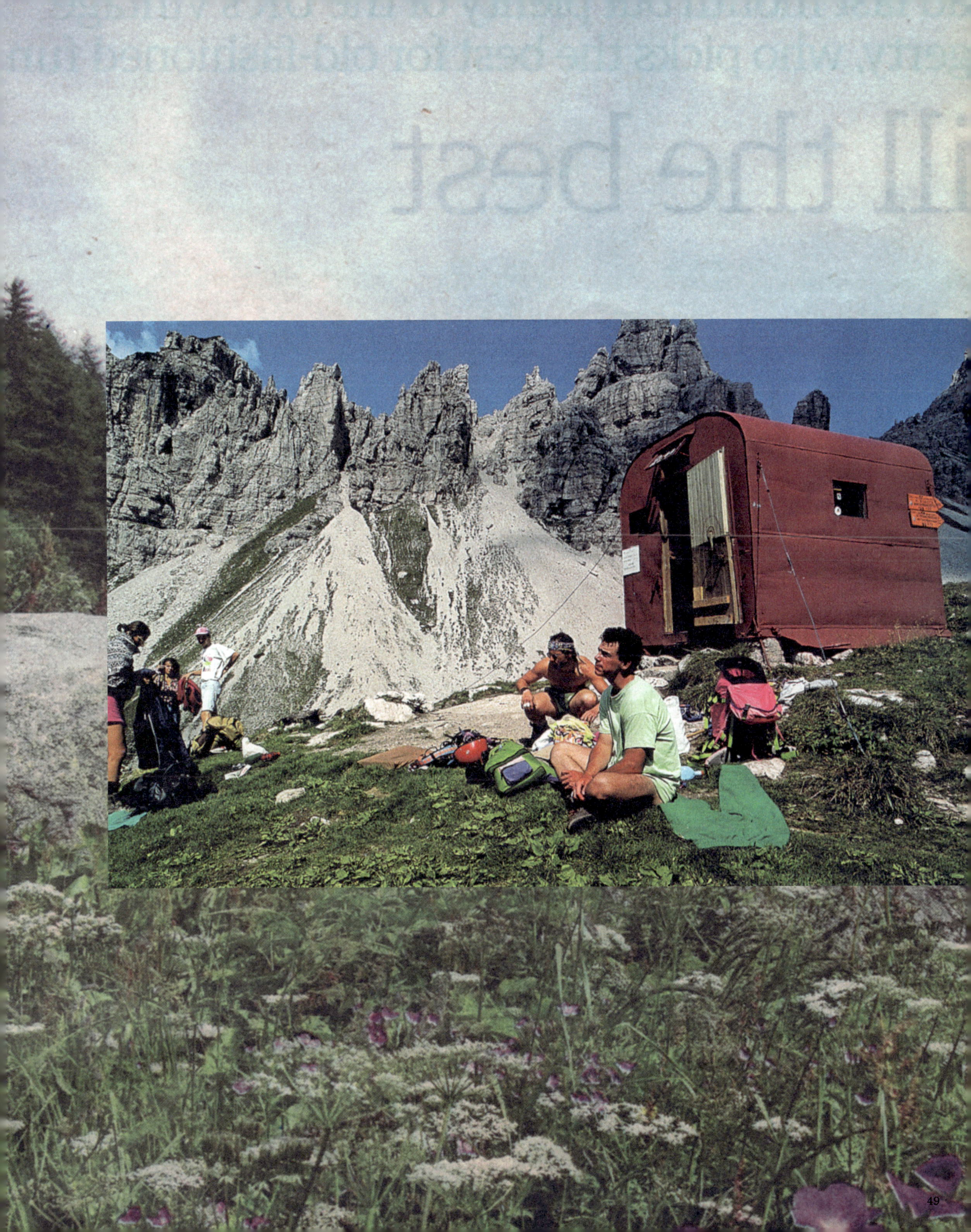

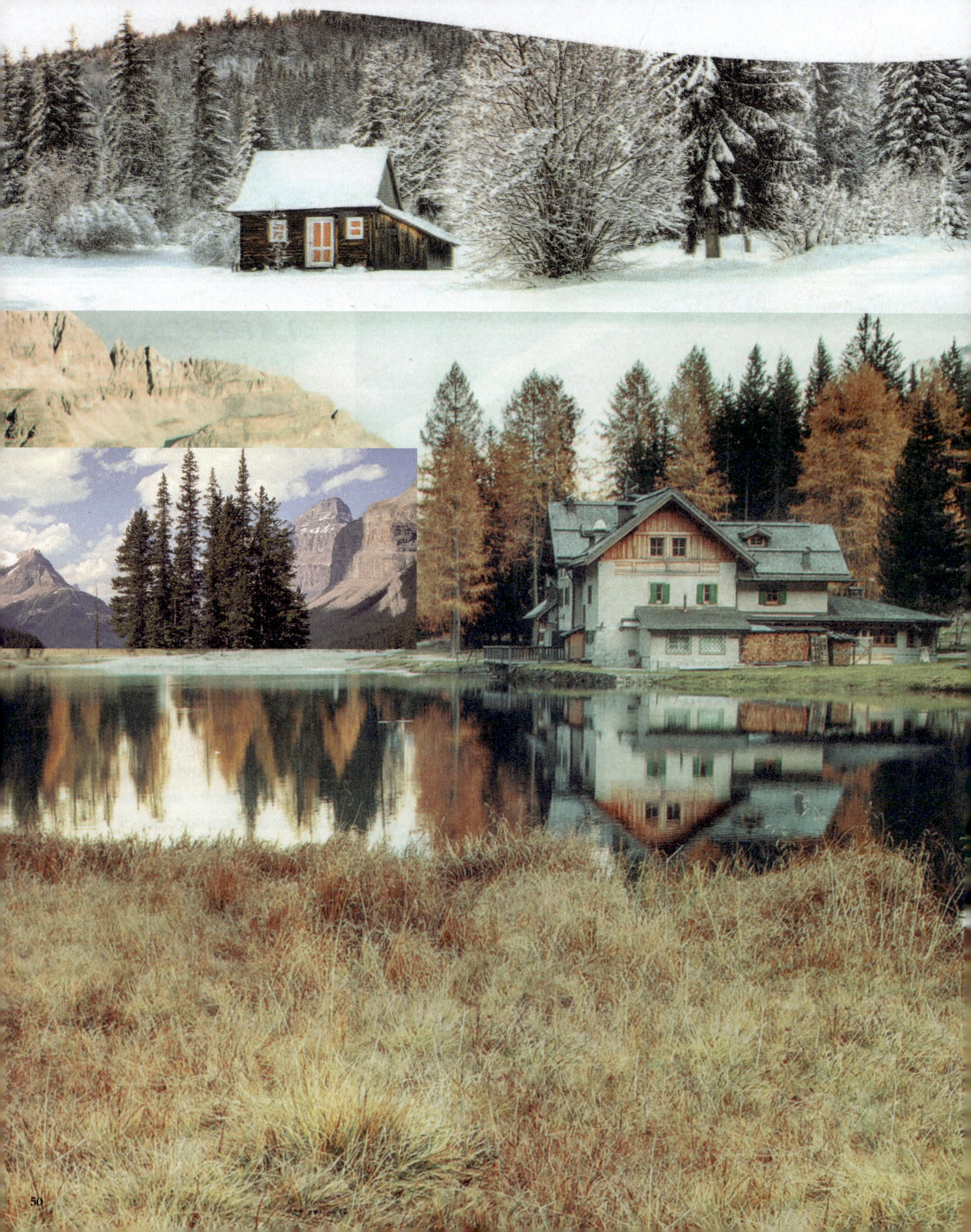

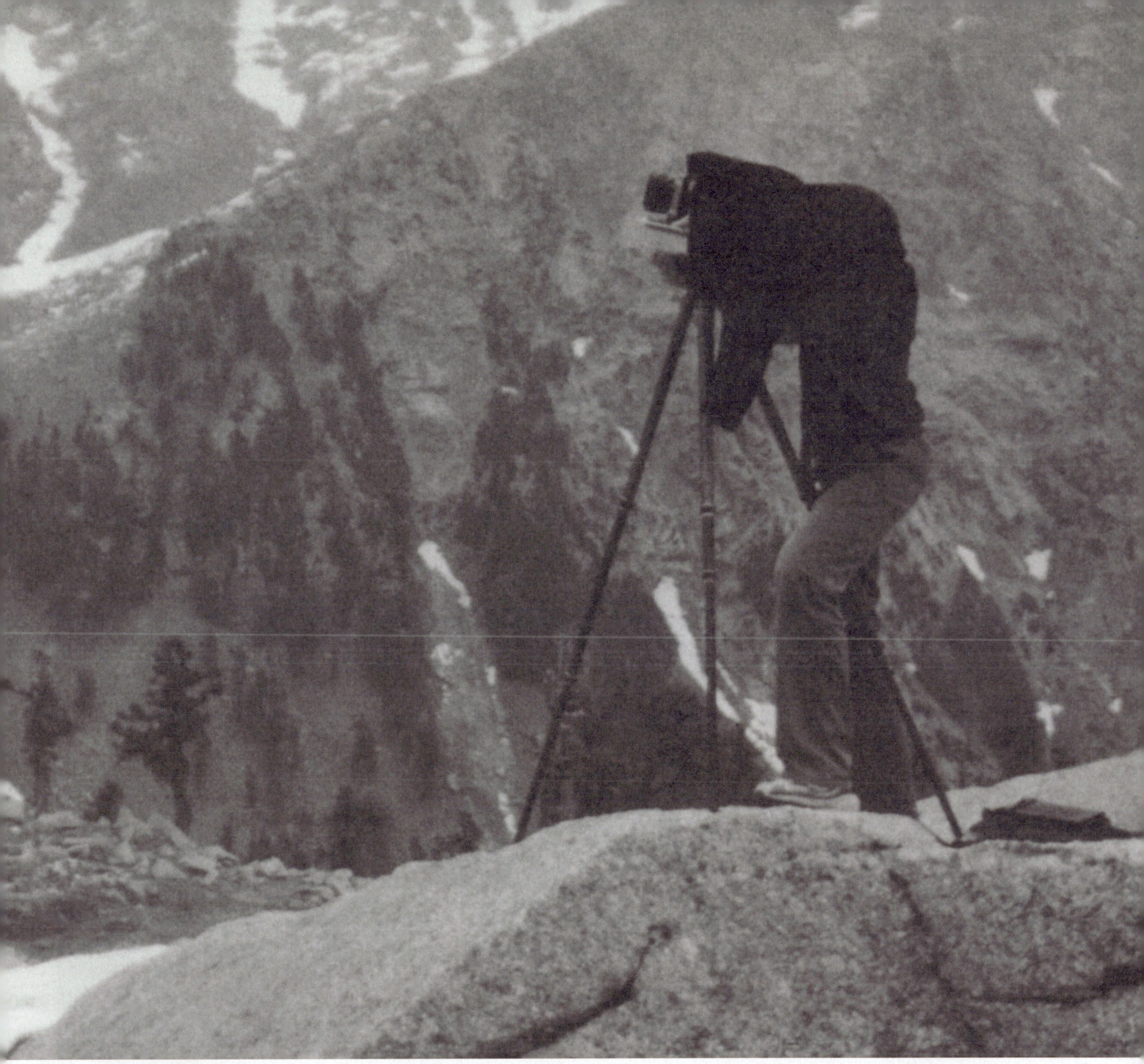

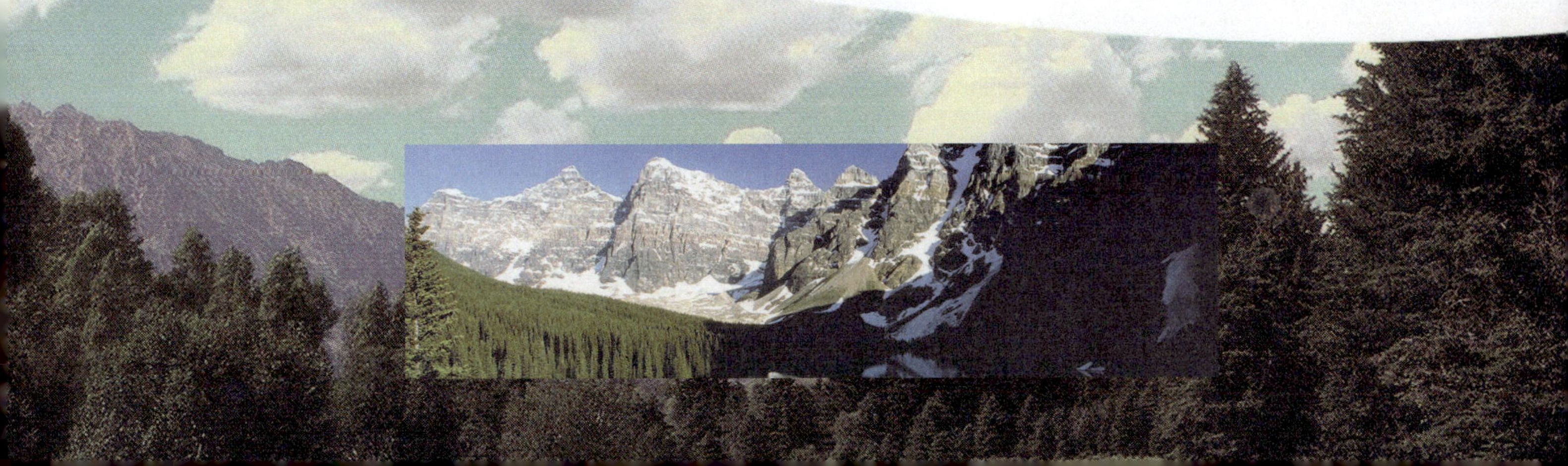

Dear Alfredo

I hope this finds you well!

As promised – some kind of landscape for your collection.

All my best,

Anne

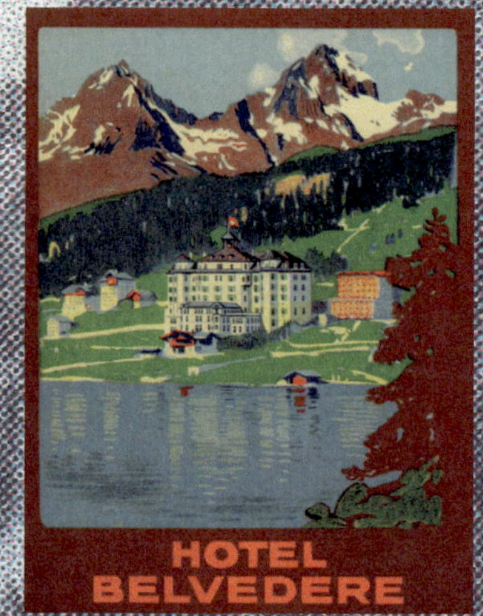

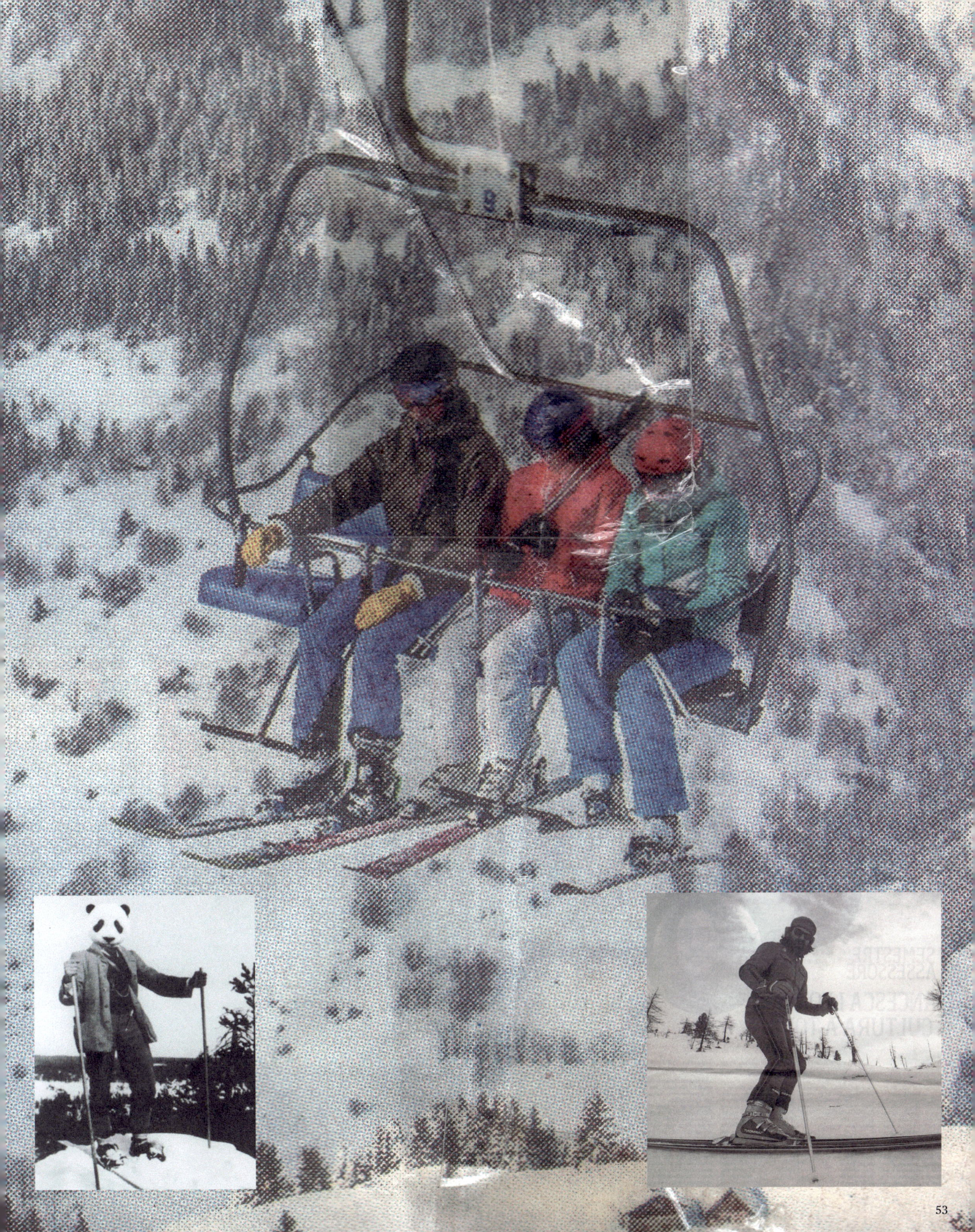

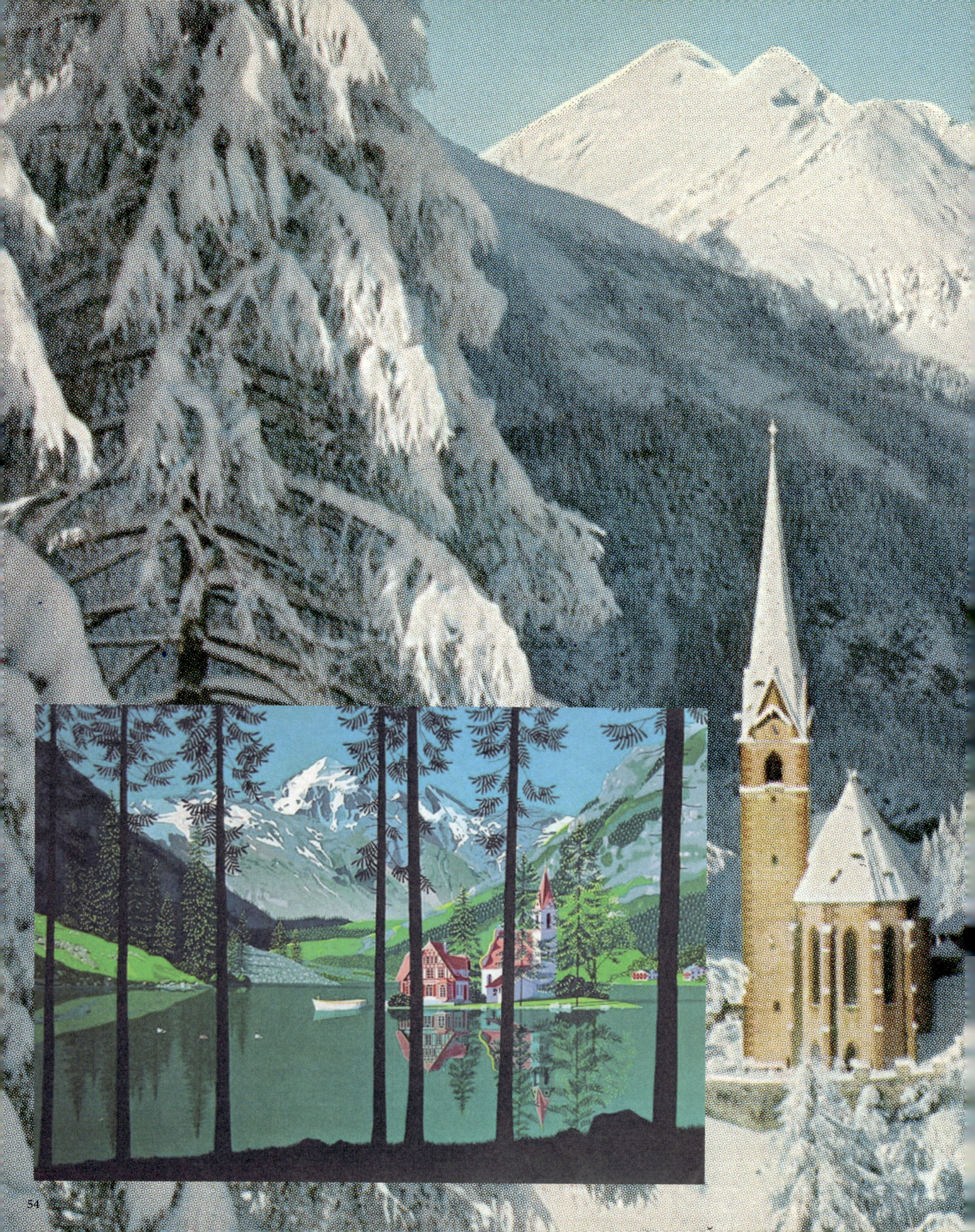

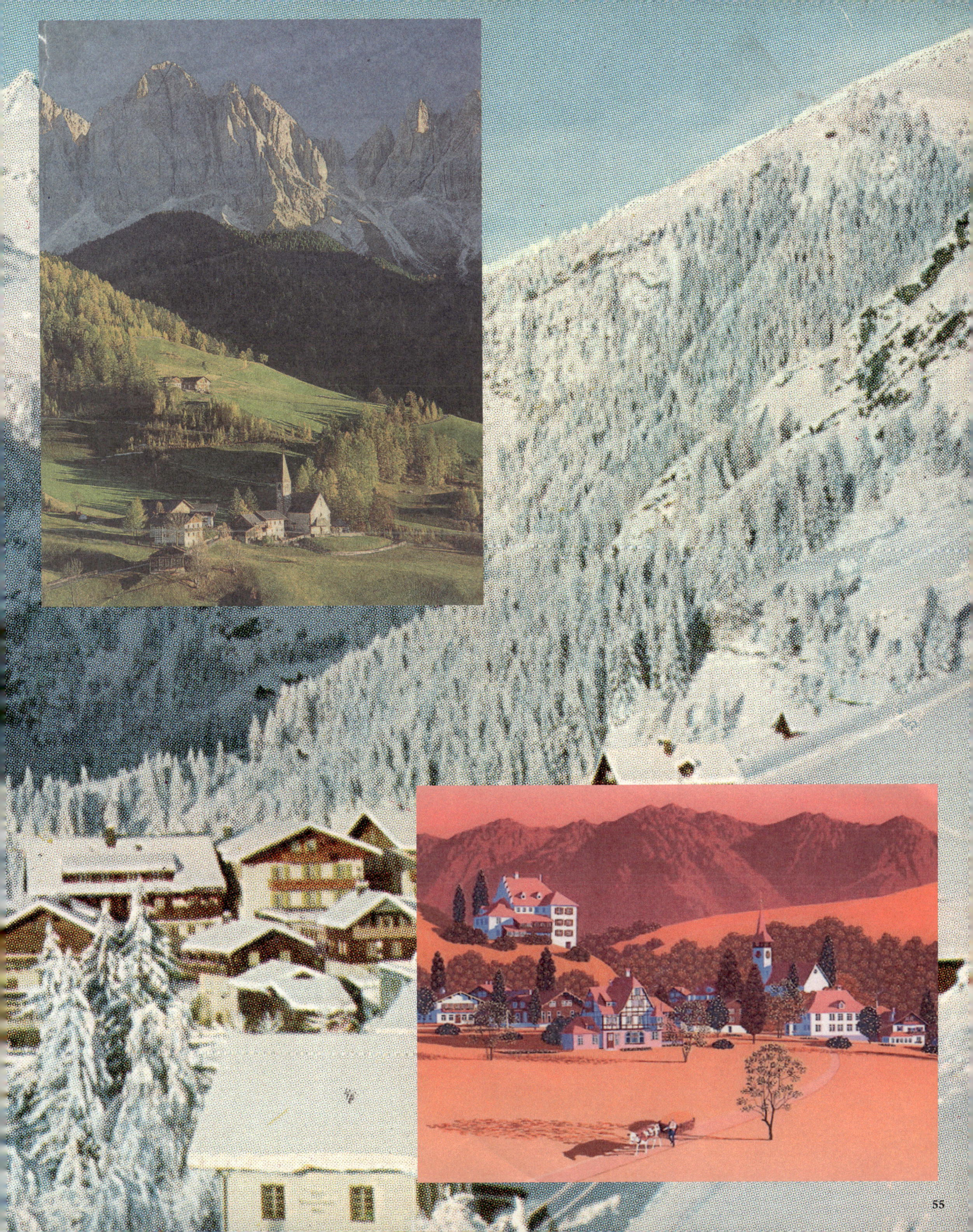

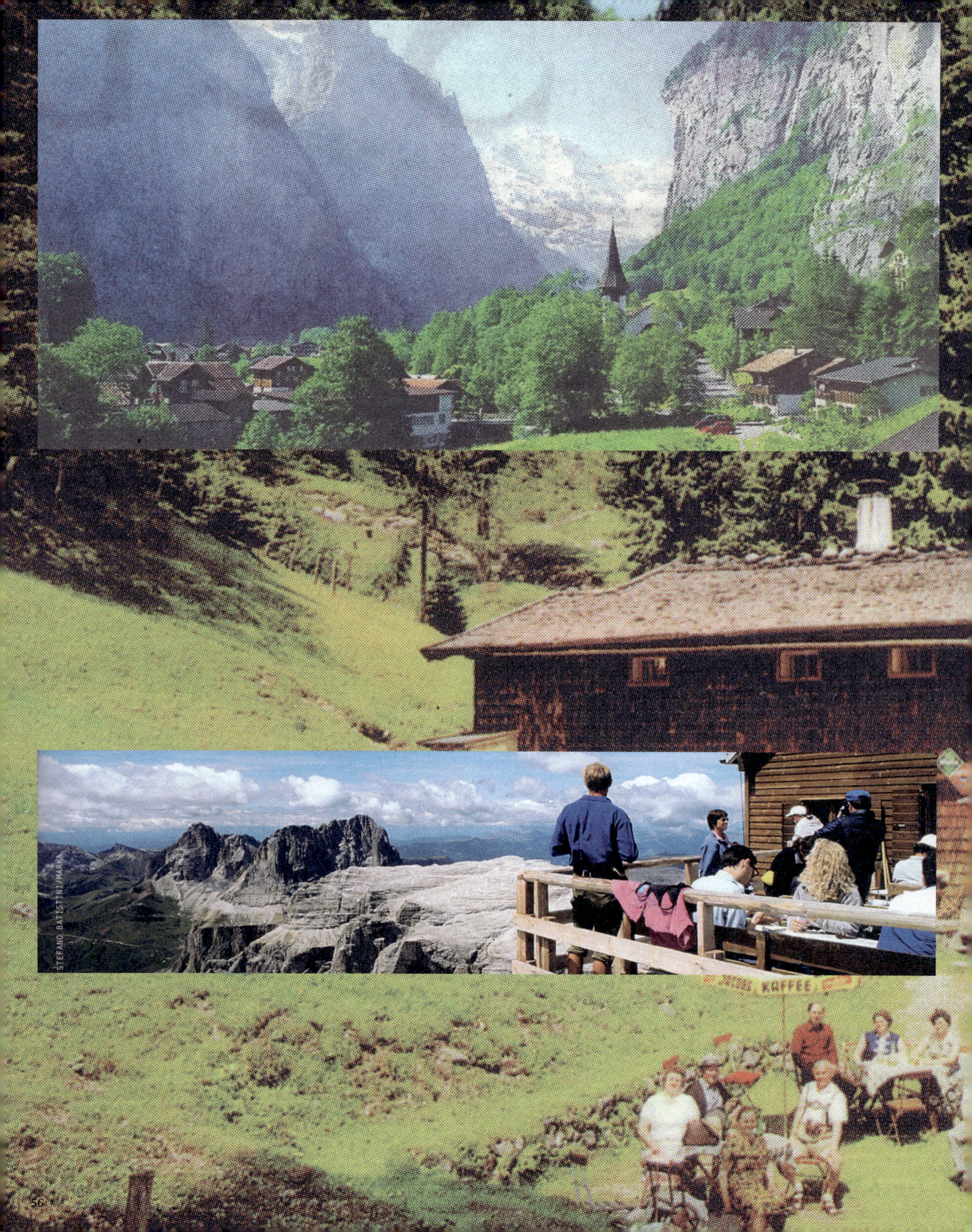
STEFANO BATTISTINI/MARKA
KAFFEE

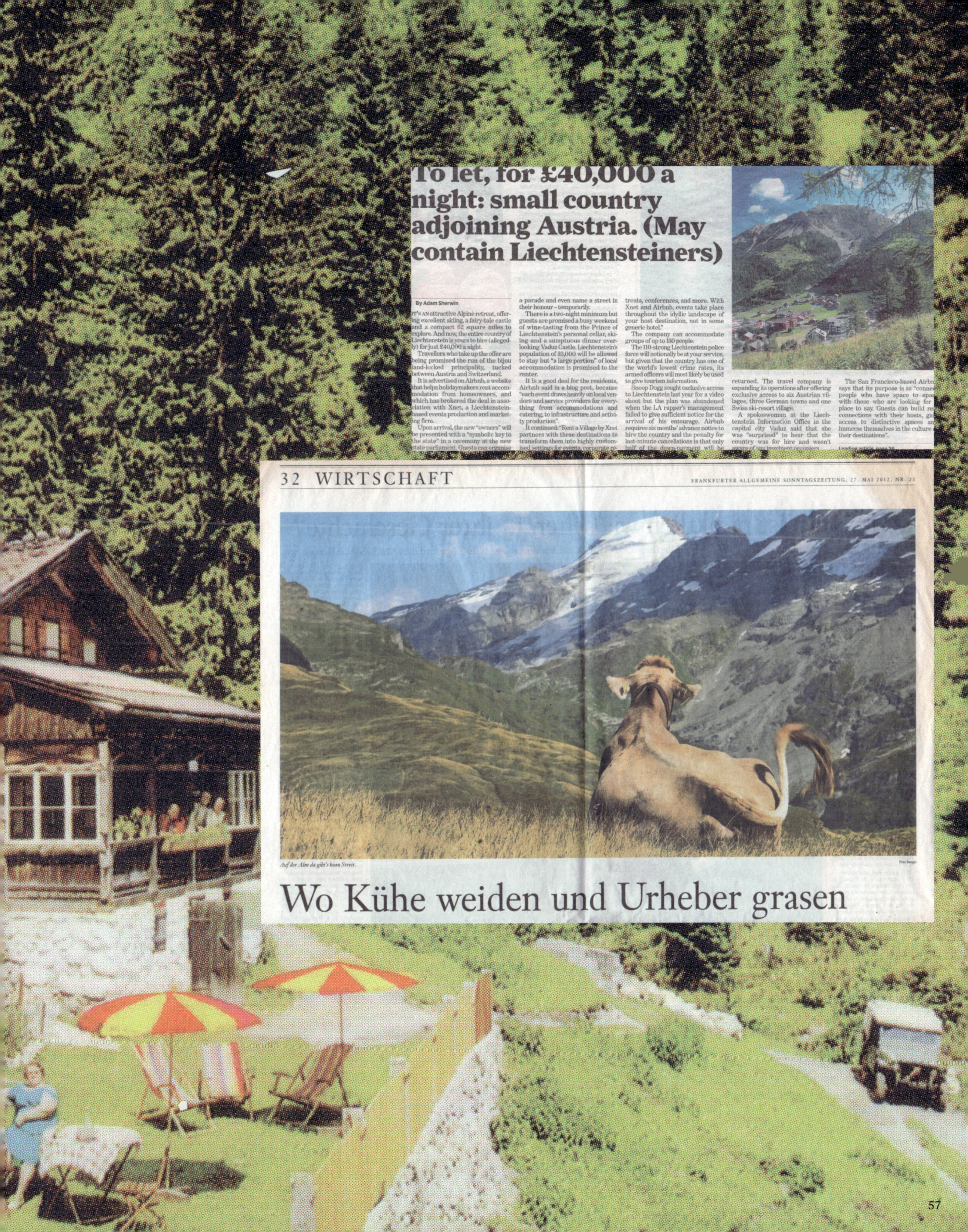

To let, for £40,000 a night: small country adjoining Austria. (May contain Liechtensteiners)

By Adam Sherwin

IT'S AN attractive Alpine retreat, offering excellent skiing, a fairy-tale castle and a compact 62 square miles to explore. And now, the entire country of Liechtenstein is yours to hire (allegedly) for just £40,000 a night.

Travellers who take up the offer are being promised the run of the bijou land-locked principality, tucked between Austria and Switzerland.

It is advertised on Airbnb, a website that helps holidaymakers rent accommodation from homeowners, and which has brokered the deal in association with Xnet, a Liechtenstein-based events production and marketing firm.

Upon arrival, the new "owners" will be presented with a "symbolic key to the state" in a ceremony at the new state parliament. Guests can organise a parade and even name a street in their honour – temporarily.

There is a two-night minimum but guests are promised a busy weekend of wine-tasting from the Prince of Liechtenstein's personal cellar, skiing and a sumptuous dinner overlooking Vaduz Castle. Liechtenstein's population of 33,000 will be allowed to stay but "a large portion" of local accommodation is promised to the renter.

It is a good deal for the residents, Airbnb said in a blog post, because "each event draws heavily on local vendors and service providers for everything from accommodations and catering, to infrastructure and activity production".

It continued: "Rent a Village by Xnet partners with these destinations to transform them into highly customised settings for events, corporate retreats, conferences, and more. With Xnet and Airbnb, events take place throughout the idyllic landscape of your host destination, not in some generic hotel."

The company can accommodate groups of up to 150 people.

The 110-strong Liechtenstein police force will notionally be at your service, but given that the country has one of the world's lowest crime rates, its armed officers will most likely be used to give tourism information.

Snoop Dogg sought exclusive access to Liechtenstein last year for a video shoot but the plan was abandoned when the LA rapper's management failed to give sufficient notice for the arrival of his entourage. Airbnb requires six months' advance notice to hire the country and the penalty for last-minute cancellations is that only half of the down-payment will be returned. The travel company is expanding its operations after offering exclusive access to six Austrian villages, three German towns and one Swiss ski-resort village.

A spokeswoman at the Liechtenstein Information Office in the capital city Vaduz said that she was "surprised" to hear that the country was for hire and wasn't aware of any imminent occupiers.

The San Francisco-based Airbnb says that its purpose is to "connect people who have space to spare with those who are looking for a place to stay. Guests can build real connections with their hosts, gain access to distinctive spaces and immerse themselves in the culture of their destinations".

Leading article, page 36

FRANKFURTER ALLGEMEINE SONNTAGSZEITUNG, 27. MAI 2012, NR. 21

Auf der Alm da gibt's koan Streit.

Foto Imago

Wo Kühe weiden und Urheber grasen

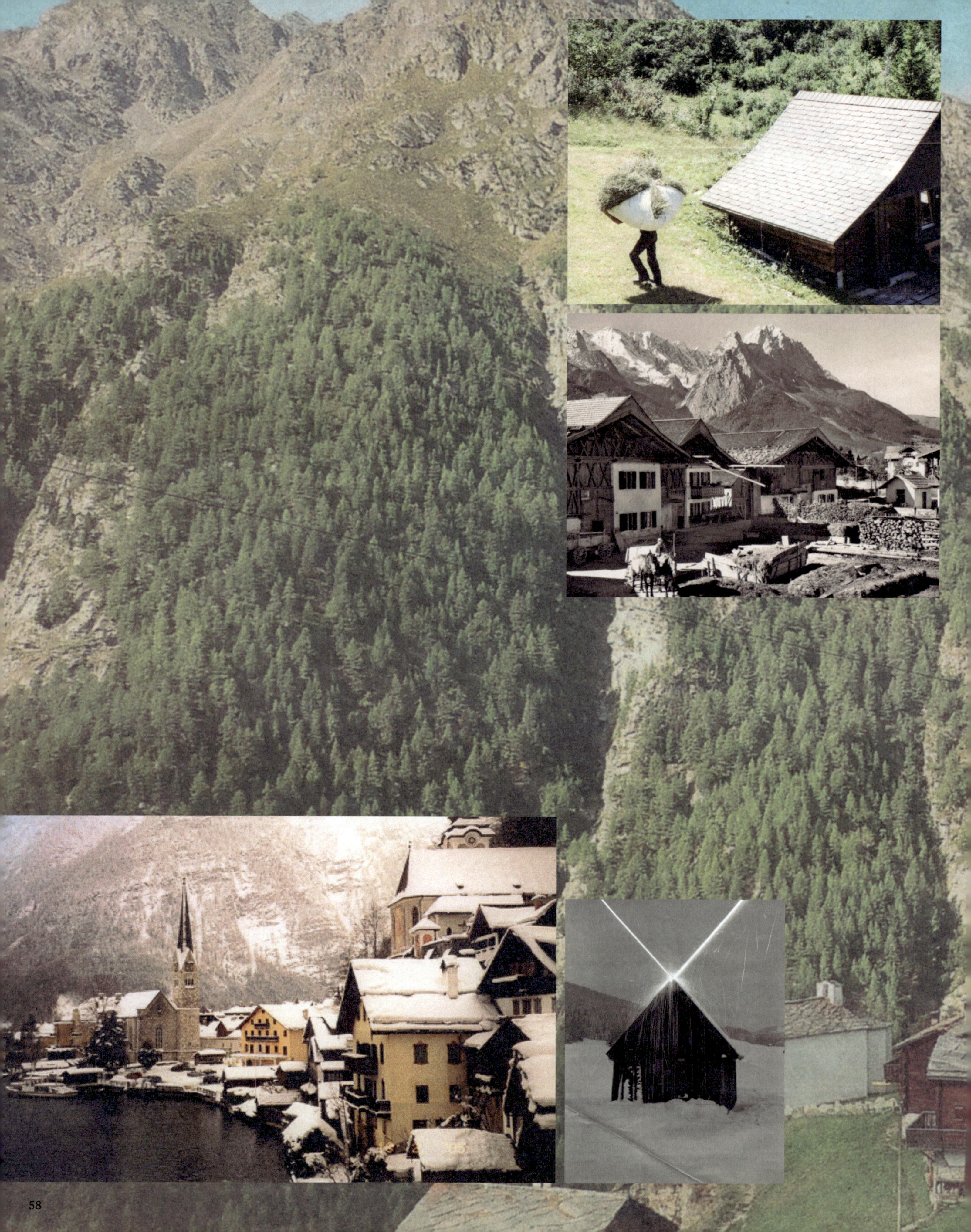

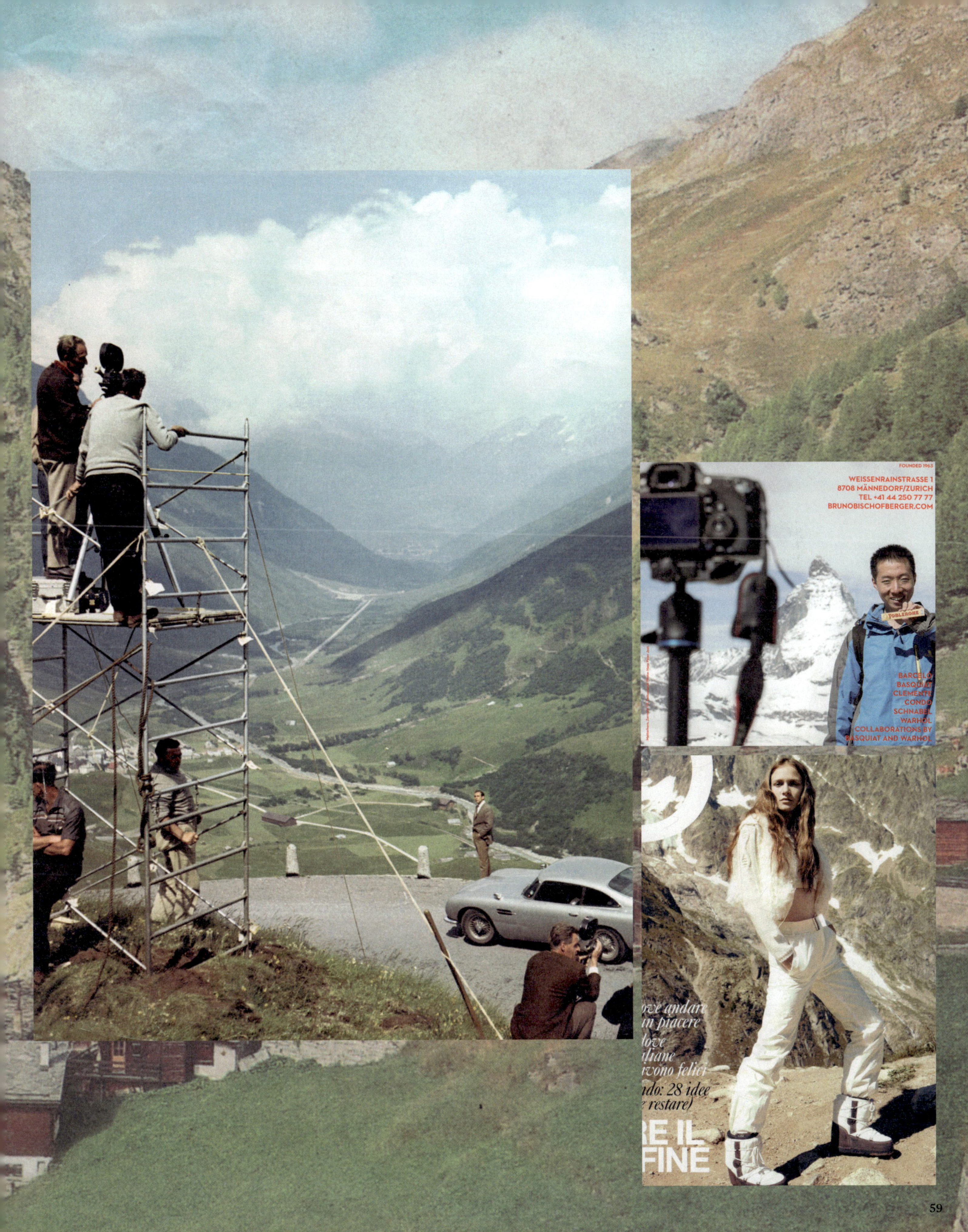
FOUNDED 1963
WEISSENRAINSTRASSE 1
8708 MÄNNEDORF/ZURICH
TEL +41 44 250 77 77
BRUNOBISCHOFBERGER.COM
TOBLERONE
BARCELO
BASQUIAT
CLEMENTE
CONDO
SCHNABEL
WARHOL
COLLABORATIONS BY
BASQUIAT AND WARHOL
ove andare
in piacere
dove
liane
ivono felici
ndo: 28 idee
e restare)
RE IL
FINE

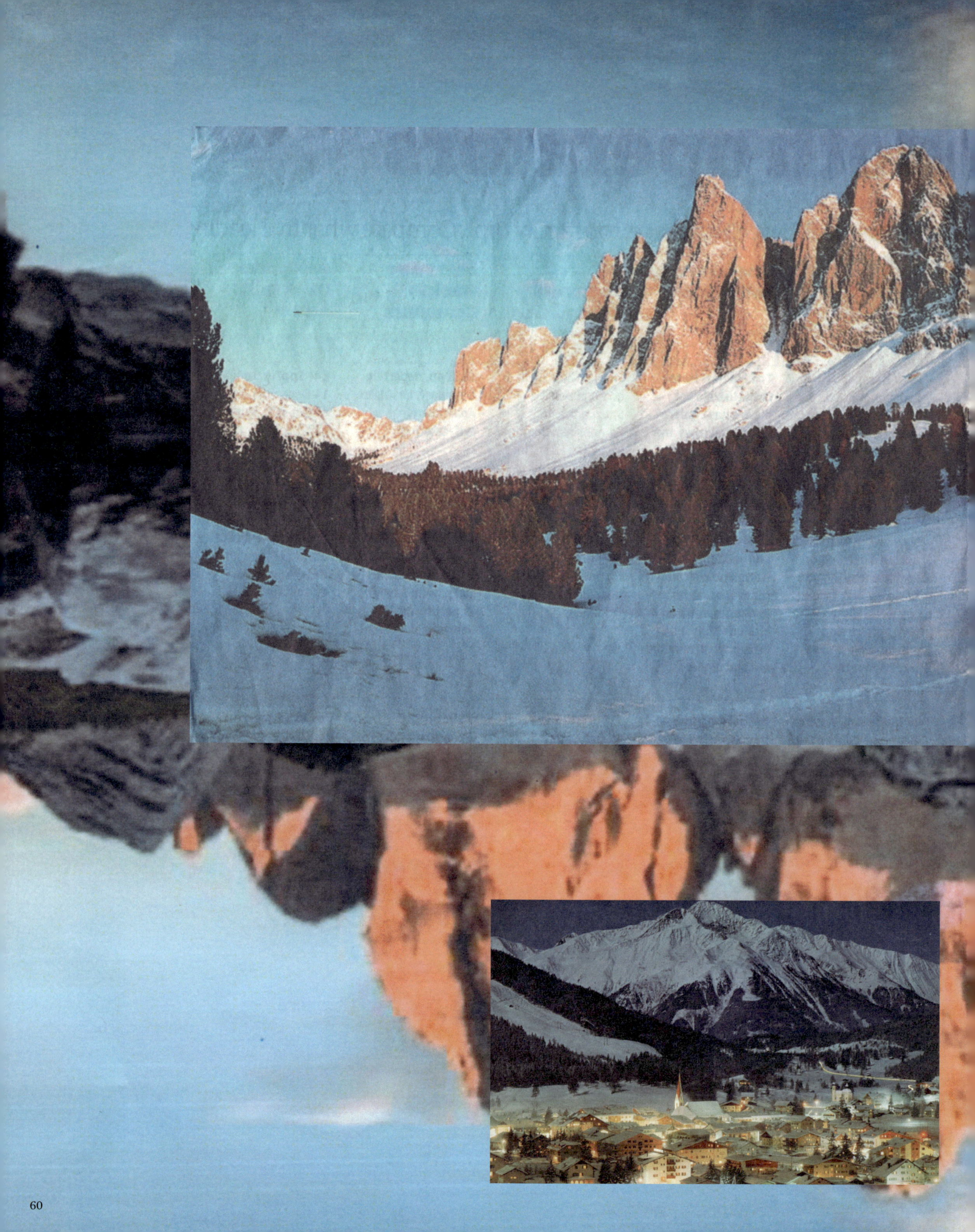

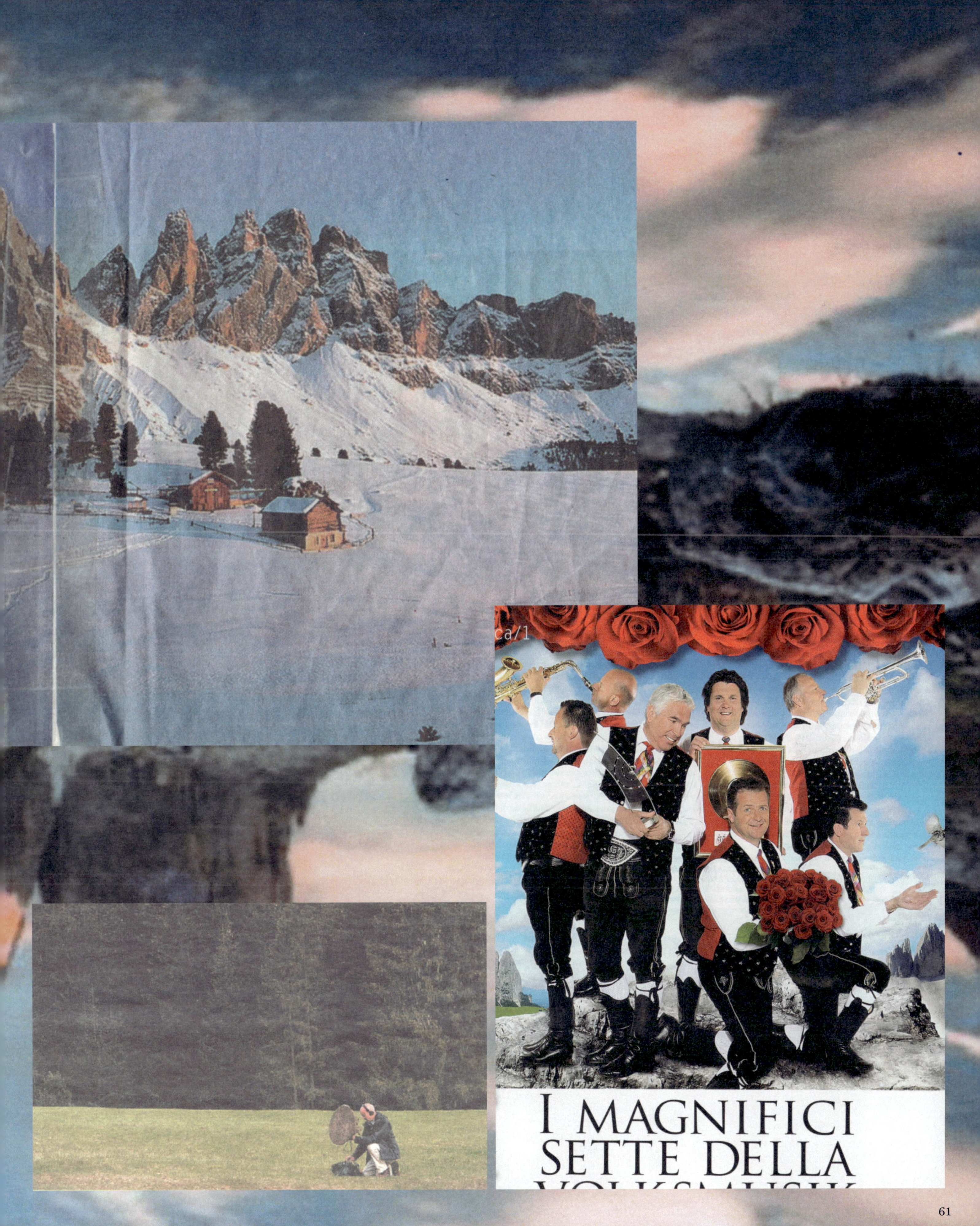
ca/1
I MAGNIFICI
SETTE DELLA

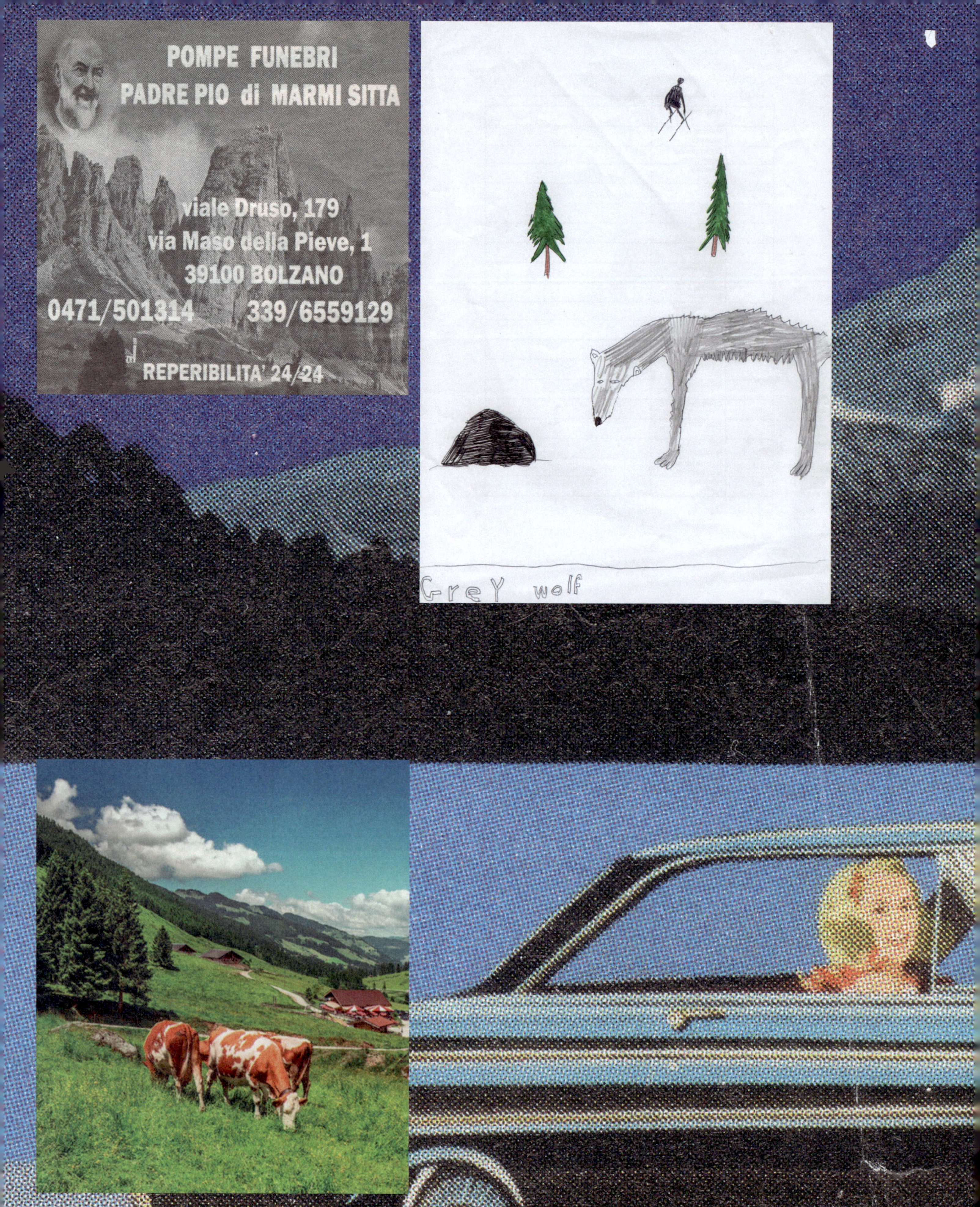

POMPE FUNEBRI
PADRE PIO di MARMI SITTA

viale Druso, 179
via Maso della Pieve, 1
39100 BOLZANO
0471/501314 339/6559129

REPERIBILITA' 24/24

Grey wolf

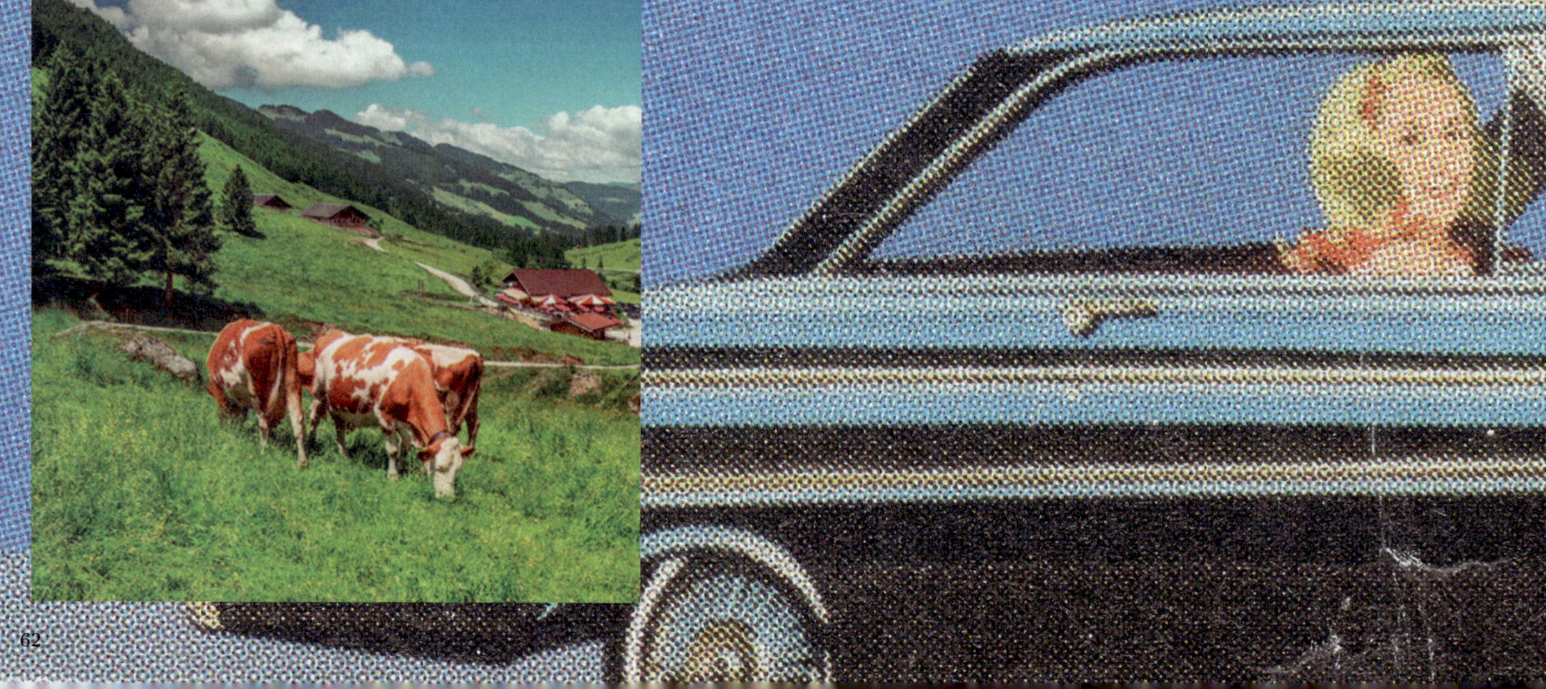

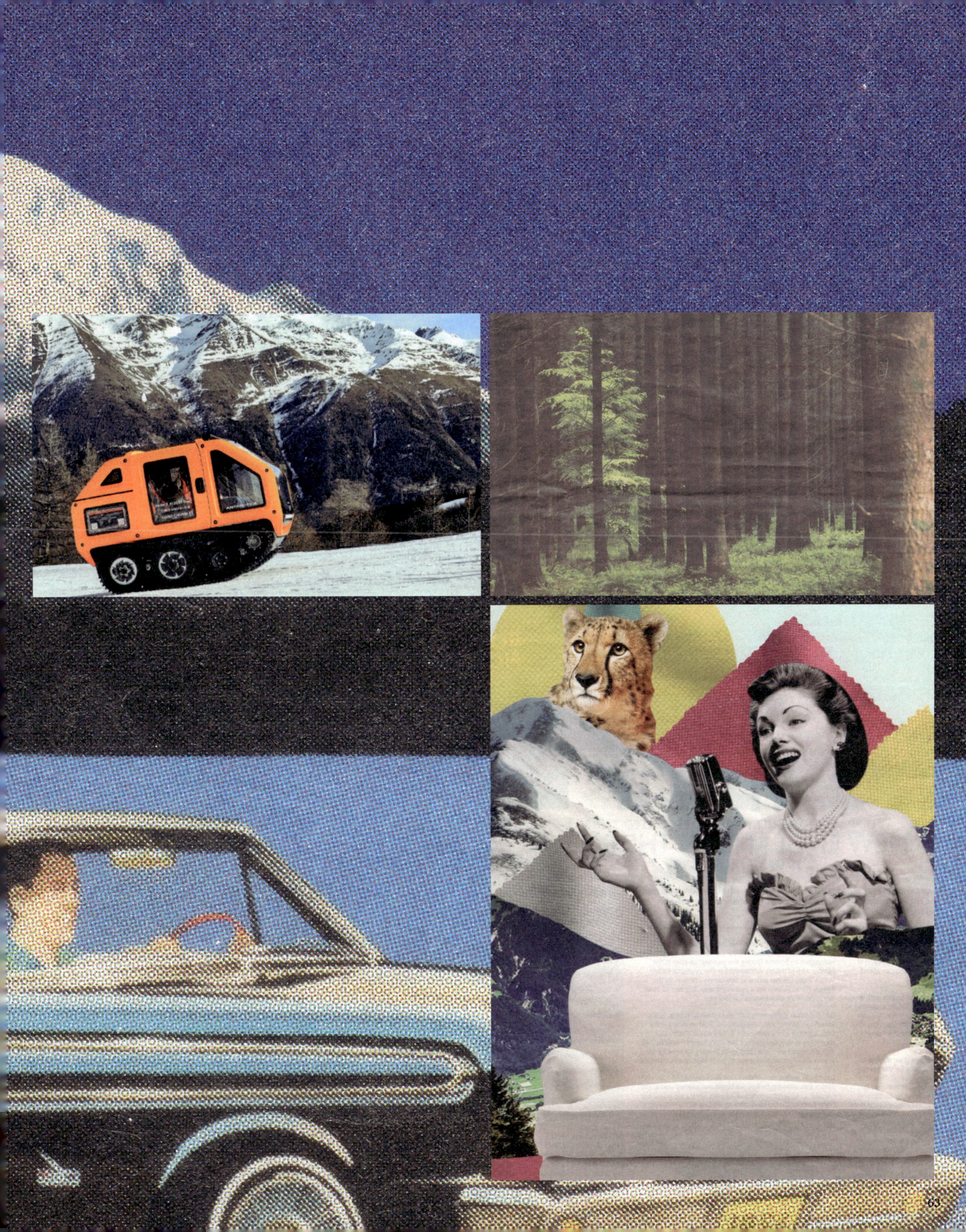

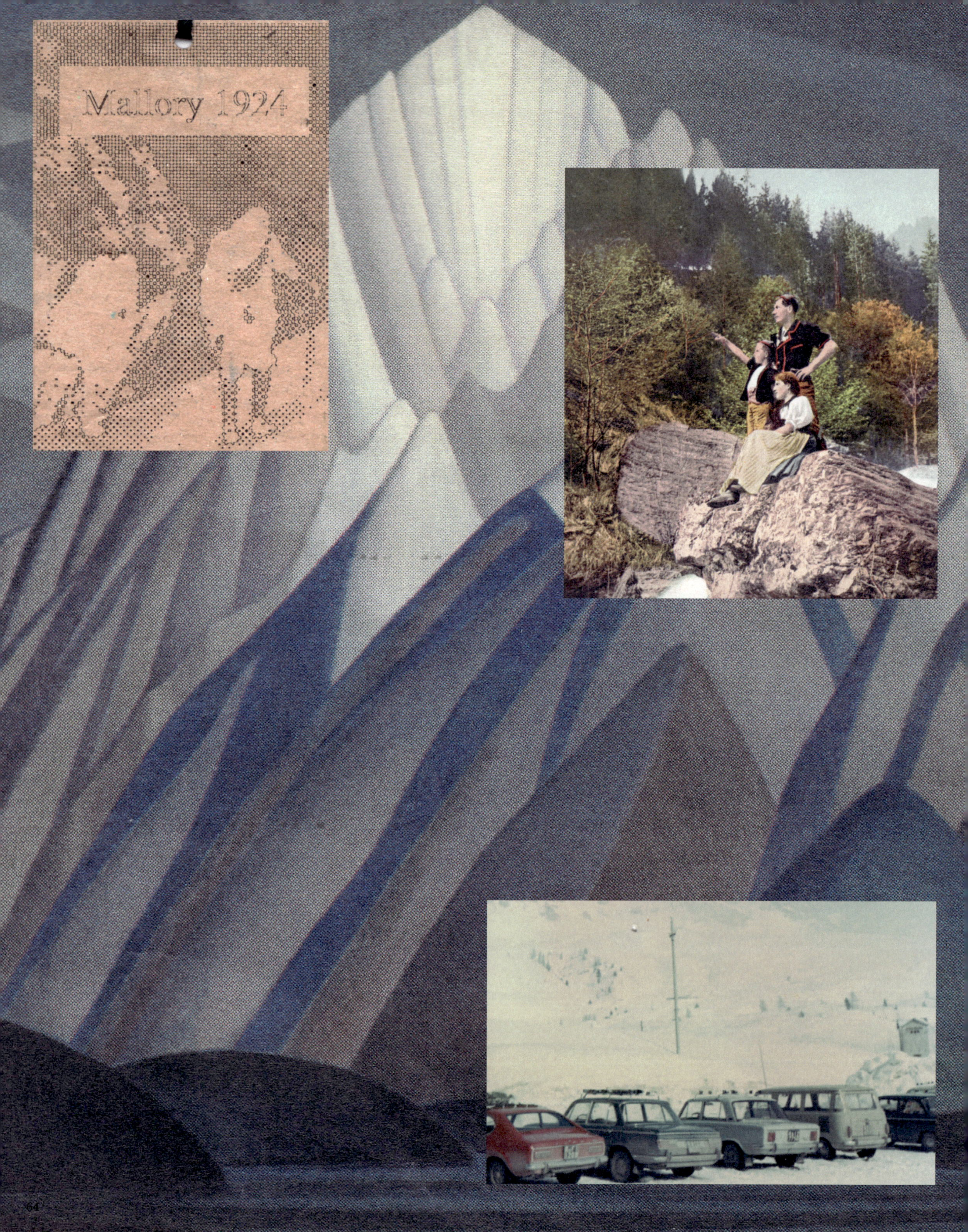
Mallory 1924

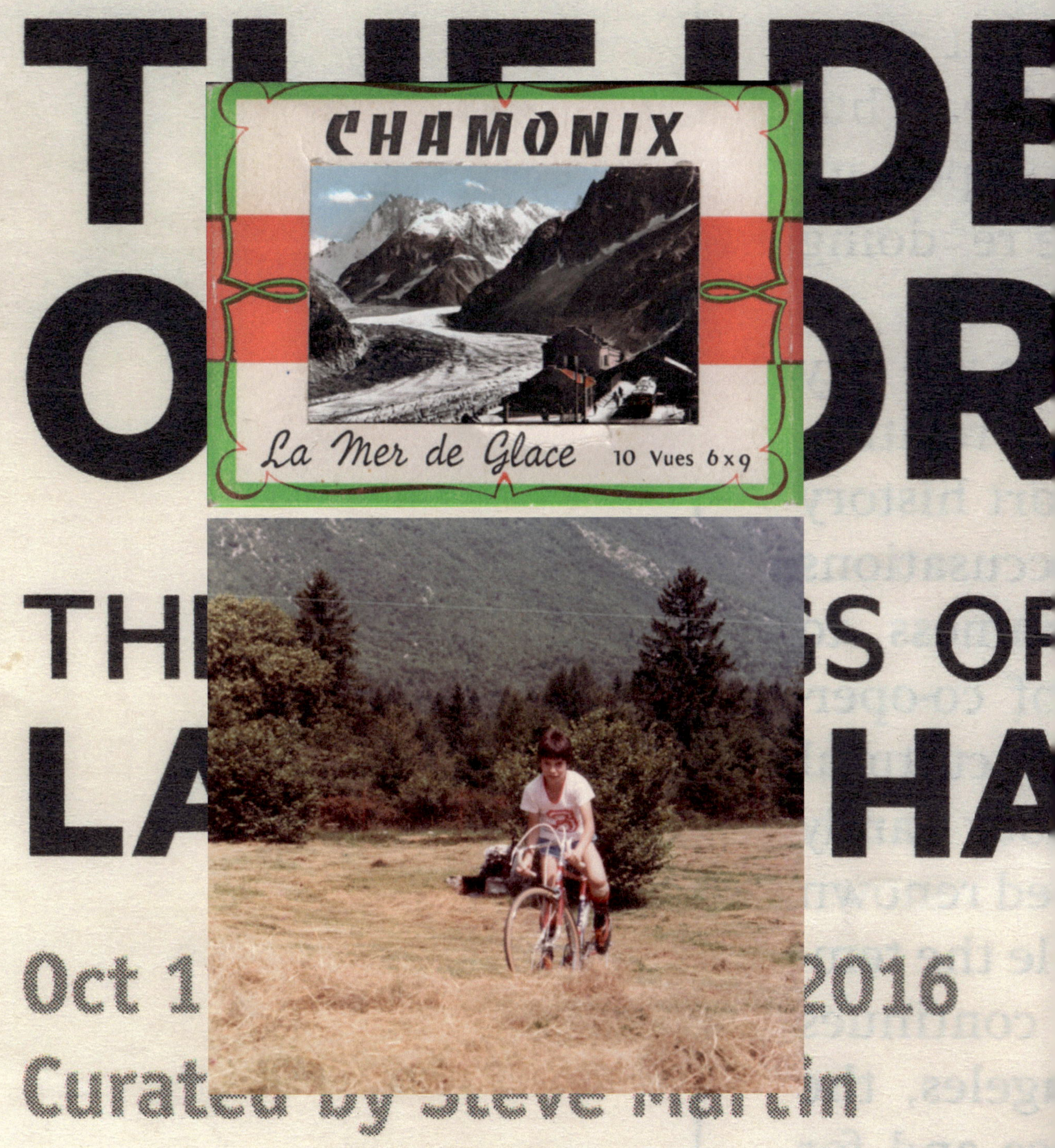

LAWREN HARRIS, *MOUNTAIN FORMS*, CA. 1926 (DETAIL). OIL C
(152.4 × 177.8 CM), COLLECTION OF IMPERIAL OIL LIMITED. © FA

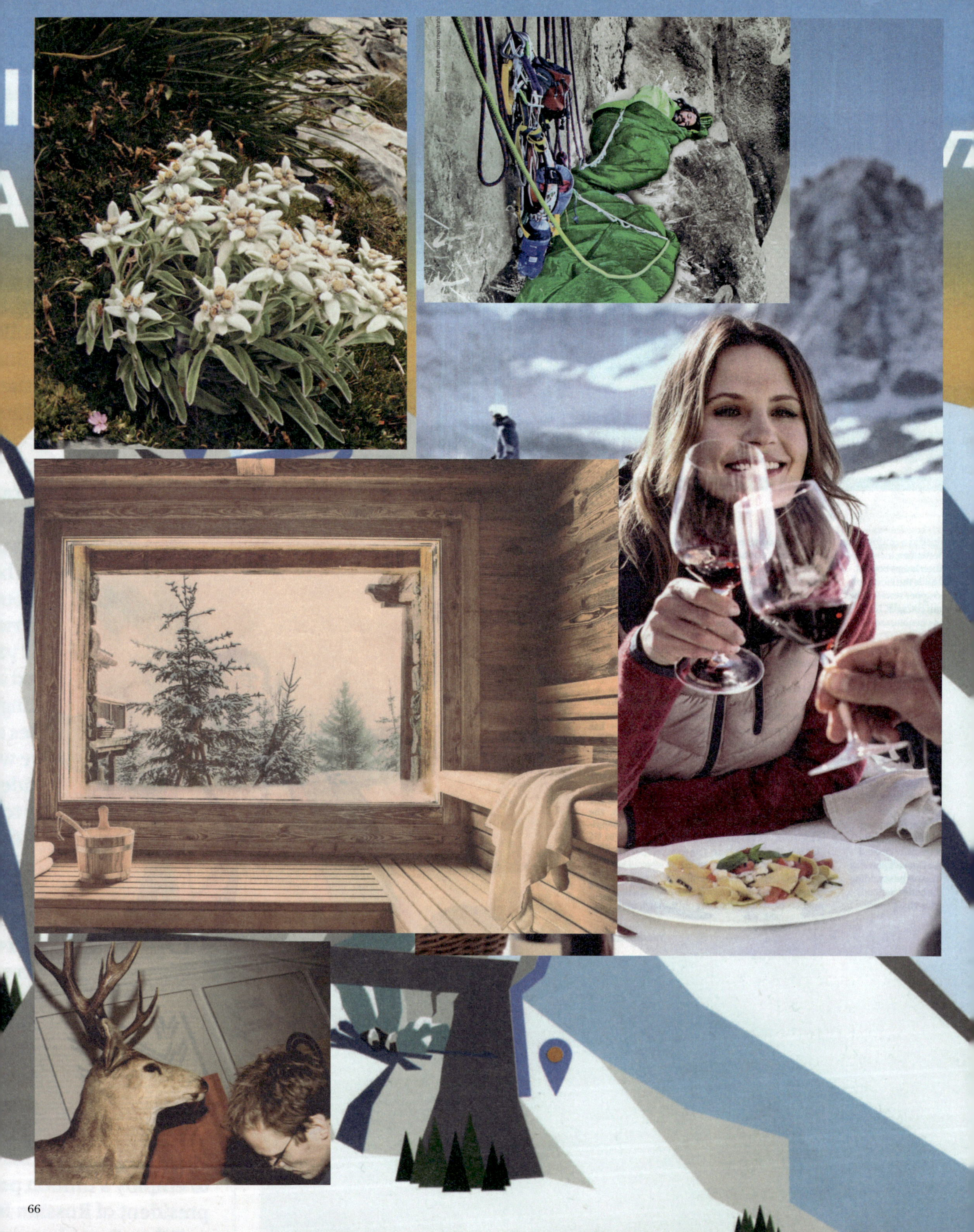

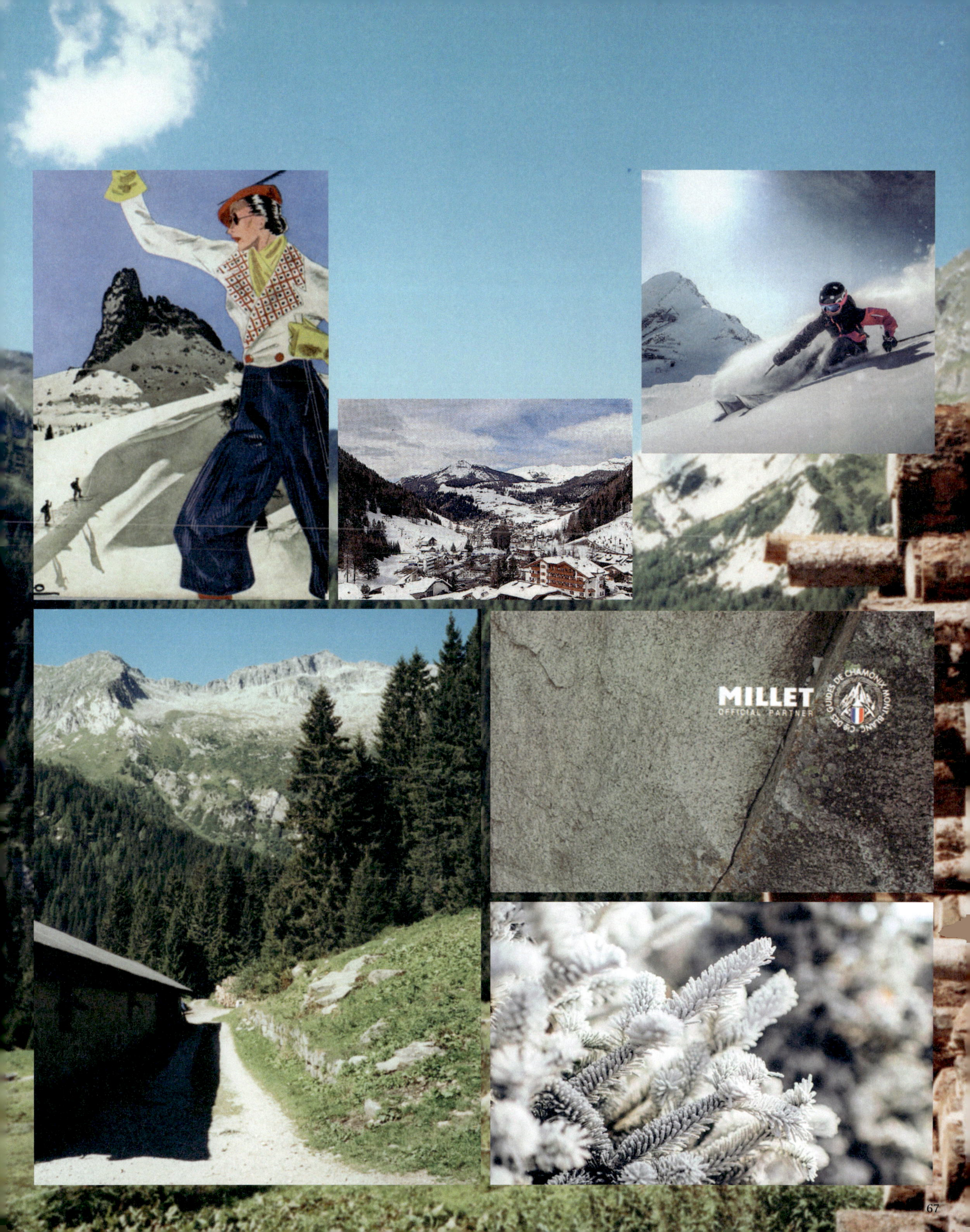
MILLET
OFFICIAL PARTNER
DES GUIDES DE CHAMONIX MONT-BLANC

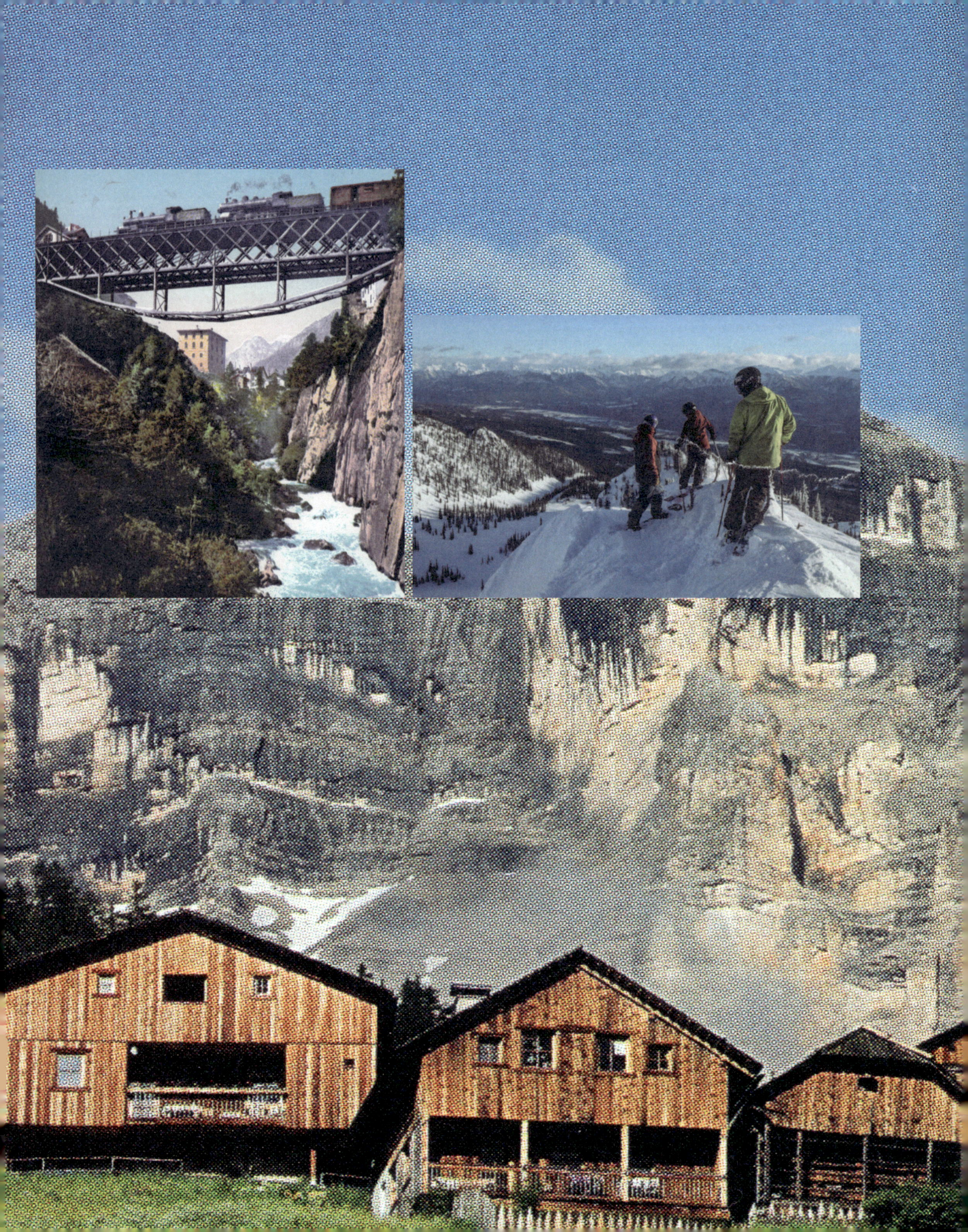

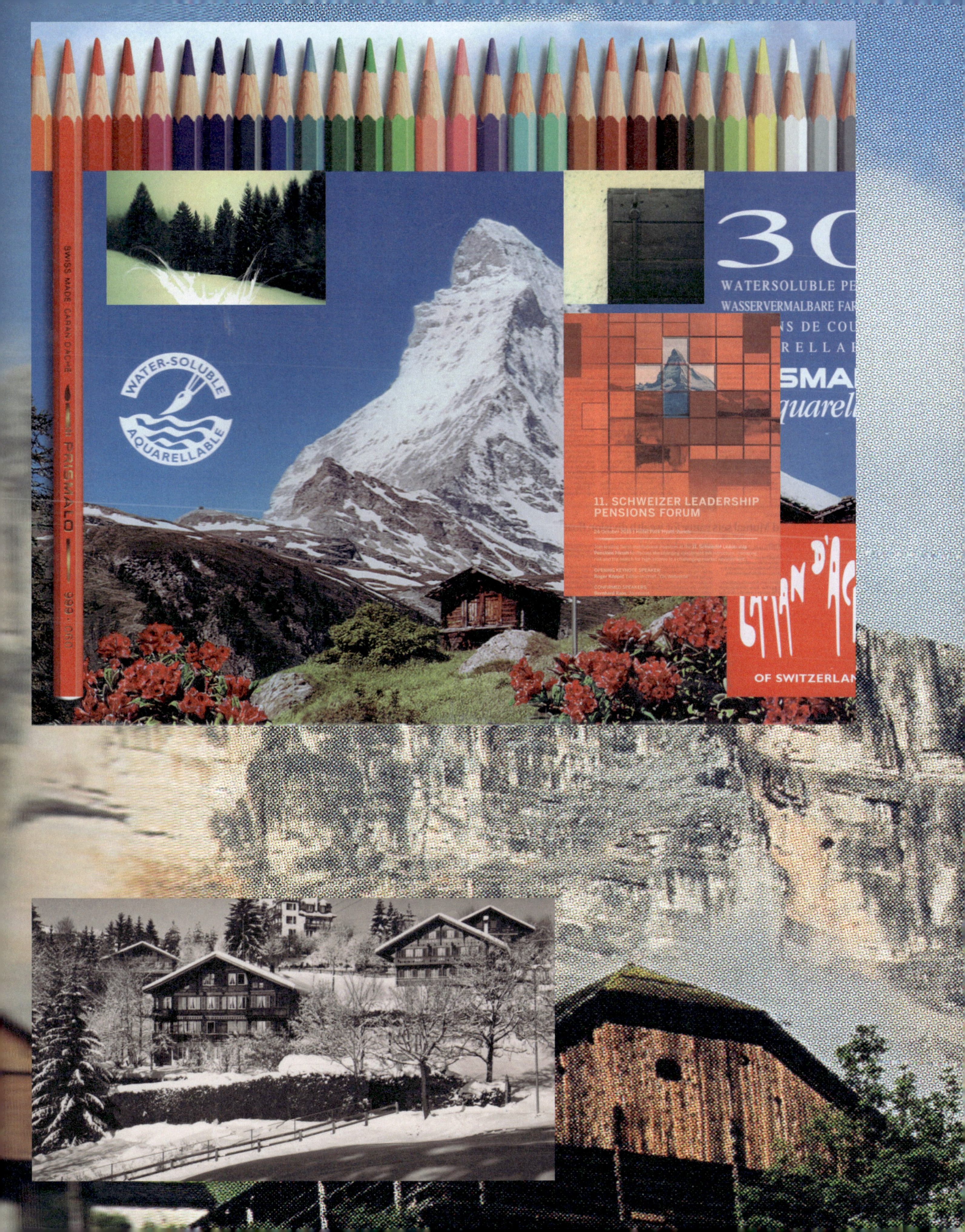

SWISS MADE CARAN D'ACHE
PRISMALO
999 · 060
WATER-SOLUBLE
AQUARELLABLE
30
WATERSOLUBLE PE
WASSERVERMALBARE FAR
NS DE COU
RELLA
SMA
quarell
11. SCHWEIZER LEADERSHIP
PENSIONS FORUM
OPENING KEYNOTE SPEAKER
CONFIRMED SPEAKERS
OF SWITZERLAN

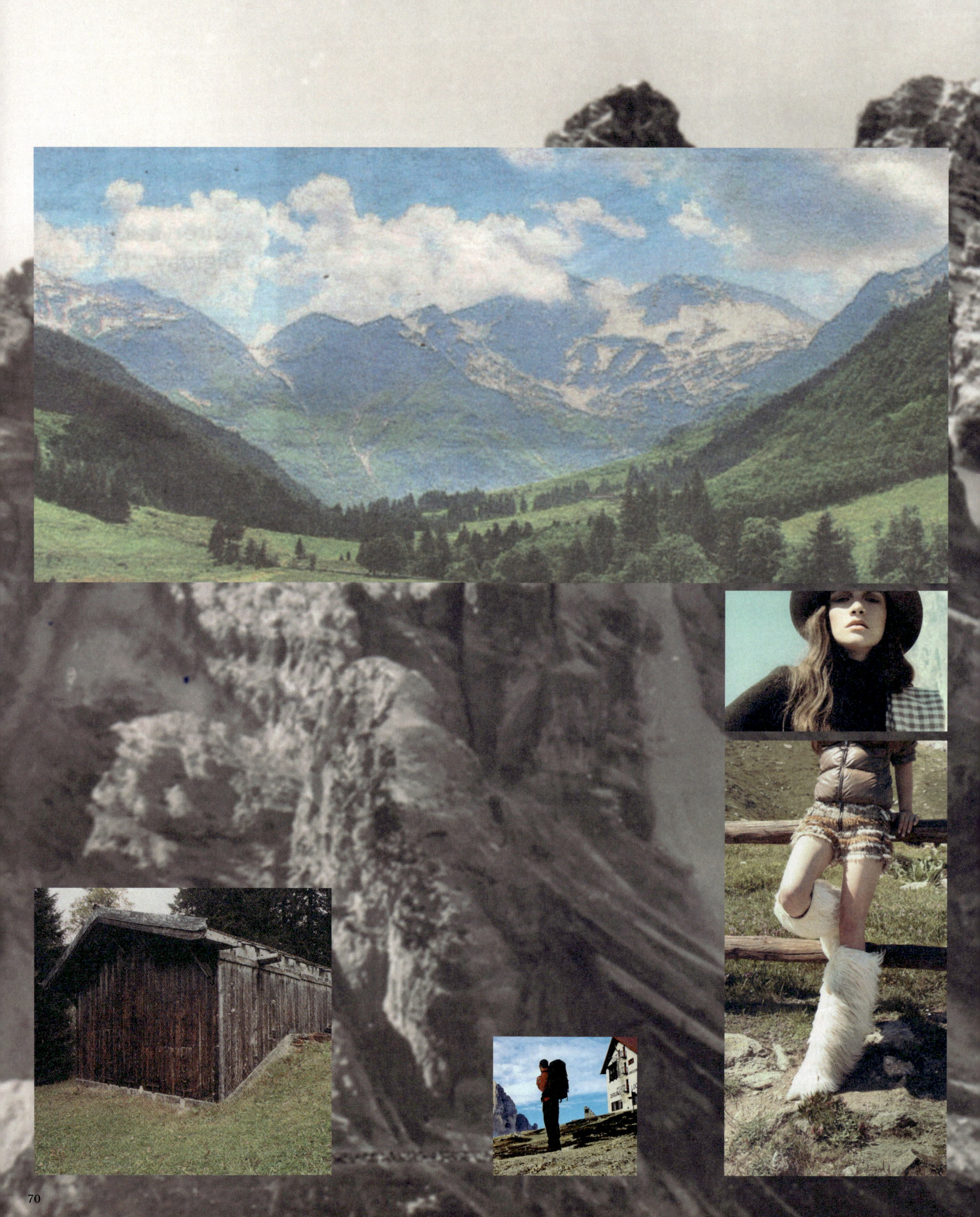

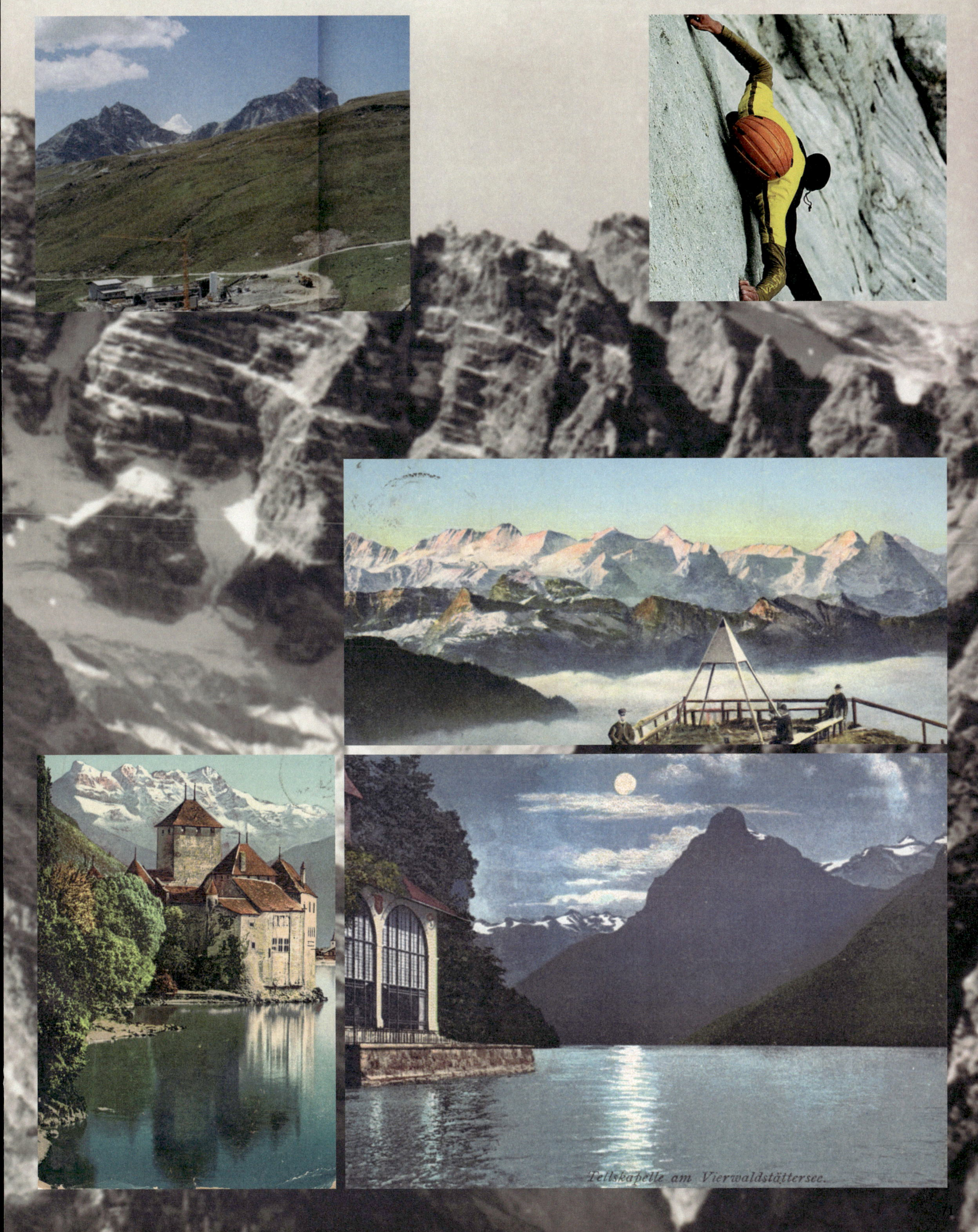
Tellskapelle am Vierwaldstättersee.

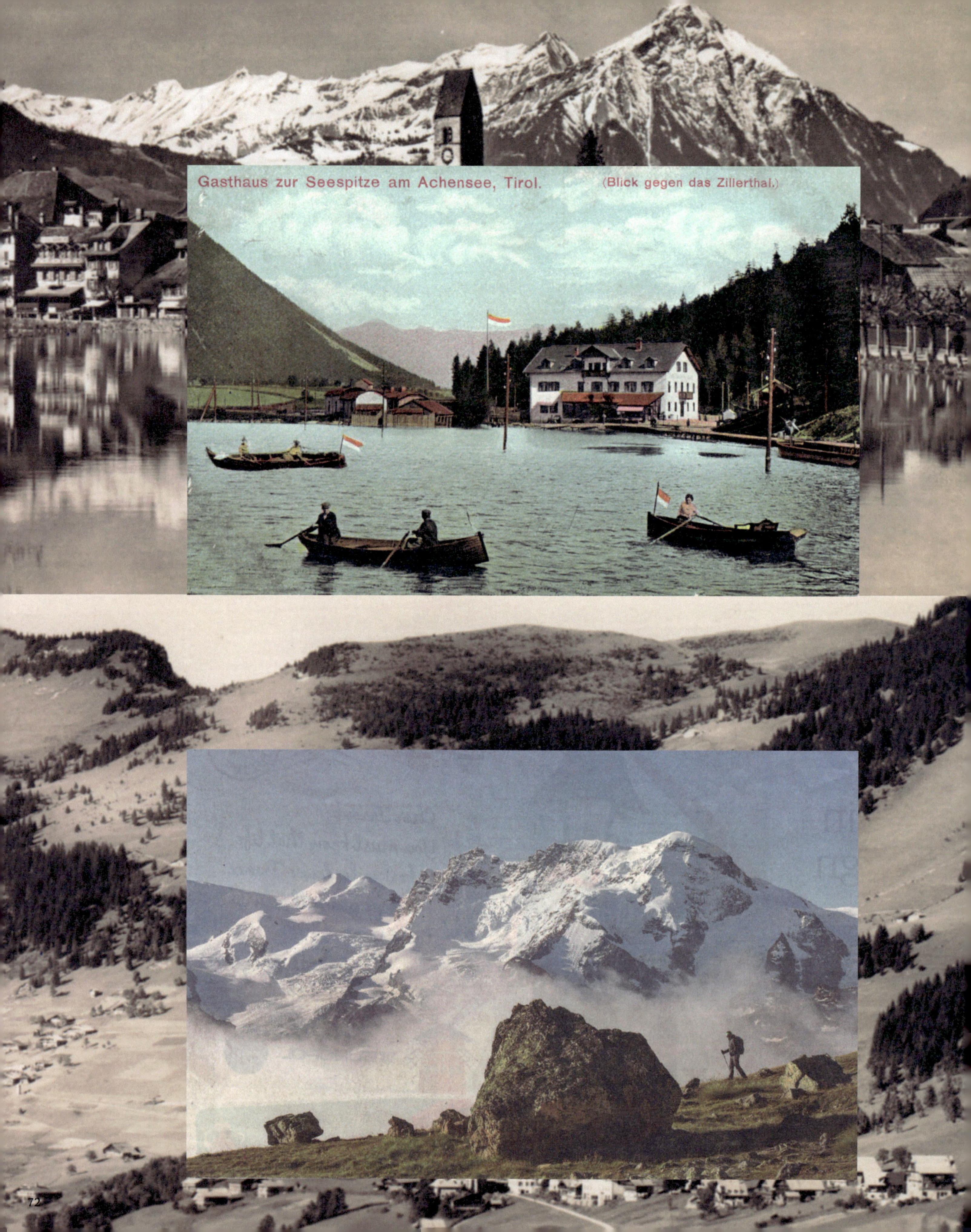
Gasthaus zur Seespitze am Achensee, Tirol.
(Blick gegen das Zillerthal.)

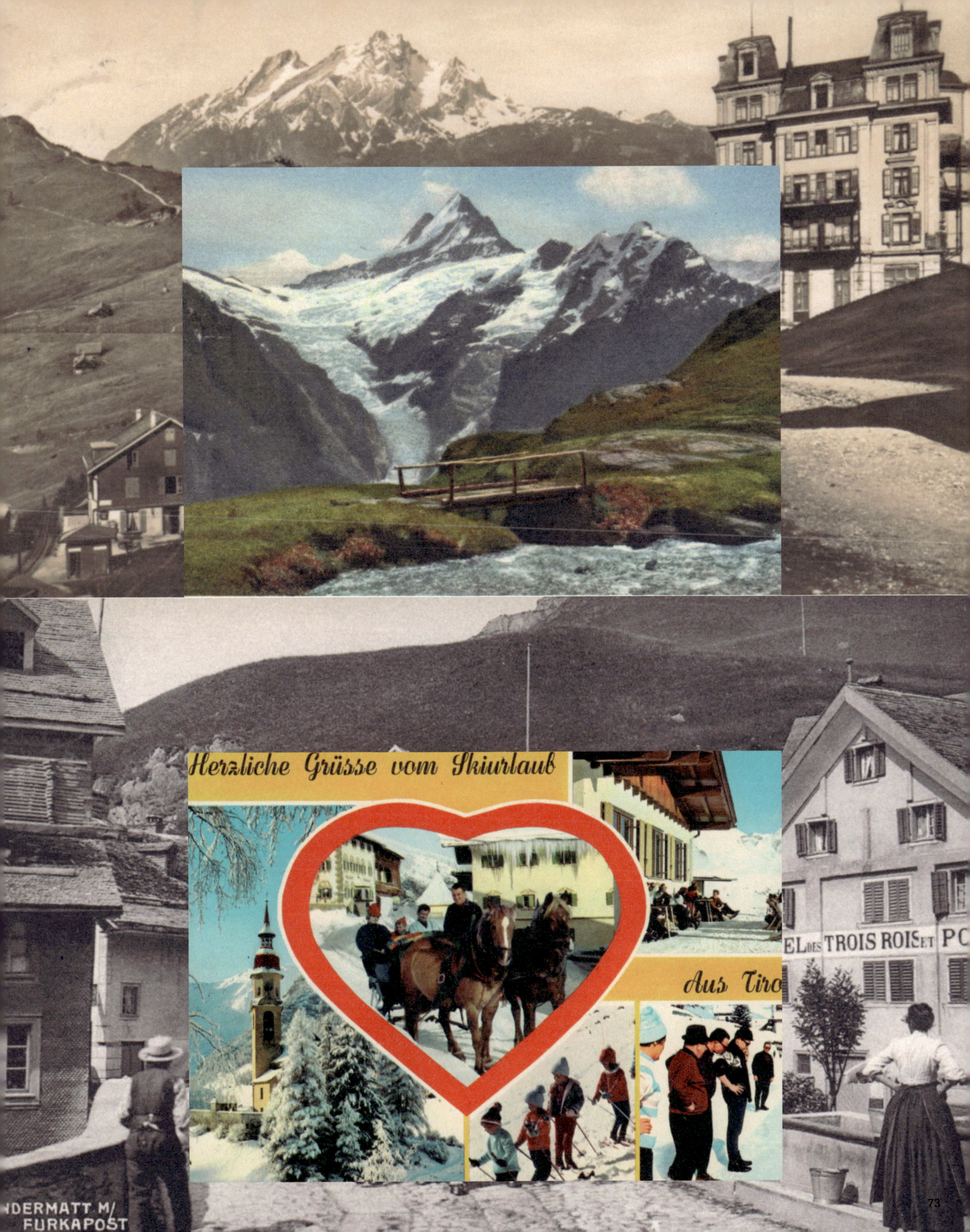
Herzliche Grüsse vom Skiurlaub
Aus Tiro
EL DES TROIS ROIS ET PO
DERMATT M/
FURKAPOST

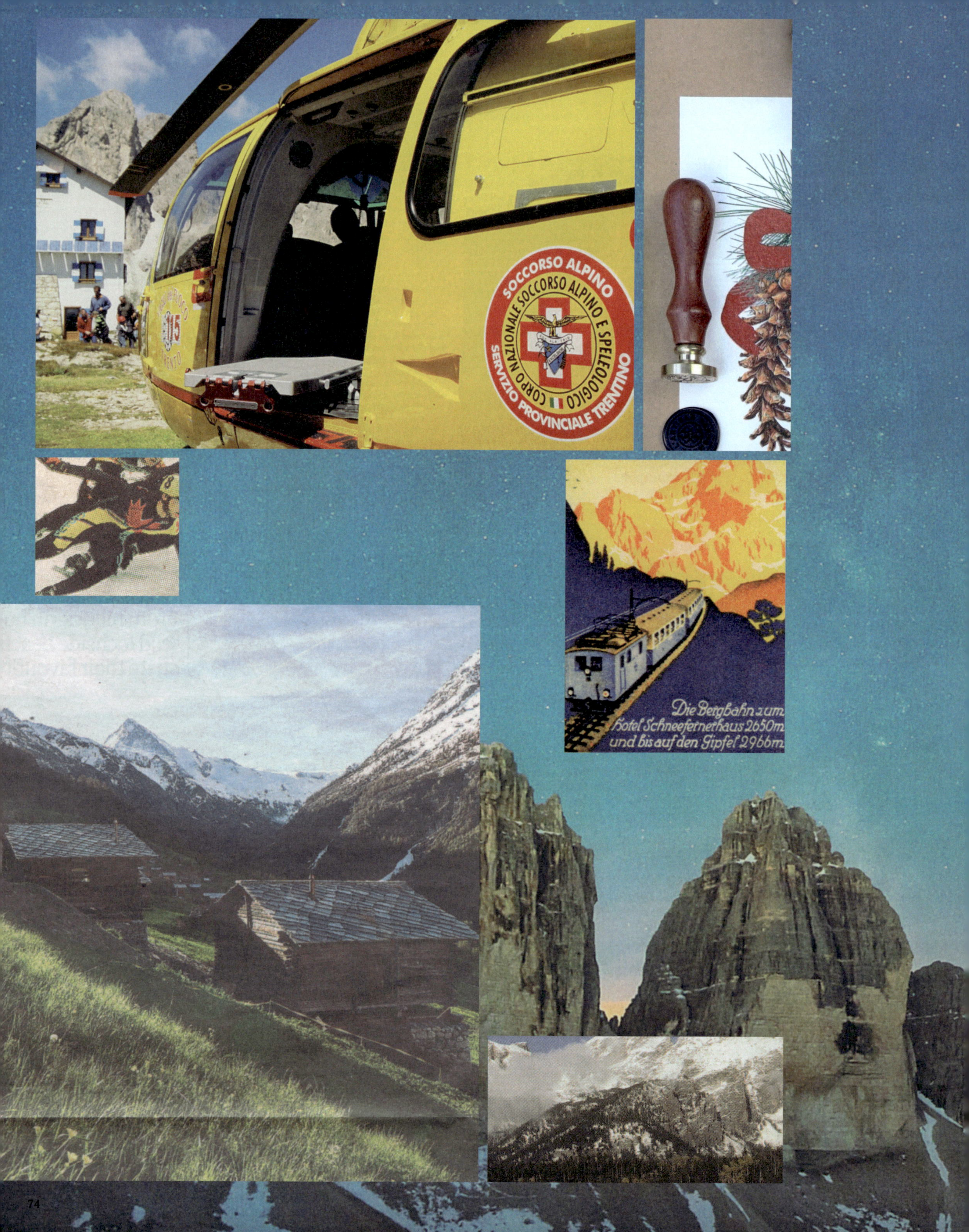
SOCCORSO ALPINO
CORPO NAZIONALE SOCCORSO ALPINO E SPELEOLOGICO
SERVIZIO PROVINCIALE TRENTINO
Die Bergbahn zum
Hotel Schneefernerhaus 2650m
und bis auf den Gipfel 2966m

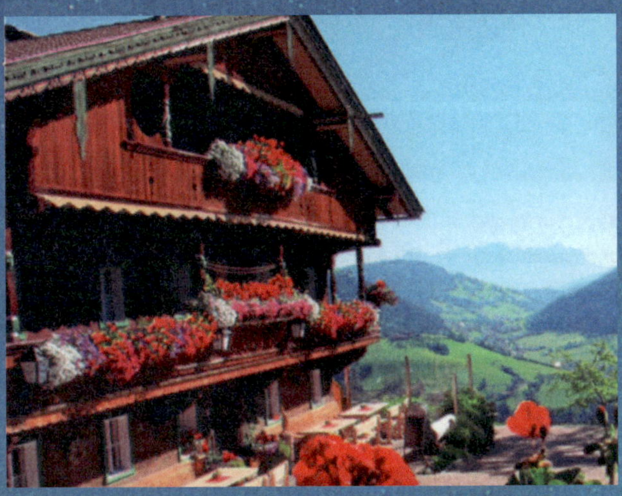

Comelico, il fronte dolomitico ha interessato div
Pallidi, tra i quali Laga
olomiti di Sesto, per u
ra. Sulle Dolomiti di S
ategica l'area delle
e Tre Cime e sullo sfo
a. Quest'ultimo, in
particolare, avrebbe potuto consentire agli italia
con un'operazione di sfondamento, di collegare
Cadore alla Val Pusteria. Dopo mesi di combatti
nell'estate del 1915 sul fronte del Monte Piana i
una logorante guerra di posizione, con le trince
degli opposti schieramenti a poche decine di m
di distanza. Dopo la disfatta di Caporetto, venne
ordinato alle trupp

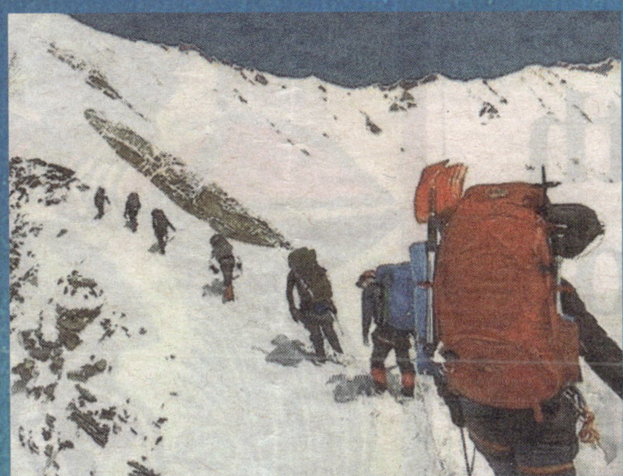

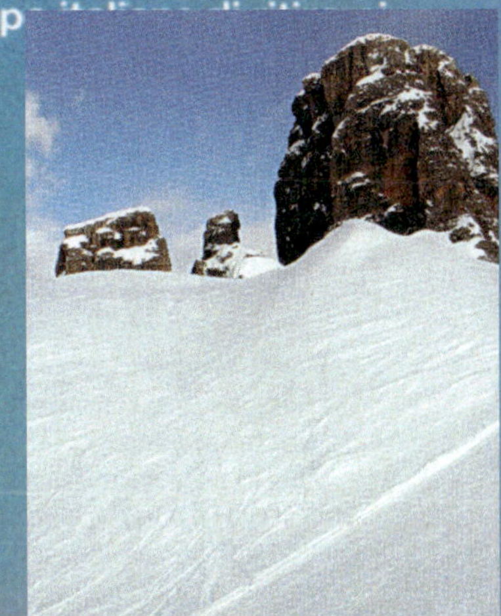

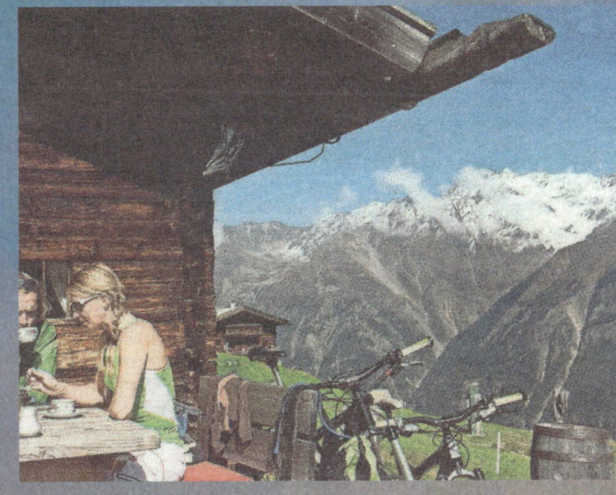

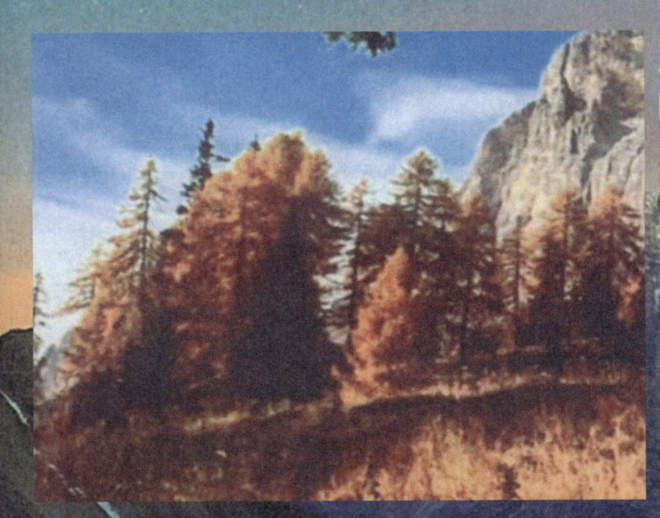

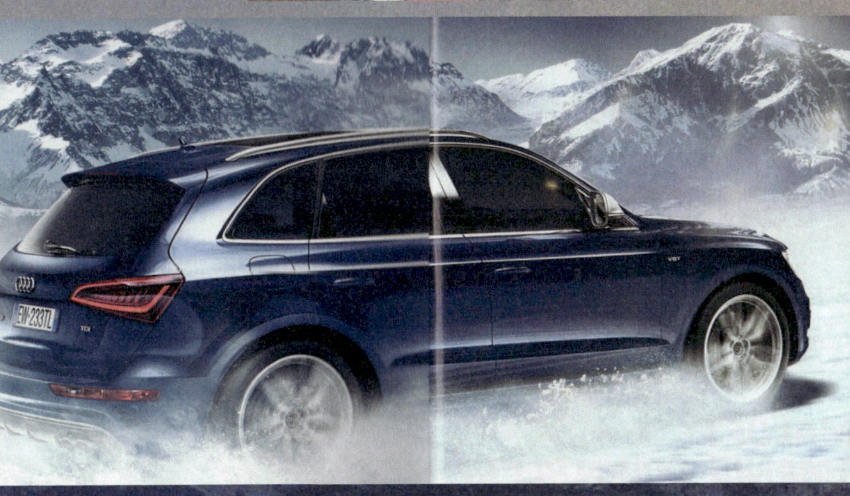

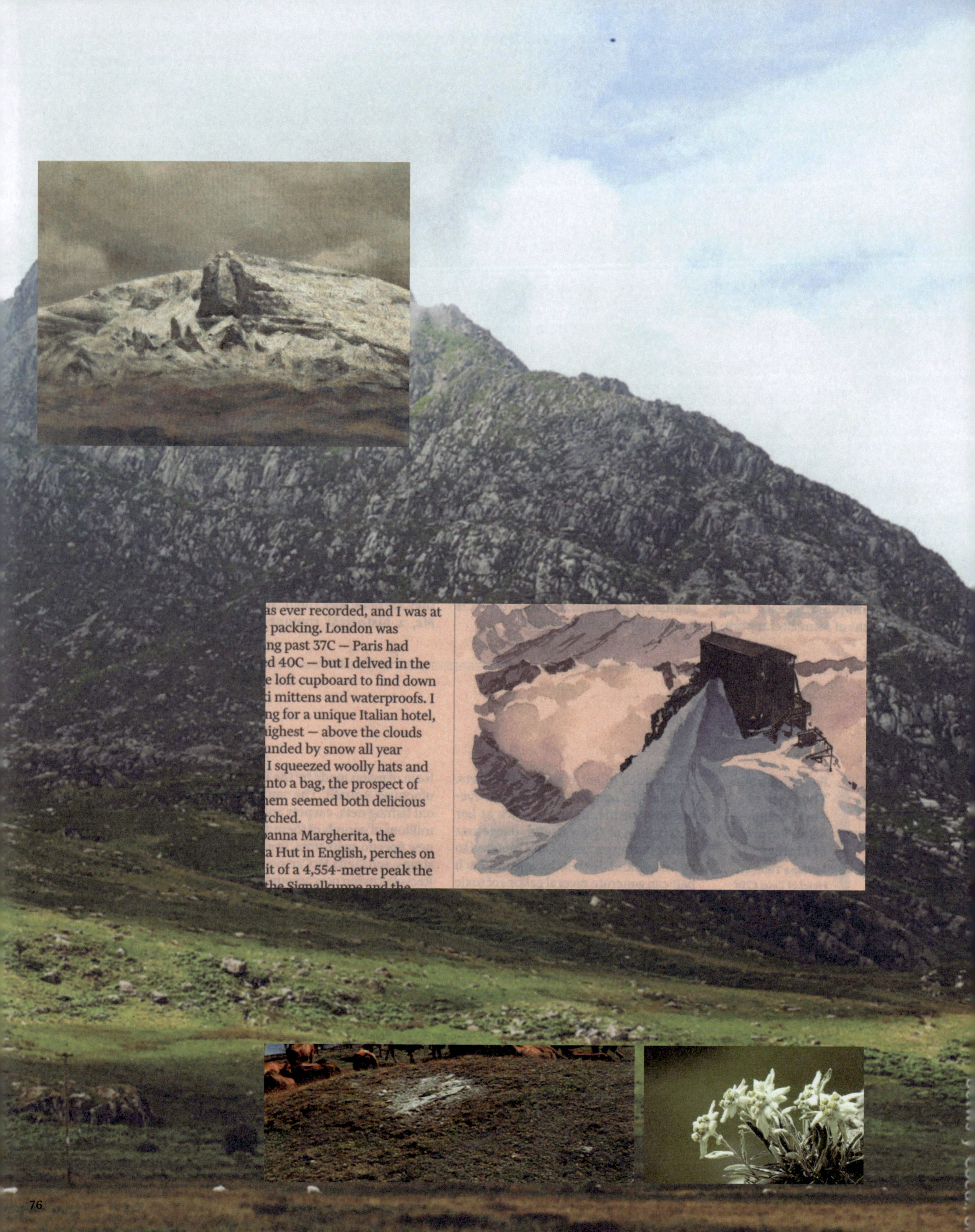

as ever recorded, and I was at
e packing. London was
ng past 37C — Paris had
d 40C — but I delved in the
e loft cupboard to find down
i mittens and waterproofs. I
ng for a unique Italian hotel,
highest — above the clouds
unded by snow all year
I squeezed woolly hats and
nto a bag, the prospect of
hem seemed both delicious
tched.
anna Margherita, the
a Hut in English, perches on
it of a 4,554-metre peak the

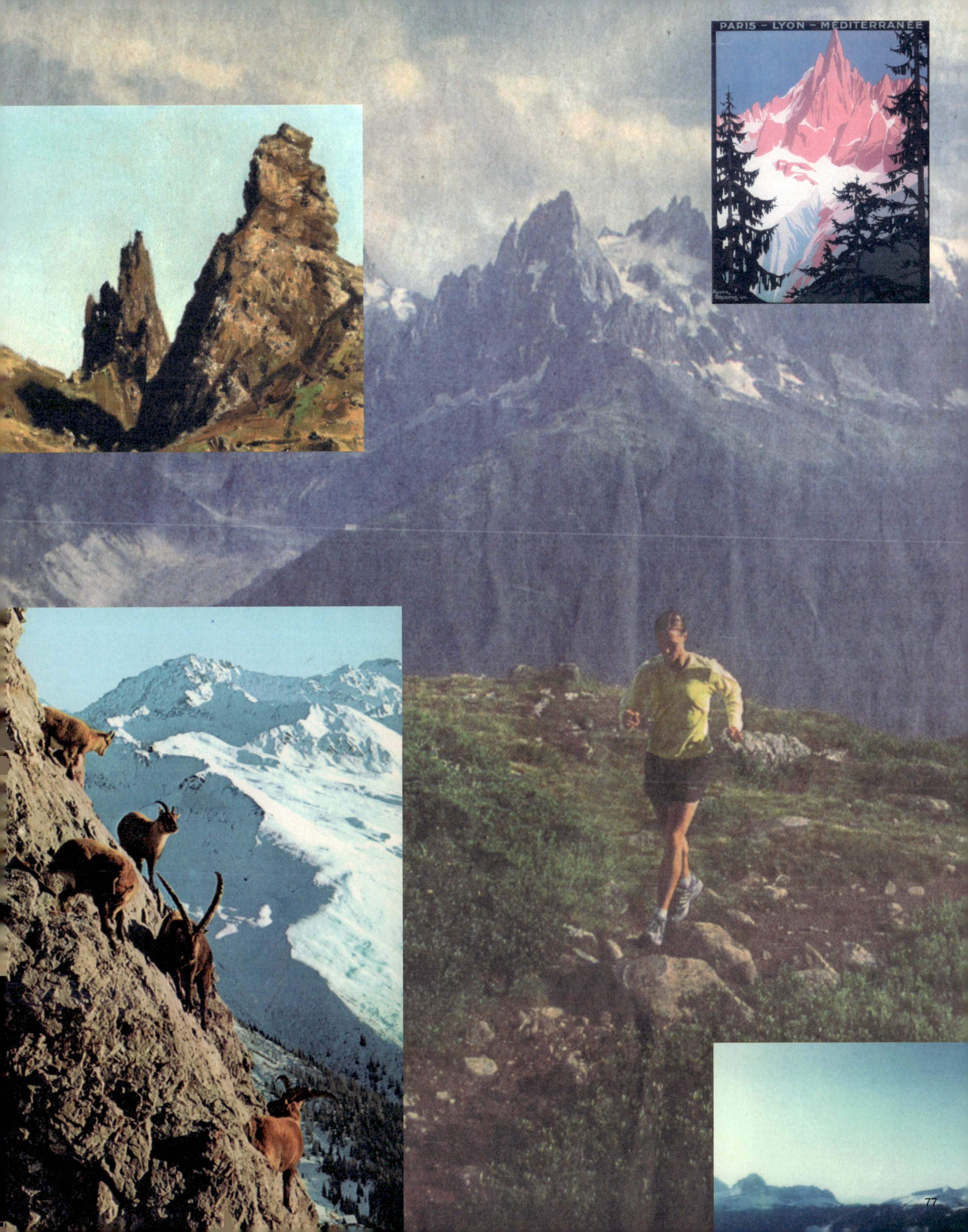
PARIS – LYON – MÉDITERRANÉE

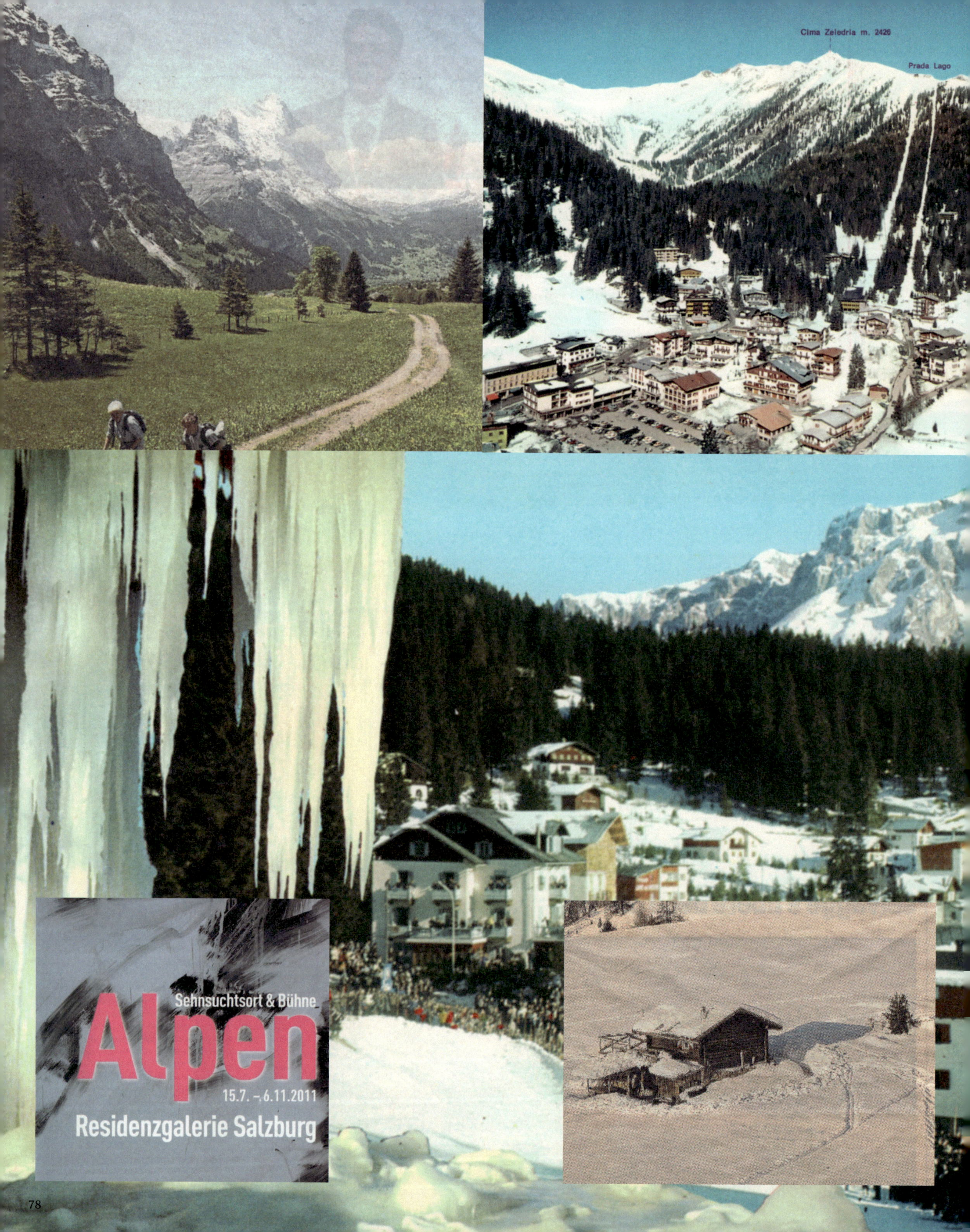
Cima Zeledria m. 2426
Prada Lago
Sehnsuchtsort & Bühne
Alpen
15.7. – 6.11.2011
Residenzgalerie Salzburg

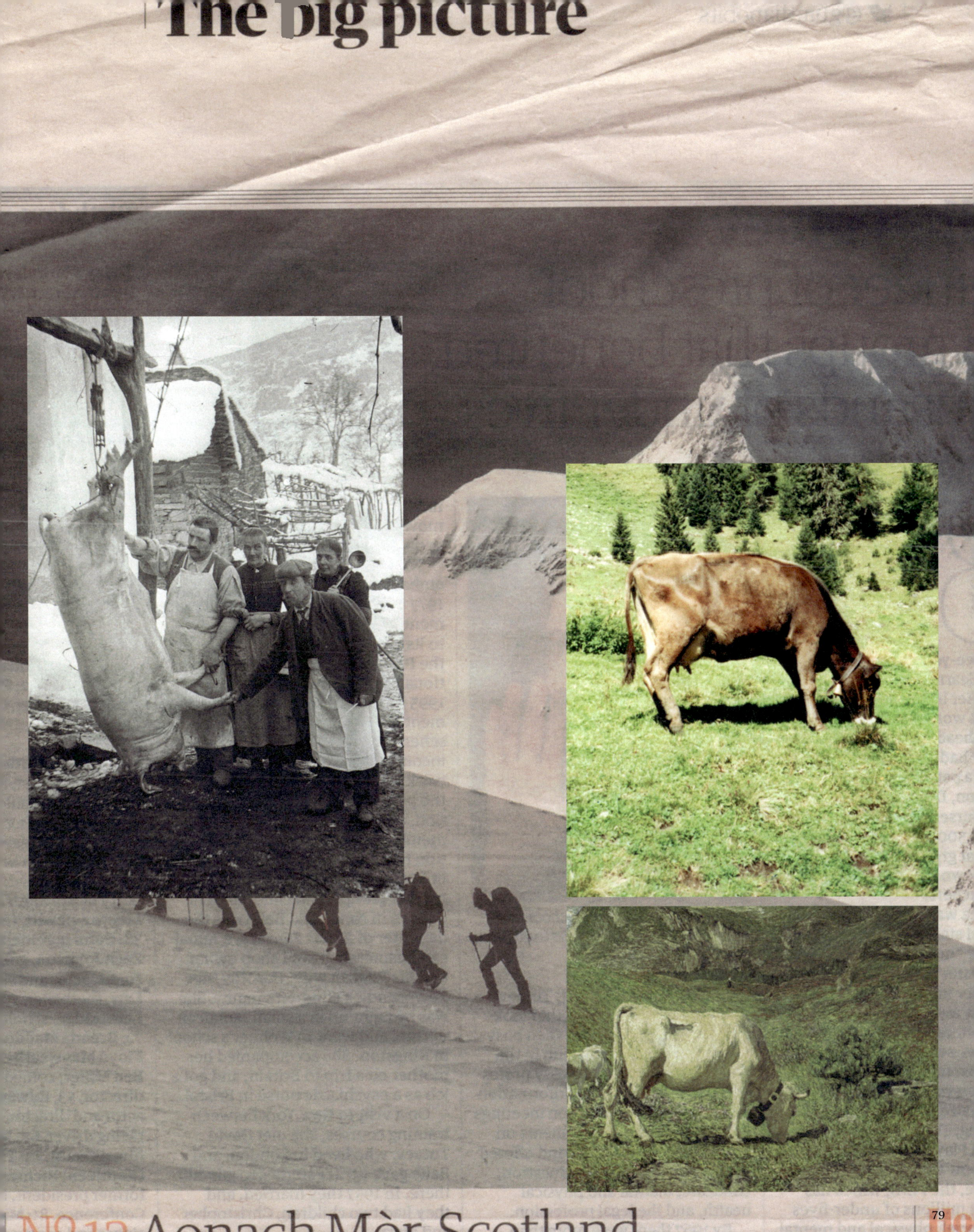
The big picture
Nº 12 Aonach Mòr Scotland

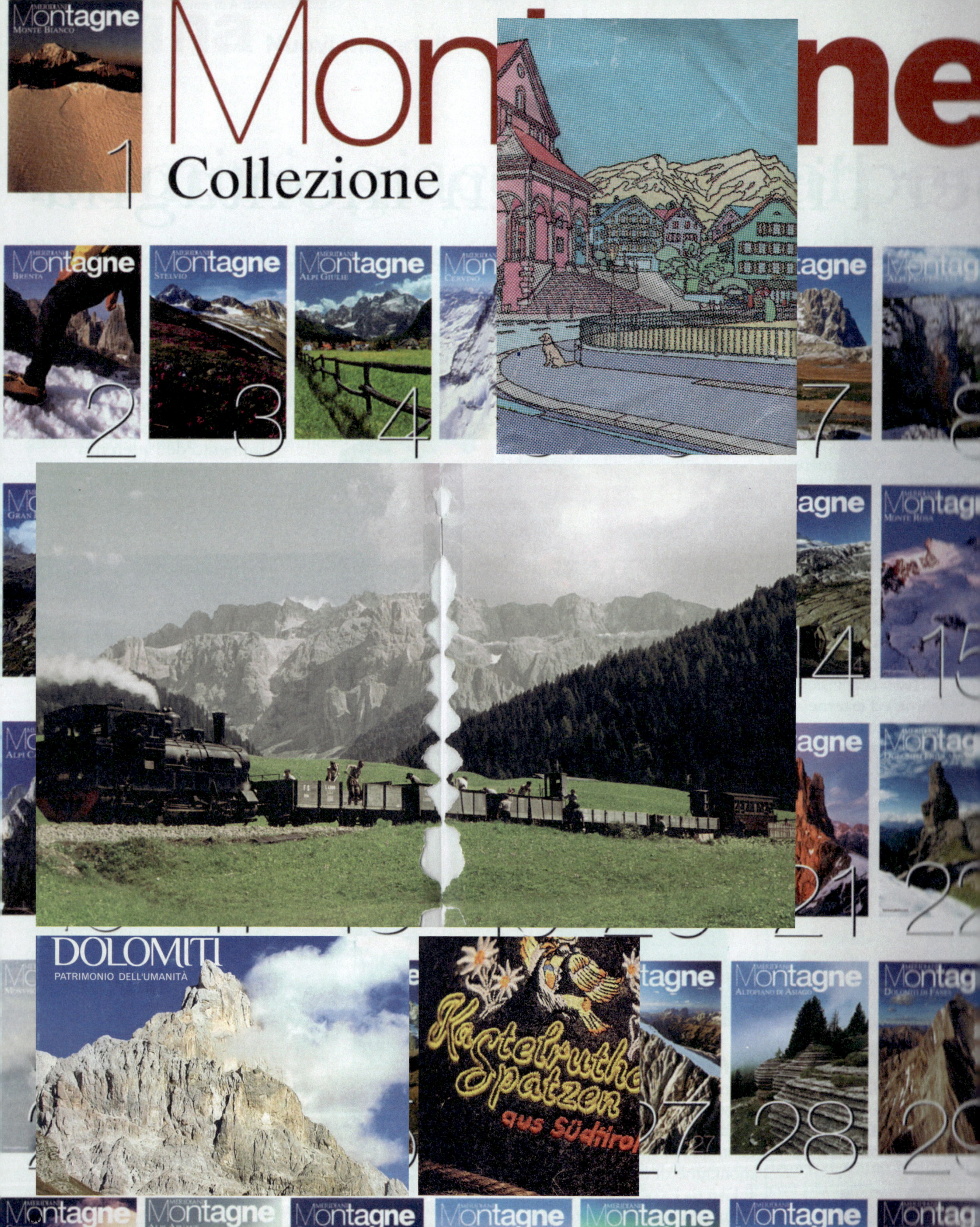
Montagne
Collezione
MERIDIANI Montagne
MONTE BIANCO
BRENTA
STELVIO
ALPI GIULIE
MONTE ROSA
ALTOPIANO DI ASIAGO
DOLOMITI
PATRIMONIO DELL'UMANITÀ
Kastelruther Spatzen
aus Südtirol

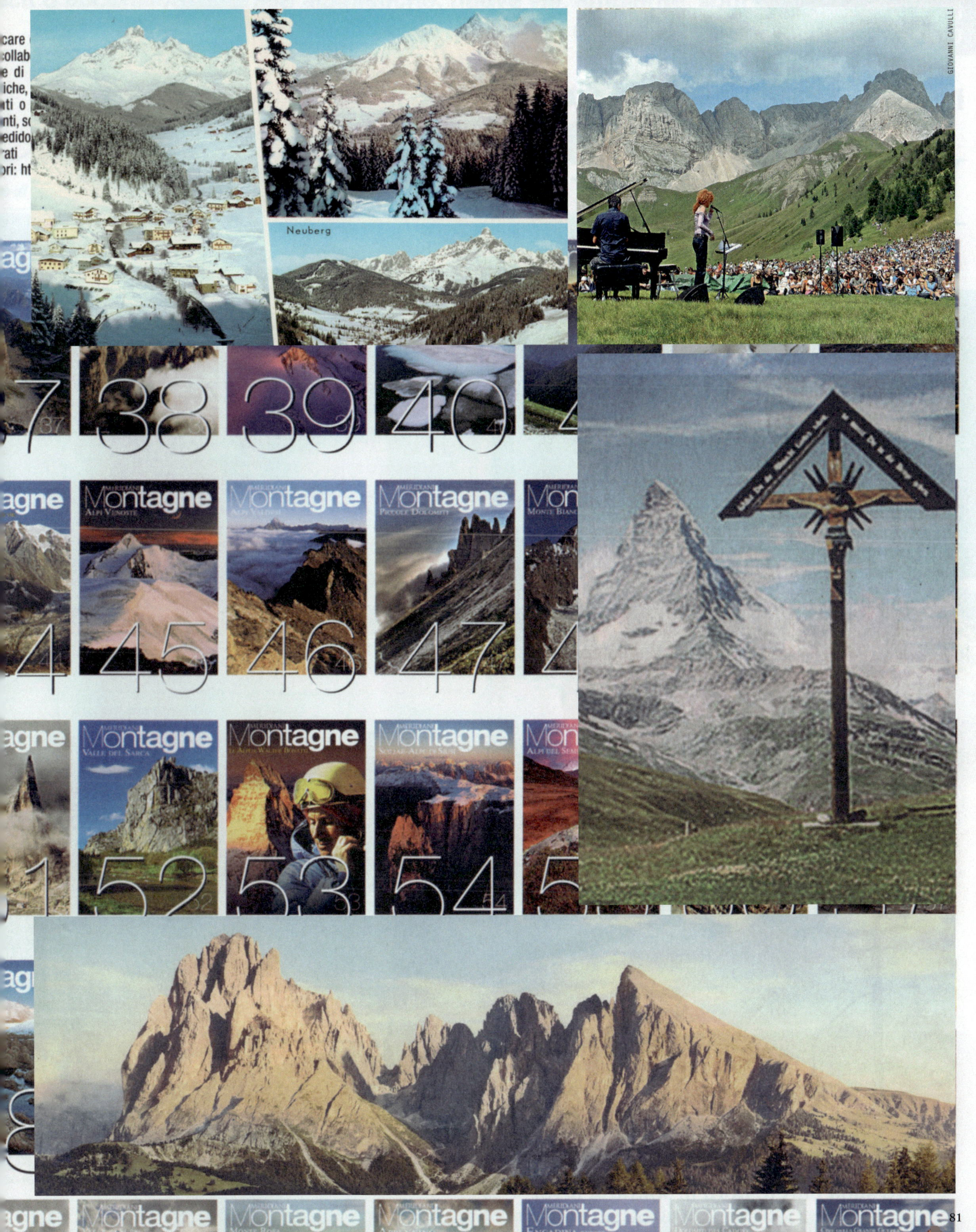
GIOVANNI CAVULLI
Neuberg
Montagne
Alpi Venoste
Montagne
Montagne
Pedole Dolomiti
Montagne
Valle del Sarca
Montagne
Montagne
Montagne
Monte Rosa
Montagne
Appennino
Montagne
Engadina estate
Montagne
Montagne

He said

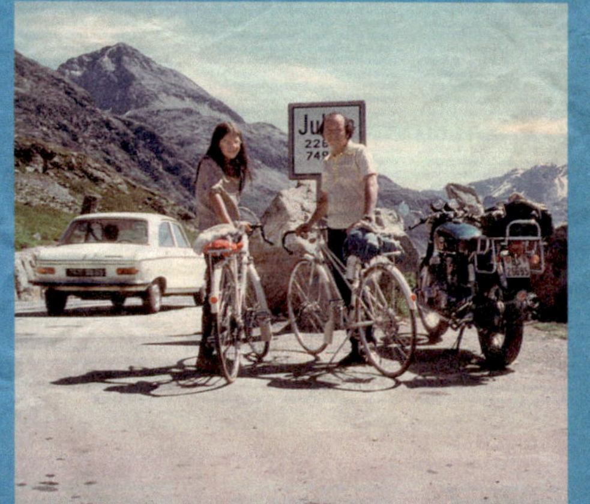

Susan Faludi's father was an ultra-competitive and occasionally violent parent. Then, after decades of estrangement, an email arrived: she was a woman. Could they rebuild their relationship?

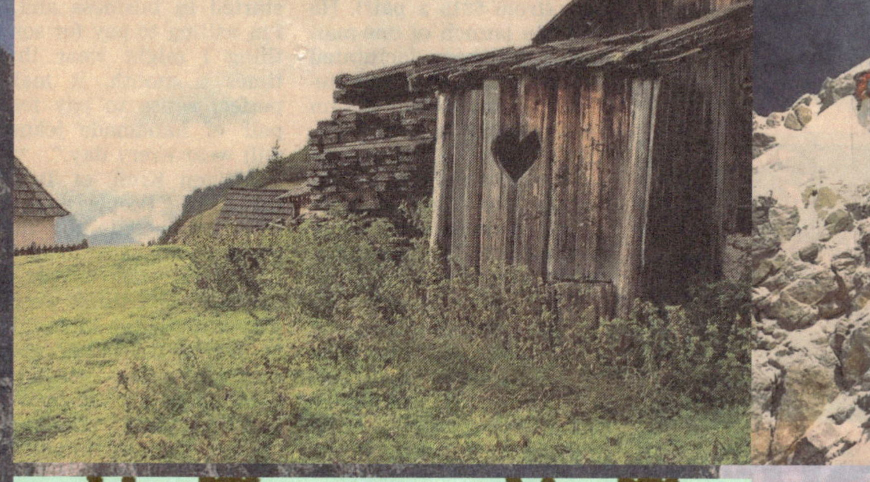

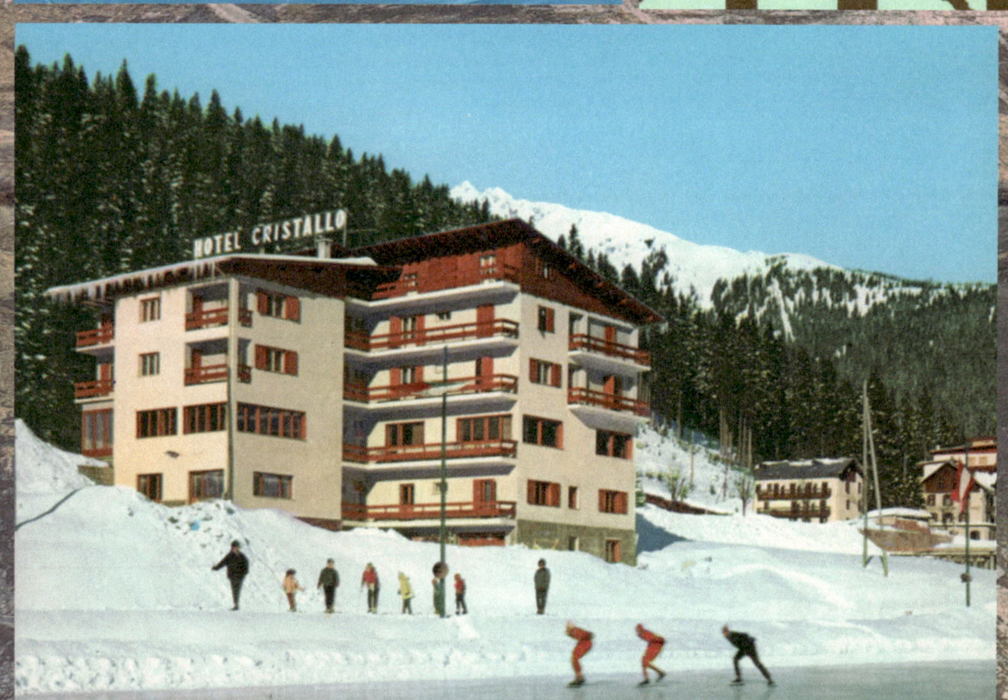

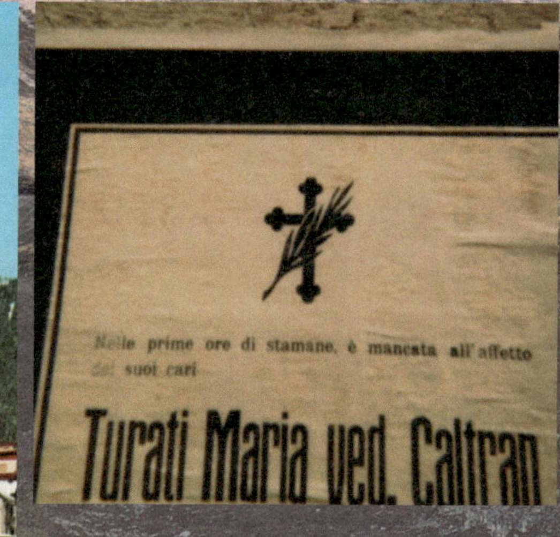

Nelle prime ore di stamane, è mancata all'affetto dei suoi cari

Turati Maria ved. Caltran

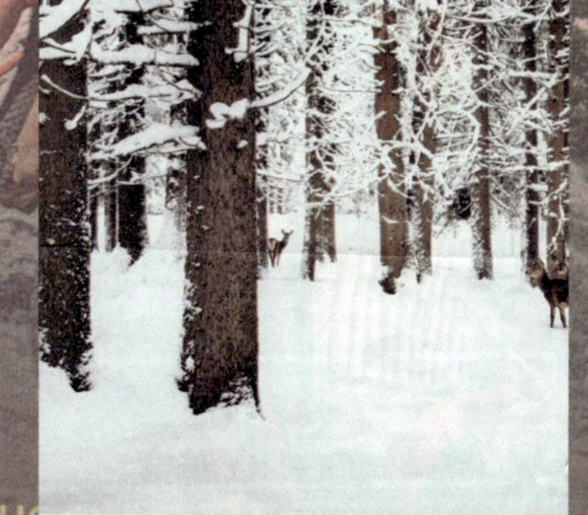

UCI

MOUNTAIN BIKE MARATHON SERIES

2 SETTEMBRE 2017

MOUNTAIN BIKE MARATHON SERIES

AURONZO MISURINA

WORLD CHAMPIONSHIP

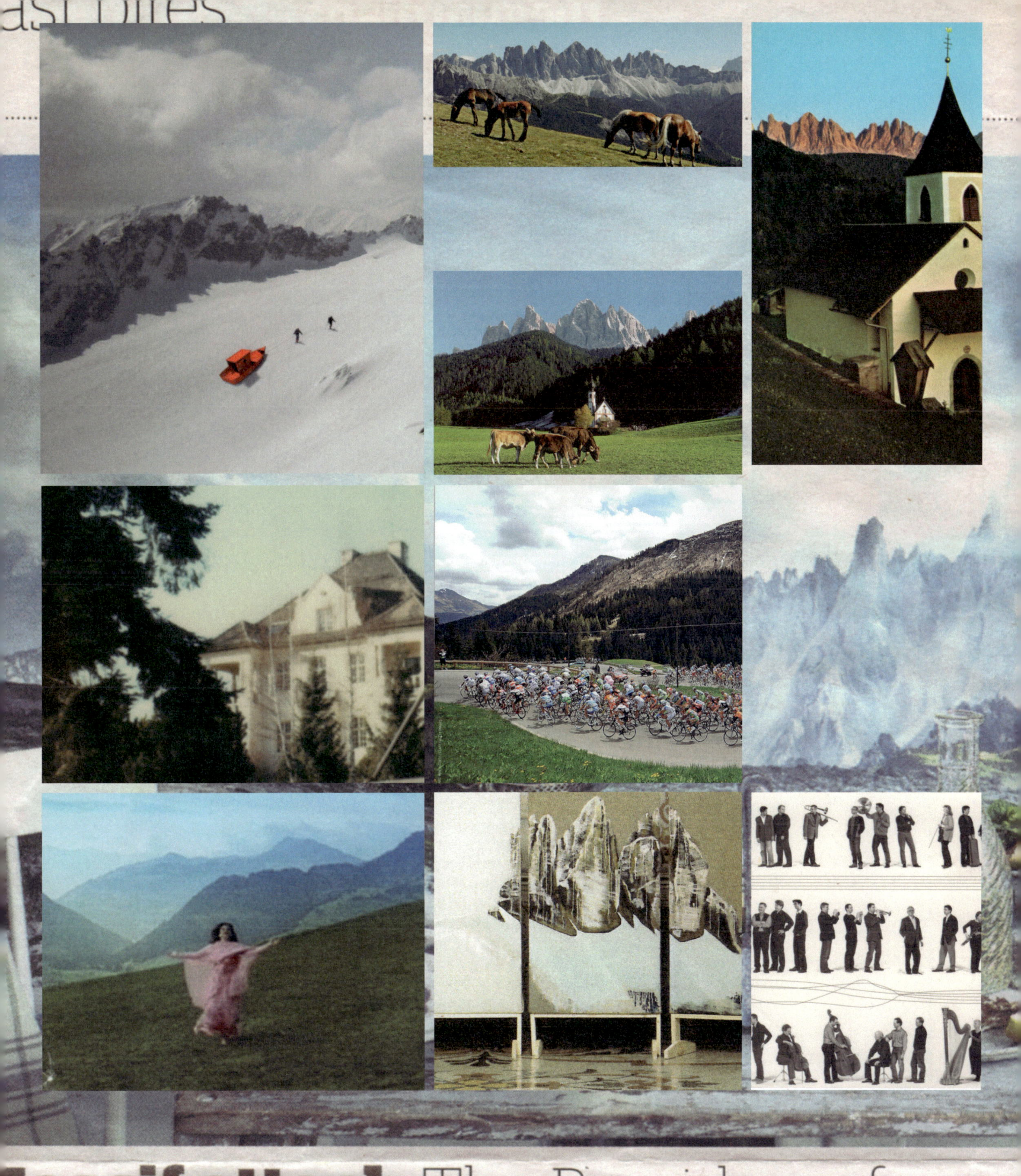

lassif attack The Providores found
o the last at a lively Tyrolean mounta

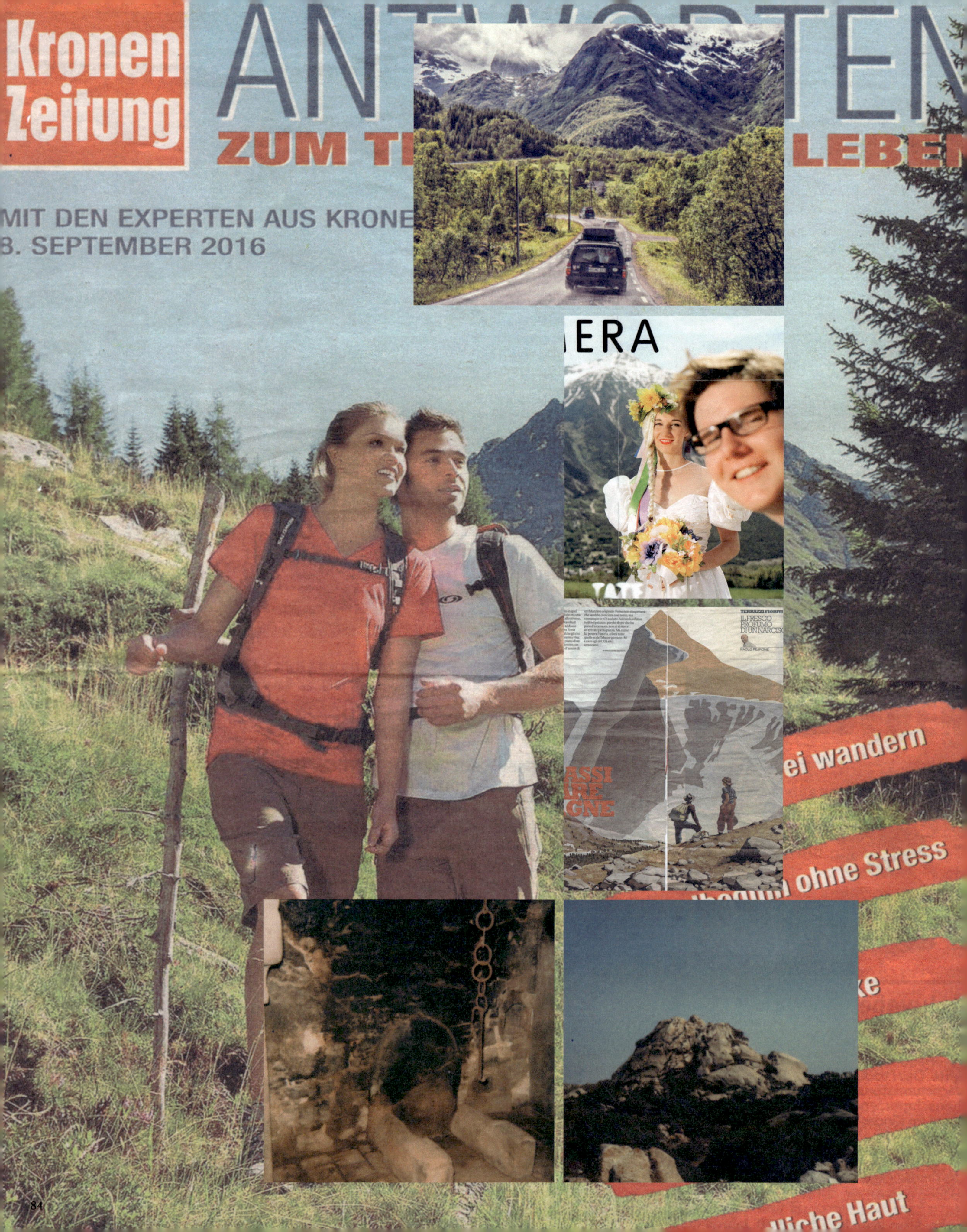
Kronen Zeitung
AN
TEN
ZUM T
LEBEN
MIT DEN EXPERTEN AUS KRONE
8. SEPTEMBER 2016
ERA
ei wandern
ohne Stress
ke
liche Haut

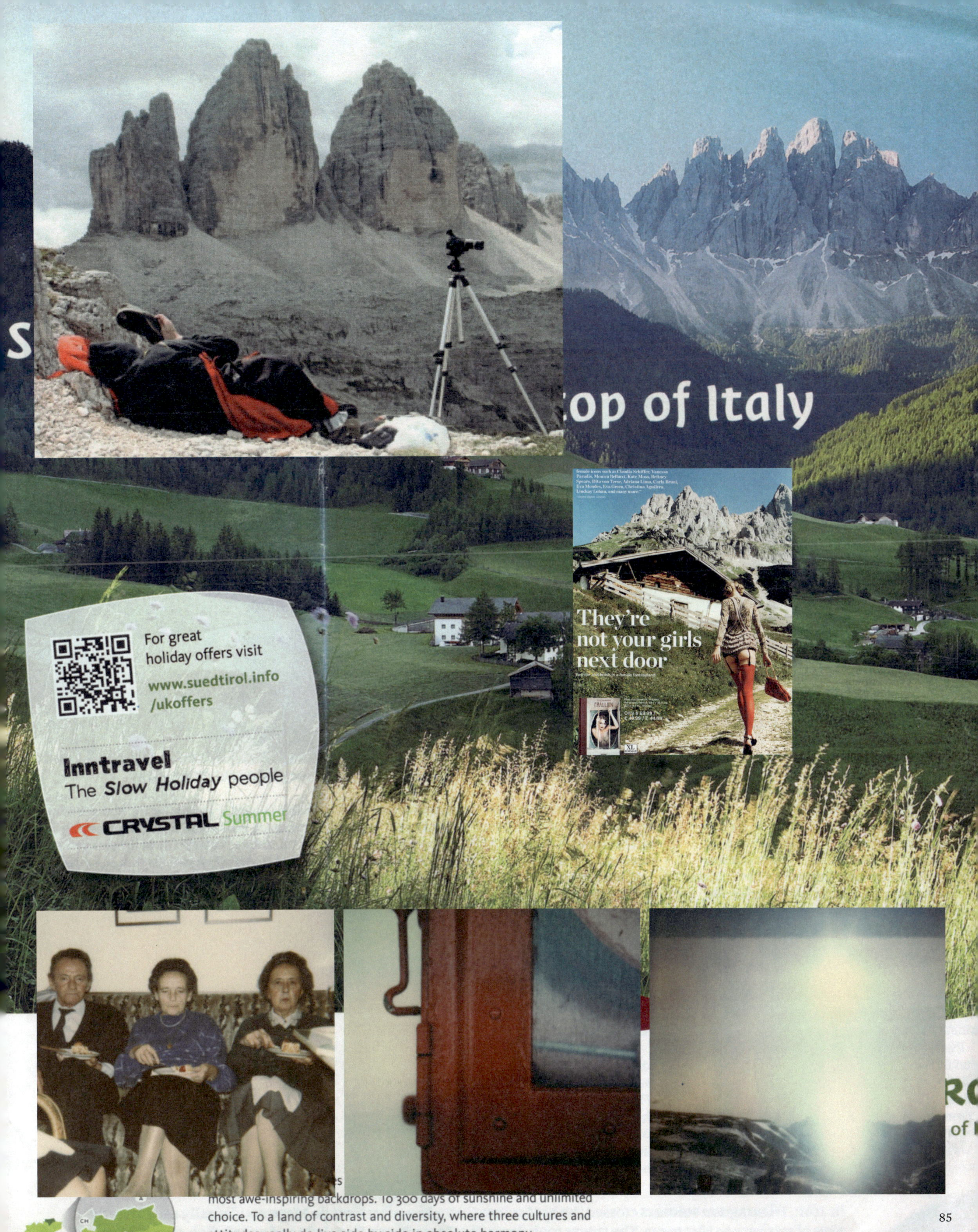

S
op of Italy
For great holiday offers visit
www.suedtirol.info /ukoffers
Inntravel
The Slow Holiday people
CRYSTAL Summer
They're not your girls next door
RO
of
s
most awe-inspiring backdrops. To 300 days of sunshine and unlimited choice. To a land of contrast and diversity, where three cultures and attitudes really do live side by side in absolute harmony.
Bolzano

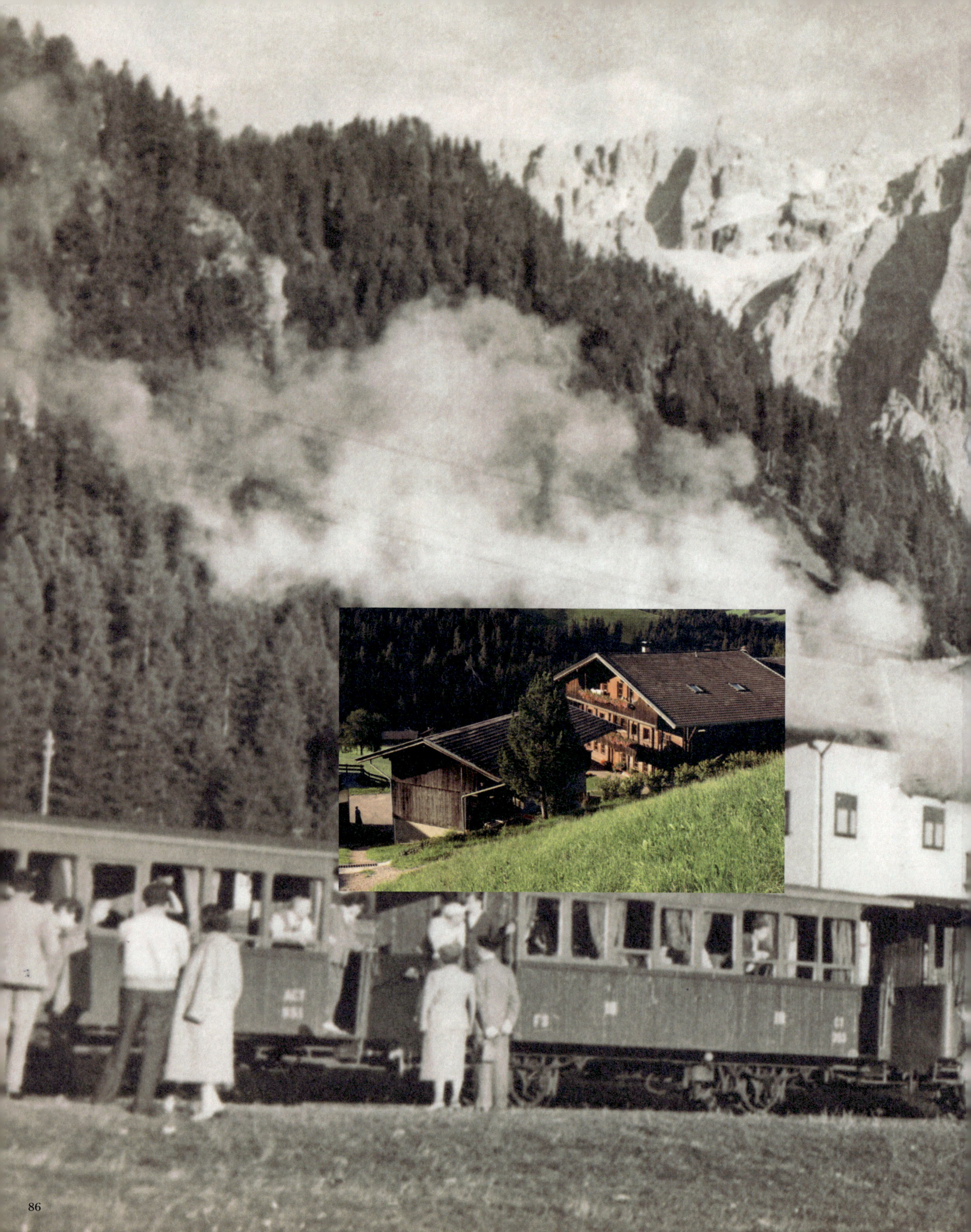

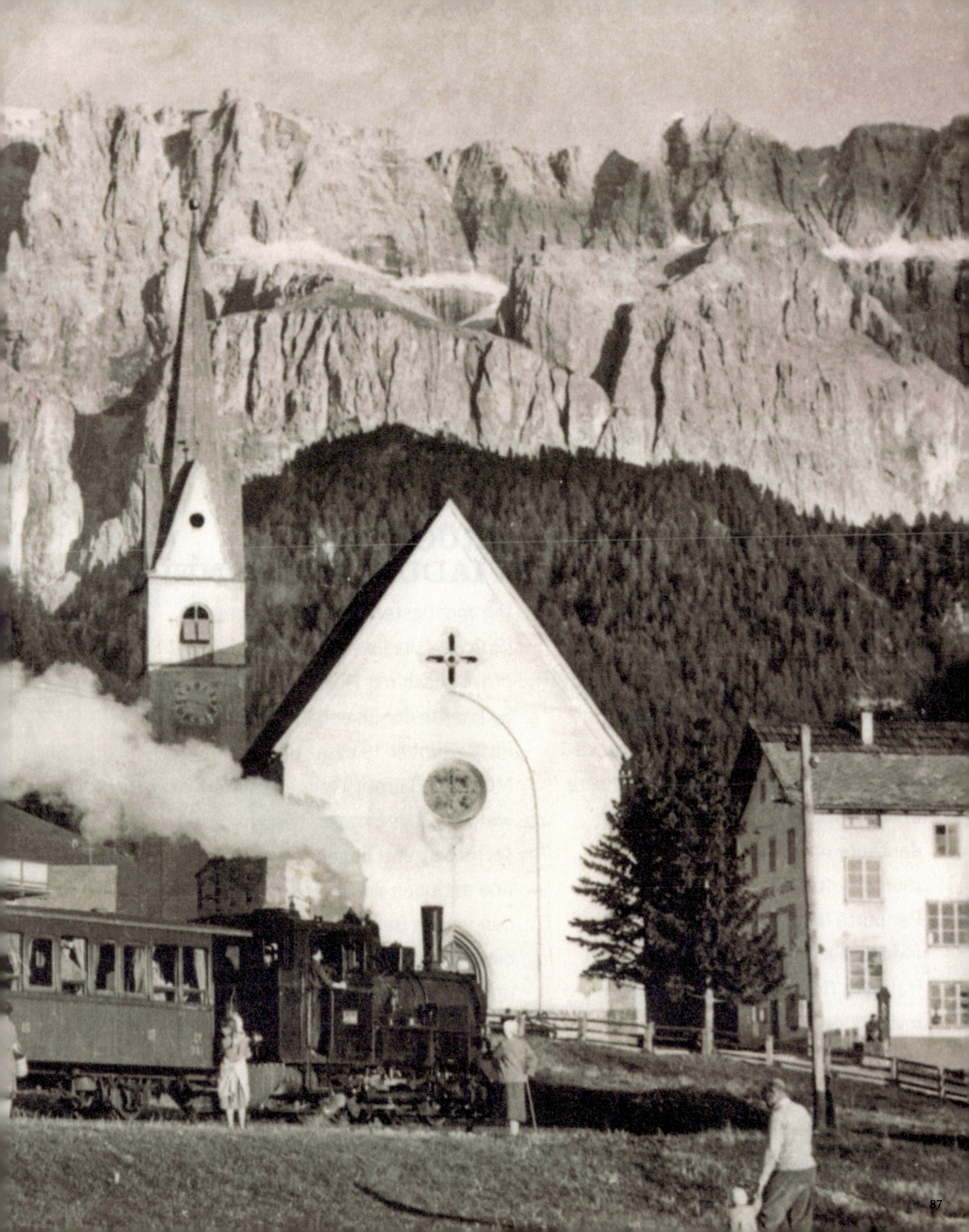

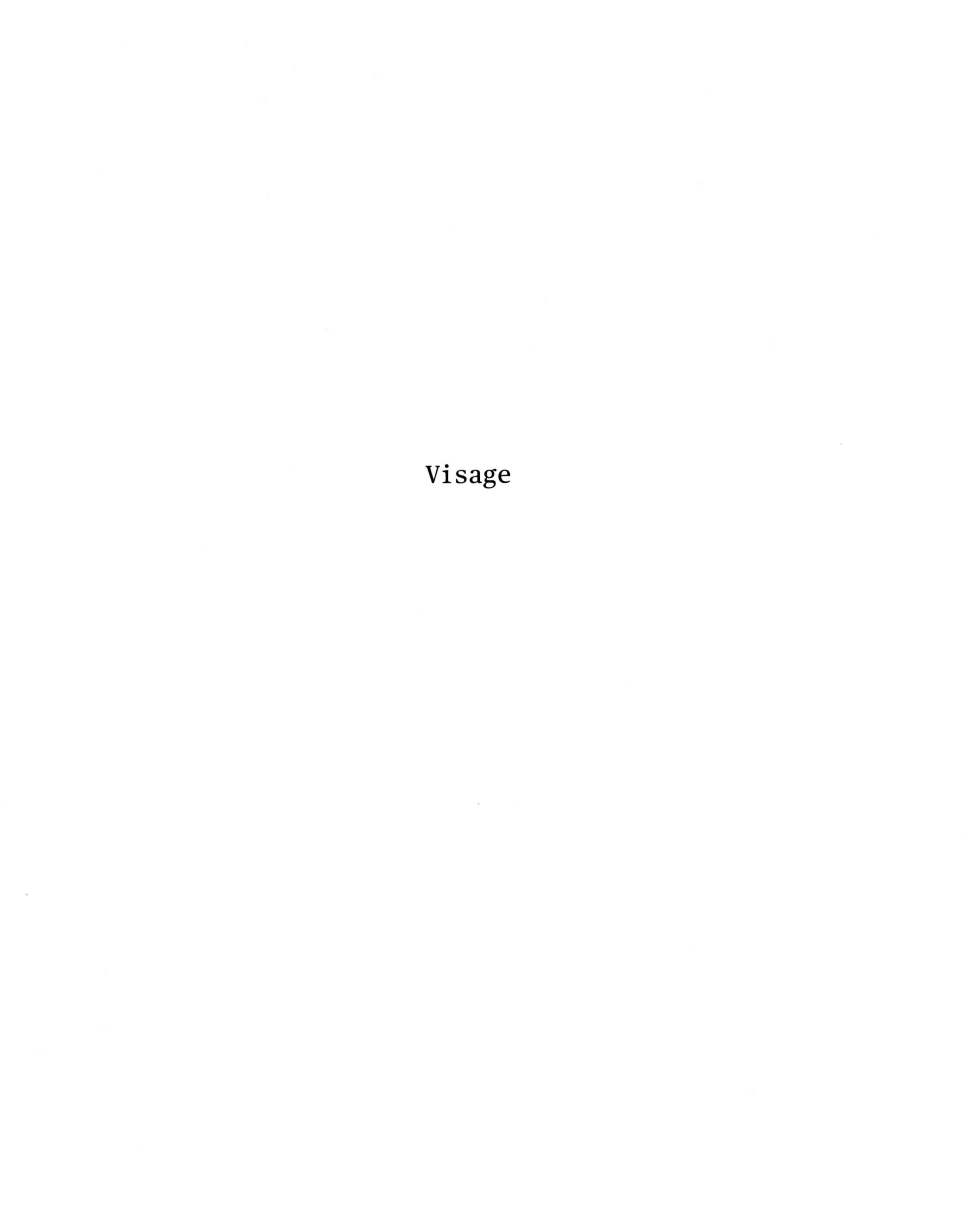

Visage

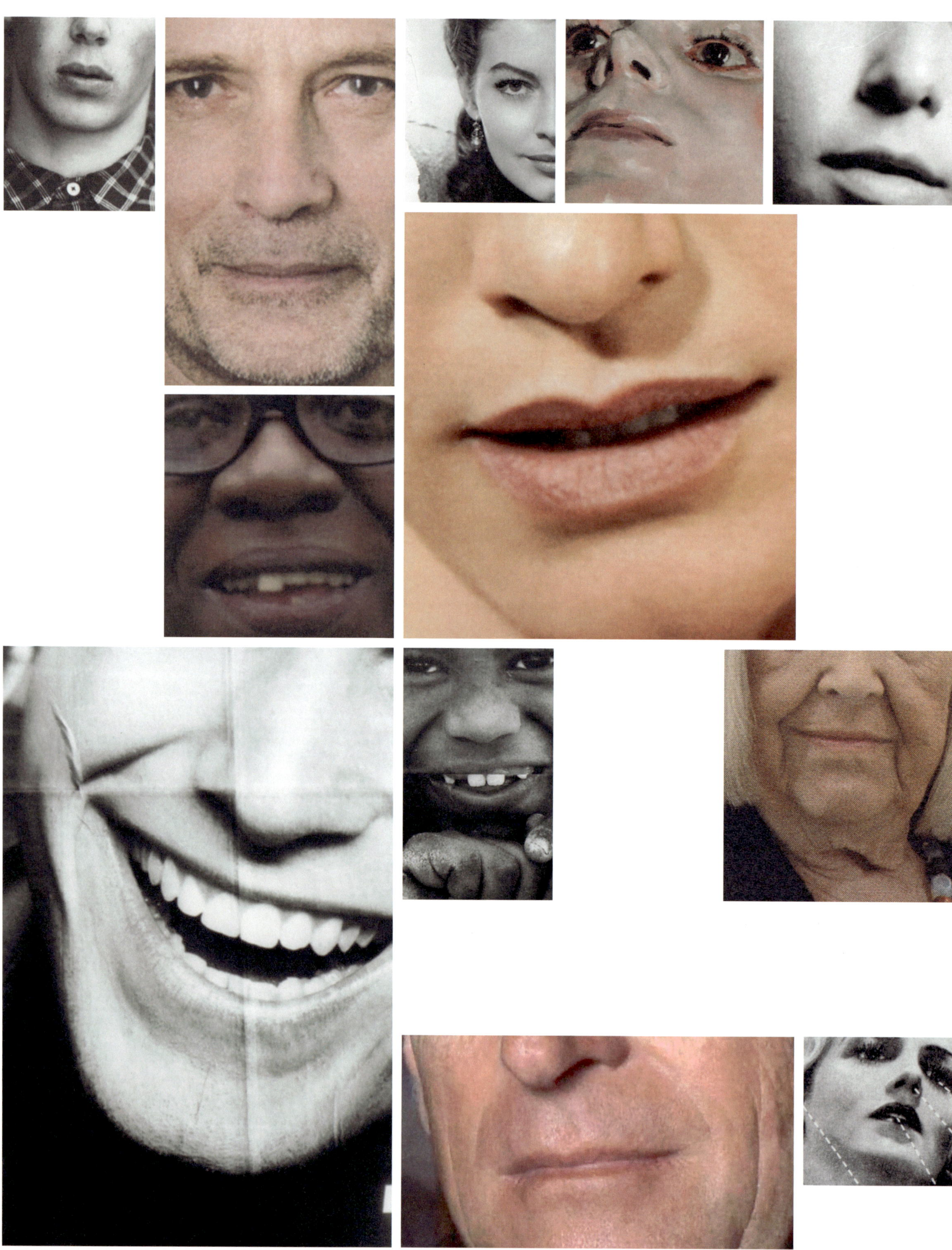

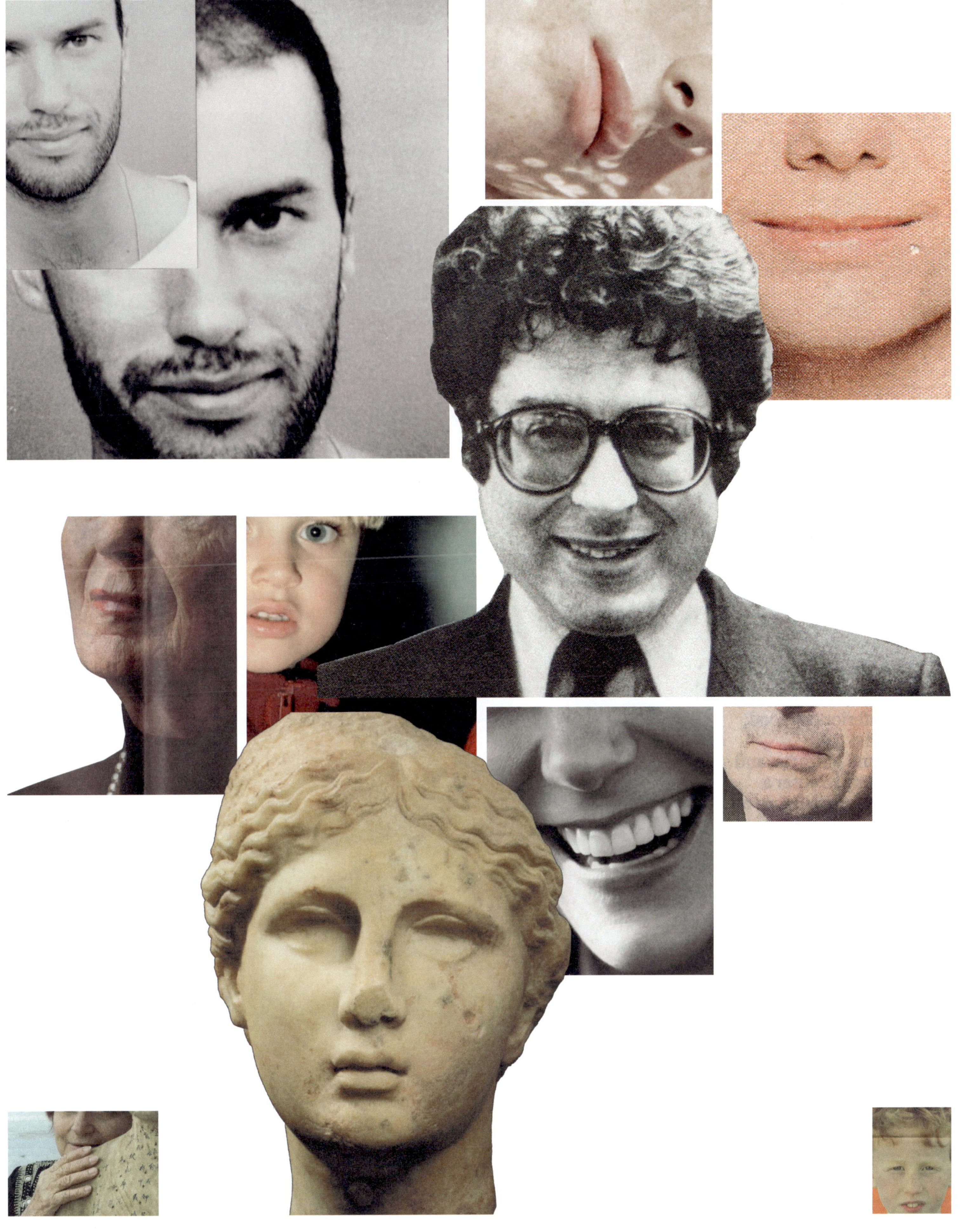

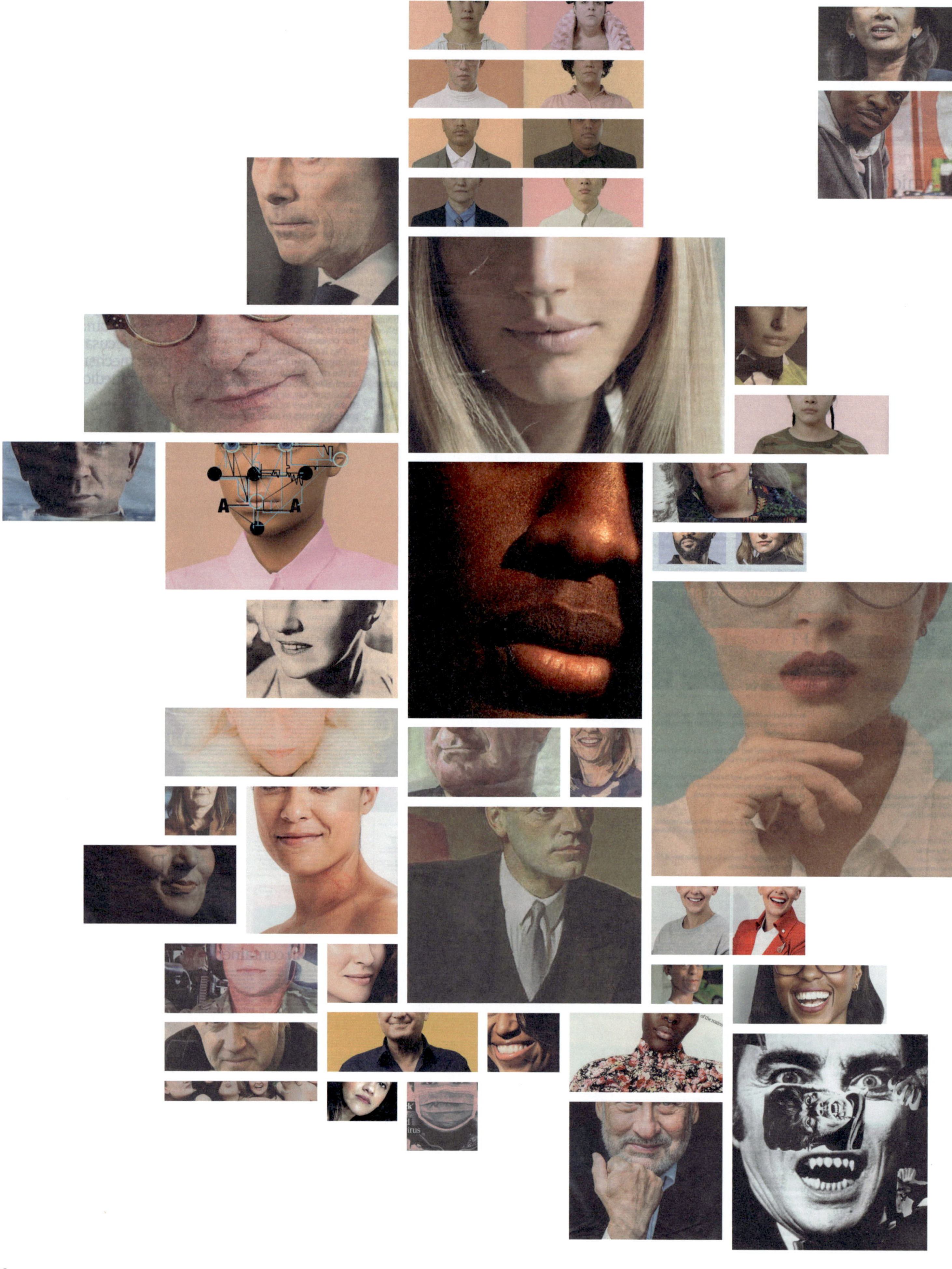

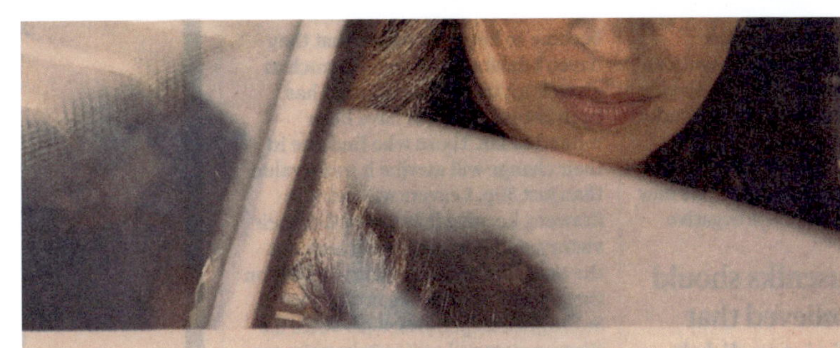

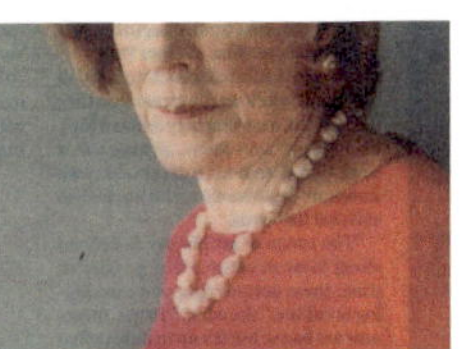

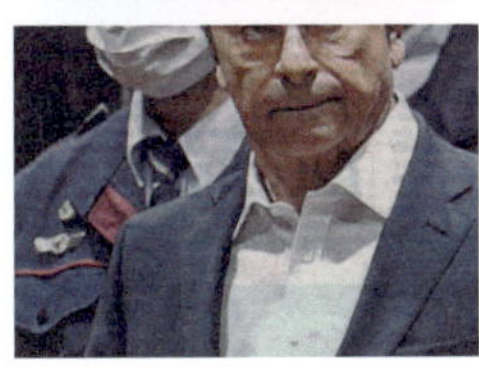

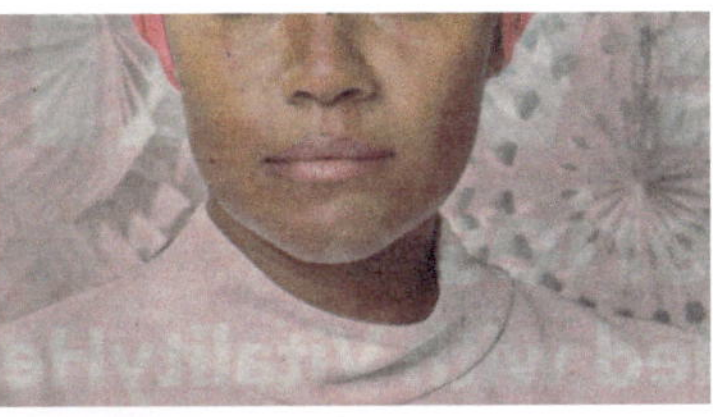

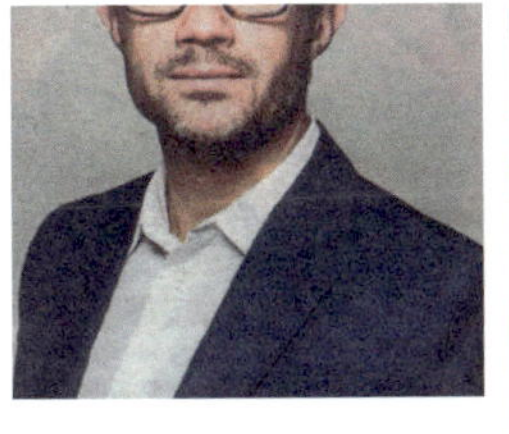

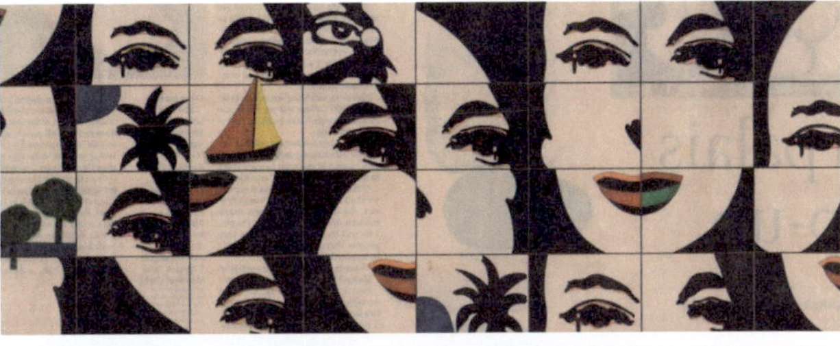

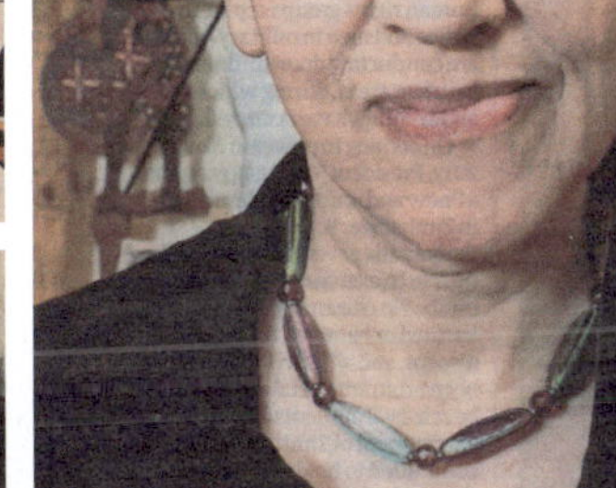

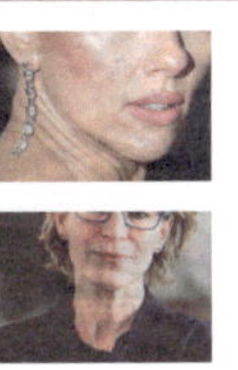

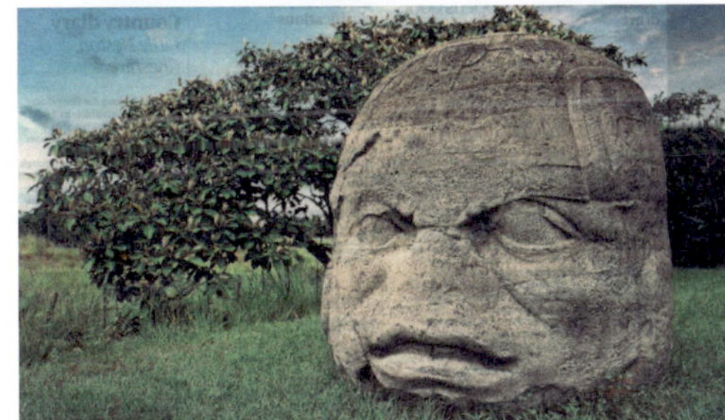

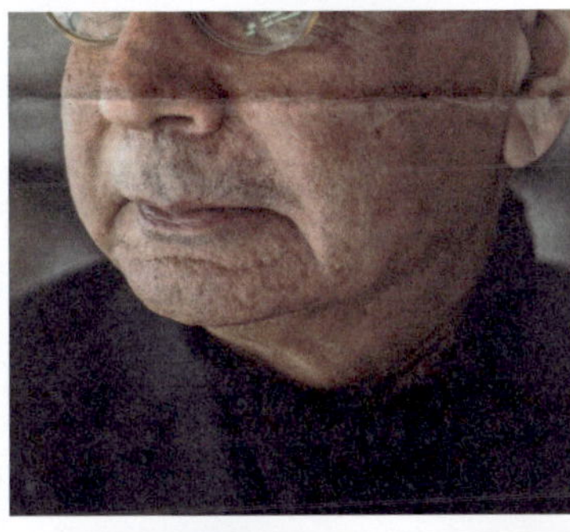

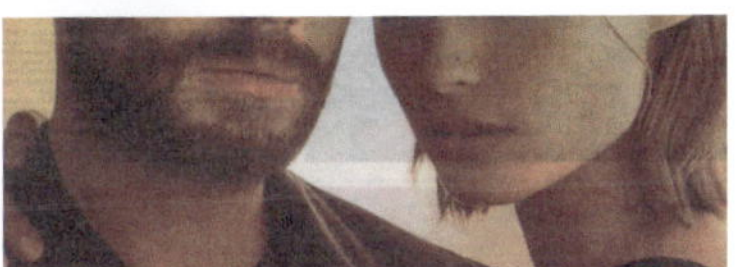

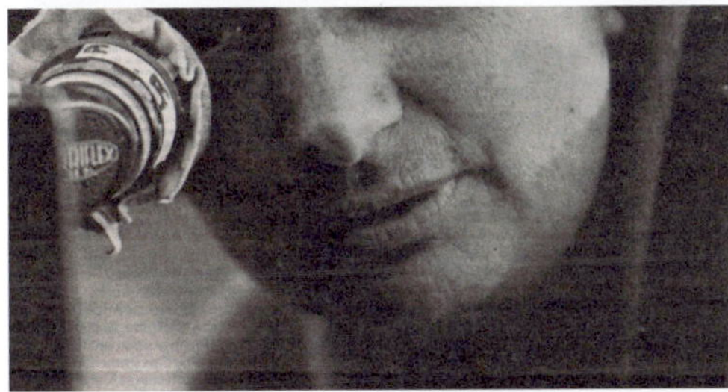

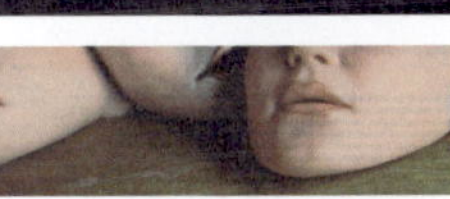

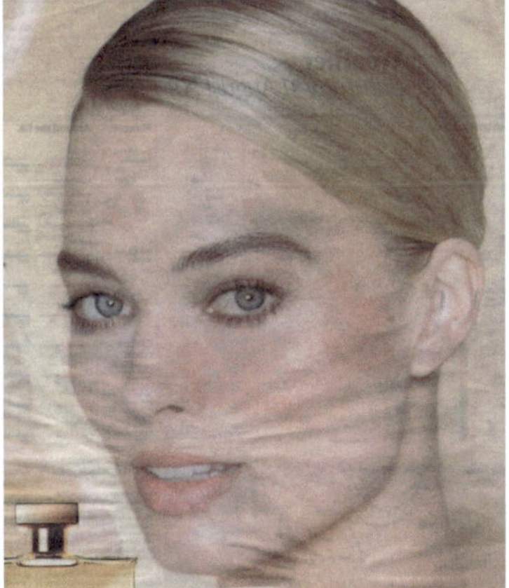

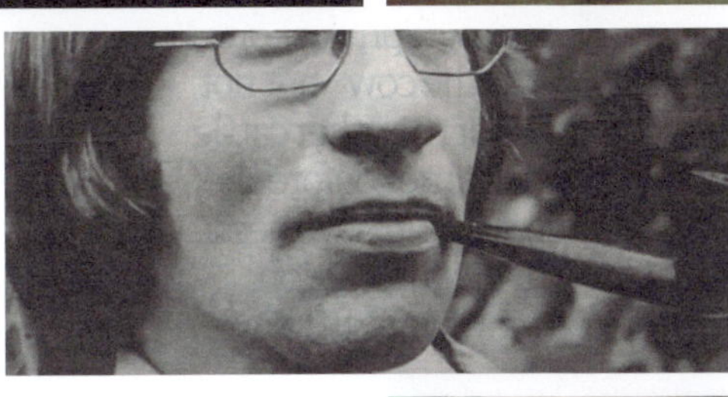

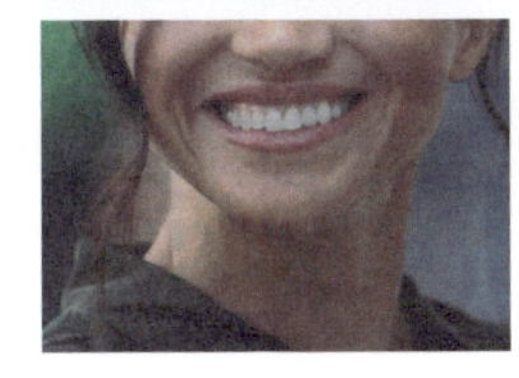

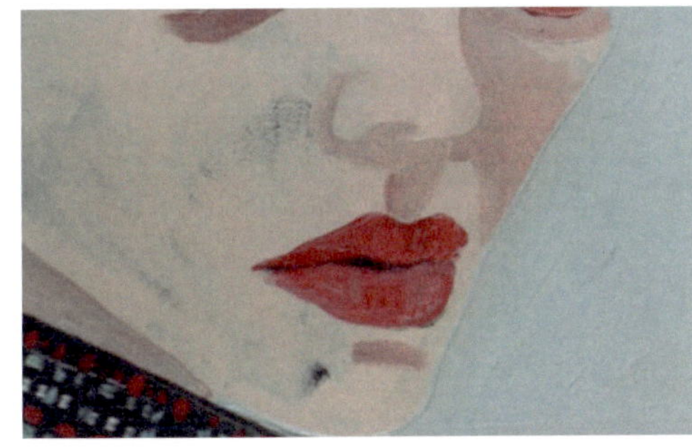

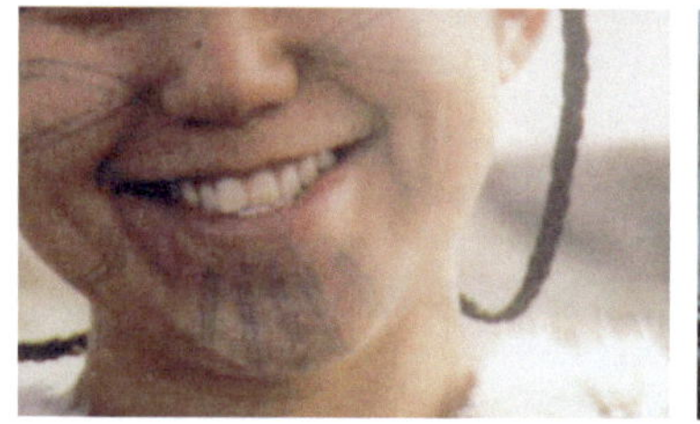
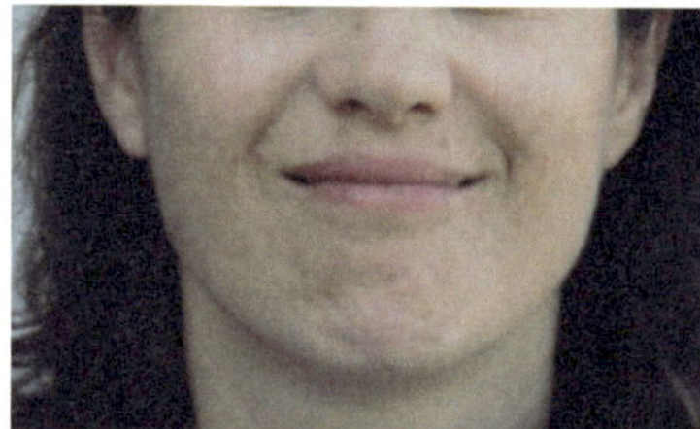
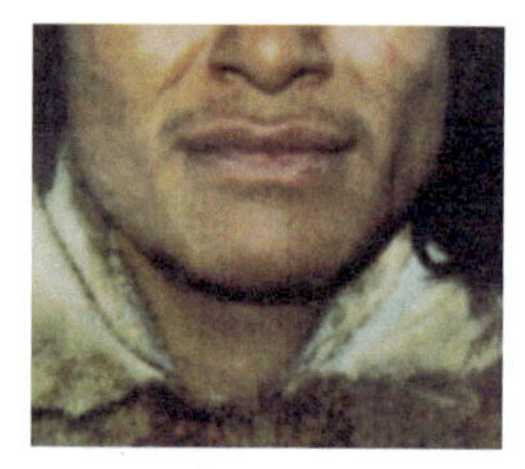
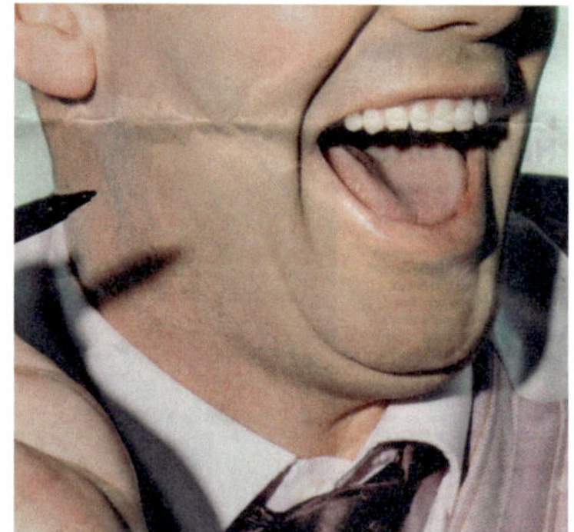
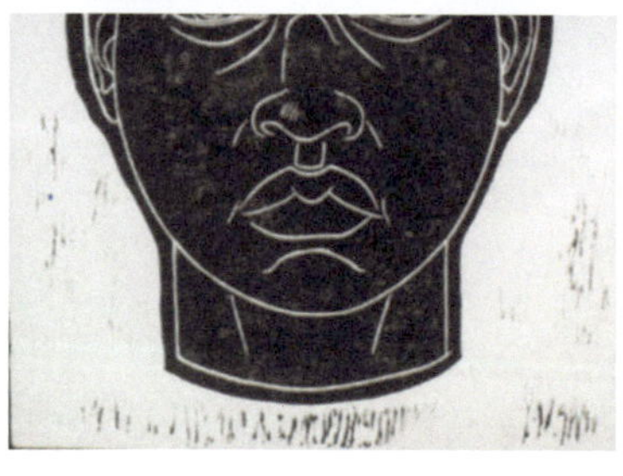
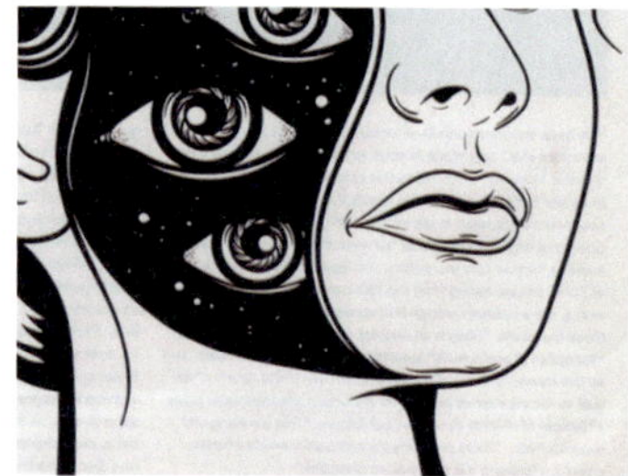
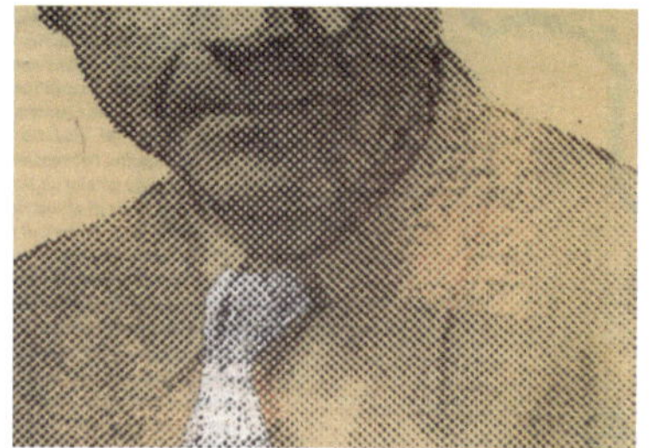
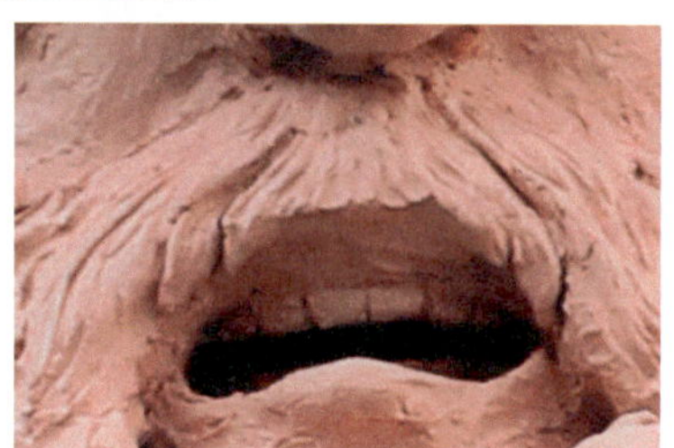
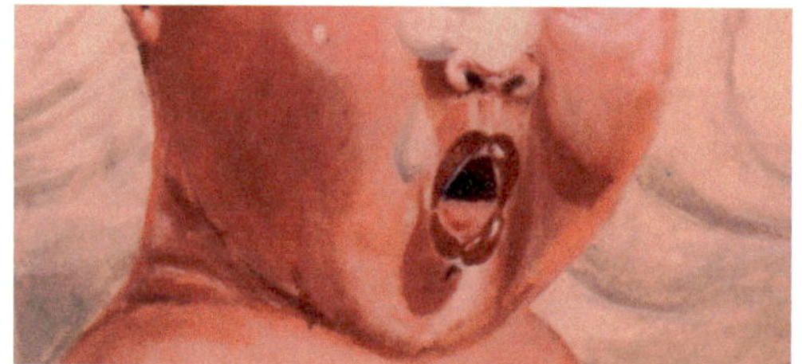
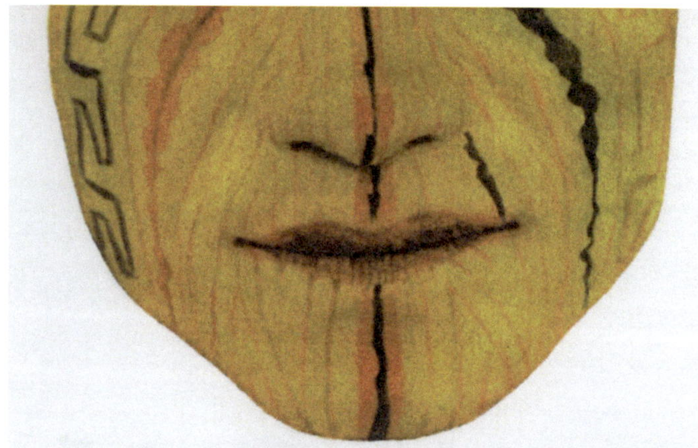
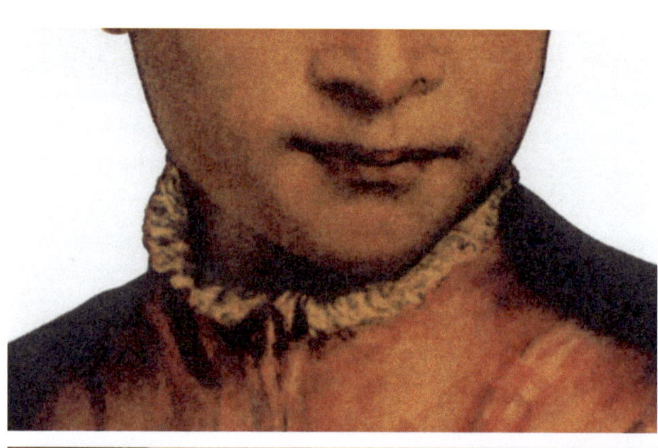
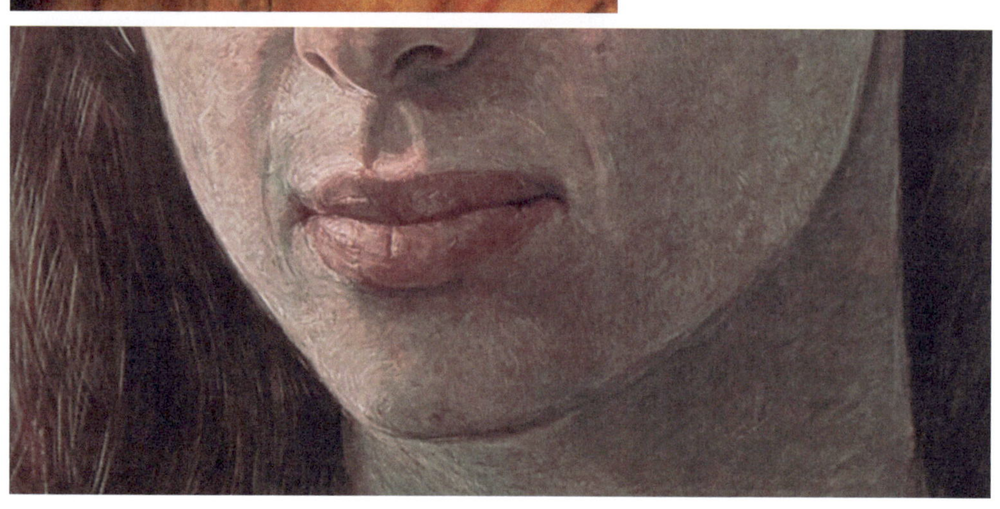
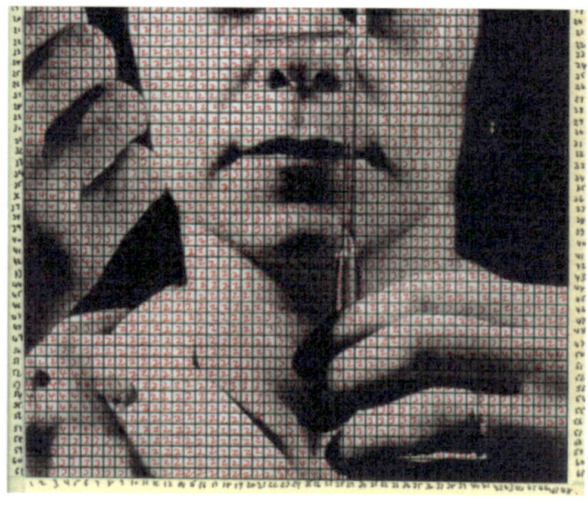
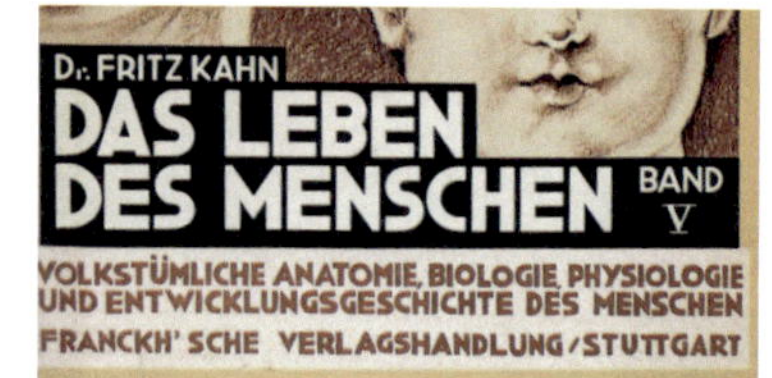
Dr. FRITZ KAHN
DAS LEBEN DES MENSCHEN
BAND V
VOLKSTÜMLICHE ANATOMIE, BIOLOGIE, PHYSIOLOGIE UND ENTWICKLUNGSGESCHICHTE DES MENSCHEN
FRANCKH'SCHE VERLAGSHANDLUNG / STUTTGART

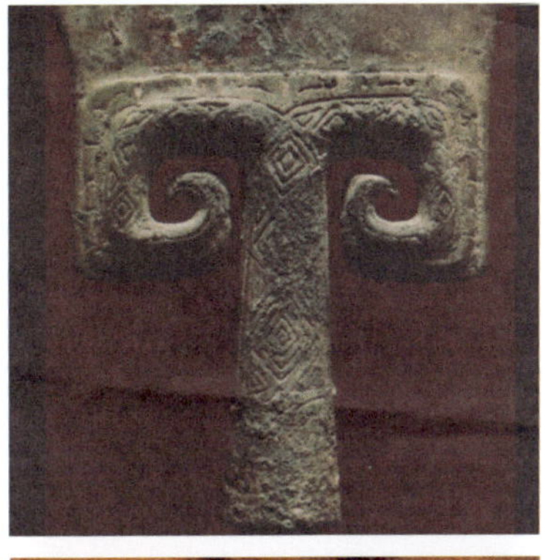

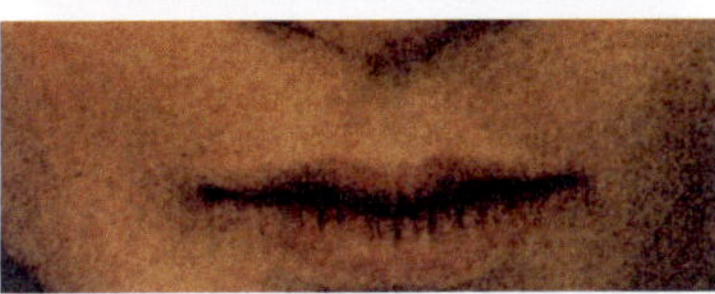

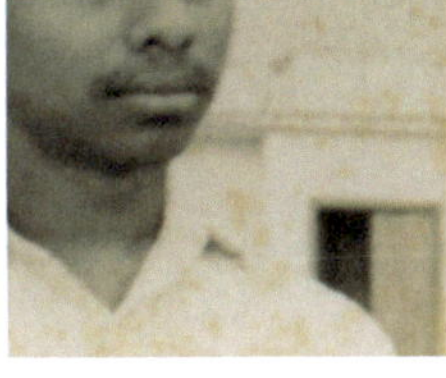

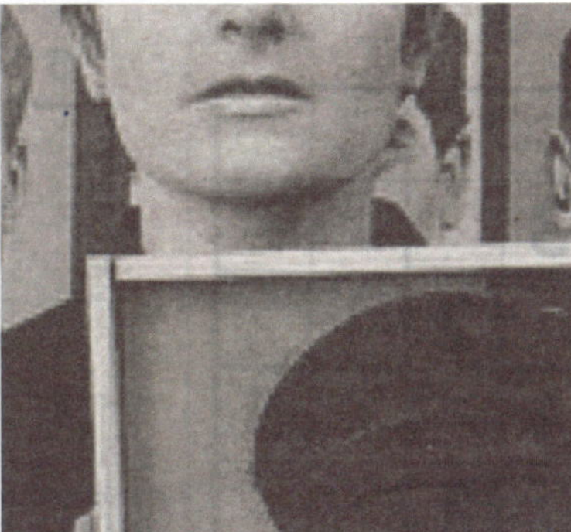

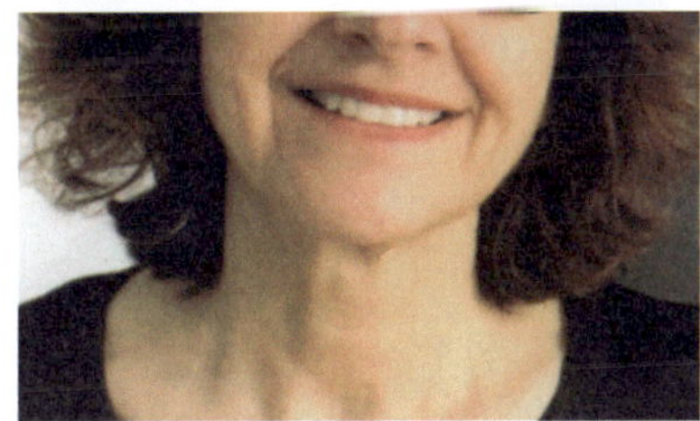

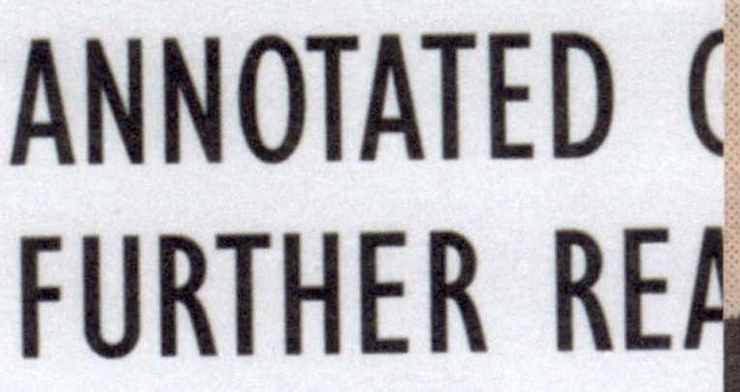

ANNOTATED C
FURTHER REA

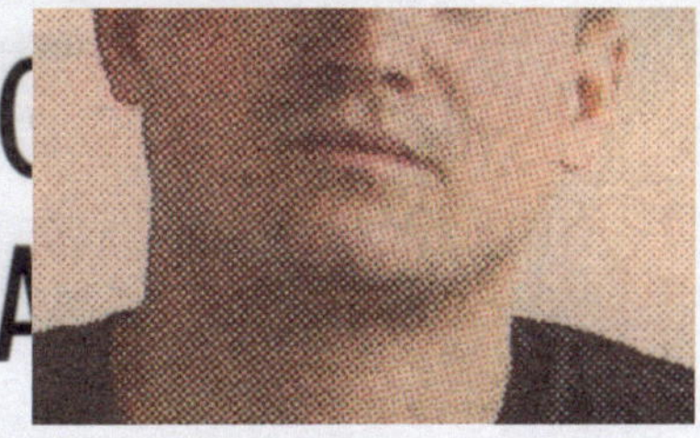

Barthes, Roland, *Image-Music-Text*, London: Fontana, 1982.
This book is a brilliant collection of essays concerning Barthes's writings on photogra
film and semiotic theory. Edited and translated by the British film theorist Stephen He
it is one of the m ... difficul
places, it shows E ... ing ab
types of photogra ... and sc
problems. Journa ... heore
discussion and cr

Barthes, Roland, *Ca*
Widely read as ... is actu
based in phenom ... experi
to examine 'the ... hy th
and criticism (it ... n wha
psychoanalysis Ja ... imagi
look from some ... at Bar
calls the *punctum* ... ay tha
original photogr ... tion o
gaze. A good complementary essay is 'The Third Meaning', whose categories of *ob*
and *obtuse* precede *studium* and *punctum* in *Camera Lucida*.

Belsey, Catherine, *A Very Short Introduction to Poststructuralism*, Oxford: Oxford Unive
Press, 2002.
This is a very good introduction to the thinking and impact of structuralism
poststructuralist arguments on the analysis of culture via images and the way we live
'inhabit' language.

Bolton, Richard, ed., *The Contest of Meaning: Critical Histories of Photography*, London:
Press, 1992.
This collection of varied critical essays deals with the avant-garde and modern 'tur
different European traditions and in USA photography, from the 1920s through t
1980s when the book was first published.

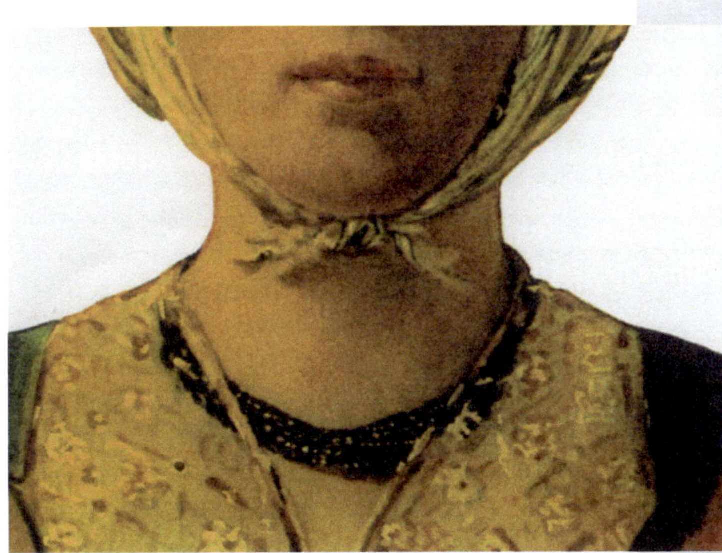

. See Sigmund Freud, *Three Essays on Sexuality*, translated by James Strachey, Pelican Freud L
Vol. 7 (Harmondsworth: Penguin, 1983).
. Jacques Lacan, *The Four Fu* ... rmondsworth: Penguin,
p115.
. See Laura Mulvey's classic ... e Cinema' in *Visual and*
Pleasures (London and Bas
. See Geoffrey Crawley, 'Co ... *ar Photography*, ed. Coli
(Bradford: National Muse ... 1989).
33. See the discussion on Jeff

Chapter 4 Looking at Por

1. On 'identity', see Stuart H ... n *Questions of Cultural I*
(London: Sage, 1996).
2. John Tagg, *The Burden of Representation* (Basingstoke: Macmillan, 1988).

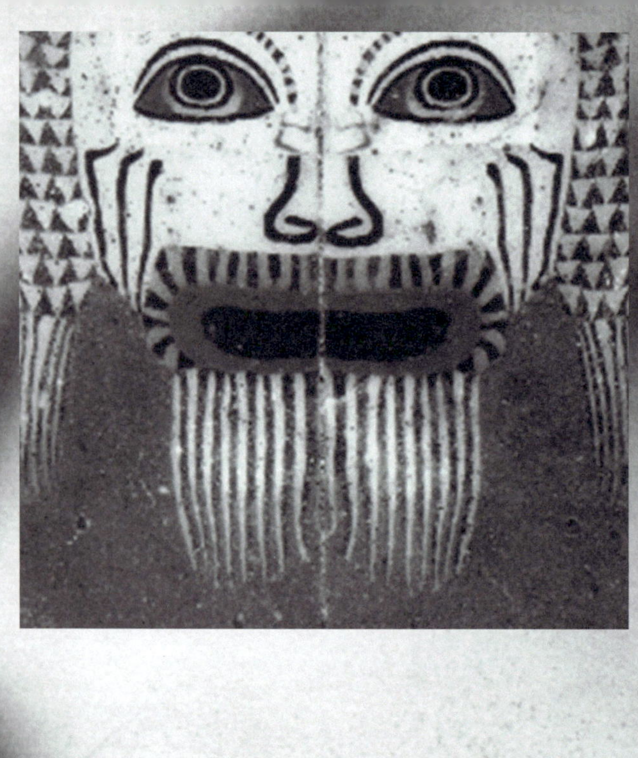
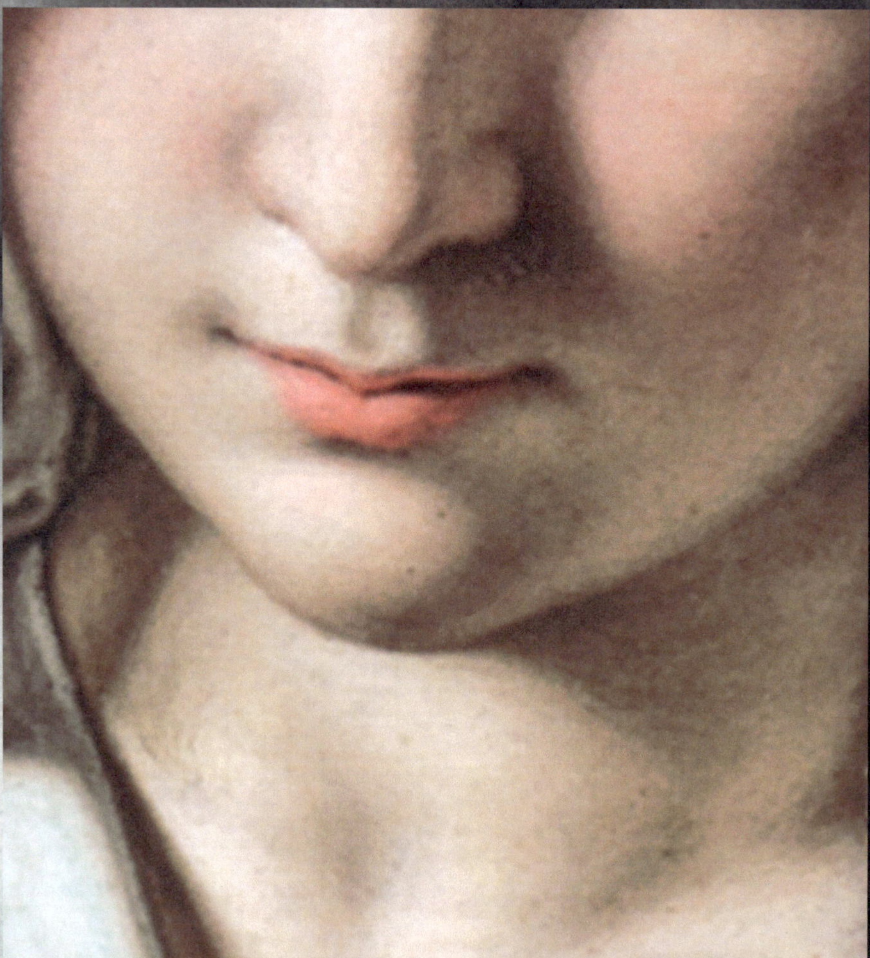
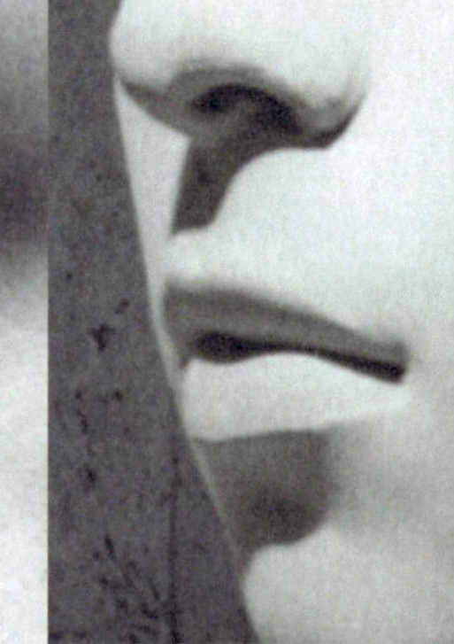
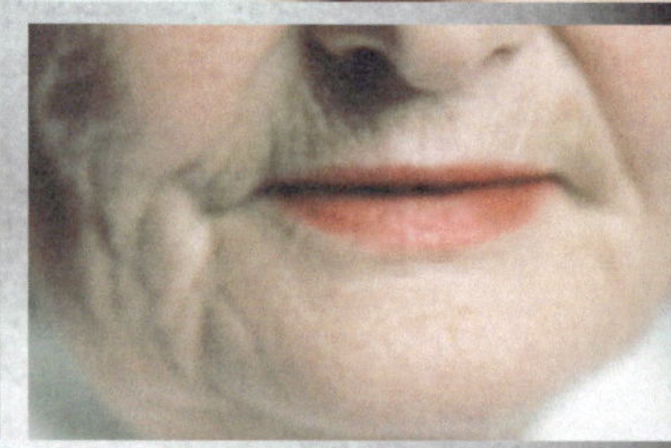
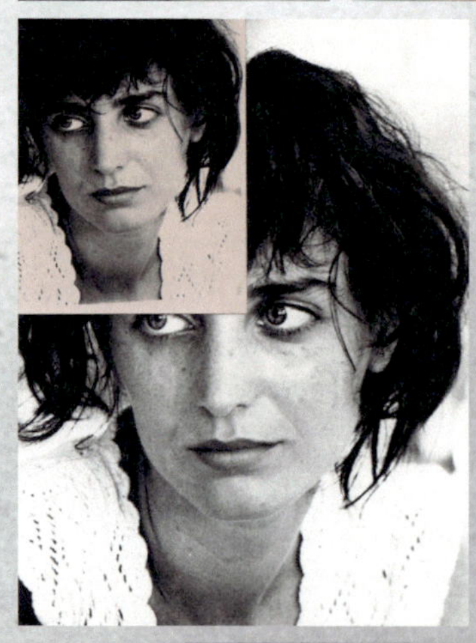
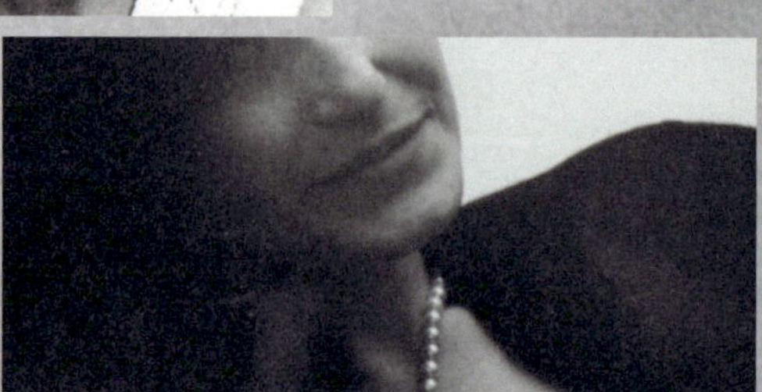
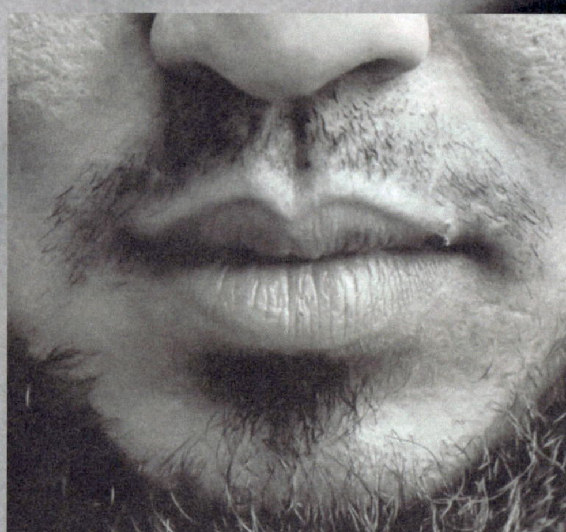
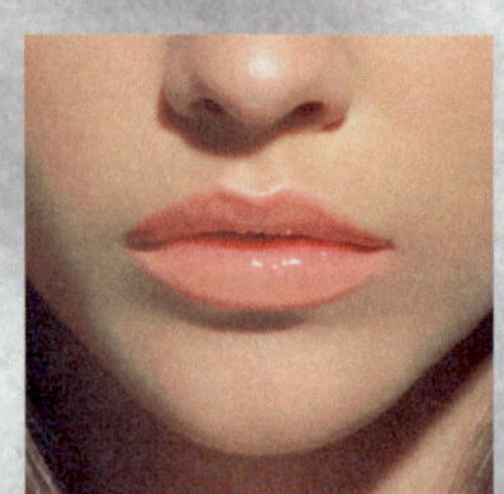

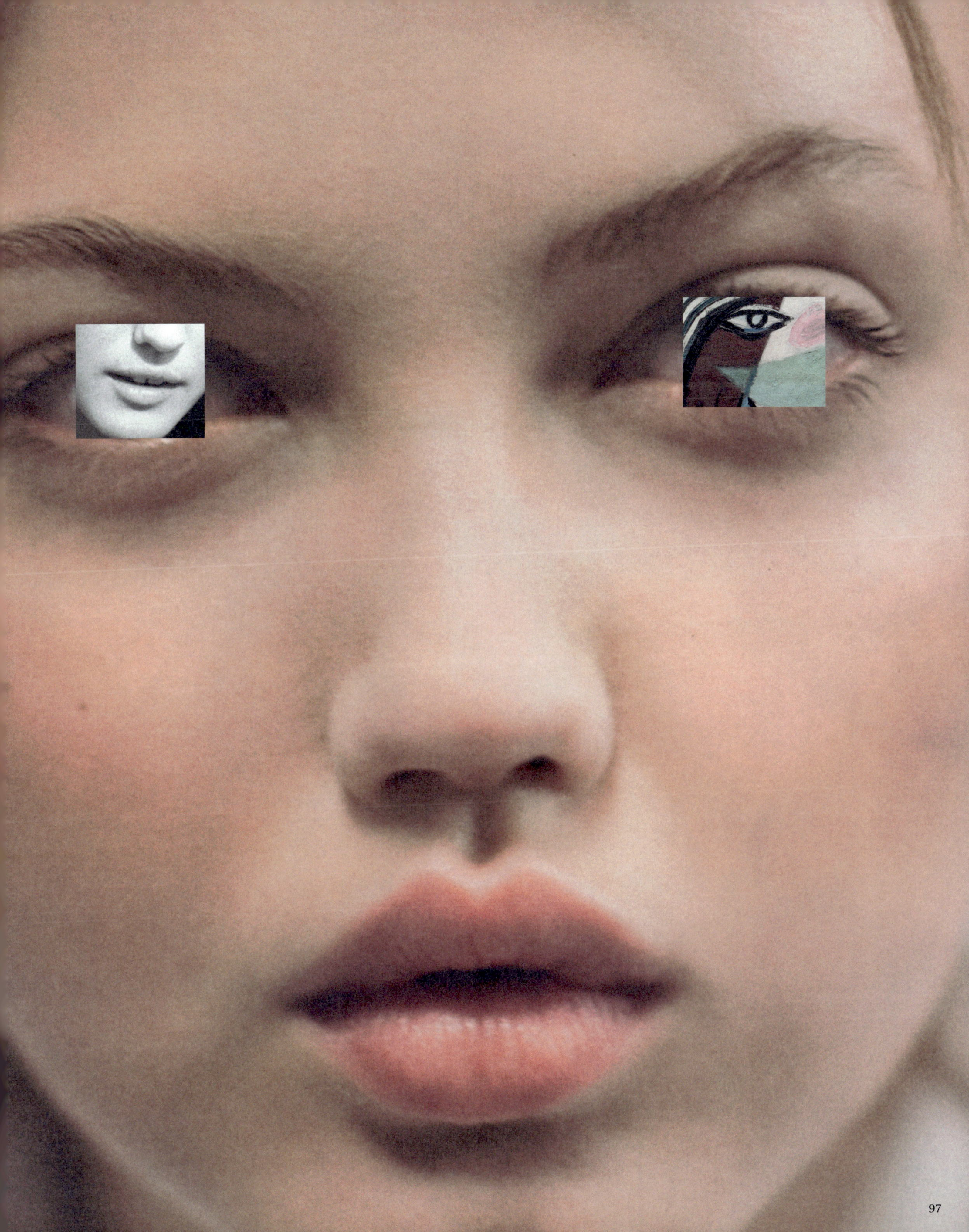

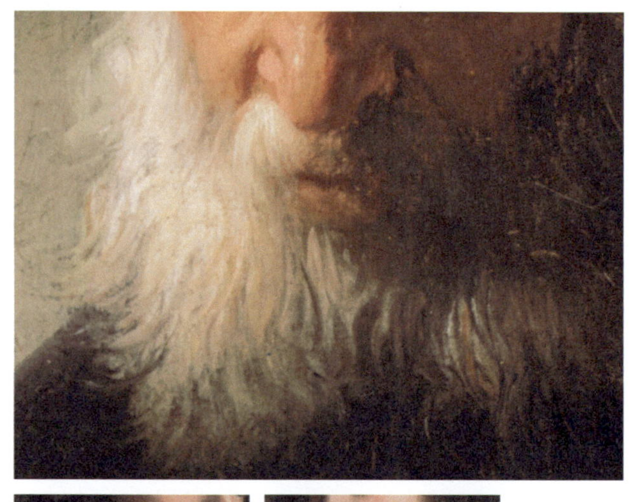
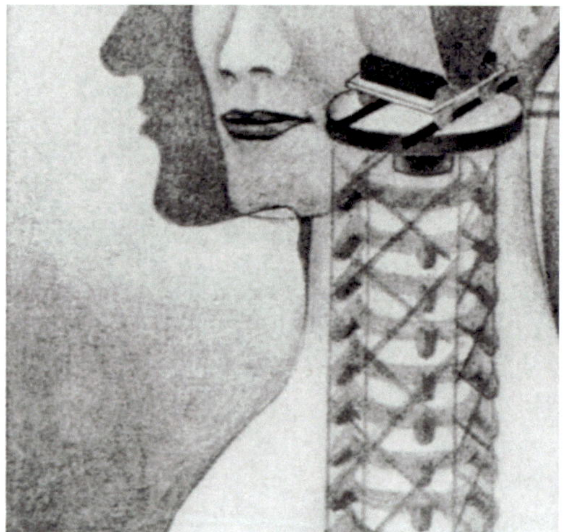
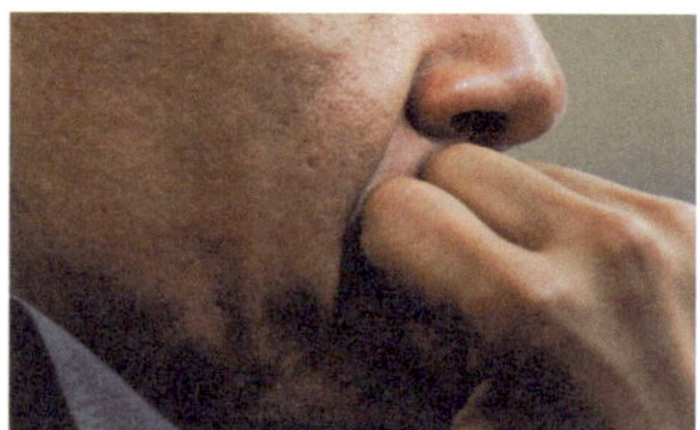
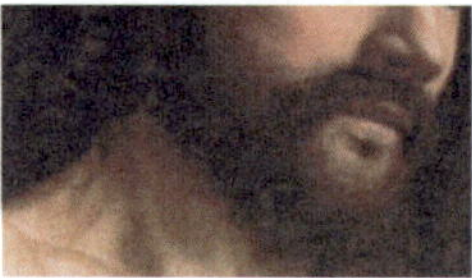
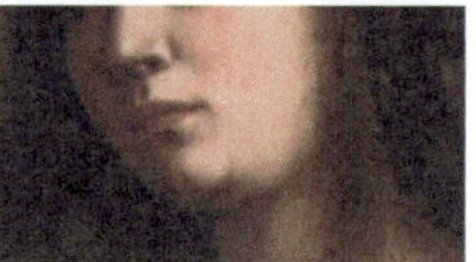
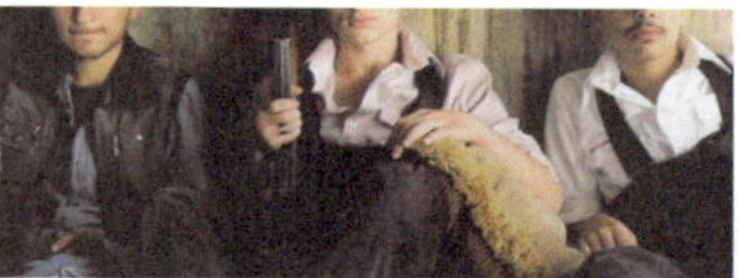
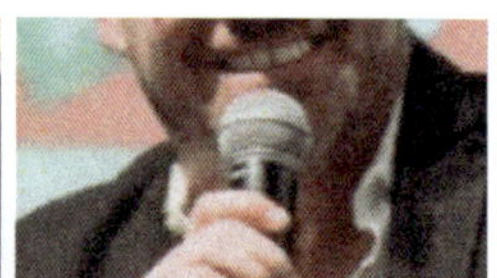
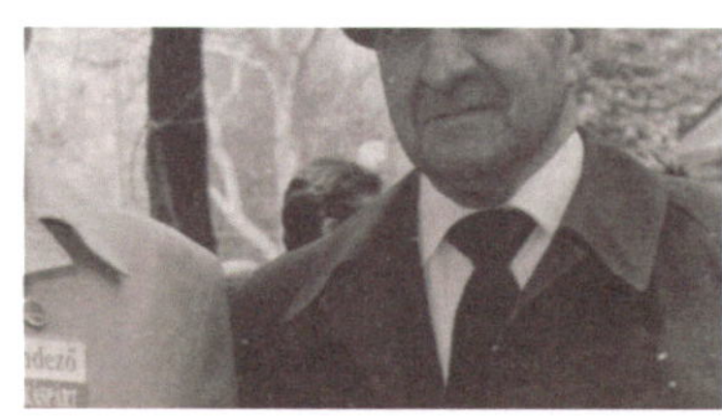
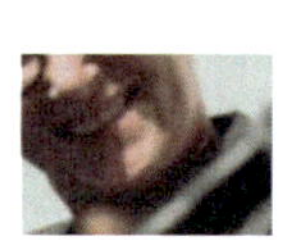
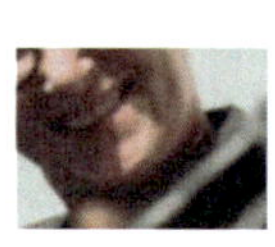
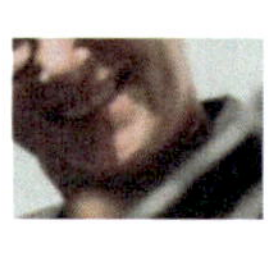
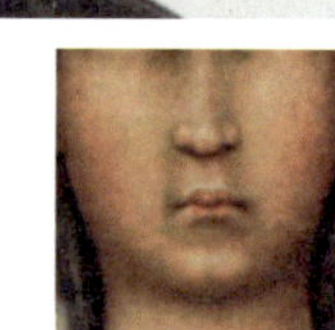
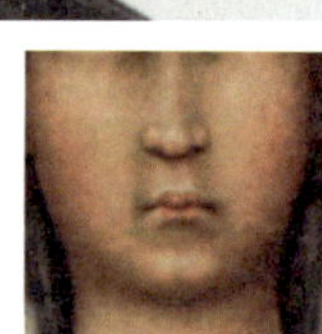
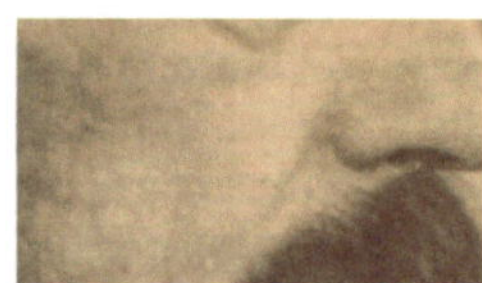
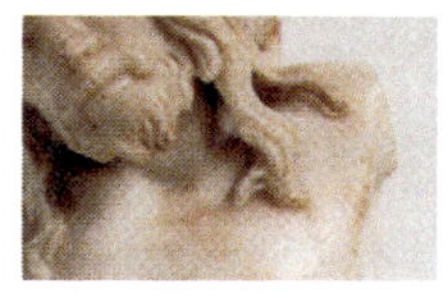
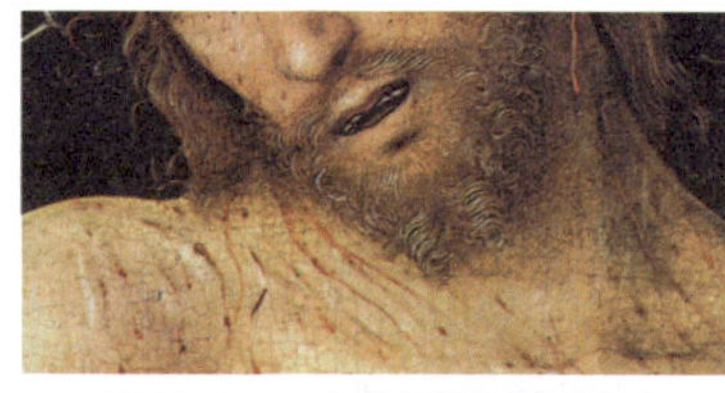
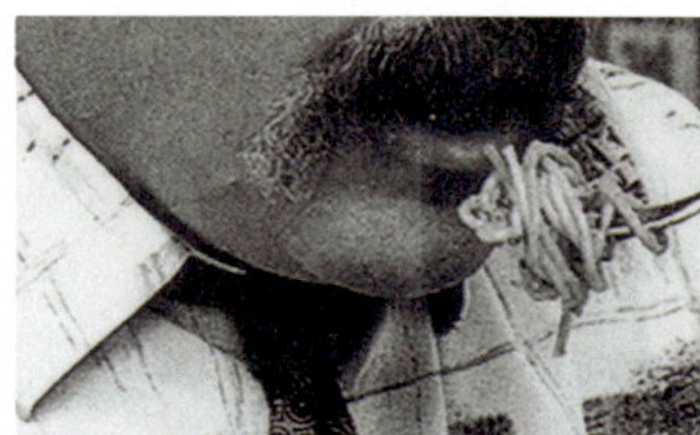
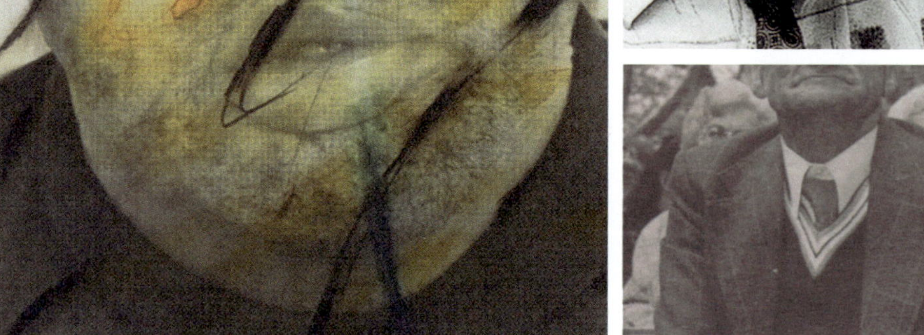
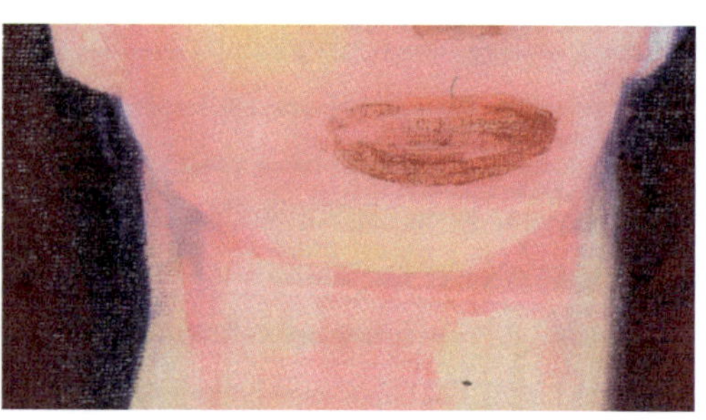

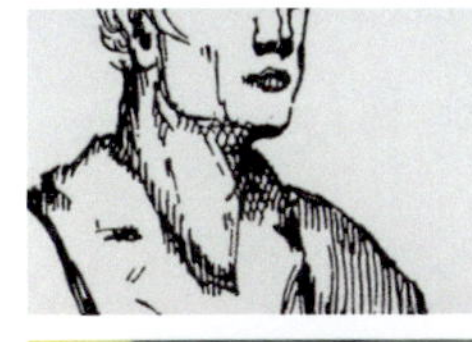
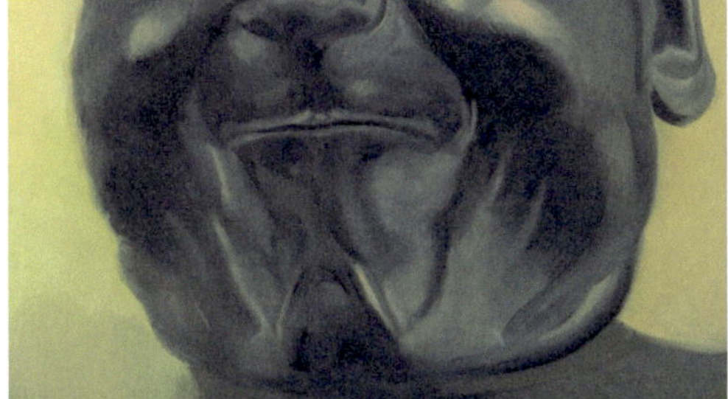
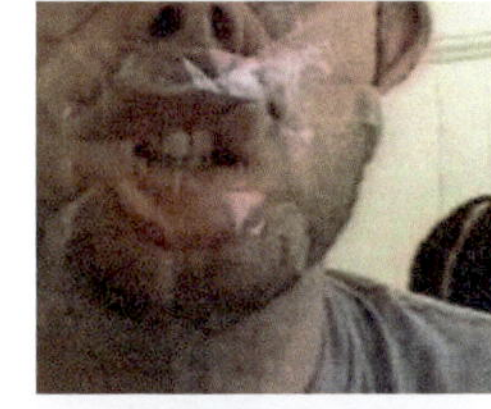
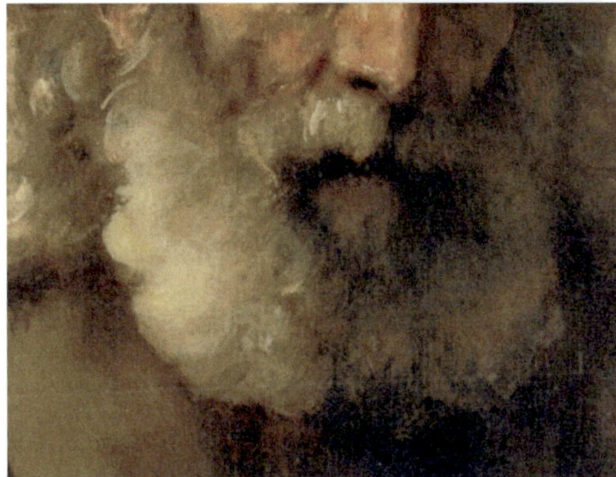
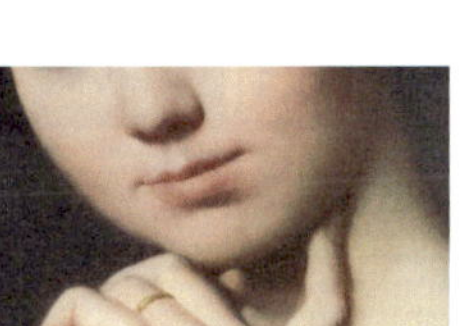
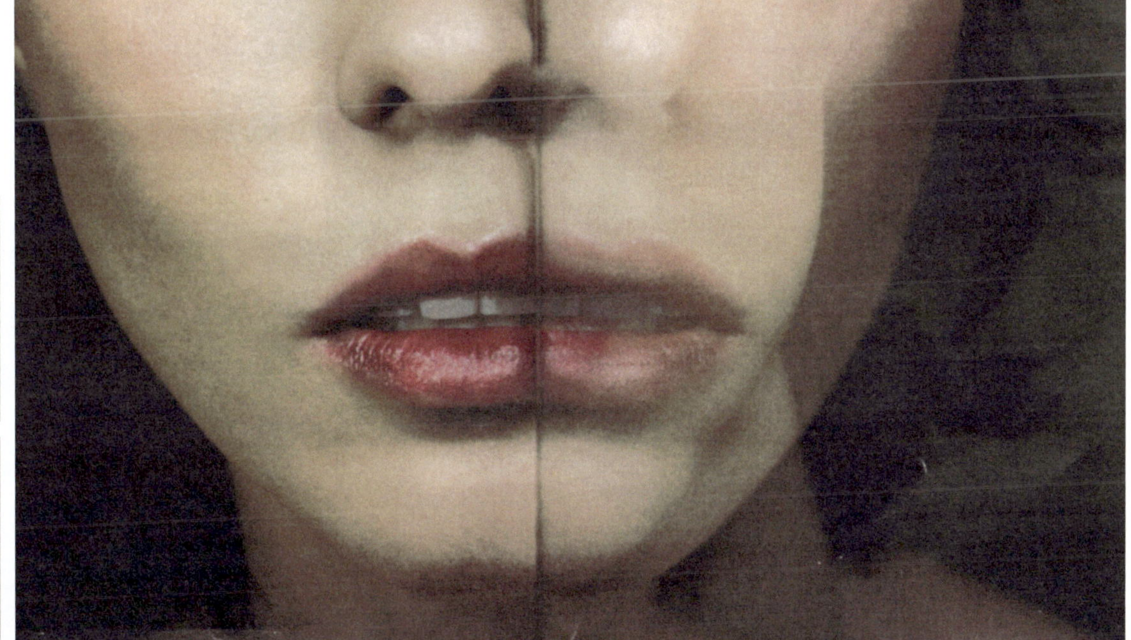
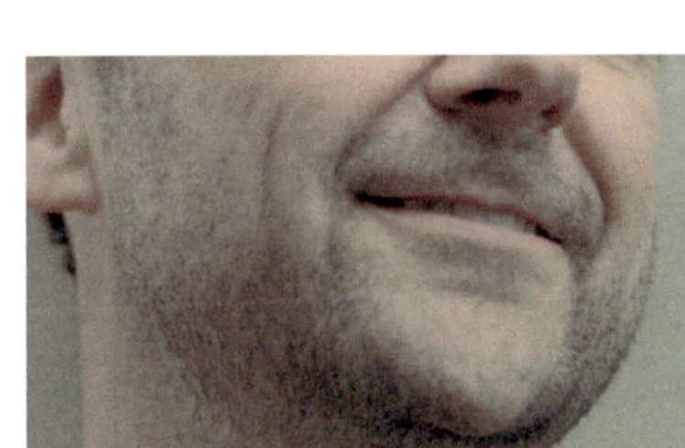
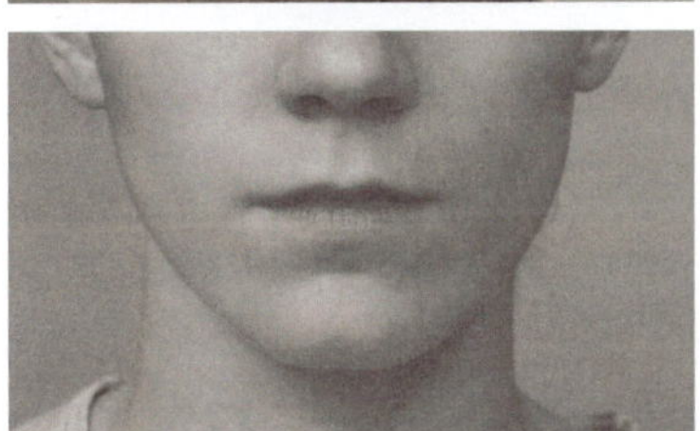
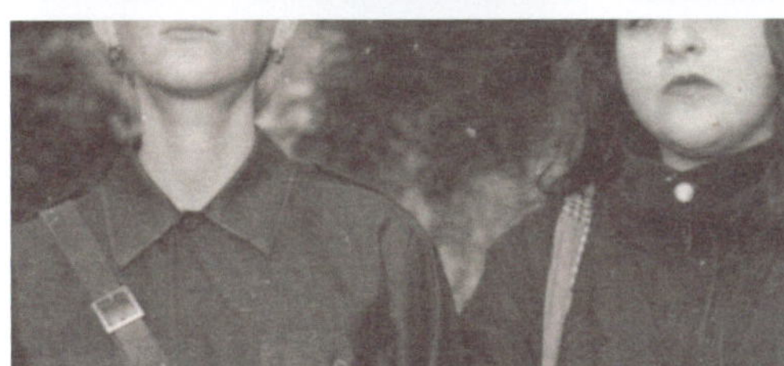
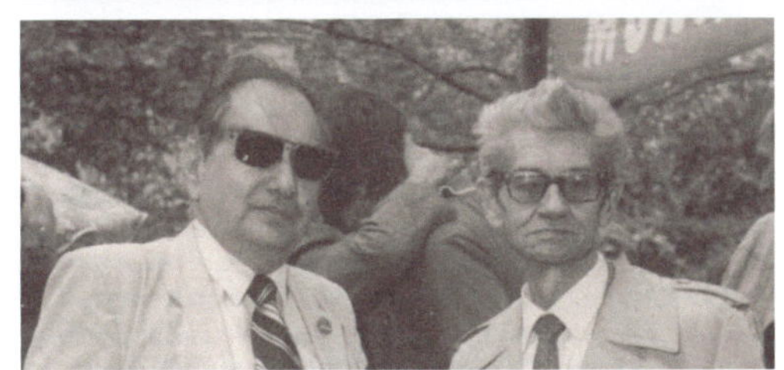
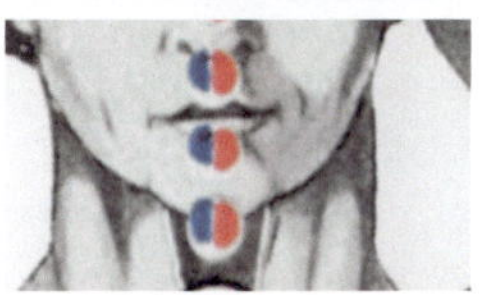
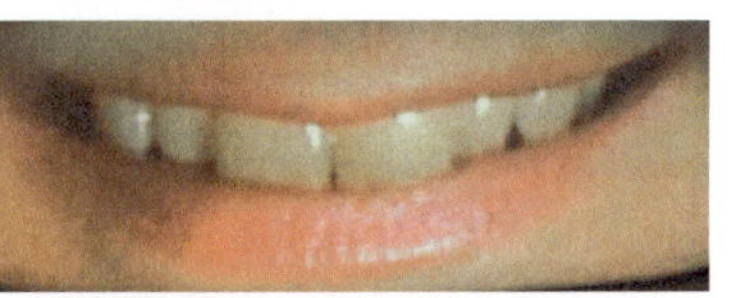
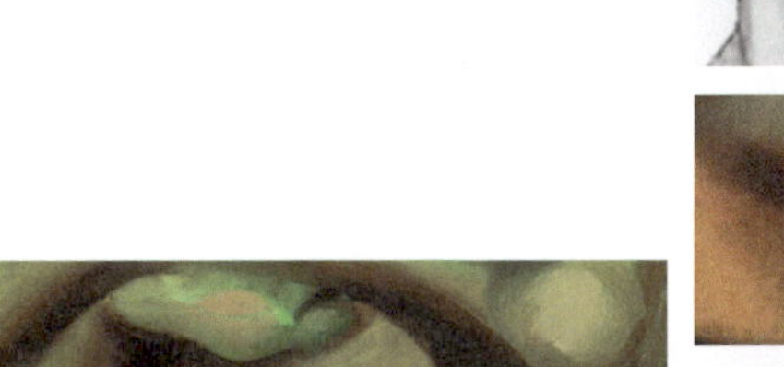
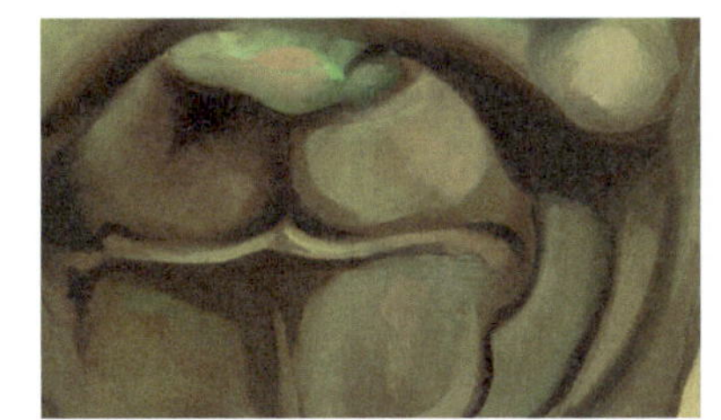
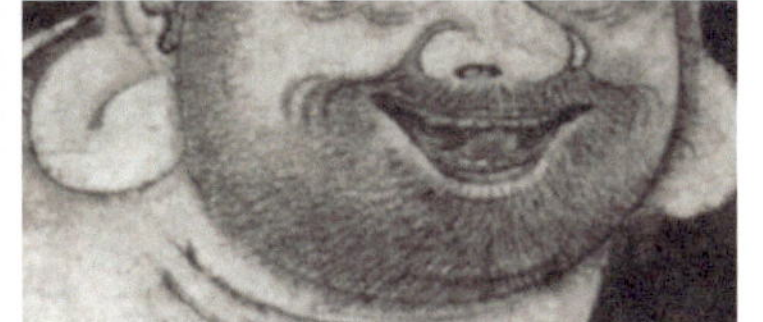

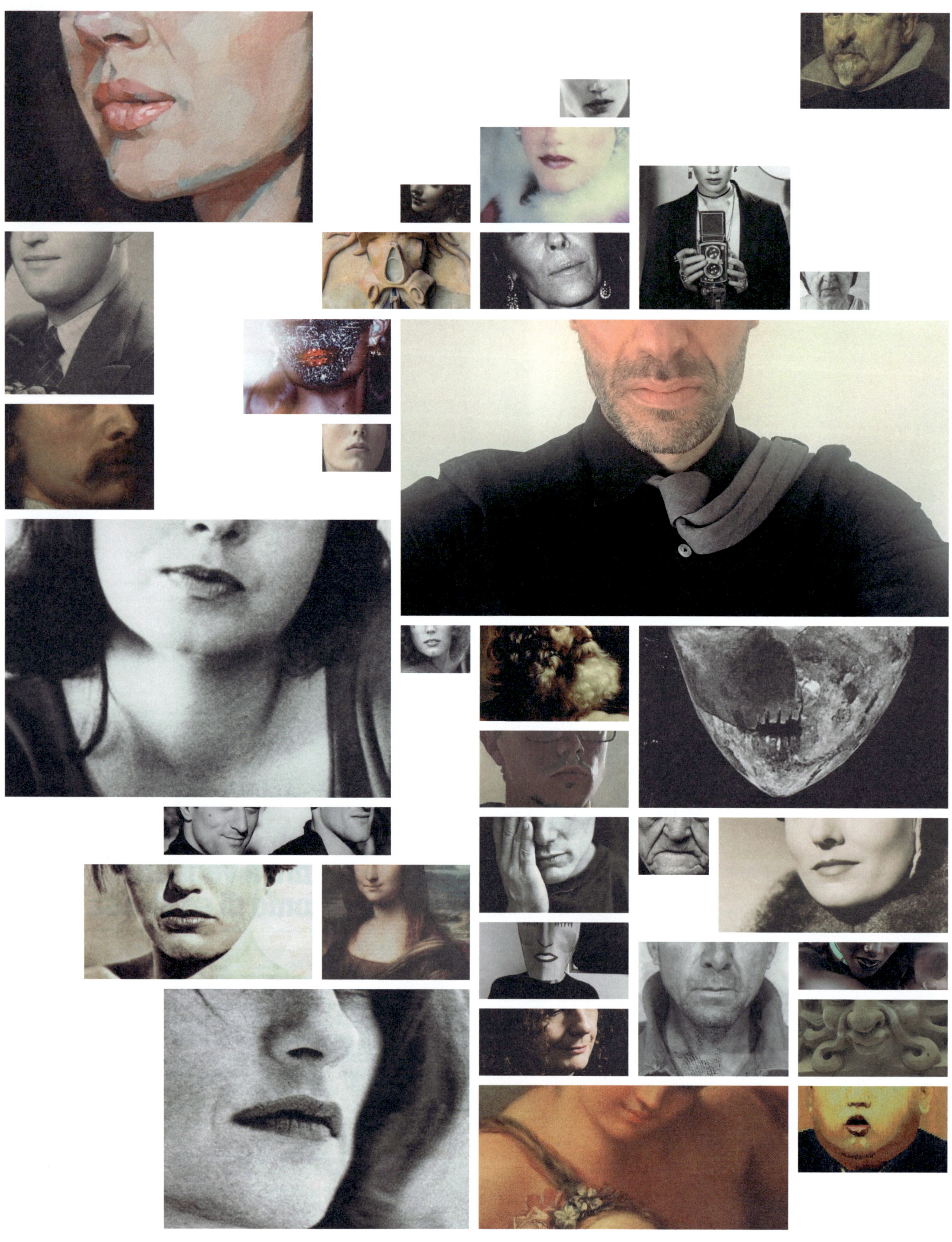

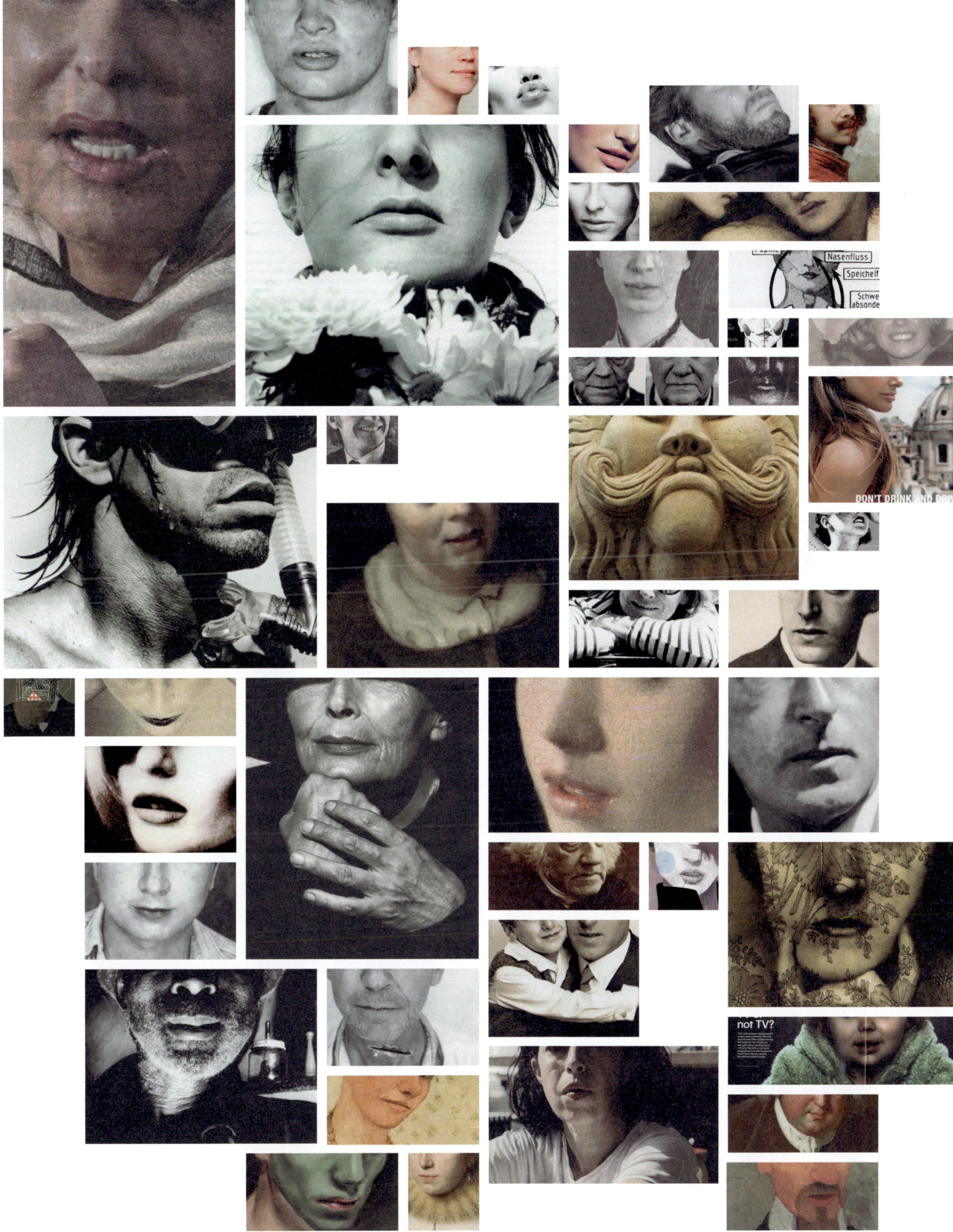
Nasenfluss
DON'T DRINK AND DRIVE
not TV?

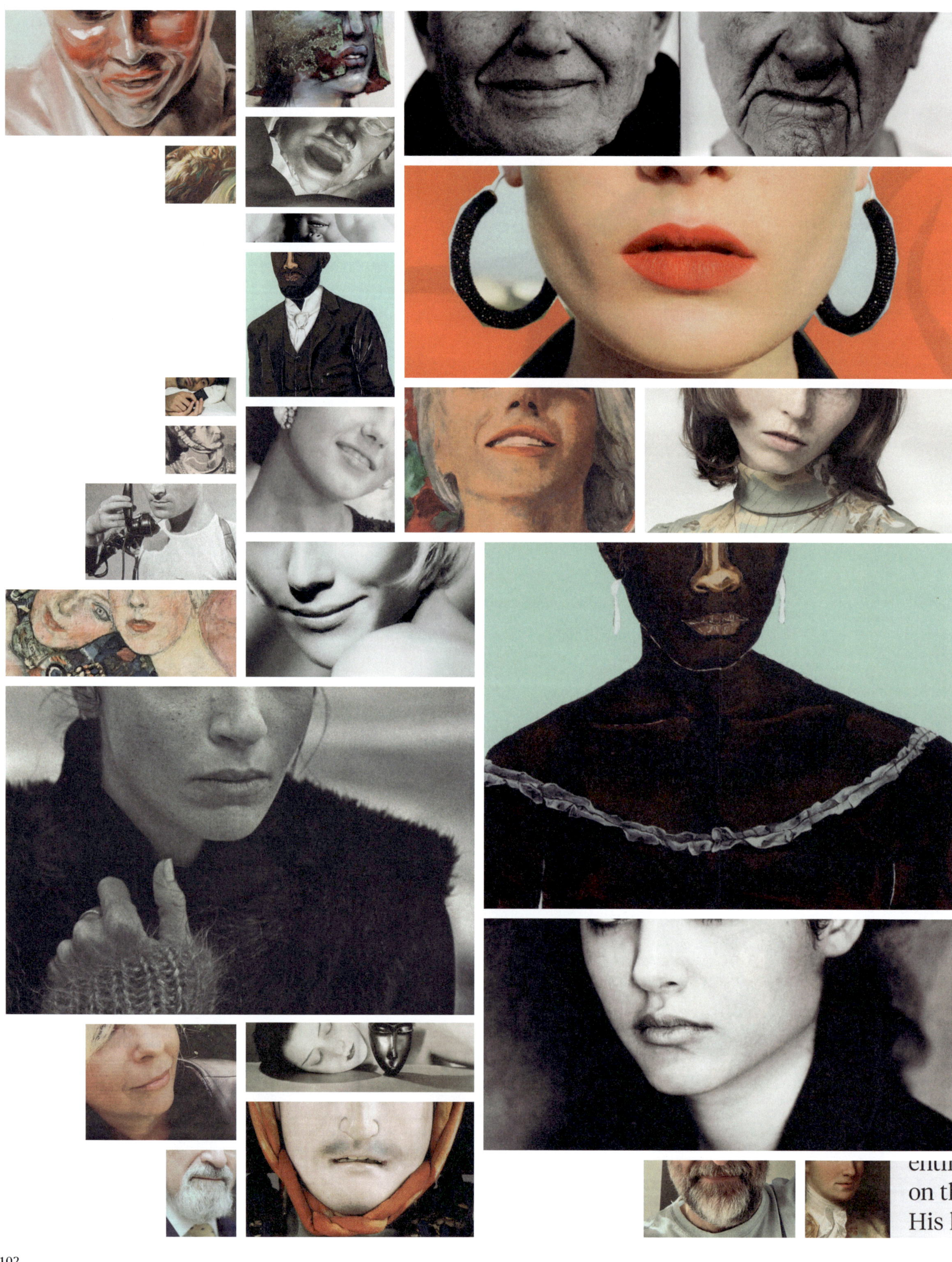
on th
His l

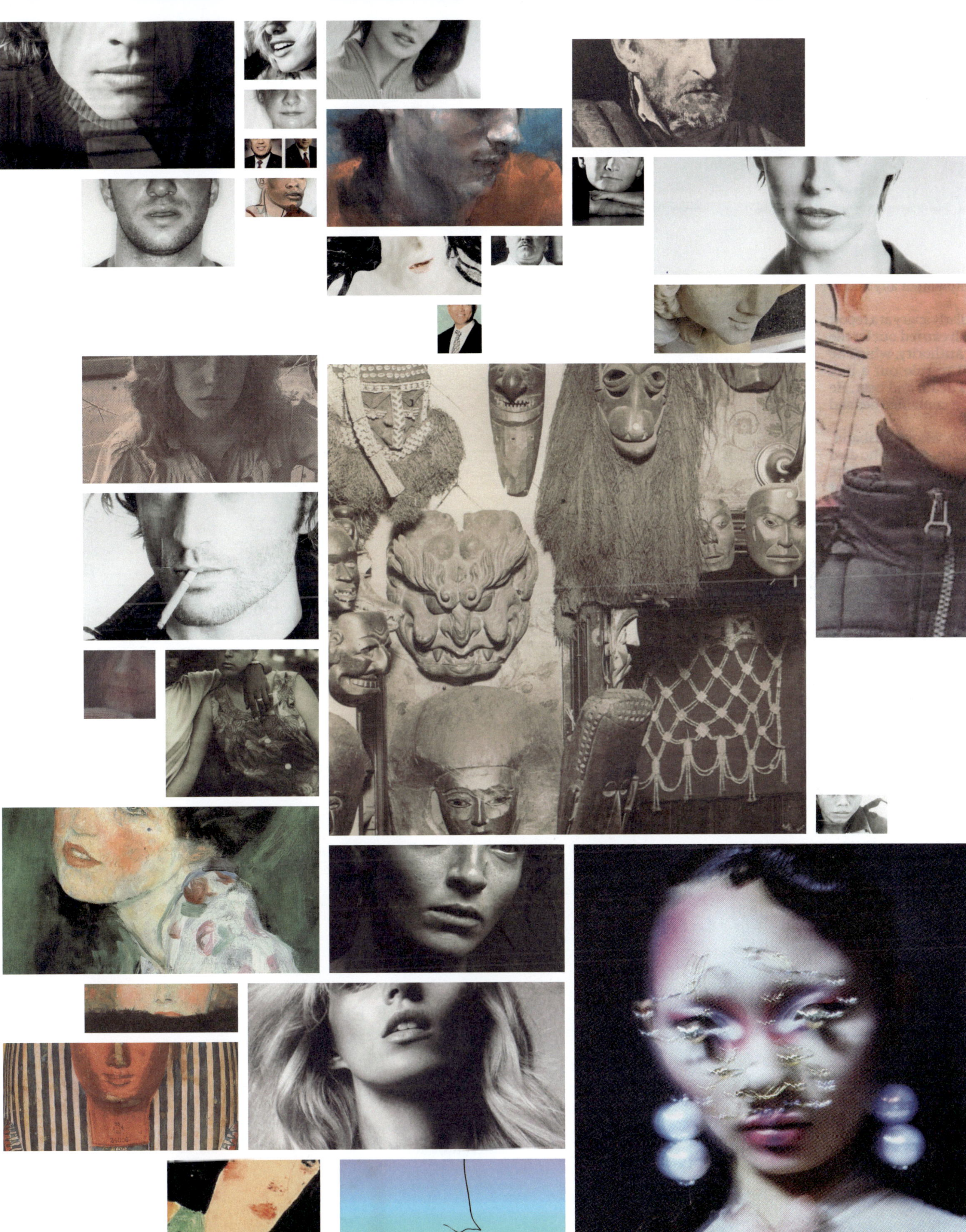

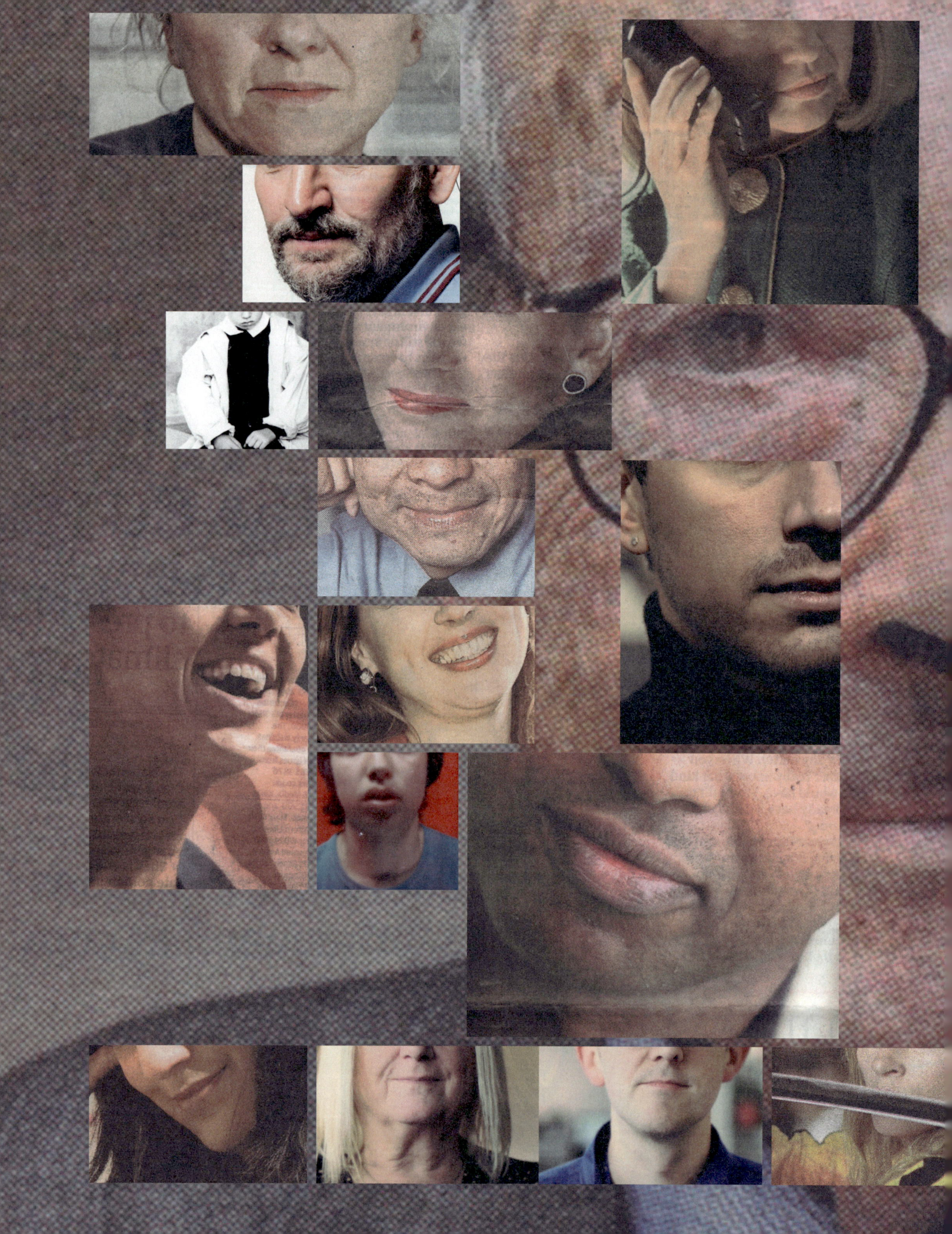

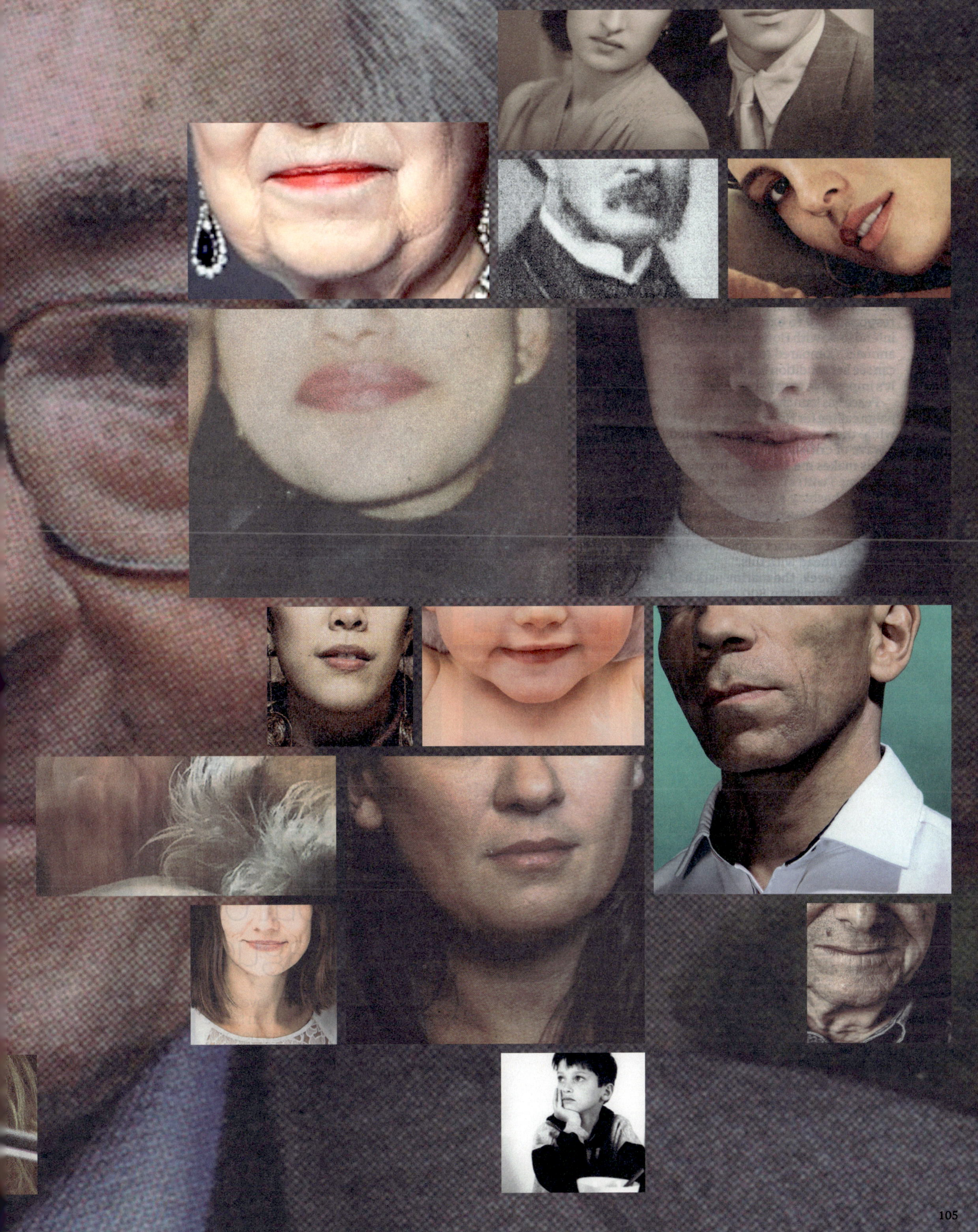

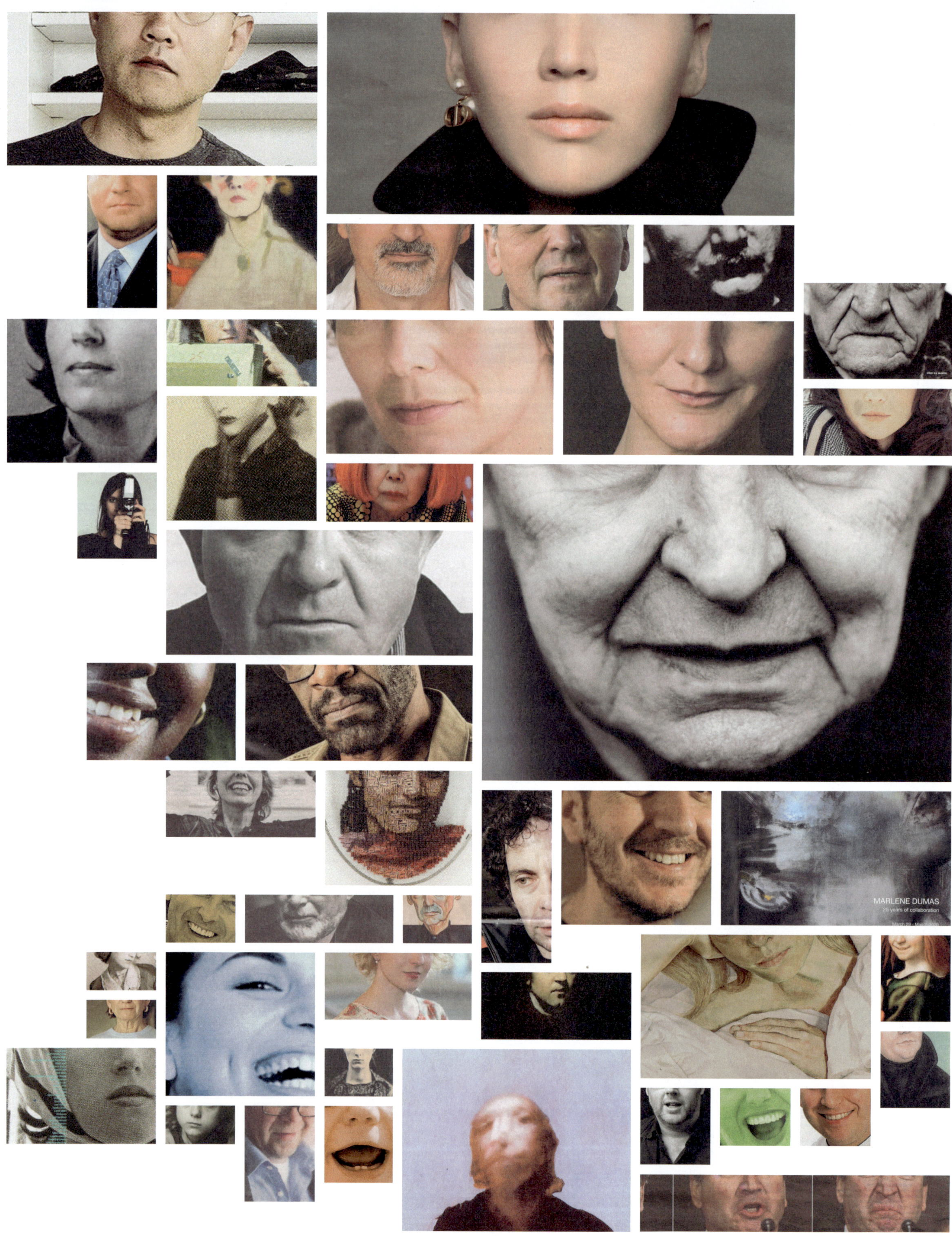
MARLENE DUMAS
25 years of collaboration

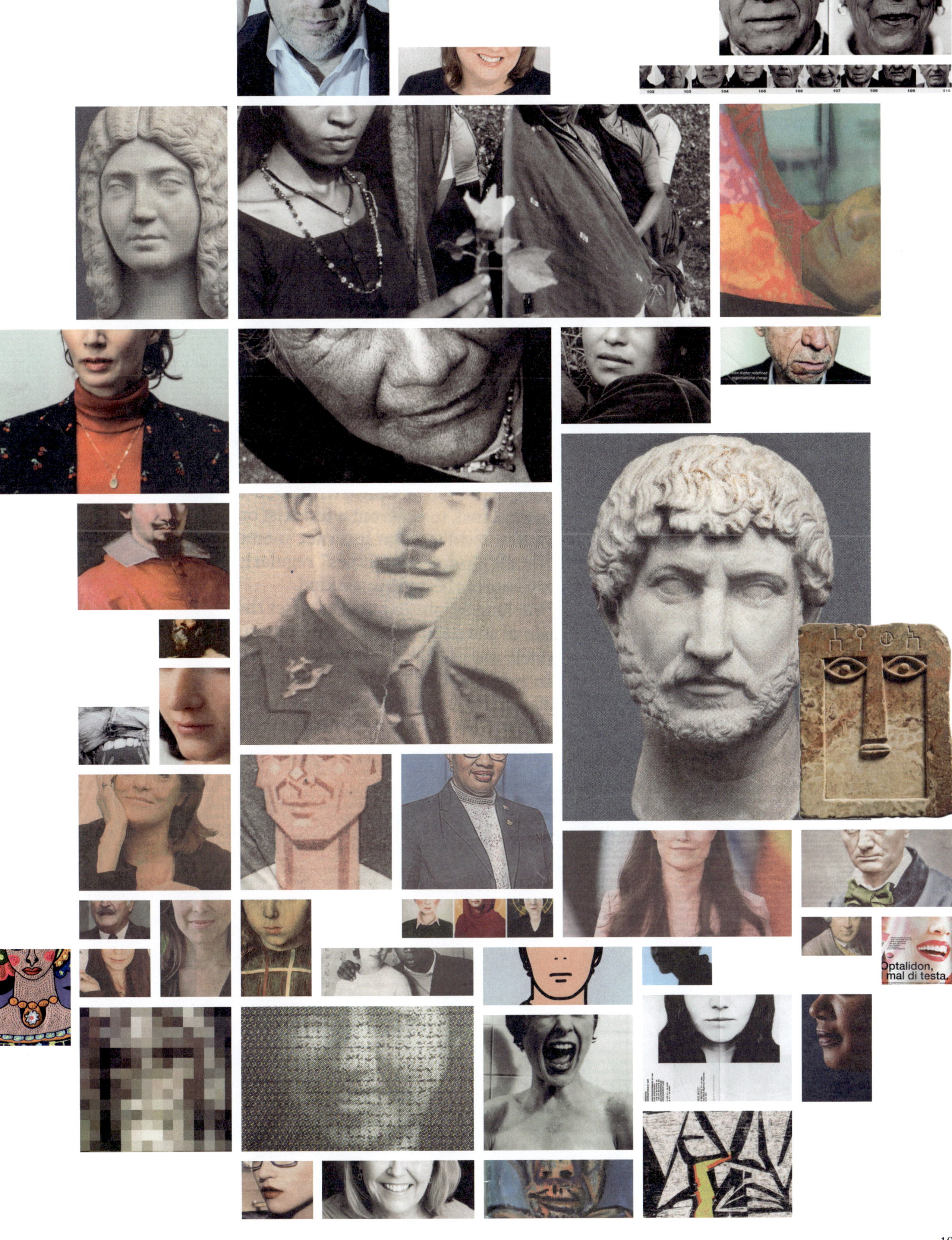
ohn Kotter redefined
organisational change
Optalidon,
mal di testa.

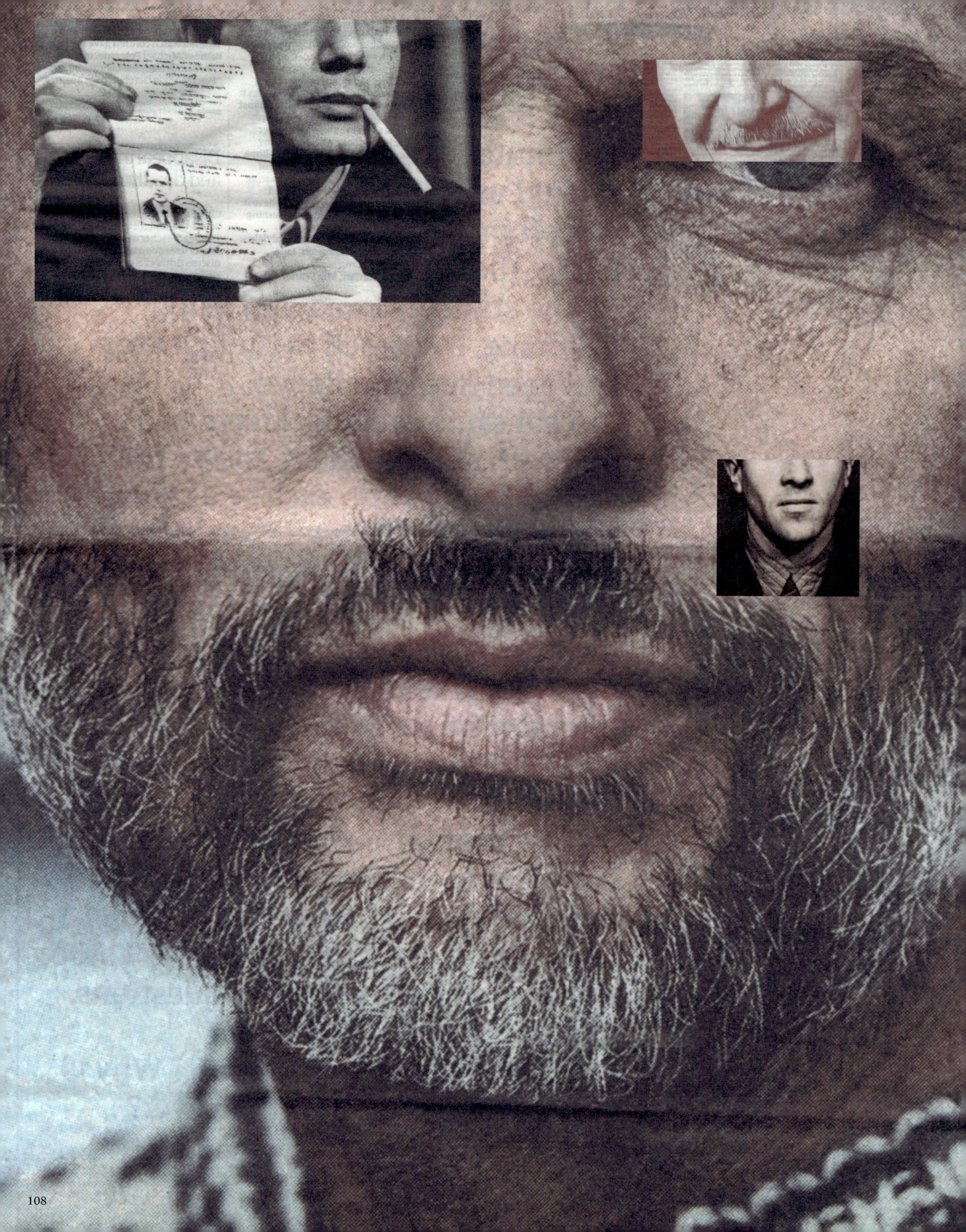

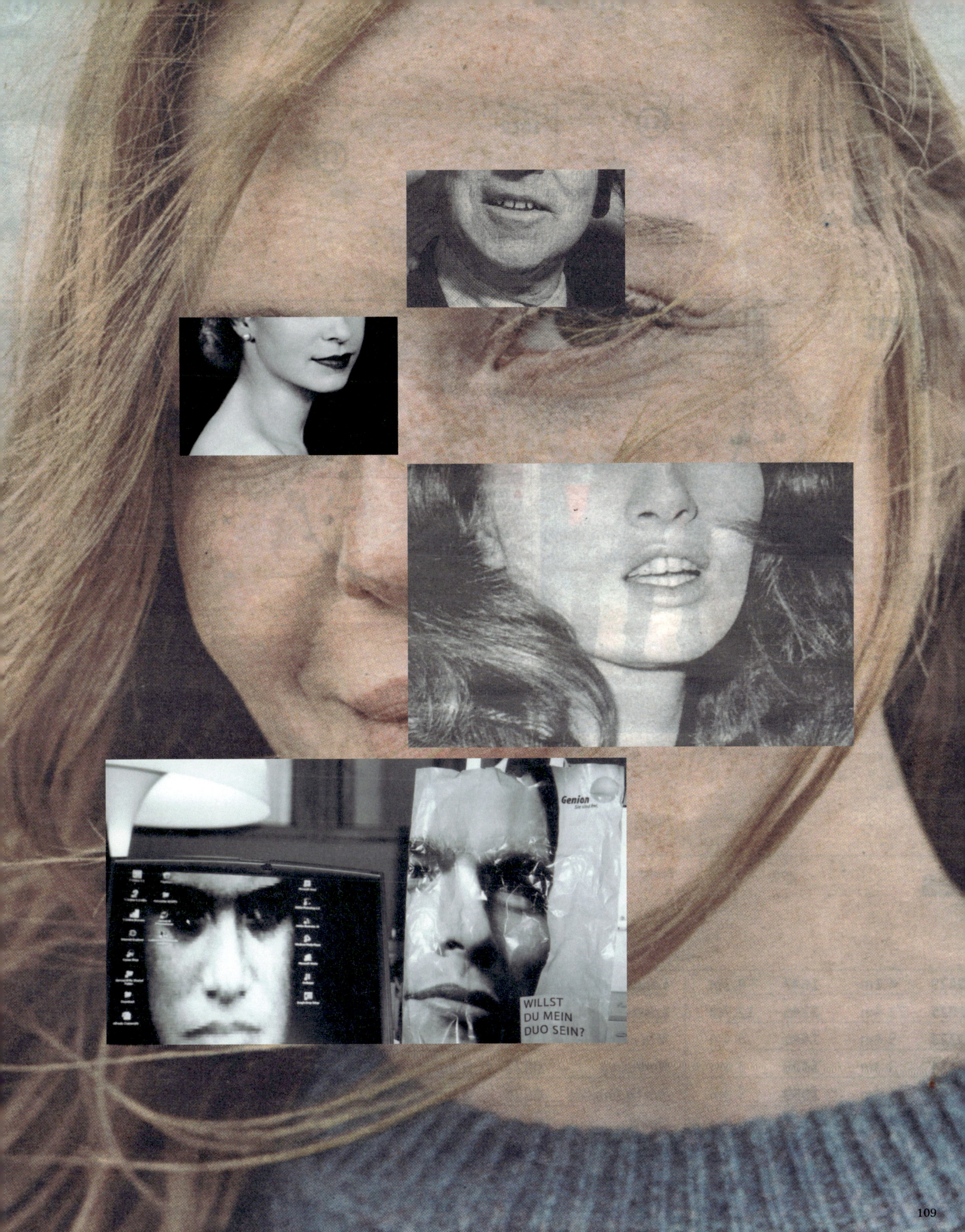
Genion
WILLST
DU MEIN
DUO SEIN?

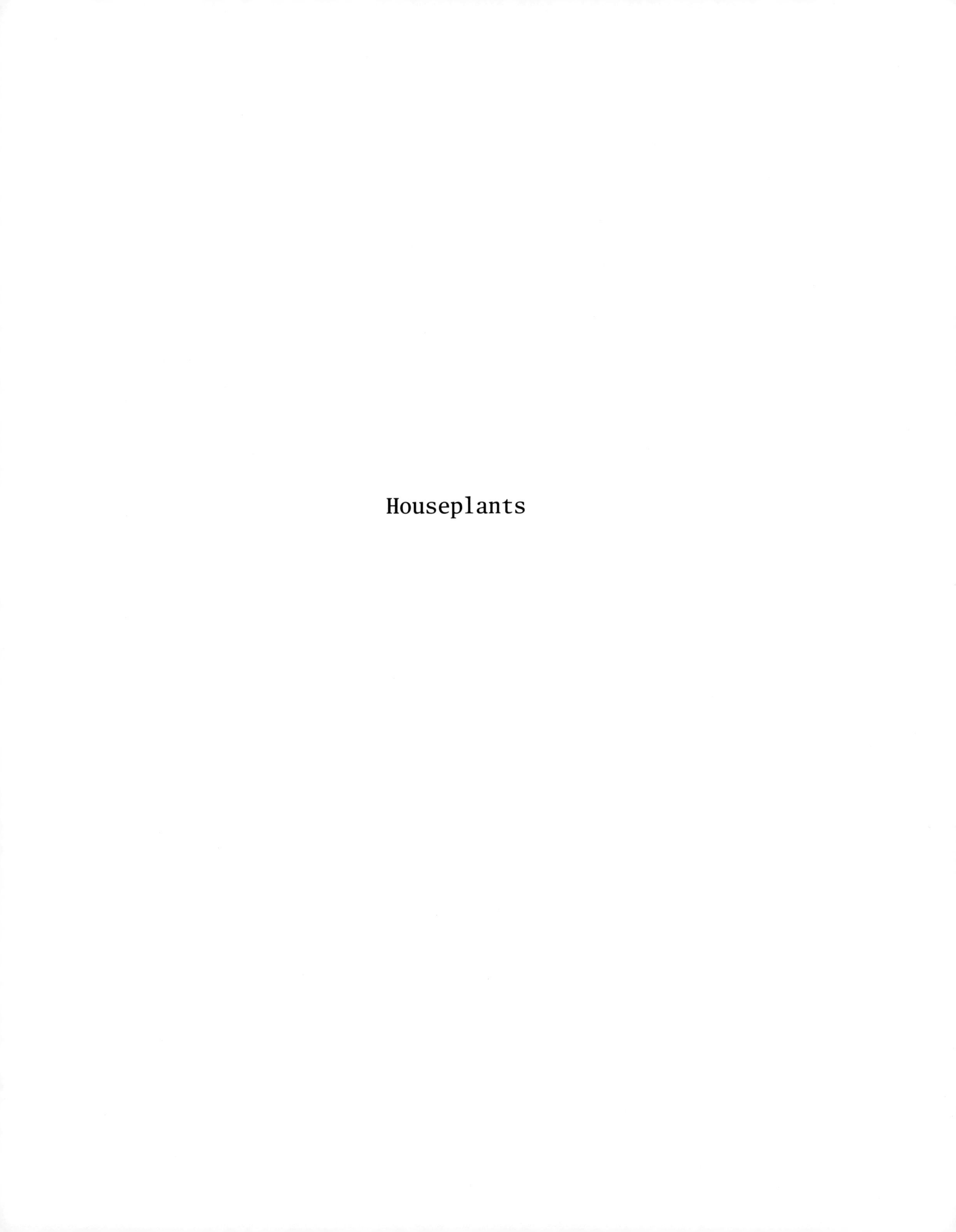

Houseplants

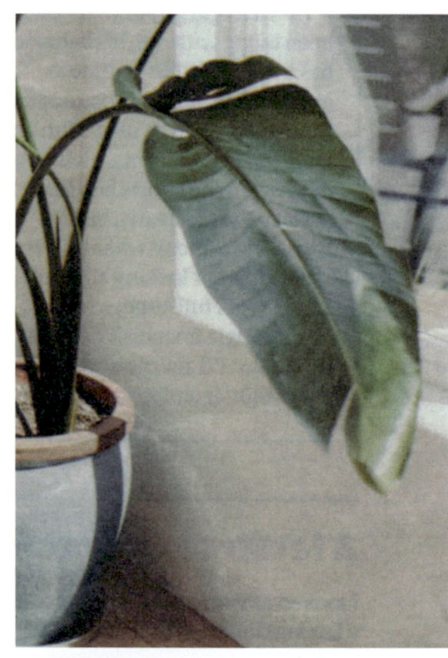
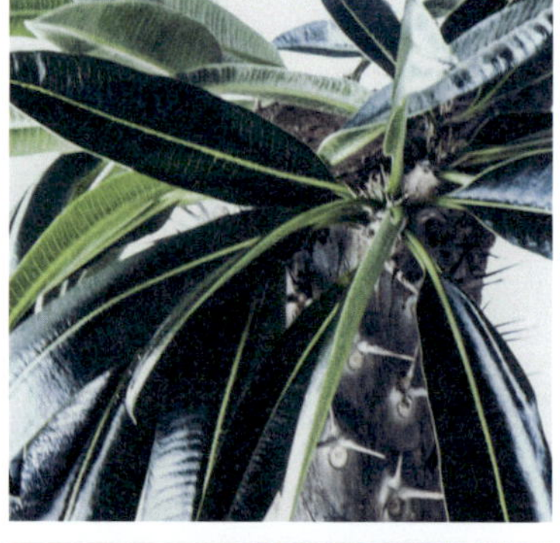
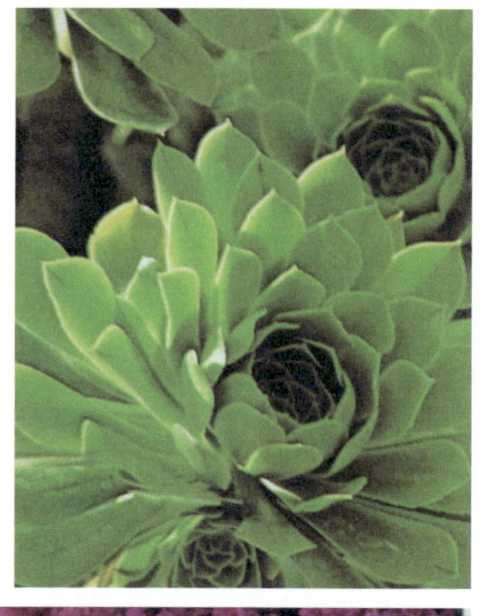
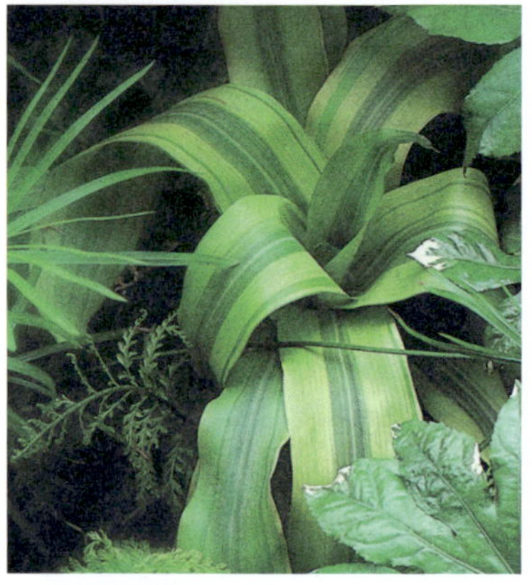
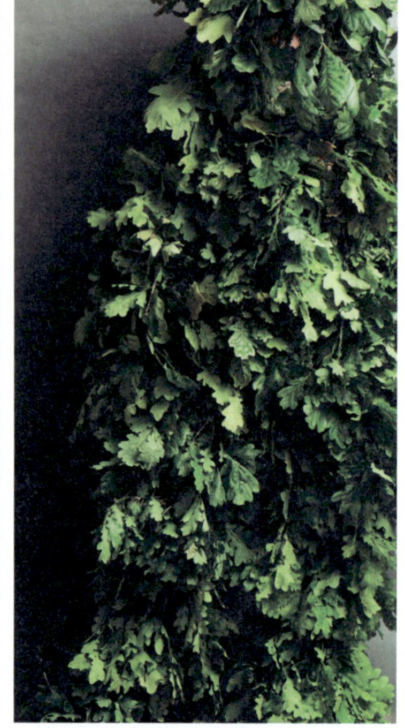
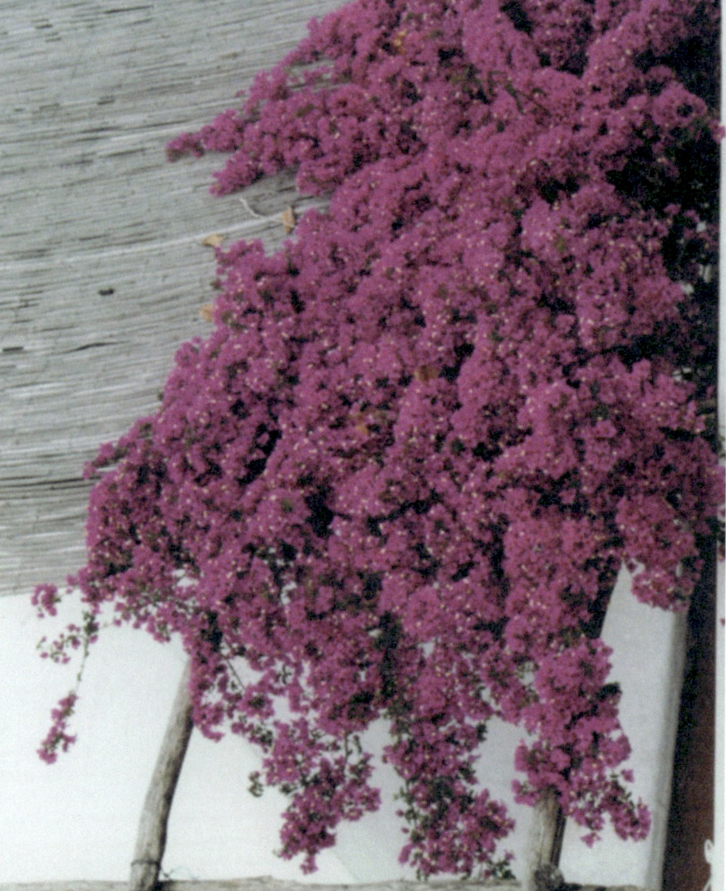
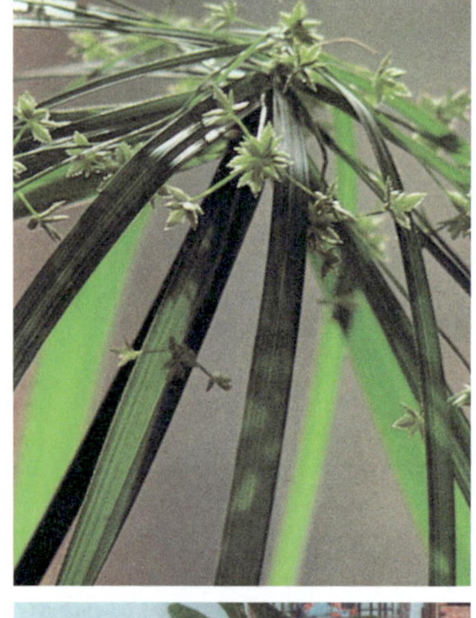
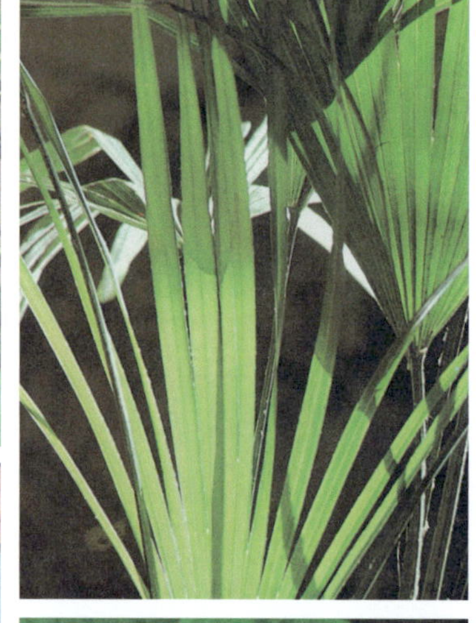
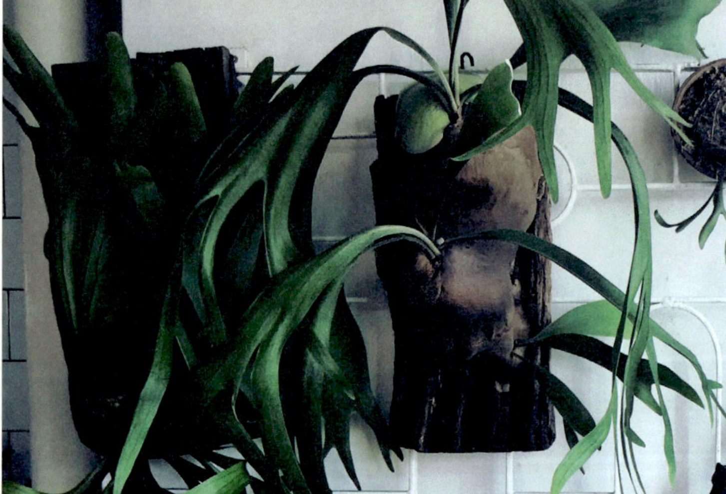
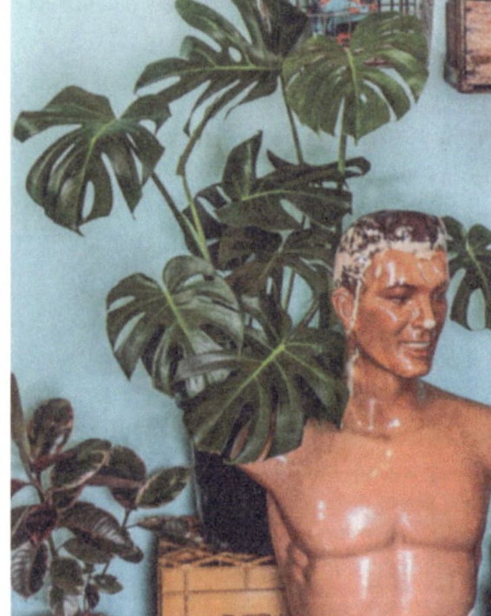
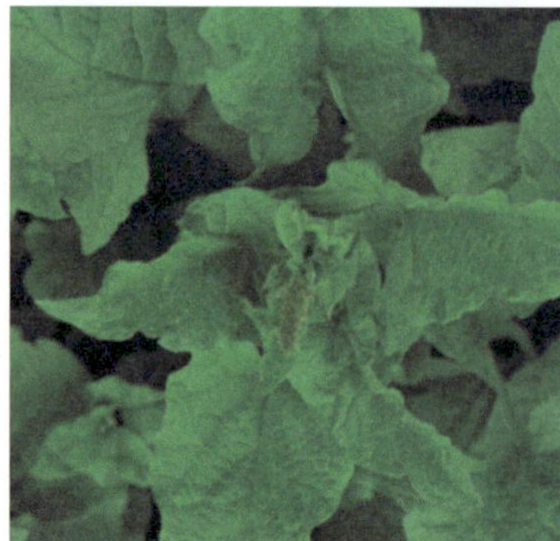

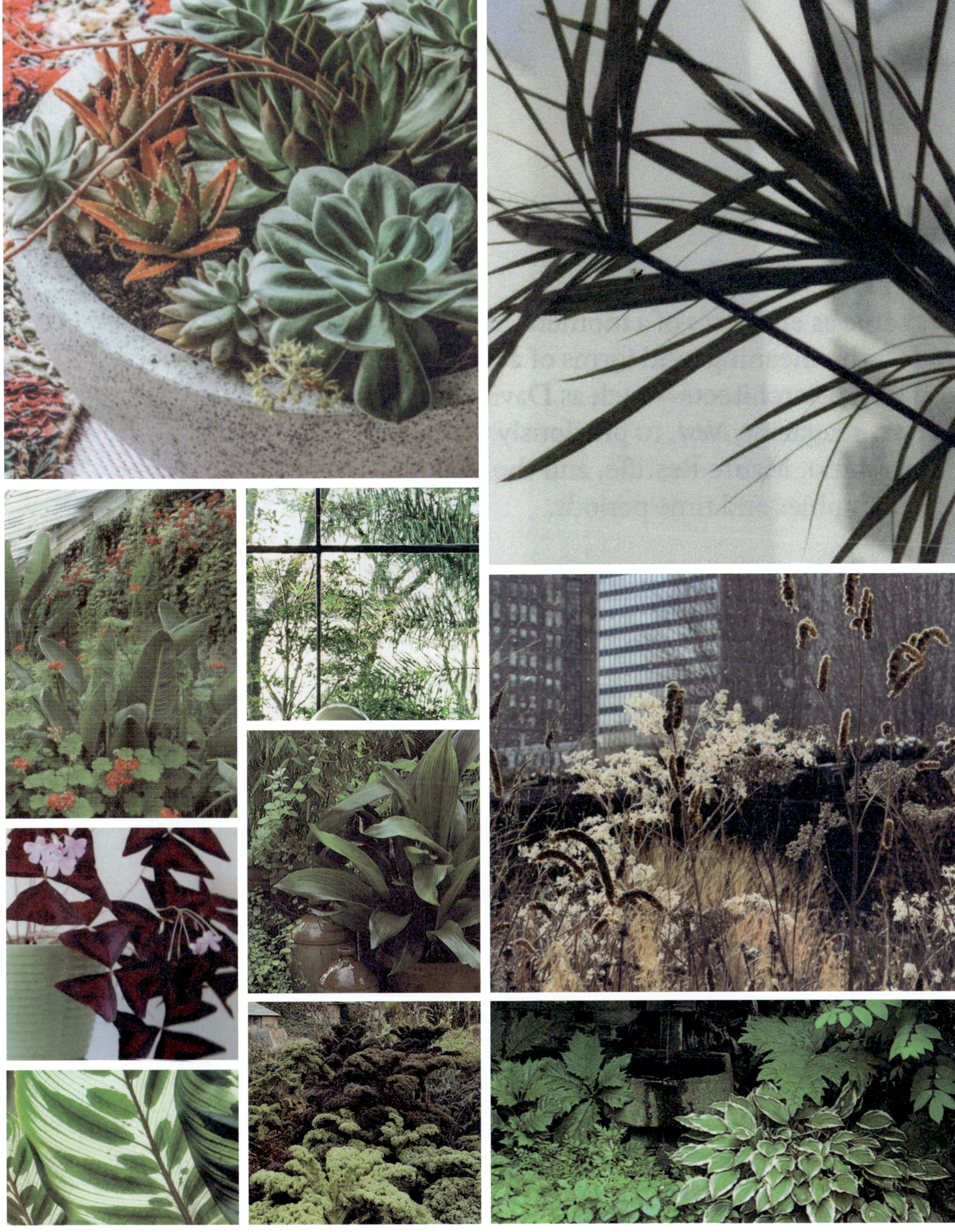

What went wrong

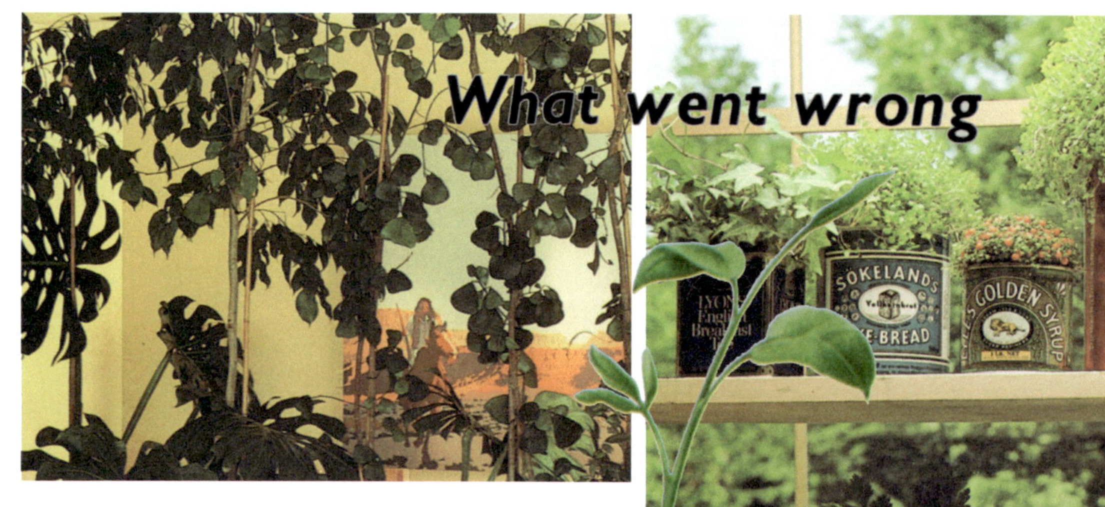

WILTING

This is a symptom of both prolonged soil dryness and waterlogging. Do *not* add more water if waterlogging is the cause; this can be due to poor soil structure or over-watering.

Another common cause of wilting is too much sun or artificial heat. Syringe leaves immediately.

DROPPING OF BUDS AND FLOWERS

The conditions which cause leaf drop can also lead to loss of buds and flowers.

Other possible reasons are movement of the pot, dryness of the air and over-watering.

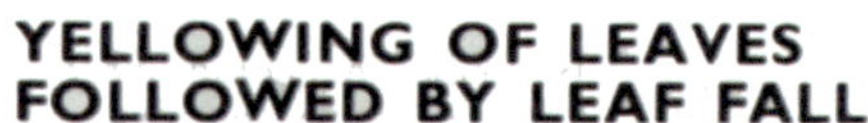

YELLOWING OF LEAVES FOLLOWED BY LEAF FALL

It is quite normal for an occasional lower leaf to turn yellow. When several leaves turn yellow and then fall, the most likely cause is over-watering or cold draughts. Dry air can also have this effect.

SUDDEN DROPPING OF LEAVES

Sudden leaf fall is generally due to a shock to the plant's system.

This may be a large drop or rise in temperature, a rapid change in light intensity or a prolonged cold draught. A sudden increase in the amount of gas in the air will have this effect. Dryness at the roots may cause leaf fall.

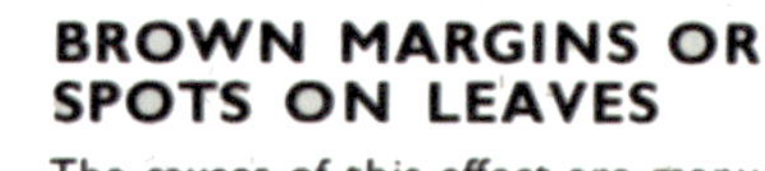

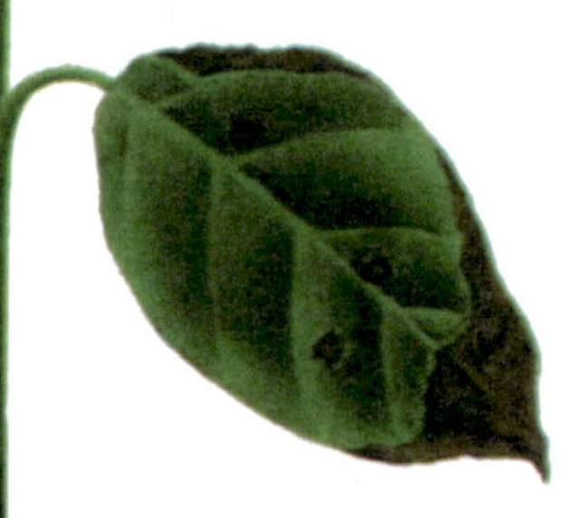

BROWN MARGINS OR SPOTS ON LEAVES

The causes of this effect are many and varied. Hot dry air is often the culprit, and other common reasons for browning are draughts, gas, over-watering, sun scorch, water splashes and overfeeding.

ROTTING OF LEAVES AND STEMS

This is due to disease attack where growing conditions are poor. The fault often lies with over-watering in winter or leaving water on the leaves at night.

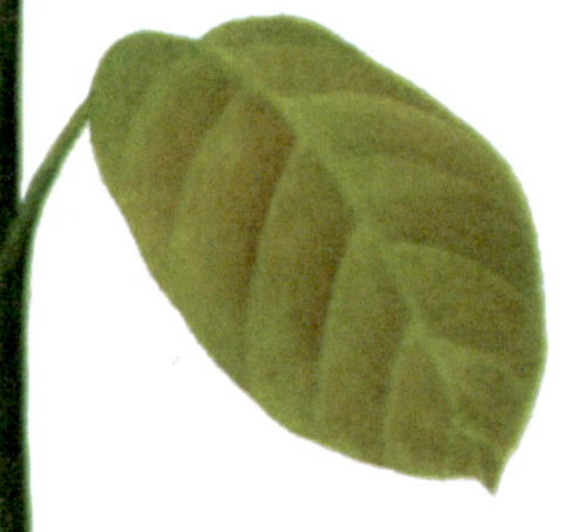

YELLOW LEAVES WHICH REMAIN FIRM AND HEALTHY

This is generally due to the use of lime in the compost used for lime-hating plants (see page 26) or the use of hard water for watering such plants.

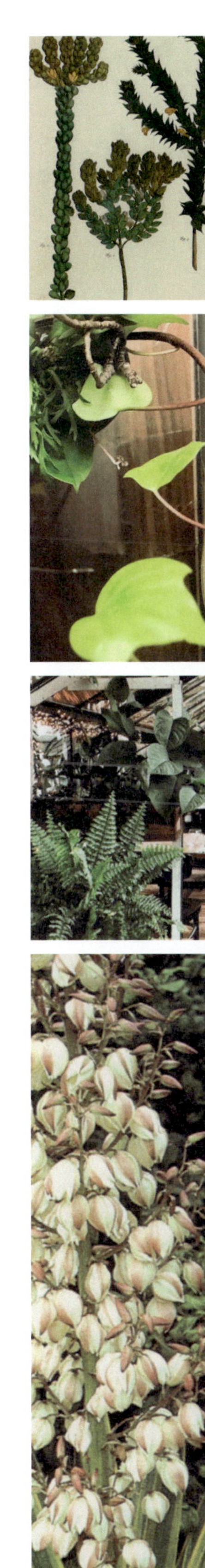

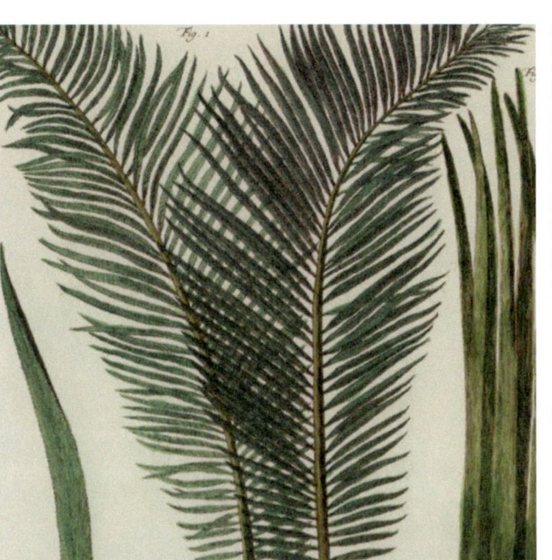

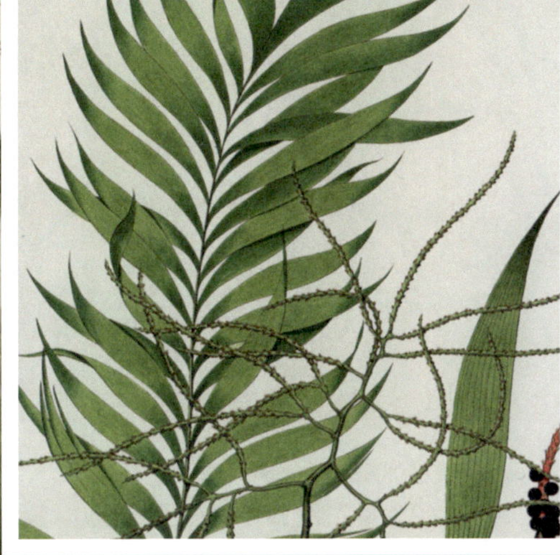

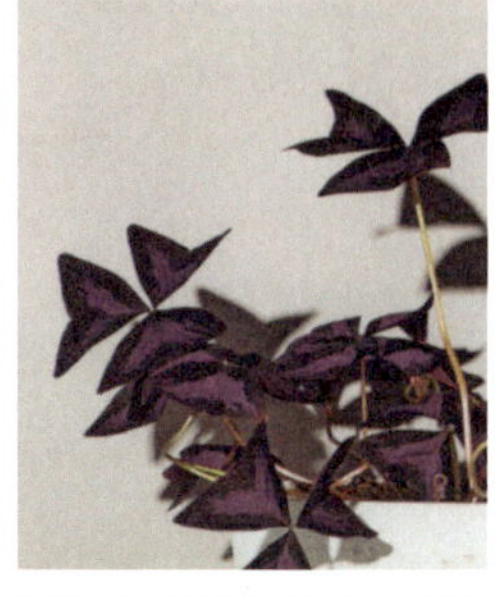

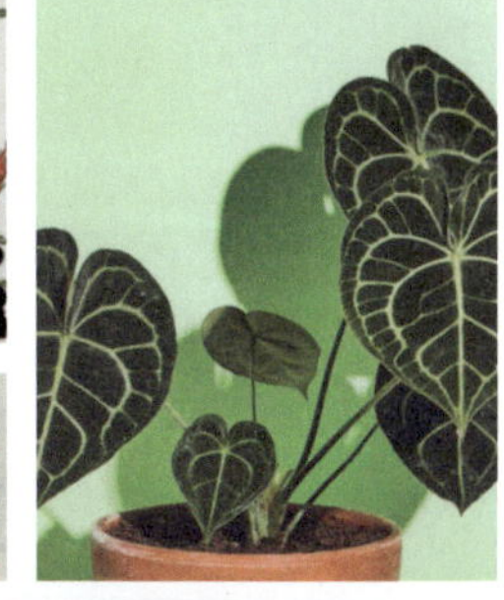

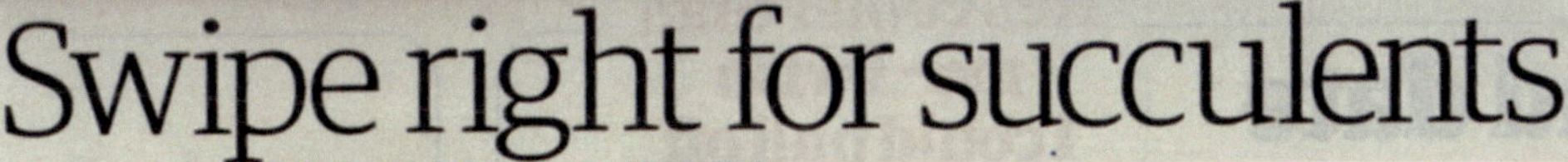

Swipe right for succulents

By Jack Wallington

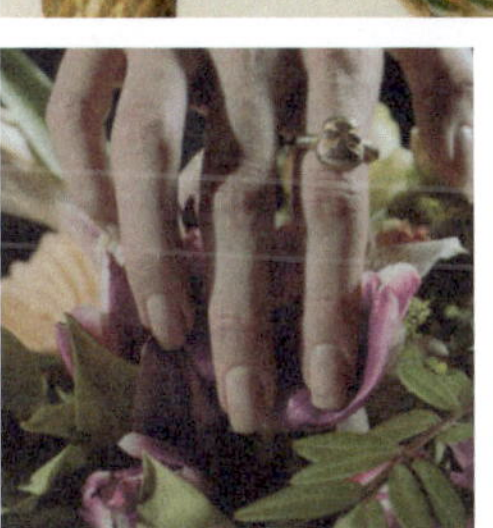

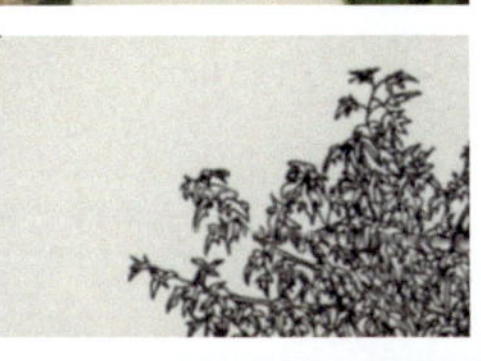

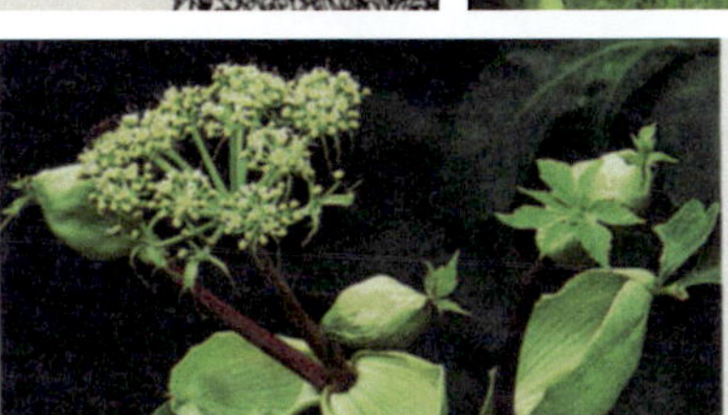

However, I wanted to find the rarer ones, steeped in the magical herbal properties offering a long life. The seed of some of these is not easy to come by, so it was with great excitement that this spring I got hold of some ashitaba, *A. keiskei* 'Koidzumi' (centre). *Ashitaba* means "tomorrow's leaf" in Japanese

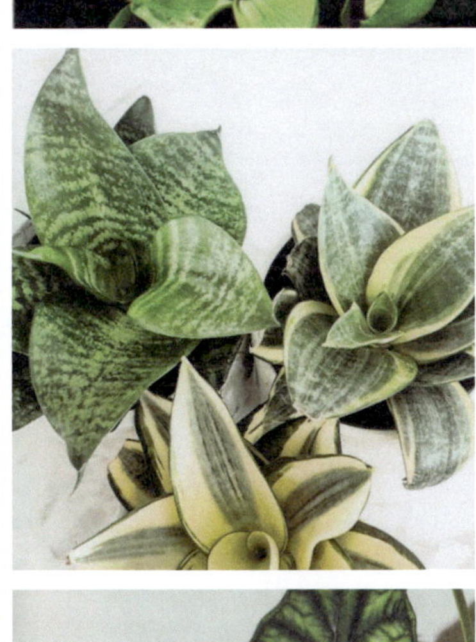

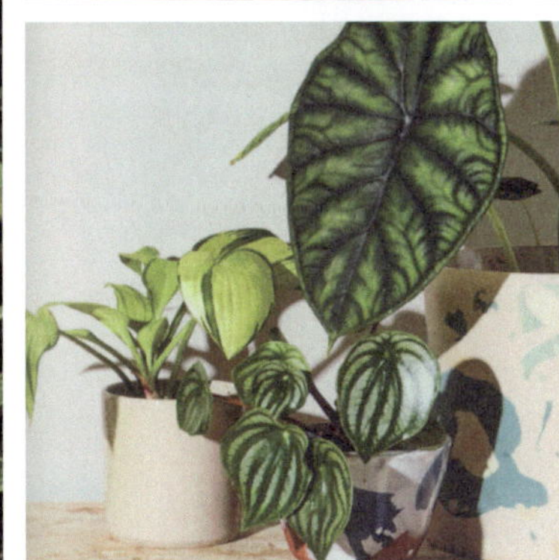

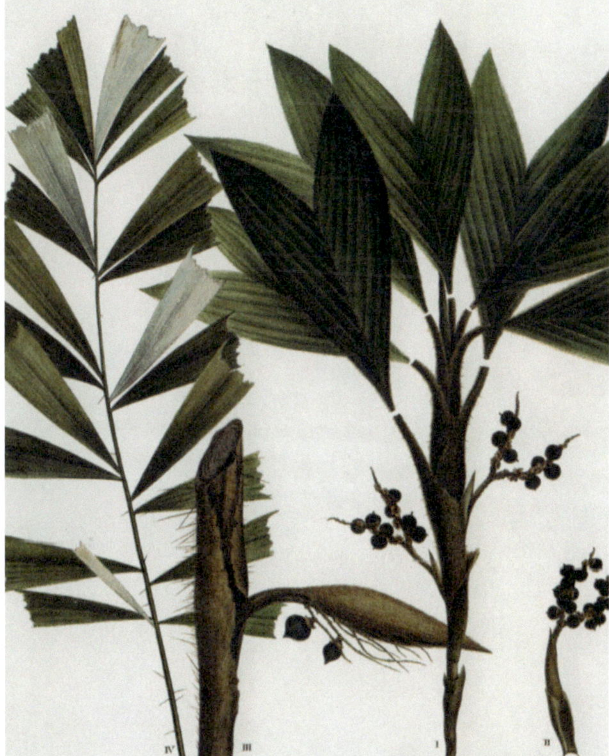

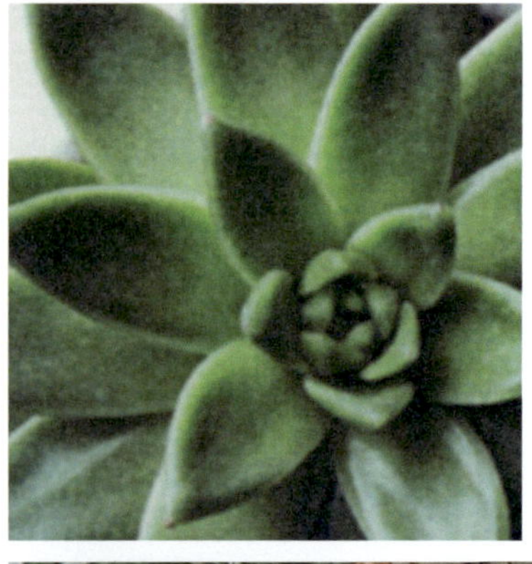

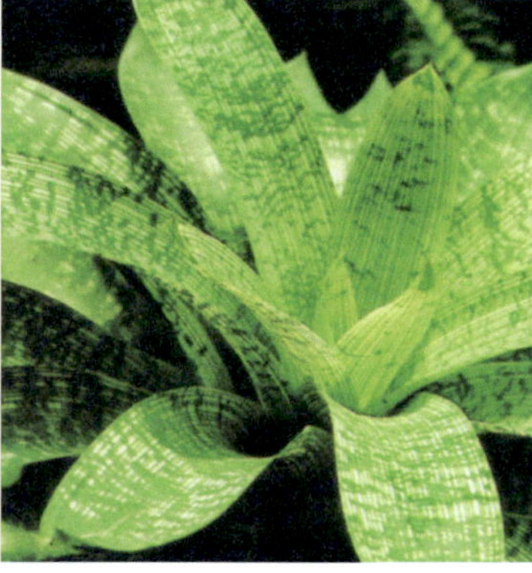

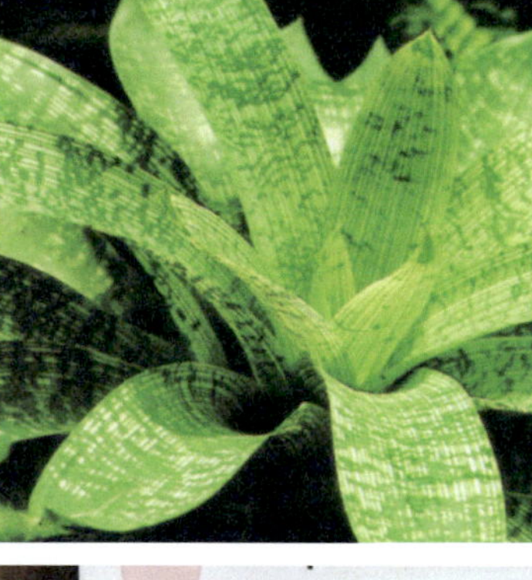

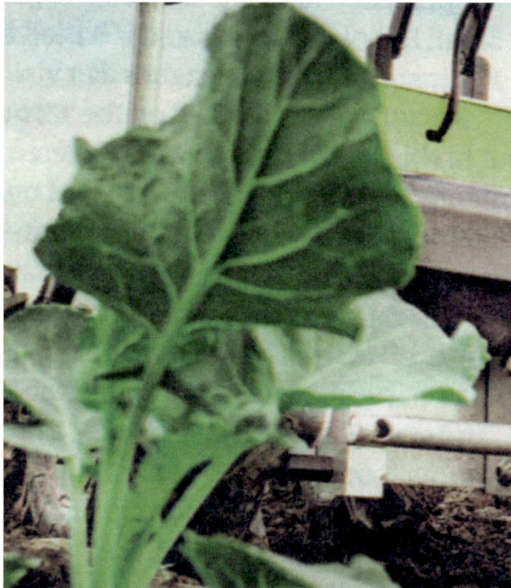

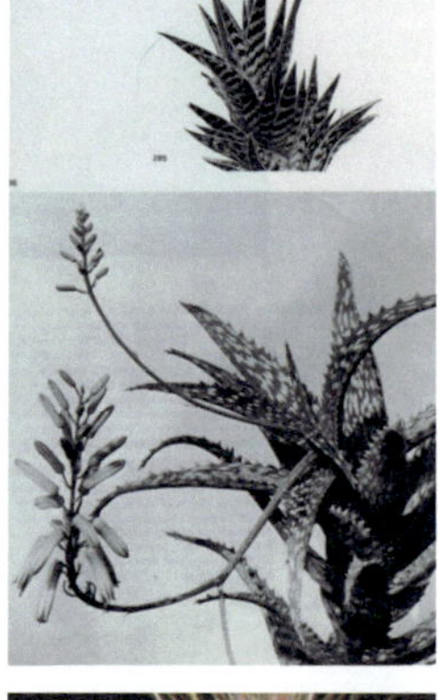

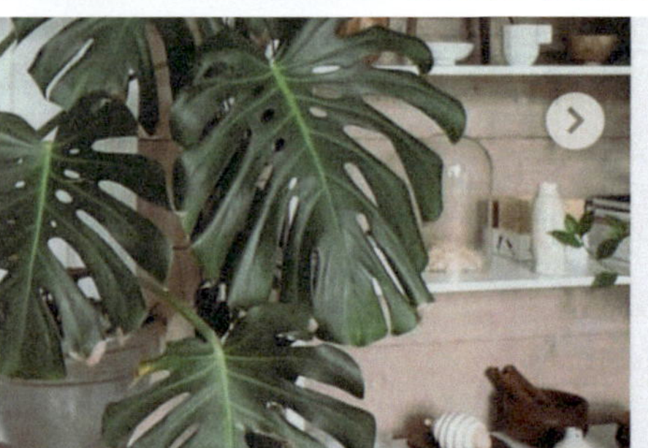

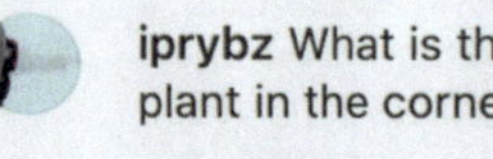

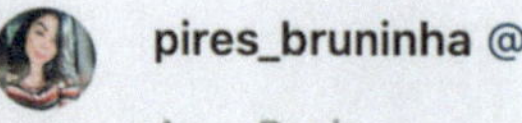

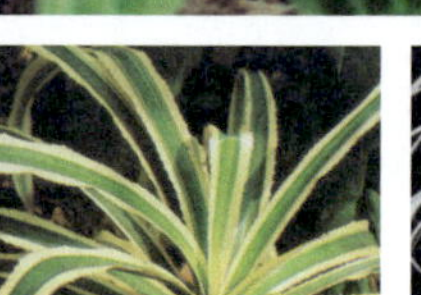

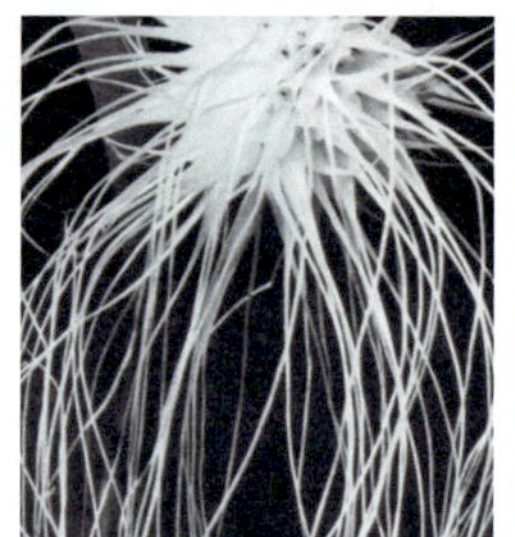

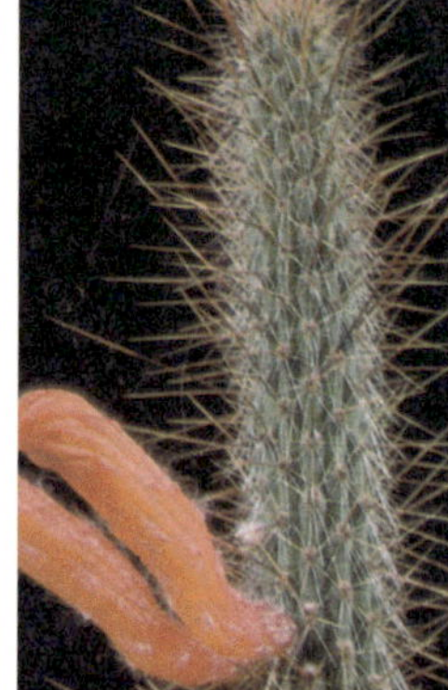

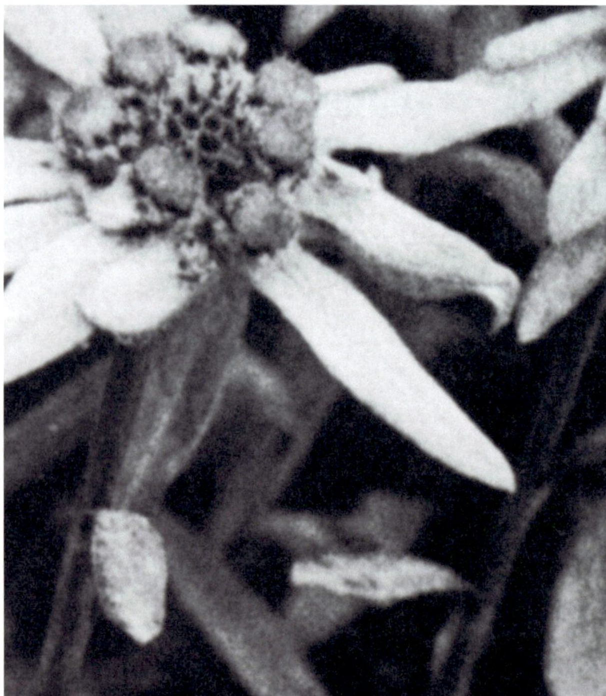

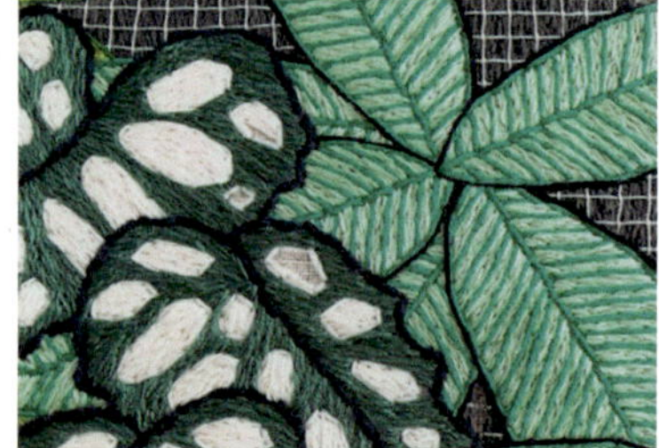

E POT GARD

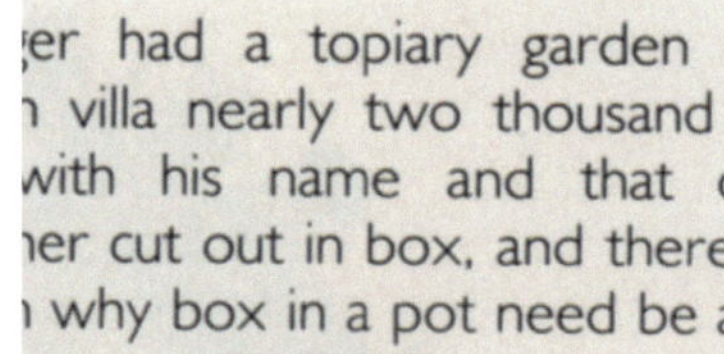

ger had a topiary garden a
n villa nearly two thousand
with his name and that o
her cut out in box, and there
n why box in a pot need be a

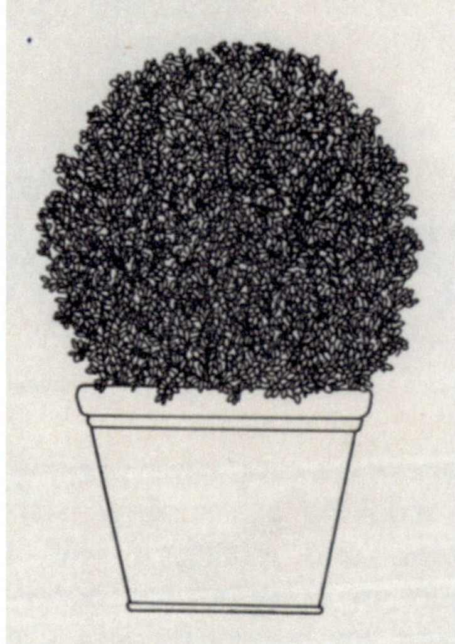

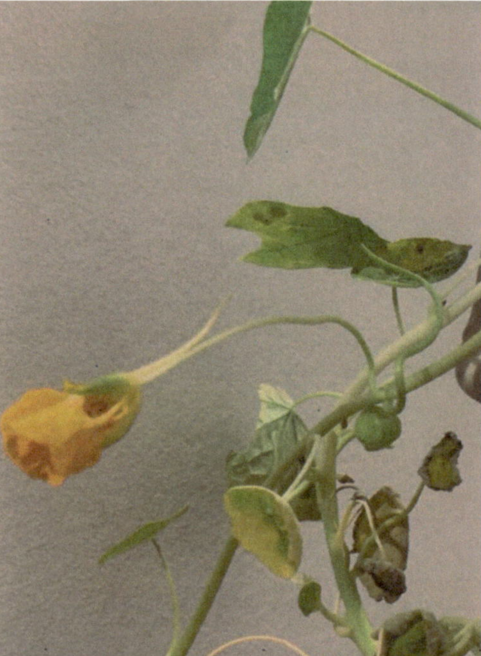

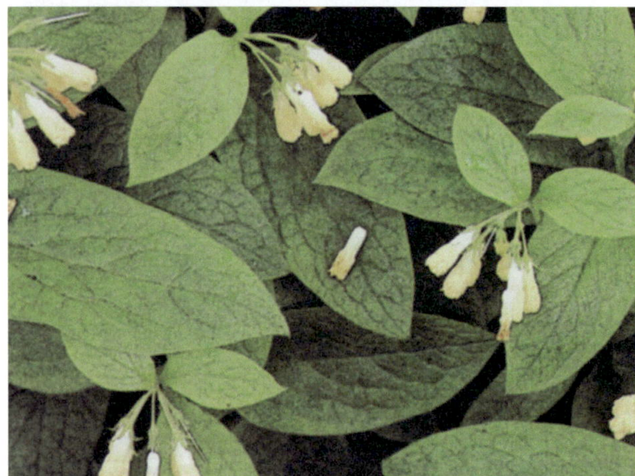

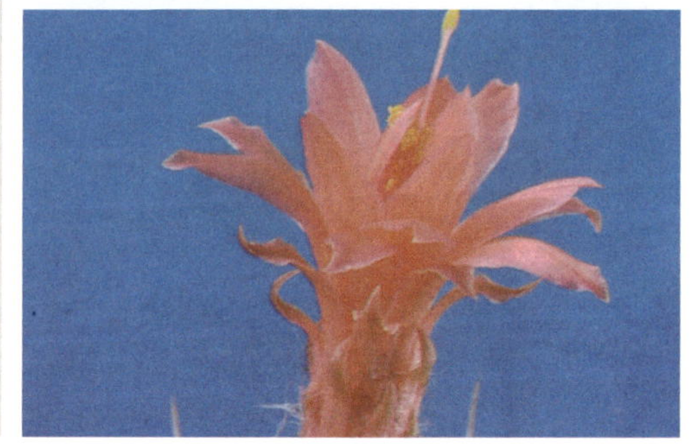

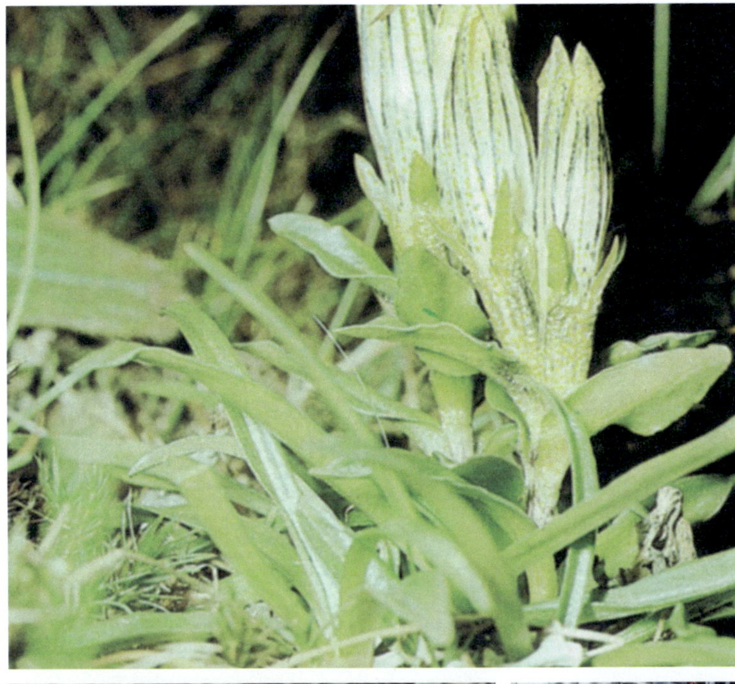

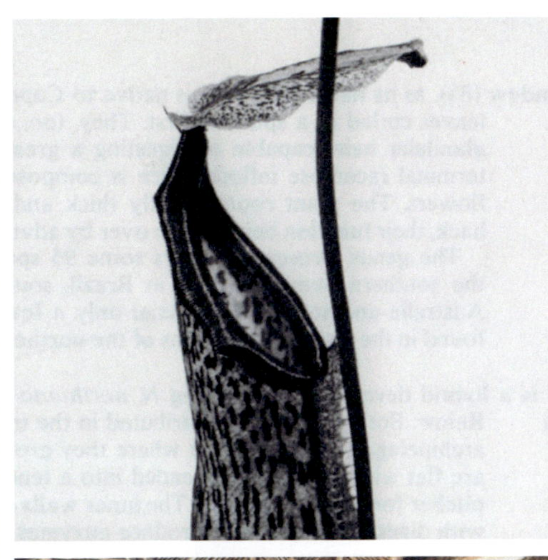

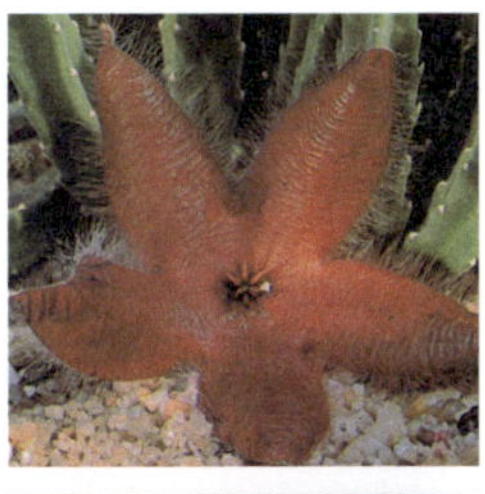

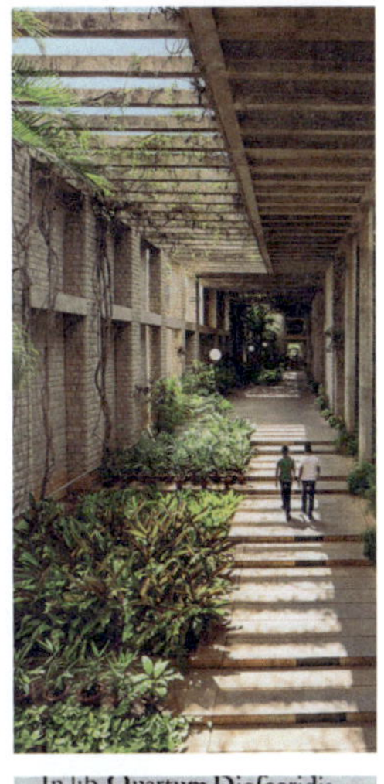

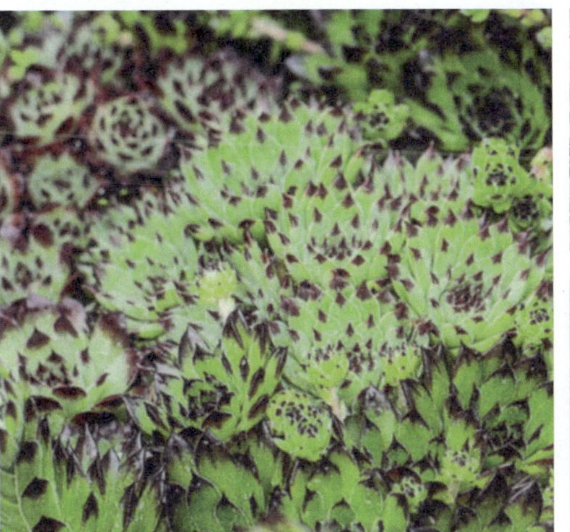

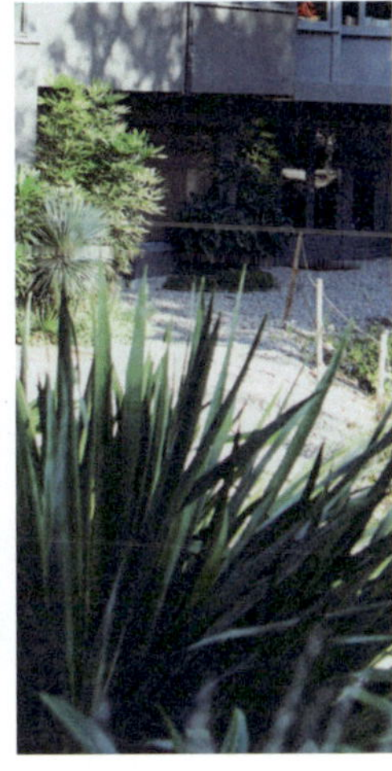

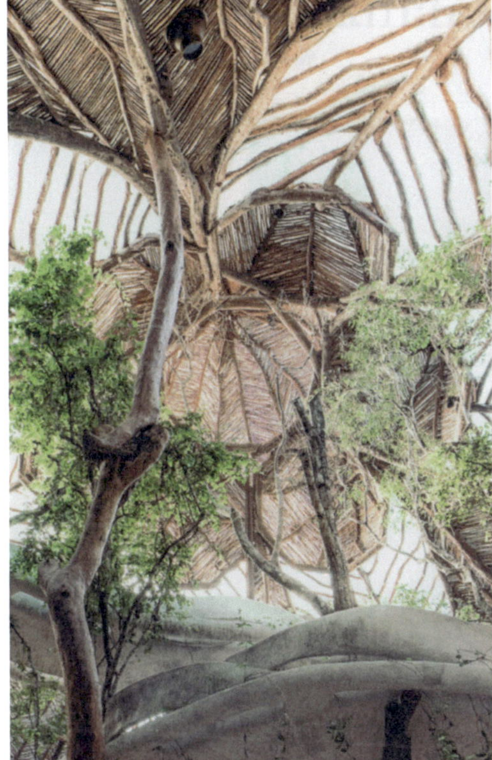

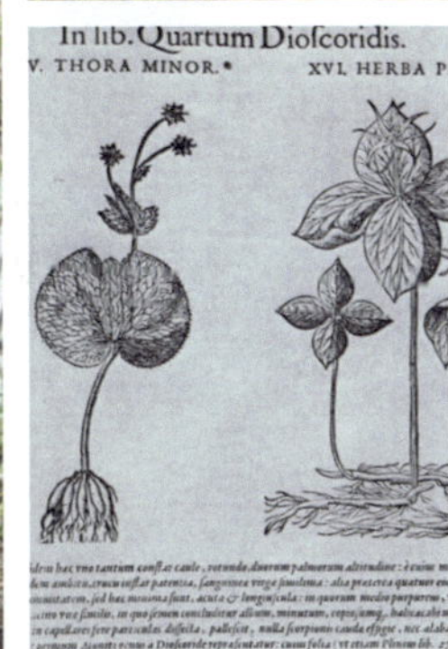

In lib. Quartum Diofcoridis.

V. THORA MINOR.*

XVI. HERBA P.

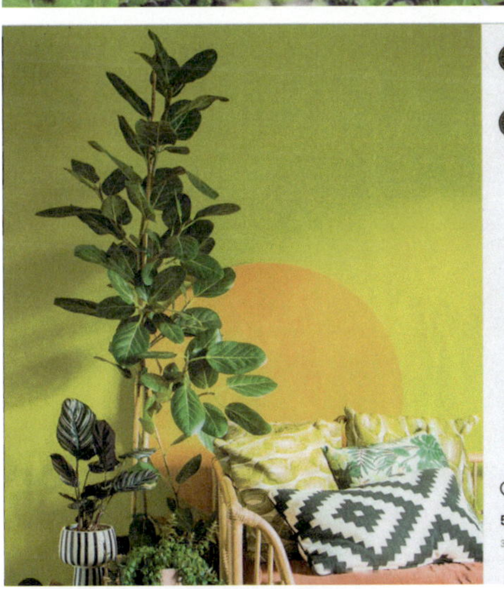

thejungalow · Following

thejungalow Our latest #plantopedia installment is here. @alecisamazing presents, The Ficus Audrey! I'm sure you've seen her around the internet constantly compared to her more popular cousins the Fiddle Leaf Fig — Ficus Lyrata — or the Rubber Plant — Ficus Elastica. This plantie is making a name for herself and is quickly coming for The Must-Have Plant title.

If you know of the struggle to keep a Fiddle Leaf Fig alive and happy, then Ficus Audrey will be a breath of fresh air! This species is a beautiful statement piece for any plant collection and is much more forgiving to environmental changes and bouts of under- or over- watering than its other ficus cousins.

5,238 likes

3 DAYS AGO

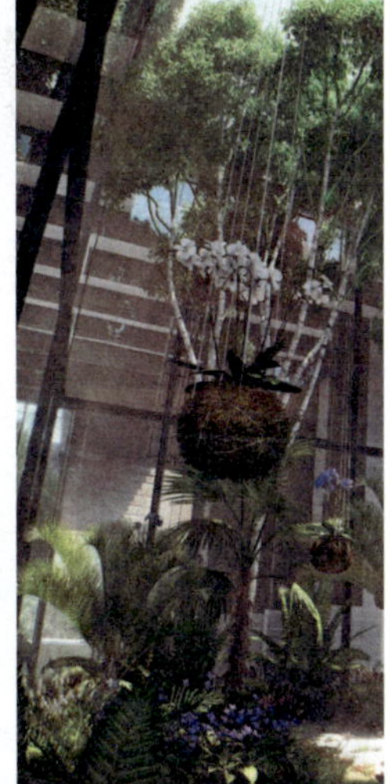

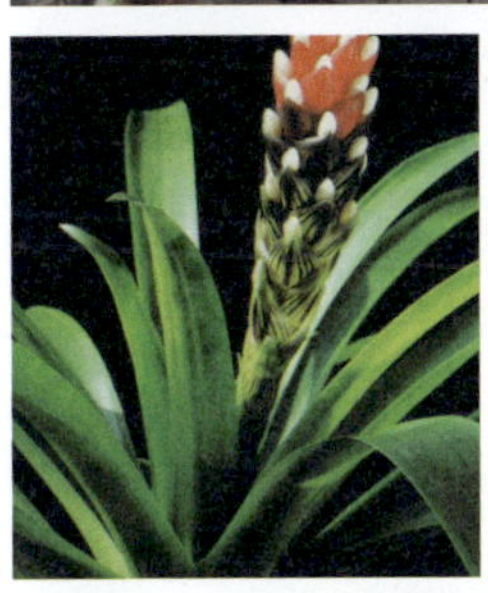

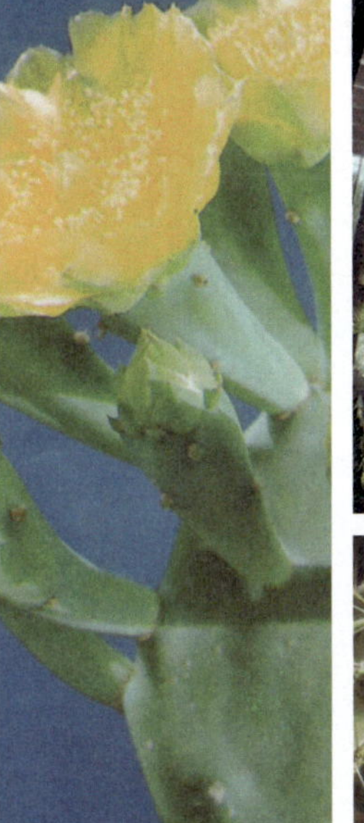

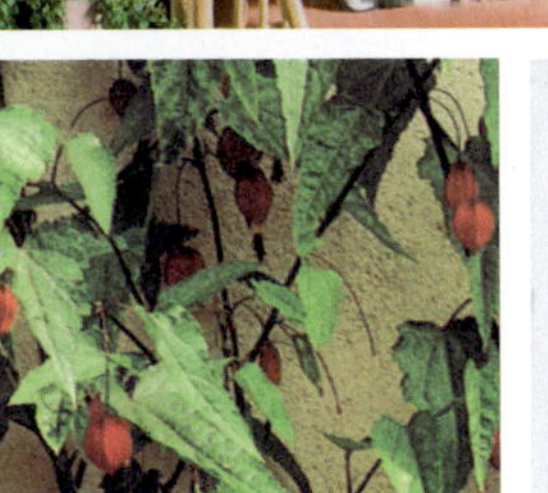

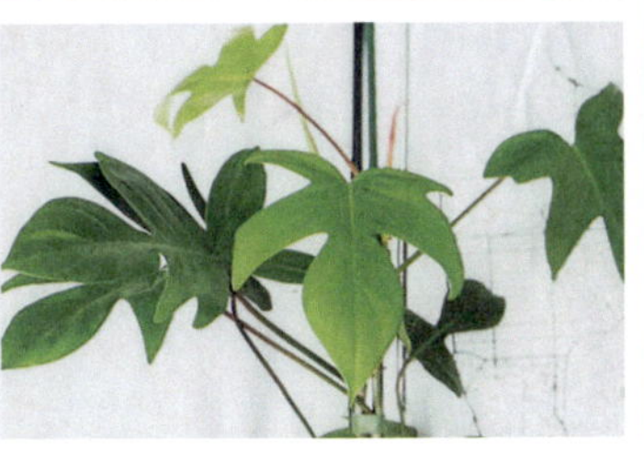

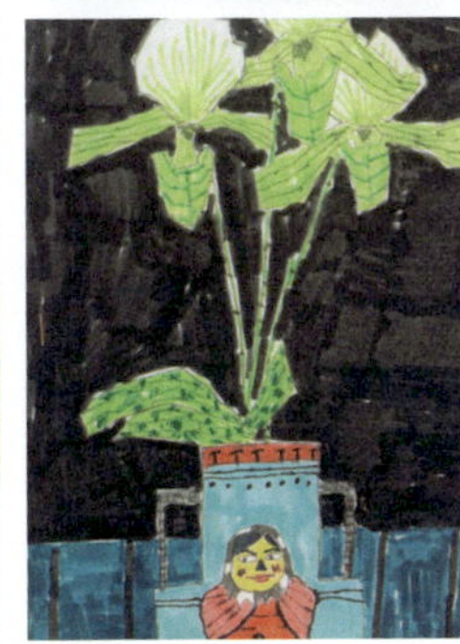

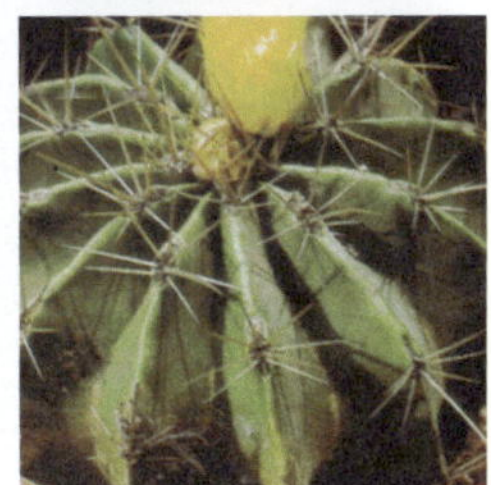

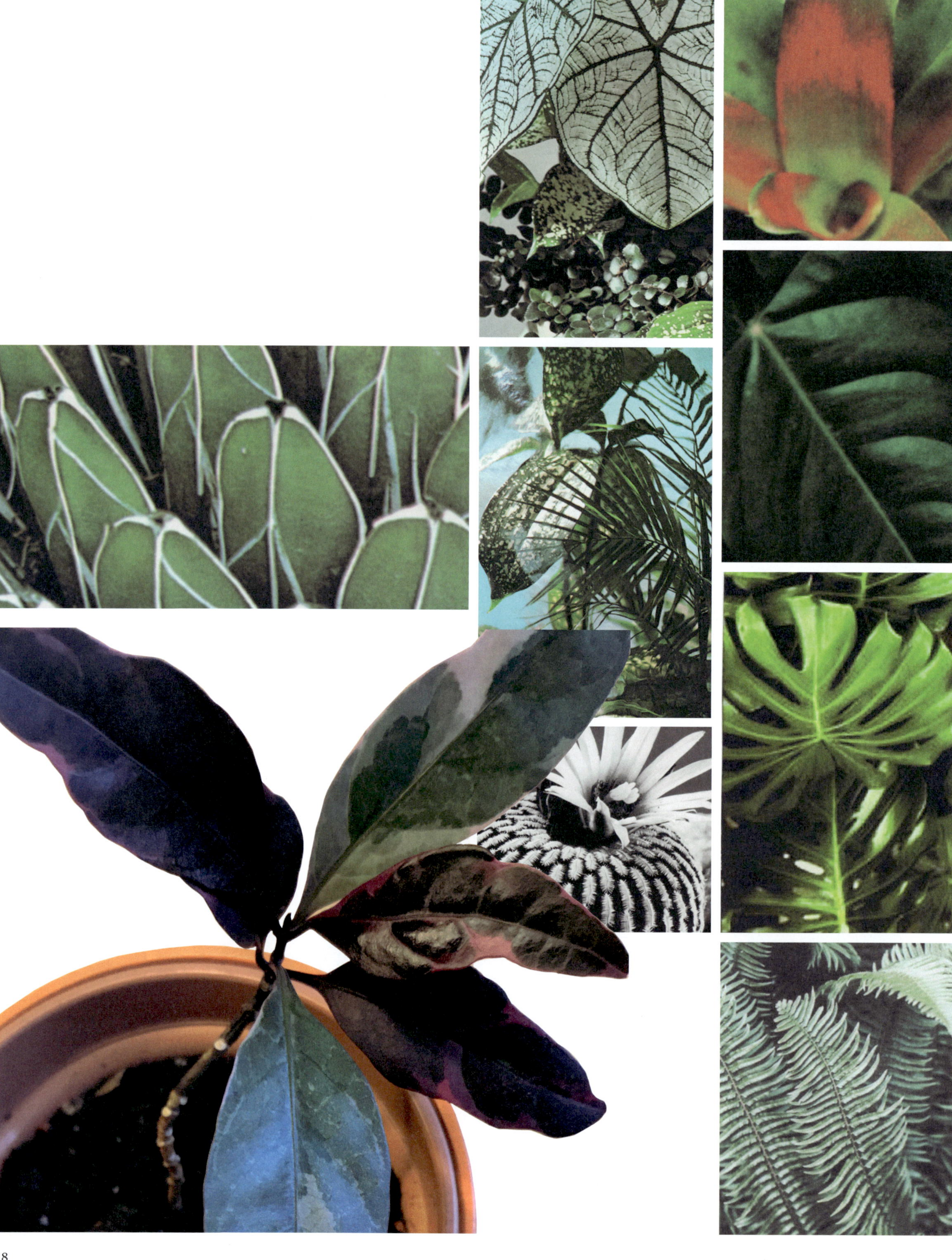

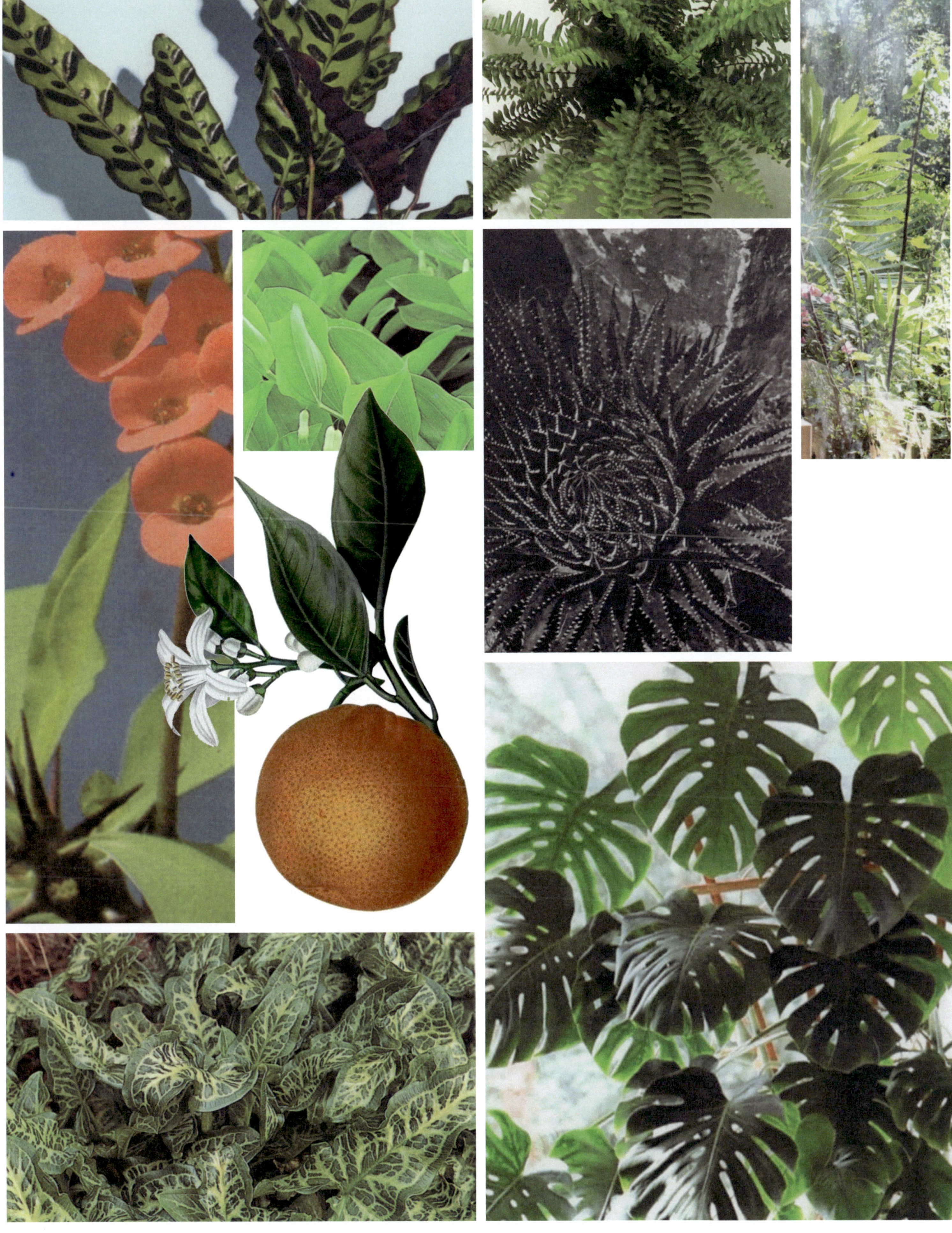

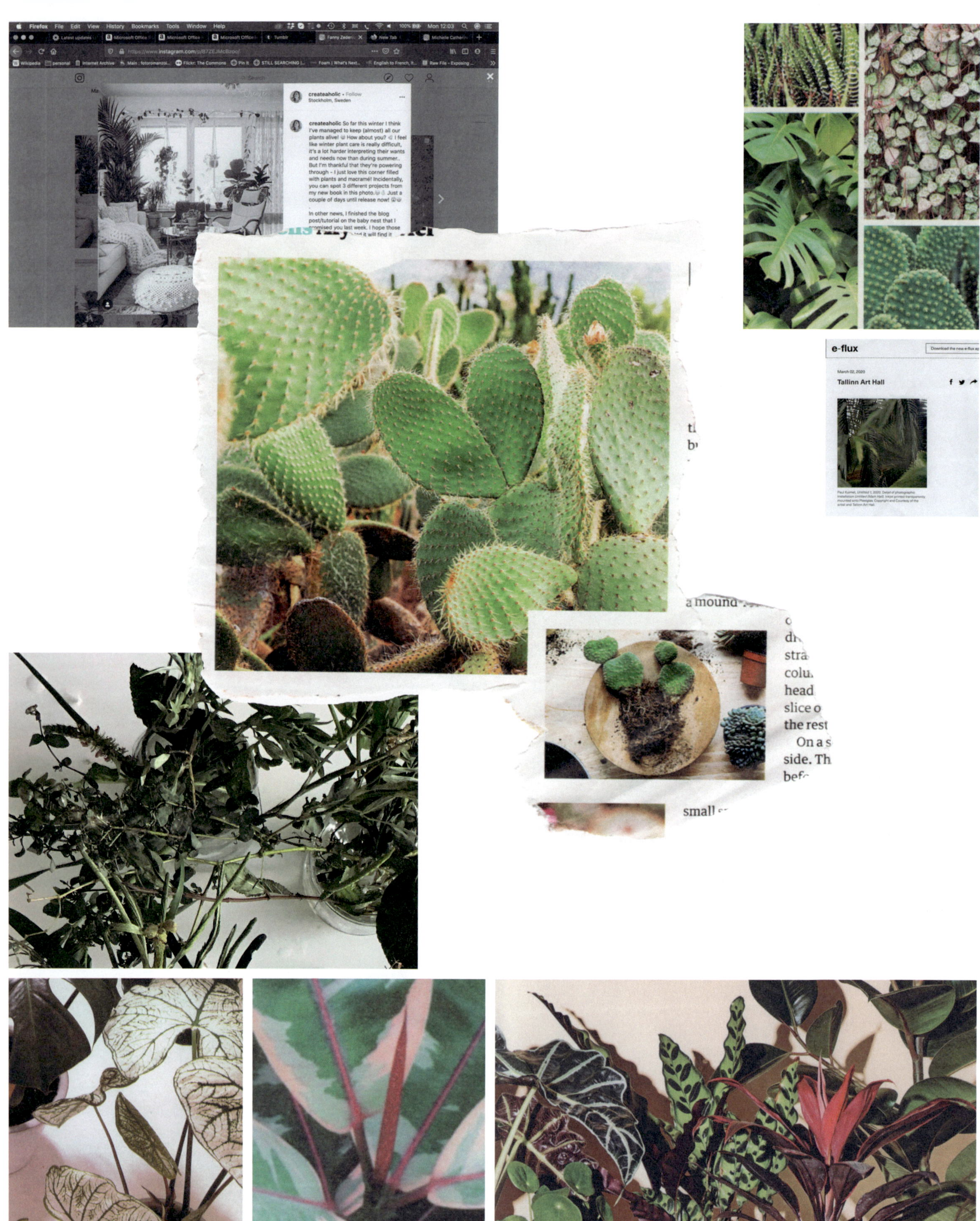
createaholic • Follow
Stockholm, Sweden
createaholic So far this winter I think I've managed to keep (almost) all our plants alive! How about you? I feel like winter plant care is really difficult, it's a lot harder interpreting their wants and needs now than during summer.. But I'm thankful that they're powering through – I just love this corner filled with plants and macramé! Incidentally, you can spot 3 different projects from my new book in this photo. Just a couple of days until release now!
In other news, I finished the blog post/tutorial on the baby nest that I
e-flux
March 02, 2020
Tallinn Art Hall
a mound
stra
head
the rest
side. Th
small

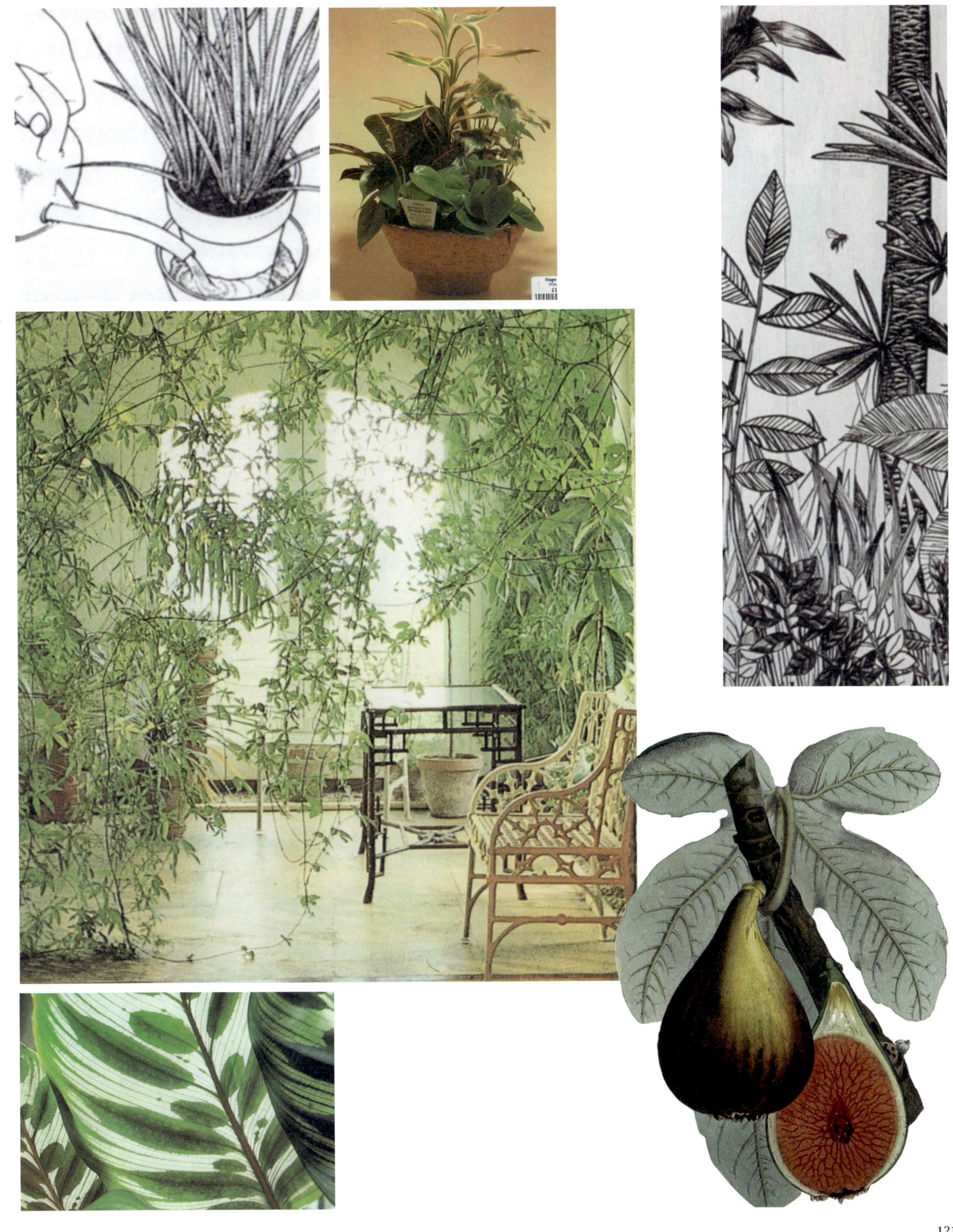

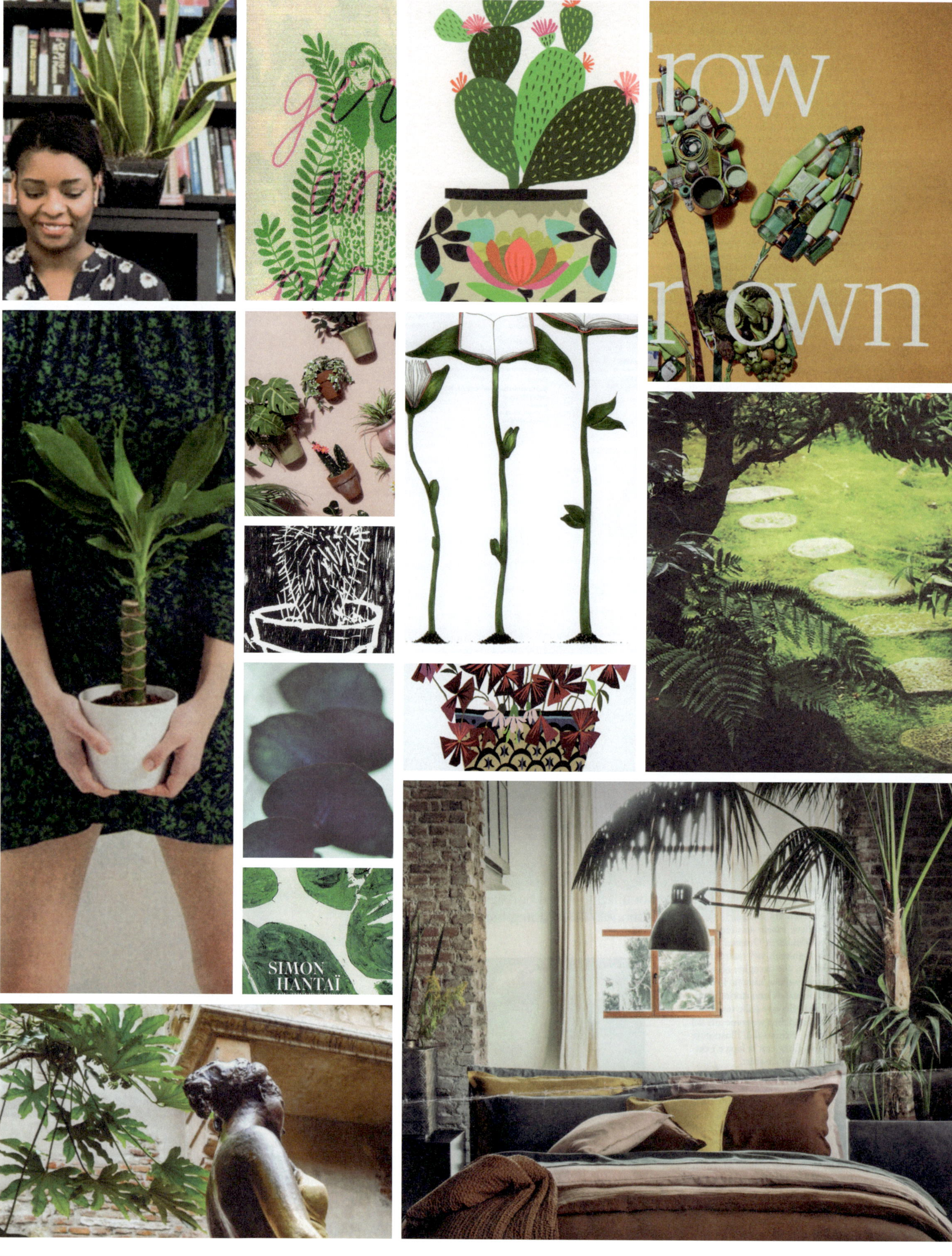
SIMON
HANTAÏ

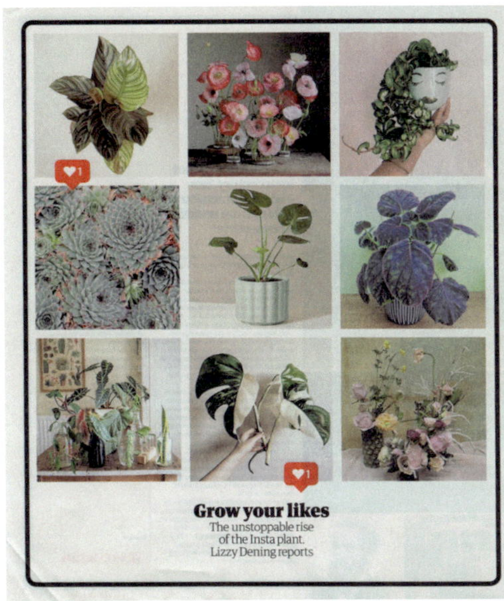
Grow your likes
The unstoppable rise of the Insta plant. Lizzy Dening reports

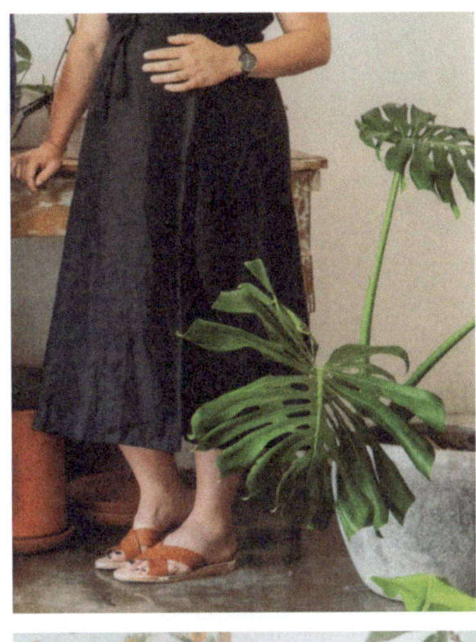

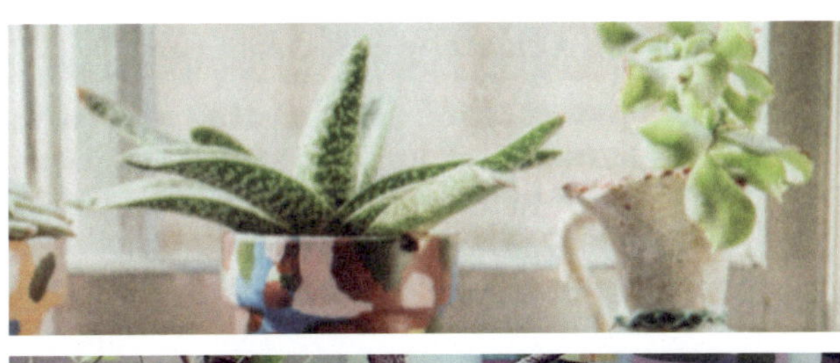

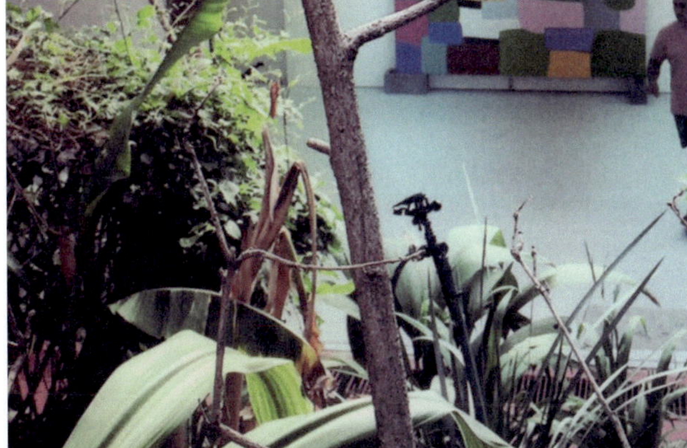

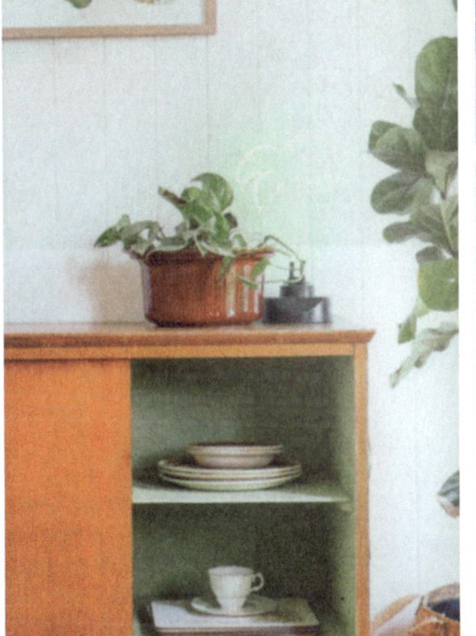

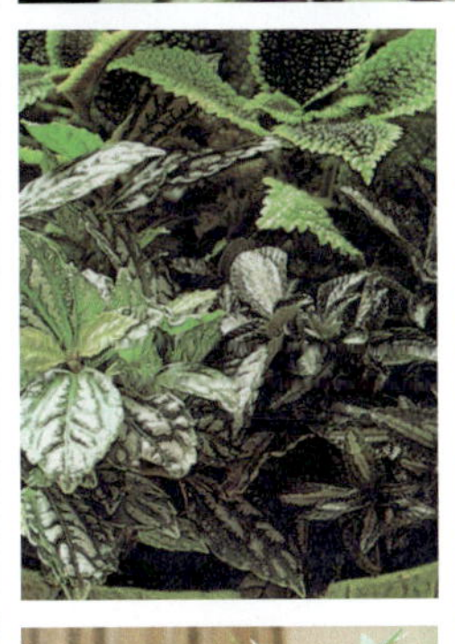

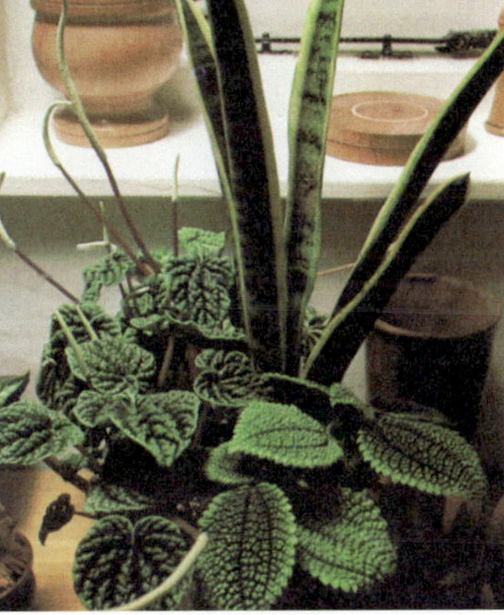

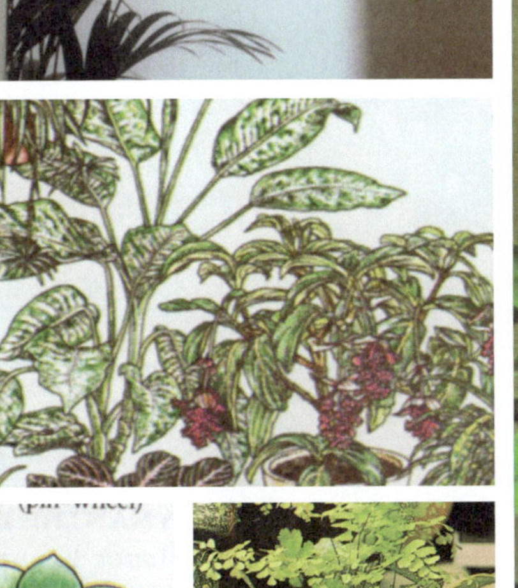

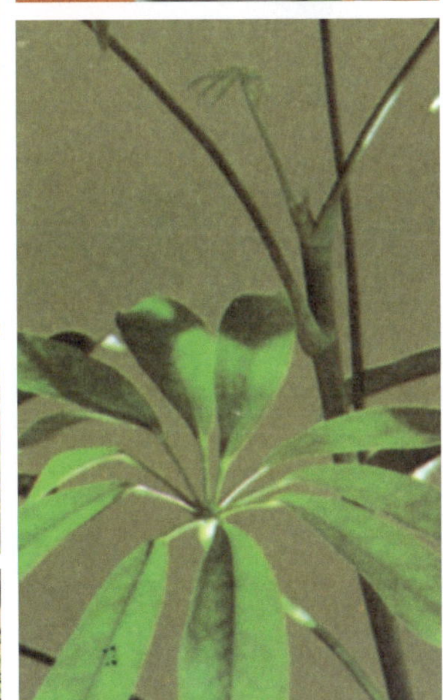

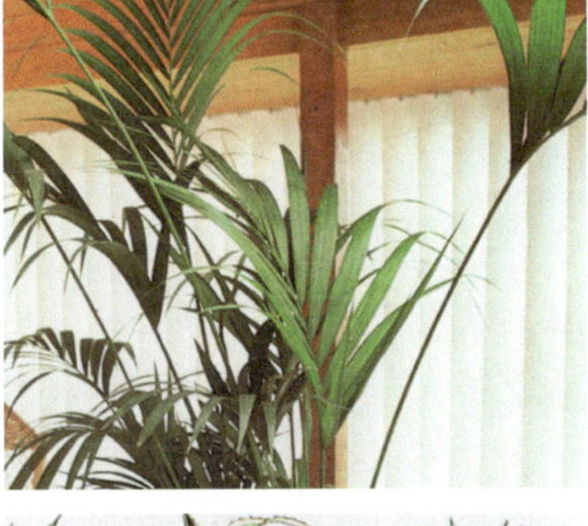

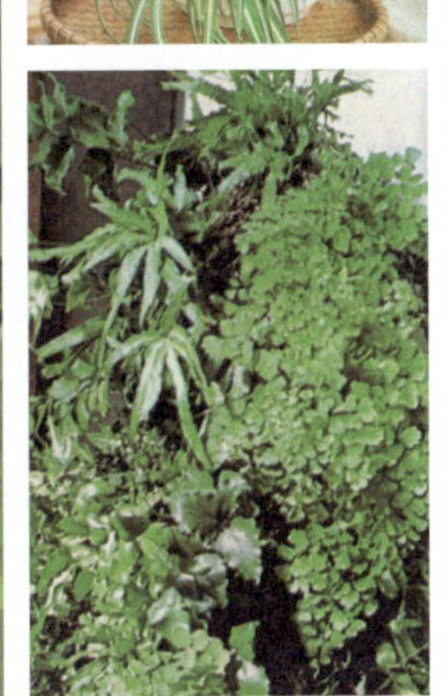

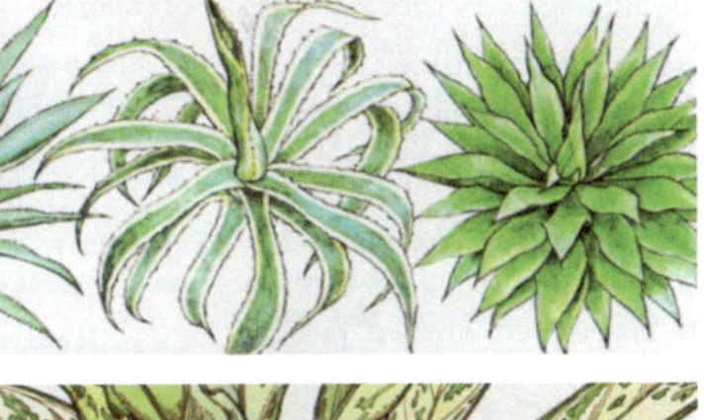

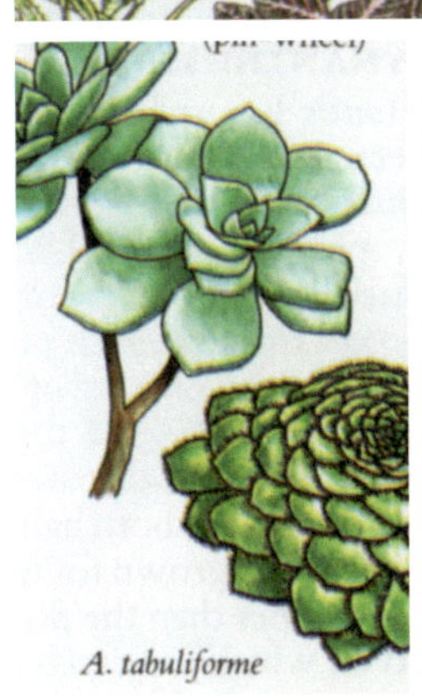
A. tabuliforme

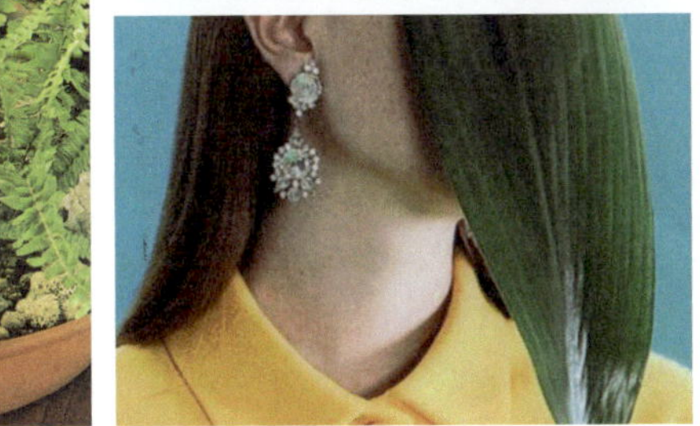

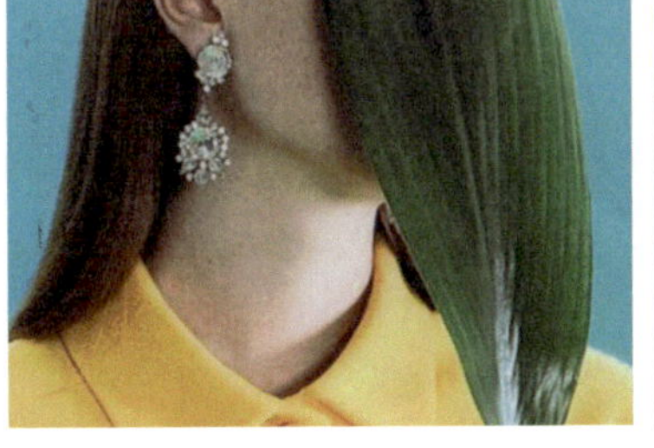

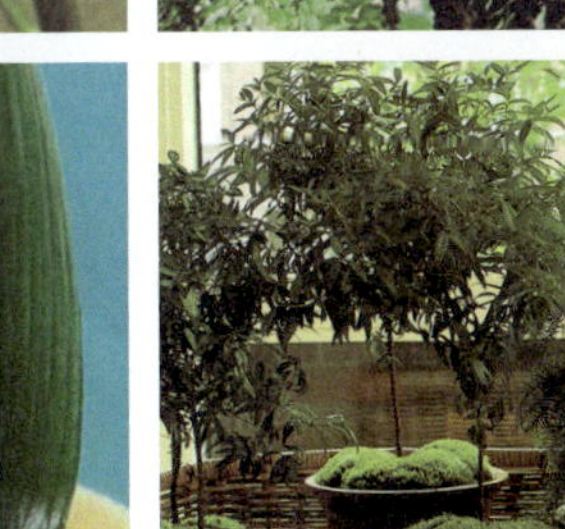

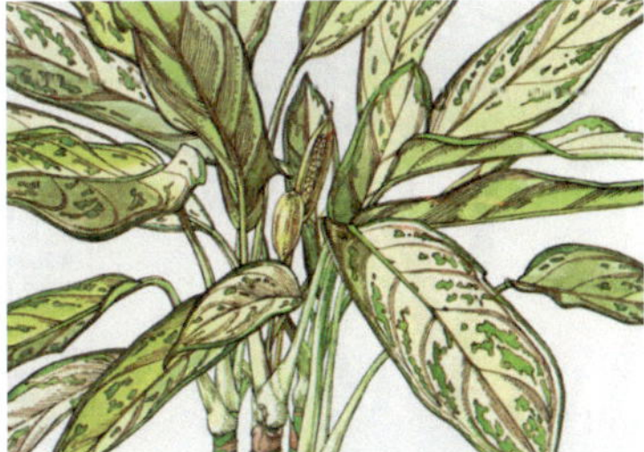

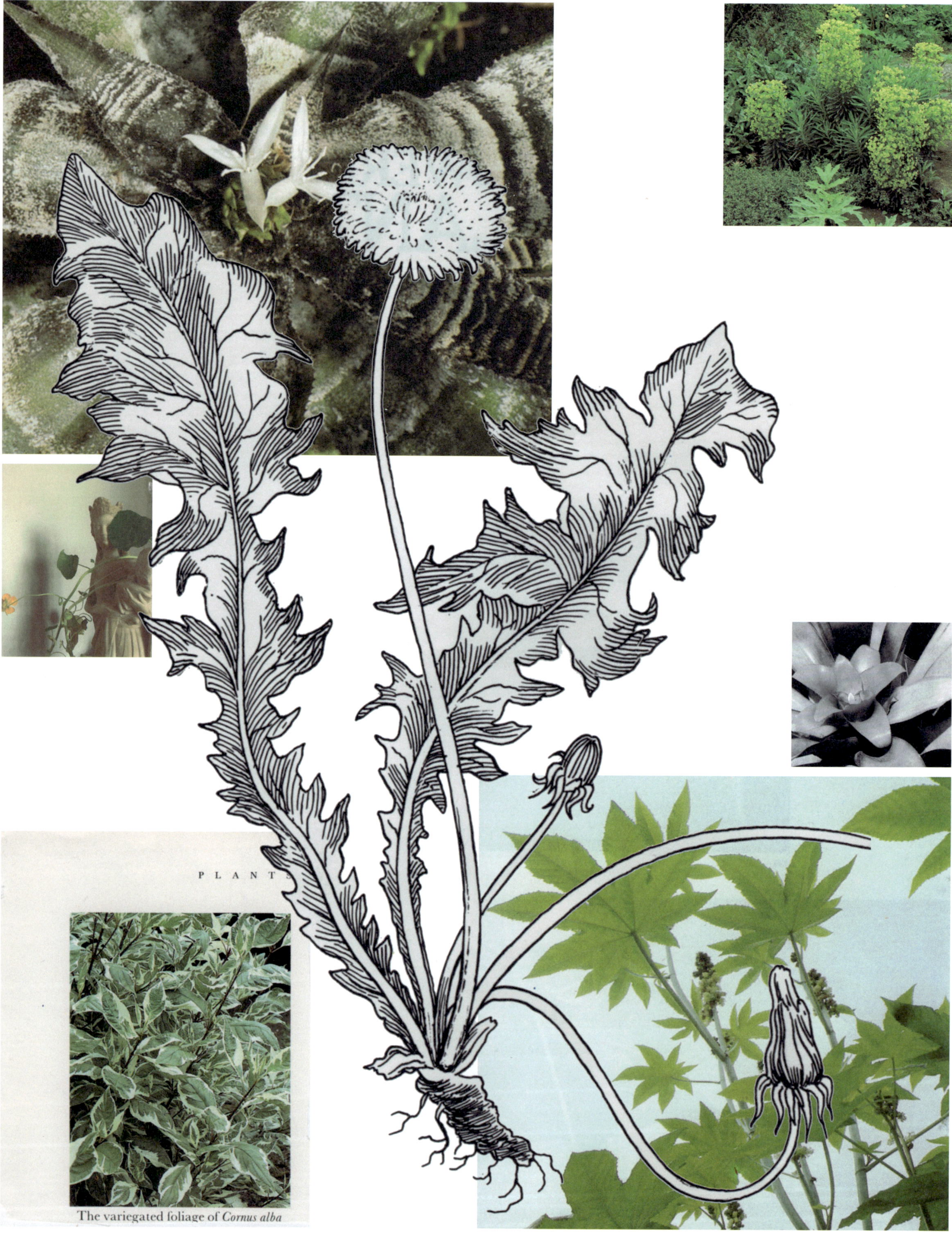

The variegated foliage of *Cornus alba*

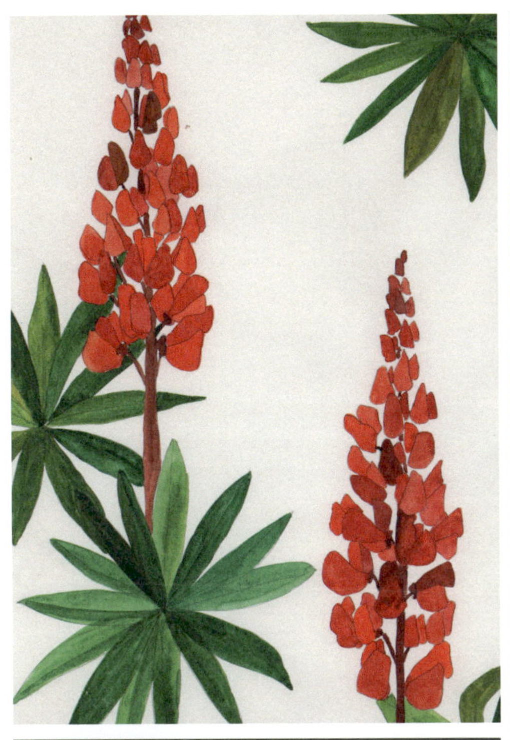

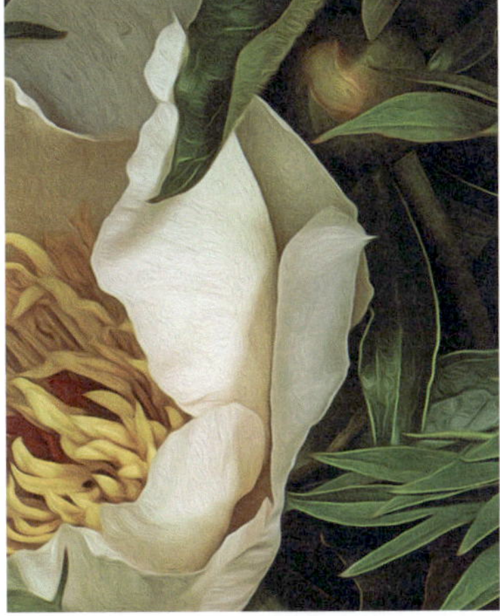

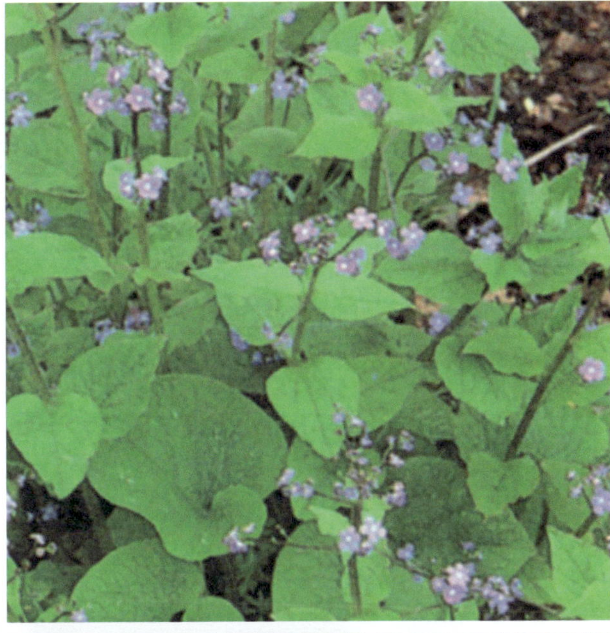

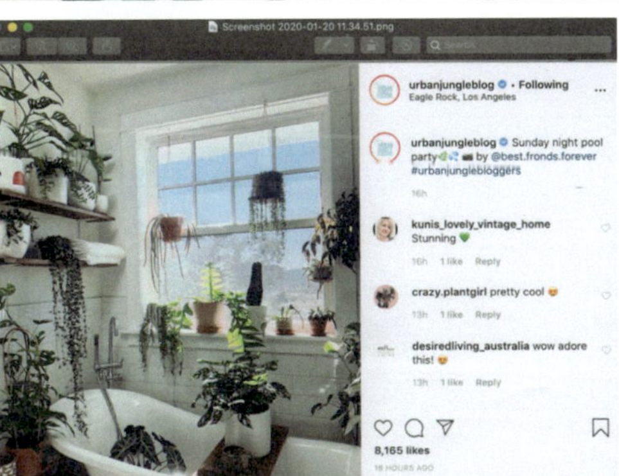
Screenshot 2020-01-20 11.34.51.png
urbanjungleblog • Following
Eagle Rock, Los Angeles
urbanjungleblog Sunday night pool party by @best.fronds.forever #urbanjunglebloggers
16h
kunis_lovely_vintage_home Stunning
16h 1 like Reply
crazy.plantgirl pretty cool
13h 1 like Reply
desiredliving_australia wow adore this!
13h 1 like Reply
8,165 likes
16 HOURS AGO
Add a comment...
Post

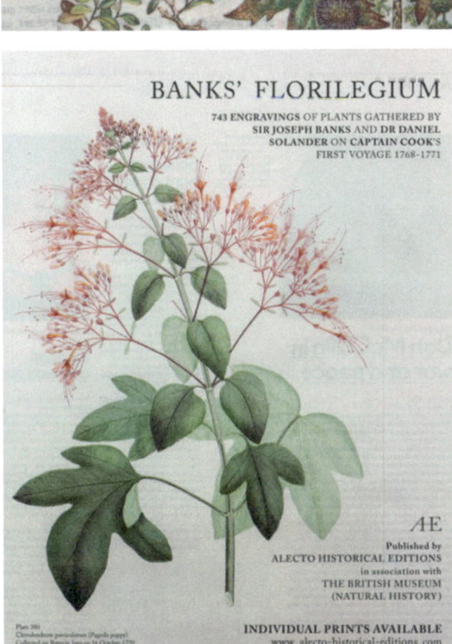
BANKS' FLORILEGIUM
743 ENGRAVINGS OF PLANTS GATHERED BY SIR JOSEPH BANKS AND DR DANIEL SOLANDER ON CAPTAIN COOK'S FIRST VOYAGE 1768-1771
ÆE
Published by
ALECTO HISTORICAL EDITIONS
in association with
THE BRITISH MUSEUM
(NATURAL HISTORY)
INDIVIDUAL PRINTS AVAILABLE
www.alecto-historical-editions.com

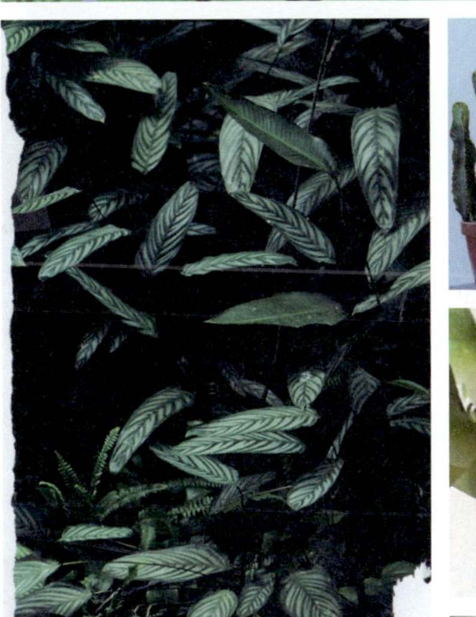

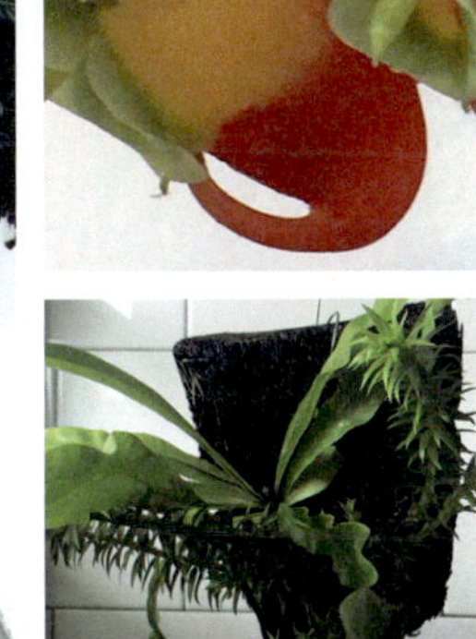

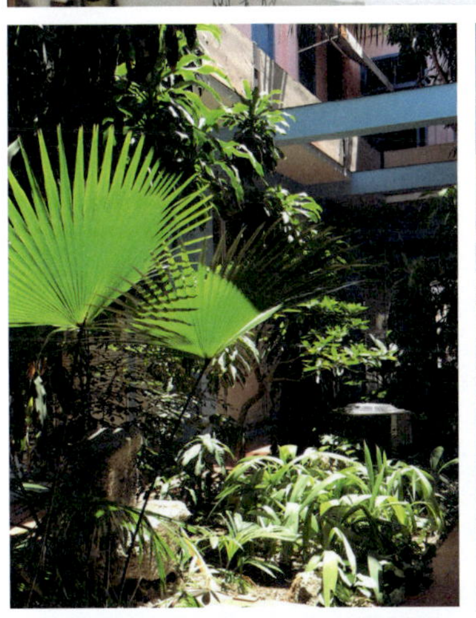

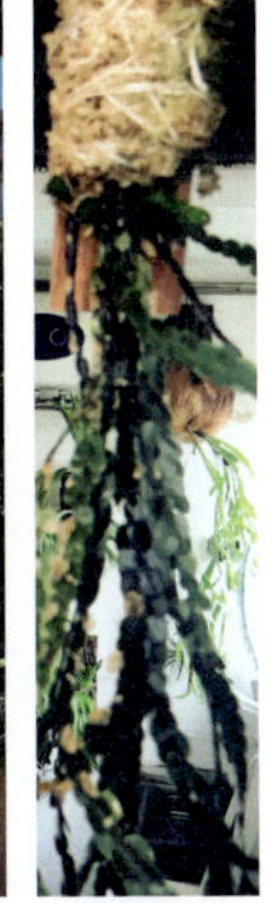

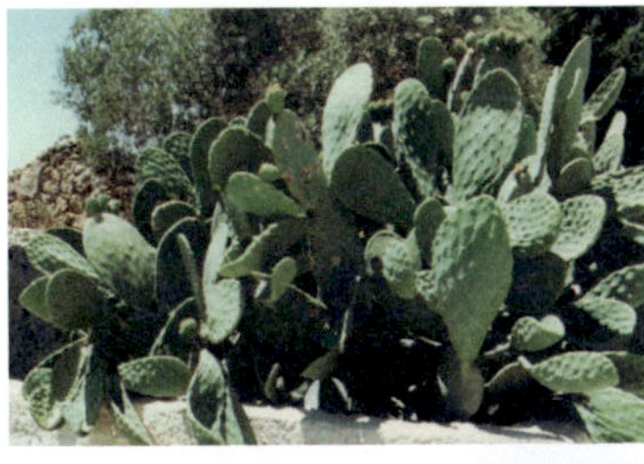

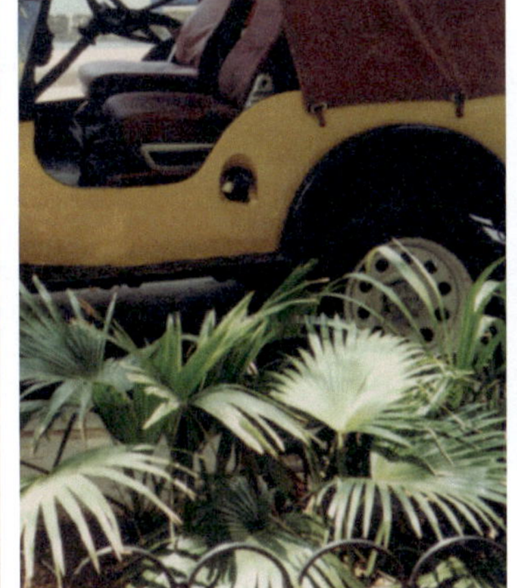

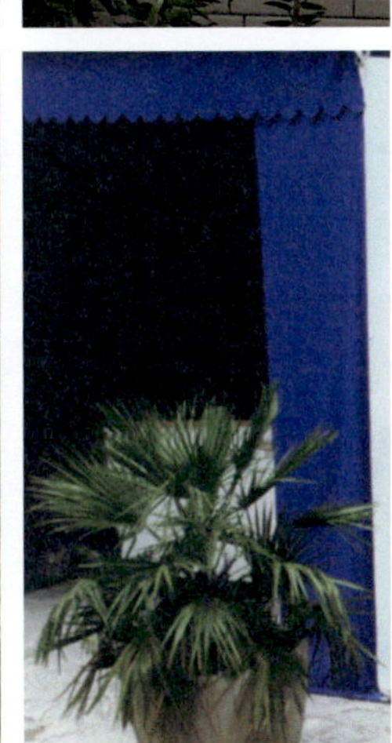

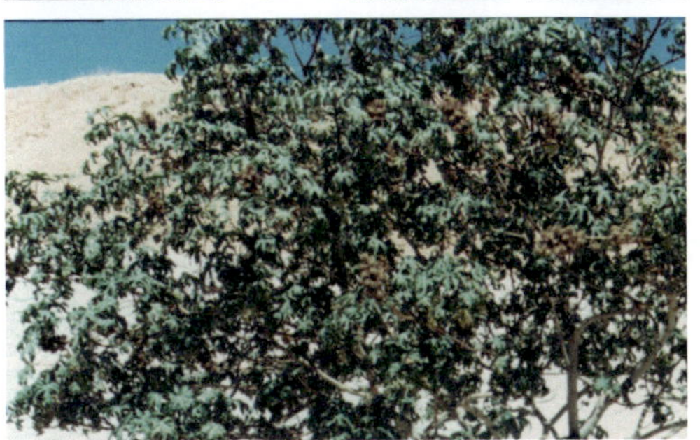

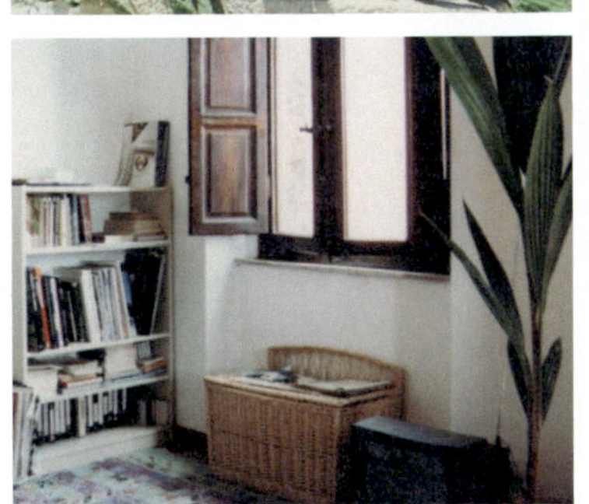

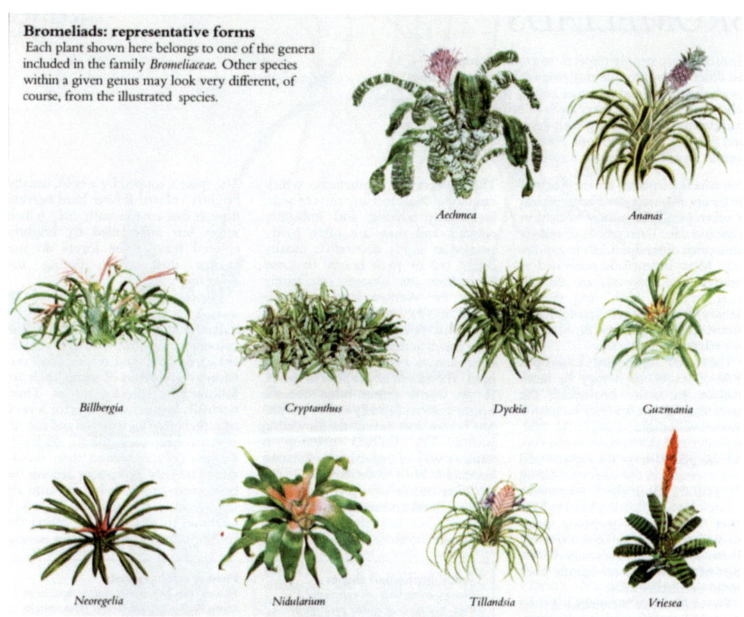

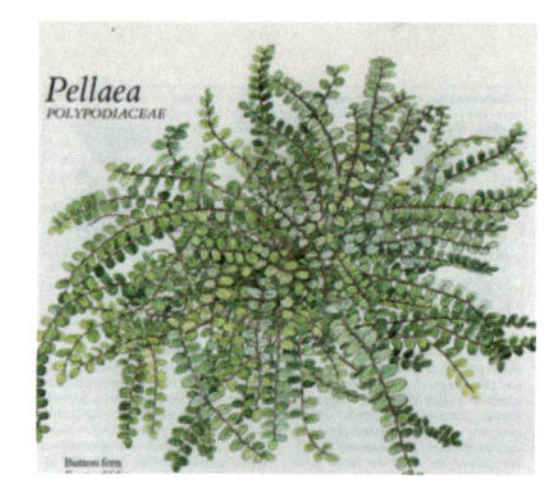

Plant this The large, silvery leaves of *Senecio* 'Angel Wings' (right) make a bold statement in a container in full sun. It's hardy down to -5C but won't like cold, wet conditions, so offer protection in winter, if necessary, or bring it inside as it also makes a great houseplant. Height and spread: 35cm x 35cm.

Try this Shady spots under trees can be tricky, but a stumpery transforms a dank corner into a cool verdant retreat. Improve the soil with leaf mould or compost, then arrange hardwood logs and stumps, planting ferns, hostas and spring bulbs such as snowdrops in the gaps between.

Click this If you want to improve your drill skills, or learn how to fix a tap, check out everywomanpower.tools, a new series of DIY video tutorials made by activists, artists and tradeswomen for women, by arts and social justice organisation Idle Women. **Jane Perrone**

The Guardian Weekend | 31 August 2019 **55**

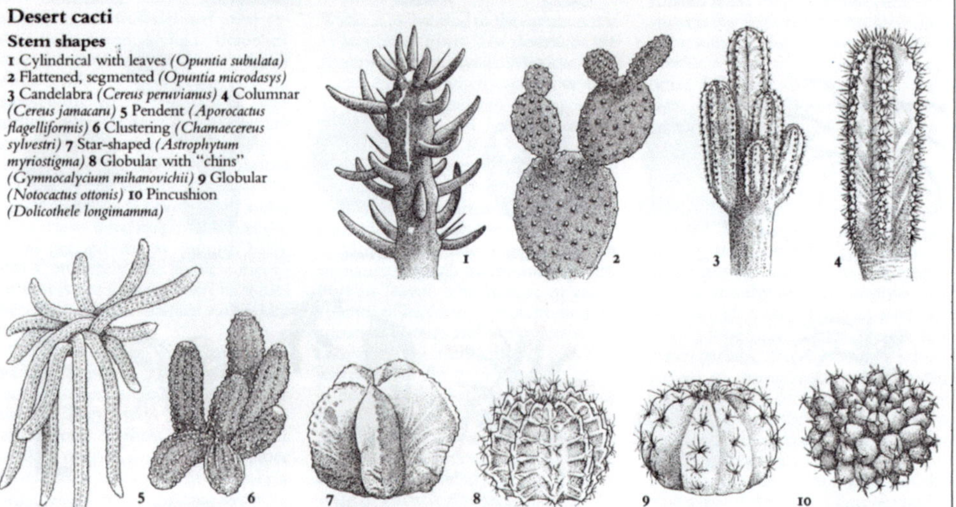

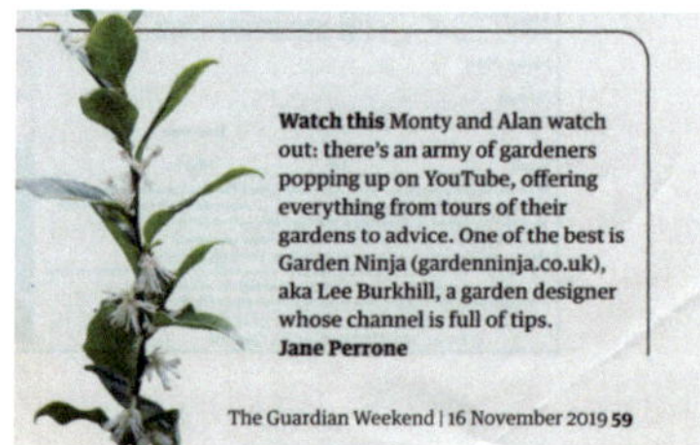
Watch this Monty and Alan watch out: there's an army of gardeners popping up on YouTube, offering everything from tours of their gardens to advice. One of the best is Garden Ninja (gardenninja.co.uk), aka Lee Burkhill, a garden designer whose channel is full of tips.
Jane Perrone

The Guardian Weekend | 16 November 2019 **59**

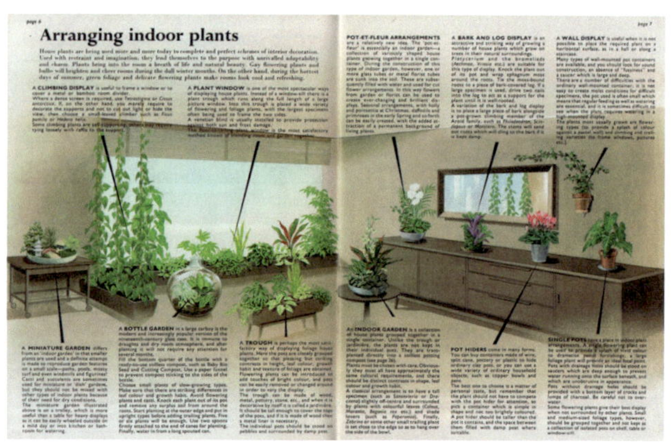

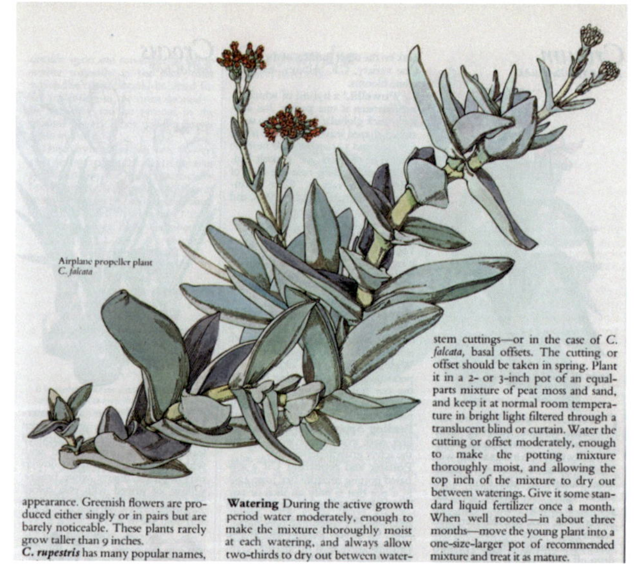

appearance. Greenish flowers are produced either singly or in pairs but are barely noticeable. These plants rarely grow taller than 9 inches.

C. rupestris has many popular names,

Watering During the active growth period water moderately, enough to make the mixture thoroughly moist at each watering, and always allow two-thirds to dry out between water-

stem cuttings—or in the case of *C. falcata,* basal offsets. The cutting or offset should be taken in spring. Plant it in a 2- or 3-inch pot of an equal-parts mixture of peat moss and sand, and keep it at normal room temperature in bright light filtered through a translucent blind or curtain. Water the cutting or offset moderately, enough to make the potting mixture thoroughly moist, and allowing the top inch of the mixture to dry out between waterings. Give it some standard liquid fertilizer once a month. When well rooted—in about three months—move the young plant into a one-size-larger pot of recommended mixture and treat it as mature.

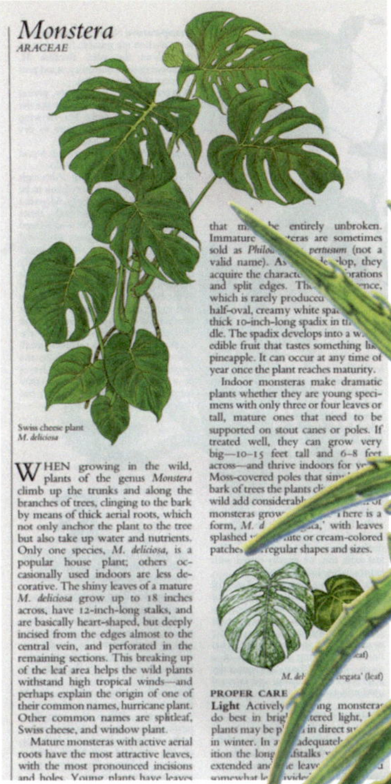

Monstera
ARACEAE

Swiss cheese plant
M. deliciosa

WHEN growing in the wild, plants of the genus *Monstera* climb up the trunks and along the branches of trees, clinging to the bark by means of thick aerial roots, which not only anchor the plant to the tree but also take up water and nutrients. Only one species, *M. deliciosa*, is a popular house plant; others occasionally used indoors are less decorative. The shiny leaves of a mature *M. deliciosa* grow up to 18 inches across, have 12-inch-long stalks, and are basically heart-shaped, but deeply incised from the edges almost to the central vein, and perforated in the remaining sections. This breaking up of the leaf area helps the wild plants withstand high tropical winds—and perhaps explain the origin of one of their common names, hurricane plant. Other common names are splitleaf, Swiss cheese, and window plant.

Mature monsteras with active aerial roots have the most attractive leaves, with the most pronounced incisions and holes. Young plants have leaves that m... be entirely unbroken. Immature ...teras are sometimes sold as *Philo... pertusum* (not a valid name). As ...de...lop, they acquire the charact... ...orations and split edges. Th... ...ence, which is rarely produced ... half-oval, creamy white spa... thick 10-inch-long spadix in th... dle. The spadix develops into a w... edible fruit that tastes something li... pineapple. It can occur at any time of year once the plant reaches maturity.

Indoor monsteras make dramatic plants whether they are young specimens with only three or four leaves or tall, mature ones that need to be supported on stout canes or poles. If treated well, they can grow very big—10–15 feet tall and 6–8 feet across—and thrive indoors for ye... Moss-covered poles that sim... bark of trees the plants cl... wild add considerabl... ...of monsteras grow... There is a form, *M. d... ...ata*,' with leaves splashed ...ite or cream-colored patches ...regular shapes and sizes.

...eaf)

M. del... ...egata' (leaf)

PROPER CARE

Light Actively ...ing monsteras do best in brig... ...tered light, ... plants may be p... ...in direct su... in winter. In a... adequatel... ition the long... ...fstalks ... extended an... ...e leav... somewhat le... ...vide...

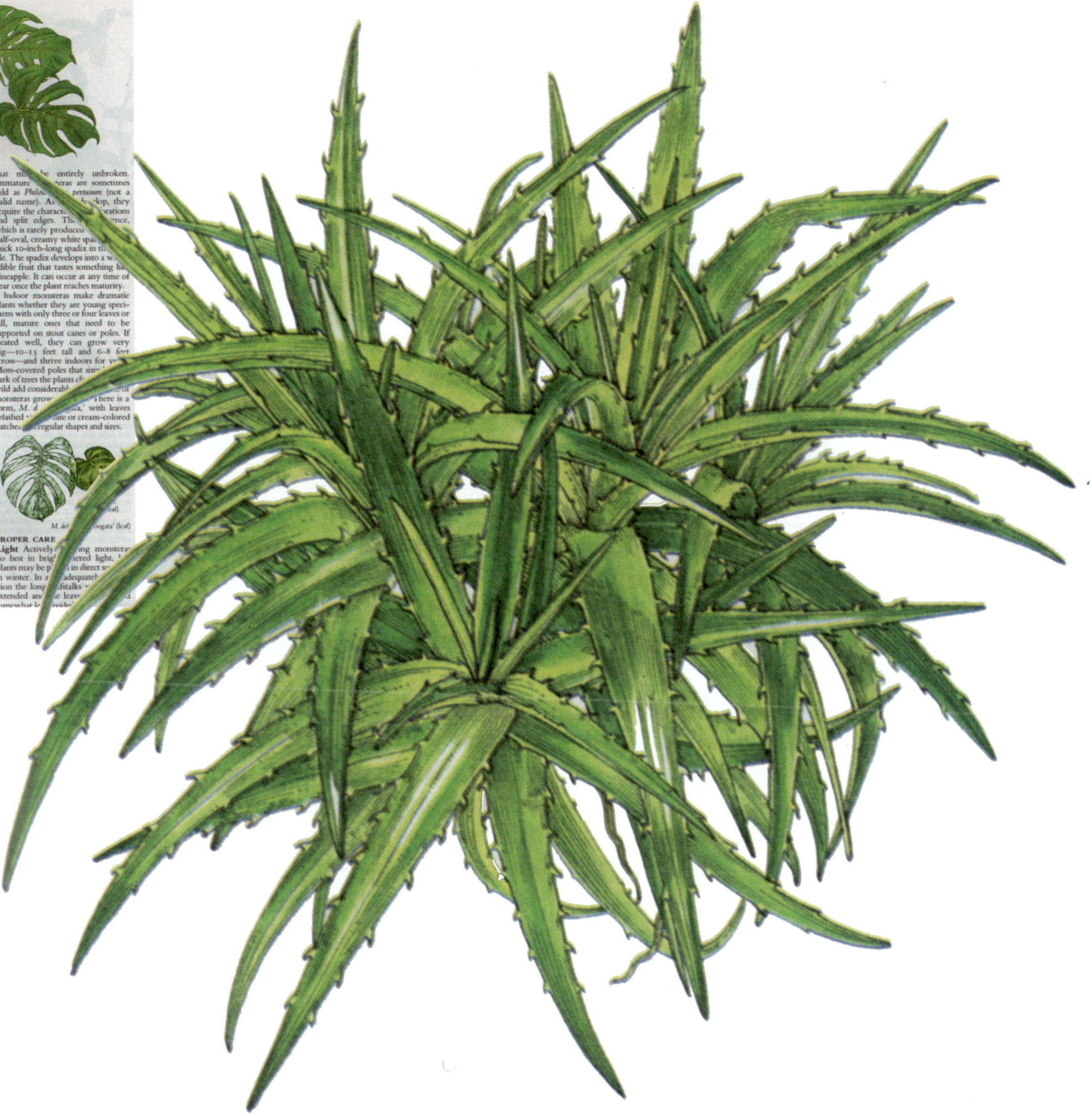

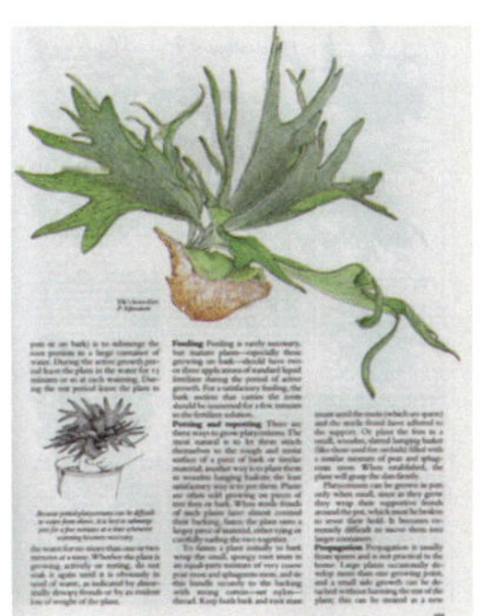

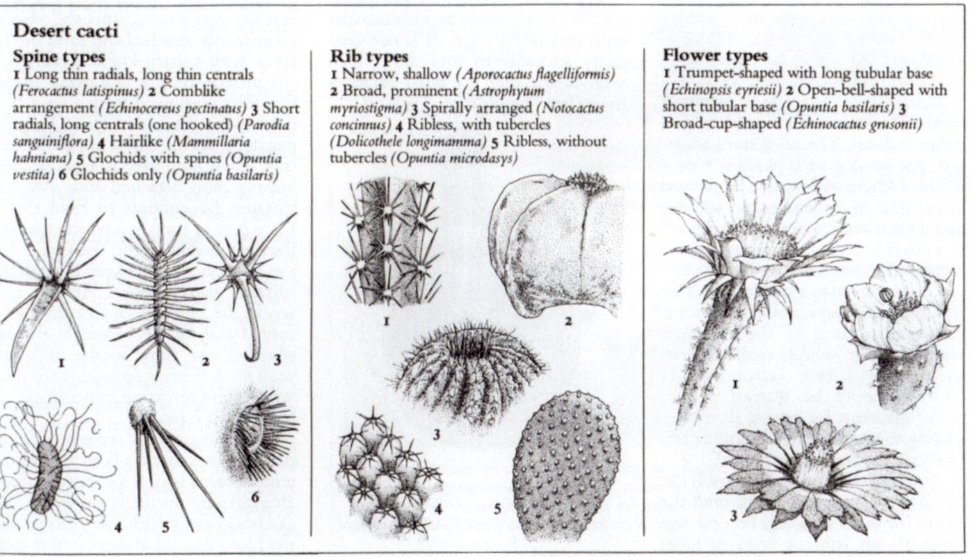

Desert cacti

Spine types
1 Long thin radials, long thin centrals *(Ferocactus latispinus)* **2** Comblike arrangement *(Echinocereus pectinatus)* **3** Short radials, long centrals (one hooked) *(Parodia sanguiniflora)* **4** Hairlike *(Mammillaria hahniana)* **5** Glochids with spines *(Opuntia vestita)* **6** Glochids only *(Opuntia basilaris)*

Rib types
1 Narrow, shallow *(Aporocactus flagelliformis)* **2** Broad, prominent *(Astrophytum myriostigma)* **3** Spirally arranged *(Notocactus concinnus)* **4** Ribless, with tubercles *(Dolicothele longimamma)* **5** Ribless, without tubercles *(Opuntia microdasys)*

Flower types
1 Trumpet-shaped with long tubular base *(Echinopsis eyriesii)* **2** Open-bell-shaped with short tubular base *(Opuntia basilaris)* **3** Broad-cup-shaped *(Echinocactus grusonii)*

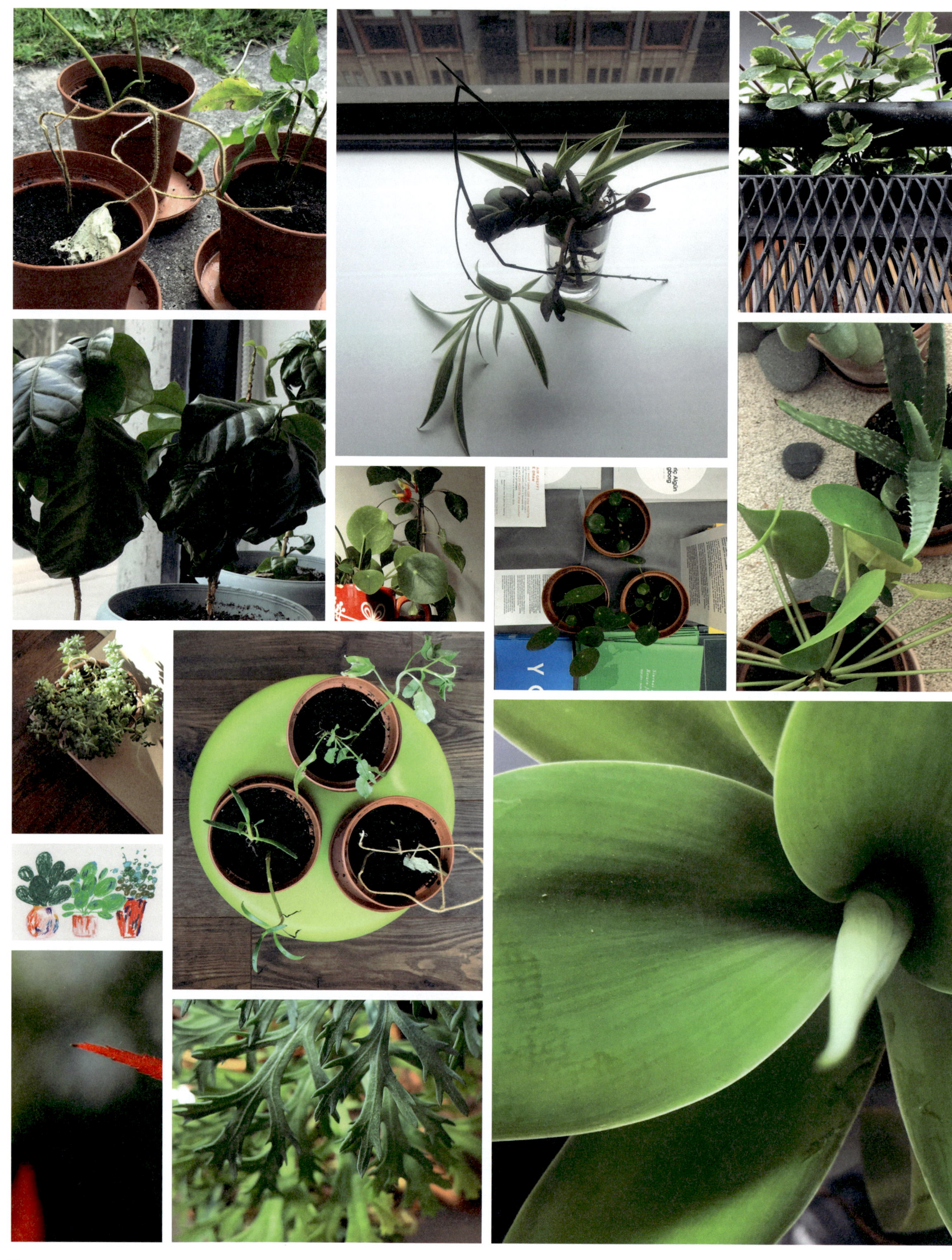

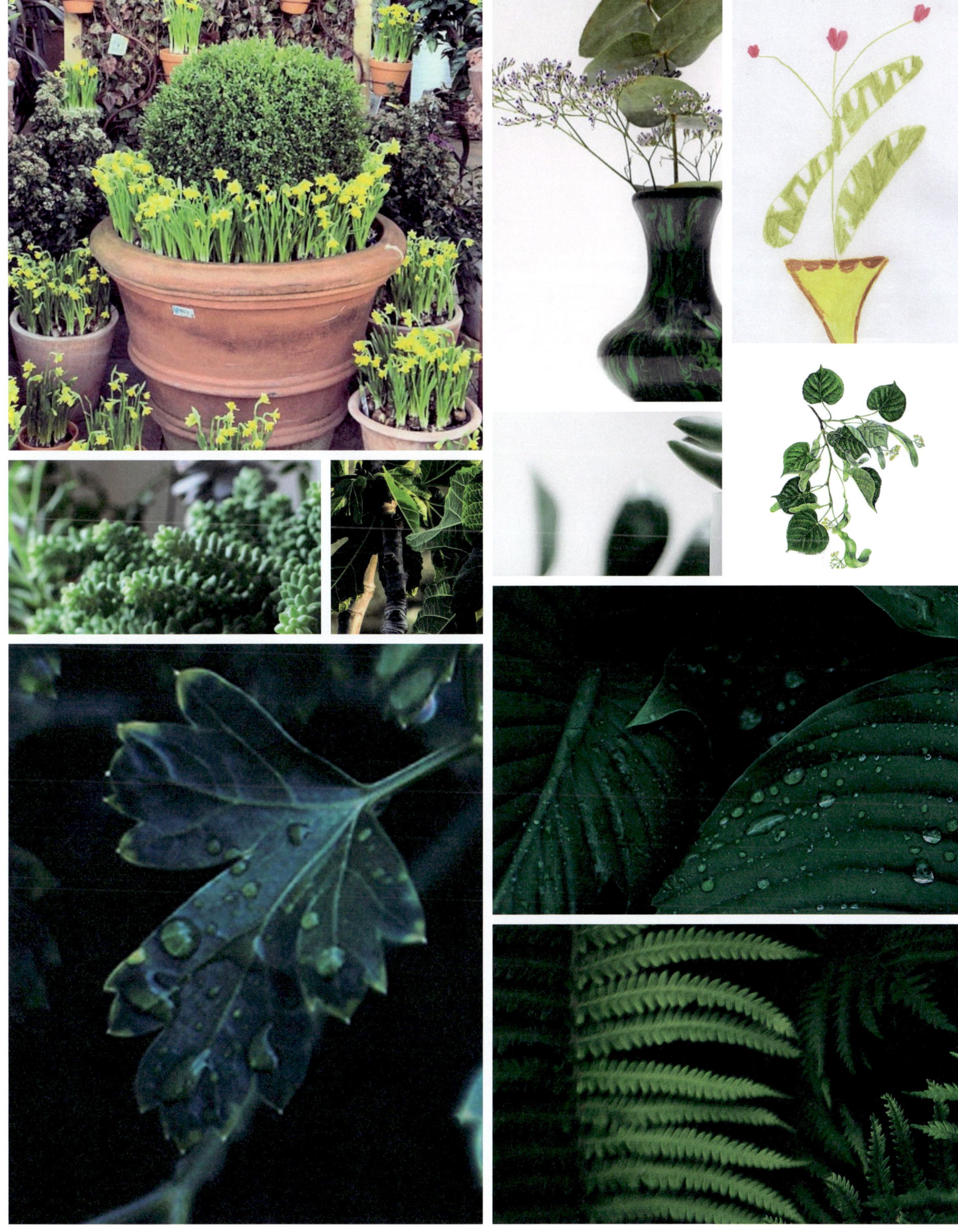

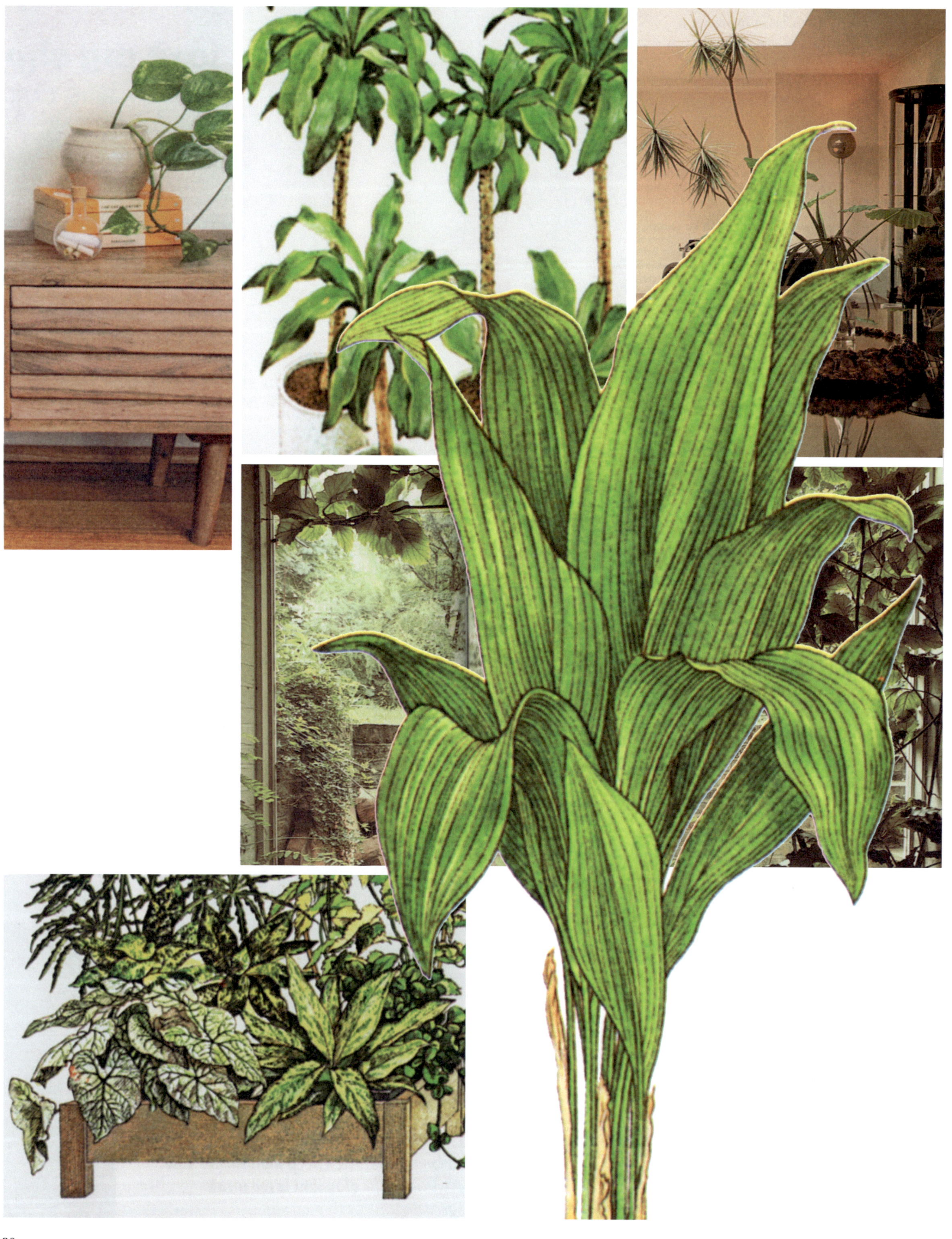

ARCHITECTURAL PLANTS

There is a whole group of plants which can be called 'architectural': they include plants beloved by architects, plants with architectural qualities and, paradoxically, plants whose feathery foliage is used as a contrast to the severity of modern architectural form. Overall, it is a group of plants that displays form and foliage rather than flowers.

Monsteras, philodendrons and rubber plants were often featured in early illustrations of modern architecture, because of their large, simple leaves. Scale, as much as form, was an important consideration, and still is. For this reason, indoor trees (see pages 68–73) are favourites; trees are large enough to make an impact on an interior, and to act as a focal point, not as clutter.

Architects and interior designers have long had a working partnership with palms. In fact, any palms that do manage to survive outdoors in temperate climates often look bedraggled; indoors, they fare better, especially in homes without central heating. In winter central heating is the main enemy of the European fan palm, Chinese fan palm, date palm, lady palm, windmill palm and desert fan palm. Other species – the fishtail palm, coconut palm, parlour palm, kentia palm and yellow palm – are more tolerant, but all these plants benefit from a humid atmosphere in warm temperatures. Although palms need bright light to flourish, lack of direct sunlight is not a problem. In nature, the young plants grow in the shade of nearby plants; small palms are generally young and need protection from direct light.

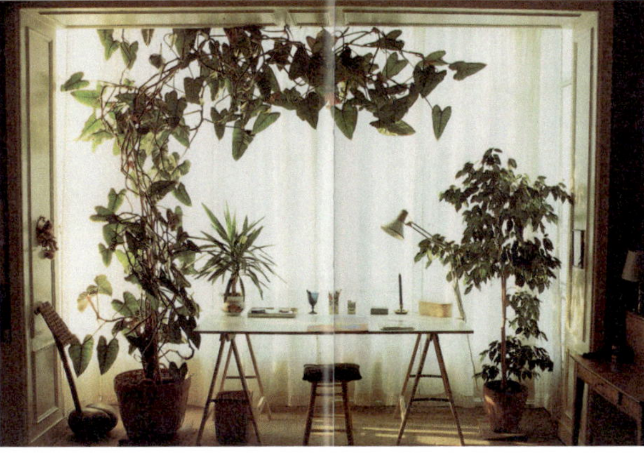

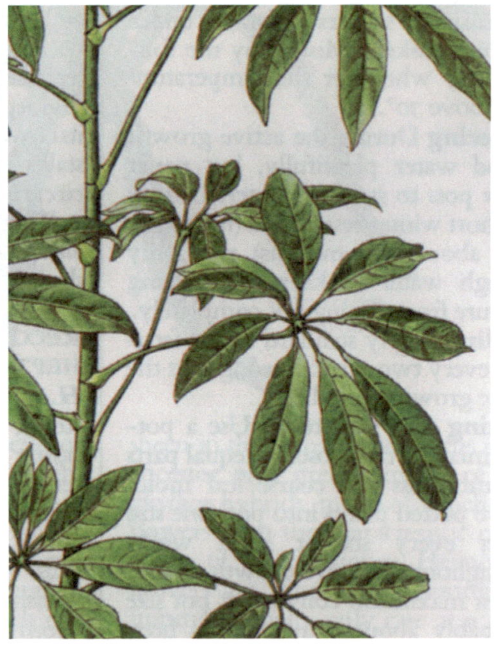

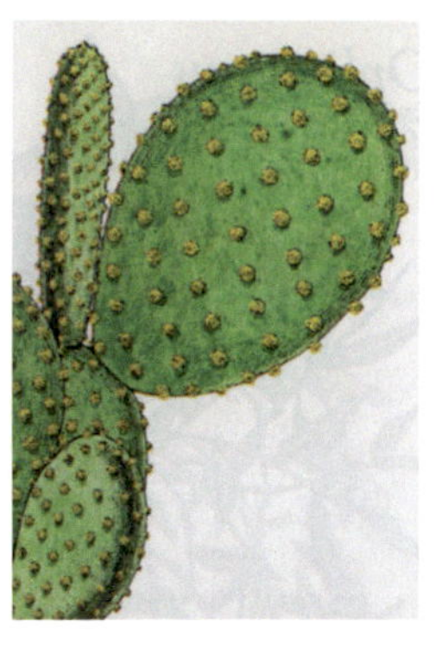

Saxifraga

SAXIFRAGACEAE

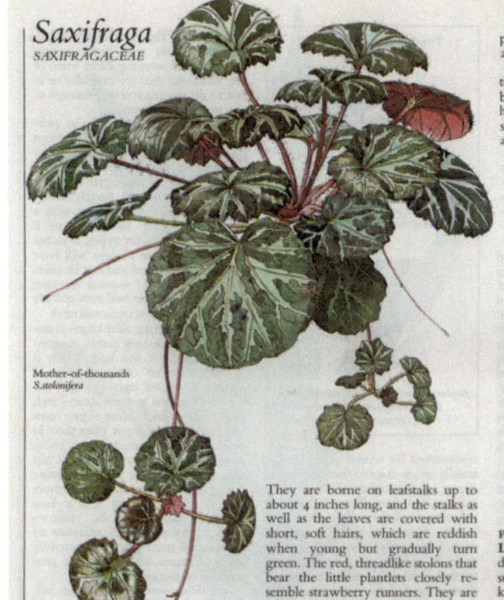

Mother-of-thousands
S.stolonifera

ONLY one species of this very large genus is suitable for use as a house plant: *S. stolonifera* (formerly known as *S. sarmentosa*), which has been aptly termed mother-of-thousands because of its many offspring. It is also known by a number of such inappropriate and misleading common names as beefsteak geranium, strawberry geranium, and strawberry begonia. It is a stemless plant that grows no more than about 9 inches tall, with loose rosettes of almost circular leaves up to 4 inches across, graceful flower spikes, and attractive trailing shoots that carry miniature plantlets. The leaves are deep olive green, roundly toothed, netted above with fine silver veining, and colored reddish purple beneath. They are borne on leafstalks up to about 4 inches long, and the stalks as well as the leaves are covered with short, soft hairs, which are reddish when young but gradually turn green. The red, threadlike stolons that bear the little plantlets closely resemble strawberry runners. They are of varying lengths (sometimes as much as 3 feet long); they emerge from the center of the plant and they occasionally divide into several threads. Some of the plantlets at the ends of stolons remain small while attached to the parent plant. Others grow larger, often attaining proportions almost as great as those of the parent plant, and can more readily be used for propagation (see below).

The flower spikes, which are up to 18 inches long, are produced in late summer. They carry loose clusters of star-shaped flowers that are white with a yellow center. Each flower is about 1 inch across, with two of its petals appreciably longer than the rest. One of the forms, *S.s.* 'Tricolor' (magic carpet), is smaller than the others, and its leaves, which have cream-colored edges, turn rose-pink if the plant is grown in good light. *S.s.* 'Tricolor' is less vigorous than the type plant in terms of both rate of growth and of plantlet production, however.

These plants are not dense enough to fill hanging baskets by themselves, but they look most attractive in small hanging pots, where their trailing shoots and decorative, colorful leaves are displayed to full advantage.

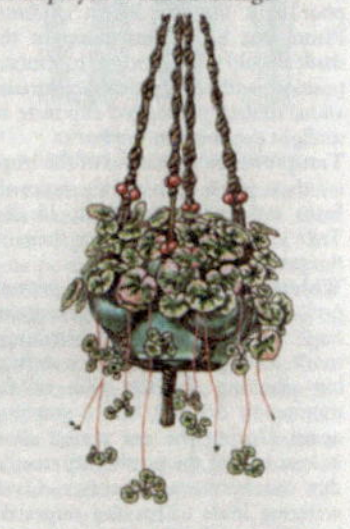

The long, threadlike stolons that bear the little plantlets of S.s. 'Tricolor' look decorative in hanging pots, but are delicate and easily damaged.

PROPER CARE

Light A little direct sunlight every day (an hour or two of early-morning sun, if possible) helps saxifrages to keep their leaf coloring, but do not place them in hot, prolonged sunshine. The variegated-leaved form *S.s.* 'Tricolor,' however, must have at least three hours a day of direct sunlight or the leafstalks will become long and spindly, and much of the leaf contrast will be lost.

Temperature *S. stolonifera* grows best in fairly cool conditions—ideally, 50°–60°F. It can, however, tolerate somewhat higher daytime temperatures during the active growth period (from spring to late fall). *S.s.* 'Tricolor' will thrive if it is kept in normally warm room temperatures throughout the year. If indoor temperatures rise above 65°, all saxifrages require high humidity. Stand potted plants on trays of pebbles kept permanently moist, and suspend dishes of water under hanging baskets. Keep plants in a well-ventilated position, but out of drafts. Minimum tolerable temperature: 40°F.

350

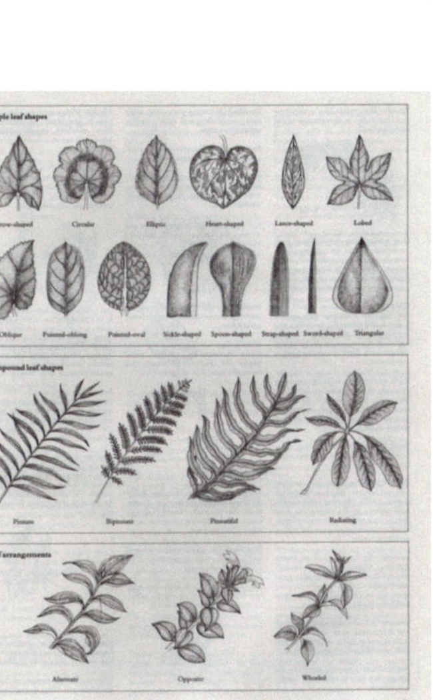

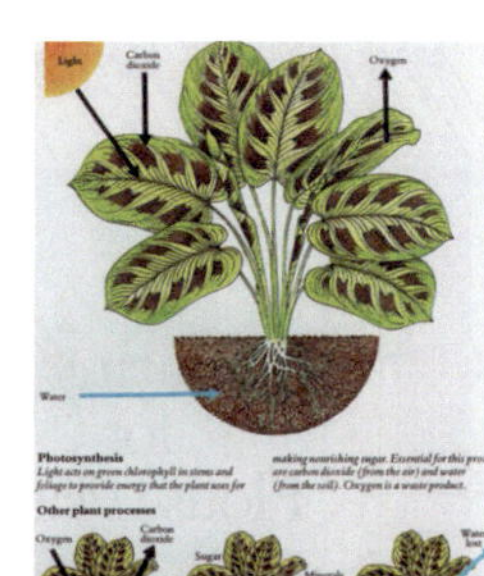

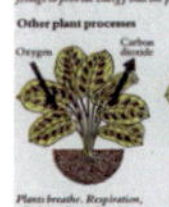

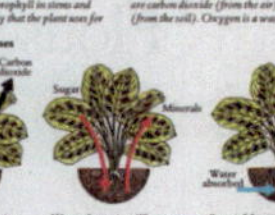

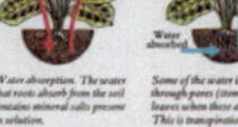

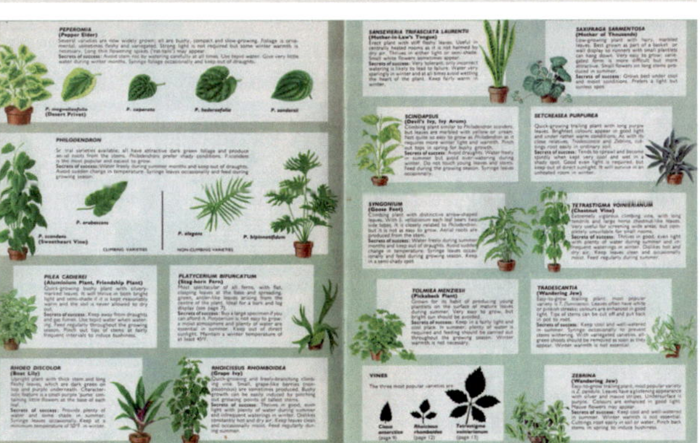

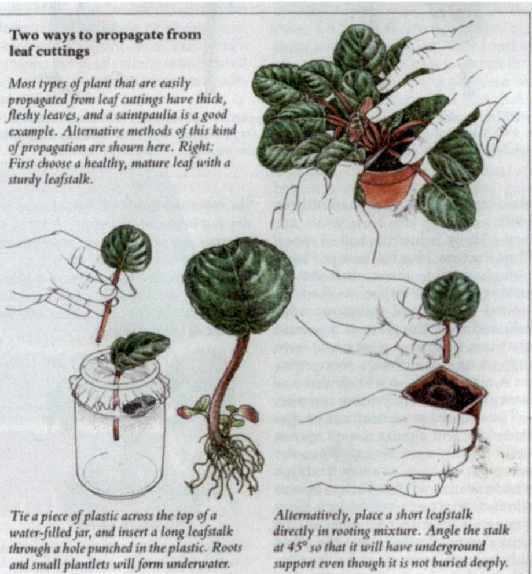

Two ways to propagate from leaf cuttings

Most types of plant that are easily propagated from leaf cuttings have thick, fleshy leaves, and a saintpaulia is a good example. Alternative methods of this kind of propagation are shown here. Right: First choose a healthy, mature leaf with a sturdy leafstalk.

Tie a piece of plastic across the top of a water-filled jar, and insert a long leafstalk through a hole punched in the plastic. Roots and small plantlets will form underwater.

Alternatively, place a short leafstalk directly in rooting mixture. Angle the stalk at 45° so that it will have underground support even though it is not buried deeply.

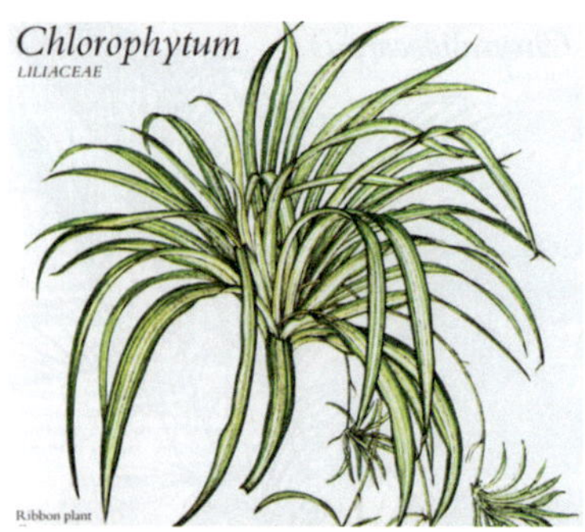

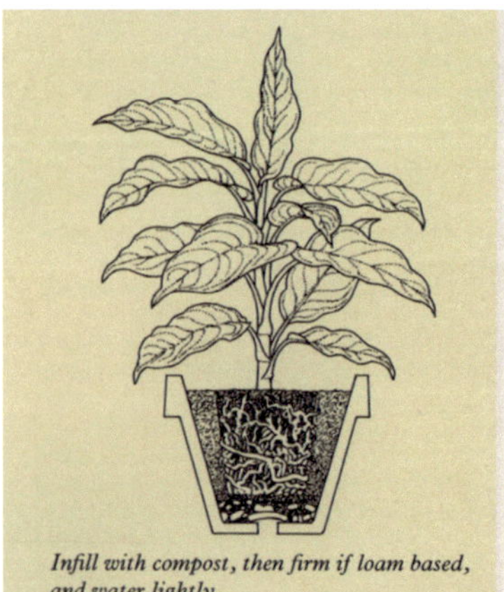

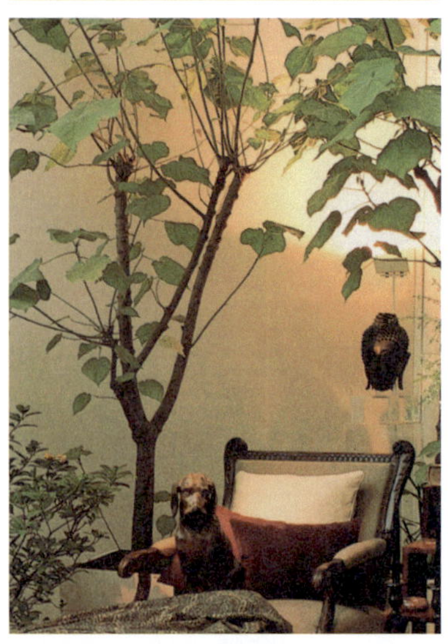

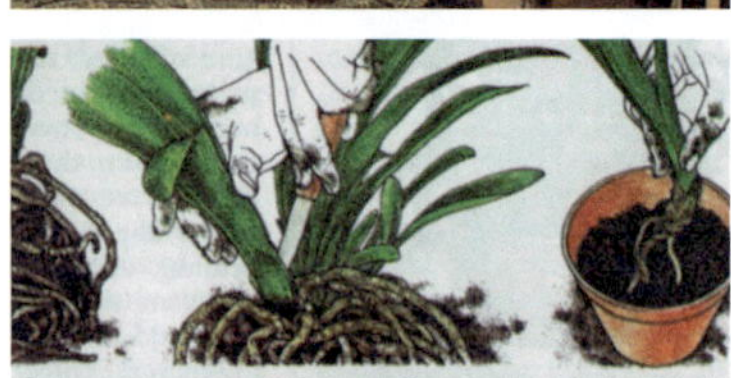

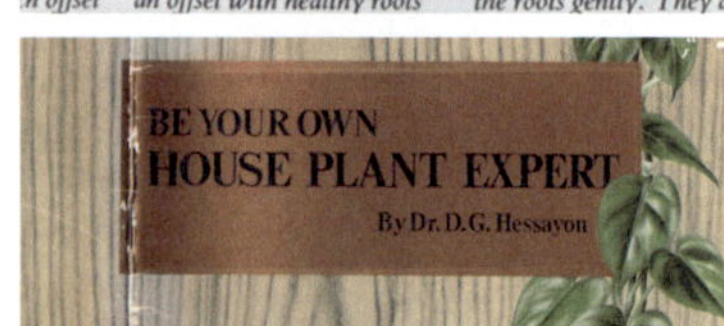

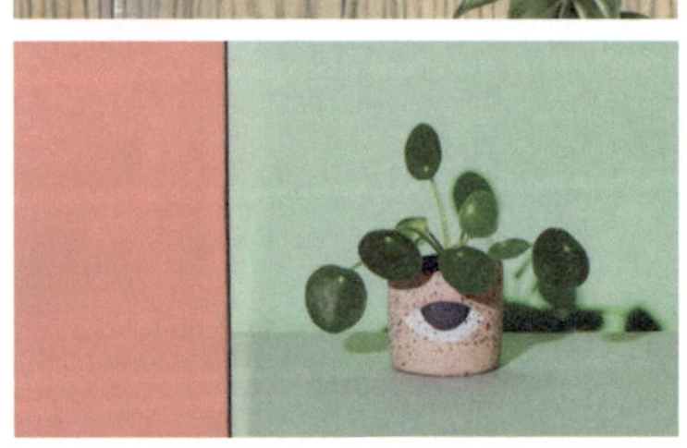

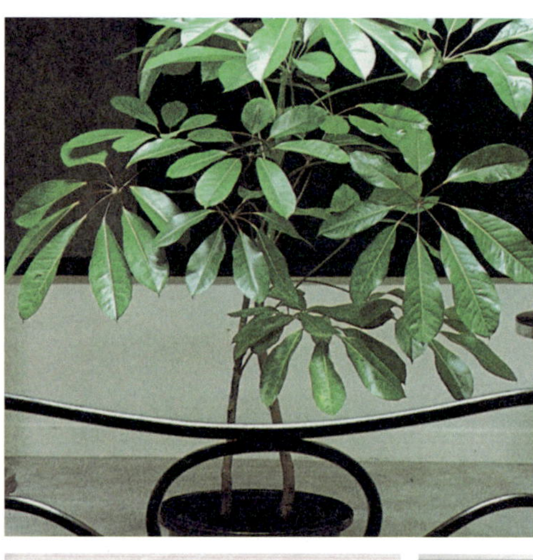

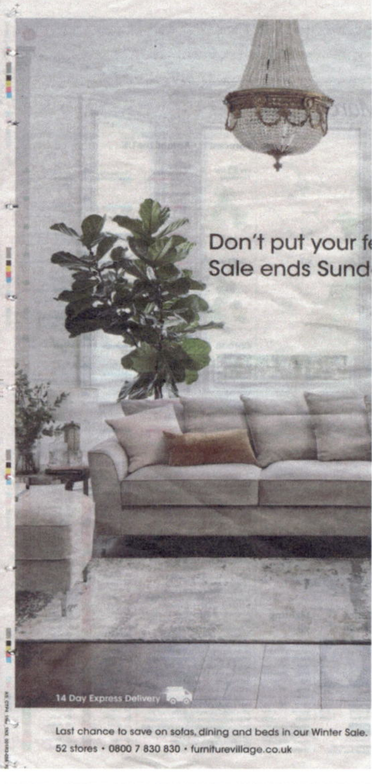

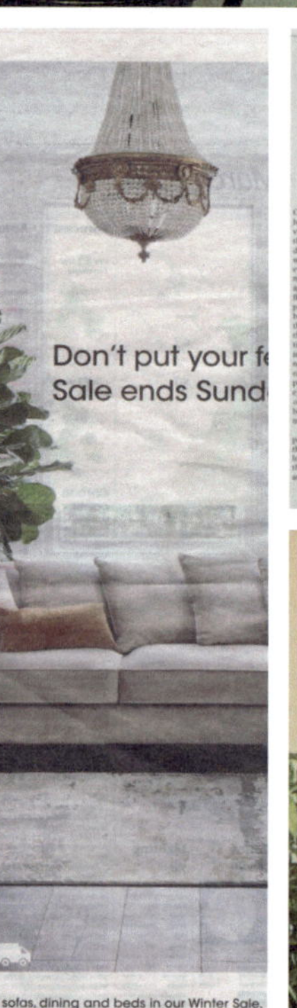

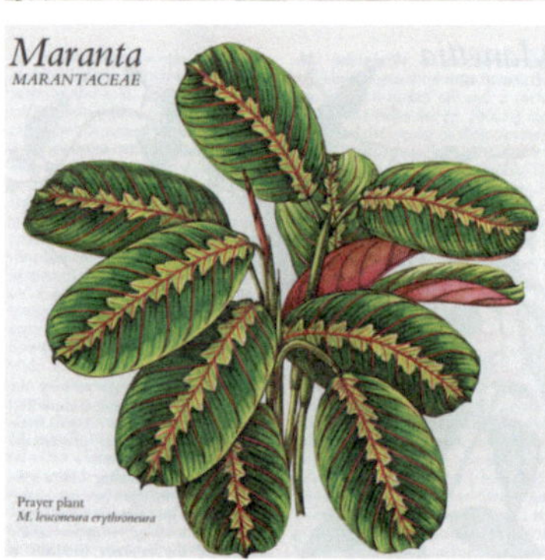

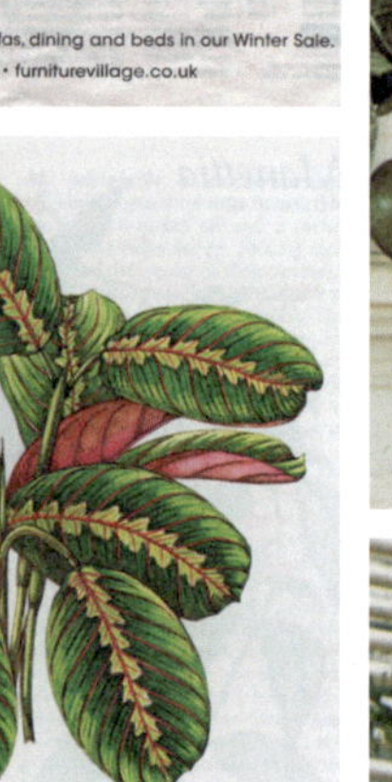

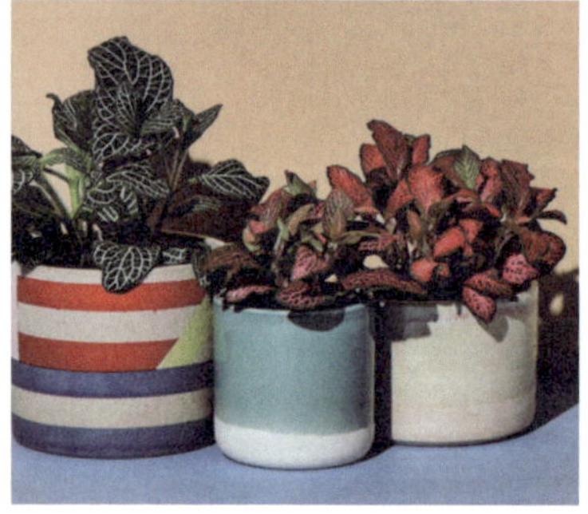

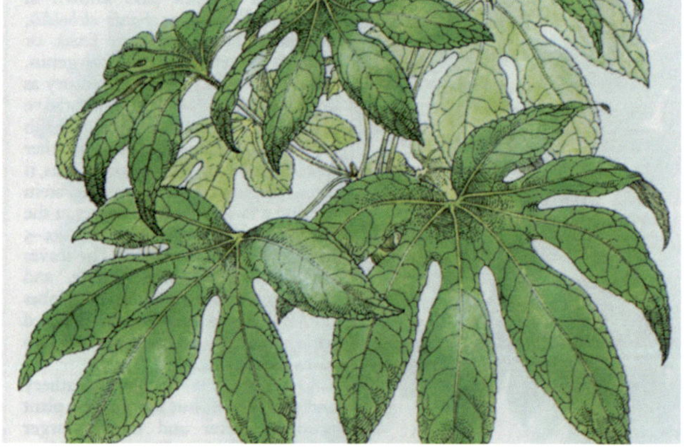

PLANTSCAPES

A house plant, like an ashtray, can theoretically be put on any horizontal surface. Unlike an ashtray, a house plant can show its displeasure by dying. It is relatively easy to match a plant to its optimum environment, but there is a definite knack to making full use of its design potential at the same time.

Of all the elements of interior design, house plants and flowers are the most visibly affected by the passage of time and their immediate environment. Wood may darken imperceptibly over the years, and wallpapers fade, but a month, a week, or even a few days in an unsuitable environment can make a huge change in the appearance of a plant or a vase of cut flowers. From that point of view, glossy photographic illustrations of interiors can be deceptive. The photographer may hire the house plants and use them wherever they look best, regardless of their horticultural requirements: the beauty of an instant is given the illusion of permanence, when, in fact, the plants are returned to the hire agency at the end of the photographic session. To the untrained eye, these pictures can be depressing: other people's house plants, as seen in books and magazines, always seem so much healthier than your own.

The horticulturalist will take the opposite view from the photographer: put the plants where they grow best, regardless of the effect on the design of a room, or the people using the room, and don't attempt to grow certain plants if the environment is less than perfect.

Most people's attitudes towards house plants and flowers fall between these two extremes. You might well go to the bother of hiring or rearranging plants for a special dinner party. And while it's unlikely that you would consciously sentence a gardenia to instant death in an unheated sun room in midwinter, you might well accept and appreciate the short-term beauty of a plant (even though, theoretically, it could live several years in a perfect environment) just because it is the perfect ornament for a special occasion. A brilliant pink anthurium will have a relatively limited life in a cool, dark hall, but the dramatic shape of its flowers, and the colour it adds, will more than justify the plant's brief existence.

In a room surrendered to plants, the pleasure derived from sitting in such an indoor jungle more than compensates for the loss of floor space. Both total commitment to plants and total ruthlessness when they overstep their allotted space are necessary.

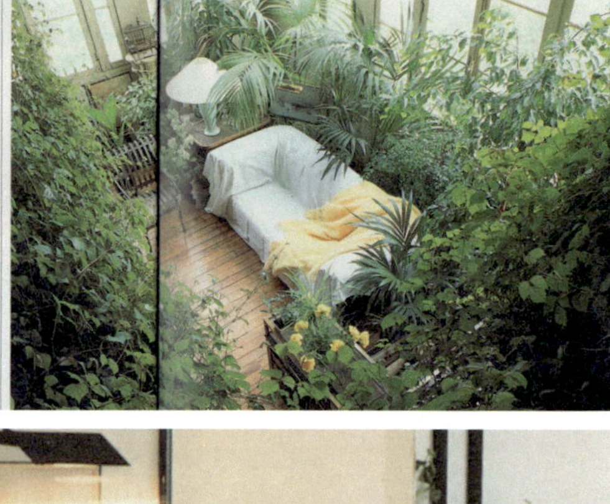

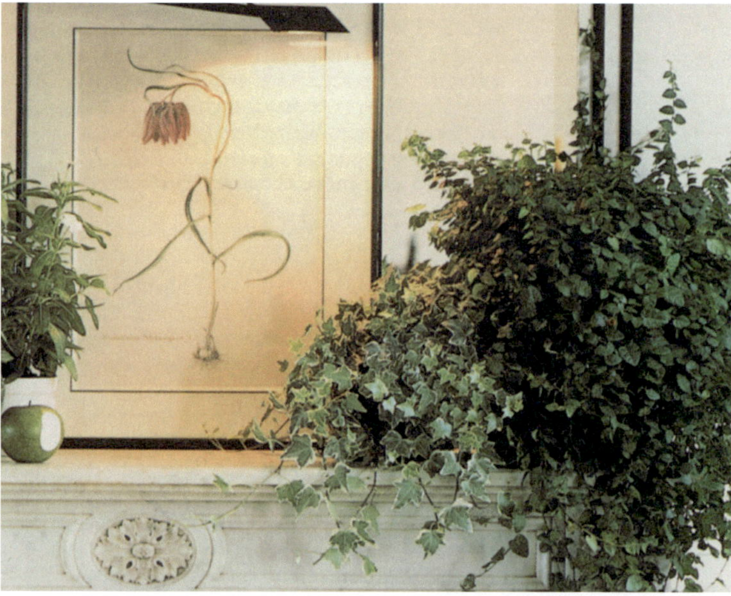

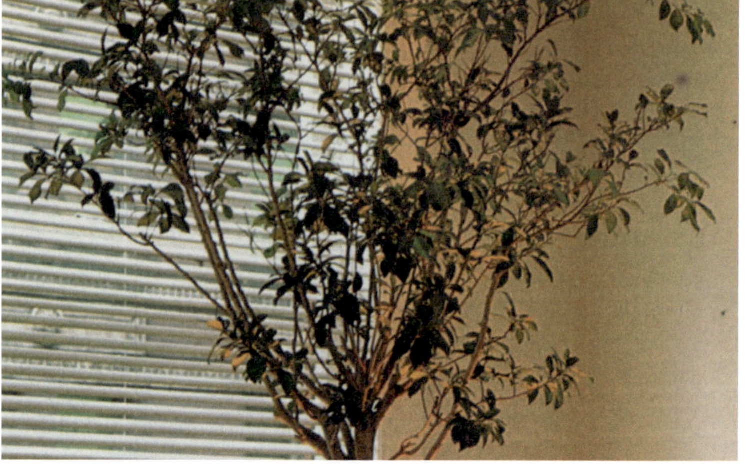

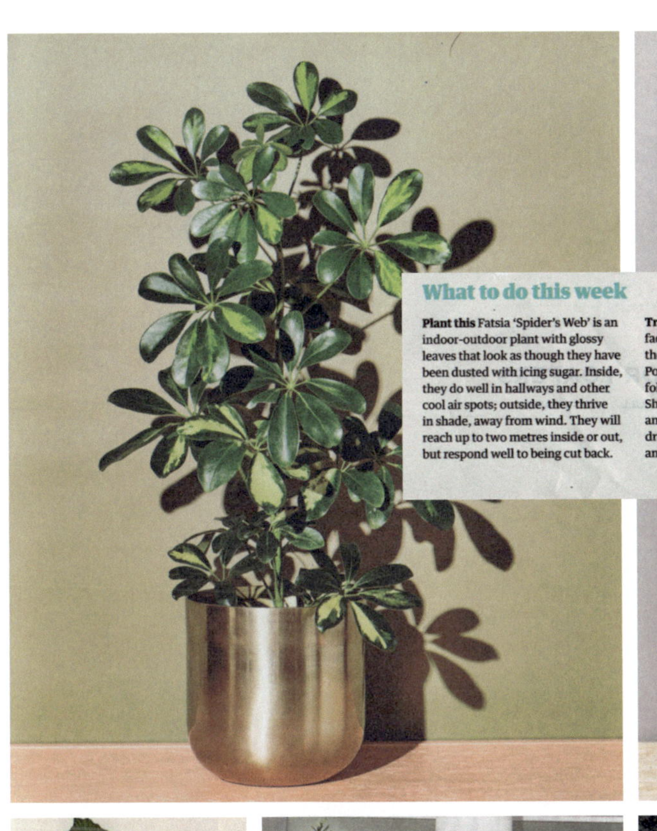

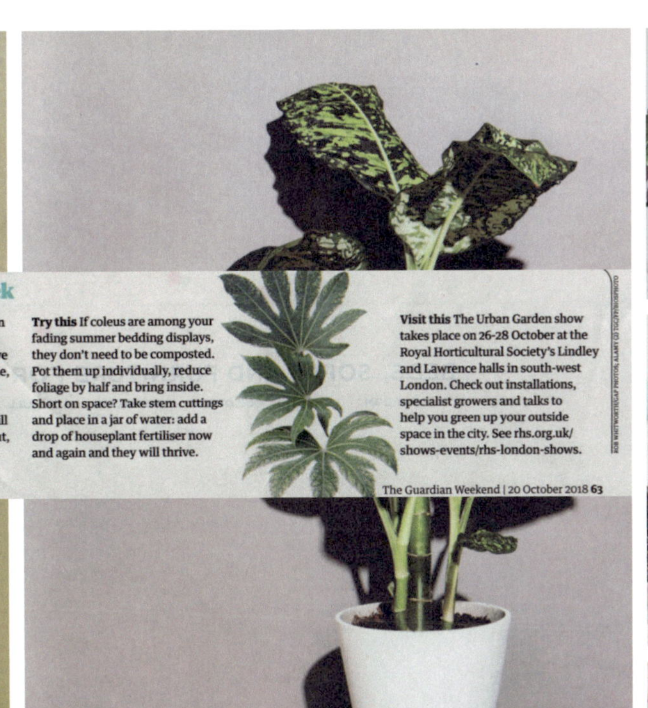

What to do this week

Plant this Fatsia 'Spider's Web' is an indoor-outdoor plant with glossy leaves that look as though they have been dusted with icing sugar. Inside, they do well in hallways and other cool air spots; outside, they thrive in shade, away from wind. They will reach up to two metres inside or out, but respond well to being cut back.

Try this If coleus are among your fading summer bedding displays, they don't need to be composted. Pot them up individually, reduce foliage by half and bring inside. Short on space? Take stem cuttings and place in a jar of water: add a drop of houseplant fertiliser now and again and they will thrive.

Visit this The Urban Garden show takes place on 26-28 October at the Royal Horticultural Society's Lindley and Lawrence halls in south-west London. Check out installations, specialist growers and talks to help you green up your outside space in the city. See rhs.org.uk/shows-events/rhs-london-shows.

The Guardian Weekend | 20 October 2018 63

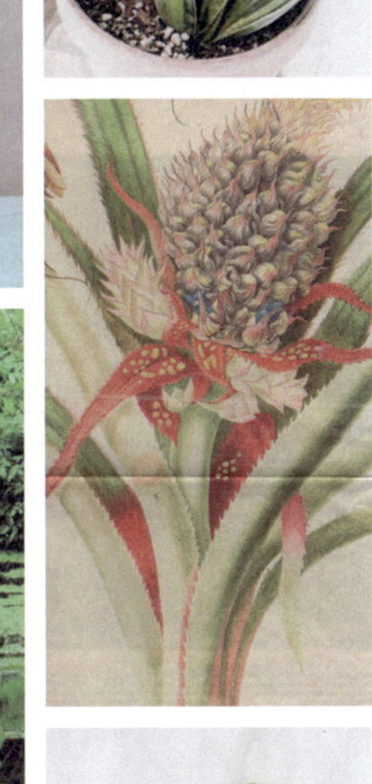

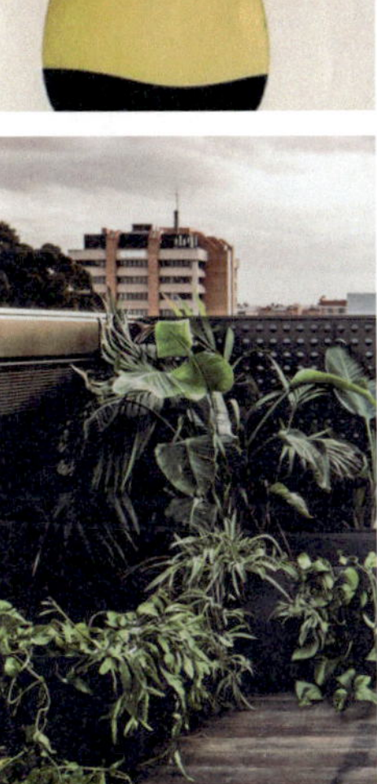

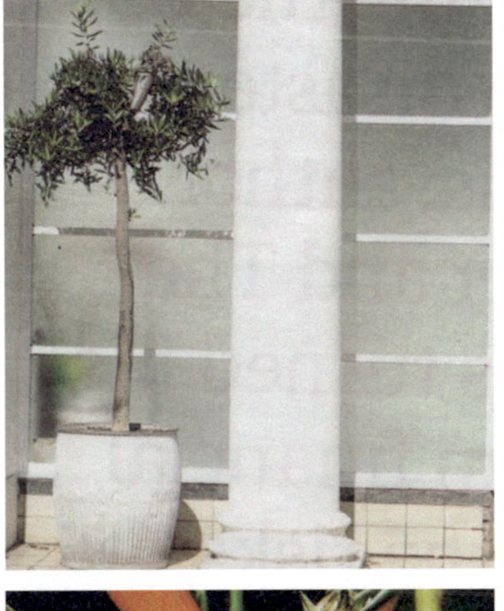

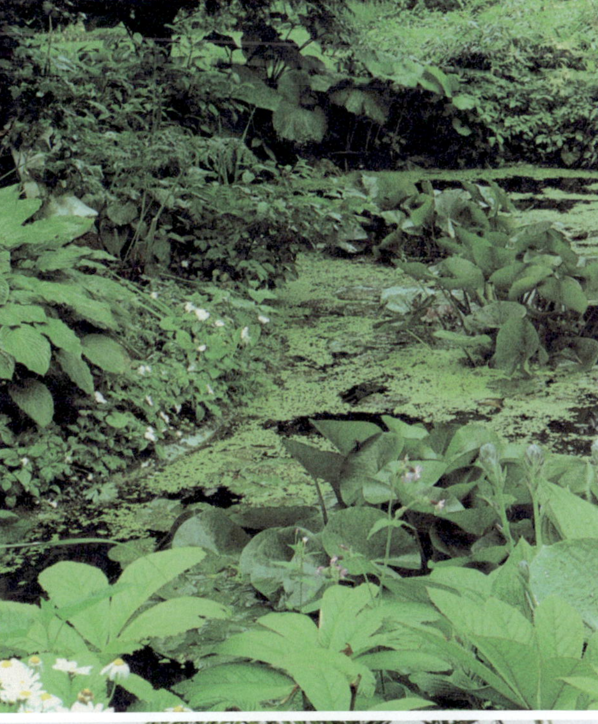

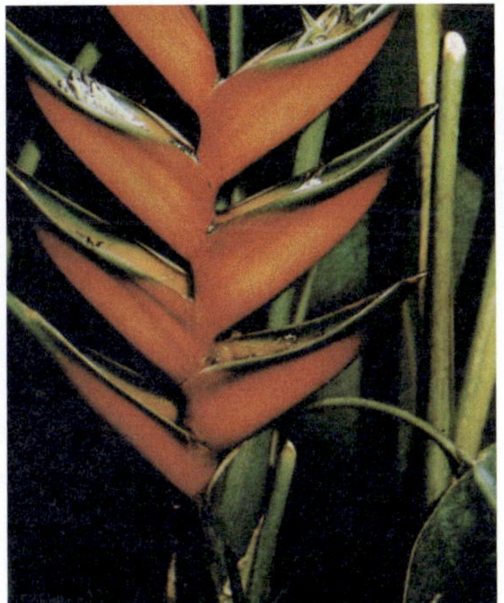

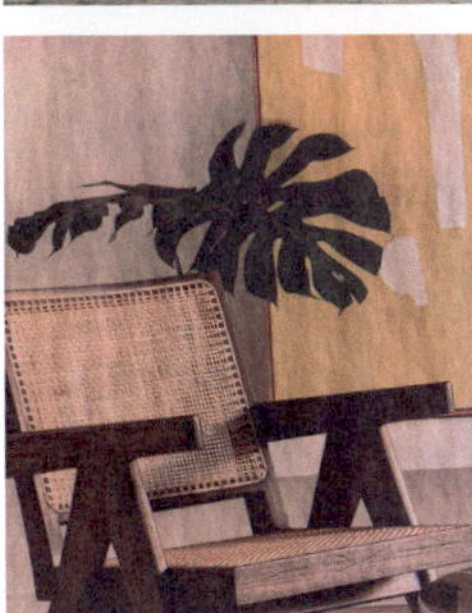

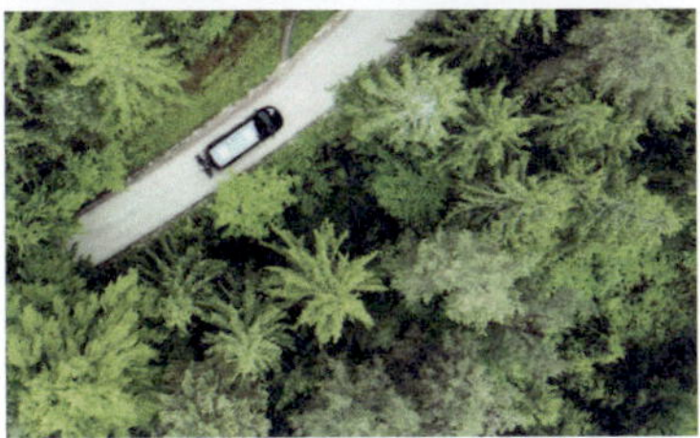

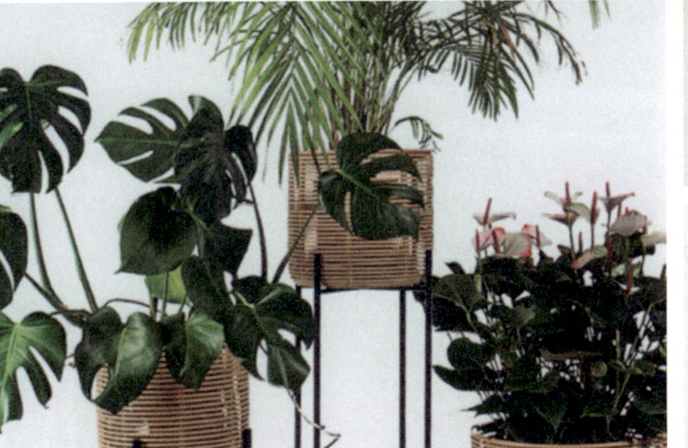

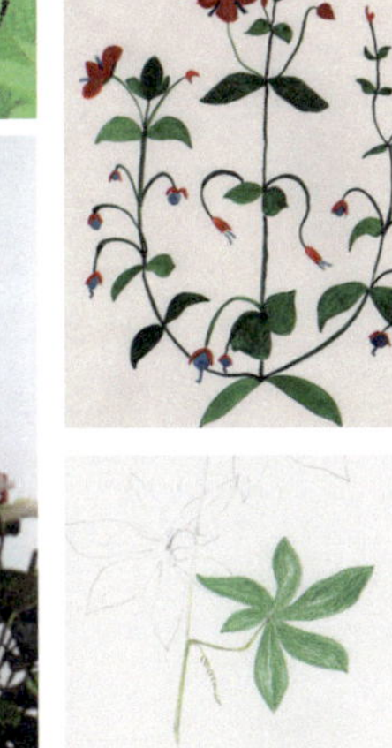

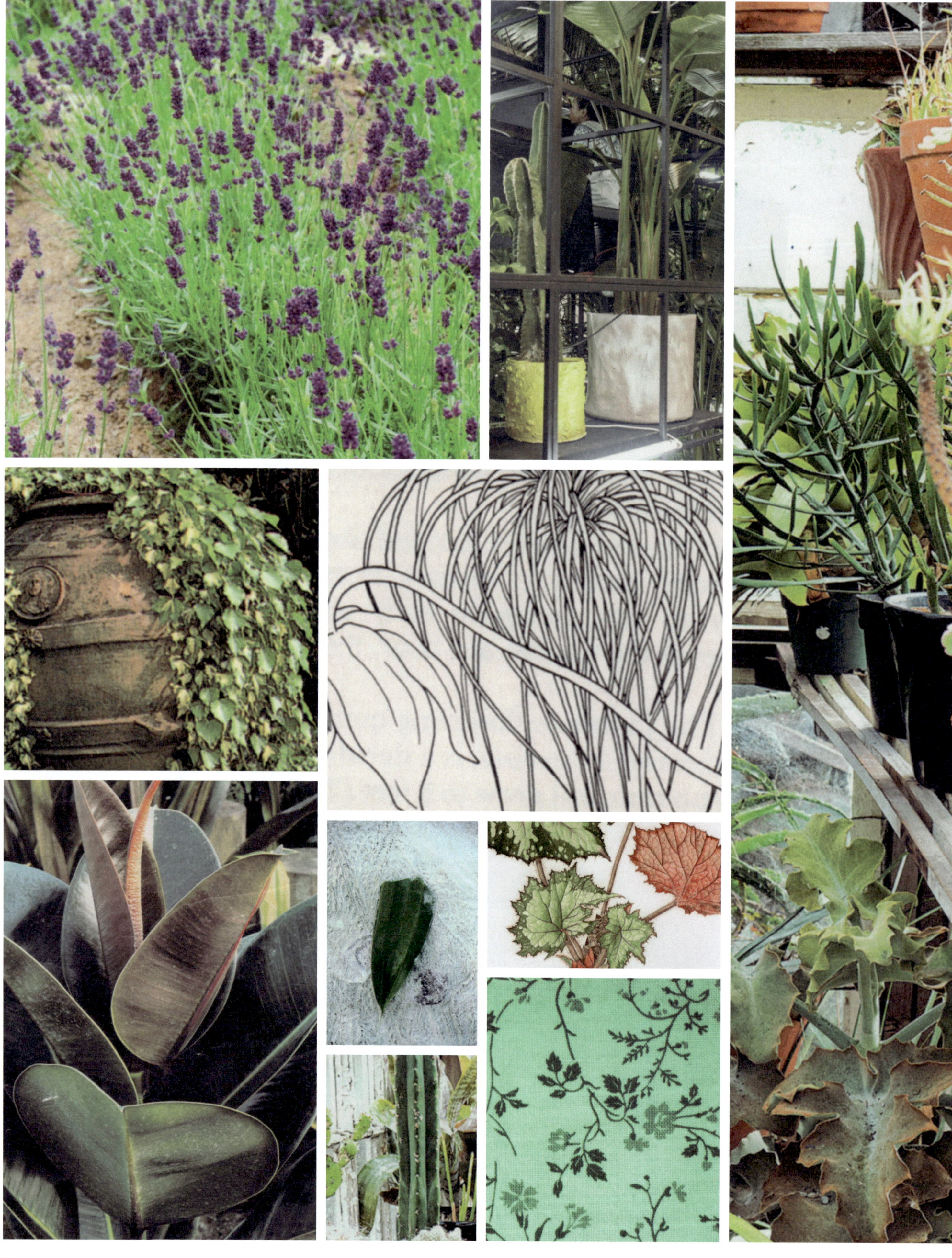

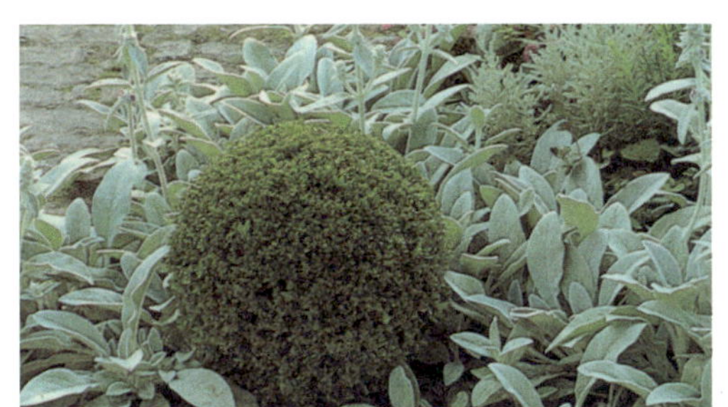
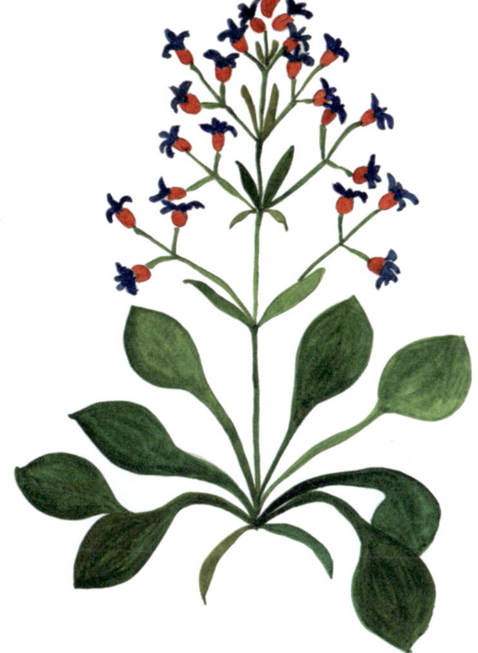
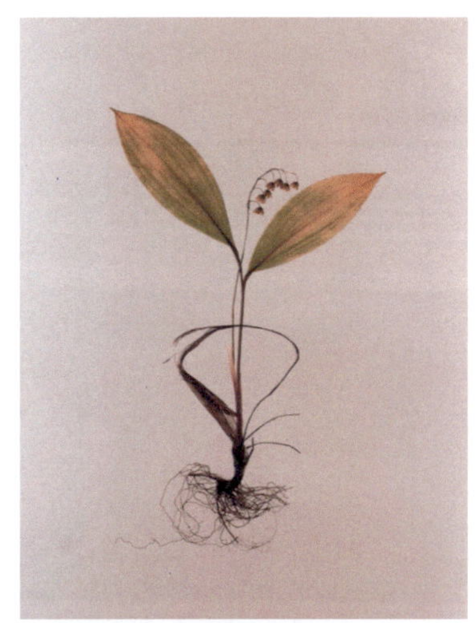
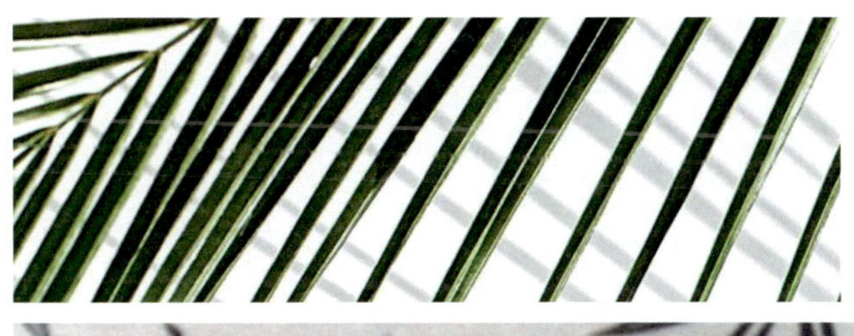
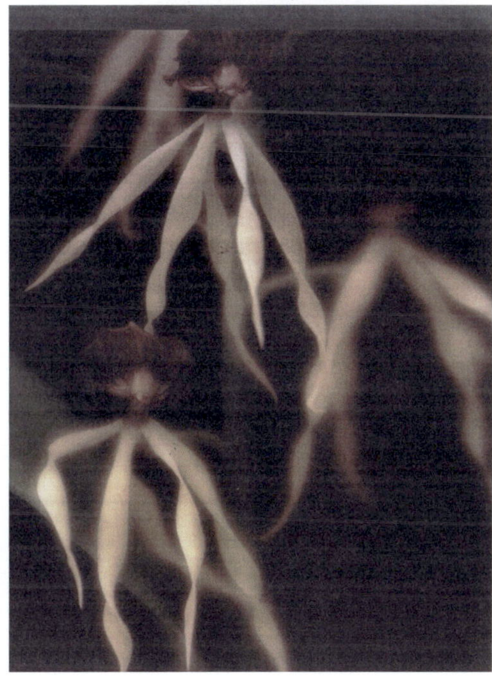
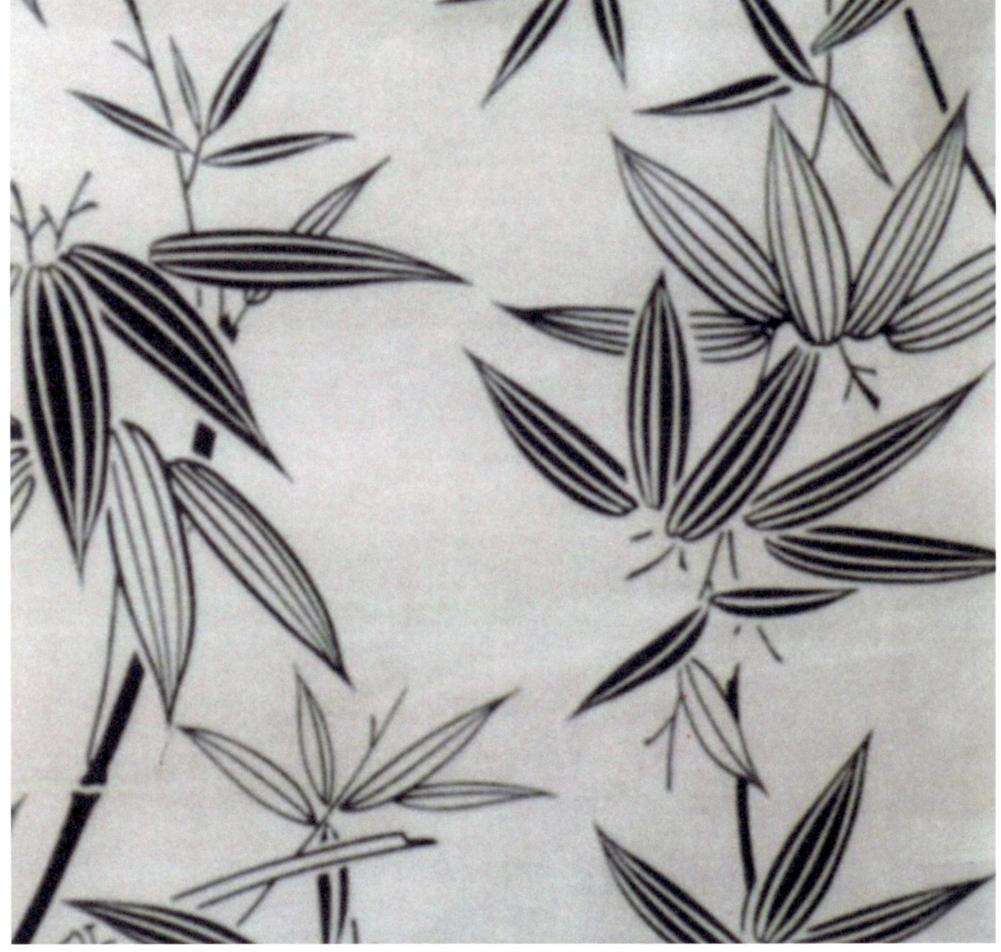

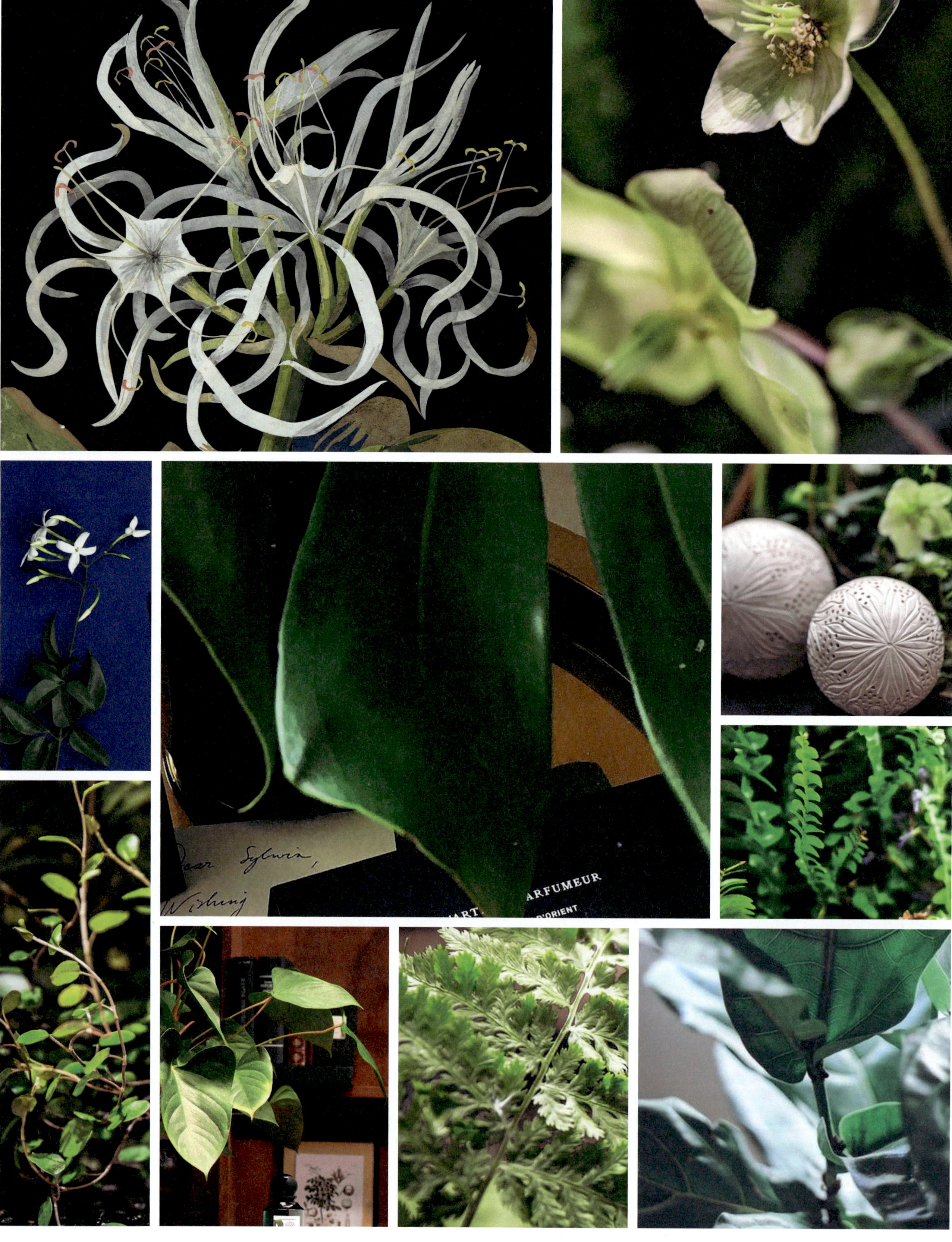

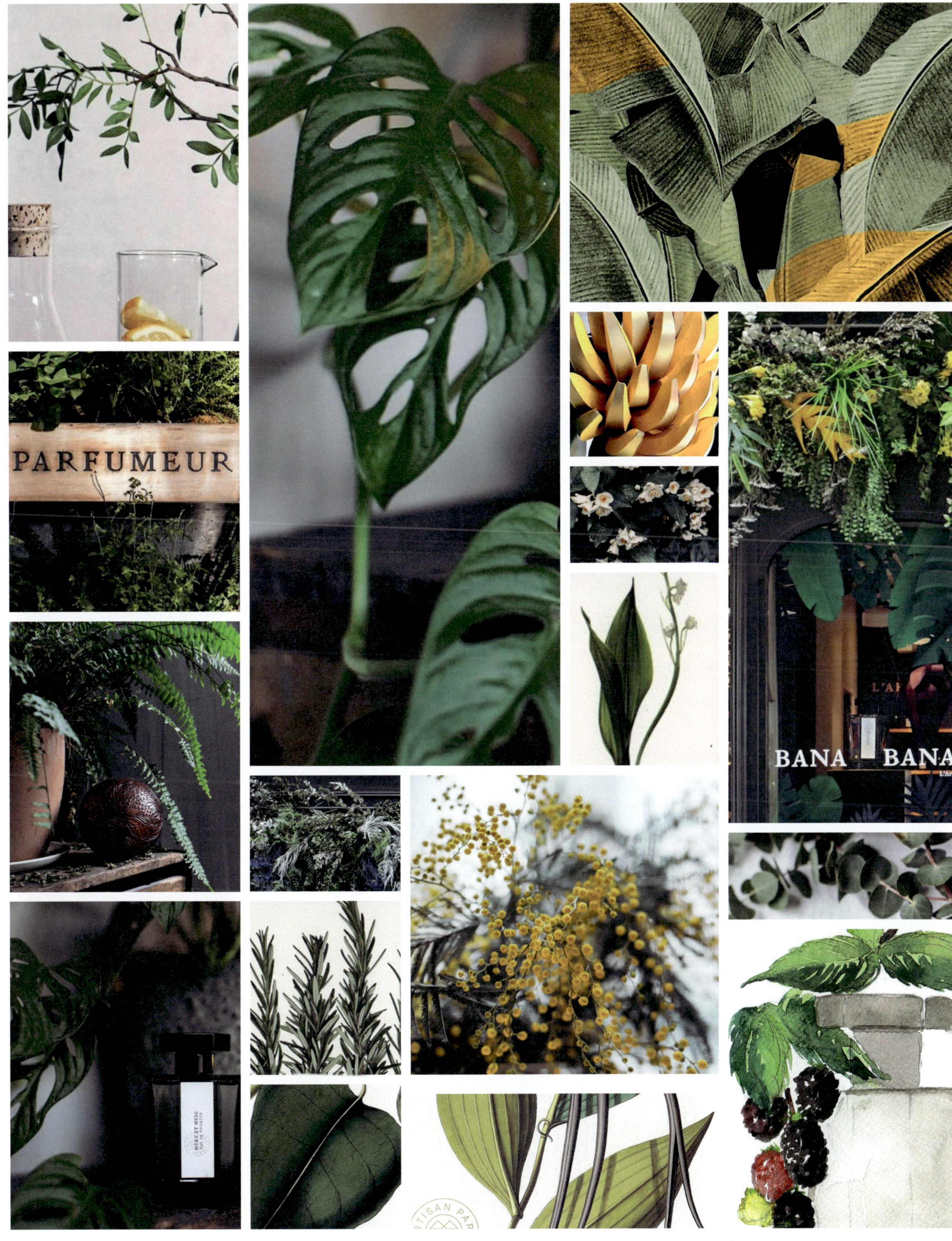
PARFUMEUR
BANA
BANA

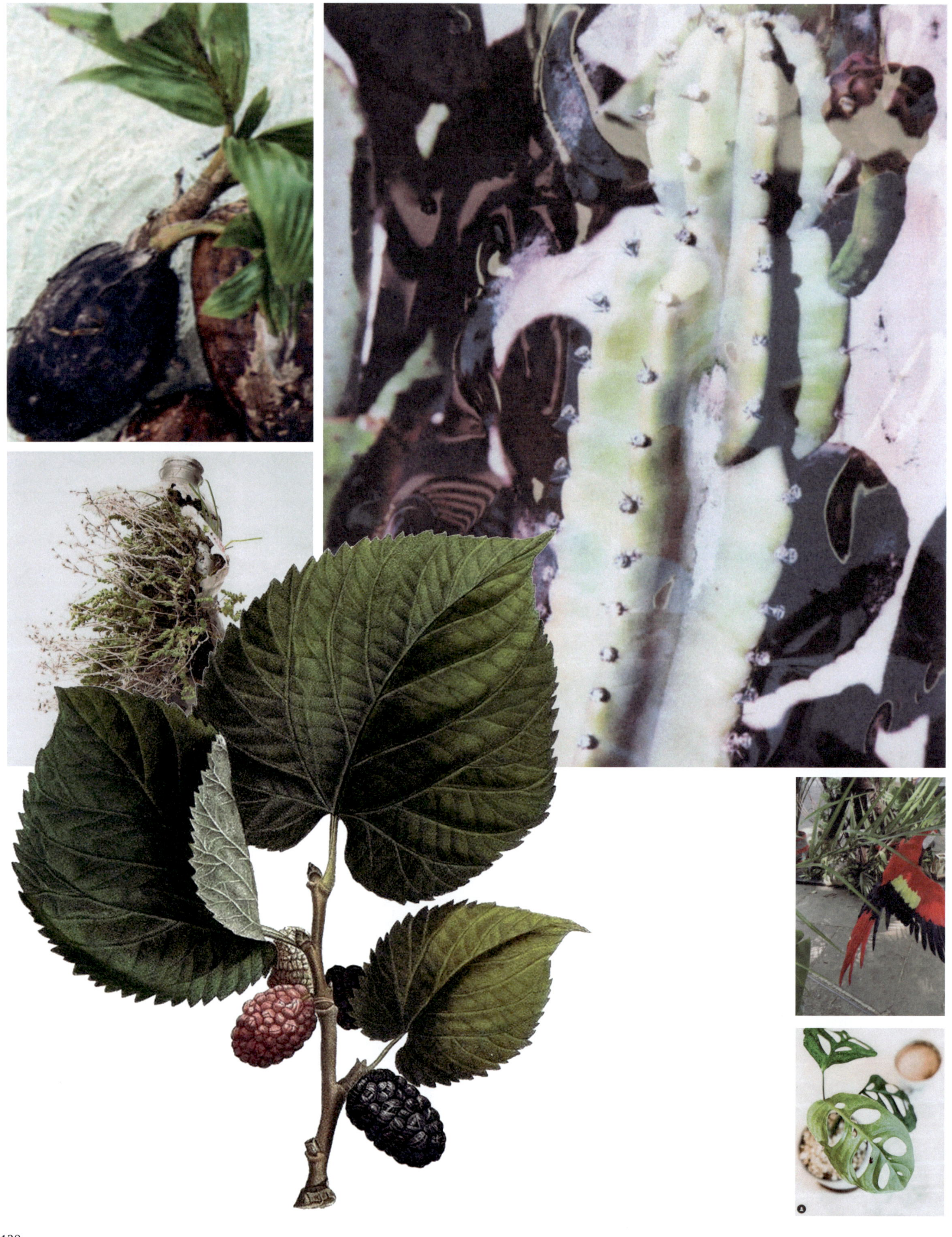

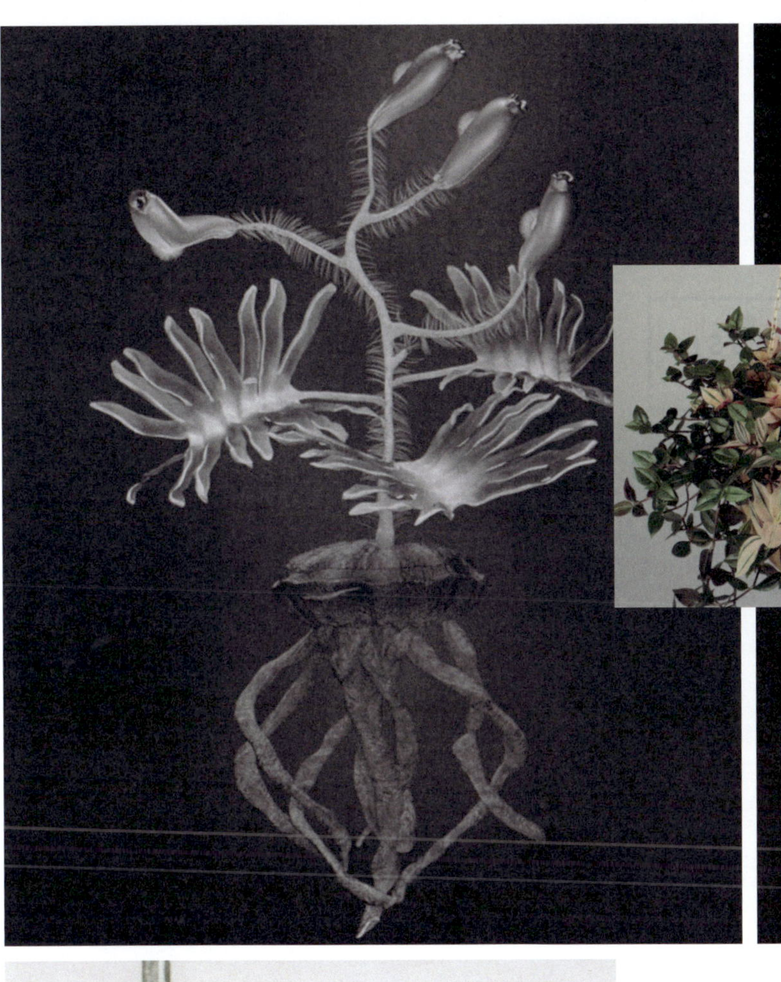

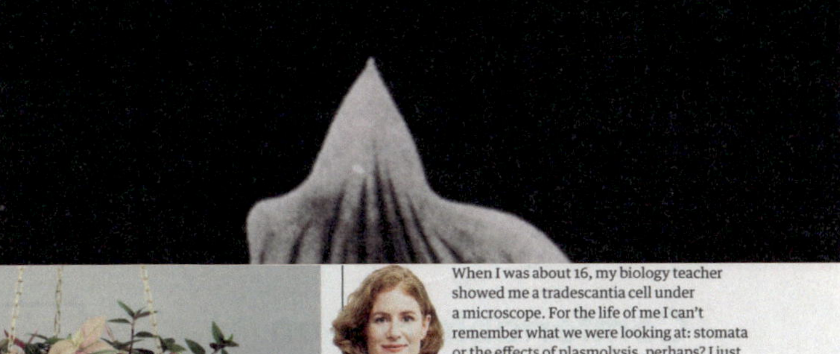

When I was about 16, my biology teacher showed me a tradescantia cell under a microscope. For the life of me I can't remember what we were looking at: stomata or the effects of plasmolysis, perhaps? I just remember looking up from the minute world of cells in this simple plant and falling headlong in love. Not long after that I took over the biology department greenhouse and the rest, as they say, is history.

If I was rewriting my past, I'd insert an orchid or a carnivorous plant, but instead I chose the one that the biology department couldn't kill. And for that reason, I'd recommend it to you, too.

Spiderworts are almost indestructible. You can take them right up to the brink (and, for any biology teacher looking for a lesson, the edge of plasmolysis) and then revive them in an hour or so. They are a very forgiving houseplant. On top of that, they really don't mind low light levels. As long as there is good ambient light they will be happy, so they are perfect for growing in north- and east-facing rooms

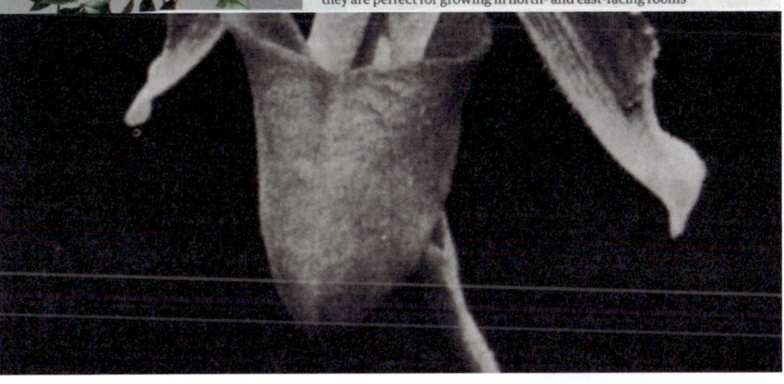

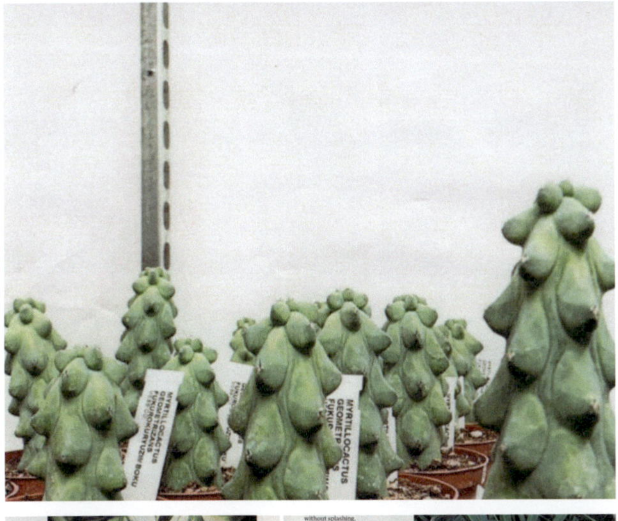

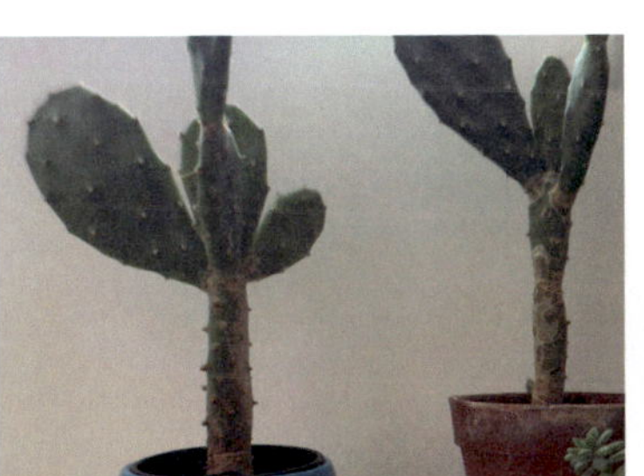

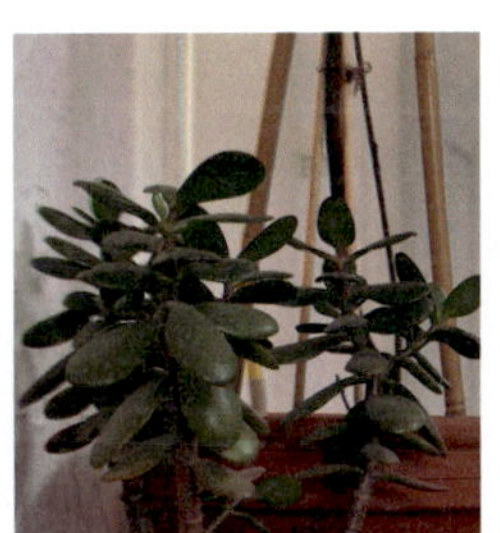

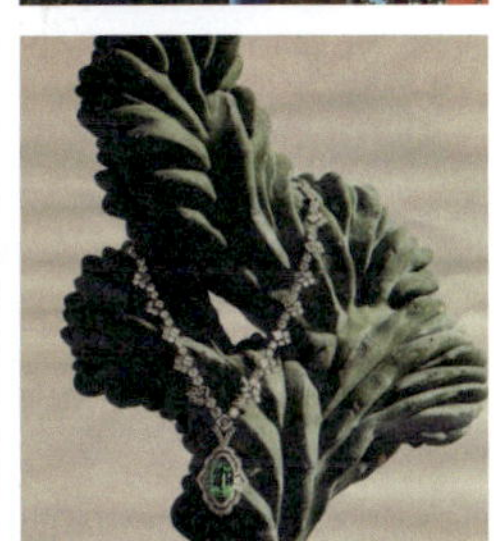

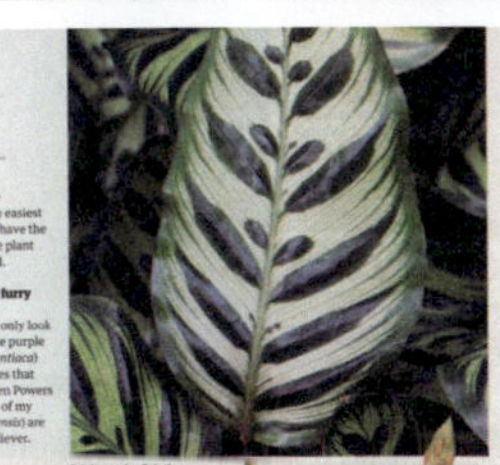

Bright sparks: Calathea makoyana (above) and Ludisia discolor (below) bring welcome colour

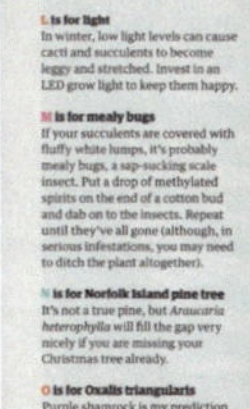

without splashing.

L is for light
In winter, low light levels can cause cacti and succulents to become leggy and stretched. Invest in an LED grow light to keep them happy.

M is for mealy bugs
If your succulents are covered with fluffy white lumps, it's probably mealy bugs, a sap-sucking scale insect. Put a drop of methylated spirits on the end of a cotton bud and dab on to the insects. Repeat until they've all gone (although, in serious infestations, you may need to ditch the plant altogether).

N is for Norfolk Island pine tree
It's not a true pine, but *Araucaria heterophylla* will fill the gap very nicely if you are missing your Christmas tree already.

O is for Oxalis triangularis
Purple shamrock is my prediction to become the must-have houseplant of 2018. Its heart-shaped leaves fit perfectly with the Pantone colour of the year, ultra violet.

P is for pebble trays
Cacti and succulents revel in dry air, but that can be problematic for other indoor plants. Misting is often recommended as a solution, but sticking pots in a tray of gravel or pebbles half-covered with water is more effective.

Q is for quarantine
If you want to avoid importing pest problems such as mealy bug (see M, above), keep any new plants in a different room from the rest of your collection for a few weeks, so you can check the arrivals for any unwanted visitors.

R is for rosary vine (Ceropegia woodii)
This trailing plant with heart-shaped, silvery leaves has a clever trick up its sleeve: the bead-like aerial tubers that grow along the stems can be snipped

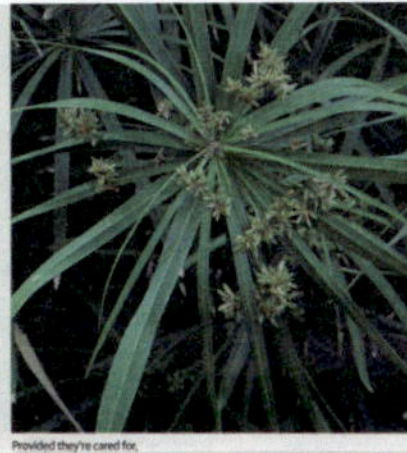

Provided they're cared for, umbrella grass (top) and succulents such as echeveria both thrive indoors

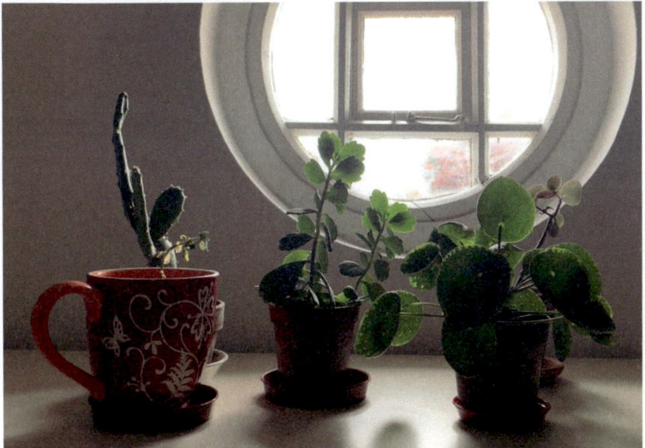

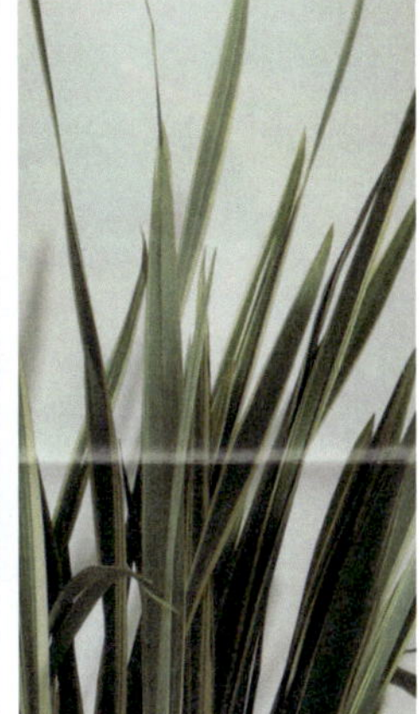

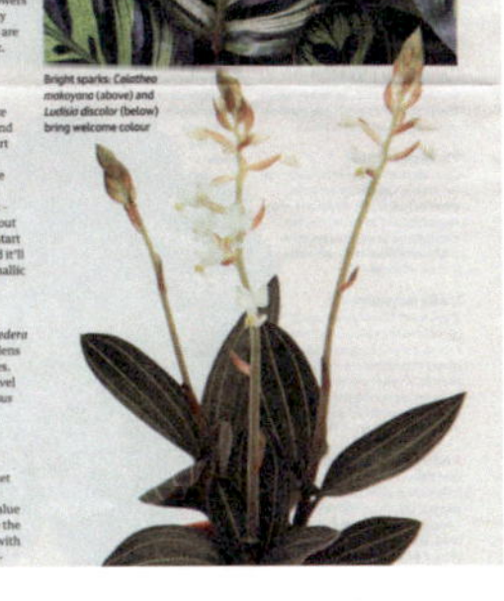

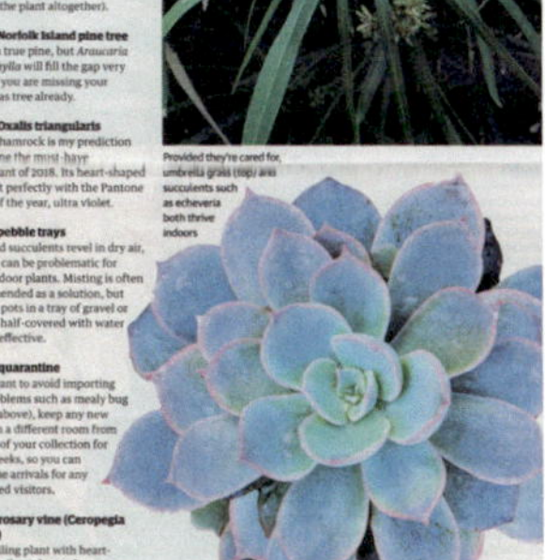

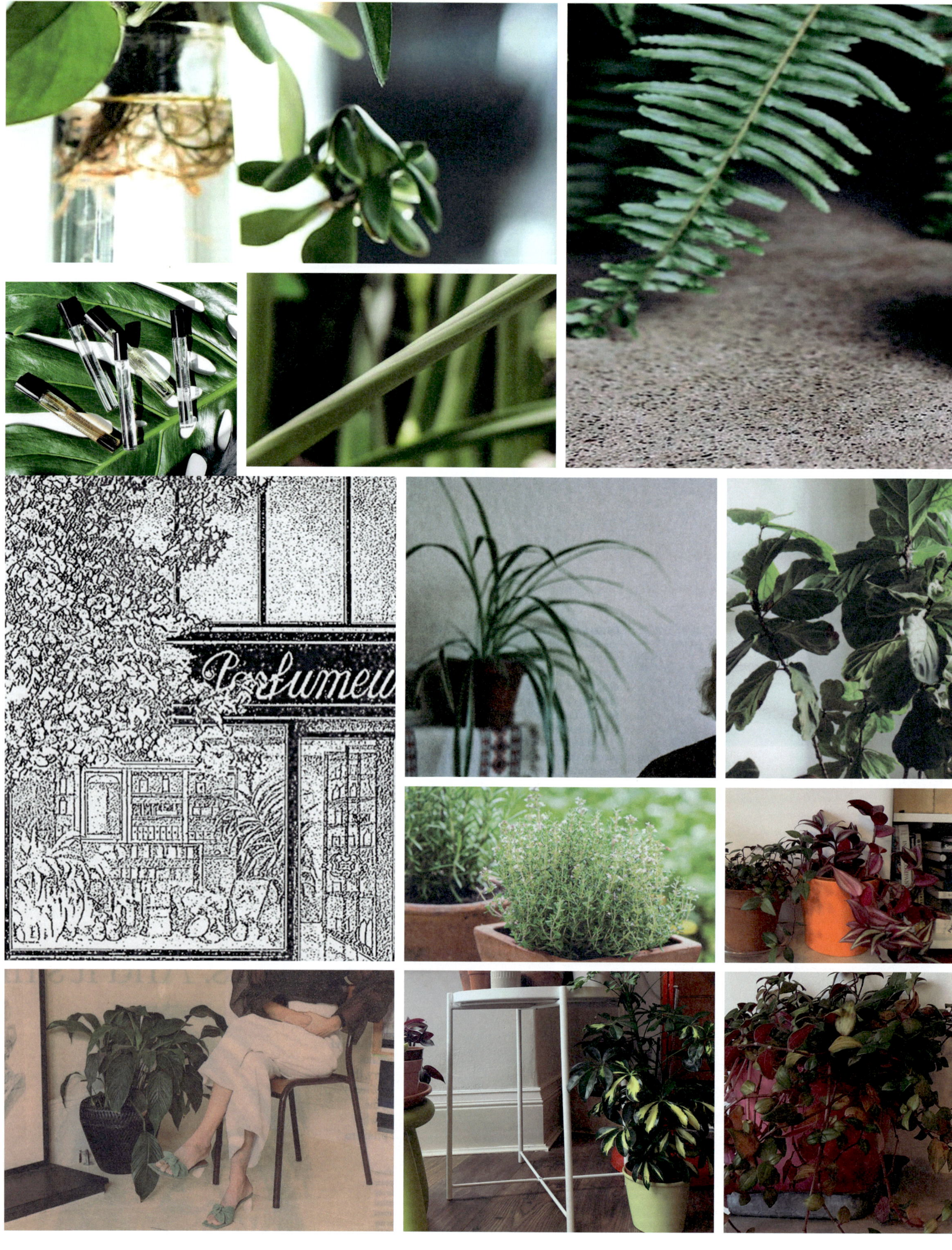

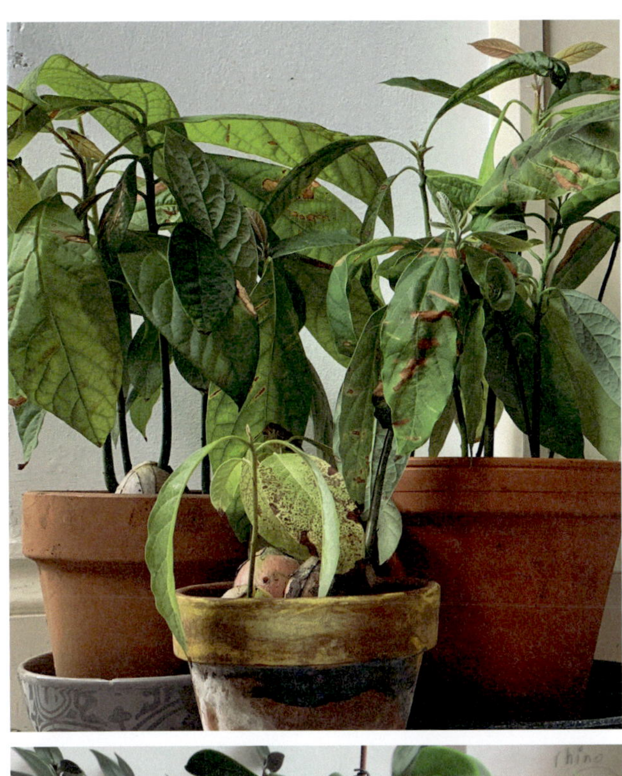

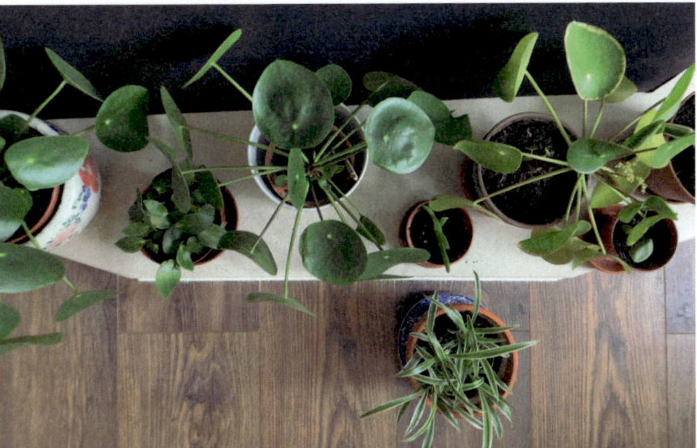

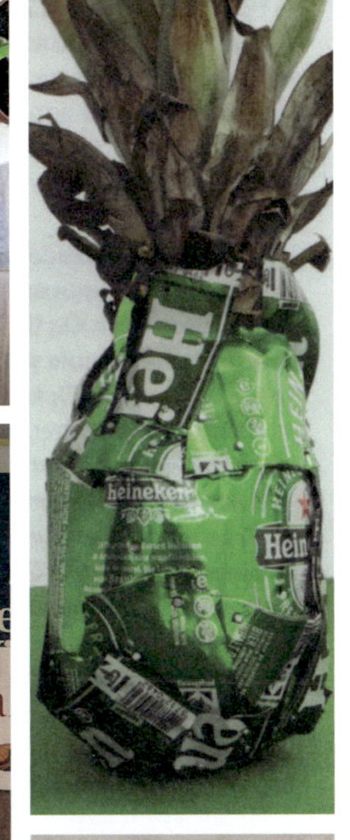
Heineken

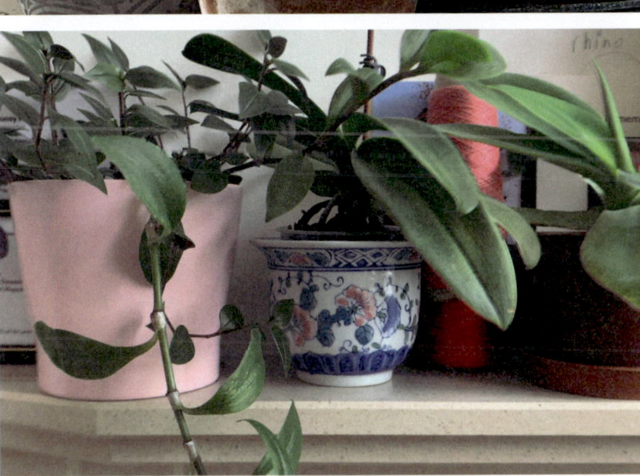

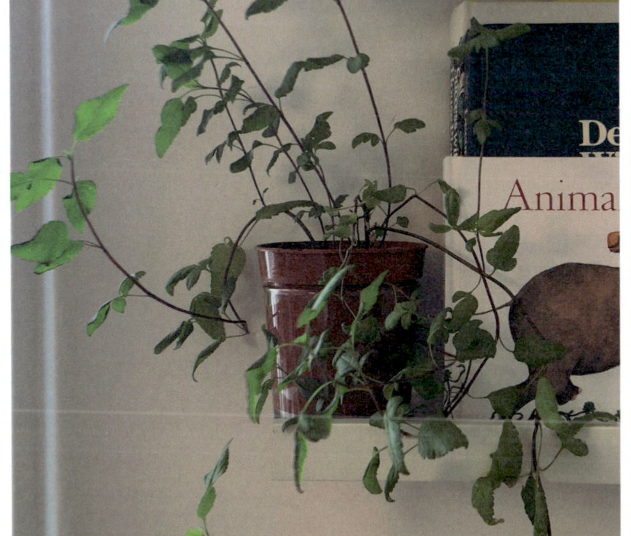
Anima

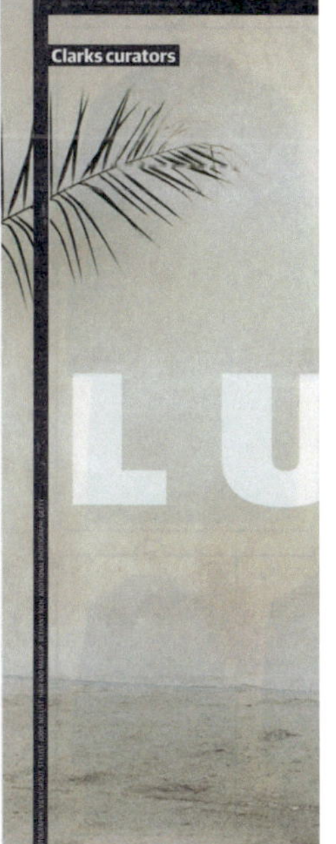
Clarks curators
LU

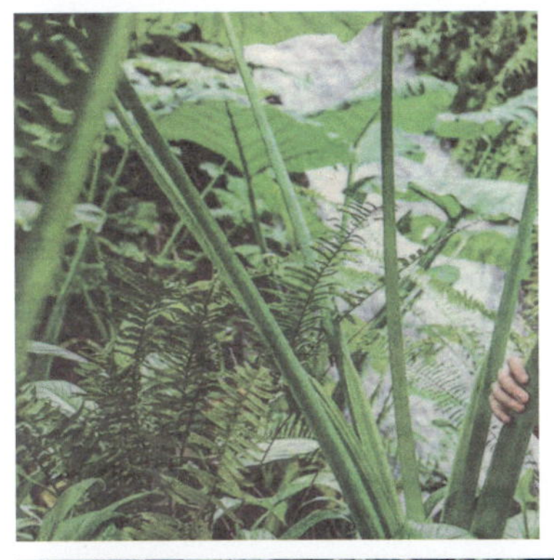

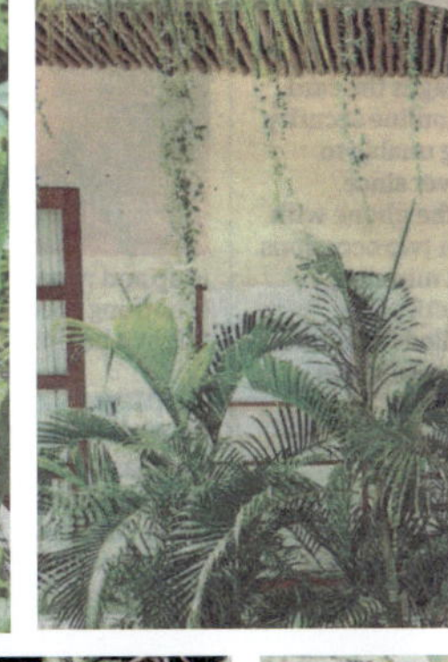

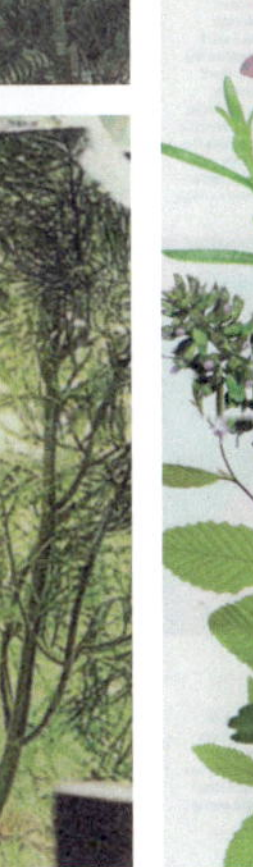

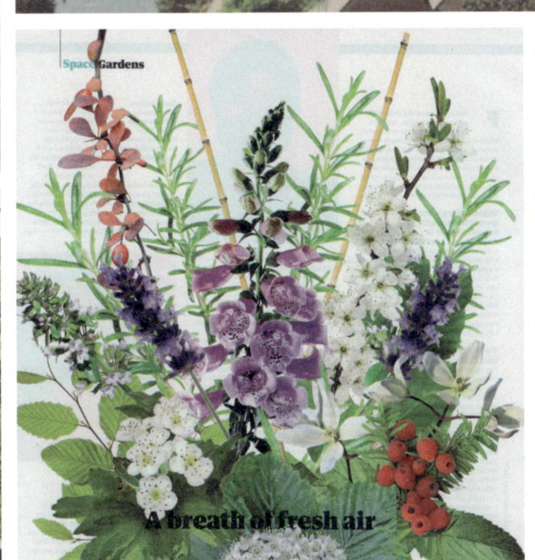
Space Gardens
A breath of fresh air

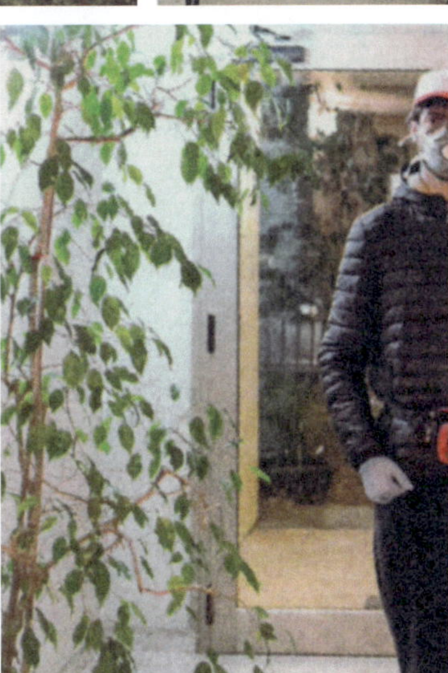

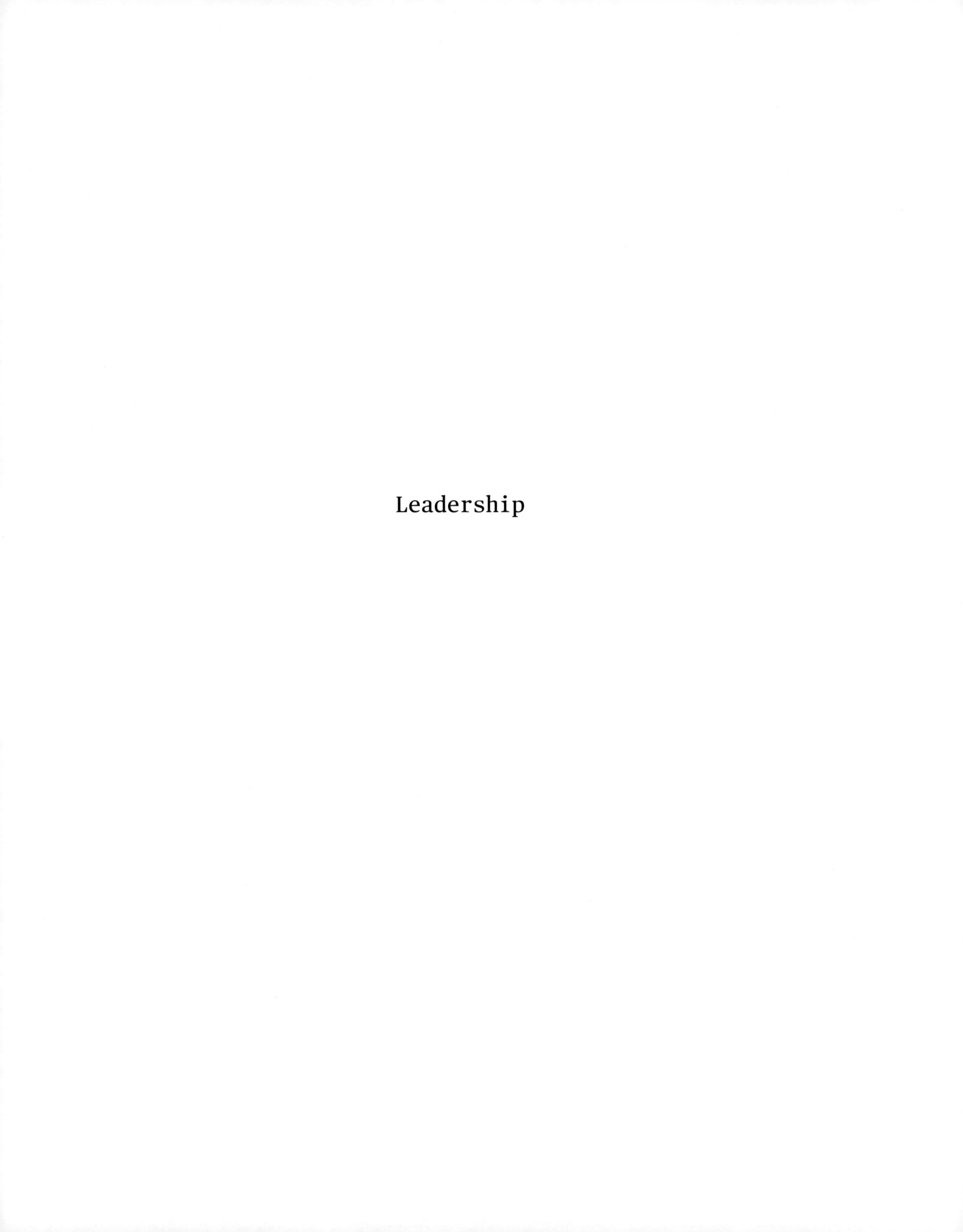

Leadership

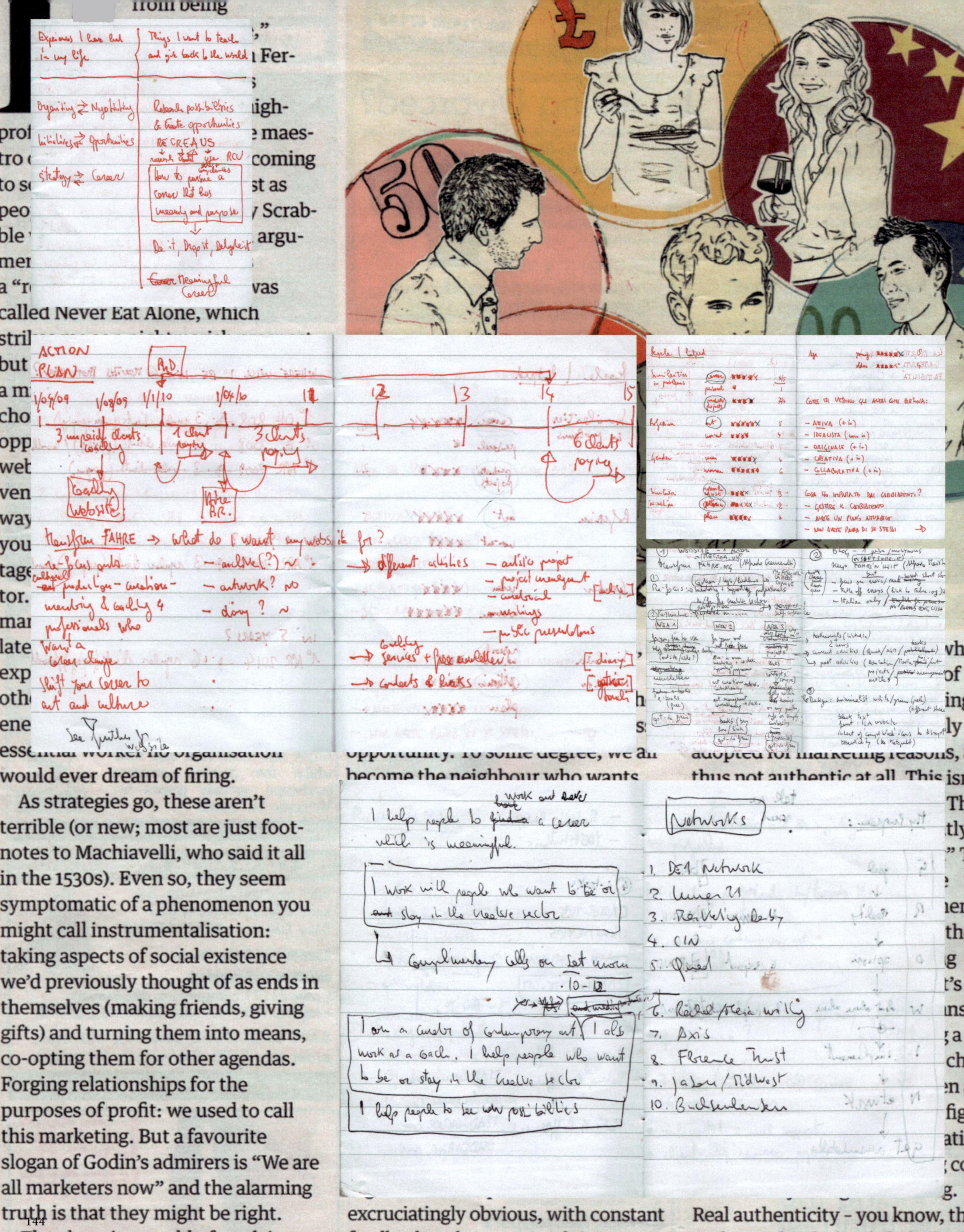

called Never Eat Alone, which

would ever dream of firing.

As strategies go, these aren't terrible (or new; most are just footnotes to Machiavelli, who said it all in the 1530s). Even so, they seem symptomatic of a phenomenon you might call instrumentalisation: taking aspects of social existence we'd previously thought of as ends in themselves (making friends, giving gifts) and turning them into means, co-opting them for other agendas. Forging relationships for the purposes of profit: we used to call this marketing. But a favourite slogan of Godin's admirers is "We are all marketers now" and the alarming truth is that they might be right.

The changing world of work is

excruciatingly obvious, with constant feedback on how you're doing.

Real authenticity – you know, the authentic kind – has left the build

MUSEUMS
US & Americas

Los Angeles museums find expe[...]

The second ed[...]
a greater colla[...]

PACIFIC STANDA[...]

Los Angeles. Of all the [...] nia curators organisi[...] second iteration of t[...] Pacific Standard Tim[...] 2017, which focuses o[...] art, Dan Cameron kn[...] better than most.

In the early 1990s, h[...] in South America. Soo[...] curator at the New Mus[...] he organised exhibition[...] es, Eugenio Dittborn, [...] Rivane Neuenschwand[...] he is organising unde[...] umbrella (PST2) for the Orange County Museum of Art, where he is chief curator, features Latin American kinetic art from the 1960s (which he [...] pired predecessor of [...] nia's Light and Space ar[...] after seeing a show or[...] at the Museo Nacional [...] Buenos Aires in 2012.

[...] on my own," Cameron says.

On the ground

[...] allowing US museums that took part to draw on their in-house expertise and archives. This time they are hiring [...]

[...] of the Getty Foundation.

Along with covering travel expenses for two dozen international scholars to join an event last October in Los Angeles, where museums shared briefs on their shows, the Getty has already distributed around $5.1m to some 40 California museums and cultural centres for "research and planning", up from about $3.7m at this stage for the first PST.

The Hammer Museum in Los Angeles' guest curator, Cecilia Fajardo-Hill, for example, has been working now for several years with the Argentin-[...]

[...] Body", a survey [...] from Latin Am[...] being scrapped [...] American Art [...] Fajardo-Hill w[...] curator), the sh[...] Hammer and [...] funding. Now, [...] Giunta is focus[...] ing Argentina, [...]

[...] secular arts. Patrick Polk, the Fowler's curator of Latin American and Caribbean popular arts, has enlisted as his co-curators Randal Johnson, a UCLA professor, and Sabrina Gledhill, a Bahia-based curator who has a doctorate in ethnic and African studies. Polk has also created a ten-person advisory board and reached out to two Afro-Brazil museums in São Paulo and Salvador as possible partners.

There are logistical challenges to be overcome by the curators, from managing different time zones to language or cultural differences. But several Latin American collaborators say that Skype, Facebook chat and online document-sharing has helped them to maintain the dialogue between face-to-face visits. "It's been surprisingly easy and smooth," [...]

Shows to travel

Many PST2 curators are lining up addition[...] shows. The Fowler Museum's curator Patr[...] for two US venues, "ideally in New York ar[...] well as European and Brazilian stops, for h[...] Pomona College Museum of Art's show th[...] Orozco's on-campus mural, *Prometheus*, [...] cially engaged art is due to travel to Mexic[...] Contemporary Art San Diego will send its [...] Lima. The Getty's show, "Luxury Arts in th[...] will travel to its co-organiser: the Met in N[...]

Art of the Amer[...]

CONTINUED FROM PAGE 17

ideas." That said, most of the collab[...] rations she is aware of are sensitive to these issues, she says.

Lowery Stokes Sims, the chief curator of the Museum of Arts and Design in [...]

[...] challenges. "In the US, people might plan six years out – that's unheard of in Latin America," says Gabriel Pérez-Barreiro, the director of the Colección [...]

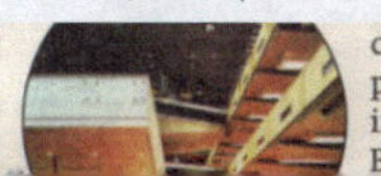

TIME SCHEDULE

	LUN	MAR	MER	GIO	VEN	SAB	DOM
7-8	get up	get up	get up	get up	get up	get up	get up
8-9	breaky	breaky	breaky	breaky	breaky	breaky	[illegible]
9-10	commute	commute	commute	commute	commute	breaky	breaky
10-11	quad	q	q	q	q	Gub	Gub
11-12	q	q	q	q	q	shopping	shopping
12-1	q	q	q	q	q	shopping	shopping
1-2	q	q	q	q	q	lunch	lunch
2-3	q	q	q	q	q	lunch	lunch
3-4	q	q	q	q	q	[illegible]	Gub
4-5	q	q	q	q	q	book/art	book/art/[illegible]
5-6	q	q	q	q	q	book/[illegible]	book/art/[illegible]
6-7	commute	commute	commute	commute	commute	Gub	Gub
7-8	dinner	dinner	dinner	dinner	dinner	dinner	dinner
8-9	Gub	Gub	Gub	Gub	Gub	Gub	Gub
9-10	Gub	Gub	Gub	Gub	Gub	Gub	Gub
10-11	book/art	book/art	book/art	book/art	book/art	film/quad	film
11-12	book/art	book/art	book/art	book/art	book/art	film/out	film
12-1	book/art	book/art	book/art	book/art	book/art	film/out	film

187
126 hrs/week:
quad 40 – 30%
family+Gub 20 – 15.5%
book/art 15 – 10%
commute 10 – 9%
breakfast 9 – 8.5%
get up 7 – 7%
dinner 7 – 7%
film/out 6 – 6%
shopping 4 – 5%

[illegible] & Carolyn Christov-Bakargiev 8.6.12

[illegible] generates spaces
space is location of the sensual, of the witness, of the embodiment.
[illegible] have place but we don't have space. We need space
space + encouraging a sense of displacement at the same time as grounding.
If you are, it is here – but you're not here, or s.where else.

The world makes facts
Art makes facts of its own different order

Kabul → under siege (exhibition)
Cairo → in a state of hope (seminar)
Kassel → being on stage (exhibition + public programme)
Banff → on retreat (workshops + [illegible] exhibition)

not only the reality of the [illegible], but the reality of the [illegible] of connections

forms of alliances → believe in [illegible] and mutual respect, not an 'interdisciplinarity'
multilateralism rather than multiculturalism

(8)

Every thing can happen with any kind of media, despite the mediation

TECHNOLOGY
(FAILS)

RADIATION → all the forms of mediation you can consider as technology
NATURAL (CHAOTIC) — HUMAN (RE)FORMED (ORDERED) (to increase survival/warfare)

– BODY (HUMAN) AS PRODUCER AS LANGUAGE
– PROSTHETIC (Mechanical extension of the body)
– REMOTE "PRESENCE" (Tele-Concept / Television–Telephone "distant")
→ ENERGY (transform energy from FORM to FORM)

– BODY (LANGUAGE)
– PROSTHETIC
– REMOTE PRESENCE
ENERGY
SOCIAL STRUCTURES – TO INCREASE SURVIVAL/WARFARE → TRICKLE DOWN [[illegible]]

As a GRANULAR LEVEL OF SOCIETY / the lowest [illegible], personal level) everything is possible. create connections, get things happen

LAW OF CAUSALITY / (IN SCIENCE/Western [illegible]) ≠ "LAW" OF SYNCHRONICITY + "CYCLING" (in [illegible]/Buddhism[illegible])

TRAY 1
urgent & important
do it now
↓
[illegible]
[illegible]
Gub

TRAY 2
urgent but not important
do if I can
↓
~~[illegible]~~ references, emails, networking

TRAY 3
important but not urgent
start now/ [illegible]
↓
[illegible] + artworks, book, articles

BIN
not important & not urgent
don't do
↓
Newsletters

(8)

Physics
Quantum Theory that all (reality) is a manifestation of energy
[dematerialisation / all is about different state + change of energy]

ENERGY (EXTERIOR OF SPHERE)
↓
LIGHT ⇄ Electro-Magnetic RADIATION [$E=mc^2$]
↓
SPIRIT

SENSUAL WORD (INTERIOR OF SPHERE)
DIALOGUE
SELF
OTHER
MEDIATION
↓
(THAT WHICH CARRIES BETWEEN)

≠

NEWTONIAN – MATERIALIST – MECHANISTIC – CARTESIAN

(2) there are many model as many people are, and its OK they are different

(3) For quantum, in system of energy there is a change, then ~~[illegible]~~ all other parts in that system that feel / experience that change

The more you give up to the social model system, the less power you have to find your own model

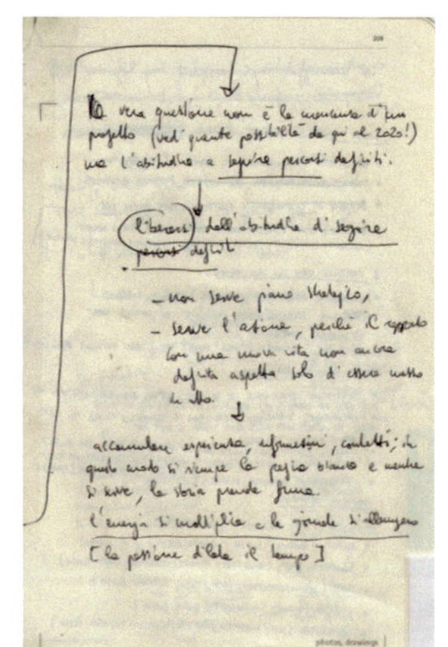

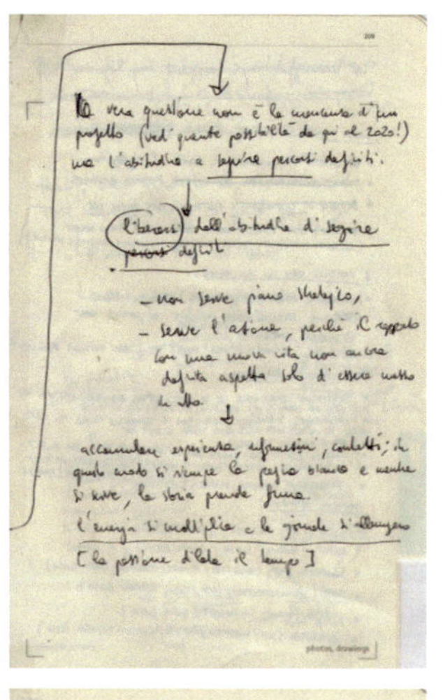

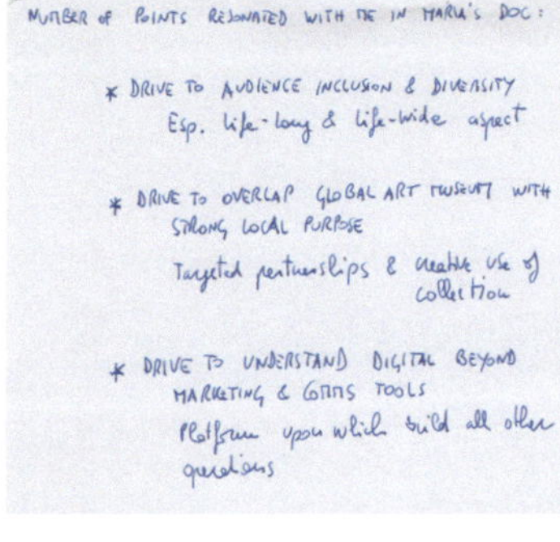

NUMBER of POINTS RESONATED WITH ME IN MARIA'S DOC:
* DRIVE TO AUDIENCE INCLUSION & DIVERSITY
Esp. life-long & life-wide aspect
* DRIVE TO OVERLAP GLOBAL ART MUSEUM WITH STRONG LOCAL PURPOSE
Targeted partnerships & creative use of collection
* DRIVE TO UNDERSTAND DIGITAL BEYOND MARKETING & COMMS TOOLS
Platform upon which build all other questions

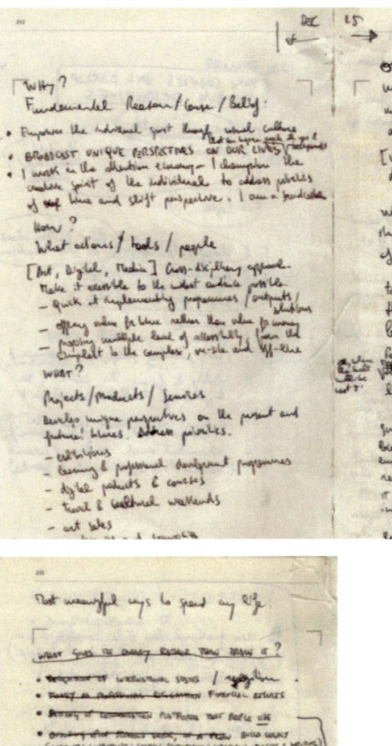

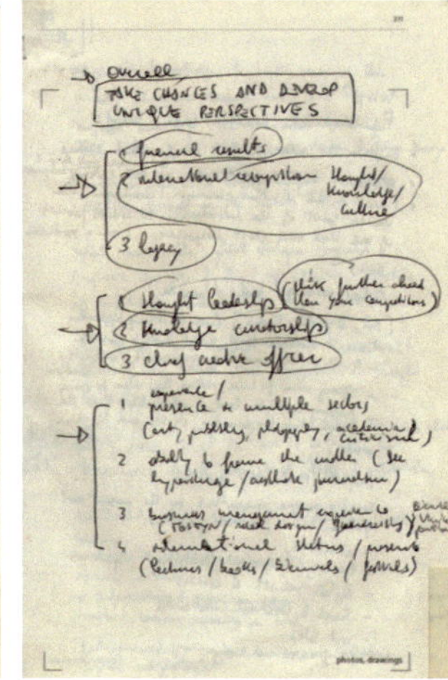

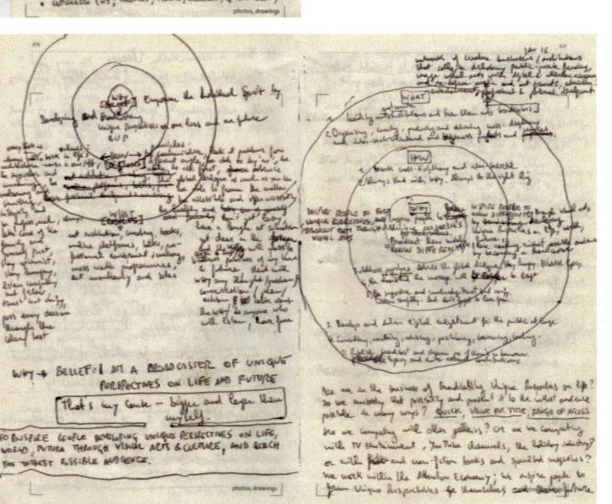

Sustained profitability depends on efficiency
you can't become efficient in crisis.

SALES – PROFIT = EXPENSES
[To be spent on your business]

Work with whatever is put in front of you

THE SOLUTION IS NOT TO TRY TO CHANGE YOUR INGRAINED HABITS, WHICH IS REALLY HARD TO PULL OFF AND NEARLY IMPOSSIBLE TO SUSTAIN, BUT INSTEAD TO CHANGE THE STRUCTURE AROUND US AND LEVERAGE THOSE HABITS.

1. USE SMALL PLATE (don't spend. Become frugal)
2. SERVE SEQUENTIALLY (profit, tax, owner comp, operating expenses – last)
3. REMOVE TEMPTATION (remove profit & tax – out of sight to remote accounts)
4. ENFORCE A RHYTHM (pay from OPEX account only on 10th + 25th each month)

After you take your profit first, your business will tell you immediately whether it can afford the expenses you are incurring; whether you are streamlined enough; whether you have the right margins.

You need to be the best at one thing you do. To become the best at something, you need to first determine what you are best at and do it a whole lot better. Take your profit first and the answers to being the best at something will reveal themselves.

Profit First just has multiple accounts at your bank so that when you log in, you know what purpose that money is meant to serve. You open your "envelope", see what you have to work with, and make your decisions. You're not changing your behavior, you're leveraging it.

TRUST THE PROCESS. THIS WORKS.

You don't have to have an answer, but you can provide a blueprint.

Not to be the one to find the answer but to start the conversation with people who then might find an answer.

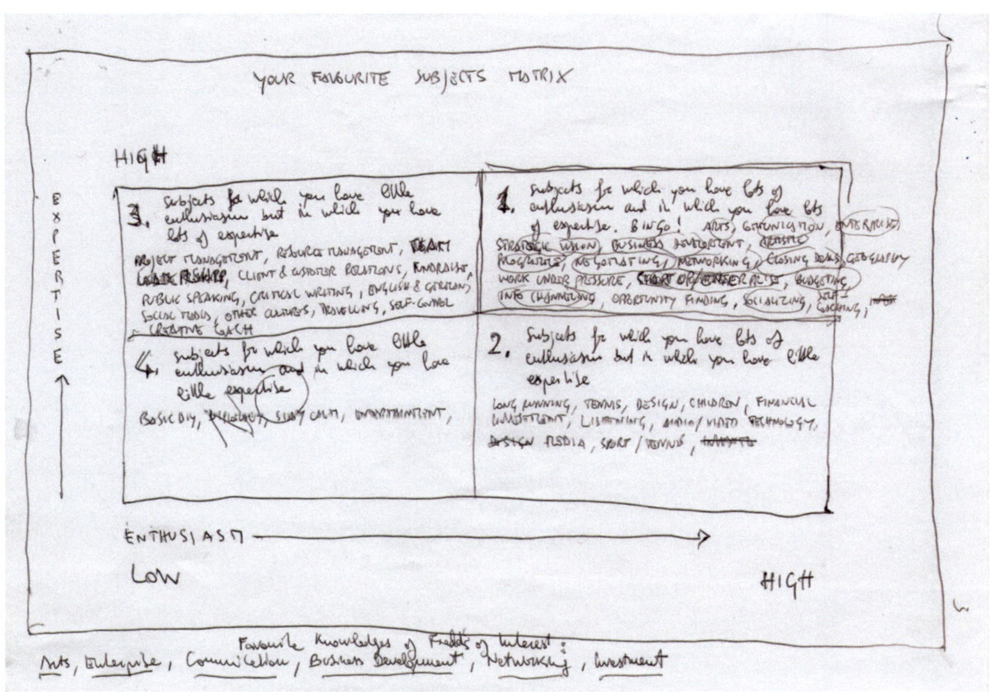

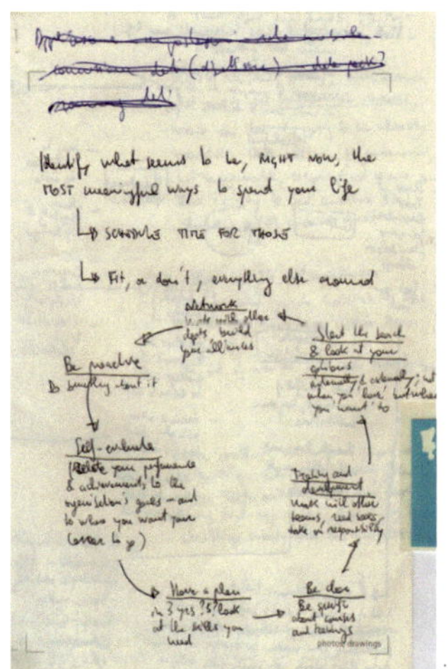

THE PROGRAMMES I DESIGN ARE RELEVANT
AND HOW WOULD I MARKET THESE

PROGRAMME – 4 STRANDS

- EXHIBITIONS – 10x pa as in 4-4-2
  - 4 EMERGENT / REGIONAL
- FILM & MUSIC
  - 3x weekly music events
- EDUCATION & PUBLIC PROGRAMMES
- LAST STRAND, REGENERATION PROGRAMME – 3 formats
  - 1x weekly
  - 1x quarterly
  - 1x annually

Regeneration:

1x weekly "COMMUNITY SUNDAYS" with 1 or more spaces given to interest & community groups: dance, choir, yoga, book club, knitting circle
[FOLKESTONE – works]

1x quarterly CREATIVE BUSINESS EVENT

1x annual FESTIVAL of CREATIVITY & DESIGN

Exhibitions:

I WOULD ORGANISE THEMATIC SEASONS, for instance, which speak the same language of the community.

- A TEXTILE THEME textile heritage from 1600 and the Flanders merchants, through the textile & fashion courses.

CHRISTINA
PETER
SHEZAD DAWOOD
SONIA DELAUNAY with 1 piece as ANCHOR for the rest

North America, where you are now chairman of

Soth

at th

have

plac

and

a dif

deve

at th

LISA

a ve

ever

que

Ton

cent

paec

bea

about what the twenty-first-century museu

would look like, both in response to a more global world and to the demands of art that had become, in some cases, outsized for mar traditional institutions. So the idea of a glob network of museums, sharing collections, w in my mind an incredibly positive developm Too many great collections sit in storage, never to see the light of day. In the collectio sharing scenario, there was also a way for th Guggenheim to annex hard-to-come-by fu for building collections – through Bilbao, for example, where the Basque government put hundreds of millions of dollars into th collection, and through Deutsche Bank, wh corporate money was leveraged to commiss artists to create works that would become pa of the collection, to the Guggenheim Las Vegas, where the State Hermitage Museum in St Petersburg and the Guggenheim formed an alliance partnership, agreeing to share parts

of th

for I

venu

of th

grea

deve

that

tion

by s

beco

cont

so t

fabu

buil

Ren

Geh

a lot

sharing partnerships develop. For me, these are the most positive developments from the

which seemed at the time to indicate a significant shift

is out of the barn, so to speak,
and we have seen some
incredibly fabulous museums
ions
a Hadid,
Piano,
se Frank
others.

tually not

ing the

essential

nuch

other than

ent show

money

f emerging

r as director,

we altered that course, first by establishing acquisition committees, whose dues went to

of the original mission of the foundation – to

ve, or abstract, art. In essence

continuity, bringing the

nsky, Malevich and Mondria

e such artists as Judd, Flavin,

angold and Ryman. The

works by predominantly

al and conceptual artists gave

epth and quality of postwar

ny ways commensurate with

gs. I think it is fair to argue

on was indeed the start of a

ement with art from the 1960

ve been a multitude of shows

s collection in venues around

ese exhibitions have provoke

olarship, as well as providing

the opportunity in many cases for the fabrica-

hadn't previously been mad

n 2010 the Guggenheim

nza Collection Initiative with

e Mellon Foundation, a very

to address the long-term

rtworks of the 1960s and 70s.

d Jeffrey Weiss, former Dia

head this initiative, as well as

rvator, and they established

advisory committee. Using

od, they are aiming to develo

ork through which to addres

stainability of other variable,

rication-based artworks of th

tion will be widely shared,

tant, I believe, because as we'

recently seen with the decision of the Flavin estate to fulfil editions that weren't made during the artist's lifetime, the rules for the preservation of this art have yet to be written. So I would argue that rather than 'dropping' the engagement, the museum took a very responsible course. As for continuing acquisitions – the future may hold some interesting possibilities should the museum decide, after the contractual time expires, to sell some of th works from the Panza Collection and reinvest the funds to broaden their holdings. They have, for example, many Rymans from 1972, and if some could be sold to purchase works from other periods of his career, this would be interesting both for the market in general as well as for representation of Ryman in the Guggenheim collection.

I also think if you look at the ongoing acquisitions programme, there has been a very strong effort to acquire works that continue the legacy of Minimalism. In 2004, for exampl I organised a show with Nancy Spector called *Singular Forms (Sometimes Repeated): Art from 19*

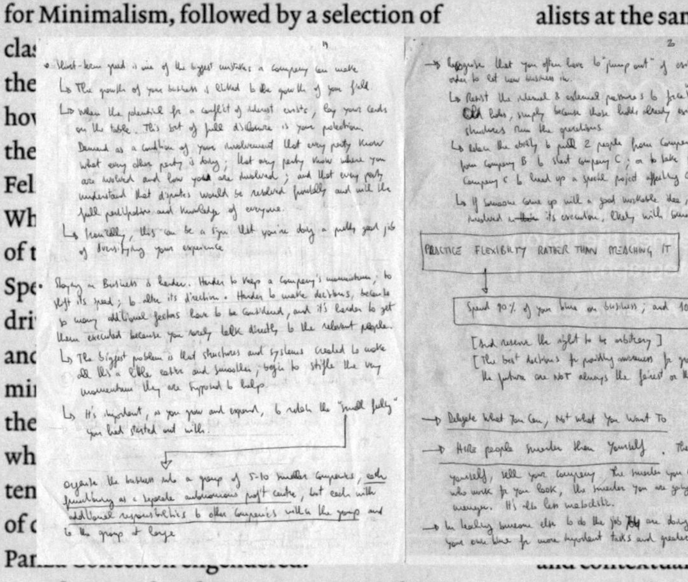

for Minimalism, followed by a selection of clas the hov the Fel Wh of t Spe dri and mi the wh ten of c Panza Collection engendered.

The mere fact that you are raising this question shows that Tom will not be remembered for one of the most significant contributions to the Guggenheim's collection building endeavour, but rather for building endeavours and the globalisation of the museum!

AR *You make a compelling and pretty convincing case. And maybe it's time to reassess that legacy. But part of the problem seems to me how and what the Guggenheim was communicating. Am I wrong or was the message constantly one of drumming up growth and globalisation, satellites and starchitects during that period? There was a sense, albeit from the outside, that the museum drifted apart from the art community. Would you just say, 'Well, Tom, the art community changed, it expanded and the museum responded and acted as a catalyst to that change'?*

LD That was exactly what I was thinking! Communication. We obviously didn't do a g in a art tab exa mu wit mu at t Eve Bui tio Plu imp to r eco in t the to l so to speak. It was an announcement that yes, we were a global museum, but we also had

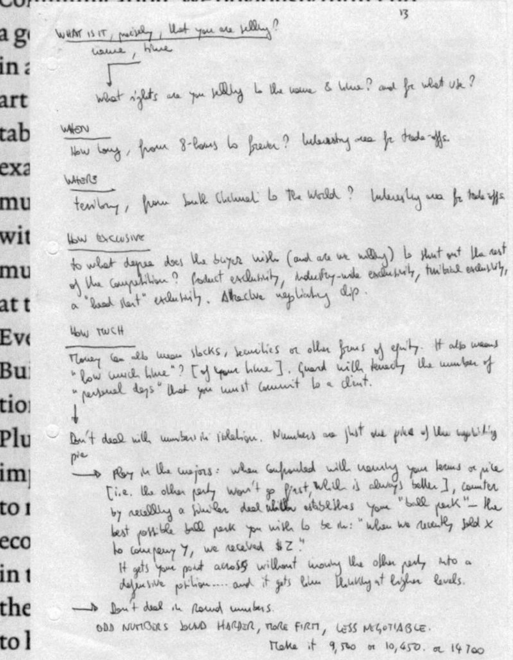

alists at the same time.

and contextualised it in a way that served the layman and the art profes

Anyway, I heartily ag reassess that legacy!

And generally corporate suppor the marketing rather than the p arm, which mean to be a real pay dollars spent. Of have to invent pro match the corporate gift, which leaves the basics underfunded. Museums are forced today to think about shows that

ming. You were a curator for many years; how do you view the health of our museums today?

facing museums yesterday – raising money. as gotten more challenging for several One of the most serious is that corpo- port has dwindled. Certainly during t was an easy thing for companies to port from their budgets. And generally most corporate support comes from the ng department rather than the philan- arm, which means there needs to be ayoff for the dollars spent. Often, ns have to invent programming to he corporate gift, which leaves the operations, acquisitions, building mmes and capital campaigns – under- Museums are forced today to think hows that will get people through the gate, because income from admission, book-

they can be more reactive to the 'zeitgeist'. The lead time for these shows is a fraction of the time it takes museums to mount an exhibition.

There are so many art experiences competing for the viewer's attention, with art fairs, bien-

Guggenheim, Carsten Höller at the New Museum…).

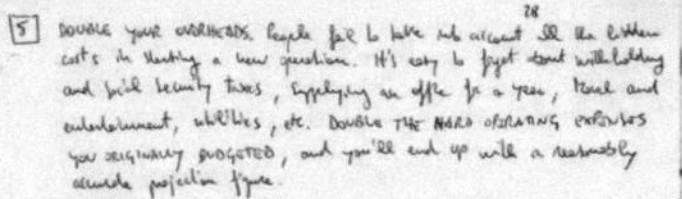

WEEKLY March 4

...ompany a...

Multination... e insight on the ultim...

By LIN WEI

Over the p... a clear shift in focus has occurred regarding Chinese outbound mergers and acquisitions, prompting unique challenges in terms of integration and deal complexity.

In tandem with China's aspirations ...ed economy ... no longer ...es sector, but rather, since about 2011, a more diverse ambit that includes technology, agriculture, consumer products, and sports and culture sectors.

Buckminster Fuller
do more with less
Lightly organize what is already there

Driven by a desire — if not need — to move up the value chain, Chinese companies now aspire to buy brands,

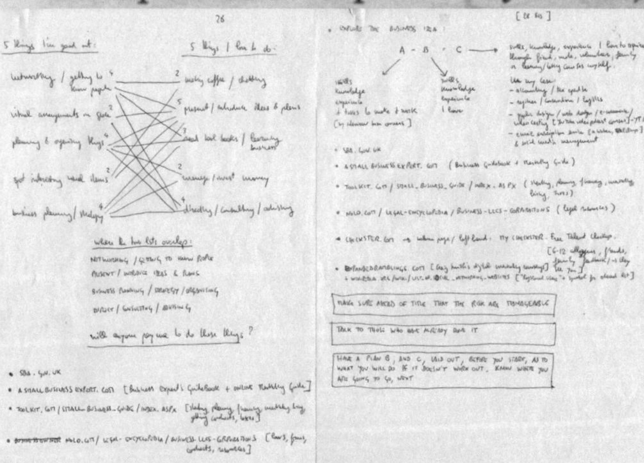

Chinese companies have generally faced two key issues related to the

...pool suited for overseas posting to manage the acquired business, and limited employer-brand visibility, presenting further difficulties in recruiting local talent abroad.

As a result, these companies have often managed acquired companies by retaining the acquired team and entrusting the business entir... the legacy management to en... continuity. This buys time for... new owner to develop a deep... understanding of the busines... after about a year or two, inte... activities may commence to a... the synergies initially planne...

This approach can be risky... buyer's agenda may differ fro... acquired management's prio... investment can often be put... back burner. Consequences c... grave for the buyer — deals m... this way can trigger a loss of... tum and result in delayed or... ized synergies. Legacy manag... accustomed to a high degree... autonomy, can resist efforts... the road to become integrate... ing it as an interference and... of distraction. Strained relat... between management and o... can ensue, damaging employee morale and overall performance.

...e s... multi... in Chi... operat... thei... en... l c... , m... gh... ma... Ch... rse...

proac

Chinese entities that expand overseas

s of
als
solid
ntities
right,
the
uni-
ovide
he
tcomes
er

ties. The … cated tea… effectively… A clear in… ture shou… the Chine… to steer t… Second… team can… set of key… ported by incentives. To reduce dependence on the legacy team, the buyer can also prepare a succession plan for senior management, by nurturing mid-level management or recruiting talent from the local job market.

This dovetails with the more recent concept of reverse integration, which is where a Chinese buyer injects its existing business in the … uired busi- … r a joint … y the legacy … rectly, reverse … n internal … lows for … ing prac- … espective … zations, such … e advanced … and the commercial platform to penetrate the China market.

Given a general expectation among Chinese companies that their outbound deals are for the benefit of the home market, the success of multinationals in China as solid operating entities in their own right, woven into the local communities, may provide insight on the ultimate outcomes for Chinese entities overseas.

That outbound deals today are … companies can further accelerate their learning curve and adapt their

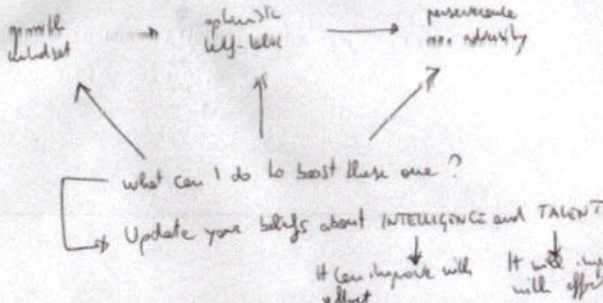

- An Artistic leader needs to be able to secure funding on faith; a Business leader needs to be able to understand and articulate a respectable curatorial vision; for these reasons, the job should ideally fall to one person.
  - → A Director / CEO / Thought leader who can make a case for that support
- Three major challenges for Directors / CEOs / Thought leaders of Art / Media / Design / Culture organizations:
  - (1) Engaging more imaginatively with audiences
  - (2) Addressing changing demographics
  - (3) Negotiating the delicate balance between the donors / patrons and the public

↓

Some of the most successful future Directors / CEOs / Thought leaders may well come from non-traditional art backgrounds: technology, journalism, community work

- MOTIVATE people through THEIR value system, not through yours.
- BE OPERATIONALLY EXCELLENT. The quality of the basic stuff is what allows you to bring about the visionary stuff.
- AGREE ON THE GAP between who you are and what is that you're going to be. Be clear. Take action on the next steps to get there.

Footfall / engagement strategy (possibilities):

- right type of exhibitions (cross-disciplinary & inter-sectoral)
- film / music / gaming sessions
- education & public programmes with "events" — see above
- engagement & participation programmes e.g. "Community Mondays", business events, Festival of Creativity & Design
- audience-centric, not audience-led. Identify target groups with appropriate / consistent message (ad agency) through appropriate / consistent channel (media agency)

Income Generation Strategy, linked with Footfall / Engagement (possibilities)

- Venue hire (film, music, gaming, community interest groups, charities, sport-health groups) in days / times where venue is less busy
- café & catering services — for general audience & for venue hire
- shop & online retail — aggressively market these
- commercial operations (prints, originals, commissions on sales for related, pop-up shows & ticketed events, online sales, print-fair, online auctions, franchise for art / music / gaming shop, franchise for streaming TV art & culture)
- patrons circles / members circles / exhibition circles
- programme support — ad hoc (Trusts & foundations, commercial galleries, makers, commercial brands i.e. gaming-film-music, publishing houses, catering businesses, national art councils, private collections, private sponsors)
- HE & academic institutions partnerships (offering public engagement & visibility for research outcome that University don't have, in exchange of co-funding agreement for departments / activities)

5 ROLES WITHIN THE CULTURAL SYSTEM IN ORDER FOR THE SYSTEM TO EXIST:

CULTURE

GUARDIANS
CONNECTORS
NOMADS
PLATFORMS

FEATURES:
- dense connectivity
- convergence of practices
- merging opposites
- focus on TIME (everything else is in plenty of supply)

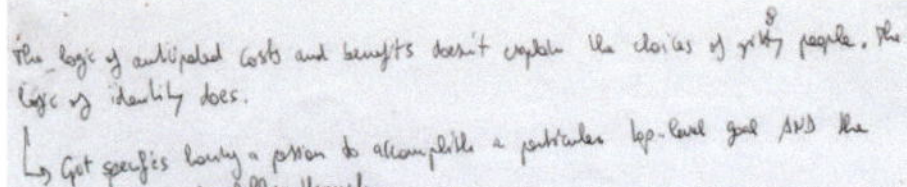

The logic of anticipated costs and benefits doesn't explain the choices of gritty people. The logic of identity does.

↳ Grit signifies having a passion to accomplish a particular top-level goal AND the perseverance to follow through.

- First, thinking of yourself as someone who is able to overcome tremendous adversity often leads to behaviours that confirm that self-conception. You have what it takes to succeed. You don't let setbacks hold you back. Grit is who you are.
- Second, in dark and desperate moments, we find that if we just keep putting one foot in front of the other, there is a way to accomplish what all reasons seem to argue against.
- Failures are going to happen, and how you deal with them may be the most important thing in whether you succeed. You need fierce resolve. You need to take responsibility.
  ↳ It takes relentless – absolutely relentless – communication. IT'S WHAT YOU SAY AND HOW YOU SAY IT. AND HOW OFTEN YOU SAY IT. Be a tireless evangelist.

Capability. Character. And How You Treat People.
Would I let them run the business?
Would I let my kids work for them?
Use mistakes and problems as opportunities to get better.
Not reasons to quit.
The style of GREAT LEADERSHIP begins with the RESPECT OF THE COMMANDER for HIS SUBORDINATES [MOST POINT]

→ Your experience is that once you have done the work to create the CLEAR VISION, it is the discipline and effort to maintain that vision that can make it all come true.

→ Your "opponent" creates challenges that help us become our best selves. Always compete. Compete in everything you do. You're either competing or you're not. Finish strong. Positive self-talk. Team first. COMPETE TEAMS EXCELLENCE. It means STRIVE TOGETHER (from the Latin). Nothing to do with another person losing.

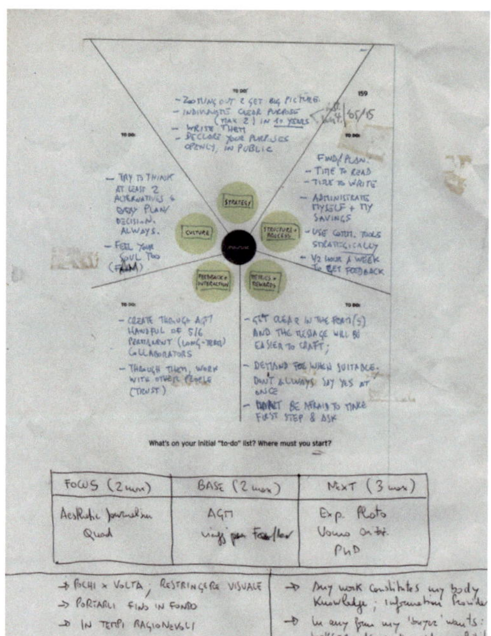

FOCUS (2 mon)	BASE (2 mos)	MIXT (3 mos)
Aesthetic journalism Quad	AGM ving" per Fowler	Exp. Photo Uomo Arte PhD

→ POCHI × VOLTA; RESTRINGERE VISUALE
→ PORTARLI FINO IN FONDO
→ IN TEMPI RAGIONEVOLI

→ Any work contributes my body knowledge; information provider
→ In any form my "buyer" wants: books – reports – audio – video – exhibitions – talks – seminars – consultancy
→ Every project as step towards fulfilment, excellence, progress

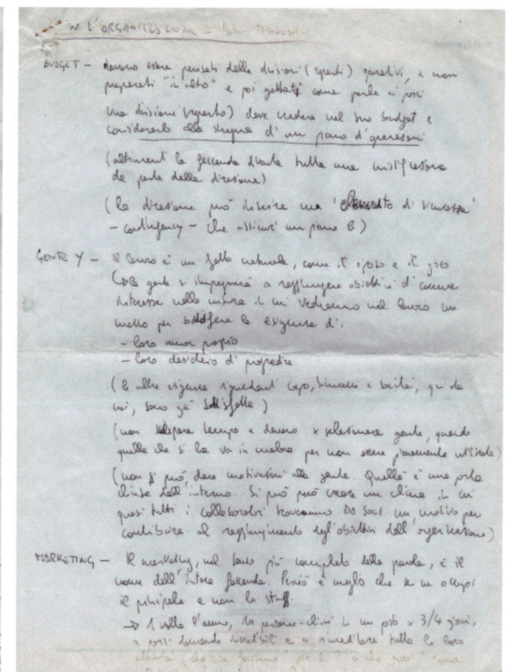

BUDGET – devono essere pensati dalla direzione (quanti) generali, e non proposti "in alto" e poi gettati come perle ai porci. Una divisione (reparto) deve credere nel suo budget e considerarlo alla stregua di un piano d'aggressione.

(attivando la fiducia dalle tutte una unità intera da parte della direzione)

(la direzione può inserire una "clausola di riserva" – contingency – che attivi un piano B)

GENTE Y – Il lavoro è un fatto naturale, come il gioco e il riposo. Le persone si impegnano a raggiungere obiettivi di comune interesse nella misura in cui vedranno nel lavoro un mezzo per soddisfare le esigenze di:
– loro amor proprio
– loro desiderio di progredire.

(le altre esigenze – quadri, capi, dirigenti e sociali, già da noi, sono già soddisfatte)

(non risparmiare tempo e denaro per selezionare gente, quindi quelle che si ha va in modo per non avere, passando all'esterno)

(non si può dare motivazione alla gente. Quello che si può fare è creare un clima in cui questi tutti i collaboratori troveranno da soli un motivo per contribuire al raggiungimento degli obiettivi dell'organizzazione)

MARKETING – Il marketing, nel senso più completo della parola, è il cuore dell'intera azienda. Perciò è meglio che se ne occupi il principale e non lo staff.

→ 1 volta al mese, la persona-chiave in un job per 3/4 giorni, …

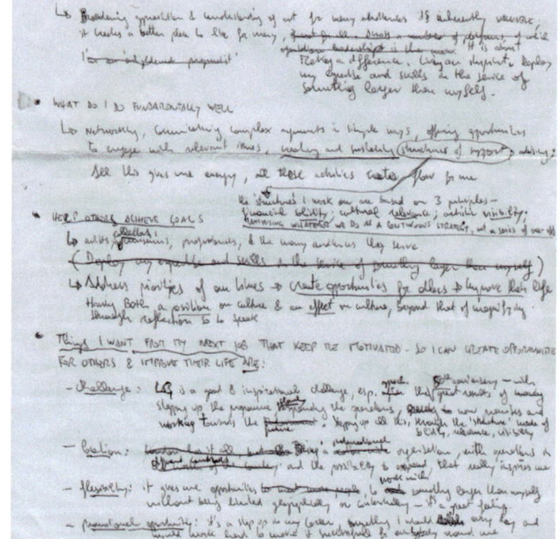

- FUNDAMENTAL REASON
- WHAT DO I DO FUNDAMENTALLY WELL
- HELP OTHERS ACHIEVE GOALS
- THINGS I WANT FROM MY NEXT JOB THAT KEEP ME MOTIVATED – SO I CAN CREATE OPPORTUNITIES FOR OTHERS & IMPROVE THEIR LIFE

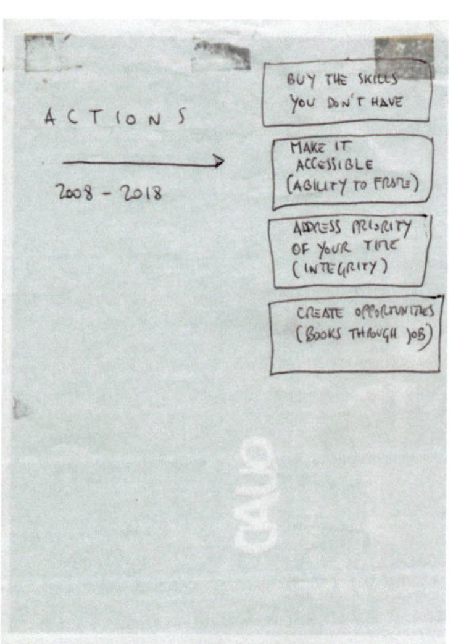

scientific knowledge vis-a-vis ethical question: Stockis

Scientific inquiry only a part of larger investigation into nature, and ultimately, human nature.
Intellect does not separate the sciences from the humanities, but combine them into a sum vastly greater than each part.
Knowing the world also from another perspective than specialised knowledge (scientific knowledge) – also combine technology & beauty.
Focus scientific knowledge on what it cannot – and should not – do
and looking for ideas that it may not work, but which would be massive if they do.
The buzzword for really big solutions and technologies is "transformative" – the internet is transformative, Skype is not.

Keith Ferrazzi · Never Eat Alone 1

- What mattered it's not "business school"; it's access to a network that could provide you with the mentorship and advice you need to help a radically growing business
  - ↳ it's not a knowledge problem, it's a people problem, with a people solution
    [MILKEN INSTITUTE'S GLOBAL CONFERENCE, Los Angeles, California]
    [Want business summit series, Powder Mountain, Eden – Salt Lake City, UTAH]
    [RENAISSANCE WEEKEND, Hilton Head, South Carolina; WEF Davos, Switzerland]
  - ↳ Today's most valuable currency is SOCIAL CAPITAL, defined as the information, expertise, trust, and total value that exist in the relationships you have
    - Success in life = The people you meet + what you create together
- Your network is your destiny. We are the people we interact with.
  Poverty isn't only a lack of financial resources, it's isolation from the kind of people who could help you make more of yourself
  You can't get there alone. In fact, you can't get very far at all.
- Success has nothing to do with class. My edge, is my INITIATIVE and DRIVE.
  When you help others, they often help you. RECIPROCITY and CARE.
  Success in ANY field, but especially in business, is about working WITH people, not against them. Business is a human enterprise, driven & determined by people.
  [↳ Foster and build relationships! Reach out to people to make a difference in people's lives as well as enrich my own.
  People do business with people they know and like. Invite those people's help in accomplishing their goal. REAL networking / connecting is about finding ways to make OTHER people more successful. WORK HARD TO GIVE MORE THAN YOU GET.
- The loyalty and security once offered by organizations can be provided by our own networks. We're all free agents now, managing our own careers across multiple jobs and companies. Because today's primary currency is information, a wide-reaching network is one of the surest ways to become and remain thought leaders of our respective fields
- You've got to be more than willing to accept generosity; Often, you've got to go out and ask for it. Introduce connections to others. Competitive edge is won by improving relationships. We live in an interdependent world. Our careers aren't paths so much as landscapes that are navigated.

We are the product of the people and networks to which we are connected.[2] Who you know determines who you are – how you feel, how you act, and what you achieve.

- It's the exercising of equity that builds equity. How can I help you?
  Relationships are solidified by trust. Institutions are built on it. The currency of real networking is not greed but generosity.
  - Business cycles ebb and flow; your friends and trusted associates remain
  - There's no point in keeping track of favours done and owed. Who cares? It's better to give before you receive. And never keep score
  - Yesterday's assistant is today's influence peddler. It's easier to get ahead in the world when those below you are happy to help you get ahead, rather than hoping for your downfall
  - Each of us is now a brand. In today's fluid economy, you must use branding to develop strong, enduring relationships with customers.
  - Contribute. Give your time, money, and expertise to your growing community of friends
- The more specific you are about what you want to do, the easier it becomes to develop a strategy to accomplish it. Part of the strategy is establishing relationships with the people who can help you get where you're going
  ↳ GOAL SETTING. Know what you want in life, and go after it.
  ↓
  MAKE GOAL SETTING A HABIT. PART OF YOUR LIFE:
  (1.) FIND YOUR PASSION
  A goal is a dream with a deadline. What's your dream?
  What's your 'blue flame' – where passion and ability converge?
  Human ambitions grow proportional to the size of their environment, the size of our dreams and the degree to which we're in touch with our mission.
  But of course the transformation of a dream into reality requires hard work and discipline. Be a disciplined dreamer with a mission.
  ↳ The kind of discipline that turns a dream into a mission, and a mission into a reality, comes down to a process of setting goals.
  See [2 BIS]
  (2.) PUTTING GOALS TO PAPER. GATHER THE SKILLS, TOOLS & MATERIAL NEEDED to turn your mission into a reality.

Twitter ← news + live
FB ← topic + place
Instagram ← images + story
↓
open up sketchbooks, for instance

~~television + radio~~

desired / guardian / museum ← offering podcasts & content "for" them
Harry Milols ← offering coverage there "for" them

Google · Twitter · FB · Snapchat ← not paid advertising

not content will bring the distribution, they now want to own publishers' content

~~FB~~, ~~Twitter~~ … (from personal accounts?)

→ they all put themselves for content providers, and treat them as such, provide content for them

Google Grant initiative – free advertising for charities $10.000 / month (upgrading to $40K / month)

FB → buying paid advertising

We are in the "business" of INSPIRATION – free inspiration and come up with creative ideas

Have OUTRAGEOUS ideas and follow them through.

- who is your most important audience?
- how can I help you achieving your goals?
- what is the population here? (county / region)
[objective question to understand the team dynamic – if they communicate with each other]

3 goals:
- promote the local county / context / institution
- promote inspiration through art
- talk about a specific theme

- You MOTIVATE people THROUGH THEIR value system; not through yours.
- You've got to be exceptional excellent in whatever you do. The quality of the basic stuff is what allows you to say about the visionary stuff.
- culture-led regeneration happens through steps
- who you are, and what it is we're going to be; agreeing on the gap, – delineating the time

- the vision and steps needs to be and feel authentic; don't wait for someone else to think and plan for it. You have to go for it. Pick up the ball and run.

	MOS	JER	HUN	PEC
RECOGNITION and LIMELIGHT	3	3	–	3
ARTISTIC and CREATIVITY	3	4	1	4
REPUTATION (INSTITUTIONAL)	3	3	2	3
ENTREPRENEURSHIP and PLANNING	4	5	4	4
MONEY	2	1	5	(2)
AUTONOMY / FREEDOM	5	1	1	2
FAMILY FRIENDLY	3	3	2	3
NICE ENVIRONM / PEOPLE	2	3	–	3
INFLUENCE / EXPERTISE	2	3	3	2
CITY CONTEXT	2	(2)	1	2
	29	28	19	28

	GAL	MOS	JER	HUN	PEC
RECOGNITION & LIMELIGHT	2	2	3	1	3
ARTISTIC & CREATIVITY	3	3	3	2	3
INSTITUTIONAL REPUTATION	3	2	3	1	2
ENTREPRENEURSHIP & PLANNING	2	3	3	3	3
MONEY	3	1	1	3	2
AUTONOMY & FREEDOM	3	4	2	3	3
FAMILY FRIENDLY	5	3	3	2	3
NICE ENVIRONMENT & PEOPLE	3	3	3	2	2
INFLUENCE & EXPERTISE	3	4	3	4	4
CITY CONTEXT	5	2	4	2	2
A.	(32)	(27)	(28)	23	27
F.	(34)	(29)	(28)	19	(28)

3

"A crowd is a tribe without a leader, and without communication. Most organizations spend their time marketing to the crowd. Smart organizations assemble the tribe. Tribes are longer lasting and more effective.

Ideas that spread win, and the ideas that are spreading are the remarkable ones. 'Good enough' stopped being good enough a long time ago → for the tribes, average can mean mediocre, not worth seeking out, boring.

Life's too short to hate what you do all day. Life's way too short to make mediocre stuff.

A true fan is a member of the tribe who cares deeply about you and your work – will cross the street to buy from you, will bring a friend to hear you, will invest a little extra to support you.

An individual artist needs only a thousand true fans in her tribe. It's enough – a 1000 fans, true fans, form a tribe – they will connect with other true fans and amplifies the noise the artist makes.

Too many organizations care about numbers, not fans. They care about hits or clicks or media mentions. What they're missing is the depth of commitment, commitment and interconnection that true fans deliver. The real win is in turning a casual fan into a true one. What they demand, in turn, is GENEROSITY and BRAVERY.

Organizations that destroy the status quo win. Individuals who push their organizations, who inspire other individuals to change the rules, thrive.

↳ Interesting side effect: creating products and services that are remarkable is fun. Doing work that's fun is engaging. Initiative = happiness.

↳ There doesn't seem to be a shortage of ideas. What's missing is the will to make the ideas happen. The idea that wins is not the best (probably) but the one with the most leaders behind it. The levers are there. The proof is here. The power is here. The only thing holding you back is your own fear.

4

↳ paraphrasing Peter Principle, in every organization everyone rises to the level at which they become paralyzed with fear. The essence of leadership is BEING AWARE OF YOUR FEAR (and seeing in the people you wish to lead). It won't go away, but awareness is the key to making progress.

The products and services that get talked about are the ones that are worth talking about (that confound expectations, etc.)

↳ How was your day?
If your answer is "fine" then I don't think you were leading.

↳ If you want to take the remarkable path, answer this one:

"HOW CAN I CREATE SOMETHING THAT CRITICS WILL CRITICIZE?"

Challenging the status quo requires a commitment, both public and private. It involves reaching out to others and putting your ideas on the line. Great leaders focus on the tribe and only the tribe – not the glory. They're generous. They exist to help the tribe find something, to enable the tribe to thrive – getting out front, making a point, challenging convention and speaking up.

Reflect the light onto your teams, your tribes. Great leaders use the attention to unite the tribe and reinforce its sense of purpose.
Leading is THE OPPOSITE of talking.

Deciding to lead NOT manage, is the critical choice. CONNECT and INSPIRE Then get out of the way.

If you're not uncomfortable in your work as a leader, it's almost certain you're

8

The secret is to listen, to value what you hear, and then to make a decision even if it contradicts the very people you are listening to. People want to be sure you heard what they said – they're less focused on whether or not you do what they said.

LISTEN, REALLY LISTEN. THEN DECIDE AND MOVE ON. Without people pushing against your quest to do something worth talking about, it's unlikely to be worth the journey. PERSIST.

A BIG PART OF leadership is THE ABILITY TO STICK with the DREAM for a long time. Long enough that the critics realize that you're going to get there one way or another … so they follow.

GREAT LEADERS EMBRACE DEVIANTS by searching for them and catching them doing something right.

⇓

FIND LEADERS (the heretics who are doing things differently and making change), and then AMPLIFY THEIR WORK, give them a platform, and help them to find followers – and things get better, they always get better.
It's simple, but it works.

I don't think we have any choice. I think we have an obligation to change the rules, to raise the bar, to play a different game, and to play it better than anyone has any right to believe is possible.

REAL LEADERS DON'T CARE ABOUT GETTING CREDIT. It's about your mission, about spreading the faith, about seeing something happen – not only do you not care about credit, you actually WANT other people to get credit.

CREDIT ISN'T THE POINT. CHANGE IS.

9

IMAGINATION IS MORE IMPORTANT THAN KNOWLEDGE
(Albert Einstein)

↳ Leaders create things that didn't exist before. They do this by giving the tribe a vision of something that could happen, but hasn't (yet).
You can't lead without imagination.

→ WHAT LEADERS DO:
THEY GIVE PEOPLE STORIES THEY CAN TELL THEMSELVES. STORIES ABOUT THE FUTURE AND ABOUT CHANGE.

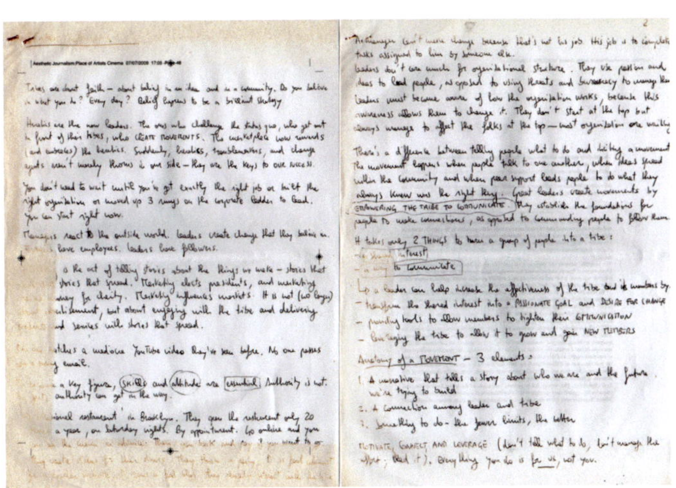

Aesthetic Journalism Place of Artists Cinema 07/07/2009 17:05 Page 48

Tribes are about faith – about belief in an idea and in a community. Do you believe in what you do? Every day? Belief happens to be a brilliant strategy.

Heretics are the new leaders. The ones who challenge the status quo, who get out in front of their tribes, who CREATE MOVEMENTS. The marketplace now rewards (and embraces) the heretics. Suddenly, leaders, troublemakers, and change agents aren't merely thorns in our side – they are the keys to our success.

You don't need to wait until you've got exactly the right job or built the right organization or moved up 3 rungs on the corporate ladder to lead. You can start right now.

Managers react to the outside world. Leaders create change that they believe in. ... have employees. Leaders have followers.

... is the act of telling stories about the things we make – stories that ... stories that spread. Marketing elects presidents, and marketing ... money for charity. Marketing influences markets. It is not (no longer) ... advertisement, but about engaging with the tribe and delivering ... and services with stories that spread.

... watches a mediocre YouTube video they've seen before. No one passes ... email.

... a key figure, skills and attitude are essential. Authority is not. ... authority can get in the way.

... restaurant' in Brooklyn. They open the restaurant only 20 ... a year, on Saturday nights. By appointment. Go online and you ...

2

A manager can't make change because that's not his job. His job is to complete tasks assigned to him by someone else.
Leaders don't care much for organizational structure. They use passion and ideas to lead people, as opposed to using threats and bureaucracy to manage them. Leaders must become aware of how the organization works, because this awareness allows them to change it. They don't start at the top but always manage to affect the folks at the top – most organization are waiting

There's a difference between telling people what to do and letting a movement. The movement happens when people talk to one another, when ideas spread within the community and when peer support leads people to do what they always knew was the right thing. Great leaders create movements by EMPOWERING THE TRIBE TO COMMUNICATE. They establish the foundations for people to make connections, as opposed to commanding people to follow them.

It takes only 2 THINGS to turn a group of people into a tribe:
– a shared interest
– a way to communicate

→ a leader can help increase the effectiveness of the tribe and its members by:
– transform the shared interest into a PASSIONATE GOAL and DESIRE FOR CHANGE
– providing tools to allow members to tighten their COMMUNICATION
– leveraging the tribe to allow it to grow and gain NEW MEMBERS

Anatomy of a MOVEMENT – 3 elements:
1. A narrative that tells a story about who we are and the future we're trying to build
2. A connection among leader and tribe
3. Something to do – the fewer limits, the better

MOTIVATE, CONNECT AND LEVERAGE (don't tell what to do, but manage the effort; lead it). Everything you do is for us, not you.

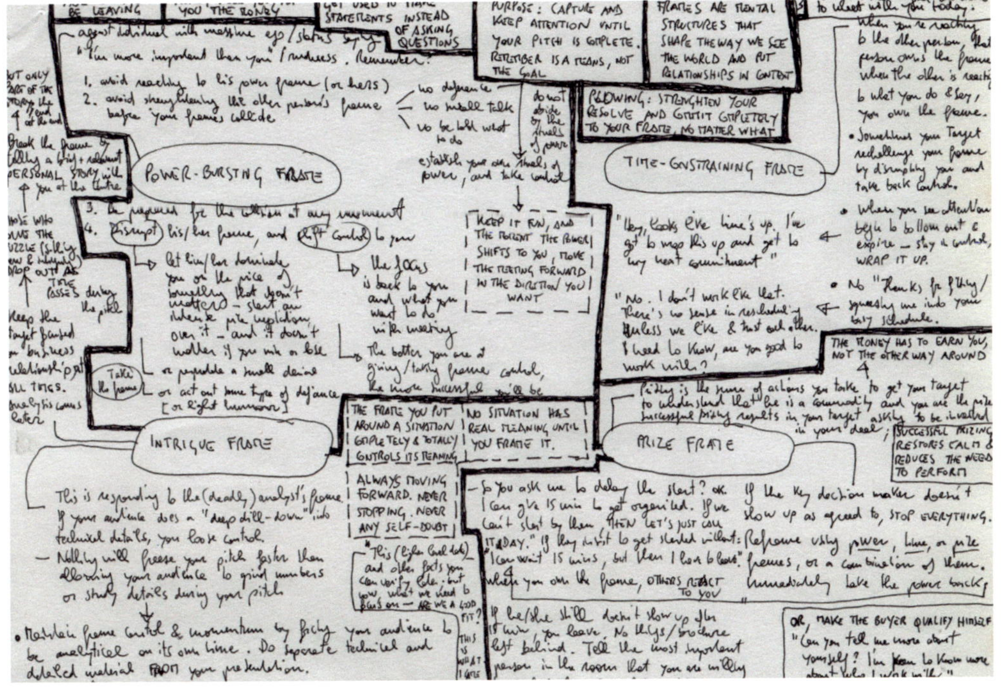

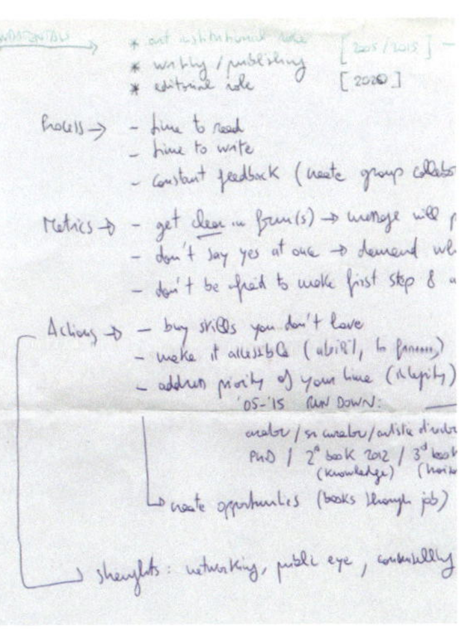

* art institutional role [2005/2015]
* writing / publishing
* editorial role [2020]

Process → – time to read
– time to write
– constant feedback (create group collabo...

Metrics → – get clear on frame(s) → manage will ...
– don't say yes at once → demand ...
– don't be afraid to make first step & ...

Actions → – buy skills you don't have
– make it accessible (...)
– address priority of your time (...)

'05-'15 RUN DOWN:
curator / sr curator / artistic director ...
PhD / 2nd book 2012 / 3rd book ...
(knowledge) ...
→ create opportunities (books through job)

strengths: networking, public eye, ...

An ideas festival is like a tribal wedding for the global elite

Next month, I will head to Colorado for the Aspen Ideas Festival, an annual current affairs conference. No surprise there; these days, politicians, academics, executives and journalists spend a considerable amount of time attending conferences: the Aspen event, the World Economic Forum's meeting in Davos, the Milken Institute's global conference in Los Angeles and countless others

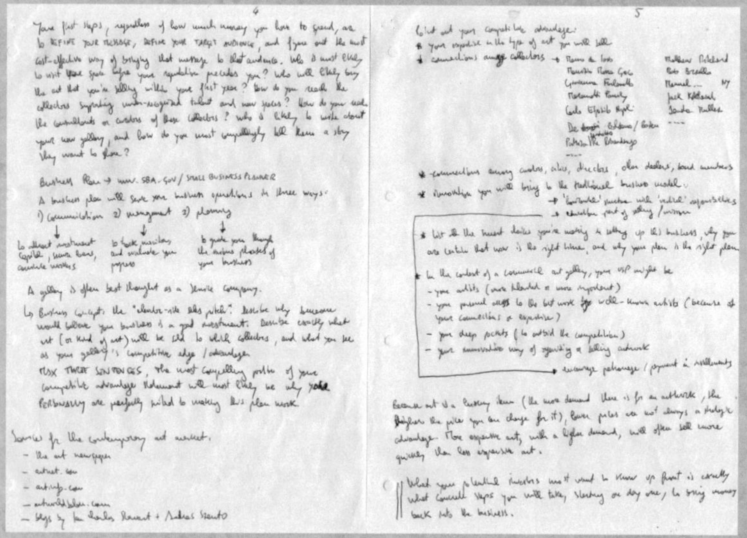

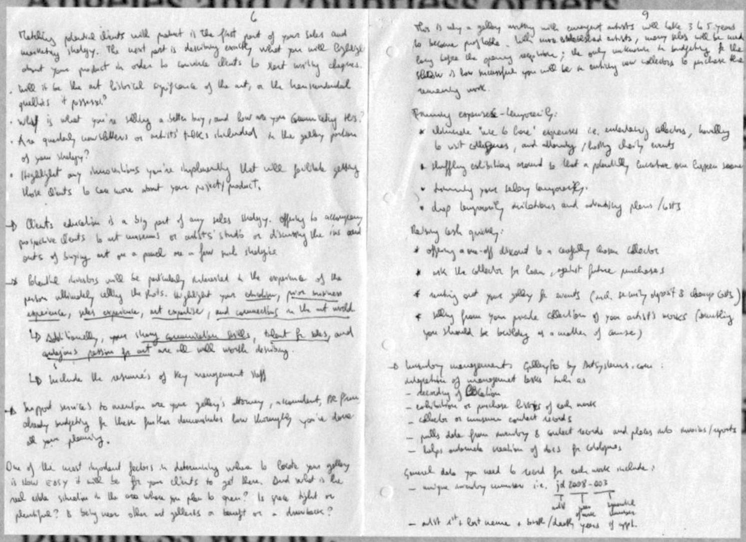

ge

of

r

is

business world.

Digital development has transformed the way media, retailing and industrial spheres work, and is now spreading into medicine and government. This ought to imply that conferen . In a world w online in need to f

When ab, the foun Forum, a ?), he predic f decades the conference business "will no longer exist" in its current form

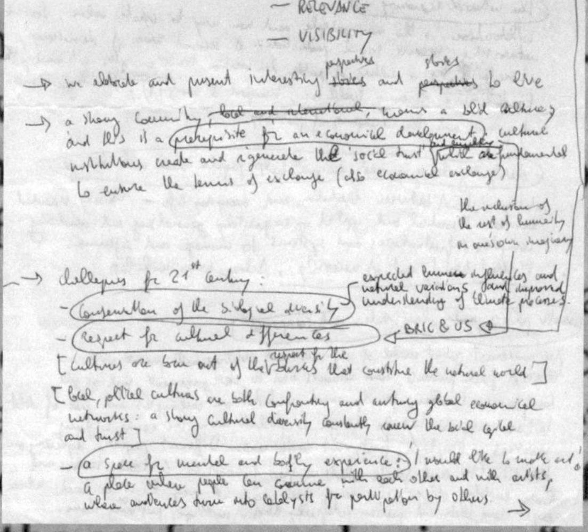

Notebook

by G

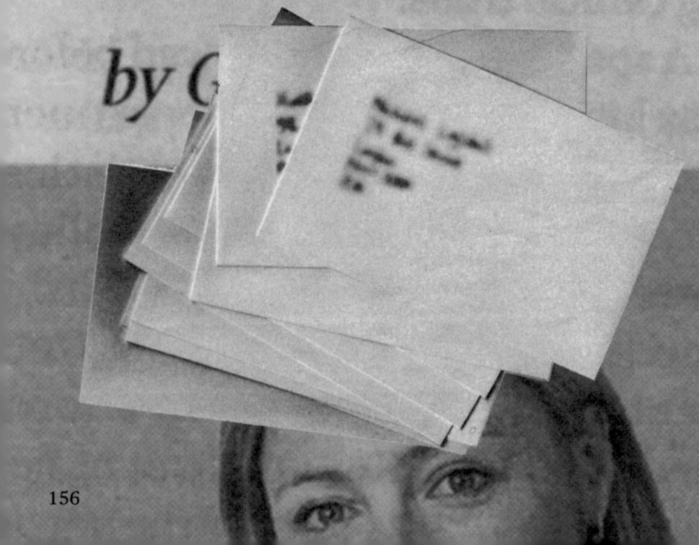

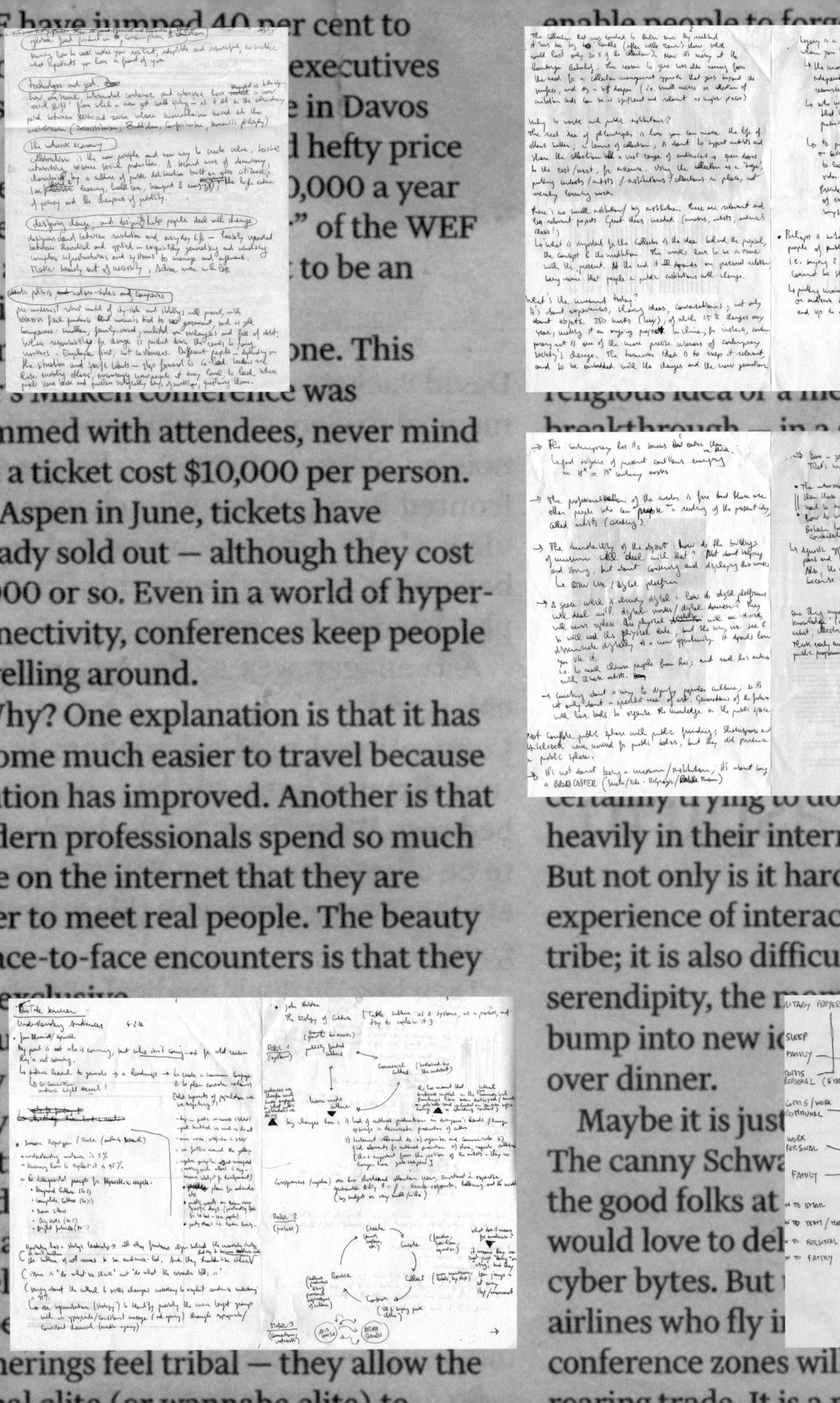
EF have jumped 40 per cent to
e in Davos
d hefty price
0,000 a year
" of the WEF
to be an
one. This
ammed with attendees, never mind
at a ticket cost $10,000 per person.
r Aspen in June, tickets have
ready sold out — although they cost
,000 or so. Even in a world of hyper-
nnectivity, conferences keep people
avelling around.
Why? One explanation is that it has
ecome much easier to travel because
iation has improved. Another is that
odern professionals spend so much
ne on the internet that they are
ger to meet real people. The beauty
face-to-face encounters is that they
atherings feel tribal — they allow the
heavily in their internet platforms.
But not only is it hard to replicate the
experience of interacting as a social
tribe; it is also difficult to produce
serendipity, the moment when people
bump into new i
over dinner.
Maybe it is just
The canny Schwa
the good folks at
would love to del
cyber bytes. But
airlines who fly i
conference zones will continue to do a

- post institutions
· not literally, but in relation State (network, and also opportunism)
· light & temporal infrastructure
you relate things to other (always contemporary, in the now)
· subjective and singular (HORWICH)
· event (periodicity) i.e. biennial.
it has a post-institutional structure

. why to choose THIS international curator rather than another?
name/fame, or good opinion, or good idea = new idea (modernism); appropriate idea (a good idea renew itself – context), or an opportunistic idea?
That's why they choose its for the 'good idea'. It has
– potency: a promise of good and appropriate exhibition
– promise is 'capitalized' one of post-Fordism (virno) or immaterial labor

relation to each other & with their own presence/position within the main collection.
→ from a passive moment/ relaying information to one of "speculation" about themes/topics/artefacts
→ devise an 'algorithm' that in turn would 'select' the works to be presented in juxtaposition to each other and shape a constellation
• narrative time vs. everyday time
• autonomous object vs autonomous experience
• art object vs documentation

ul Haq, in the 1980s, the government promoted violent *jihad* as a state policy and spread Islamist extremism. Ms Jalal spells out too, without labouring it, how American worries about the cold war and then Islamist terrorism helped to give the army a free hand and many resources for controlling domestic affairs.

Ms Fair's focus is on the army's "strategic culture", as she tries to explain why the generals behave as they do. She has pored over decades' worth of official army publications and she concludes, gloomily, that they are driven not by an urge to promote national security, but by ideology. Their main motivation is to resist and weaken Hindu-dominated India in whatever way possible; they see India as an exis threat. Ms Fair says that Pakistan thus best understood as a "purely state", one that would consume wh territory, aid or other benefits it can would never seek peace with th enemy, since giving up hostility even the best circumstances wou tantamount to defeat.

When it comes to advice, the a differ widely. Ms Jalal thinks Ame should keep on engaging and fu nuclear-armed Pakistan, rather tha "untold consequences" by isolat Outsiders can help to preserve a sp moderates in the country and lin disruption that might spread abro Fair's opinion is bolder. Elsewhere s depicted the army, in view of its ab extract funds from America, as a m "self licking ice-cream cone". She now urges Westerners to stop paying for this and to dare, instead, to "let Pakistan fail". The country has endured so many crises and shown "a very stable instability" over the years. It will not collapse now. The

should know

Zero to One: Notes on Start-Ups or How to Build the Future. By Peter Thiel with Blake Masters. *Crown Business; 210 pages; $27. Virgin Books; £16.99*

CONTRARIANISM and controversy have long been the hallmarks of Peter Thiel, the co-founder of PayPal and Palantir, and the first outside investor in Facebook. He has made headlines advocating seasteading (building new cities in or under the oceans), urging students to drop out of education to start companies and

How long will you be on the phone.

talism are opposites".

The book's title sums up the main argument, that truly valuable innovation occurs not through incremental change but by creating something out of nothing, something entirely new. That will require

says, and not "Randian" prime movers' who claim to be independent of everybody around them."

Nor, despite his optimism about the future, does Mr Thiel fully share Ray Kurzweil's techno-Utopianism: the "Singularity", a future of superhuman artificial intelligence, may be near, but it is not inevitable. Instead, he says, "We cannot take for granted that the future will be better, and that means we need to work to create it today." Quite so. Crisply written, rational and practical, "Zero to One" should be read not just by aspiring entrepreneurs but by anyone seeking a thoughtful alternative to the current pervasive gloom about the prospects for the world. ■

-Israel peace treaty of 1978

led terms

Days in September: Carter, Begin, at Camp David. By Lawrence *opf; 345 pages; $27.95. To be in Britain by Oneworld in November*

ra of appalling violence in the East, from Libya to Iraq, one ve expected a book by Lawrence explain how it all got so bad. An ork, "The Looming Tower", is one est accounts of the birth of al-Qaeda and its attack on America on September 11th 2001. Instead "Thirteen Days in September" looks back at a fleeting moment when things might have turned out for the better.

In his retelling of the summit at Camp

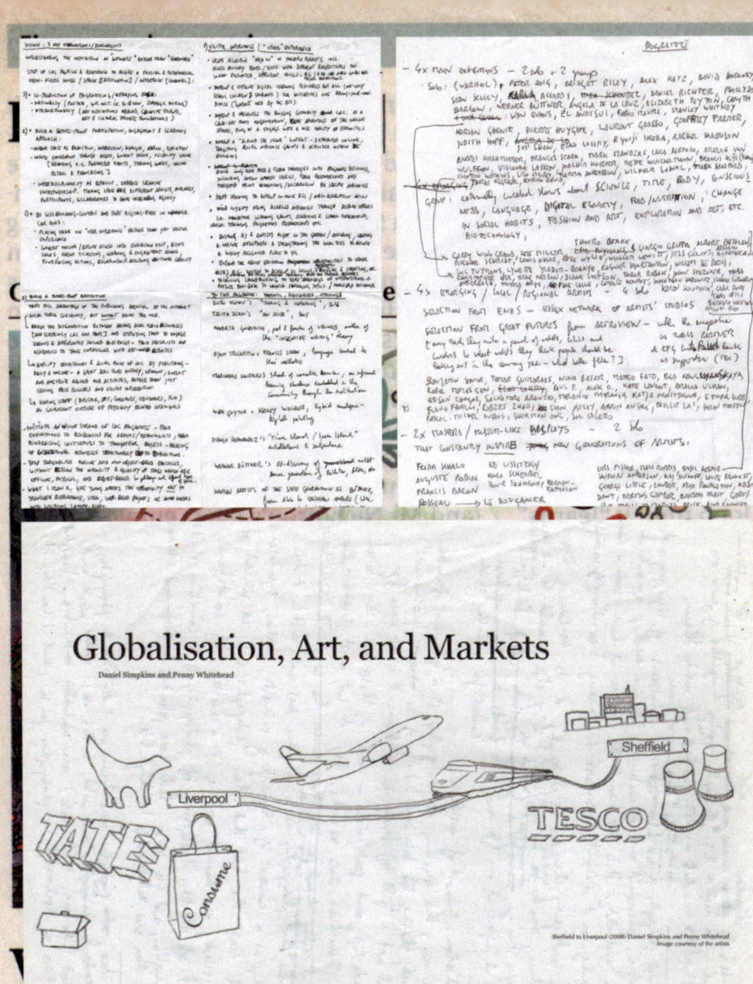

long tail

niche interest only, the aggregate
For example, since a minority of
jority of music sales, the fact that s
load tripled between 2000 and 20
of those new songs may be by ma

Joel Waldfogel of the Univers
understates the internet's contrib
products is much harder to pred
ducts such as shoes or soda. Sea
vague idea what book, film or song will be a hit. A major record label can sign only a fraction of the artists available, knowing full well it will unwittingly reject a future superstar.

Thanks to cheap digital recording technology, file sharing, YouTube, streaming music and social media, however, barriers to entry have been dismantled. Artists can now record and distribute a song without signing to a major label. Independent labels have proliferated, and they are taking on the artists passed over by major labels. Hit songs are still a lottery, but the public gets three times as many lottery tickets.

This seems at odds with the collapse in recorded music revenue since 2000 which suggests declining, not rising, music industry output. Mr Waldfogel says that is misleading: because of piracy, revenue understates how much music the public has really consumed. He calculates the quality of songs recorded since then has been either stable (based on the number that made it onto critics' "best-of" lists) or significantly improved (based on the pattern of sales and airplay). This is corroborated by the success of indie-affiliated bands such as Arcade Fire and Mumford & Sons. Indie labels' share of the Billboard top 200 selling albums grew from 13% in 2001 to 35% in 2010. Mr Waldfogel and a co-author reckon that tripling the selection of songs available has

lower and more uniform. And the selection available to consumers would increase.

Identifying those benefits has been challenging. Online prices have proved to be surprisingly diverse. And while the selection of products online is indeed vast, many are niche products such as self-published books for which demand is scant to non-existent. E-commerce is still a net plus. But papers presented at this year's meeting of the American Economic Association demon-

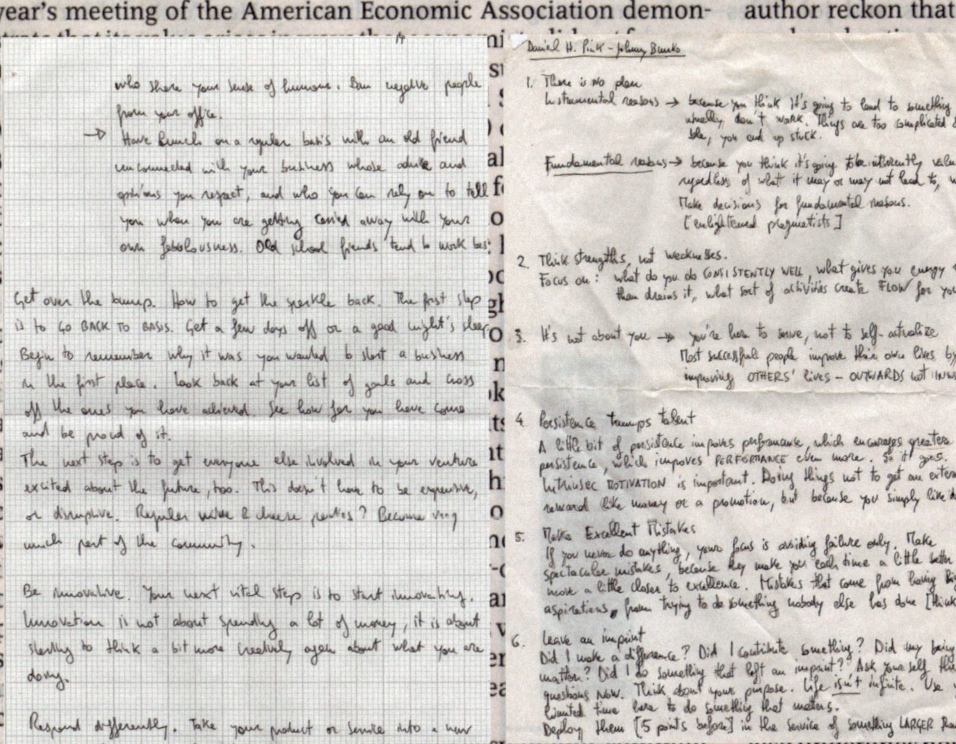

who share your sense of humour. Ban negative people from your office.

→ Have lunch on a regular basis with an old friend unconnected with your business whose advice and opinions you respect, and who you can rely on to tell you when you are getting carried away with your own fabulousness. Old school friends tend to work best.

Get over the bump. How to get the sparkle back. The first step is to GO BACK TO BASIS. Get a few days off or a good night's sleep. Begin to remember why it was you wanted to start a business in the first place. Look back at your list of goals and cross off the ones you have achieved. See how far you have come and be proud of it.
The next step is to get everyone else involved in your venture excited about the future, too. This doesn't have to be expensive, or disruptive. Regular wine & cheese parties? Become very much part of the community.

Be innovative. Your next vital step is to start innovating. Innovation is not about spending a lot of money, it is about starting to think a bit more creatively again about what you are doing.

Respond differently. Take your product or service into a new

Daniel H. Pink – Johnny Bunko

1. There is no plan
Instrumental reasons → because you think it's going to lead to something else, ultimately, don't work. Things are too complicated & unpredictable, you end up stuck.
Fundamental reasons → because you think it's going to be inherently valuable, regardless of what it may or may not lead to, WORK.
Make decisions for fundamental reasons.
[enlightened pragmatists]

2. Think strengths, not weaknesses.
Focus on: what do you do CONSISTENTLY WELL, what gives you energy rather than drains it, what sort of activities create FLOW for you.

3. It's not about you → you're here to serve, not to self-actualize
Most successful people improve their own lives by improving OTHERS' lives – OUTWARDS not INWARDS

4. Persistence trumps talent
A little bit of persistence improves performance, which encourages greater persistence, which improves PERFORMANCE even more. So it goes.
Intrinsic MOTIVATION is important. Doing things not to get an external reward like money or a promotion, but because you simply like doing it.

5. Make Excellent Mistakes
If you never do anything, your focus is avoiding failure only. Make spectacular mistakes, because they make you each time a little better and move a little closer to excellence. Mistakes that come from having high aspirations, from trying to do something nobody else has done [think big].

6. Leave an imprint
Did I make a difference? Did I contribute something? Did my being here matter? Did I do something that left an imprint? Ask yourself these questions NOW. Think about your purpose. Life isn't infinite. Use your limited time here to do something that matters.
Deploy them [5 points before] in the service of something LARGER than yourself

START WITH WHY – Simon Sinek

Great leaders who are able to inspire give people a sense of purpose / belonging that has little to do with any external incentive or benefit to be gained.
↳ For those who are inspired, the motivation to act is DEEPLY PERSONAL. They act for the good of the whole not because they have to, but because they want to.

Organisations that achieve more, get more out of fewer people and resources, ones with an outsized amount of influence, build products and companies, even recruit people that all fit based on the original intention.

There are only two ways to influence human behaviour: you can manipulate it or you can inspire it. Manipulations work, but don't produce loyalty. All too often it's not the systems that fail but the ability to maintain them. That's why the motivation to act has to be deeply personal in employees and customers.
↳ Often, just like the "habitual dieter", company managers never have the time and money to do it right the first time, but they always have the time and money to do it again.

Leadership, instead, requires people to stick with you through thick and thin; it is ability to rally people not for a single event, but for years. There is a big difference between repeat business and loyalty – between doing business with you multiple times and being willing to turn down a better product / price to continue doing business with you. It all starts from the INSIDE OUT. It all starts with WHY.

WHAT a person, organisation or company does, products or services or functions, it's easy to identify.

HOW they do what they do is often given to explain how something is different or better – the differentiating factors.

WHY is your purpose, cause or belief. Why does your company exist? Why do you get out of bed every morning? Why should anyone care?

The inspired organisations go from the WHY to the WHAT, INSIDE → OUT.

These benefits are less likely to hold for easy-to-find, commoditised products; online prices of popular, usually in-print, books were less dispersed and closer to offline prices.

also underlines how far away measures like GDP are from capturing the benefits of the internet. ■

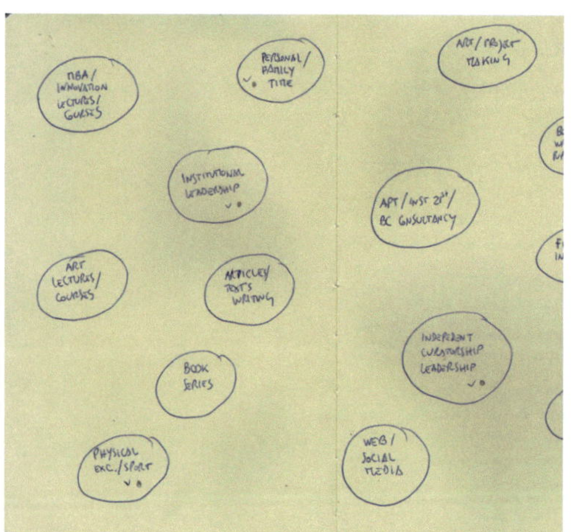

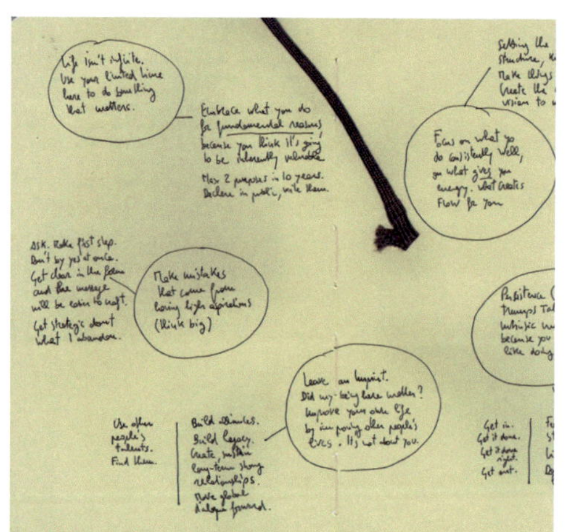

25

(3) leaders encourage reflective backtalk. You never know what you say until you hear the response. For instance, the backtalk from the spouse, the trusted person, is reflective because it allows the leader to learn, to find out more about himself.

(4) leaders encourage dissent. The organisational corollary of reflective backtalk. leaders need around them 'variance sensors' who can tell them the difference between what is expected and what is really going on.

(5) leaders possess the Nobel factor: optimism, faith, and hope.

(6) leaders understand the Pygmalion effect in management. – What managers expect of their subordinates and the way they treat them largely determine their performance and career progress. – A unique characteristic of superior managers is the ability to create high performance expectations that subordinates fulfill. – Subordinates appear to do what they believe they are expected to do.
If you expect great things, your associates will give them to you. But STRETCH, DON'T STRAIN (be realistic about expectations). PRETEND YOU'RE TRAINING FOR THE OLYMPICS. If you pull a muscle in today's game, you sit on the bench for tomorrow's. Stretch the person a little, but don't let them fall short too many times.

(7) leaders have what I think of as the Gretzky Factor – a certain "touch". It's not as important to know where the puck [in ice hockey] is now as to KNOW WHERE IT WILL BE. leaders have that sense of where the culture is going to be, where the organisation must be if it is to grow.

(8) leaders see the long view. They have patience. 10-15-25-30 years plan.

26

(9) leaders understand stakeholder symmetry. They know they must balance the competing claims of all the groups with a stake in the corporation.
Stakeholder symmetry is the first principle followed by the best corporations.
Consider not only the wonderful world outside the organisation but also what is going on in your immediate vicinity.

(10) leaders create strategic alliances and partnerships. The shrewd leaders of the future are going to recognize the significance of creating alliances with other organisations whose fates are correlated with their own.
The next generation of leaders will have certain things in common:
- broad education
- boundless curiosity
- boundless enthusiasm
- belief in people and teamwork
- willingness to take risks
- devotion to long-term growth rather than short-term profit
- commitment to excellence
- readiness
- virtue
- vision

→ It's much easier to express yourself than to deny yourself. And much more rewarding, too.

cfr. KORN / FERRY

23

- Not surrendering to the context, but mastering it, and eventually conquering it.
FIVE QUALITIES IN A NEW LEADER:
'technical competence'
people skills
conceptual skills
judgement and taste
character

Great leaders are people who understand the prevailing culture, even though much of the culture is latent, existing only in people's minds and dreams, or their unconscious.
But understanding is only the first step. The great leaders are those who take the next step, to change the culture.

it's only through changing something that one truly comes to understand it.

Chaos is the beginning, not the end. Chaos is the source of energy and momentum.

So:
- Think strategically and invest in the future – but keep the numbers up
- Be entrepreneurial and take risks – but don't cost the business anything by failing
- Continue to do everything you're currently doing but better – and spend more time communicating with employees, serving on teams, and launching new projects.
- Know every detail of your business – but delegate more responsibility to others
- Become passionately dedicated to "visions" and fanatically committed to carrying them out – but be flexible, responsive, and able to change direction quickly
- Speak up, be a leader, set the direction – but be participative, listen well, cooperate
- Throw yourself wholeheartedly into the entrepreneurial game and the long hours it takes – and stay fit
- Succeed, succeed, succeed – and raise terrific children

24

10 FACTORS FOR COPING WITH CHANGE, FORGING A NEW FUTURE, AND CREATING LEARNING ORGANISATIONS:

(1) leaders manage the dream. Create a compelling vision, one that takes people to a new place, and then translate that vision into reality
[define the mission ⇒ first, define reality; last, say thank you; in between you're a servant]
- Communicating the vision (40 % of time communicating the organisation's credo ⇒ "challenge meetings" going through the credo lines to see what changes need to be made)
make company 1% better in 100 different ways than its competitors
create a model with identify [illegible] 'moments of truth'
- Recruiting meticulously
- Rewarding
- Retraining
- Reorganizing → not △ but ○○○ – organisational space i.e. special, [illegible] project (CPH → NYC)
↓ involve all people who have to do with this segment in a SELF-MANAGED, AUTONOMOUS WORK GROUP WITH A GAIN-SHARING PLAN
(the whole corporation structured in terms of small, egalitarian groups)
(participating in whatever increment of profits that particular [illegible] brings in)

- Tomorrow's person leads through a vision, a shared set of values, a shared objective. The defining quality of a leader IS THE CAPACITY TO CREATE AND REALIZE A VISION. The responsibility is to transform the vision into reality. In doing so, he transforms his dominion [sector/field].

(2) leaders embrace error. Be not afraid to make mistakes, and admit them you do. This creates an atmosphere in which risk taking is encouraged. The only mistake is to do nothing. Failure is not the crime. Low aim is.

8

Anyone in business (as in personal life) who simply accepts conventional wisdom may reach the top of a bureaucratic organization, but he will never use his particular talents to their fullest, and if he ever confronts his life, he will suffer the shock of failed aspirations – at the very least.

↳ Innovative learning must replace maintenance / shock learning. The principal components of innovative learning are:

- Anticipation (being active and imaginative rather than habitual)
- learning by listening to others
- Participation: shaping events

It implies that you trust yourself, that you be self-directed in life and work. In innovative learning, one must not only recognize existing contexts, but be capable of imagining future contexts. You have to be able to envision in fairly concrete terms what ought to be done or what you want to do or where you want to go. A certain amount of conceptualization is required. It's not unlike planning a trip. First you have to figure out where you want to go. Then you have to devise a mode of transportation (if no one's done the journey before, you may have to make it up). You have to establish a certain amount of flexibility in organizing people to go with you. You have to know from the beginning how much baggage you have to haul, and how light you can travel. It requires a combination of historical perspective, vision, and institutional appreciation – what its texture is, what its possibilities are.

Innovative learning is a dialogue that begins with curiosity and is fueled by knowledge, leading to understanding. We become free to express ourselves, rather than endlessly trying to prove ourselves. We anticipate things as they can be, and participate in making things happen.

There is nothing you can do about your early life now, except to understand it. You can, however, do everything about the rest of your life. A combination of MOTIVATION, CHARACTER, AND OPPORTUNITY. Most talent remains undeveloped.

10

The essence of creativity is not the possession of some special talent, it is much more the ability to play. If you can't take the risk of saying or doing something wrong, your creativity goes right out of the window. Mistakes are not 'bad', but they are virtually synonymous with growth and progress.

↳ You have to get 80 or 85 % of information and analysis and then take your best shot and go on to something else. You'll blow it now and then, but you also develop a momentum and a pace that gets to be exciting.

↳ It's ok to make mistakes, as long as you make them in good conscience and you're doing the best you can at that moment. I'm not afraid to make a mistake, and I'm not afraid to say afterward, 'Boy, that was a mistake. Let's try something else.' I think that wins people over. I can also say, 'You have a better idea than I have. Let's do your idea.'

↳ Create a climate that encourages people to take risks. All business is making decisions, and if you don't make decisions, you won't have any failures. The hardest job I have is getting people to make decisions. If you make that same decision wrong again, I'll fire you. But I hope you'll make a lot of others, and that you'll understand there are going to be more failures than successes. It's important to encourage dissent and embrace error.

If you haven't failed, you haven't tried very hard. There are lessons in everything, and if you are fully deployed, you will learn most of them. Experiences aren't truly yours until you think about them, analyze them, examine them, question them, reflect on them, and finally understand them. Use your experiences. Be the designer.

The primary pull is the vision. You are simply passionately compelled to make it come about. A compelling vision combined with a unique ability to manage risk is the magic behind successful entrepreneurs.

une

Jenn
grie
to sa
she now owns, writes
And

Y

live. A
What

If yo
to the
busin
third
chief
profit

"I'm
who v
before she took the top job. "I'd always
wante
leapt a

Wea
a drap
secon
office
pany
Foster
cance

"Th
what I
But I
don't
she sa
very s
in the

Just
Chester in the northwest of England,
ITC sp
the C
other
Briton
want s

Fou
for ho
event
and E
findin
best s
might
Cliff ir
ten ite

The
hotel,
area t
pets a
rated with beach themes and motiva-
tional quotations such as Oscar Wilde's
"I have the simplest tastes. I am always

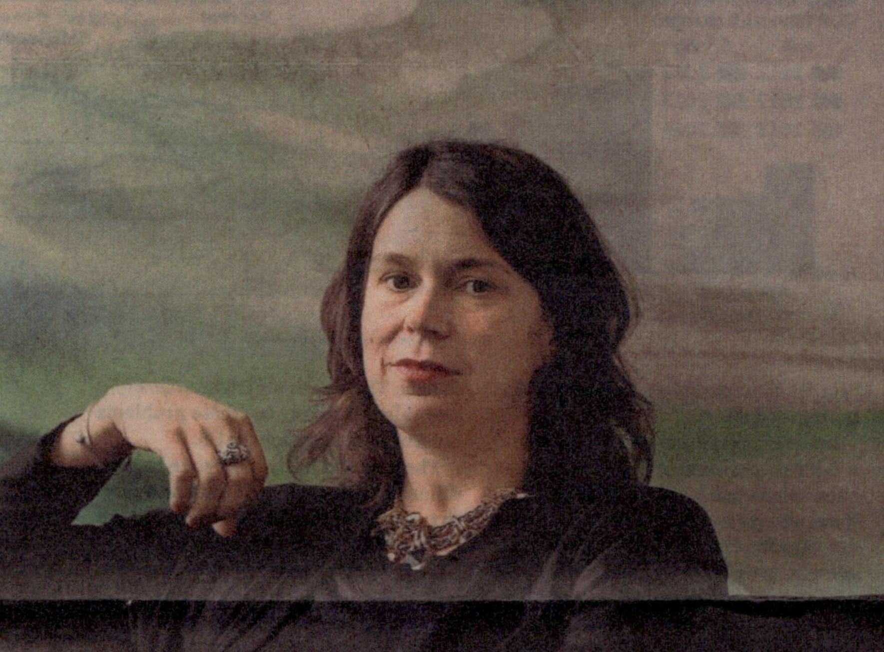

tumultuous first few months
executive.

...ing how she came to take over
Foster, she says: "He gave me
...est thing anybody could have
– belief . . . He trusted me with
...ion and with his children's
...ce. He was always incredibly
...he just had a gut feeling I could
do it and he went with it."

...time of Mr Foster's death, the
had taken hold and bookings
...tkinson had to win over staff
...king 44 out of 140 redundant.
...ery difficult. You have to put
... of the many above those of the
... was about the business surviv-
...e time, people question and
they come to respect you if you
...he right reasons," she says. "It
...aking of me, really."

Selling up, moving on

...ort of June Foster, widow of the
...f ITC Luxury Travel, has been
...nnifer Atkinson. "[Jennifer] has
...ethos but changed what was
... keep up with the times," Mrs
Foster says. In August Mrs Foster, whose
three children did not want to be
involved in the business, agreed to sell

She had to contend with RBS's Global Restructuring Group, the arm of the troubled lender that dealt with clients it deemed to be struggling. The unit is being shut down after criticism of the way it treated small corporate customers, with claims it forced some out of business by levying extra charges and withdrawing lending, though RBS has denied any wrongdoing. The Scottish bank was itself under huge pressure to collect bad debts.

"I still have the scars," Ms Atkinson says, recalling the constant phone calls and demands for detailed financial information. "It wasn't a great experience. But we traded out of a bad situation very quickly."

Although ITC had no debt, it collected millions in advance payments from credit cards. Its bank would have been liable to repay these had ITC gone bankrupt but Ms Atkinson says the company was always paid before settling bills with hotels and airlines so cash flow was not a problem.

After hitting a low of 80, staff numbers are back above 100. Turnover has increased from £33m in 2008 to £47m in 2014, with £1.4m earnings before interest, tax, depreciation and amorti-

Paul Pindar, who s
chief executive of Cap
outsourced service pr
has acquired a stake a
chairman from Mrs F
who bought more tha
while expanding Capit
will buy complementa

When Mr Pindar
treated themselves
cruise in the Caribbe
expected to return h
ness deal. But Ms Atkir
was on board and pit
dinner. "I never miss
says Ms Atkinson, wh
ing for 12 months for f
agement buyout of ITC

The luxury travel
mented and many ow
looking to retire. Saga,
cialist, recently bough
online luxury travel ag

While the travel s
online – ITC has one hi
Chester – Ms Atkinson
scope for traditional s
term relationships. "
get better prices book
don't. We have the v
counts at the very be

6 – After every encounter & communication, leave the customer feeling better about (her)himself and the world around them than they were when you got there → LIFT

Also – think – whom would you rather be selling to – a skeptical & pessimistic person or an accepting & optimistic person?

CREATE THE TRIBE YOUR DESIRED CUSTOMERS ARE EAGER TO BE A MEMBER OF

→ the affluent's devotion to membership in smaller & smaller elite and therefore profoundly exclusionary tribes – remember

Include these forces [validation of superiority] & fully incorporate them into your marketing

7 – Emotional Factors for the affluent:

- Insecurity
- Fear of being found failures
- Desperate not to commit a faux pas / acceptance validation
- Feeling emotional emptiness
- Giving selves respect & recognition for hard work through purchasing
- What's the point of being rich → pride & model from / of exclusive cliques

Give serious thought to how you present your services, business & products in sync with these

8 – Break the chains that bind in your own mind. Re-assess what you are doing, for whom, at what level.

Starbucks does not define itself as a coffee shop or a coffee house. It describes itself as being in the "third-place business" –

In short, the price is (not tied) to its product; but to that experience

Somewhere in the process there is the opportunity to alter the experience and the way the buyer FEELS about it. It begins with determining the feelings you want to create for the buyer: security & peace of mind & validation

"How can you make two months' salary last forever?" What DeBeers did for diamonds, anyone can do for anything. De Beers recognized the problem with its mundane commodity, so it took the radical move of ignoring inherent value altogether, and made the product ritualistic & metaphoric, its purchase mandatory without practical purpose

MARKETING TO VALUES IS MORE POWERFUL THAN THE MARKETING OF PRODUCTS

→ It's about selling aspirations & emotionally fulfillments with finesse

9 – Make Yourself Magnetic to the

- Develop, display & convey a PROFOUND POSITION OF EXPERTISE, good judgement, understanding, professional & competence.

  THE MOST TRUSTWORTHY OF ADVISORS

- Relieve your affluent clients of time pressure, anxiety, day-to-day hassle.

  CREATE PRIVILEGE & LUXURY-LEVEL GAIN FOR THEM

- Give them Acceptance, Approval, and They are extremely responsive to those who celebrate their success & respect as earned.

  Take PHILOSOPHICAL POSITIONS THAT COUNTER the constant criticism they receive from most other quarters.

→ BUT MAKE SURE THAT:

1. Decide EXACTLY who you want as a customer
2. Be sure you have positioned your offer for that customer

Profit First – Mike Michalowicz

Revenue is vanity, profit is sanity, and cash is king

→ your job is to maximize profit, regardless of the current size of your business

→ Focus on profit, and you'll discover new ways to both streamline & grow your business. It doesn't work the other way around.

Growing first and hoping to find profit in the process is not the way. REVERSE ENGINEER THE PROFIT. Take profit first. You need to fix profit first, Then grow.

FIGURE OUT THE THINGS THAT MAKE PROFIT AND DUMP THE THINGS THAT DON'T. When you focus on profit first, you inevitably figure out how to make profit consistently.

Most of the time, we can't discern profitable income from debt-generating income.

BE THE WORLD'S BEST AT ONE THING, mastering the process of delivering perfectly and super-efficiently; don't end up doing a greater variety of things and becoming less and less efficient at each step

10 – Redraw your map. Focus more on the ideal customer than on self-imposed limitations

The more affluent the customer / client, the less concerned with convenience and the more s/he is willing to conduct business at a distance, import from afar, or travel to places to get exactly what s/he wants and what s/he believes to be the best of a category.

The most valuable asset is a LIST of high-value customers and prospective customers who invite and welcome communication from you

→ All wealth is derived from business BASED ON SYSTEMS. Doing perhaps boring but diligent work, developing a system that produces consistent results, and sticking to it

→ Have an operation system but also a more valuable marketing systems. Spend more per prospective customer

Alter your 'advertising' from being service- or product-directed to be CUSTOMER / CLIENT-DIRECTED

↓

Build a database of people who've stepped forward, raised their hands, and identified themselves as interested prospects.

11 – The "seven" Pillars of Authority Marketing

- The higher up in income you go, the more you're paid for WHO YOU ARE, rather than what you do

  Or, affluent individuals will be drawn in to what you do by who you are. Your background, story, and authority credentials will drive the conversation far more than simply stating what you do.

  To get on the radar of affluent people, you need to author a book. You will better understand the rationale behind authority. Writing a book AIMED AT YOUR TARGET AUDIENCE

12 – When producing a story that includes testimonials, "heroes", START WITH THE END IN MIND.

What is your objective for this story? Is it indoctrination of your principles? Is it to help current customers to buy more? Is it to help prospective clients overcome an objection? Is it to help people see that your service worked for someone just like them?

→ Keep your objective and your target reader in mind as you write

→ Include elements that make your "hero" likable and relatable

→ Be transparent / credible re difficulties / stumbles / solutions / advances

→ Point you / your service as the guide and give a plan or ideas for the reader to follow

Ultimately you want to wrap up the story with the transformation of your 'hero'. Paint a picture of what the reader can experience, too

13 – To be successful as a coach or consultant you must have an "info business" at the front end

This gets to a view of selling as performance art. As such it has to be planned, scripted, physically choreographed, rehearsed and performed.

DESIGN THE MOST EFFECTIVE LANGUAGE AND CHOREOGRAPHY POSSIBLE, and INSIST ON ITS IMPLEMENTATION

→ Figure out the biggest & most common 'problems' your clients experience when it comes to your "thing"

→ Offer some form of consultation where you address all those issues

→ Talk about the problems in your marketing. Show the client you understand them

→ Position yourself as the expert. Position your consultation as the solution to their problems

If you can transform their experience you're on to a winner.

Make your business about something. TAKE A STAND FOR SOMETHING. Bring to it your ideas, convictions & values

Authority = Expertise × Celebrity → High visibility

ACE Formula

Few understand the power of PERSONAL BRAND, as opposed to corporate brand. Authority levels the playing field. By focusing your attention on your authority, you essentially become your own individual brand.

This is even true in big business. People aren't buying from Berkshire Hathaway, they are buying Warren Buffett. People buy from people, regardless of the industry.

→ INVEST IN BUILDING THE INDIVIDUAL AUTHORITY OF ITS FIGUREHEAD

If the prospect doesn't trust you, they will not buy from you. Authority accelerates trust.

By building authority through third-party affirmation of your skills, you create the right perception — NOTE: IN THE EYES OF THE PEOPLE WHO CAN AND WILL GIVE YOU MONEY. Narrow the focus to those you can do business with.

- PR / Media / Speaking

The media agenda is to create compelling stories that their viewers / listeners / readers want to consume. You must become part & parcel to the compelling stories that media outlets want to tell, THEN they will want to feature you

When you share your thought leadership on stage, you are perceived as an authority by your listeners, and convey authority objectively. You don't speak for the sake of speaker fees, but for the sake of putting yourself in front of the right people, who have the capacity to do business with you

- Events

If you pull people's attention away from their day-to-day to come to you and give you their undivided attention, you succeed in building your authority

→ BE CLIENT-CENTRIC, NOT COMPANY-CENTRIC

The (affluent) client doesn't care about your story. They care about their own.

made it possible for Lowe's to run a business at this scale more efficiently. For instance, they write, it has allowed the group to employ directly more truckers because it could monitor their movements more easily.

But apart from the privacy implications of constantly monitoring, it is not realistic for many organisations, from banks to accountancy groups, to impose such large-scale oversight on staff whose work is more flexible or cerebral. For companies that need to put "boots on the ground" — such as G4S, the world's third largest listed private-sector employer with 618,000 employees in six continents, or Sodexo, with more than 420,000 workers in 80 countries — it may be simply impractical. Instead, companies must use structural means to maintain control.

Initially, most companies are led by the founder and a small team. But as they grow, the need to create a structure becomes more pressing.

Growth spurt

As they grew into multinationals, for instance, big companies such as Unilever, the consumer products group, tended to work on the basis of decentralised country managers reporting up

Mintzberg, the management calls Mr Gulliver's reasoning "You can't excuse [scan- saying we have so many es. You . . . have got to be on nd to have a sense of what your ion is all about."

research, Professor Mintzberg dowed John Cleghorn, then cutive of Royal Bank of Canada,

Too b manage

'Can I know what every one of 257,000 people is doing? Clearly I can't'

Stuart Gulliver, pictured

'You can't excuse scandals by saying we have so many employees. You . . . have got to be on the ground to have a sense of what your organisation is all about'

Henry Mintzberg, management writer

'Wars are won not

hen relatively simple factories expand.

llel, the limited liability com-

icism for mishandling some contracts, last year decided to focus only on public sector work. But G4S, which has come

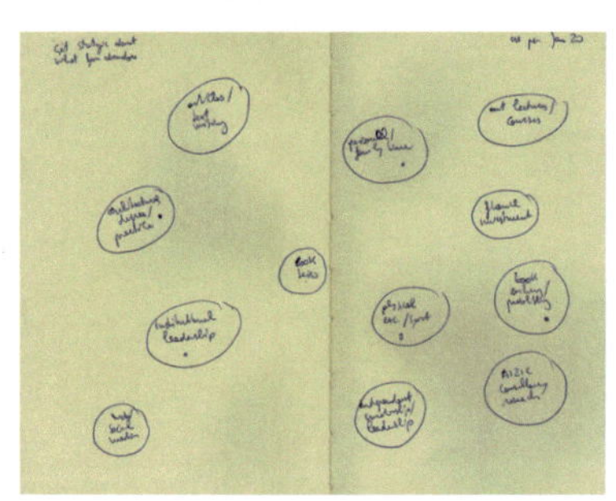

5

- There's no better way to learn something, and become an expert at it, than to have to teach it.

IN SHORT, forget your job title and forget your job description. STARTING TODAY, YOU'VE GOT TO FIGURE OUT WHAT EXCEPTIONAL EXPERTISE YOU'RE GOING TO MASTER THAT WILL PROVIDE REAL VALUE TO YOUR NETWORK AND YOUR COMPANY.

How do you start?

- Find someone who has already connected the dots and become an expert of their content.
- Connect the dots on your own.

1. Get out in front and analyze the trends and opportunities ON THE CUTTING EDGE. Shape a foresight that gives you and your business the flexibility to adapt to change. Trend spotters, knowledge brokers, change agents; identify the people in your business who always seem to be out in front, and use all the relationship skills you have to connect with them. Read everything you can. Create a carefully curated news feed. Eventually, all this knowledge will build on itself, and you'll start making connections others aren't.
2. Ask seemingly stupid questions. If you ask questions that are like no other, you get results that are unlike any that the world has seen. Greatest innovations come from that.
3. Know yourself and your talent. Develop an expertise that highlights your strengths to overcome your weaknesses. DO NOT WORK OBSESSIVELY ON THE SKILLS AND TALENTS I LACK, BUT FOCUS AND CULTIVATE MY STRENGTHS SO THAT MY WEAKNESSES MATTER LESS. 80/20 RULE.
4. Always learn. You have to learn more to earn more. All content creators are readers, or at least deep questioners or connectionalists. Create a program of self-development, incl. books & magazines, curated news feeds, 5x conferences a year, 1x course a year, developing relationships with the leaders in my field.

16

6. Expose yourself to unusual experiences. Stimulate your creativity. Different experiences give rise to different tools. Learn about things that are out of the mainstream. Take a deep and boundless curiosity about things outside your profession and comfort zone.
7. Don't get discouraged. Face rejections on a regular basis in a holistic way. They're part of your journey. If you're going to be creative, cutting edge, out of the mainstream, you'd better get used to rockin' the boat. Passion keeps you going through the rough times, come hell or high water — and hell will come. Be persistent and committed through cultural changes and challenges. Focus on the results and keep your eyes open for what is happening on the edges of your industry.
8. Know the new technology. You don't need to be a technologist, but you do need to understand the impact of technology on your business and be able to leverage it to your benefit. Adopt a tech geek, or at least hire / sire one.
9. Develop a niche. Individuals that gain renown establish themselves within a carefully selected market niche that they can realistically hope to dominate. Choose to focus on the one area that is least attended to.
10. Follow the money. Creativity is worthless if it can't be applied. MANTRA: This will MAKE US MORE MONEY. The life blood of any company is sales and cash flow. All great ideas are meaningless in business until someone pays for them.

- Powerful content communicated in a compelling story can energize your network to help you achieve your mission.

The most gripping stories are those COVERED WITH IDENTITY — who we are, where we've come from, and where we're going. They tap into something common to all people. The more we care for the happiness of others through wellbeing, beauty and meaningful relationship, the greater our own sense of wellbeing becomes. Appeal to your cause by appealing to everyone's cause.

FIGURE OUT HOW TO SPIN YOUR YARN IN A FASHION THAT (A) IS SIMPLE TO UNDERSTAND

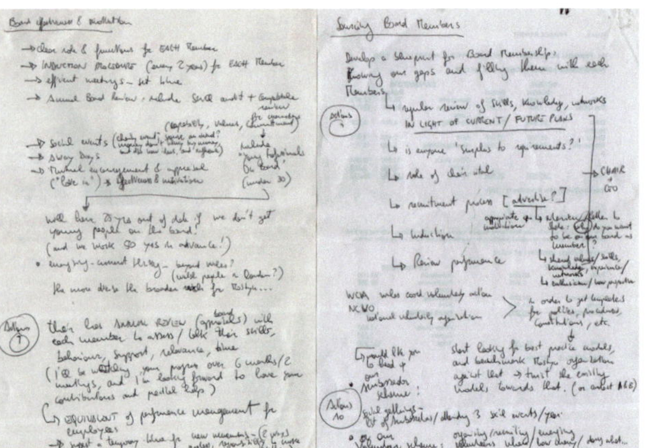

16

… serendipity — "How to get lucky".
… a social framework early in career — diversity!
… creates talent, forging projects of mutual passion with others. [illegible]
… yourself firmly at the geographic center of your business. [illegible]
… a highly visible leader in philanthropic organizations and associations.
… will opportunities.

… luck serendipity. CHANGE IS THE CONSTANT. It's not what you know; it's … you're able to know the new and right things:

… FOSTER JUXTAPOSITIONS OF SMART PEOPLE WHO WOULD NORMALLY NEVER HAVE … UNITY TO TALK TO ONE ANOTHER BUT IF THEY DID WOULD CREATE AMAZING …

… Collect art. I am a people collector. Surround yourself with geniuses. … on "to-dos" and more on "to-meets". And get busy. Take action.

… worth talking to and, even better, worth talking about … want to spend an hour eating lunch with this person? [the airport question]

question used to choose one person over a pool of equally talented candidates

schedule time into your schedule to keep up with what's going on in the world. NYT, WSJ, Guardian, Economist

People don't hire people they like, they hire people who they think can make them and their companies better: someone with an EXPANDED VIEW OF THE WORLD. Be aware of your intellectual property and what you have to say that others might benefit from.

… OTHERS, YOU HAVE TO SPEAK BEYOND YOURSELF. Get attention for your desire … the world. Expertise is your differentiation, the message that will make … and unique. Being known for something is respect. Have a unique POV.

Content is a cause — the unique subject matter on which you are the authority. What will set you apart is the relentlessness you bring to LEARNING and PRESENTING and SELLING your content.

Come up with the credible and unique Point of View that people are ready to buy.

1 — Immerse yourself in the subject. Become a voracious reader. Talk to specialists.
2 — Sometimes you can simply appropriate another person's innovative ideas and become a leader in distilling and applying those ideas. Other times, you have to develop the content from scratch — take all the disparate dots of information and connect them in a way others had not. Creativity is making connections that everyone else has almost thought of.
3 — Redefine your activity [e.g. a marketing company rather than a videogame company]. Realize how your customers may not be the end users, but, for instance, the companies who want access to end users. What you produce may be less a product than a medium itself, able to deliver / shape any kind of message one wanted to send.
4 — That's your unique Point of view. Perfect a resounding pitch.
5 — Get attention. Journalists are hungry for ideas. The story doesn't have to involve my company or me. I'm just building the credibility I'll need when the day comes to make my own pitch. Offer a great story. Create a story about your company and the ideas & controversies that readers / watchers will care about. That's your content. Then share it. You CANNOT outsource this to PR.

What if you are the brand?

SEE ABOVE — 5 POINTS. The same approach / process to make a business standing in the marketplace can be applied to make you noteworthy to your network & beyond. A UNIQUE POINT OF VIEW IS ONE OF THE ONLY WAYS TO ENSURE THAT FROM NOW ON YOU'LL HAVE A JOB.

- In our information economy, we frame our competitive advantage in terms of knowledge and innovation. TODAY'S market values CREATIVITY over mere competence, and EXPERTISE over general knowledge.

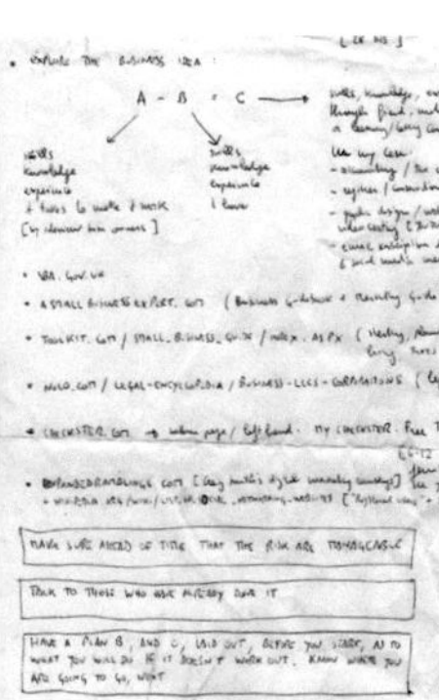

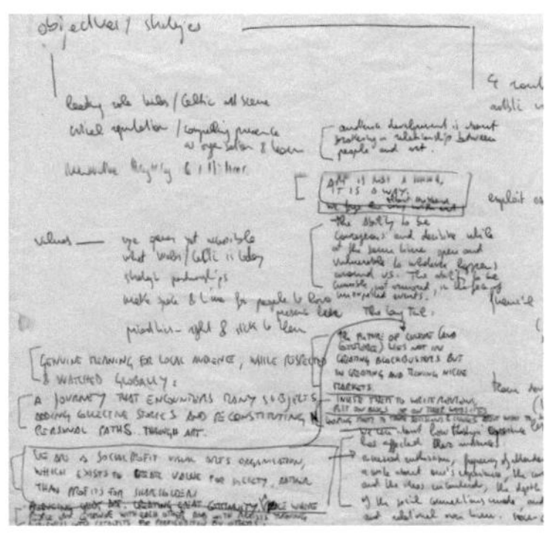

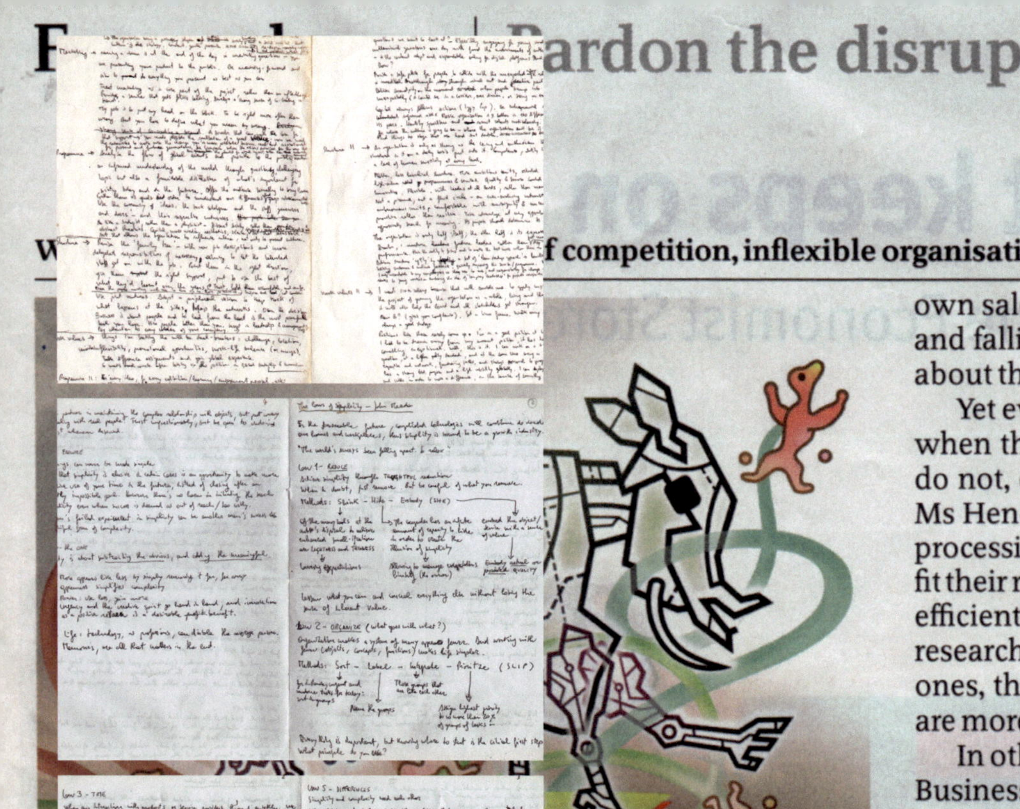

Pardon the disrupti

f competition, inflexible organisation

own sales a
and falling
about the l
Yet ever
when the t
do not, eco
Ms Hender
processing
fit their resp
efficiently
research. W
ones, this s
are more ra

In other research with Sarah Kaplan of the Whar Business, Ms Henderson considers why older firm pursue new technologies. Many of them have syster detect and respond to changing market conditions nologies. But they have also built up a system of inc sure employees meet existing goals. Systems design age consistency and efficiency in the production o goods or services might be a powerful deterrent to e tion or creative thinking about new markets, regard the corporate memos say.

One still might expect more adaptability give enough threat, argues Ms Henderson in another with Timothy Bresnahan of Stanford University Greenstein of Northwestern University. Establishe point out, can always set up loosely affiliated "entr

I for the new is the essence
ought it one of the nastier
q Schumpeter, an Austrian economist, cast "creative destruction" in more positive light, as the only route to sustained growth. In the 1990s Clayton Christensen, a professor at Harvard Business School, gave the notion a modern sheen with his theory of "disruptive innovation". The term is now everywhere. Uber is said to be disrupting th business, Cronuts are disrupting breakfast and Twitter is dis ing communication.

A disruptive innovation, in Mr Christensen's work, is a specific thing: a new technology that is inferior in certain res to existing ones, but has other desirable attributes. He cites inch floppy disks, which could store more data than smaller
b nted because they were too bi
e ters. By the same token, publi
o ere wrong-footed by the adve
o as initially of lower quality. S
d netheless ended up displacing
the size of a firm and its capa
i onship between the two. Yet t
i s ought to enjoy big advantage
w l employees, infrastructure a
r to share costs among produc
w e as capable as new entrants o
c Yet research by Rebecca Hend
o nds that the money old firms i
evolving industries devote to research brings much lower returns than the research budgets of their younger rivals.*

usin
cult
inno
l riva
com
elop
han
ecau
ame
bein
s in
ole, v
eso
con
ver.
, Jo
Wh
suggests that survival often comes down to what the erative commercialisation". Once it becomes clear

occupied by that notion at the moment: the only way to p

arke

omp

n "t

pape

s su

o ign

ill le

mn

ts. Y

adin

ter L

o ye

he m

ut b

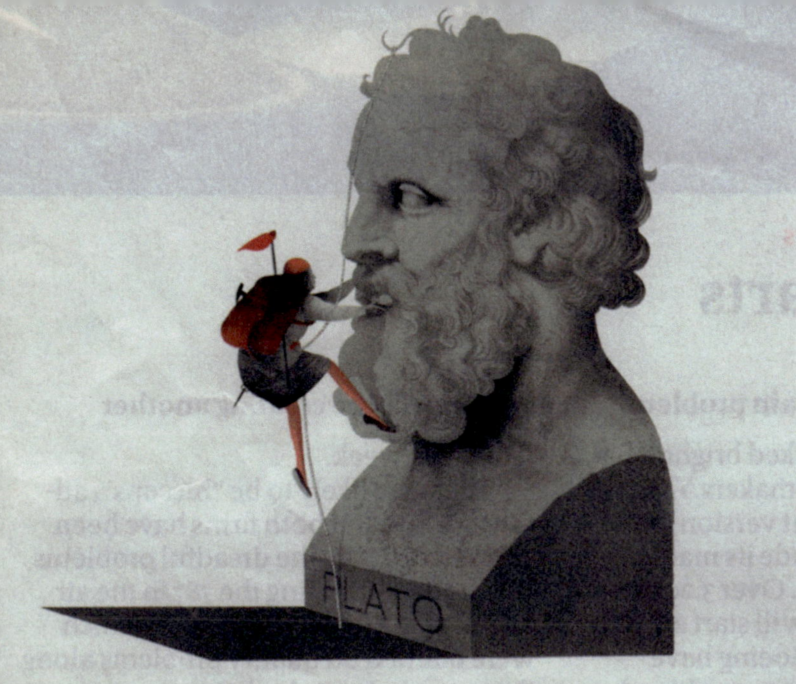

alliances with reference to marriage alliances in Jane Aust

Inward-bound courses would do something even m portant than this: they would provide high-flyers with b anchor and a refuge. High-flyers risk becoming so obsesse material success that they ignore their families or break t Philosophy-based courses would help executives overcon obsession with status symbols. It is difficult to measur worth in terms of how many toys you accumulate wh have immersed yourself in Plato. Distracted bosses wou benefit from leaving aside all those e-mails, tweets and Li updates to focus on a few things that truly matter.

IT IS hard to rise to the top in business without doing an outward-bound course. You spend a precious weekend in sweaty activity—kayaking, climbing, abseiling and the like. You endure lectures on testing character and building trust. And then you scarper home as fast as you can. These strange rituals may produce a few war stories to be told over a drink. But in general they do nothing more than enrich the companies that arrange them.

It is time to replace this rite of managerial passage with something much more powerful: inward-bound courses. Rather than grappling with nature, business leaders would grapple with big ideas. Rather than proving their leadership abilities by leading people across a ravine, they would do so by leading them across an intellectual chasm. The format would be simple. A handful of future leaders would gather in an isolated hotel and devote themselves to studying great books. They would be deprived of electronic distractions. During the day a tutor would ensure their noses stay in their tomes; in the would be encouraged to relate wh

It is easy to poke fun at the ide tives to read the classics. One coul up titles that might pique their int or "Accenture Shrugged", perhaps ality types: "Apologia Pro Vita Sua and "Crime and Punishment" fo imagining what Nietzschean co would look like. Or Kierkegaardia

Then there are practical questi sion-makers rather than cogitator time to spend on idle thought? Ho American CEOs studied philosop one of the founders of LinkedIn, at Oxford University and briefly c demic before choosing the life of executives clearly have enough tim fests such as Davos, where the corporate clichés about "stakeh Surely they have enough time for

Inward-bound courses would do wonders for "thought leadership". There are good reasons why the business world is so pre-

Looking for answers

The business world has been groping towards inward courses for years. Many successful CEOs have made a p preserving time for reflection: Bill Gates, when running soft, used to retreat to an isolated cottage for a week and m on a big subject; and Jack Welch set aside an hour a day fo tracted thinking at GE. Clay Christensen of Harvard B School was so shocked at how many of his contemporari ed up divorced or in prison that he devised a course calle

mos

k.

ions

me

s m

eter

thir

er a

nd

w p

o in

as t

hilo

s wh

hey

ecti

prov

npti

inte

hilo

und

offer the prospect of filling the mind while forming bon fellow-strivers. They are an idea whose time has come. ■

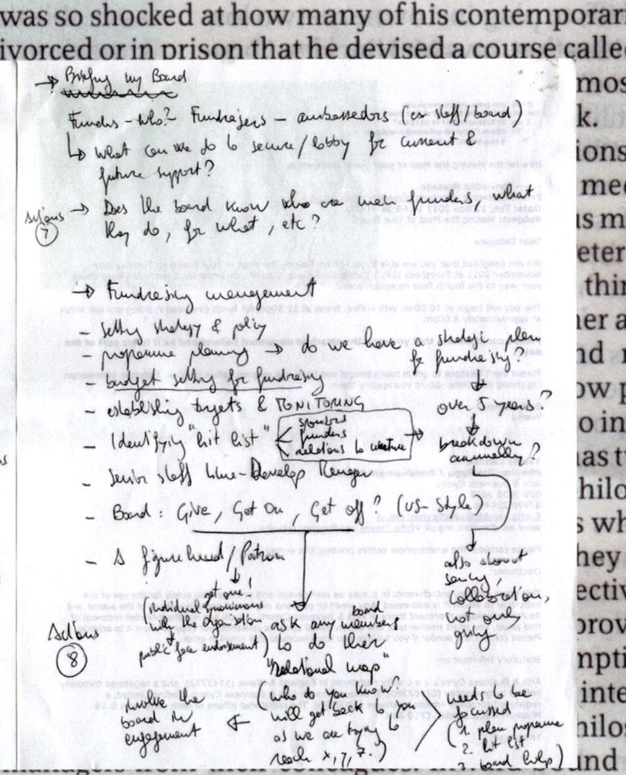

Public policy & Board

Fundraising & Board

Briefing my Board

Funders - who? Fundraisers - ambassadors (ex staff/board)

→ Fundraising management

- Setting strategy & policy

- Budget setting for fundraising

- Board: Give, Get On, Get off? (US-Style)

of space; and the uselessness of Europe's

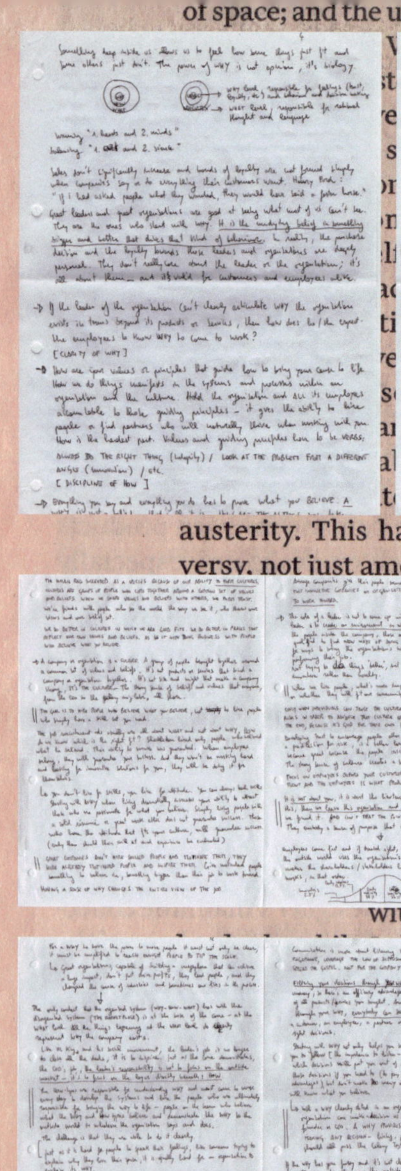

austerity. This has provoked controversy, not just among US venture capi-

with the sou

moved to the
n her father
usion physi-
ty. "I sound
cent Italian.
Italian and
cooked Italian." She does the same with

an literature
king on the
ests included
ize-winning
bed develop
nging, intel-
ay in Italian:
mamma soja
utiful in its
mother's eyes'). I say how great my parents are. Every mother is beautiful in their daughter's eyes."

Mazzucato studied history and international relations at Tufts University in Massachusetts but was increasingly drawn to economic history and theory, which she pursued at the New School for Social Research in New York, home to generations of radical intellectuals. Her doctorate was on technological change,

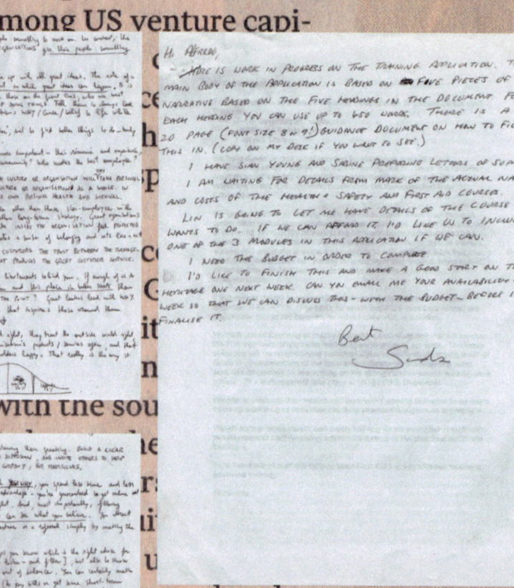

Euston Road, London NW1

Hi Alfredo,

Here is work in progress on the training application. The main body of the application is based on five pieces of narrative based on the five headings in the document. For each heading you can use up to 650 words. There is a 20 page (font size 8 or 9!) guidance document on how to fill this in. (copy on my desk if you want to see.)

I have Sian Young and Sabine preparing letters of support.

I am waiting for details from Mark of the actual nature and costs of the Health & Safety and First Aid courses.

Lin is going to let me have details of the course she wants to do. If we can afford it, I'd like us to include one of the 3 modules in this application if we can.

I need the budget in order to complete.

I'd like to finish this and make a good start on the heritage one next week. Can you email me your availability next week so that we can discuss this - with the budget - before I finalise it.

Best

Sendz

illy-Fumé x2 £80.00

2 £4.00

Total (including service) £177.50

An evening with Simon Schama

The art historian and FT contributing editor's upcoming book *The Face of Britain: A History of the Nation through its Portraits*

government spending would produc
ronger, more competitive, more inn
tive economies — a conclusion at od
with much of her research.

"So my mission was to change th
ve more sustai
h, rather tha
tive growth, the
nd where growt
. "If we actual
tries that hav
tion-led growt
ve governme
we square tha
discourse?"

As Mazzucato explains it, the trad-
tional way of framing the debate abou
wealth creation is to picture the privat
sector as a magnificent lion caged by th
public sector. Remove the bars, and th
lion roams and roars. In fact, she argue
private sector companies are rarel
lions; far more often they are kitten
Managers tend to be more concerne
with cutting costs, buying back thei
shares and maximising their shar

pimpini architetto
035223052 tel.fax.
3483559083
02509060162 | C.F. PMPGRL60M20A271N

~~Organisation~~ ~~Structural~~ & ~~Strategical~~ Approach

STRATEGICAL APPROACH

Teams within the institution can each be responsible for budget allocation and decision-making; ACCOUNTABLE but NOT micro-managed by the Director.
Injecting this level of autonomy directly creates ownership - an essential ingredient for entrepreneurial behaviour, and a yardstick for improving performance

We have all our money-budget documents, but where are all our time-budget documents?
Choosing how time is spent in the organisation is crucial - especially when we're drawing attention away from the core business to play around with something. BUDGETING TIME IS ESSENTIAL

We're talking about uniting people at an emotional level - belonging to a team that together is working to create better and more accessible public collections of contemporary art, and to lead the market on intelligence around collecting opening the access to private collections.

The SECRET IS IN KNOWING WHICH NICHE(S) WE'RE AN AUTHORITATIVE institutional member of, and finding the SPACE where that community resides.
Also, cultural institutions aren't limited to the one niche - we can project ourselves as CLUSTER of interconnecting brands/values appealing to different niche markets.

Our success depends on our ABILITY to continually IDENTIFY

ey ar
velop
rth.
thes
h lar
ut th
, as a
ilure.
," sh
crea
ecla
ion t
oal c
, an
ome
nicon
. "Yo

ven Silicon Valley's much
fabled tech entrepreneurs ar

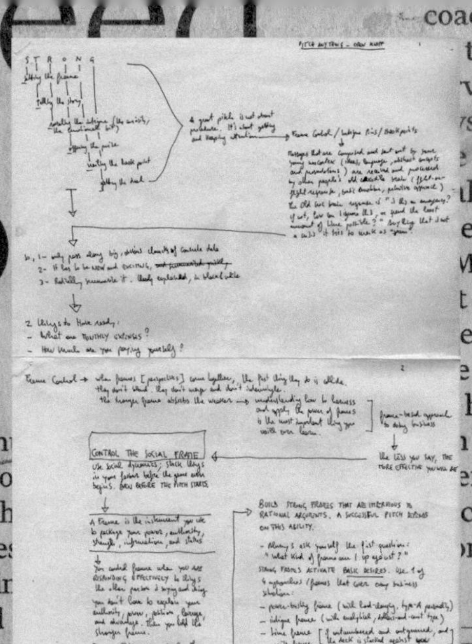

d m
ng o
nt h
nves
ed in
all
ent
eally
” she says. “It is an incredibly
mission-oriented role.”
of the original engines of Silicon
’s creativity, she argues, was the
se Advanced Research Projects
y (Darpa), founded by President
t Ei... following
arm... et Union’s
of t... Darpa, run
US... fense, has
pum... llars into
g-ed... as instru-
l in... internet.
ding... e publicly
l Na... Health has
l a similar role in nurturing the
harmaceuticals industry. The
nced Research Projects Agency-
y (Arpa-E), set up by President
k Obama and run by the US
tment of Energy, is designed to
ate green technology.
zucato points to the critical role
by government agencies in other
mies, such as China, Brazil, Ger-
Denmark, and Israel, where the
not just acting as a market regula-
is actively creating and shaping
ts. For instance, the Yozma prone in Israel that provided the fund-
d expertise to create the so-called
up nation”. “My whole point to
ss is, ‘Hello, if you want to make
in the future, you had better
stand where the profits are coming
This is a pro-business story. This is
out socialism,” she says.
arguments stray into more radi-
ritory as we discuss how the fruits

coach,” she says. Referring to a speech
the British prime minister to Con-
rvative party supporters in 2011, she
ys: “They are constantly told they are
problem. [David] Cameron was
lly explicit: civil servants are the
emies of enterprise’. That’s dumb.”
Mazzucato has a rare chance to help
t some of her theories into practice in
ew field: extraterrestrial space. She is
e of several economists advising Nasa
how the private and public sectors
n share their responsibilities and co-
erate in Low Earth Orbit (LEO). “It’s
cinating. It gave me goosebumps as
on as they talked to me about it.”

blanch when I register that the wine that Mazzucato ordered cost £40 a glass. For the record, it was a 2006 Pouilly-Fumé Blanc de Fume by Didier Dagueneau and it tasted pretty good. It is only later that I spot they have made a hash of the bill, failing to charge for several dishes (an oversight later settled by the FT).

As Mazzucato would doubtless have observed, the private sector does not do everything right.

John Thornhill is deputy editor of the FT

Innovation in the UK — what's the problem? See FT Weekend Magazine

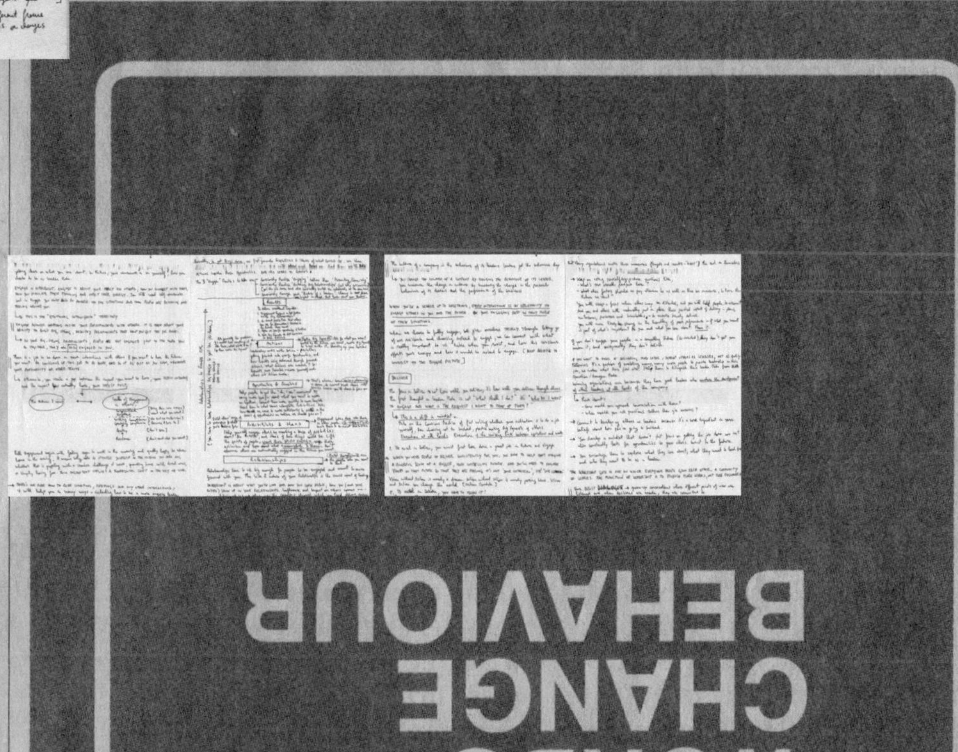

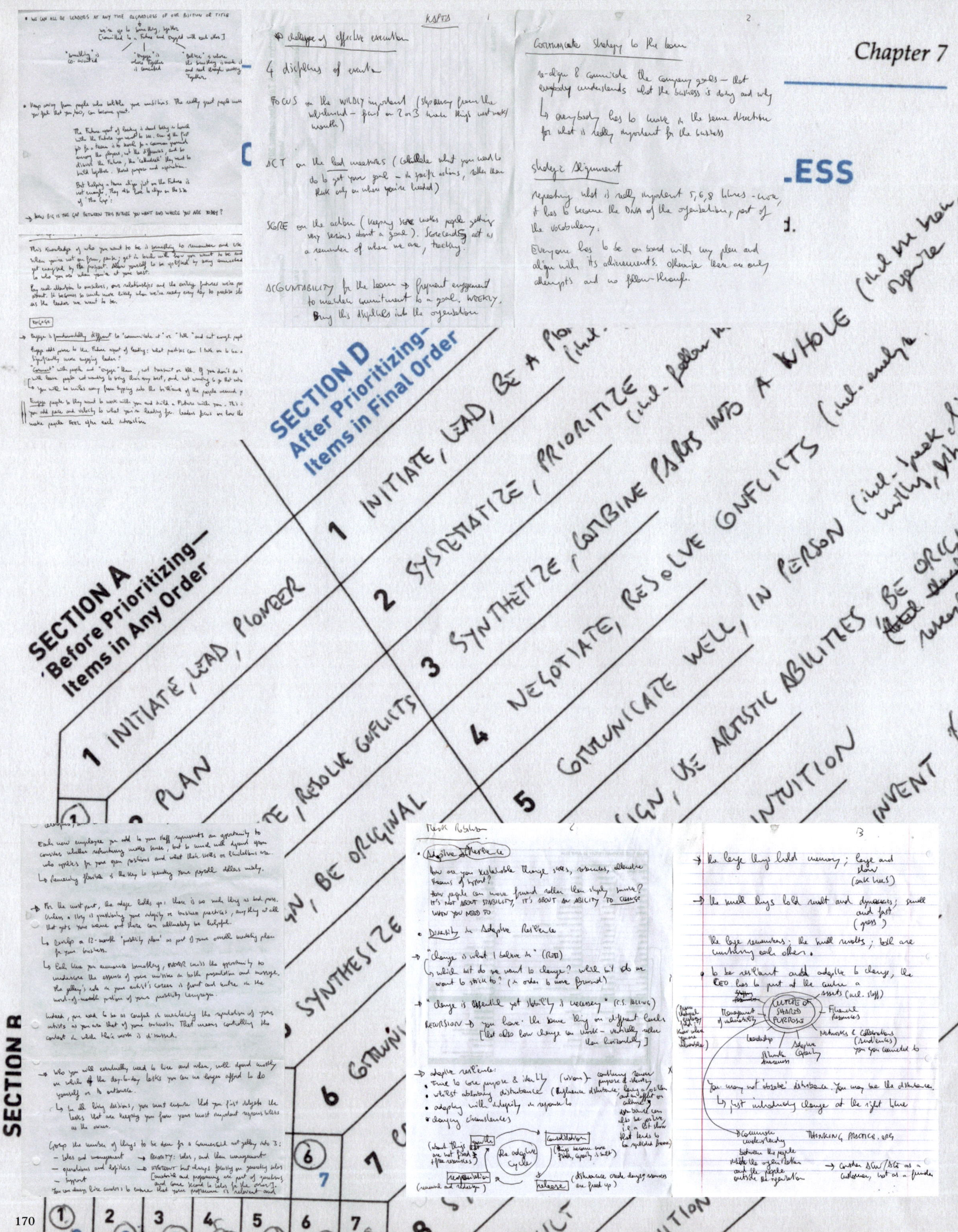
SECTION D
After Prioritizing—
Items in Final Order
1 INITIATE, LEAD, BE A PIO
2 SYSTEMATIZE, PRIORITIZE
3 SYNTHETIZE, COMBINE PARTS INTO A WHOLE
4 NEGOTIATE, RESOLVE CONFLICTS
5 COMMUNICATE WELL, IN PERSON
SECTION A
Before Prioritizing—
Items in Any Order
1 INITIATE, LEAD, PIONEER
PLAN
RESOLVE CONFLICTS
BE ORIGINAL
SYNTHESIZE
USE ARTISTIC ABILITIES
INTUITION
INVENT
SECTION B
Communicate strategy to the team
Strategic Alignment
CULTURE OF SHARED PURPOSE
THINKING PRACTICE.ORG

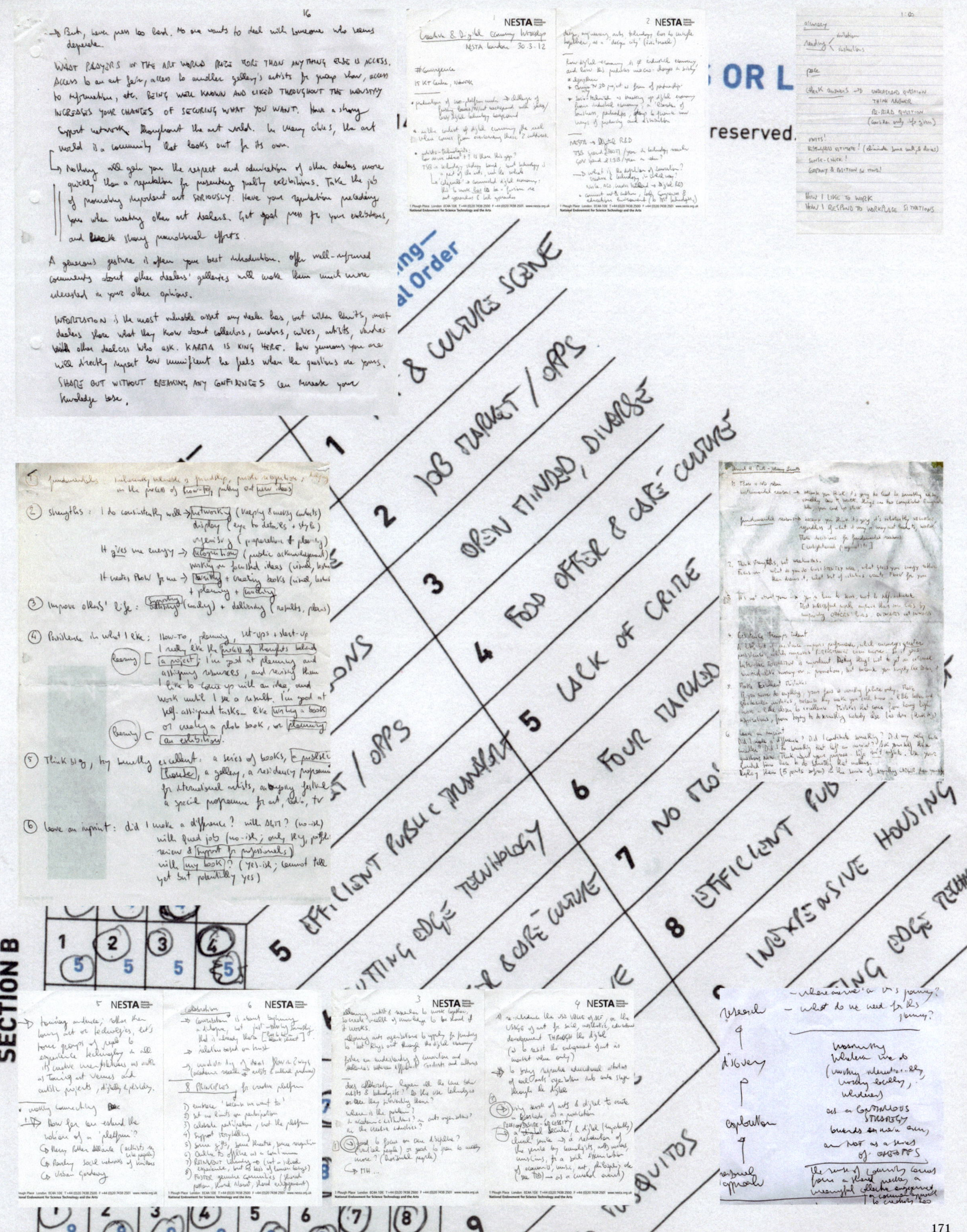
16
→ But, never press too hard. No one wants to deal with someone who seems desperate.
WHAT PRAYERS IN THE ART WORLD PRIZE MORE THAN ANYTHING ELSE IS ACCESS. Access to an art fair, access to another gallery's artists for group show, access to information, etc. BEING WELL KNOWN AND LIKED THROUGHOUT THE INDUSTRY INCREASES YOUR CHANCES OF SECURING WHAT YOU WANT. Have a strong support network throughout the art world. In many cities, the art world is a community that looks out for its own.
→ Nothing will gain you the respect and admiration of other dealers more quickly than a reputation for presenting quality exhibitions. Take the job of promoting important art SERIOUSLY. Have your reputation preceding you when meeting other art dealers. Get good press for your exhibitions, and show strong promotional efforts.
A generous gesture is often your best introduction. Offer well-informed comments about other dealers' galleries will make them much more interested in your other opinions.
INFORMATION is the most valuable asset any dealer has, but within limits, most dealers share what they know about collectors, curators, critics, artists, venues with other dealers who ask. KARMA IS KING HERE. How generous you are will directly impact how munificent he feels when the questions are yours.
SHARE OUT WITHOUT BREAKING ANY CONFIDENCES can increase your knowledge base.
OR L
reserved.
& CULTURE SCENE
1
2 JOB MARKET / OPPS
3 OPEN MINDED, DIVERSE
4 FOOD OFFER & CAFE CULTURE
5 LACK OF CRIME
6 FOUR MARKED
7 NO STO'
8 EFFICIENT PUB
INEXPENSIVE HOUSING
EFFICIENT PUBLIC TRANSPORT
CUTTING EDGE TECHNOLOGY
5 EFFICIENT
NO MOSQUITOS
SECTION B

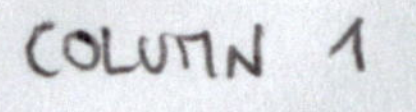

COLUMN 1	COLUMN 2	COLUMN 3	COLUMN 4
Places I have worked so far in my life	Kinds of people there who drove me nuts – describe what about them drove you nuts	Kinds of people I'd prefer not to have to work with – which is worst? next? (in order)	
Centre Sciale	Arrogant / So Tutto Io	1a MICROMANAGER	
Gimenedo	Lento / Slow		
	Burocrat / Pessecente		
	Too-ironic / sarcastic		
	Constant moaner	2a CONSTANTLY MOANING	2b. POSITIVE ATTITUDE PROBLEM-SOLVING
	Too polite / cruel		
	Self-obsessed / all about him or her		
	Bulley / Brioso		TEAM PLAYER
	Constantly cleaning up / team spirit "Offer"	3a	
Spenwater Ltd	Condescendent / feel patronising / superior		
CPS	Ineffective / Messy /		
		6a BUREAUCRAT	6b. CAN-DO ATTITUDE

Mind

This column will change your life

Your next big idea is still out there, says Oliver Burkeman

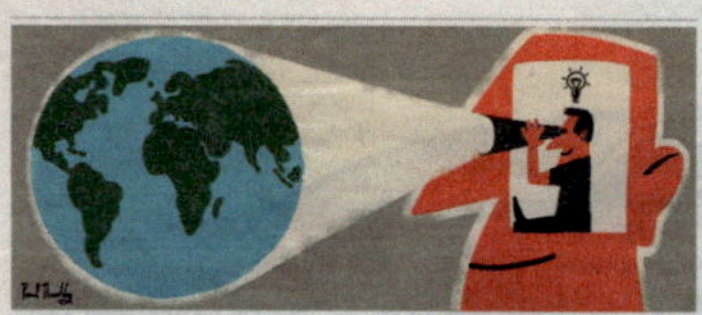

The problem with the world today, says the Silicon Valley investor Peter Thiel, is that we've lost faith that there's anything truly big or exciting left to be discovered. I've been rude about Thiel before, mainly because he's an easily mockable libertarian who plans to live to 120, or even "solve death", and wants to build floating cities far from the reach of government. Even so, in a month when the tech world is losing its mind about adding live video to Twitter (because if there's one thing we need, it's a reason to spend more time on Twitter), it's hard not to admire the scale of his ambition. …

92 Business books quarterly

Information technology

The right mix

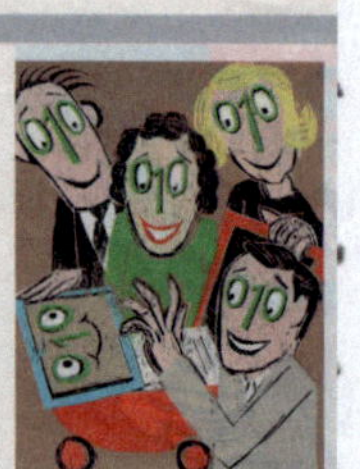
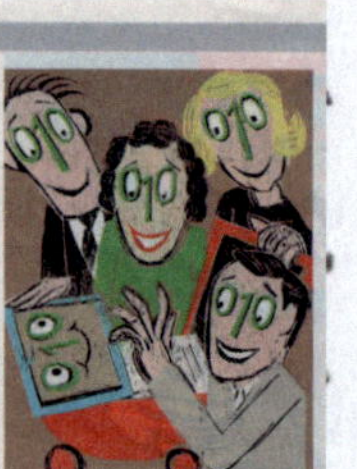

The Innovators: How a Group of Hackers, Geniuses and Geeks Created the Digital Revolution. By Walter Isaacson. *Simon & Schuster; 542 pages; $35 and £20*

Consult any encyclopedia and you will find Charles Babbage credited with having conceived the first automatic digital computer. Dig deeper, however, and it quickly becomes apparent that Babbage had a lot of help. …

We must make theatre accessible to everybody

Before the summer, we decided to knock down the walls to Sheffield Theatres. Not literally. But we knew we had to intensify our efforts to open up to our buildings to everyone. …

FFARWELIO / FAREWELL

CROESAWU / WELCOME

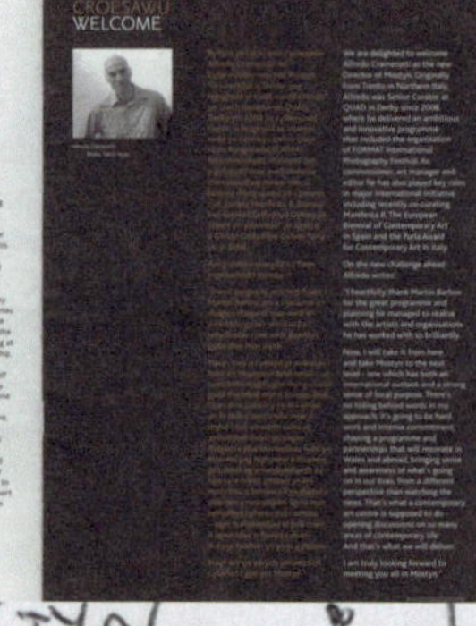

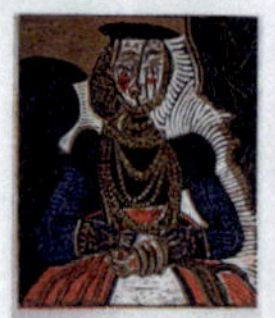
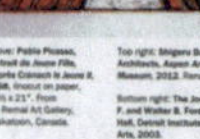
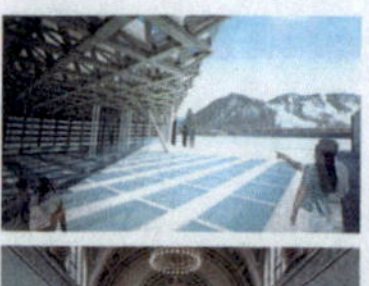

The Economist September 6th 2014

Schumpeter | Over the horizon

Three issues that should preoccupy managers in the next 50 years

For most people a 50th anniversary is an excuse for a party. For the men and women of McKinsey it is an excuse for a conference. Earlier this year the consulting firm decided to celebrate half a century of the *McKinsey Quarterly* by arranging a gathering of some of the world's leading business thinkers and asking them to look forward to the next 50 years of management. …

MATERIAL WORLD – *Material World* by Perri Lewis. Perri Lewis makes it her task to bring the world of making into the 21st century. With the help of luminaries from the worlds of art, craft, design and fashion she shares her knowledge and advice. RRP £18.99 *Our price £14.99*

START IT UP – *Start It up* by Luke Johnson. Learn how to find the right idea and get the best from everyone you meet on the way. Compressing two decades of success to reveal the realities of running your own business. RRP £12.99 *Our price £10.39*

30 Sec…

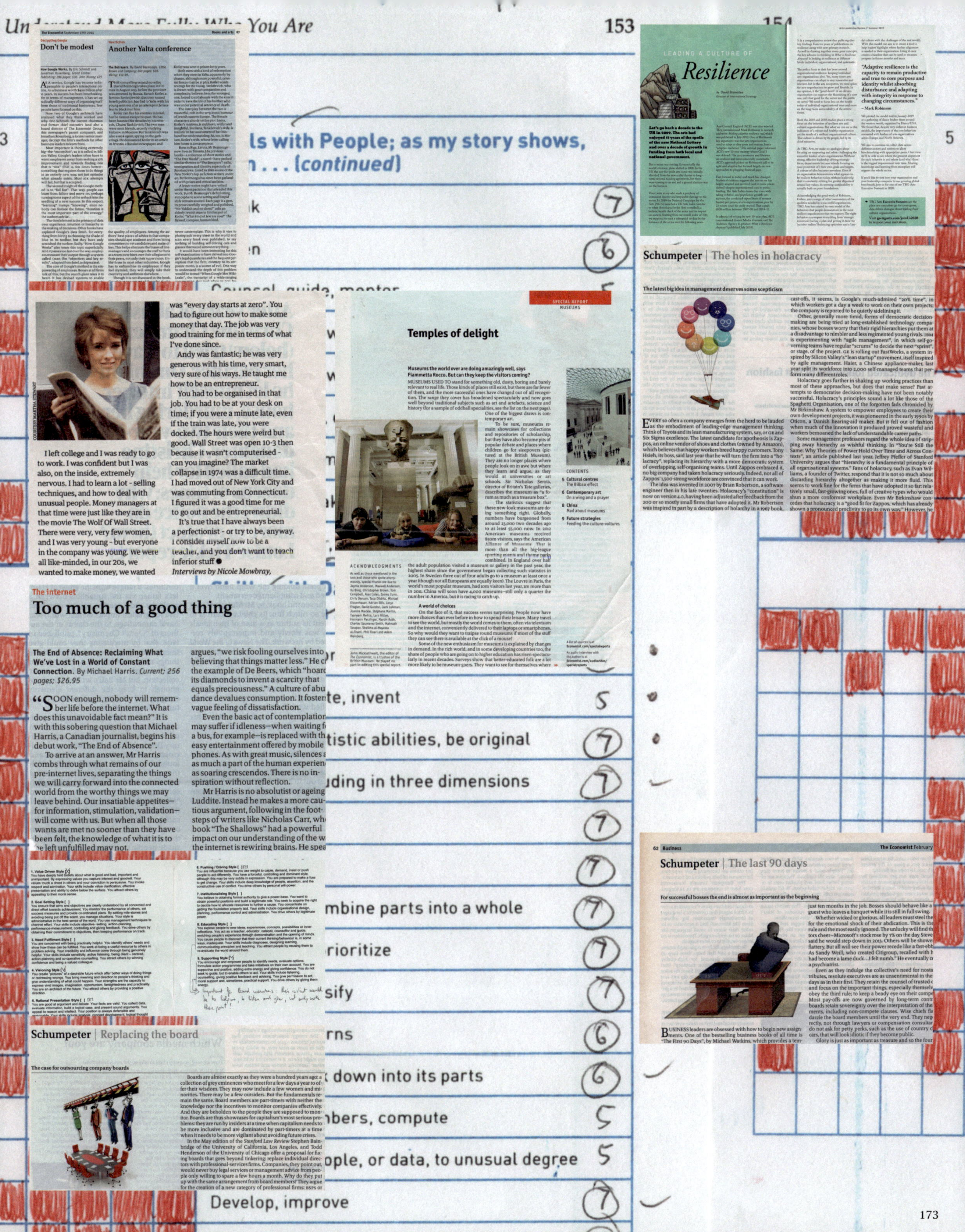
Don't be modest
Another Yalta conference
Leading a culture of Resilience
Schumpeter | The holes in holacracy
The latest big idea in management deserves some scepticism
Temples of delight
Too much of a good thing
The End of Absence: Reclaiming What We've Lost in a World of Constant Connection. By Michael Harris.
Schumpeter | Replacing the board
The case for outsourcing company boards
Schumpeter | The last 90 days
For successful bosses the end is almost as important as the beginning
Interviews by Nicole Mowbray
Develop, improve

Most meaningful ways to spend my life:

ancora presidente, dice: «In entrambe vige l'idea che sia meglio discutere su una domanda e lasciarla senza risposta piuttosto che dare una risposta senza discuterne».

WRITERREPLIES

Let the egos play on

Professional Manager catches up with **Itay Talgam**, author of *The Ignorant Maestro*

What inspired the book?
In addition to conducting symphony orchestras, I've spent the past 20 years meeting diverse groups of people – from businessmen to schoolchildren – to discuss the concept of leadership from this unique perspective of conducting. It's something different and I have found myself supplying this distant mirror where people can see themselves in a fresh light.

You mention how one of the similarities between businesses and orchestras is that you have lots of big egos. What's the best way to deal with this?
You don't want an orchestra or a conductor without an ego: it is something that drives you to unleash your potential – but it doesn't have to make you arrogant. The challenge is to find a way to let people express themselves, without putting aside this artistic ego, in a way that harmonises the contribution of so many other people. That's the leadership challenge.

So, as Carlos Kleiber said, you shouldn't over-manage the 'egos' but, rather, help them?
Exactly; just give them the best conditions possible so they can thrive – don't be too controlling.

You're a champion of the theory that 'an ignorant can teach another ignorant what he does not know himself'. How does that work?
The best way to support someone is to assume this position of ignorance. If you know where they are supposed to be going, you will lead them that way – and performance can never be anything other than what you imagine. Just think: what if you, out of this ignorance, have no expectation but to listen – and what you hear is something you could never have imagined. The role of a leader, much like that of an educator, is mostly to support the willpower of his people. If they encounter a problem, you have to find a way not to solve it for them: let them achieve it and help them not to give up.

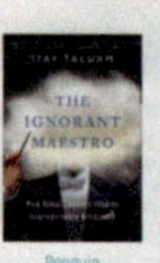

Penguin £14.99

What do you hope managers will achieve from your book?
There may be a wider spectrum of leadership or behaviour that managers never knew about. Don't approach the book from a defensive point of view but rather as an opportunity that will enlarge your scope of leadership skill. People think they should only change if they've been doing something wrong – and it comes with guilt or remorse. I want to avoid that negativity. If you are negative to yourself, you will be negative to those around you.

What can the music industry

VIEWPOINTS ON BUSINESS SENSE

"My job is to be chief cheerleader and chief storyteller..."

How do you go from flipping burgers to heading a communications giant? By not being in a hurry, says O2 CEO **Ronan Dunne**

AS THE HEAD of telecommunications giant O2, Ronan Dunne is paid to keep a lot of plates spinning. There are high-pressure pitches to big-name suppliers, mentoring and after-dinner speaking, all alongside running a national mobile network. But he definitely doesn't run the O2 arena. That's someone else's job – as he often has to remind people...

Things often don't go to plan
"Originally, I wanted to be a lawyer, but the year I sat my State Exams, the examiners went on strike. So Terry O'Rourke, then managing partner of Touche Ross (now Deloitte), contacted our college to see if any students caught in the strikes wanted to pursue accountancy rather than wait. I jumped at the offer and, at 22, was a qualified accountant. Now, I'm glad those examiners went on strike."

Find positivity in unlikely places
"O2 suffered one of its biggest network outages in July 2012. The network went down for 19 hours, leaving millions without service. Every media organisation in the country rang to see if I'd resigned. It was the toughest time of my life, but it was also a positive one. It got nasty on social media, but the good humour of our social-media team meant that customers started defending them."

Don't wait to do good
"In my early 20s, I thought I needed to be in a hurry for everything: personal development, career, financial gain. When I first embarked on my career path – which began in McDonald's, flipping burgers – I assumed that hard graft should be where I focused my energies, but spending time mentoring someone or volunteering on a local project is just as rewarding."

Go with it
"Being the boss can create some amusing situations. For example, when people you meet at business events assume that I'm the boss of the O2 (entertainment arena). After the third or fourth question about what a certain artist is really like or how many litres of beer are sold, I often don't have the heart to tell them what I really do. It's when they then ask for tickets to a sold-out gig that I have to own up."

VITAL STATISTICS

NAME Ronan Dunne
NATIONALITY Irish
EDUCATION Blackrock College, Ireland
FAMILY Wife and one daughter
CAREER 1981-87, Touche Ross (Deloitte); 1987-94, manager, Banque Nationale de Paris plc; 1994-96, deputy treasurer, Waste Management International plc; 1996-2000, director of treasury, NFC plc; 2000-01, head of strategic finance, Exel plc; 2001-05, joined O2 as head of finance; currently CEO at O2

Hire people better than you
"I used to be finance director here at O2 and when I was appointed chief executive, I made a point of hiring someone to take my place who would be better at it than I was. The important thing wasn't massaging my ego, it was about getting the right person for the job. When you do that, it liberates you to be the best leader you can be."

Be innovative
"In 2007, there was a lot of excitement about the new iPhone, and Apple was negotiating with a competitor over a big deal. The talks had been going on for months, but we had an opportunity to speak with them. The temptation was to go and talk figures. We decided to make life-size mock-ups of our retail stores and literally showed how we would engage with our customers and build an experience for them. It won us the deal."

Take your time
"Sometimes, when you get that first, big promotion, you're keen to show how you can make bold, quick decisions. But a far more empowering course of action can be to say: 'I can't make a decision on this, because I don't know all the facts.' I did this in my days as finance director, when someone came to us with a seemingly great way of offering our customers cheap international dialling. Our marketing people loved it, but it just didn't sit well with me. We took a different approach in the end and it worked out better for everyone."

AS TOLD TO SIMEON DE LA TORRE ILLUSTRATION GREYGOUAR

112

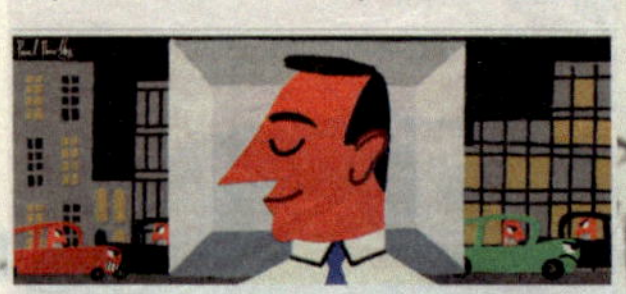

o like le g & ays

The Flower

"That One Piece of Paper"

PETAL 2
My Preferred Kinds of People to Work With:
1
2
3
4
5
My Holland Code:

PETAL 3
What I Can Do and Love to Do (My Favorite Transferable Skills):
1
2
3
4
5
6
7
8
9
10

PETAL 7
My Goal, Purpose, or Mission in Life (or my philosophy about life):

PETAL 1
My Favorite Knowledges or Fields of Interest:
1
2
3
4
5

PETAL 6
My Preferred Place(s) to Live (sooner or later):
1
2
3
(4)
(5)

PETAL 4
My Favorite Working Conditions:
1
2
3
4
5

PETAL 5
Level of Responsibility I'd Like:

My Preferred Salary Range:

Other Rewards Hoped For:

On the menu. Catering cash

Arts institutions dish up foodies' revenue

Theatres and museums are raising their restaurant game to attract bigger audiences

NATALIE WHITTLE

On Friday and Saturday evenings, Londoners can sit down to a three-course, £47.50 dinner to savour the likes of confit and grilled Welsh lamb belly with barbecued cucumber, cooked by a chef who has toiled at Michelin-starred stoves.

It sounds like any number of ambitious restaurants in the capital, but this one, with a pop-up menu created by winners of the Young British Foodies awards, is perched on the top floor of Tate Modern.

Like Somerset House, which has just installed chef Skye Gyngell's elegantly expensive Spring restaurant, or the National Theatre, whose ex-Ivy chef recently opened its new restaurant House, the Tate has spotted a way to reach revenue through its visitors' stomachs. Andrew Downs, operations manager for Tate Modern's in-house catering, says: "We want to let people know that as a gallery caterer we're doing some amazing things . . . We return profit to the gallery and [with the YBF menu] we hope to have our restaurant full of foodie people, keen to try the produce."

The month-long weekend YBF menu, by ex-Noma chef Tomos Parry, hints at a desire to experiment.

Chloe Scott-Moncrieff, co-founder of ...

'Twenty years ago there was a tendency for food to be at canteen level . . . it should be as serious as the art'

Skye Gyngell, who won a Michelin star at Petersham Nurseries, is behind the elegantly expensive Spring restaurant at Somerset House in London

life ... ums, ... als ... ely/really ... in a week ... get feedback

– through them, work with other people (trust)

It won't be popular – but if you follow your instincts rather than the pack, you'll avoid being trampled

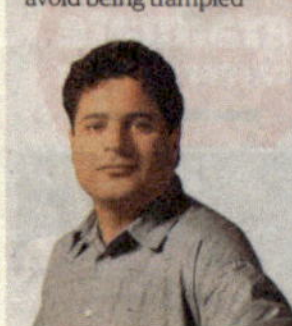

'Every person who tries to do real innovation is going to be tempted by money, greed and acceptance'

step and ask

Body & mind Oliver Burkeman

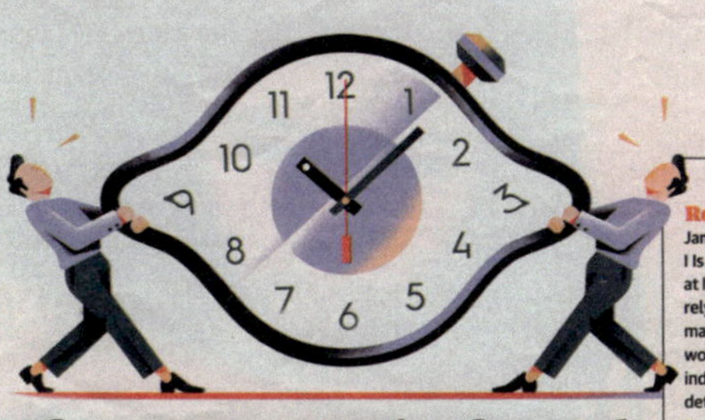

If you move a meeting forward, what does that really mean?

Read this
James Geary's book I Is An Other looks at how greatly we rely on metaphor to make sense of the world around us – indeed, it even helps determine what we see in the first place

We talk about time in confusing ways - as anyone who's ever tried to move a meeting with me "forward" a few days will be able to testify. With my dying breath, I'll maintain that this means moving it into the future, forward along the timeline I picture projecting into the distance from where I'm standing. Yet most people, I have learned, actually think that this means holding the meeting sooner, metaphorically pulling it forward towards them. The Aymara people of the Andes see the future behind them and the past in front; some rural Papuans see the future lying uphill. And a new study from Italy, reported on the Research Digest blog, adds an intriguing detail: it found that Italians who have been blind since birth or early childhood don't generally conceive of the past as behind them, or the future in front. (No doubt they can *talk* this way as well as anyone; the study was designed to elicit instinctive associations.) Nor do they think of an event in two months' time as "closer" than one two months ago. But sighted people do, which makes sense: the space up ahead is in front of our eyes, while the space behind takes effort to see.

All of which is a reminder of how odd it is that we think of time using spatial metaphors at all - indeed, that it seems virtually impossible not to. Ask me about the coming month and I can't help picturing a sequence of little boxes, like a calendar; ask me what I did yesterday and my eyes shoot upwards, as I consult a "space" somewhere behind my head. Your specific images may not match mine, but anthropologists suggest that the basic metaphor - "time is space" - is a cultural universal. Which a pity, in a way, because I'm pretty sure it makes our experience of tim[e] more anguished than it needs to be.

Take busyness: for me, the feeling of overwhelm is bound up with a sense of time as a physical container, too small for the tasks I need to cram in. (The anthropologist Edward Hall once said that Americans see time as an endless conveyor belt, carrying bottles that must be filled; if one passes by unfilled, time's been wasted.) When you stop and notic[e] that's just a metaphor, it's liberatin[g]. There is no container and thus no need to fret about whether it'll pro[ve] big enough. There's just you, in th[is] moment of time, and all you can d[o] is use it as best you can.

Such metaphors also trick us into thinking we control time more than we do. After all, mortgage notwithstanding, I really do own my physical space; it's up to me how I use it. But as the blogger David Cain points out, we never really have time: "The time we 'have' is never where we are, and we can never see it, unlike anything else we have." Any number of things might disrupt your plans, and eventually death certainly will. So treating time as if you own it is a recipe for stress.

We probably can't abandon these metaphors, and besides, they are useful. But it's worth remembering also that they're only metaphors. Wouldn't that be the wisest approach, going forward?

about your purpose. Life isn't
–. Use your limited time here to
…lly that matters.

…o plan really; work/embrace
…do for fundamental reasons,
…n think it's going to be inherently
… . Make decisions for fundamental,
…mental, reasons (not because you
think it's going to lead somewhere else).
Otherwise, you'll end up stuck.

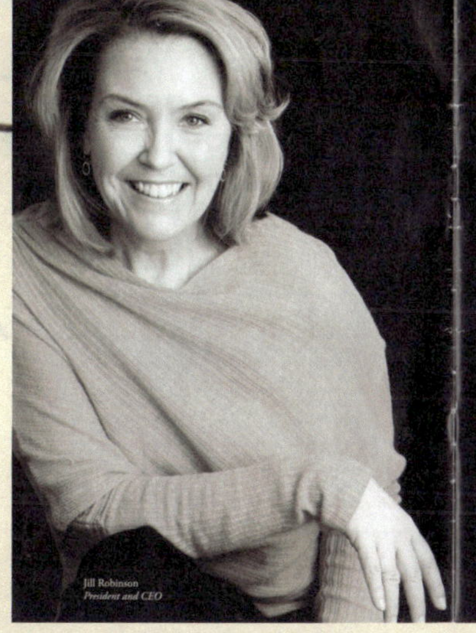

Jill Robinson
President and CEO

Welcome

Those of you who follow us on social media, read our blog, and work with us know that we're obsessed with translating data into action that gets results. And, action — consequential action — requires leadership.

Leadership is responsible for understanding the environment, listening, making decisions, and ultimately motivating the action that gets results. Results that go beyond the immediate now and start to shift the functional culture of an organization to operate in a nimbler way.

Right now, I'm obsessed with leaders who initially drive organizations to sustainability, and then move them beyond that curve to the resilience that will be required in the next decade. Developing a resilient organization requires some level of grit, I think. Angela Duckworth in her book, *Grit: the Power of Passion and Perseverance*, says that grit requires passion for your organization and its purpose, investing in practice to grow your leadership skills, and BELIEF that the hard work will have an impact. Take a moment and ask yourself: Are you cultivating your personal grit? Are you building grit with your team and at your institution? As leaders we must make time to develop ourselves, and dialogue with our peers can be an accelerator. I've developed Arts Leadership Book Club with hopes that we might provide these experiences in a low investment but high-impact way for you. I encourage you to join us for the November Book Club (see page 6 for more information).

In May, I completed TRG's 20th Executive Summit, this time in Colorado. The leaders that joined me agreed: resilience is now the name of the game, and resilience requires grit. We talked about my awakening to the concept of The Long Now as the Notre Dame Cathedral burned. And indeed, it was the long game that we talked about and focused on, while recognizing that there are urgent challenges facing us today. For instance, there's **a clear need to ensure that arts and culture is more relevant to more people everywhere.** Equity, diversity, inclusion…every organization we talk to has local and national pressures right now with which they're grappling. There are change management issues, funding challenges, and organizational identity conversations that are pre-occupying, motivating, and also threatening. The ability to navigate and lead these necessary changes requires grit.

Thinking just a bit further out, in just 10 years, the aging of Boomers combined with the size of the Generation X cohort (which is 10-15% smaller) will result in a smaller population pool at the target age for arts and cultural participation. This shift, combined with differences in the ways Millennials expect to engage, is resulting in real and affecting changes. These changes are already starting to show up in the way we communicate, raise money, and nurture long-term relationships with our communities.

"Grit requires passion for your organization and its purpose, investing in practice to grow your leadership skills and belief."

We recently published our 2019 Generational Analysis which creates a compelling argument that if your organization isn't already acting in new ways to address coming generational changes, it's behind the curve. And if you're *leading* your institution, it means you're behind the curve.

We've taken the next step in our work around understanding generational behaviors. Jim DeGood's article, *Becoming a "Master Gardener" of Audience Cultivation*, on page 20 digs into why we think it is so important to engage Generation X as one part of a larger strategy in building a more resilient organization for tomorrow.

Those of us serving this sector believe in the power of arts and culture to drive new approaches, to embrace failure (and success!), and lead us into new ways of thinking in our communities and nations. That is why the organizations you're part of matter so much. And, why you and your professional development matter so much. If resiliency requires resilient behaviors from us as leaders, then we must adopt them.

Learning from the octopus

Reading your report on the decentralised control system and brainpower of certain cephalopods, especially the octopus ("Tentacles that think", August 15th), brought to mind an outside-the-box analysis of what we can learn from nature about protecting ourselves from terrorist threats, natural disaster and pandemics.

In "Learning from the Octopus" the late Rafe Sagarin, a marine ecologist and security analyst at the University of Arizona, developed these ideas in a provocative work documenting the way that certain natural species have survived in a world of predators, adversaries and surprise attacks. His conclusions stress the importance of adaptable, flexible control systems, decentralised decision-making, redundant capabilities and symbiotic relationships with potential enemies.

CHESTER CROCKER
Professor of strategic studies
Georgetown University
Washington, DC

3.
Make excellent mistak…
do anything, your focus …
only. Make mistakes …
having high aspirations, from trying to do

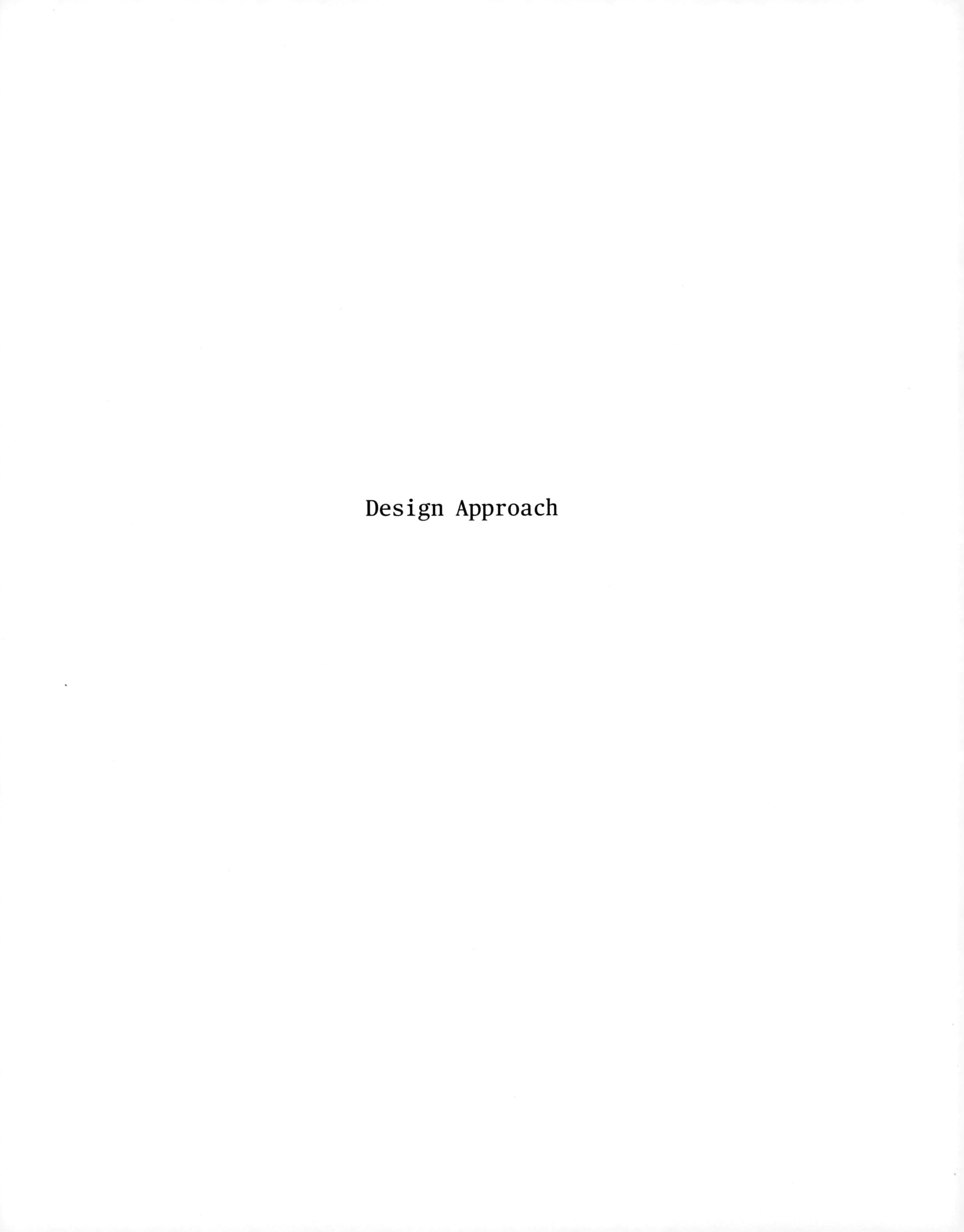

Design Approach

there are many details to be worked out. A circular fou
dation is built around the city to take the thrust of t
roof. A preassembled skin is laid flat on the ground a
inflated. After this the construction of the city procee
as if under normal conditions. The enclosure dome has
free span of 2 km (1.24 miles) and a height of 240
(790 ft), and is made with a double-layered plastic sk
within a strong cable net of specially prepared and i
pregnated high-strength polyester fibres. The dome sha
will be able to resist severe storms and its form preve
snow accumulations. The city can accommodate betwe
fifteen thousand and forty-five thousand people. T
residential areas are interspersed with kindergartens a
schools around the inside periphery of the dome. T
main street of the city begins at the main traffic inters
tion on the outside, crosses the business section, and e
at the city centre with its municipal auditorium, theatr
city administration, churches, hotels, apartments, tou
and shopping centre and high schools. A pedestri
system connects administration, residence and recr
tional areas. The administration, located at the entra
to the city, is the headquarters for land exploration a

The characteristic feature of austere arrangement is this:—It requires that the words should be like columns firmly planted and placed in strong positions, so that each word should be seen on every side, and that the parts should be appreciable distances from one another, being separated by perceptible intervals. It does not in the least shrink from using frequently harsh sound-clashings which jar on the ear; like blocks of building stone that are laid together unworked, blocks that are not square and smooth, but preserve their natural roughness and irregularity. It is prone for the most part to expansion by means of great, spacious words. It objects to being confined to short syllables, except under occasional stress of necessity.[56]

Antoine Dansaertstraat 190
1000 Brussel

(advertisement)

139
Art Fair
11–16/6

REALITY EXTENDE

JAKOB KUDSK STEENSEN AND KATHERI
IN CONVERSATION WITH BEN VICK

rian Zijlstra, *Altea*, inkjet print, 30 × 30 cm, 1958

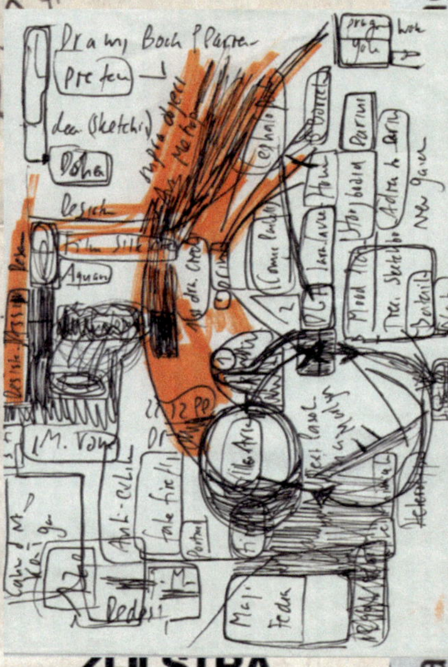

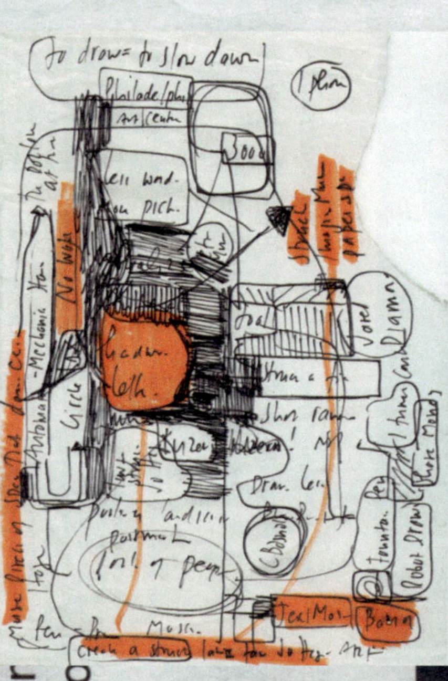

Mot

SSELS, MAY 2013 – For the last show
e season I invited Marian Zijlstra, a
friend since many years, to present
lection of photographs taken in the
s and Sixties. Zijlstra (°1933, Amster-
studied photography at the Kunst-
rheidschool in Amsterdam (which later
me the Gerrit Rietveld Academie) and
r Carel Blazer and Ad Windig. She
in Amsterdam but has spent long pe-
in Mexico in the Fifties and Sixties

where she photographed mostly people in public spaces throughout the country. She has very rarely exhibited her work, one of the few occasions was a group show at the Stedelijk Museum in 1967, a competition entitled 'Fotoprijs Amsterdam'. The selection of 27 photographs was made in collaboration with Ben Krewinkel and the prints, all in black and white, were realised by Michael Windig (De Verbeelding), son of her former teacher. The show is her first solo presentation and is entiteld *Terugblik. 1950–1970 (Looking Back. 1950–1970)*.

ZIJLSTRA

TERUGBLIK
1950–1970

Jan Mot
Rue Antoine Dansaertstraat 190
1000 Brussels, Belgium

YERING AND SEPARATION 65

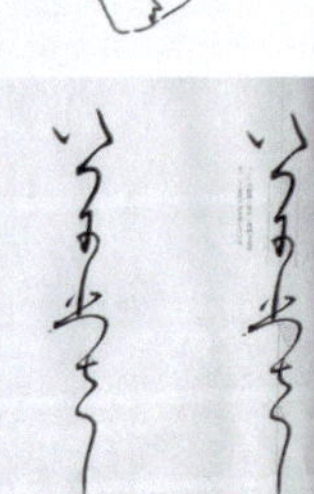

VENEZIA
8 APRILE · 1932/X · 28 OTTOBRE

MAGGIO
NGRESSO
D'ARTE

IUGNO
NFERENZE

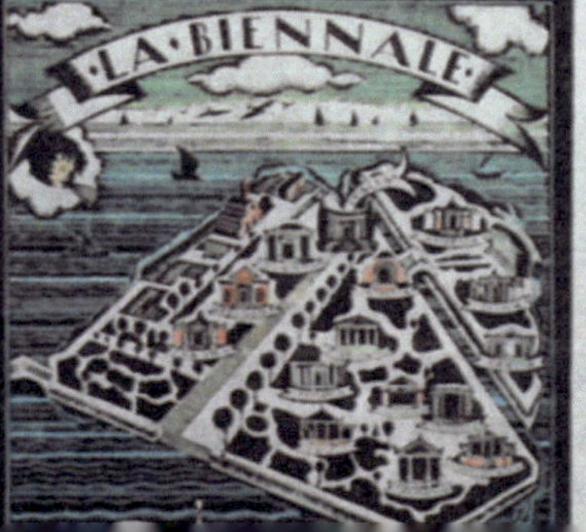

AGOSTO
FESTIVAL DEL
CINEMA

SETTEMBRE
FESTIVAL DI
MUSICA

NARRATIVES OF SPACE AND TIME

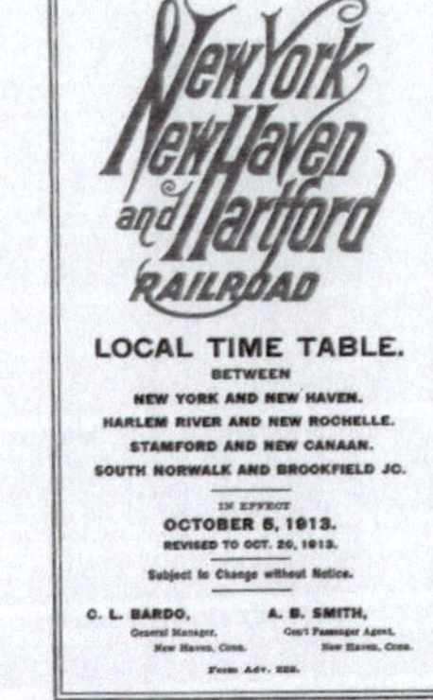

orted con-
raceful but
tined, are
ne-book
uch as the

[5] Center for Design and Typography
Cooper Union, "Matthew Carter: B
Centennial," *Type & Technology Mo
graph*, 1 (1982). Ani Stern did the in

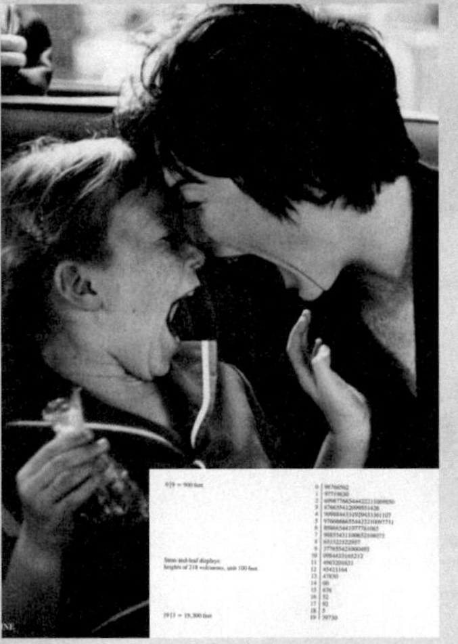

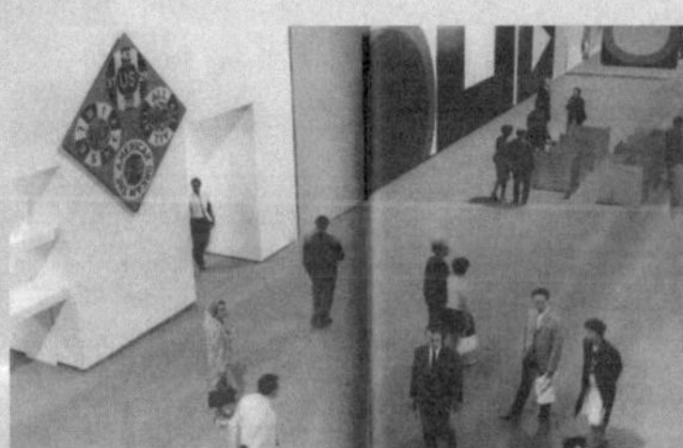

CRIMINAL ACTIVITY OF GOVERNMENT INFORMANTS

CRIME	CARDINALE	LOFARO	MALONEY	POLISI	SENATORE	FORONJY	CURRO
MURDER	X	X					
ATTEMPTED MURDER		X	X				
HEROIN POSSESSION AND SALE	X	X		X			X
COCAINE POSSESSION AND SALE	X		X	X			
MARIJUANA POSSESSION AND SALE							X
GAMBLING BUSINESS		X		X		X	
ARMED ROBBERIES	X		X	X	X		X
LOANSHARKING		X		X			
KIDNAPPING			X	X			
EXTORTION			X	X			
ASSAULT	X		X	X			X
POSSESSION OF DANGEROUS WEAPONS	X	X	X	X	X		X
PERJURY		X				X	
COUNTERFEITING					X	X	
BANK ROBBERY			X	X			
ARMED HIJACKING				X	X		
STOLEN FINANCIAL DOCUMENTS			X	X	X		
TAX EVASION				X		X	
BURGLARIES	X	X		X	X		
BRIBERY		X		X			
THEFT: AUTO, MONEY, OTHER			X	X	X	X	X
BAIL JUMPING AND ESCAPE			X	X			
INSURANCE FRAUDS					X	X	
FORGERIES				X	X		
PISTOL WHIPPING A PRIEST	X						
SEXUAL ASSAULT ON MINOR							X
RECKLESS ENDANGERMENT							X

Large Paintings by American, Br
and European Artists selected
Gimpel Fils *F.B.A. G*

My heart usually sinks, I must confess, wh
I am asked to wander through the somewha
bidding rooms of this gallery. First, most
painters on show can be said to have 'arrive
there is no need for a lot of critical panegyri
of that wisdom after the event), and secon
should certainly visit the gallery if only f
Alan Davie's. Well spaced, it offers an ex
opportunity to deepen our acquaintance
Davie's work. Out of the disparate organism
beautifully painted passages there emerges a
cal presence that retains a certain aura of
ence or allusion which adds to the tensions
'meanings', yet the central meaning is nev
vealed, too many disruptive ambiguities of
morphoses take place. One feels that only I
exceptional command of his medium hold in
ance these demonstrations of power and vi
One clearly sees what happens when a p
'cuts loose' like Appel. Another painter who
out well is Larry Rivers, and *New York* w
combined automatism and an acute ration
manipulation of paint has created a style b
the dissembling and facile proliferation of
which are brought into a perfectly collusive
Hassel Smith is a painter who risks all on
Structure is dictated by the dimensions
needs to make themselves and their neighb
shapes felt. I particularly enjoyed *Trium*
Gargoylism. There are several later wor
Matta, a characteristic Gear, two collages
string composition by Irwin. There is neve
much to be said for using pieces of torn pap
substitute for the paint tube. A fluid abs
by Hamilton Frazer, an untitled piece of

BRIDGET RILEY *Fall* emulsion on board 55½ x
Gallery One.

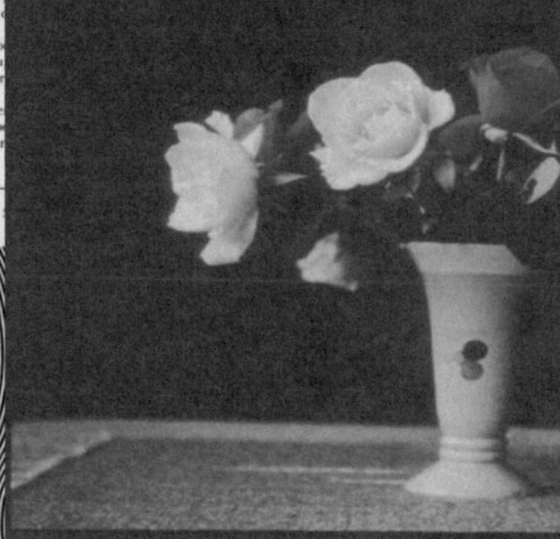

FEBRUARY

25 26 27 28

I ORIEL
KEBLE
CHRIST CHURCH
PEMBROKE
ORIEL II
EXETER
BRASENOSE
WORCESTER
LINCOLN
NEW COLLEGE
QUEEN'S
ST CATHERINE'S
II SEH
WADHAM
HERTFORD
UNIVERSITY
BALLIOL
TRINITY
MAGDALEN
WOLFSON
ST JOHN'S
KEBLE II
OSLER HOUSE
ST PETER'S
III JESUS
CHRIST CHURCH II
ORIEL III
EXETER II
CORPUS CHRISTI
LINCOLN II
LMH
MERTON
WORCESTER II
PEMBROKE II
BRASENOSE II
ST CATHERINE'S II
IV UNIVERSITY II
MANSFIELD
NEW COLLEGE II
ST JOHN'S II
ST ANNE'S
HERTFORD II
QUEEN'S II
BALLIOL II
SEH II
WADHAM II
JESUS II
WOLFSON II
V WORCESTER III
ST JOHN'S III
REGENT'S PARK
EXETER III
ORIEL IV
ORIEL V
LINACRE
LMH II
KEBLE III
TRINITY II
WADHAM III
JESUS III
VI ORIEL VI
ST PETER'S II
CHRIST CHURCH III
QUEEN'S III
TRINITY III
NEW COLLEGE III
ST CATHERINE'S III
HERTFORD III
LMH III
MERTON II
BRASENOSE III
MAGDALEN II
VII NEW COLLEGE IV
HERTFORD IV
SEH III
CHRIST CHURCH IV
ST JOHN'S IV
WORCESTER IV
QUEEN'S IV
ST PETER'S III
BRASENOSE IV
BRASENOSE V
ST ANNE'S II
SEH IV
ST ANNE'S III

WOMEN
I OSLER HOUSE
ST HUGH'S
ST CATHERINE'S
SOMERVILLE
LMH
ST HILDA'S
WADHAM
UNIVERSITY
WORCESTER
BALLIOL
JESUS
BRASENOSE
II ST ANNE'S
PEMBROKE
ST HUGH'S II
TRINITY
KEBLE
WOLFSON
NEW COLLEGE
LINCOLN
CORPUS CHRISTI
QUEEN'S
EXETER
HERTFORD
III SEH
SOMERVILLE II
CHRIST CHURCH
ST HILDA'S II
ST HUGH'S III
ST PETER'S
MAGDALEN
MERTON
ST JOHN'S
ST JOHN'S II
SEH II
PEMBROKE II
IV ST HUGH'S IV
NEW COLLEGE II
ST HUGH'S V
KEBLE II
HERTFORD II
WADHAM II
ORIEL
BRASENOSE II
LMH II
OSLER HOUSE II
CHRIST CHURCH II
LINCOLN II
QUEEN'S II

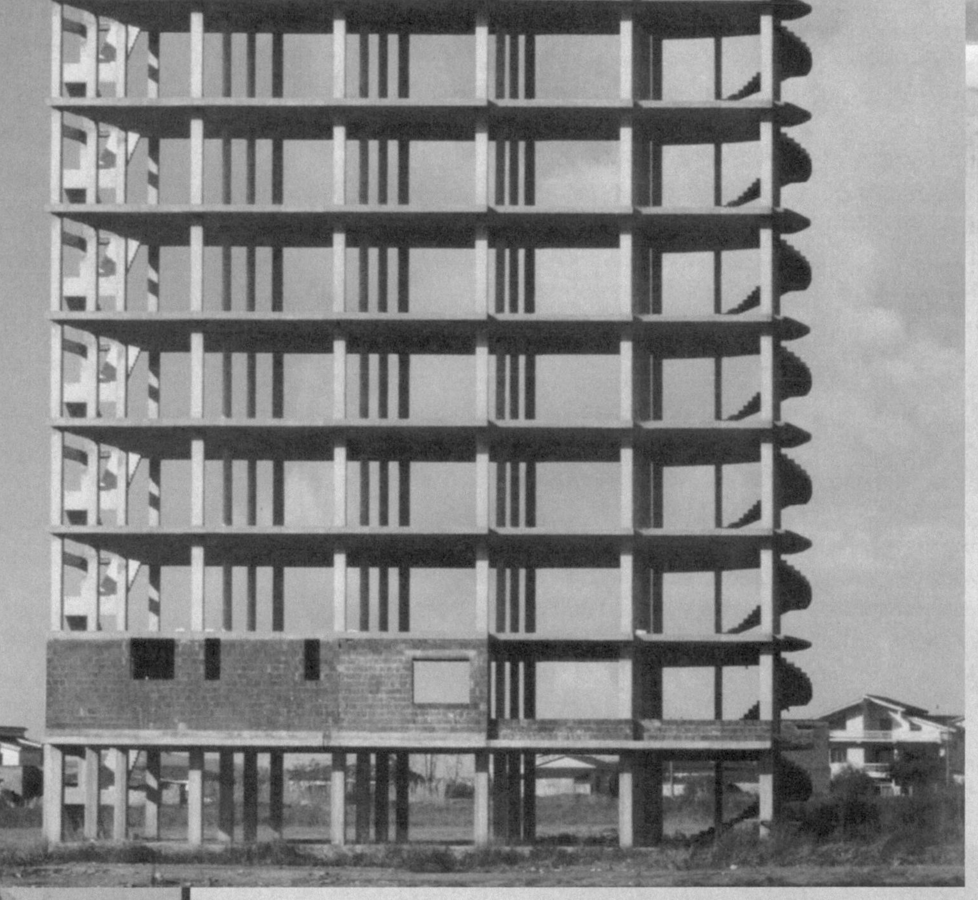

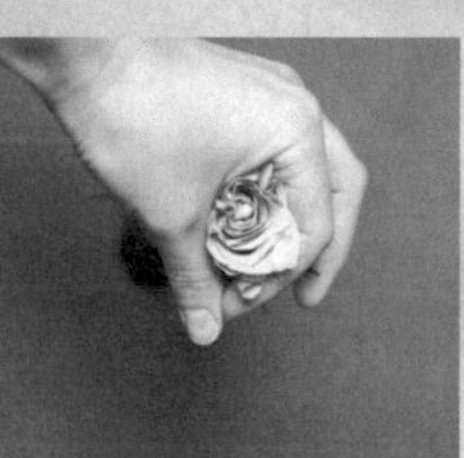

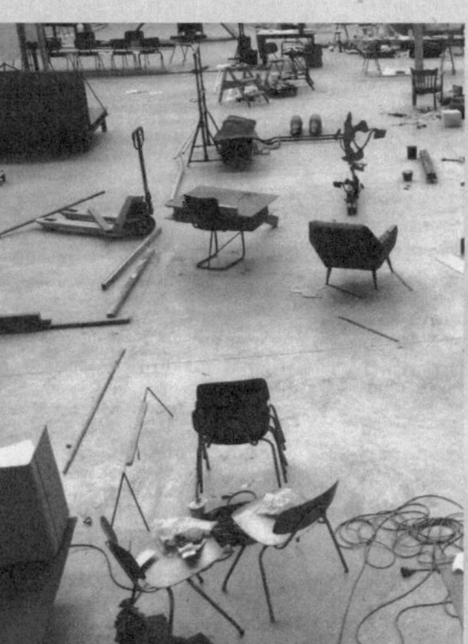

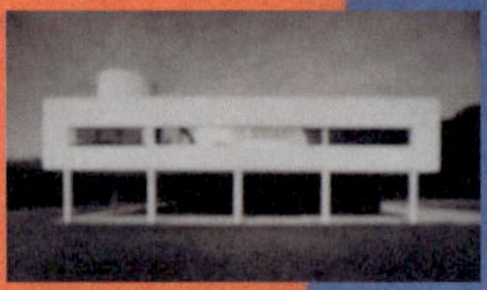

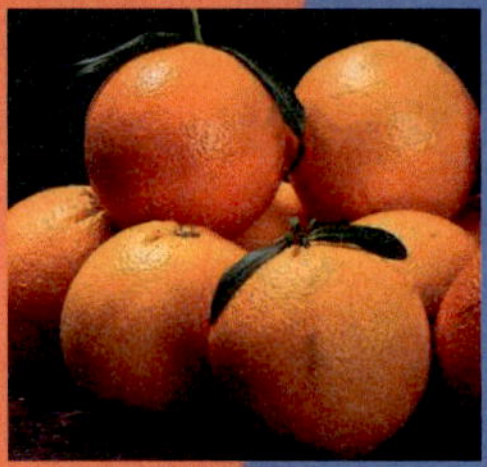

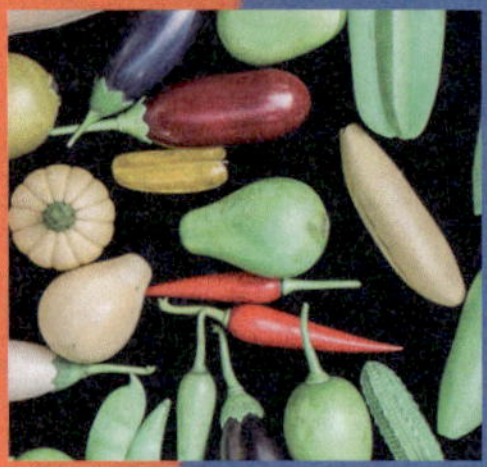

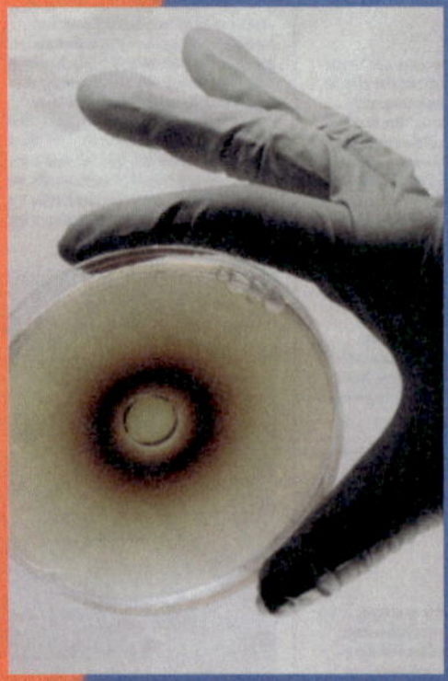

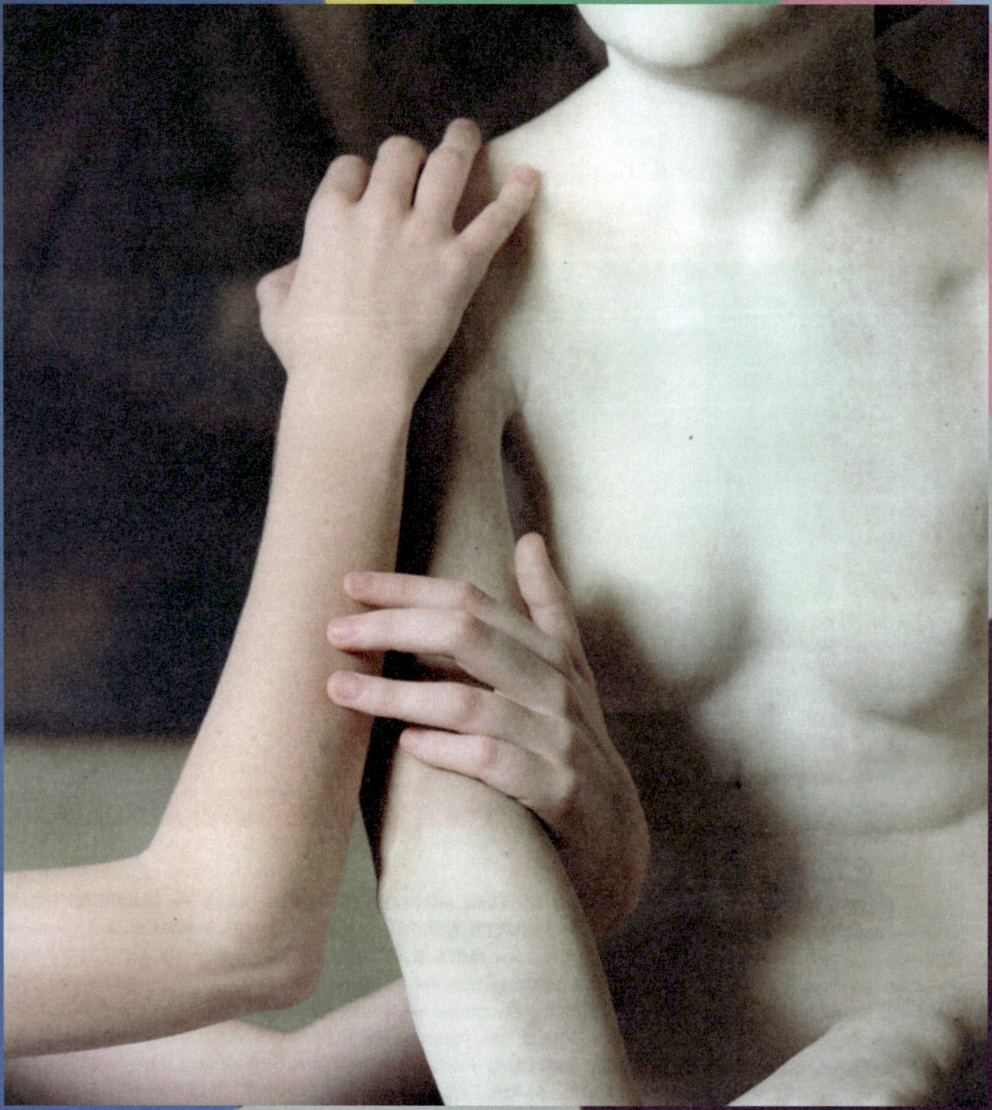

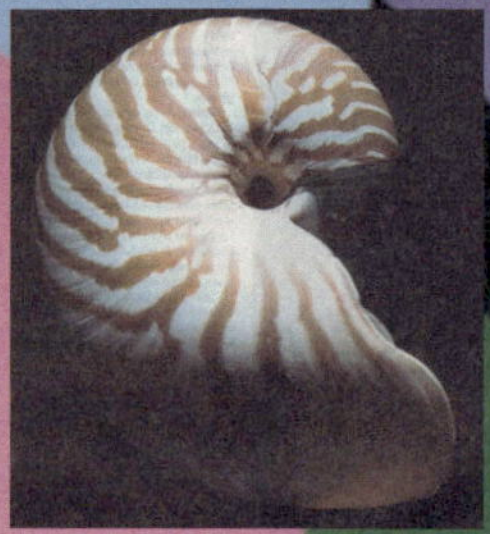

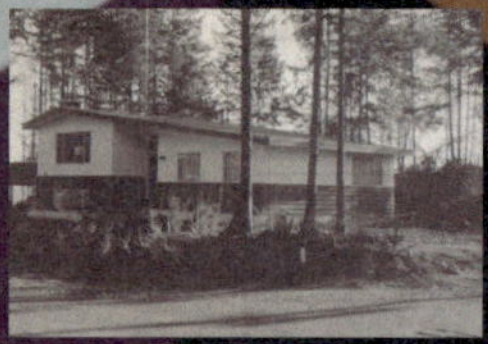

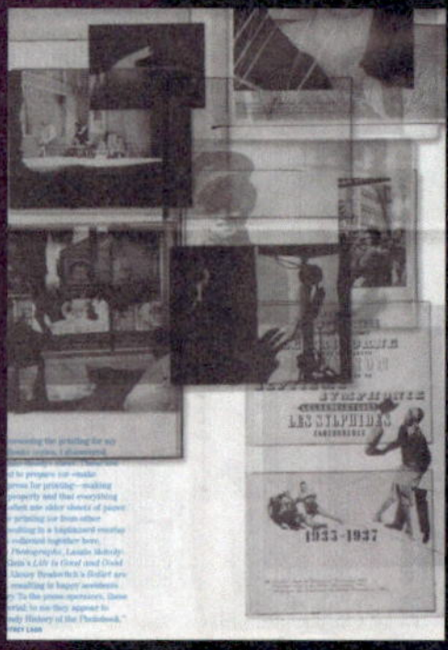

THE WHITE REVIEW is a quarterly journal featuring fiction, poetry, reportage, essays and artwork, alongside interviews with writers and artists.

thewhitereview.org

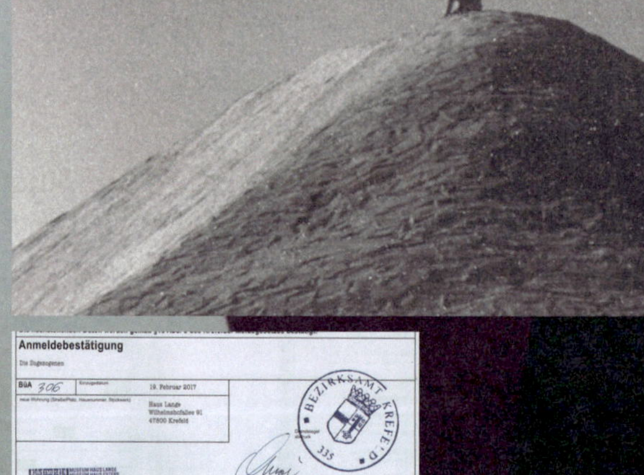

Anmeldebestätigung

Die Zugezogenen

BüA 306 — 19. Februar 2017

Haus Lange
Wilhelmshofallee 91
47800 Krefeld

BEZIRKSAMT KREFELD 335

Krefeld, den 19.02.2017

Elmgreen & Dragset
Die Zugezogenen

19. Februar - 27. August 2017 /
February 19 - August 27, 2017

Museum Haus Lange
Wilhelmshofallee 91
47800 Krefeld
Di - So 11 - 17 Uhr /
Tue - Sun 11a.m. - 5 p.m.

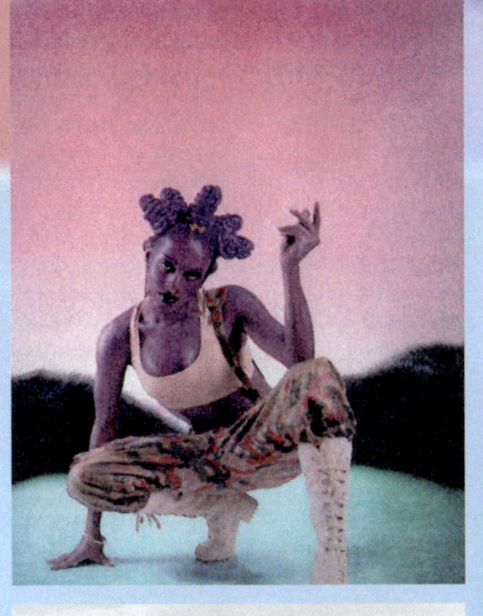

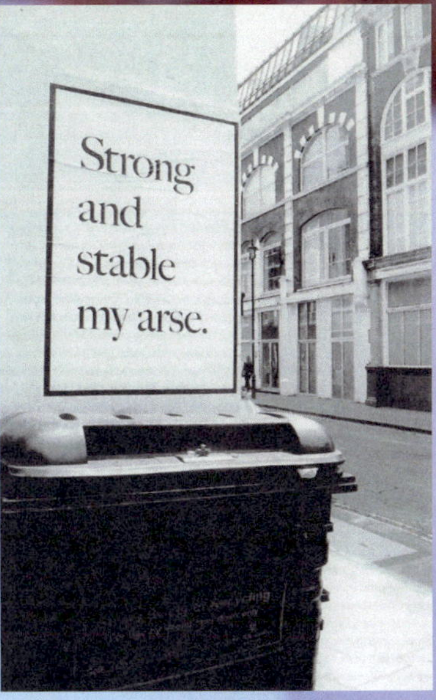

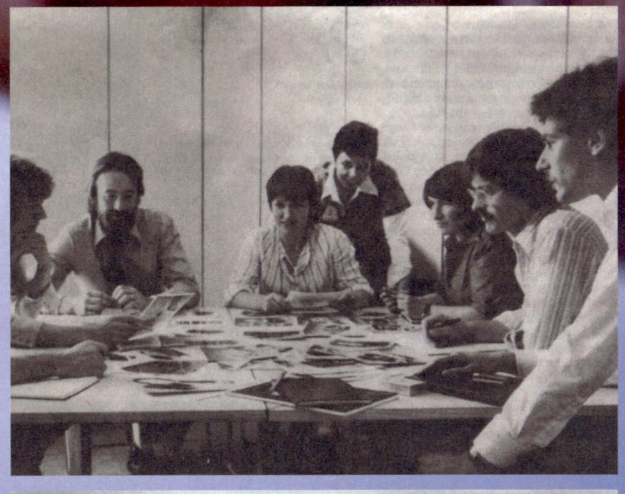

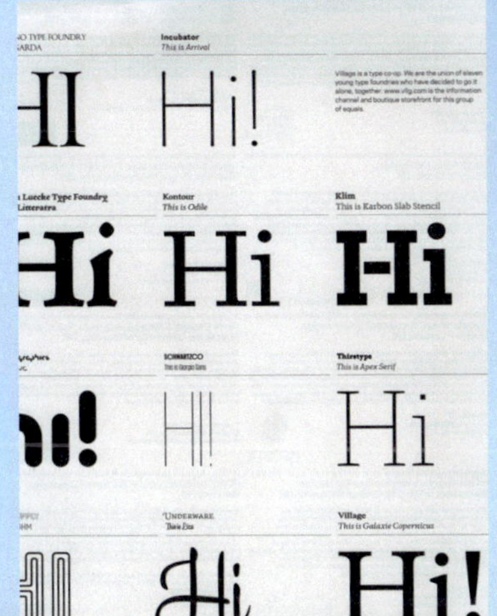

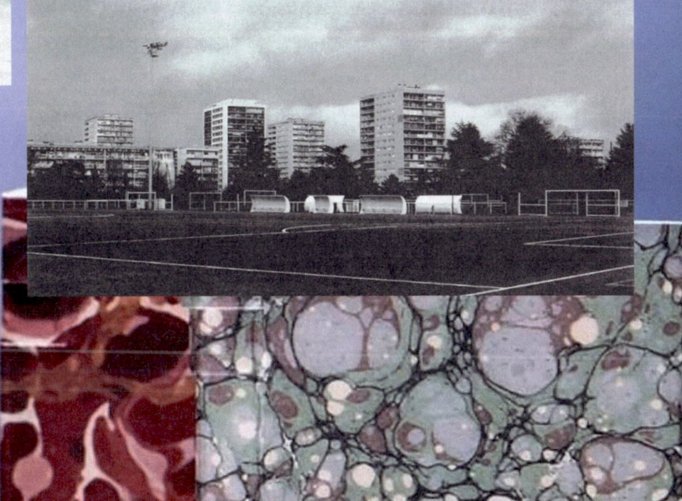

PAUL CHAN

$$\frac{\partial u_i}{\partial x_j} = \rho f_i + \frac{\partial}{\partial x_j}\left[-p\delta_{ij} + \mu\left(\frac{\partial u_i}{\partial x_j}+\frac{\partial u_j}{\partial x_i}\right) - \rho\overline{u_i' u_j'}\right].$$

THE BATHER'S DILEMMA

∴

9/12-10/19

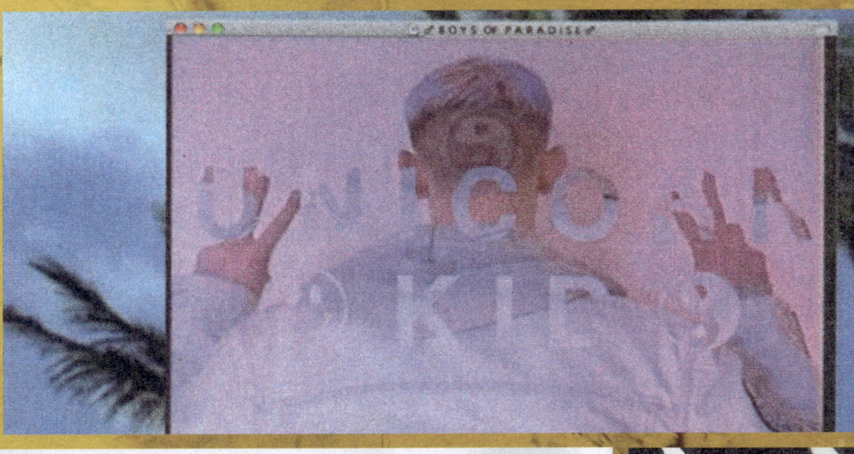

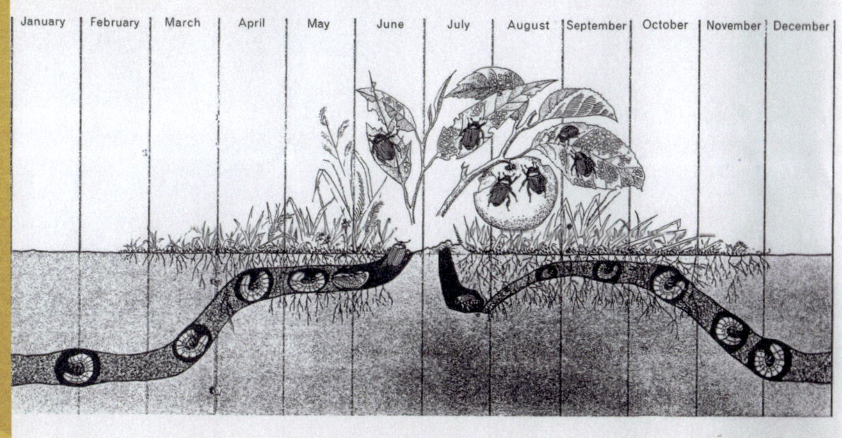

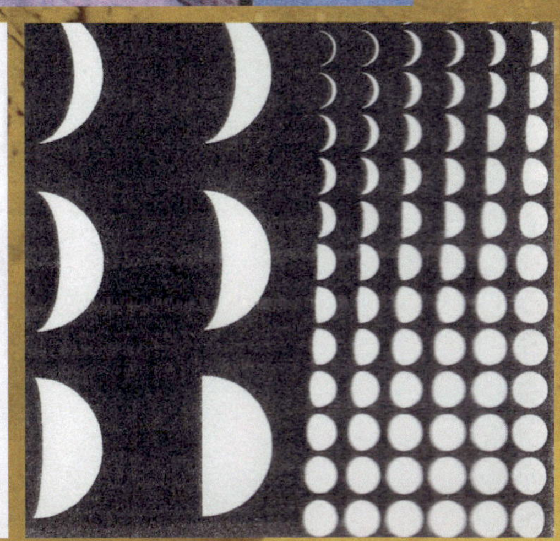

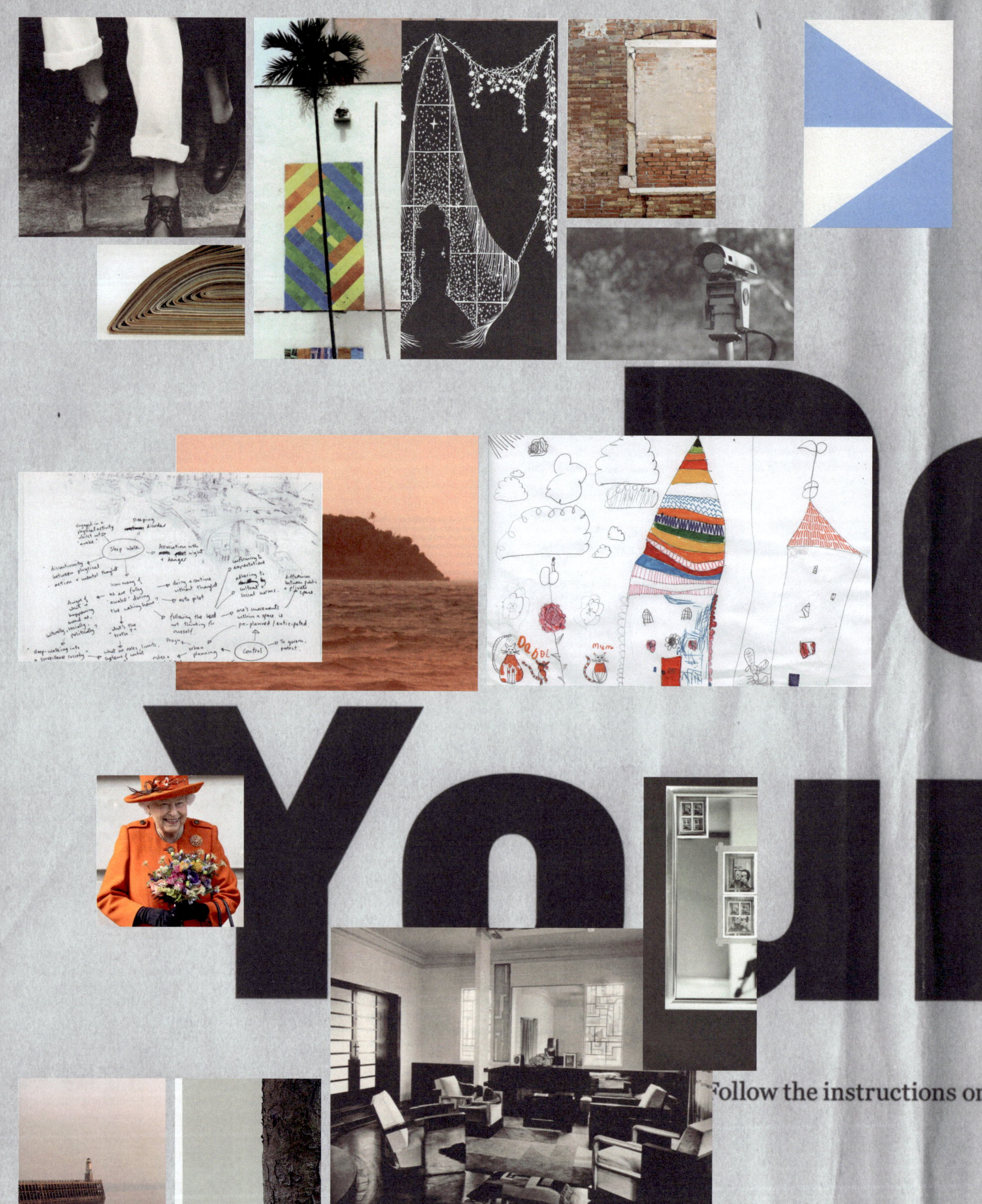
Follow the instructions or

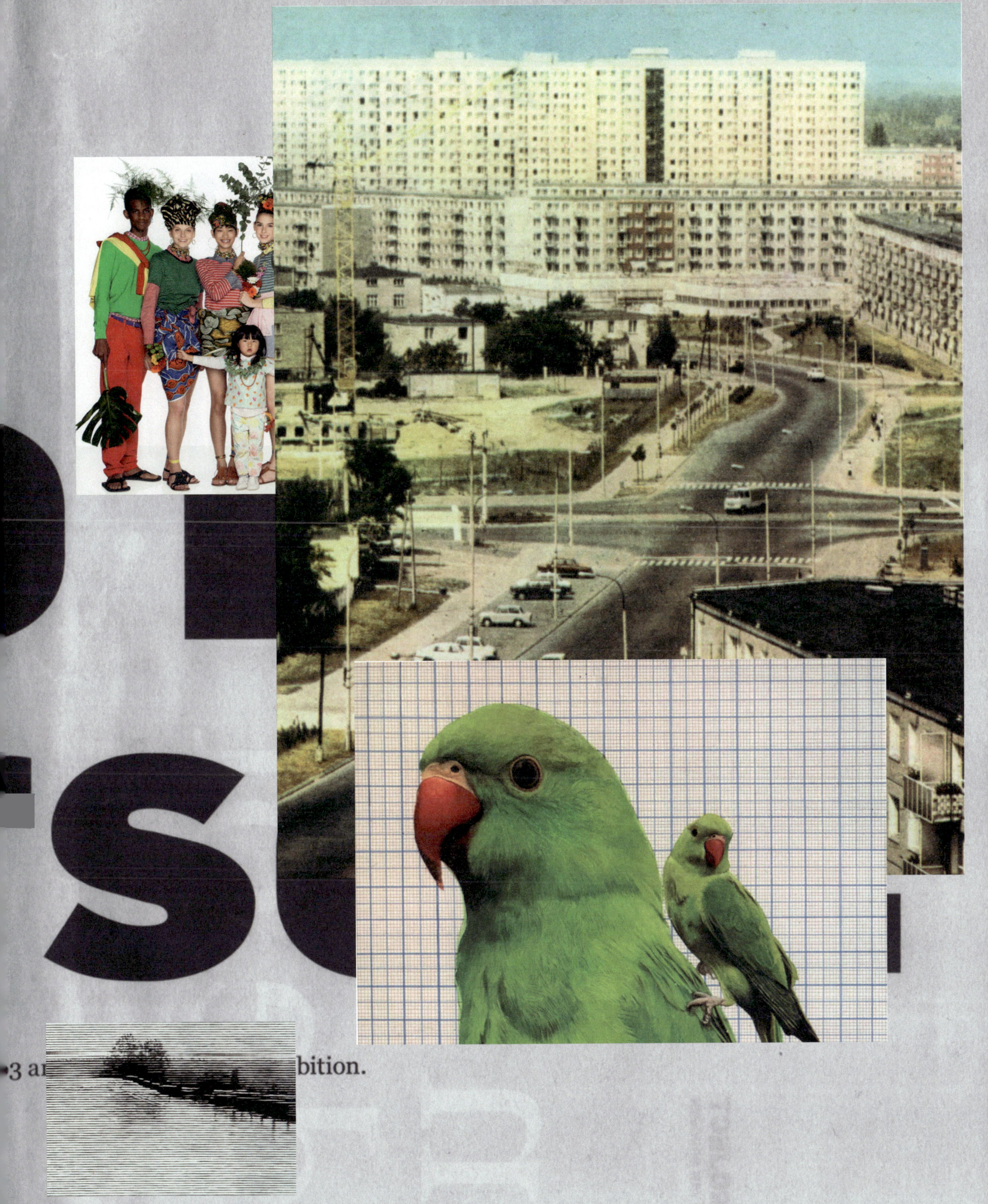

It's about your essence.
Trust in yourself.

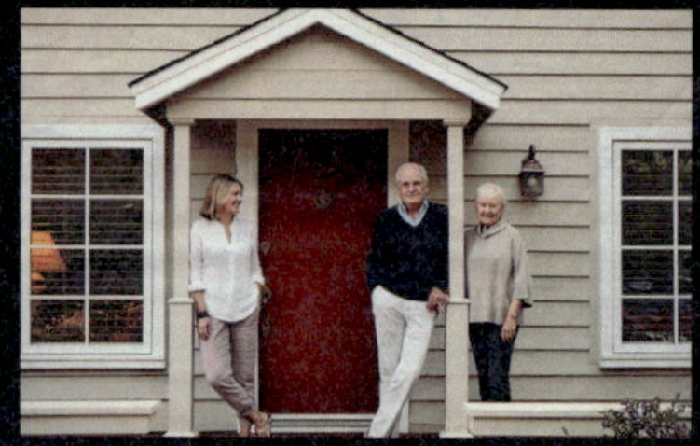

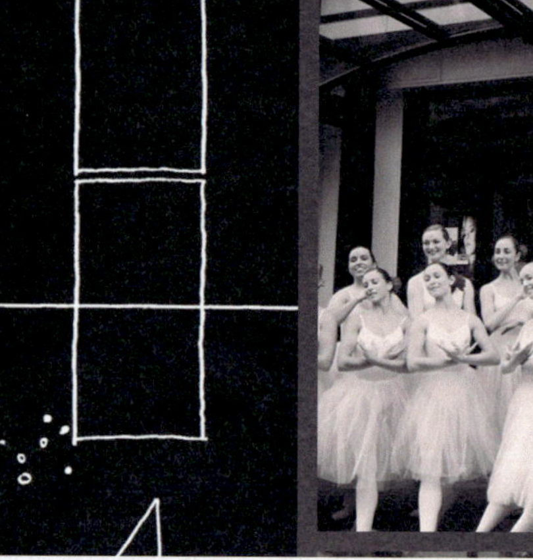

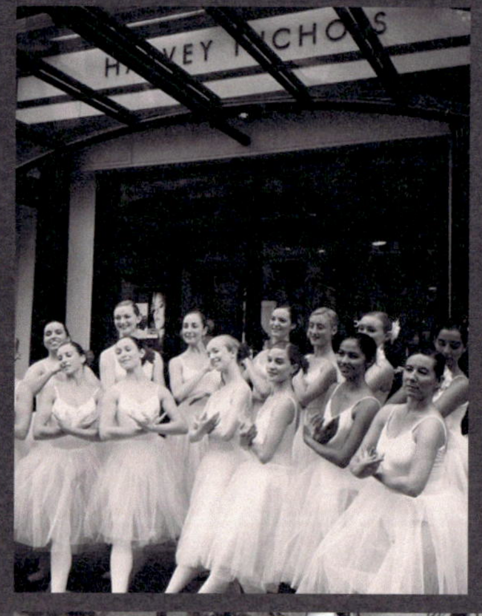

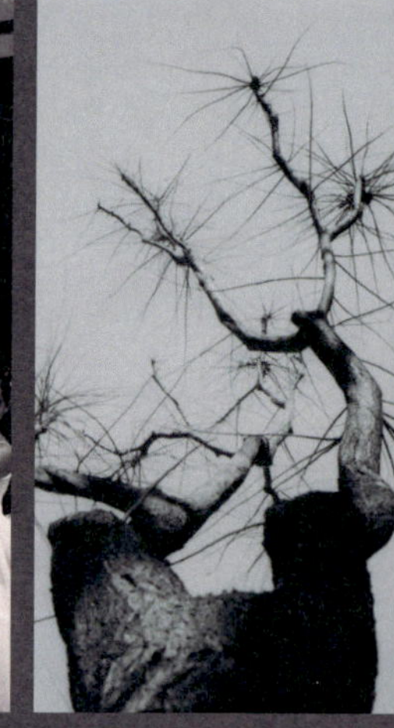

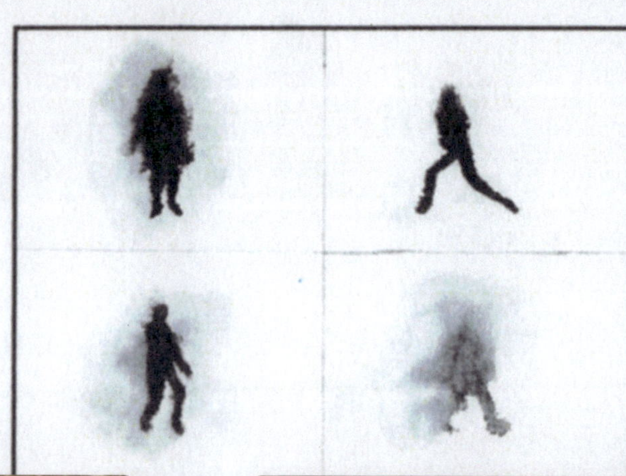

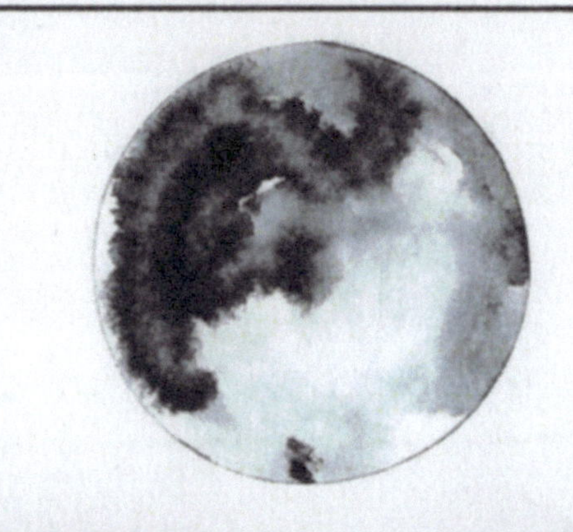

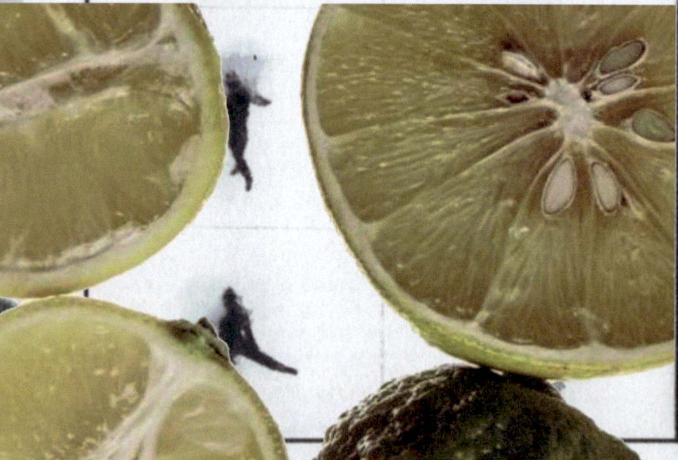

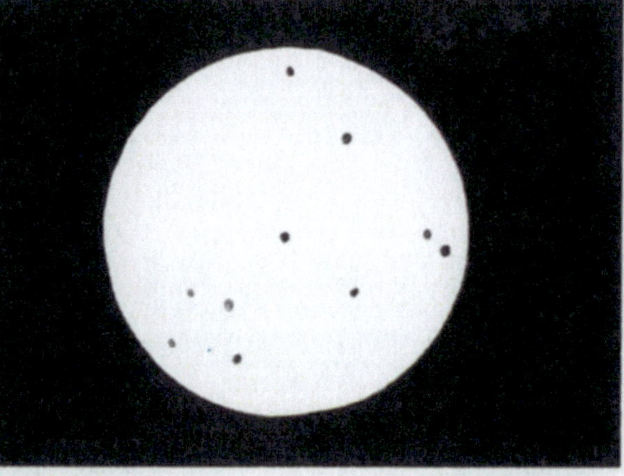

...ama Press, 2016). From *The Dancer at Midnight*, 2012.

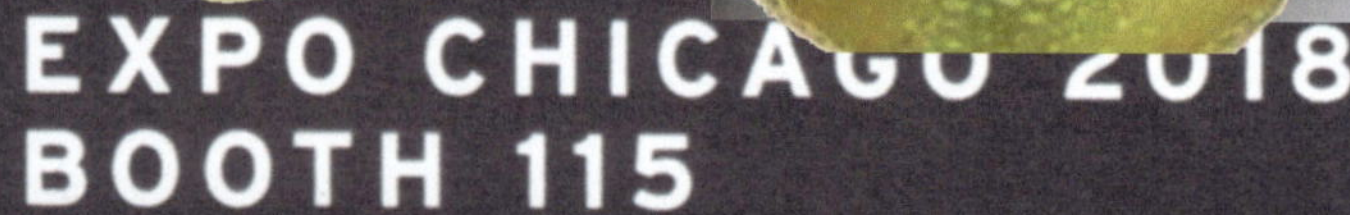

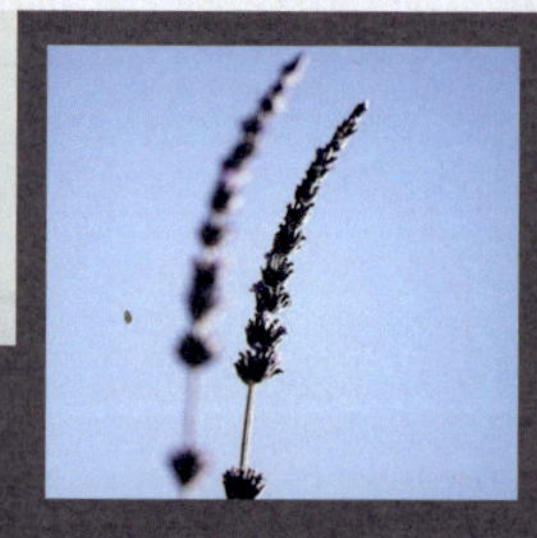

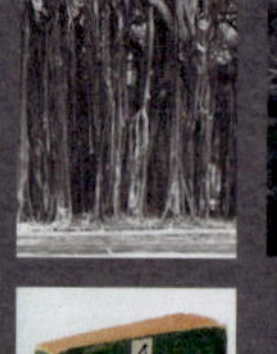

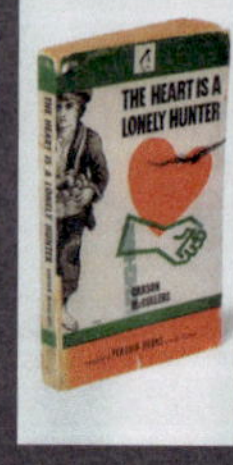

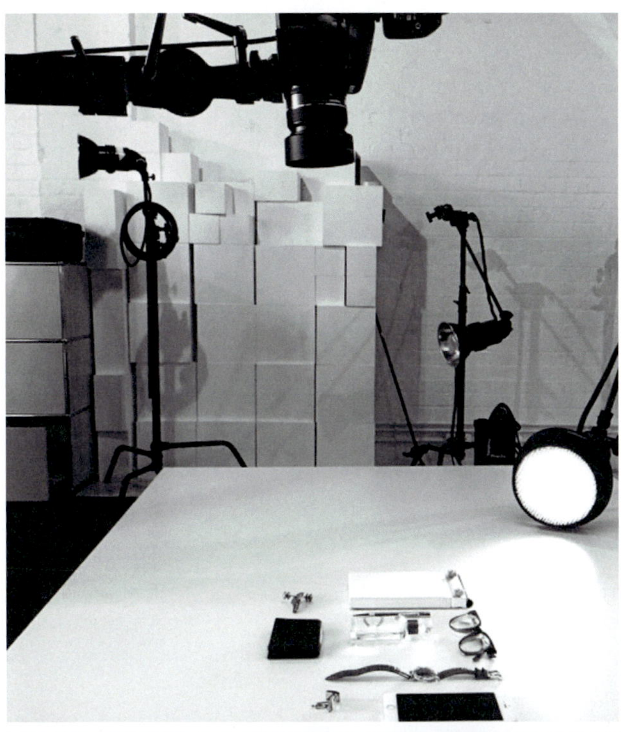

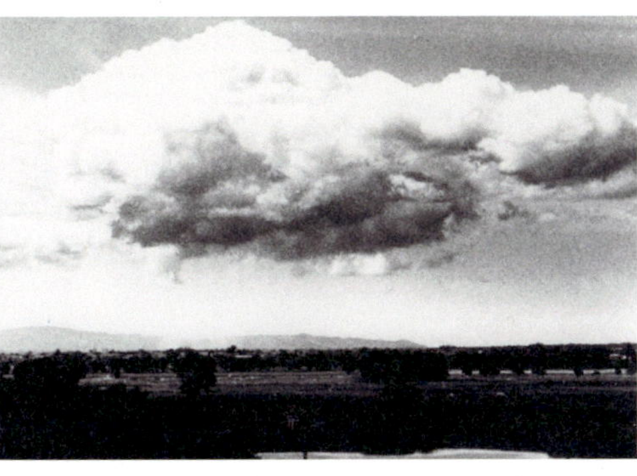

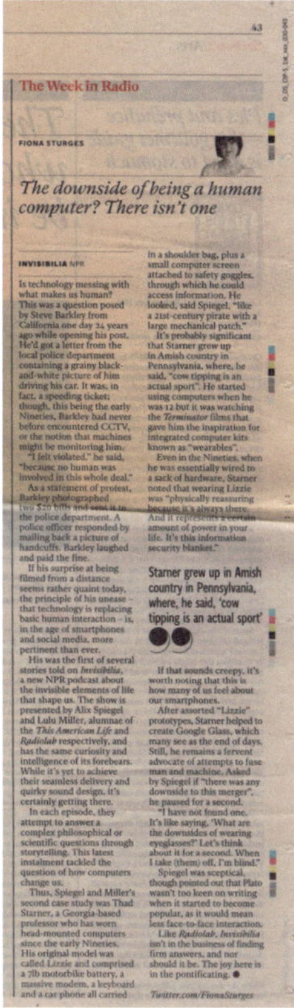

43

The Week in Radio

FIONA STURGES

The downside of being a human computer? There isn't one

INVISIBILIA NPR

Is technology messing with what makes us human? This was a question posed by Steve Barkley from California one day 24 years ago while opening his post. He'd got a letter from the local police department containing a grainy black-and-white picture of him driving his car. It was, in fact, a speeding ticket; though, this being the early Nineties, Barkley had never before encountered CCTV, or the notion that machines might be monitoring him.

"I felt violated," he said, "because no human was involved in this whole deal."

As a statement of protest, Barkley photographed two \$20 bills and sent it to the police department. A police officer responded by mailing back a picture of handcuffs. Barkley laughed and paid the fine.

If his surprise at being filmed from a distance seems rather quaint today, the principle of his unease – that technology is replacing basic human interaction – is, in the age of smartphones and social media, more pertinent than ever.

His was the first of several stories told on *Invisibilia*, a new NPR podcast about the invisible elements of life that shape us. The show is presented by Alix Spiegel and Lulu Miller, alumnae of the *This American Life* and *Radiolab* respectively, and has the same curiosity and intelligence of its forebears. While it's yet to achieve their seamless delivery and quirky sound design, it's certainly getting there.

In each episode, they attempt to answer a complex philosophical or scientific questions through storytelling. This latest instalment tackled the question of how computers change us.

Thus, Spiegel and Miller's second case study was Thad Starner, a Georgia-based professor who has worn head-mounted computers since the early Nineties. His original model was called Lizzie and comprised a 7lb motorbike battery, a massive modem, a keyboard and a car phone all carried in a shoulder bag, plus a small computer screen attached to safety goggles, through which he could access information. He looked, said Spiegel, "like a 21st-century pirate with a large mechanical patch."

It's probably significant that Starner grew up in Amish country in Pennsylvania, where, he said, "cow tipping is an actual sport". He started using computers when he was 12 but it was watching the *Terminator* films that gave him the inspiration for integrated computer kits known as "wearables".

Even in the Nineties, when he was essentially wired to a sack of hardware, Starner noted that wearing Lizzie was "physically reassuring because it's always there. And it represents a certain amount of power in your life. It's this information security blanket."

Starner grew up in Amish country in Pennsylvania, where, he said, 'cow tipping is an actual sport'

If that sounds creepy, it's worth noting that this is how many of us feel about our smartphones.

After assorted "Lizzie" prototypes, Starner helped to create Google Glass, which many see as the end of days. Still, he remains a fervent advocate of attempts to fuse man and machine. Asked by Spiegel if "there was any downside to this merger", he paused for a second.

"I have not found one. It's like saying, 'What are the downsides of wearing eyeglasses?' Let's think about it for a second. When I take (them) off, I'm blind."

Spiegel was sceptical, though pointed out that Plato wasn't too keen on writing when it started to become popular, as it would mean less face-to-face interaction.

Like *Radiolab*, *Invisibilia* isn't in the business of finding firm answers, and nor should it be. The joy here is in the pontificating. ●

Twitter.com/FionaSturges

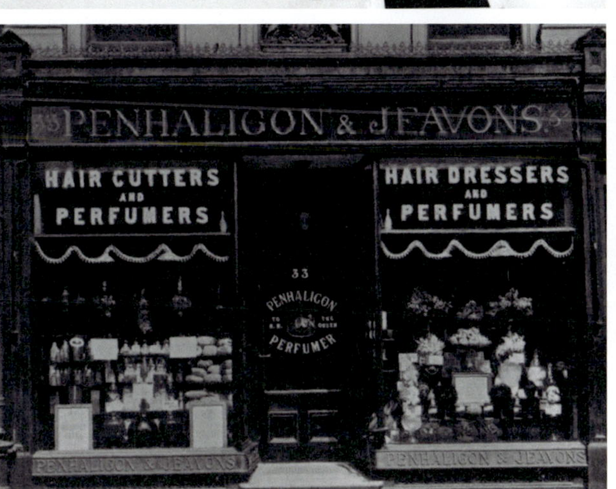

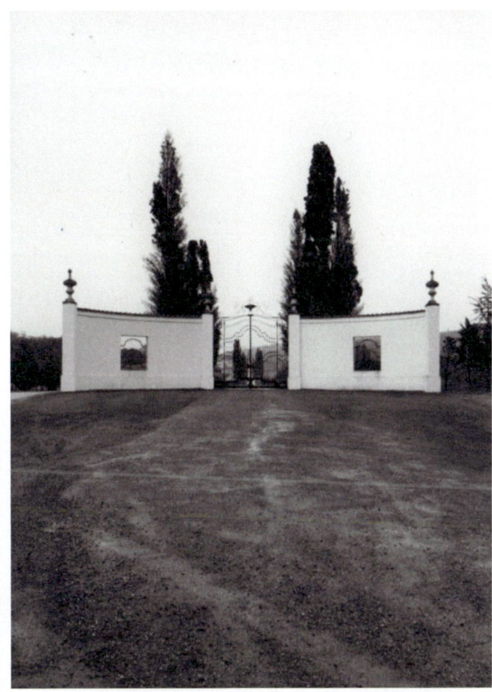

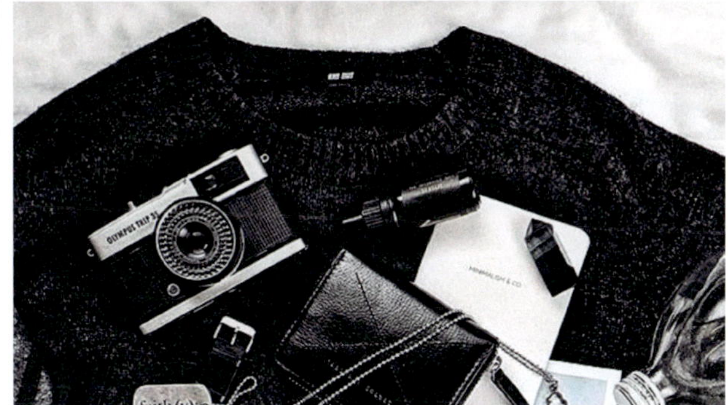

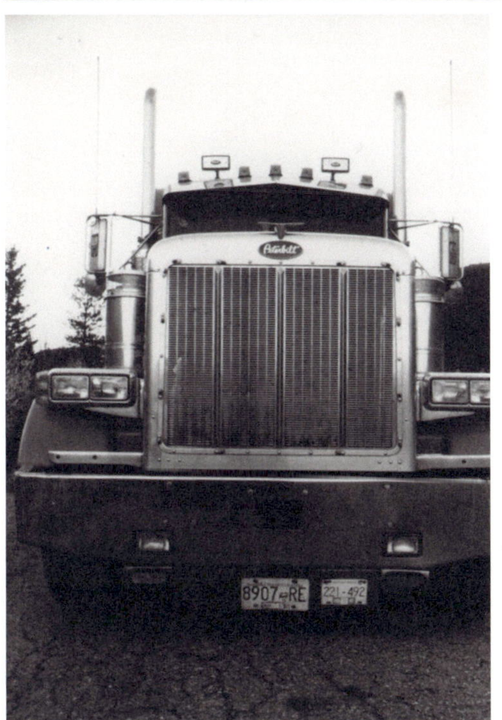

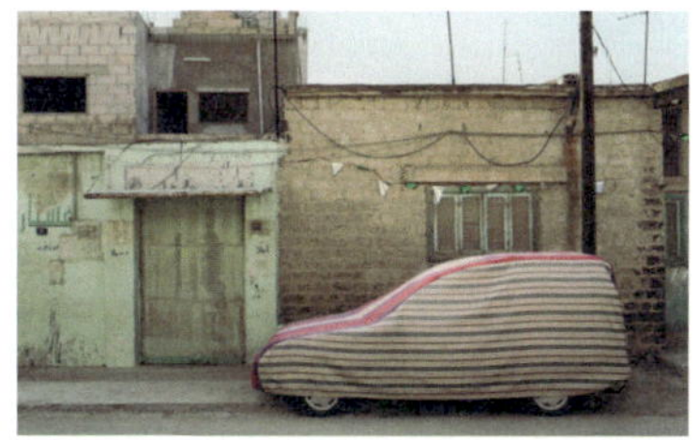

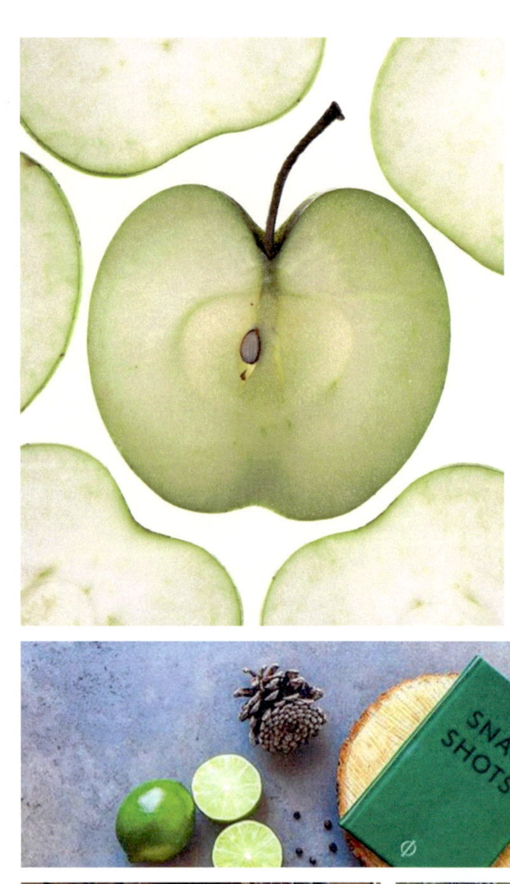
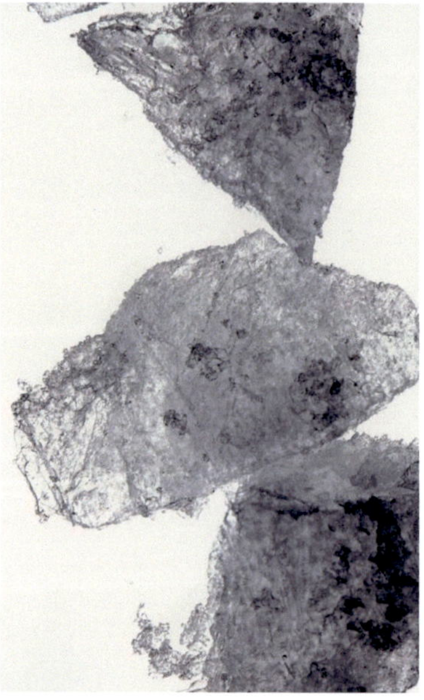
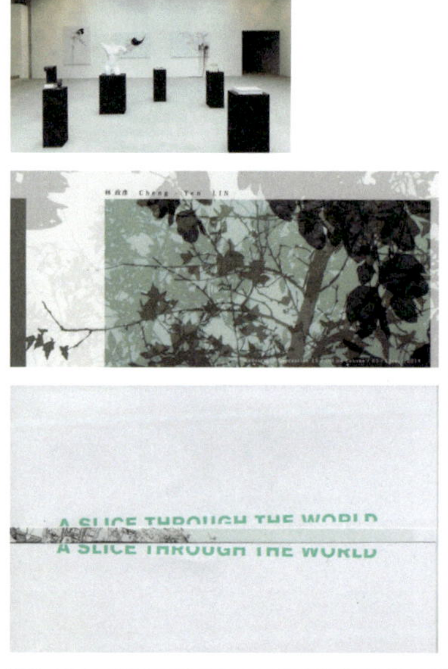
A SLICE THROUGH THE WORLD
A SLICE THROUGH THE WORLD
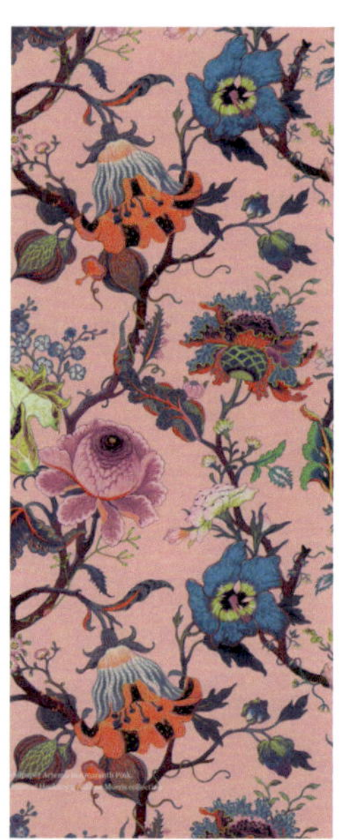
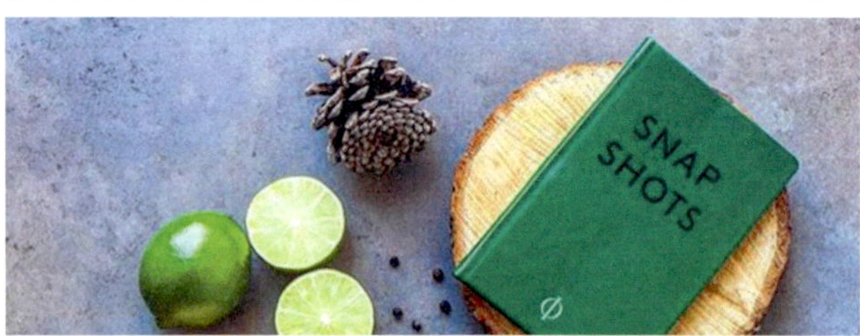
SNAP SHOTS
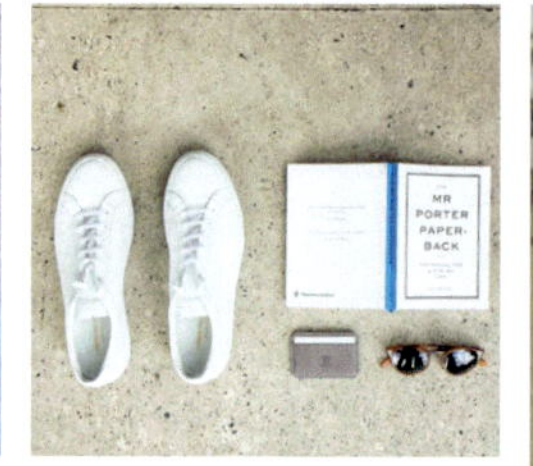
MR PORTER PAPER-BACK
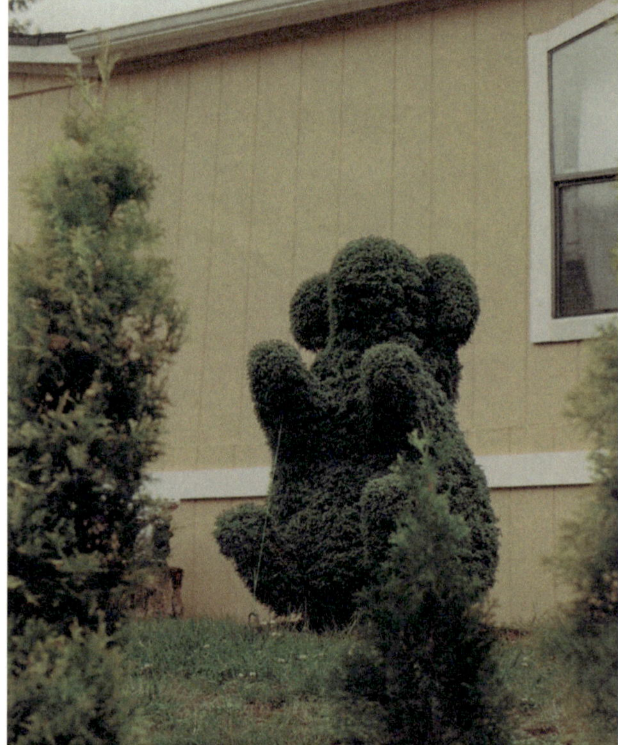
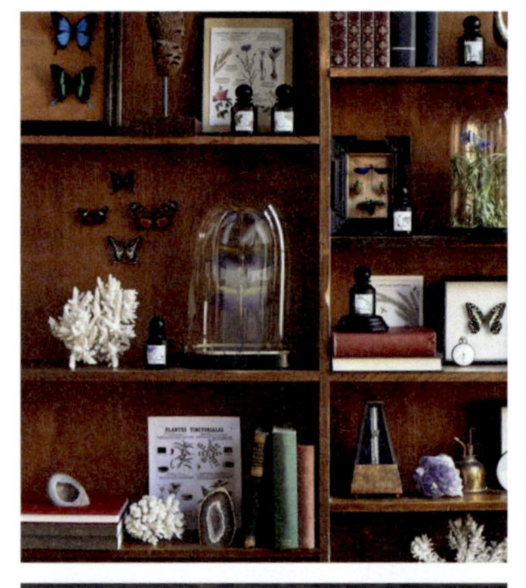
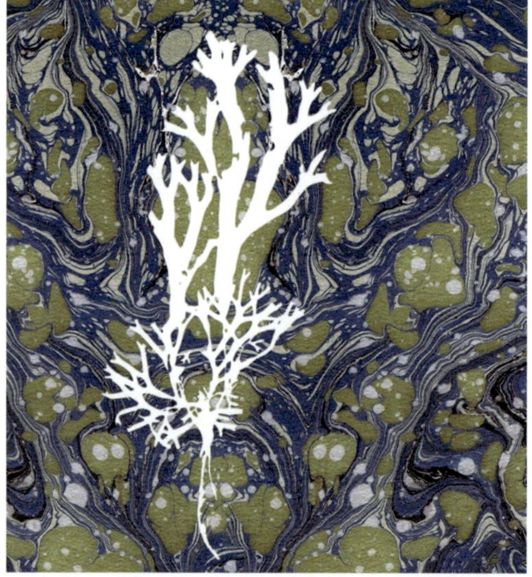
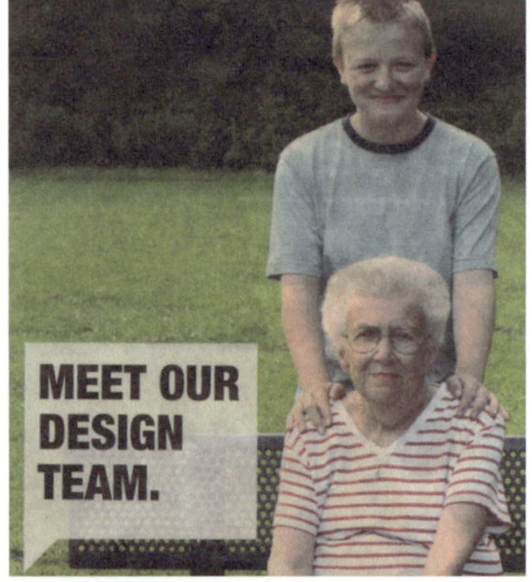
MEET OUR DESIGN TEAM.
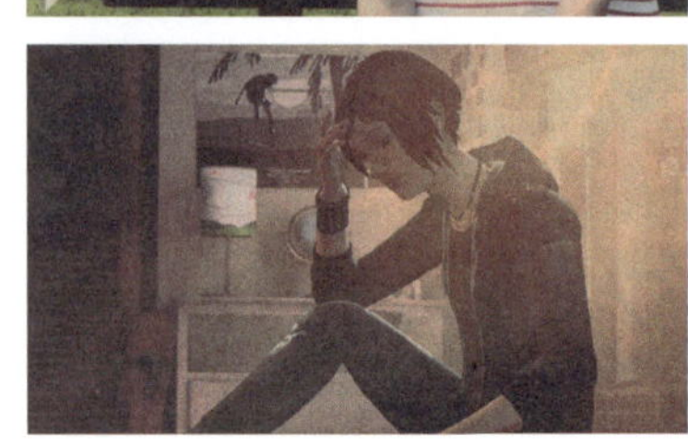
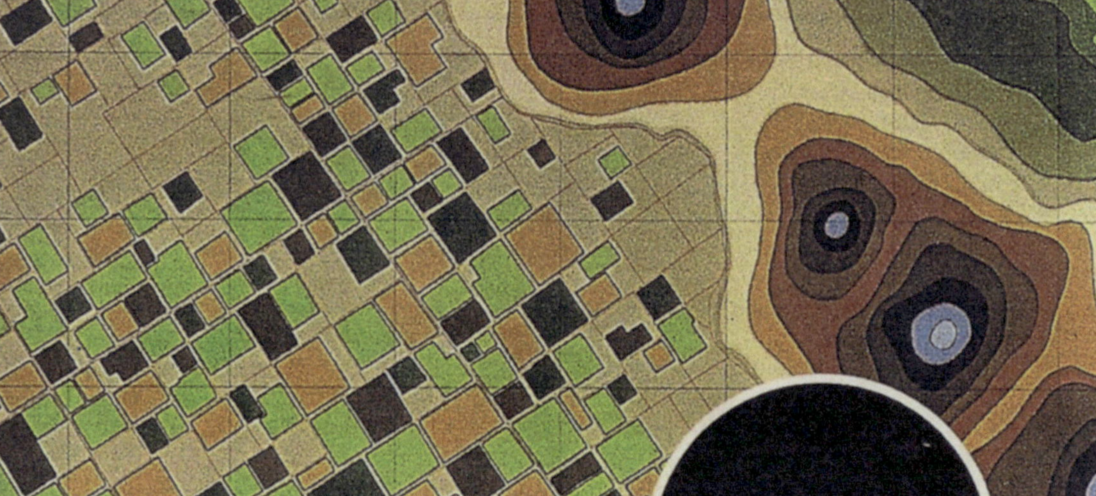

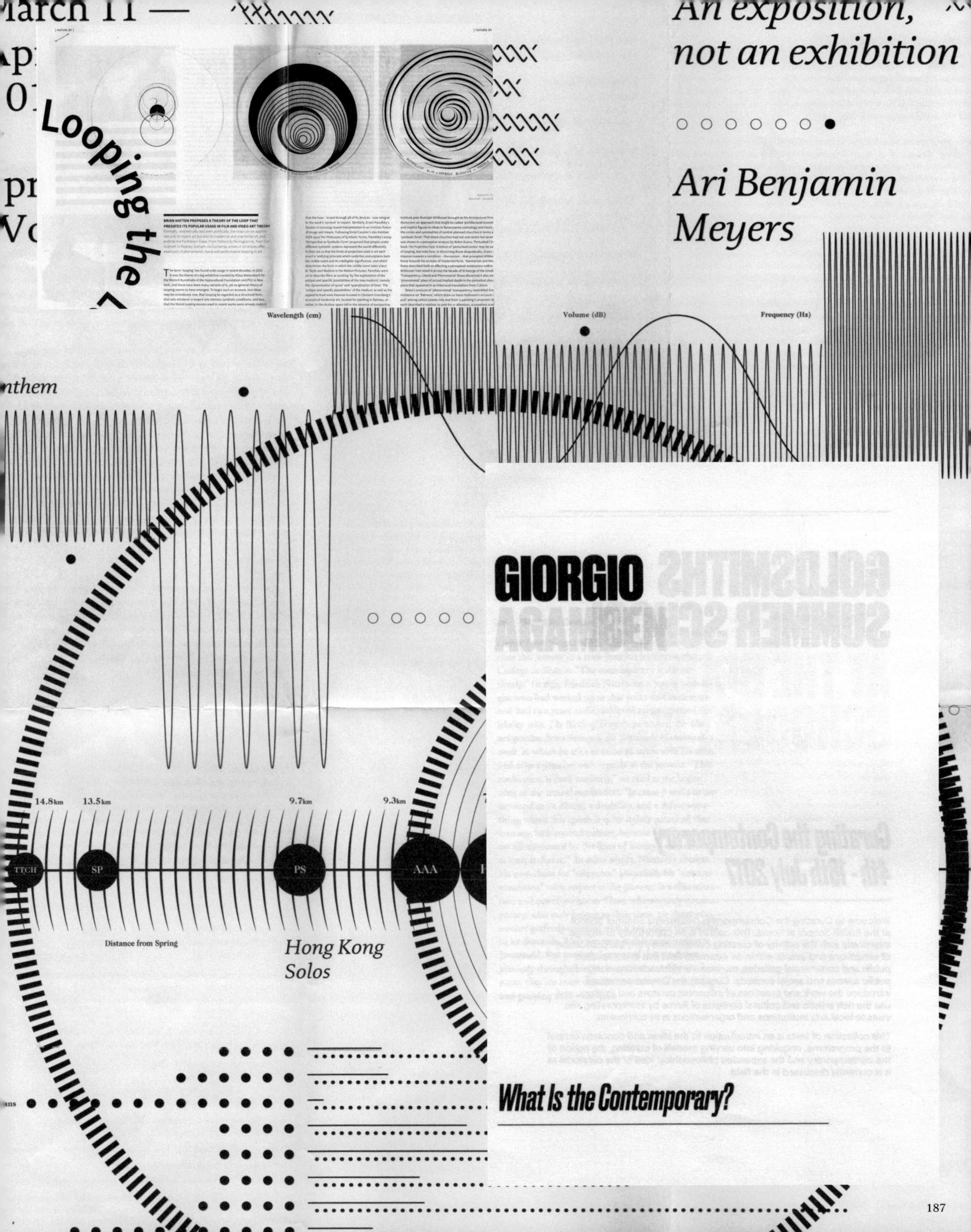

An exposition, not an exhibition
Ari Benjamin Meyers
Looping the
Wavelength (cm)
Volume (dB)
Frequency (Hz)
14.8km
13.5km
9.7km
9.3km
TTCH
SP
PS
AAA
Distance from Spring
Hong Kong Solos
GIORGIO
AGAMBEN
What Is the Contemporary?

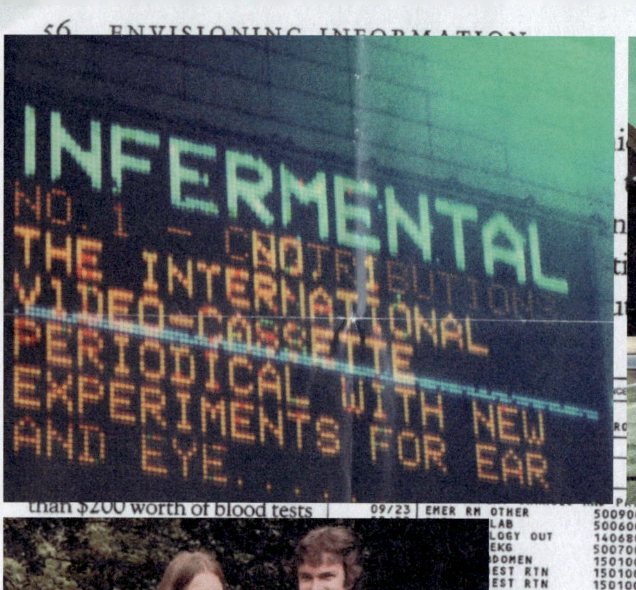

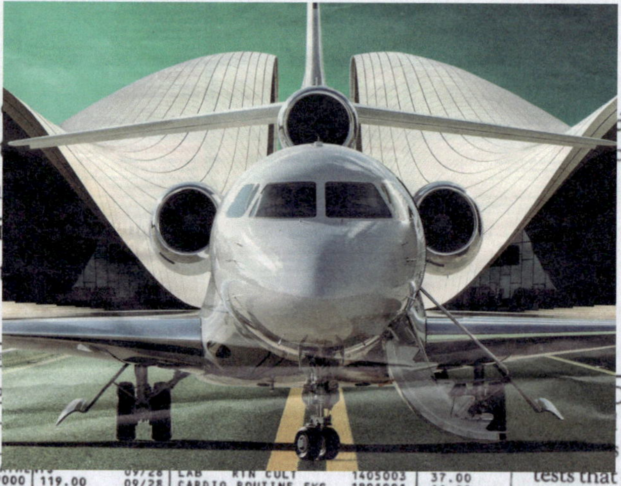

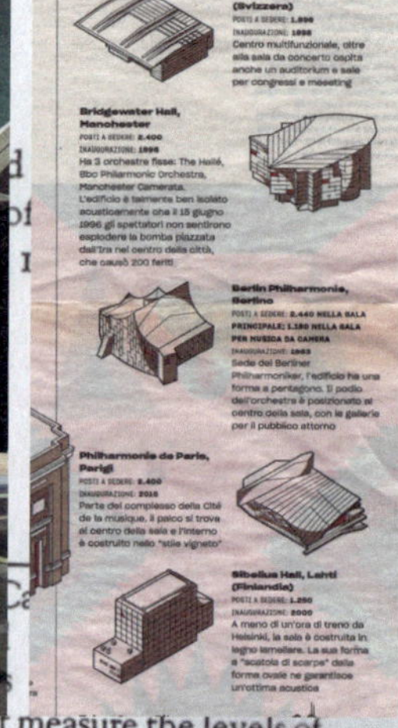

than $200 worth of blood tests

09/23	EMER RM OTHER	5009000	119.00	
	LAB	5006000	172.00	
	…LOGY OUT	1406800	35.00	
	EKG	5007000	61.00	
	…DOMEN	1501001	58.00	
	…EST RTN	1501009	58.00	
	…EST RTN	1501009	58.00	
	…EST RTN	1501009	58.00	
	…ARMACY	2601000	2.25	
	…PHARMACY	5002000	46.00	

09/28	LAB RTN CULT	1405003	37.00
09/28	CARDIO ROUTINE EKG	1801001	61.00
09/28	BLD BK GROUP RH	1701002	28.00
09/28	BLD BK X MATCH	1701006	46.00
09/28	BLD BK ANTIBDY SCRN	1701004	23.00
09/28	X-RAY CHEST-BED	1501128	74.00
09/28	X-RAY CHEST-BED	1501128	74.00
09/28	PHARMACY	2601000	11.00
09/28	PHAR IV SOLUTIONS	2601003	13.50
09/28	PHAR IV SOLUTIONS	2601003	50.00

tests that measure the levels of sodium, potassium, and six other chemicals in her blood. The hospital charges Mrs. K ____ $31 for each Chem-8.

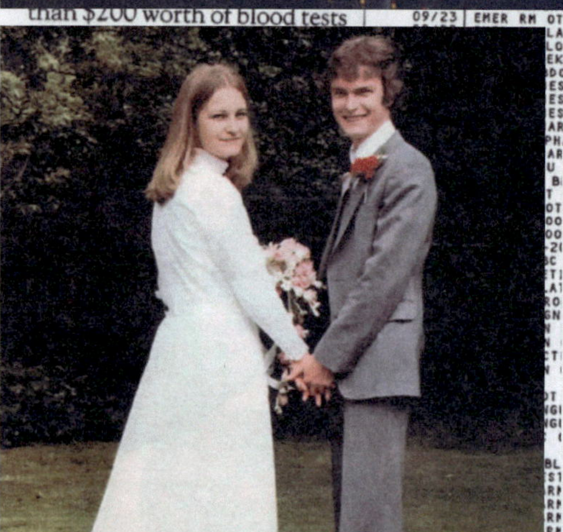

SHELF-IMPROVEMENT

The coronavirus pandemic has prompted a surge in sales of DIY products as many of us finally get around to doing all those jobs we didn't have time for before lockdown. Self-confessed procrastinator *Neville Hawcock* celebrates the new-found urge to repair – but will he ever get around to fixing his own shed?

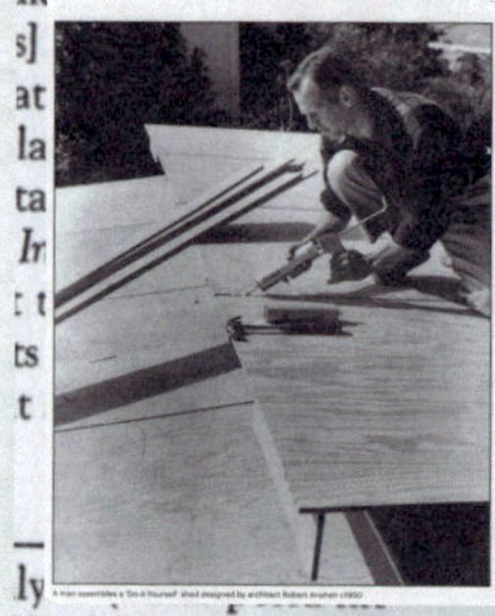

average ICU rates in the country: $632 a d
the average i
developed i
provide tech
port systems
traordinary
ing. An inh
monitor ("
mont") is being used to keep a
close check
oxygen in he
the attentio
in the ICU
might alread

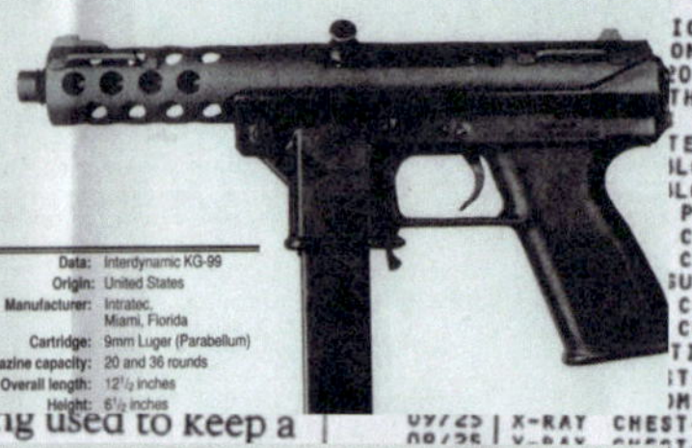

Her kidneys are fail-

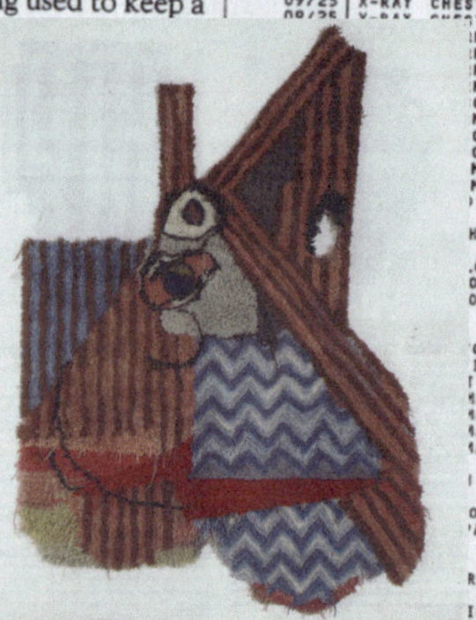

09/25 X-RAY CHEST-BED	1501128	74.00	
09/25 X-RAY CHEST-BED	1501128	74.00	
…MACY	2601000	13.50	
…MACY	2601000	39.00	
…MACY	2601000	3.70	
…MACY	2601000	16.50	
…OLUTIONS	2601003	16.00	
…MACY	2601000	2.50	
…OLUTIONS	2601003	13.50	
…OLUTIONS	2601003	13.50	
…MACY	2601000	3.35	
…MACY	2601000	2.25	
… GAS MONT	2101014	354.00	
		500.00	
…H DETER	1404011	17.00	
	1401111	31.00	
…OOD CT	1402101	L7.00	
…ODIUM	1401077	27.00	
…OTASS	1401076	27.00	
	1402099	15.00	
	1401111	31.00	
…CIN TROUG	1401112	27.00	
…INE EKG	1801001	61.00	
…T BED	1501128	74.00	
…MACY	2601000	31.20	
…MACY	2601000	3.70	
…MACY	2601000	13.50	
…MACY	2601000	39.00	
	1401111	31.00	
… DETER	1404011	17.00	
	1402099	15.00	
…OOD CT	1402101	17.00	
…AR THROM	1404001	27.00	
	1401111	31.00	
	1401104	31.00	
…RY OUT	1401800	10.00	
… CULT	1405007	40.00	
…INE EKG	1801001	61.00	
…BDY SCRN	1701004	23.00	
…N FEE	1701028	69.00	
…SOLUTIONS	2601003	37.50	
09/27 PHAR IV SOLUTIONS	2601003		
27 PHAR IV SOLU…			
27 PHAR IV SOLU…			
27 PHAR IV SOLU…			
27 PHARMAC…			
27 PHARMAC…			
27 PHARMAC…			
27 PHARMAC…			
27 PHARMAC…			
27 PHARMAC…			
27 PHARMAC…			
27 PACK CE 250 P…			
27 25 NSA 50MU P…			
27 INFUSION PUMP			
27 INHAL RESPIRAT…			
27 ROOM ICU			
28 OPER OP RM 1…			
28 LAB OCC BLO…			
28 LAB GENTAMYCIN…			
28 LAB DIFF	1402099	15.00	

09/29	INHAL BLOOD GAS MONT	2101034	354.00
09/29	INHAL BLOOD GAS MONT	2101034	354.00
09/29	ROOM ICU		500.00
09/30	LAB AUTO BLOOD CT	1402101	17.00
09/30	LAB CHEM-8	1401111	31.00
09/30	LAB CHEM-8	1401111	31.00
09/30	LAB DIFF	1402099	15.00
09/30	SP HEM COAG STDY COM	1602007	239.00
09/30	SP HEMATOLOGY	1600000	49.00
09/30	SP HEM RETIC CT	1602046	17.00
09/30	SP HEM CBC	1602010	28.00
09/30	LAB BACTERIA SM	1405011	16.00
09/30	LAB ACT PAR THROM	1404001	27.00
09/30	LAB PROTH DETER	1404011	17.00
09/30	LAB FIBRIN QUAN	1404007	40.00
09/30	LAB AUTO BLOOD CT	1402101	17.00
09/30	LAB CHEM-20	1401104	31.00
09/30	LAB TBC CULT	1405014	42.00
09/30	LAB CHEM-20	1401104	31.00
09/30	LAB RTN CULT	1405003	37.00
09/30	LAB RTN CULT	1405003	37.00
09/30	BLD BK ADMIN FEE	1701028	207.00
09/30	X-RAY CHEST-BED	1501128	74.00
09/30	X-RAY CHEST-BED	1501128	74.00
09/30	PHAR IV SOLUTIONS	2601003	16.00
09/30	PHARMACY	2601000	39.00
09/30	PHAR IV SOLUTIONS	2601003	21.00
09/30	PHAR IV SOLUTIONS	2601003	16.00
09/30	PHARMACY	2601000	3.70
09/30	PHARMACY	2601000	13.50
09/30	PHARMACY	2601000	11.00
09/30	PHARMACY	2601000	2.25
09/30	PHAR IV SOLUTIONS	2601000	21.00
09/30	PHAR IV SOLUTIONS	2601000	21.00
09/30	PHAR IV SOLUTIONS	2601003	18.50
09/30	PHARMACY	2601000	2.50
09/30	PLAT CONC PROC FEE	1701014	180.00
09/30	FRSH FR PLA PROC FEE	1701019	26.00
09/30	INHAL RESPIRATOR	2102015	119.00
09/30	DRESSING SET-DISP.	2708041	7.00
09/30	VEST RESTRAINT	2709032	12.00
09/30	INHAL BLOOD GAS MONT	2101034	354.00
10/02	PHARMACY	2601000	27.20

kidney dialy
respirators
systems for
time, but ca
lying disease
beginning to question this
practice. A r
George Was
sity Medic
cluded: "Su
resources are
aggressive bu
attempts to a

Mrs. K ____
a high fever.
sent culture
urine, and spu
find out why
gentamicin (
troug"), a pov
Such strong
toxic side effe
kills bacteria
cause kidney

Mrs. K ____
vest restrain
used in Intensive Care to keep

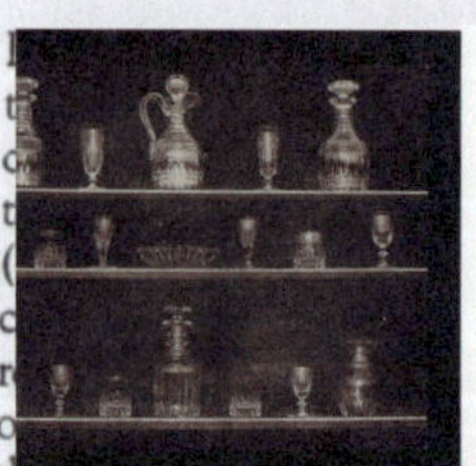

the machine for about $15,000.

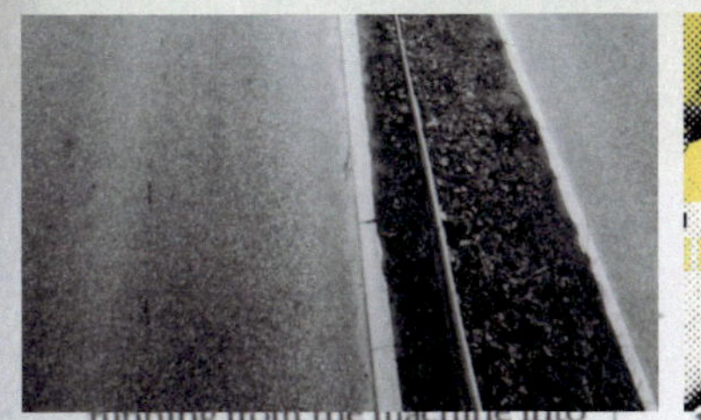

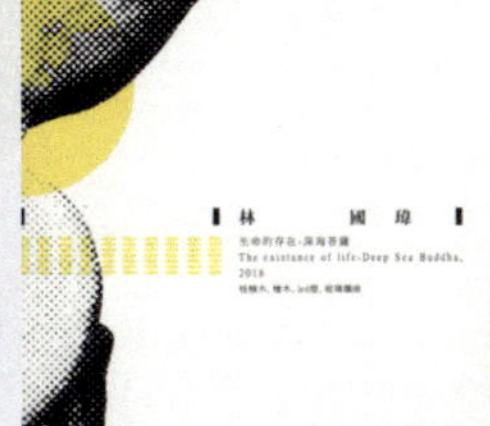

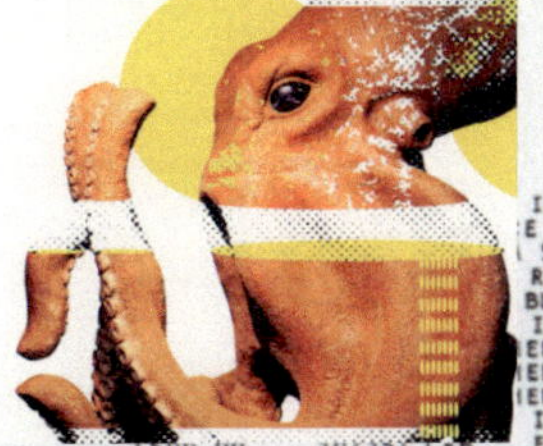

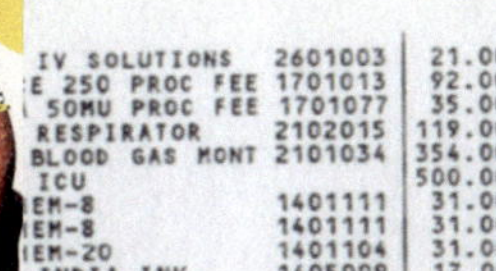

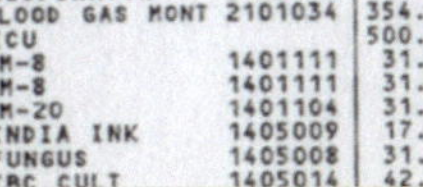

	IV SOLUTIONS	2601003	21.00
	E 250 PROC FEE	1701013	92.00
	SOMU PROC FEE	1701077	35.00
	RESPIRATOR	2102015	119.00
	BLOOD GAS MONT	2101034	354.00
	ICU		500.00
	EM-8	1401111	31.00
	EM-8	1401111	31.00
	EM-20	1401104	31.00
	INDIA INK	1405009	17.00
	FUNGUS	1405008	31.00
	TBC CULT	1405014	42.00

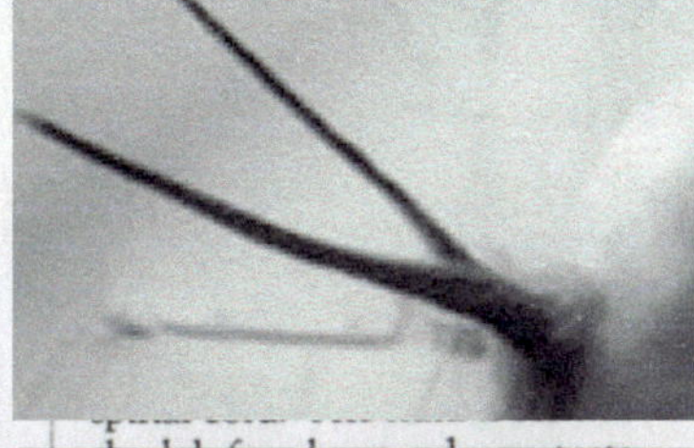

running from the machine into

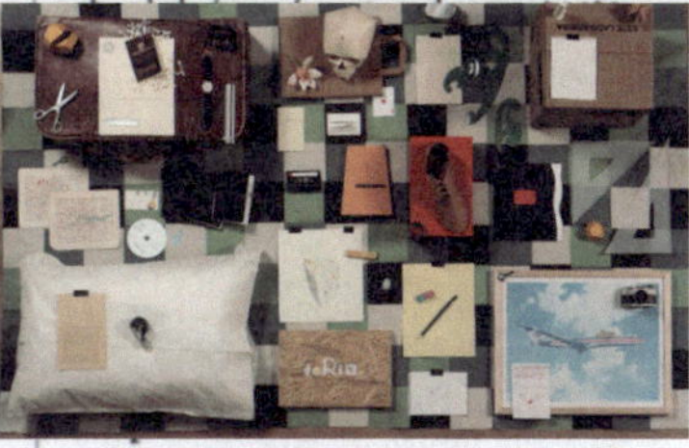

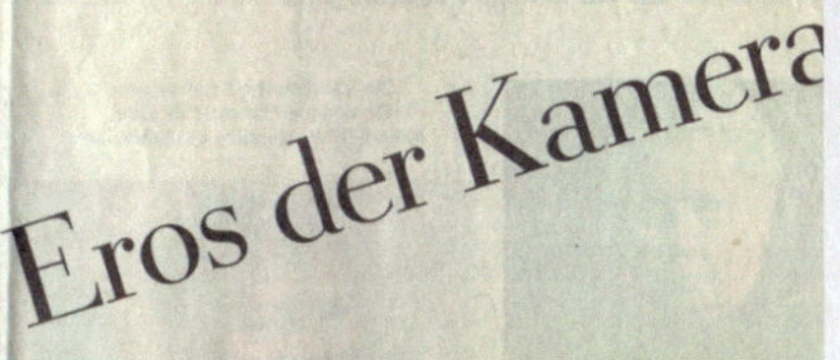

Eros der Kamera

Die Berliner Doppelausstellung »Am Set« dokumentiert Filmkunst in Fotografien

VON ALEXANDER CAMMANN

10/17 | X-RAY CHEST-BED 1501128 | 74.00

Weeks of halfway technology have given the doctors time for testing. The doctors may even have diagnosed what is wrong with Mrs. K _____; it is hard to say. But the ICU and its technology have not given

the cost of fresh blood plasma

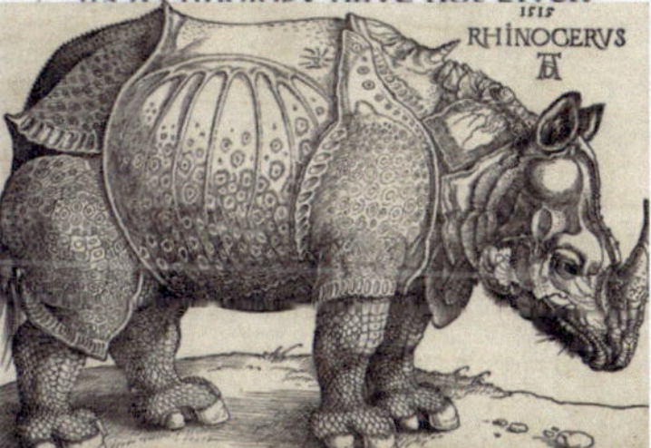

poured in.

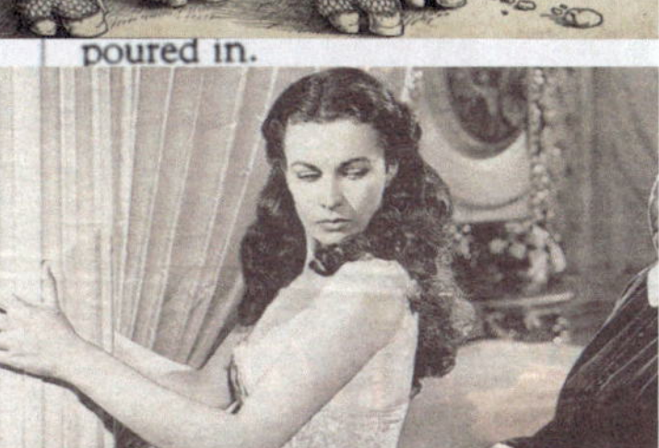

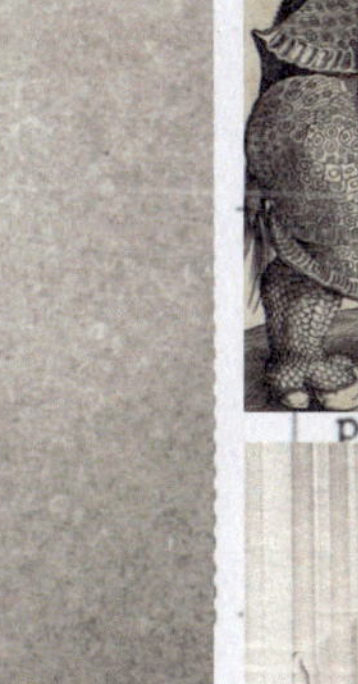

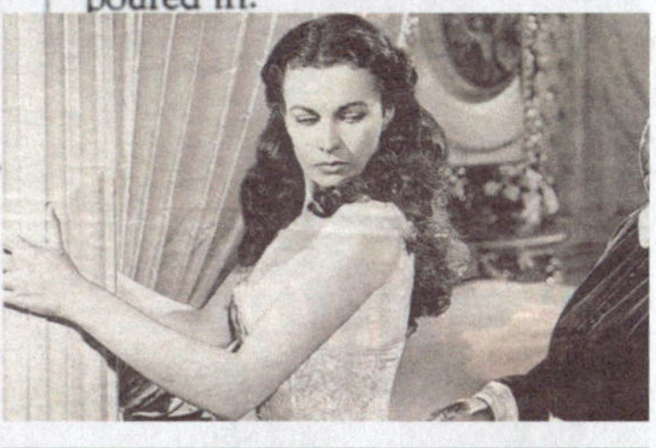

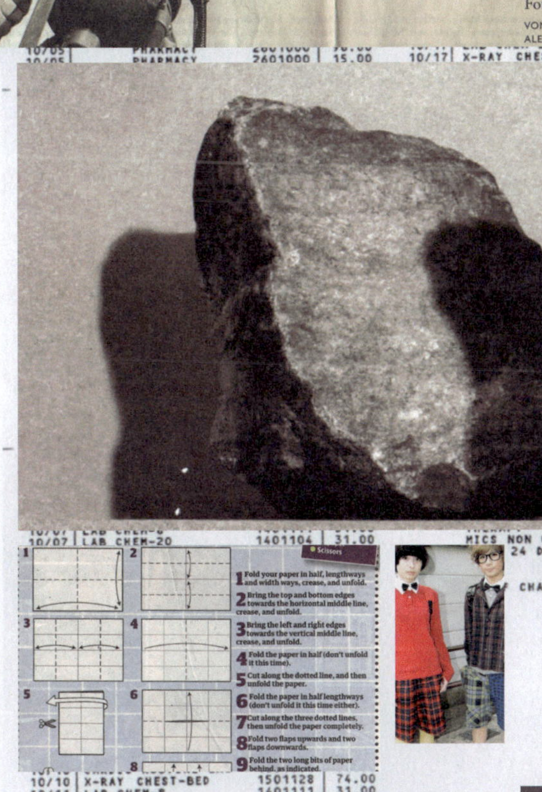

10/07 | LAB CHEM-20 1401104 | 31.00

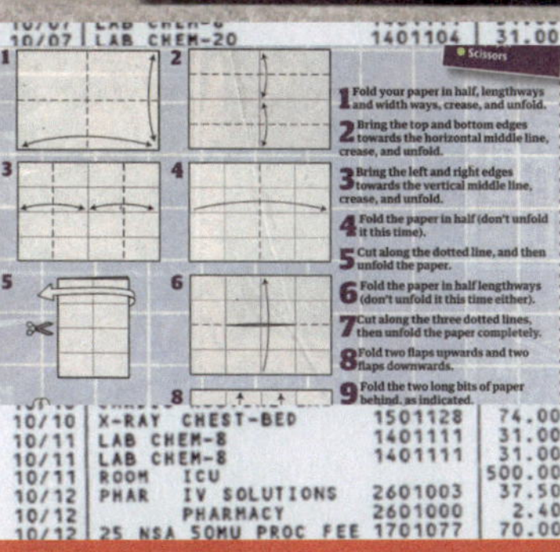

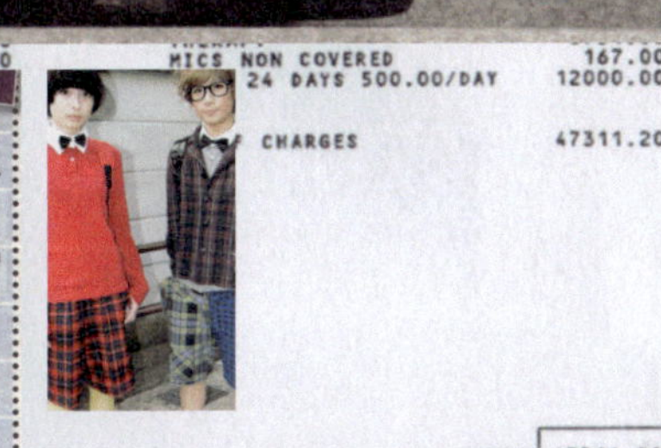

MICS NON COVERED	167.00
24 DAYS 500.00/DAY	12000.00
CHARGES	47311.20
TOTAL	47311.20

10/10	X-RAY CHEST-BED	1501128	74.00
10/11	LAB CHEM-8	1401111	31.00
10/11	LAB CHEM-8	1401111	31.00
10/11	ROOM ICU		500.00
10/12	PHAR IV SOLUTIONS	2601003	37.50
10/12	PHARMACY	2601000	2.40
10/12	25 NSA SOMU PROC FEE	1701077	70.00

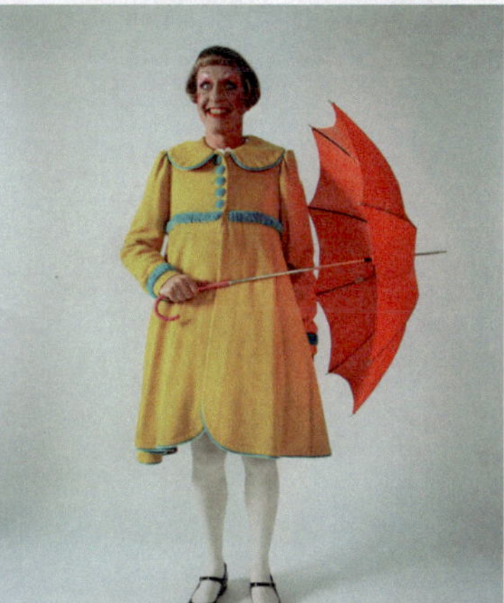

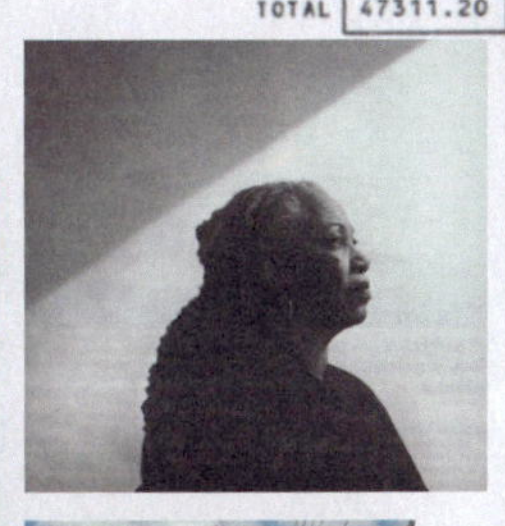

tors have "tagged" her red blood cells with a radioactive isotope. Using a camera that picks up the isotope, the doctors can watch the passage

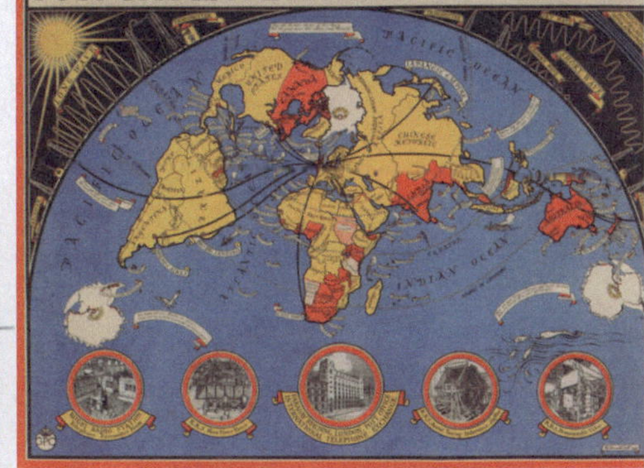

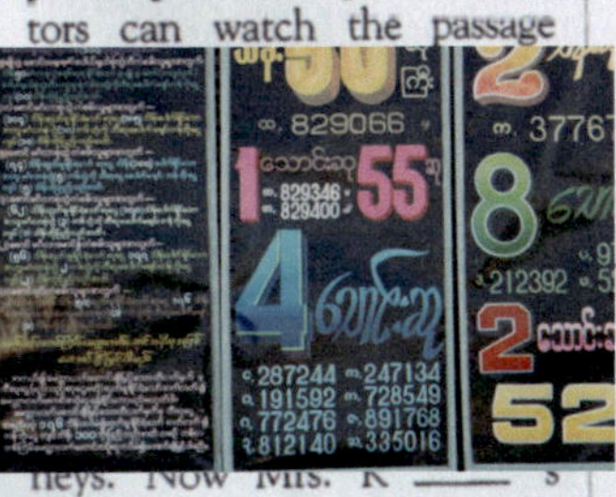

neys. Now Mrs. K _____'s heart seems to be going.

10/13	PHARMACY	2601000	14.50
10/13	PHARMACY	2601000	2.40

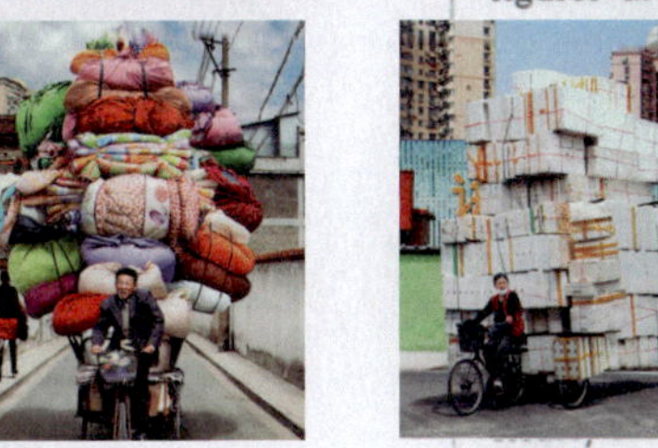

22 billion on f this, $135.5 nt on hospital e 56,241 ICU e the one Mrs. t alive in, and n was spent for t represented ent of the gross national product.

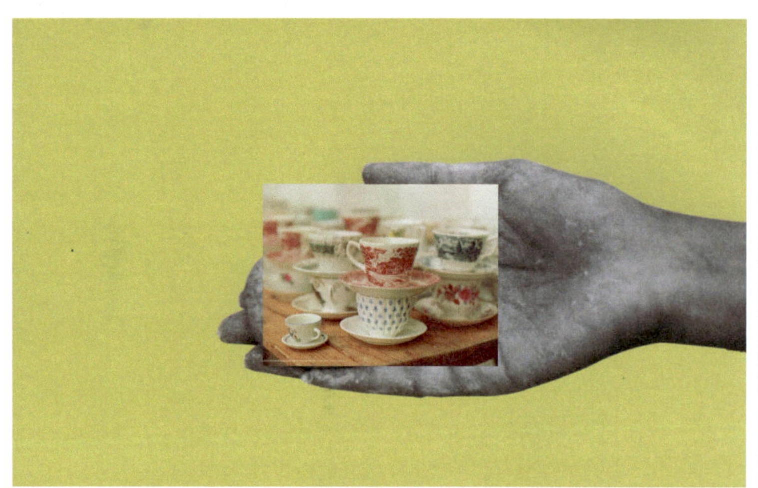

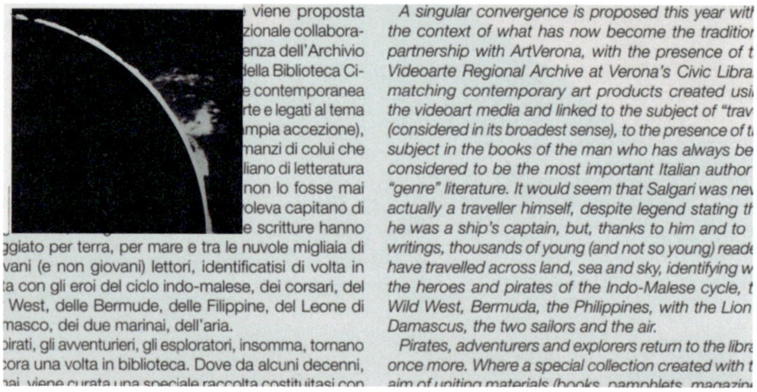

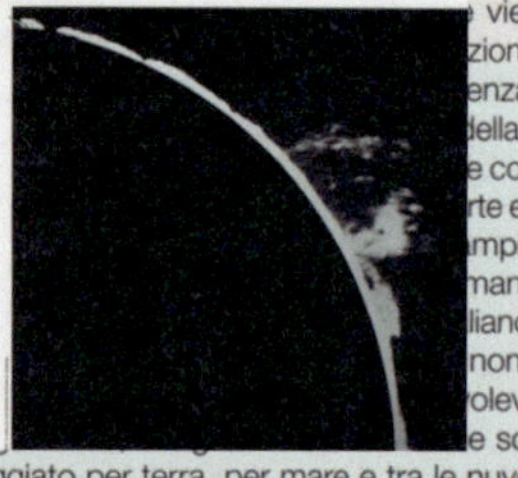

viene proposta
zionale collabora-
enza dell'Archivio
della Biblioteca Ci-
e contemporanea
rte e legati al tema
mpia accezione),
manzi di colui che
liano di letteratura
non lo fosse mai
oleva capitano di
e scritture hanno
ggiato per terra, per mare e tra le nuvole migliaia di
vani (e non giovani) lettori, identificatisi di volta in
ta con gli eroi del ciclo indo-malese, dei corsari, del
West, delle Bermude, delle Filippine, del Leone di
masco, dei due marinai, dell'aria.
pirati, gli avventurieri, gli esploratori, insomma, tornano
cora una volta in biblioteca. Dove da alcuni decenni,

*A singular convergence is proposed this year wit
the context of what has now become the traditio
partnership with ArtVerona, with the presence of t
Videoarte Regional Archive at Verona's Civic Libra
matching contemporary art products created usi
the videoart media and linked to the subject of "trav
(considered in its broadest sense), to the presence of t
subject in the books of the man who has always be
considered to be the most important Italian author
"genre" literature. It would seem that Salgari was ne
actually a traveller himself, despite legend stating t
he was a ship's captain, but, thanks to him and to
writings, thousands of young (and not so young) read
have travelled across land, sea and sky, identifying w
the heroes and pirates of the Indo-Malese cycle, t
Wild West, Bermuda, the Philippines, with the Lion
Damascus, the two sailors and the air.*
*Pirates, adventurers and explorers return to the libr
once more. Where a special collection created with t*

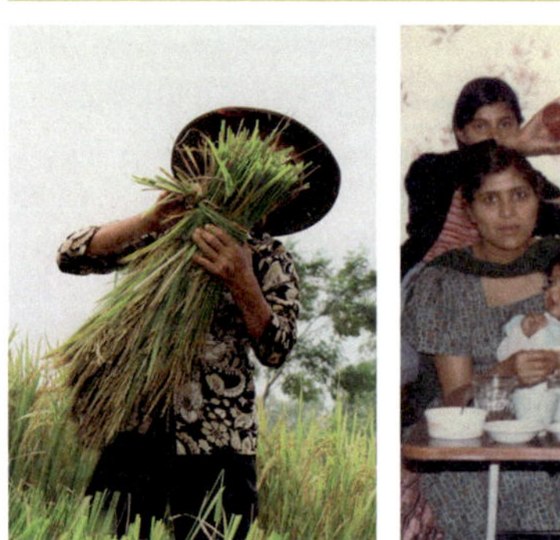

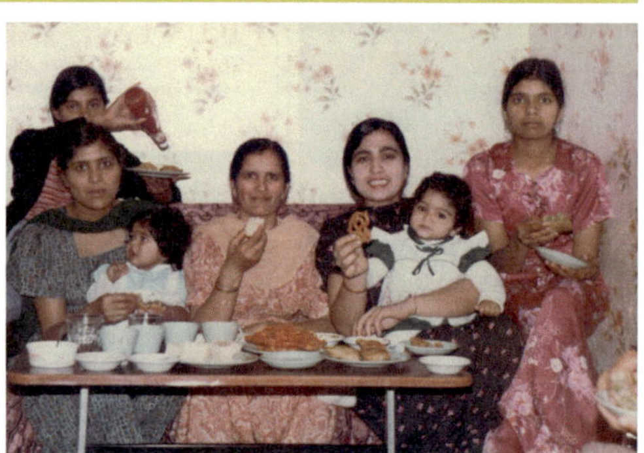

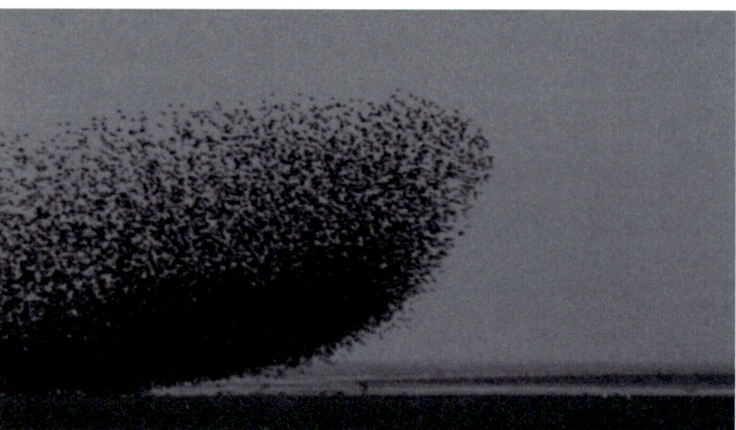

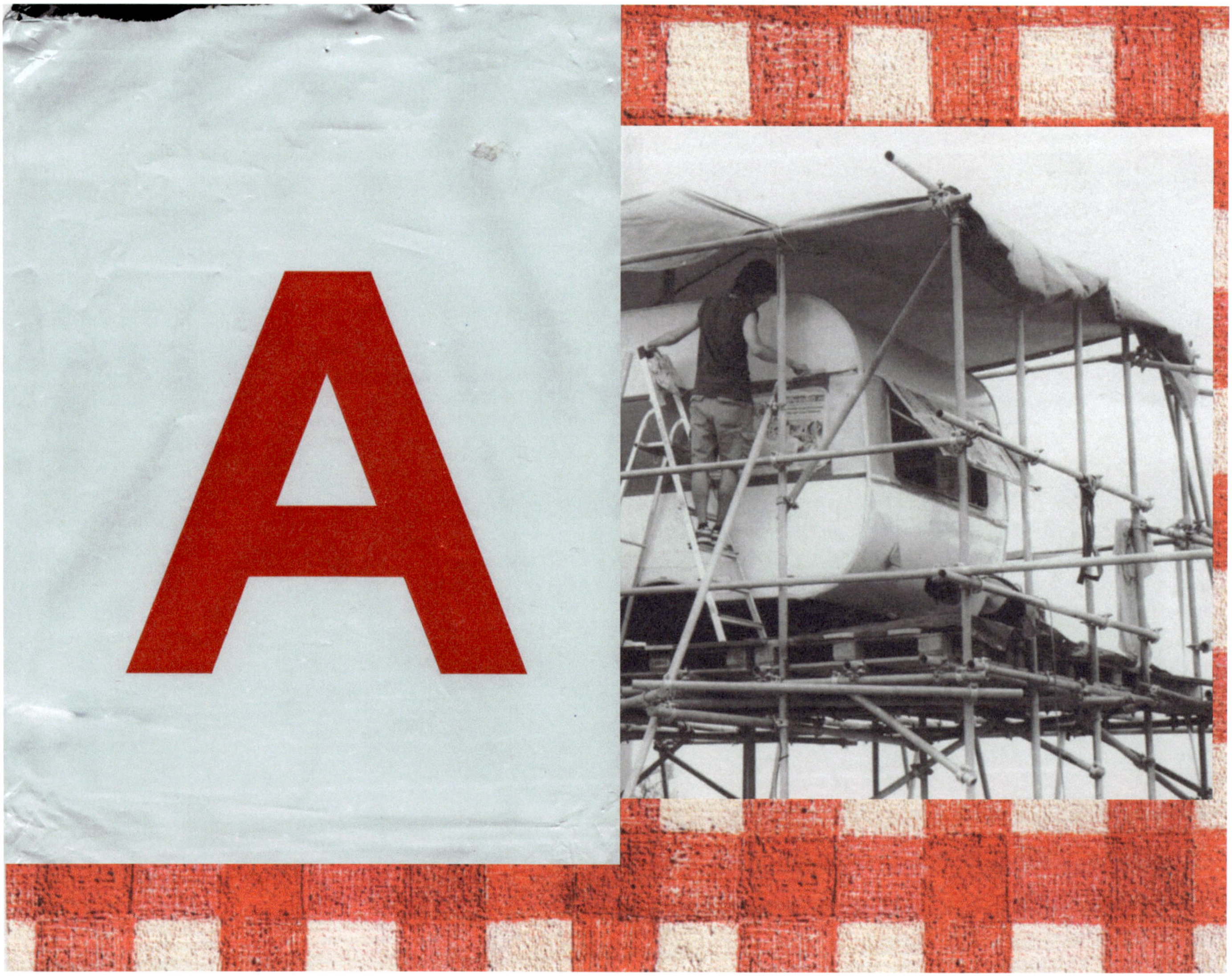

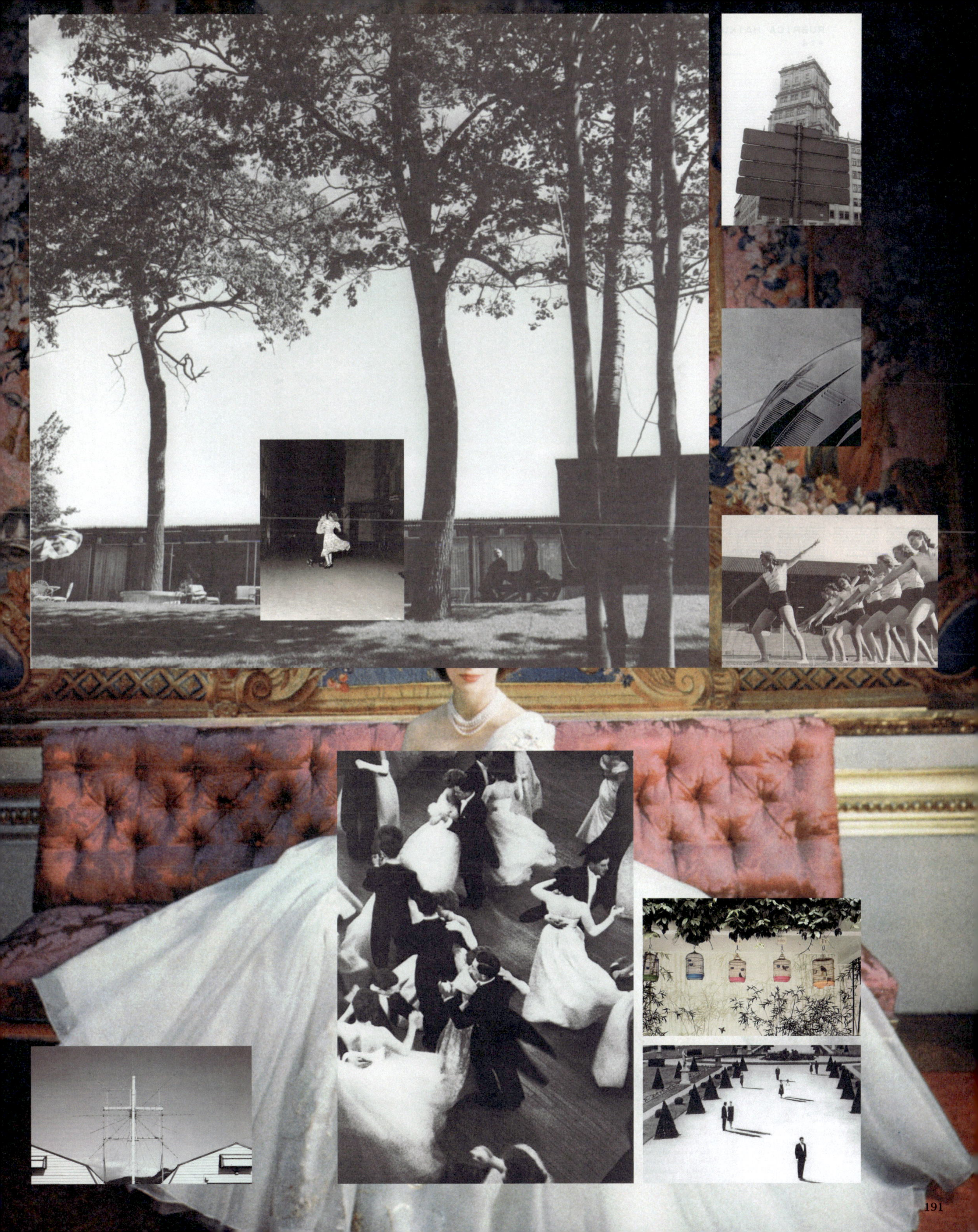

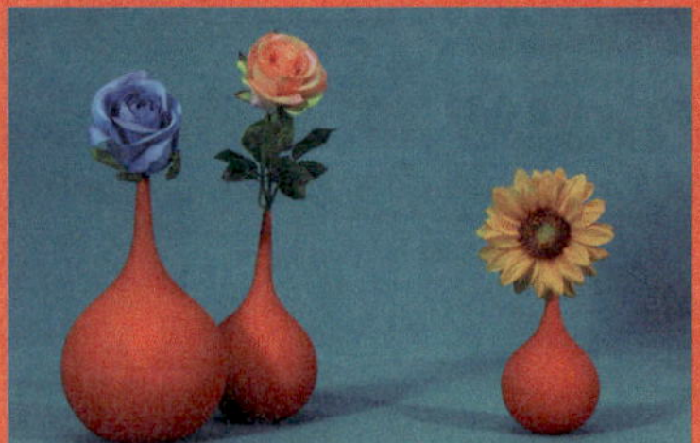
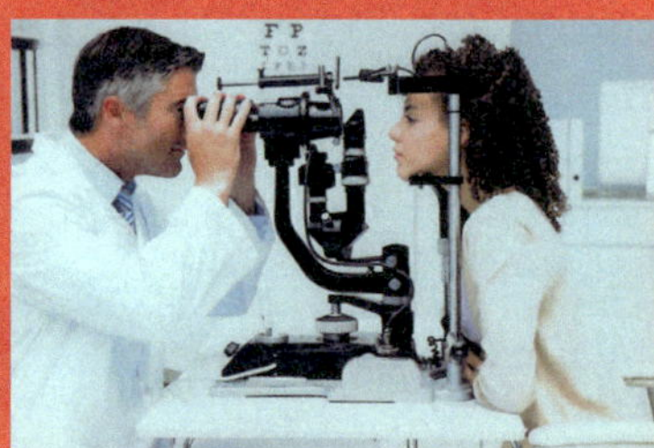
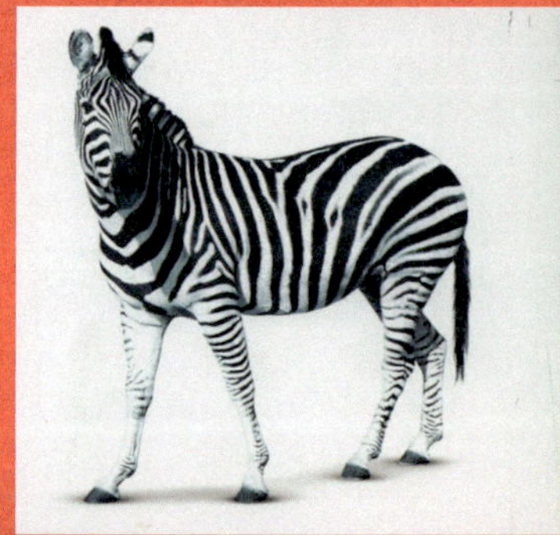

OUT

NOW!

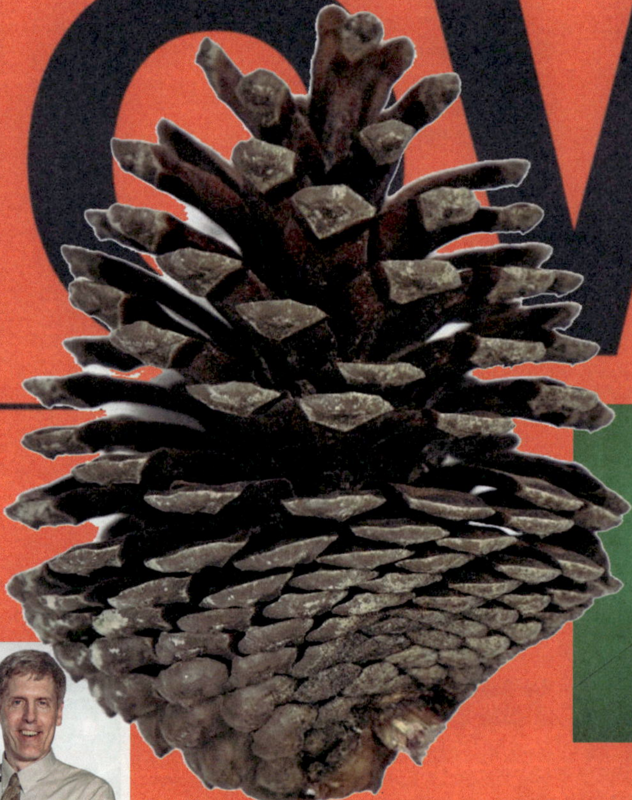

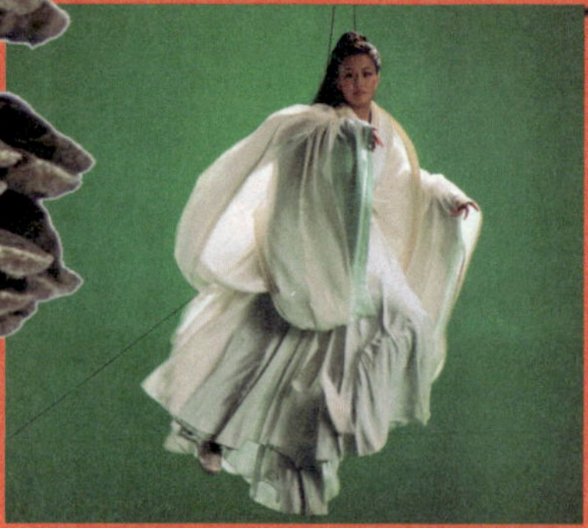

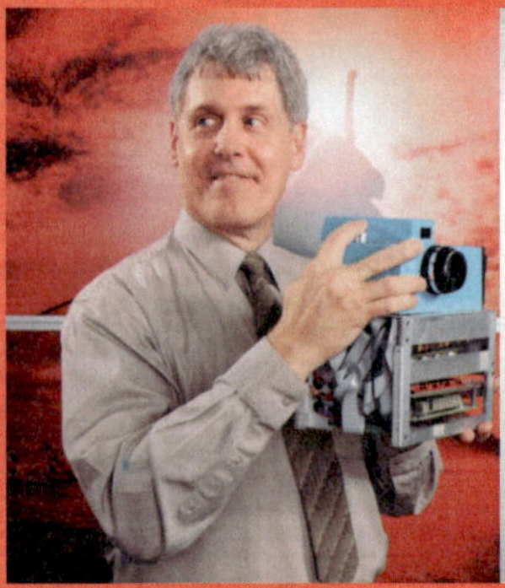

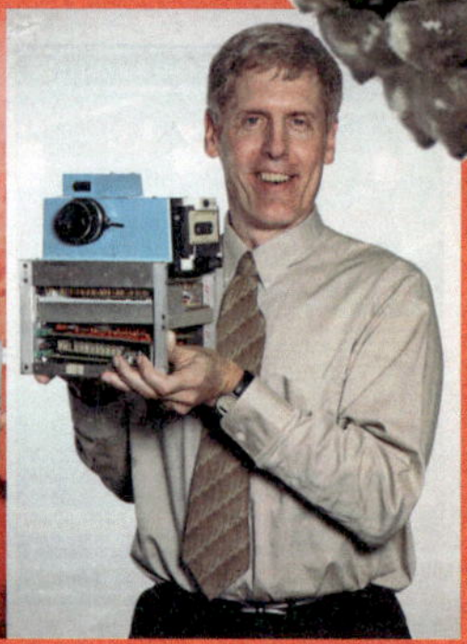

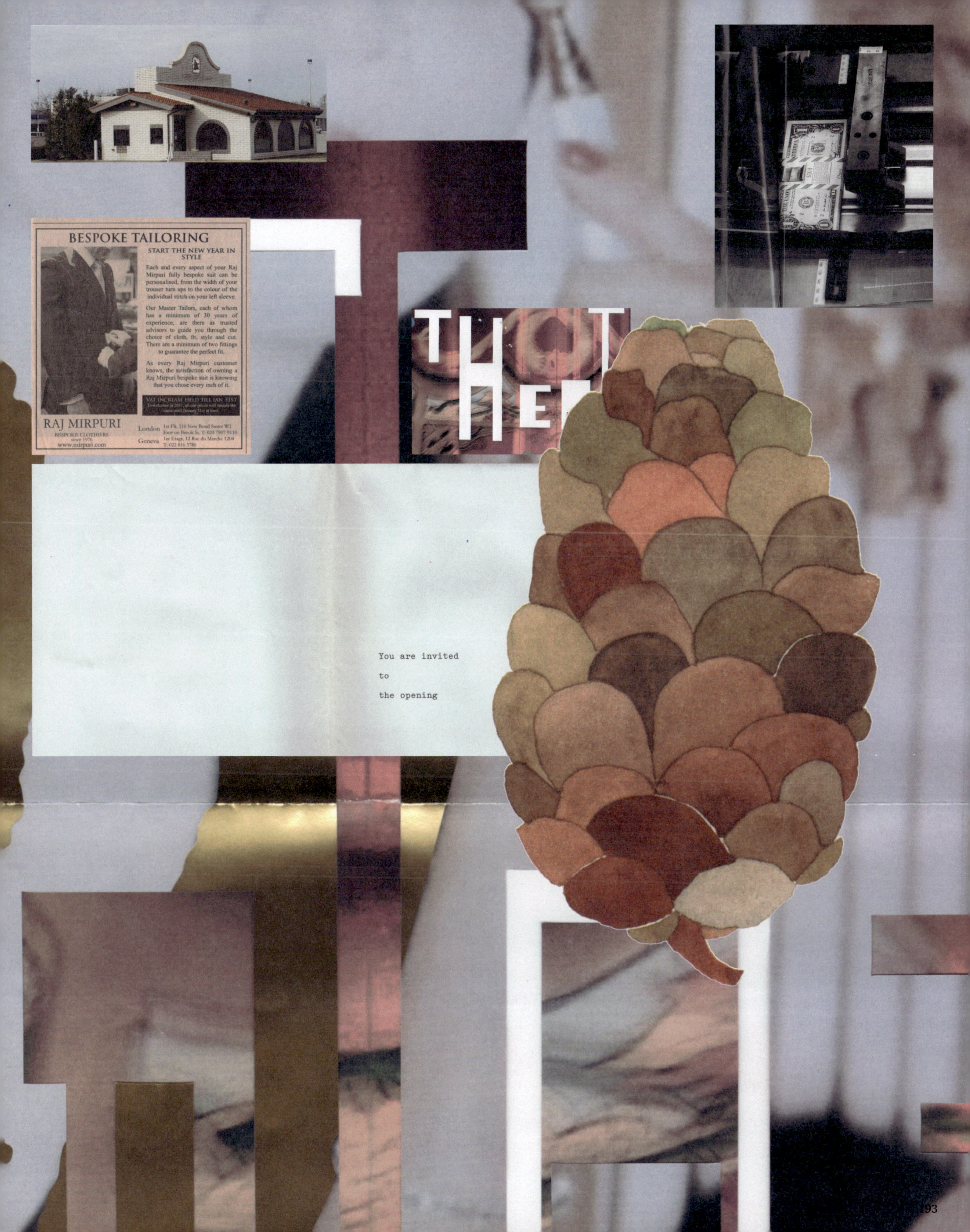
BESPOKE TAILORING
START THE NEW YEAR IN STYLE
Each and every aspect of your Raj Mirpuri fully bespoke suit can be personalised, from the width of your trouser turn ups to the colour of the individual stitch on your left sleeve.
Our Master Tailors, each of whom has a minimum of 30 years of experience, are there as trusted advisors to guide you through the choice of cloth, fit, style and cut. There are a minimum of two fittings to guarantee the perfect fit.
As every Raj Mirpuri customer knows, the satisfaction of owning a Raj Mirpuri bespoke suit is knowing that you chose every inch of it.
VAT INCREASE HELD TILL JAN 31ST
RAJ MIRPURI
BESPOKE CLOTHIERS
since 1976
www.mirpuri.com
London 1st Flr, 110 New Bond Street W1
Entr on Brook St. T: 020 7907 9110
Geneva 1er Etage, 12 Rue du Marche 1204
T: 022 816 3780
You are invited
to
the opening

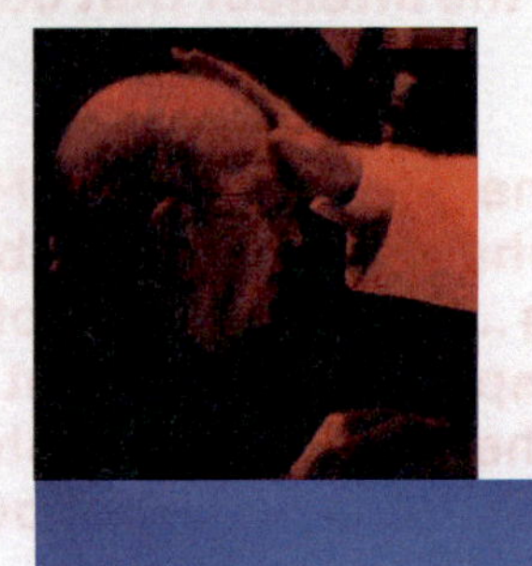

NOVEMBER 29 IS:

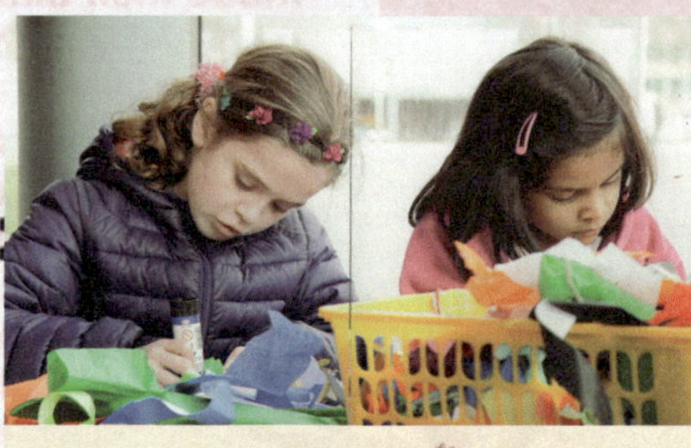

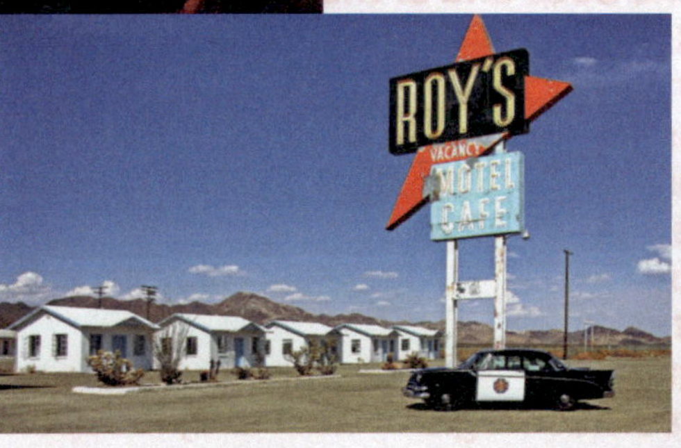

DO

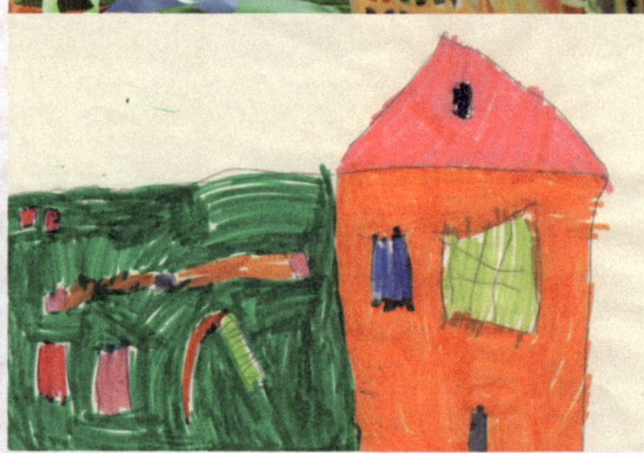

N NG

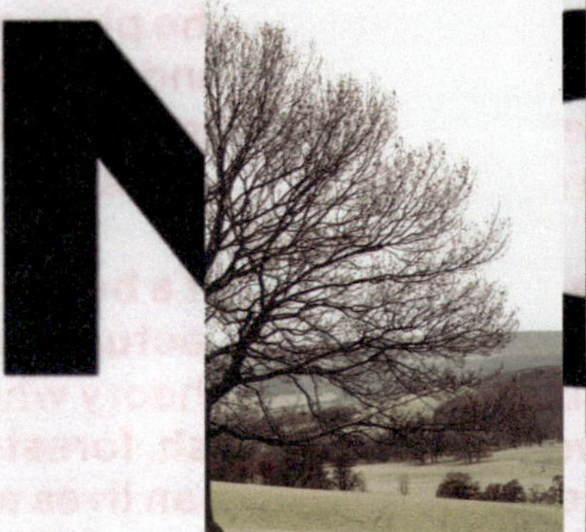

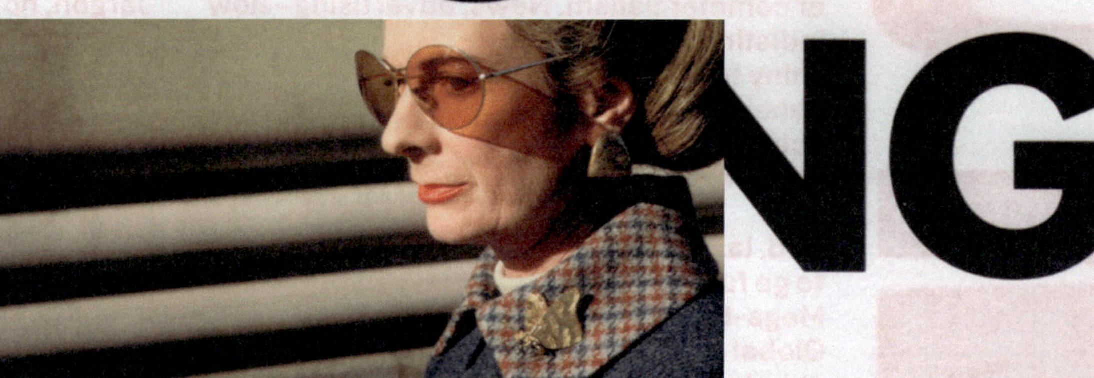

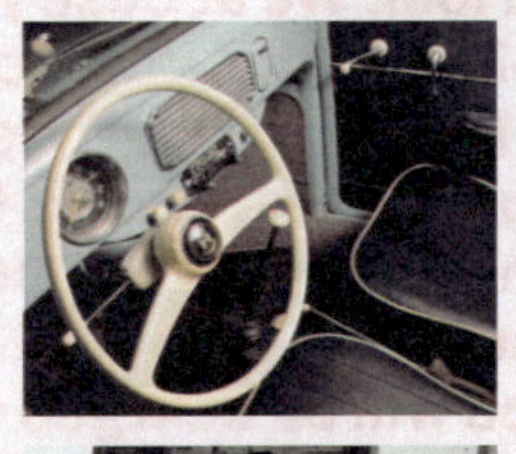

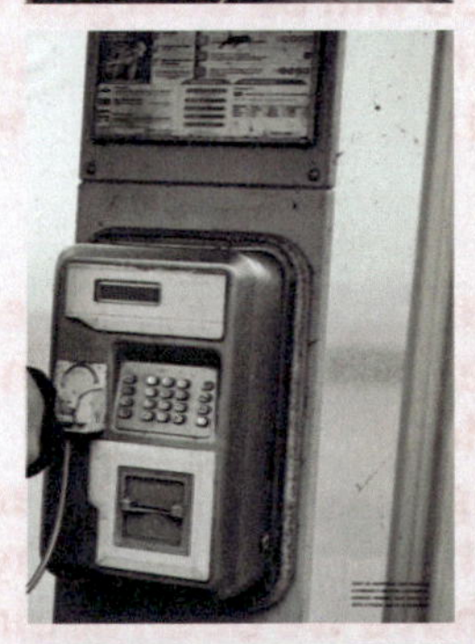

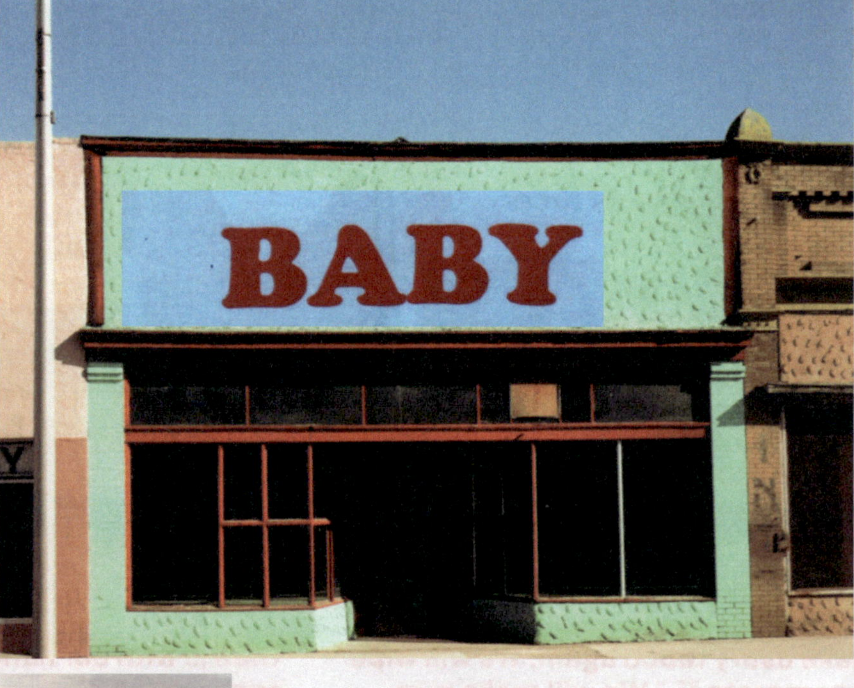

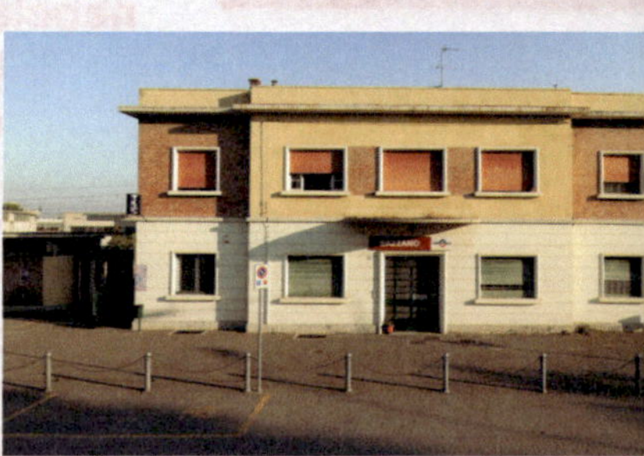

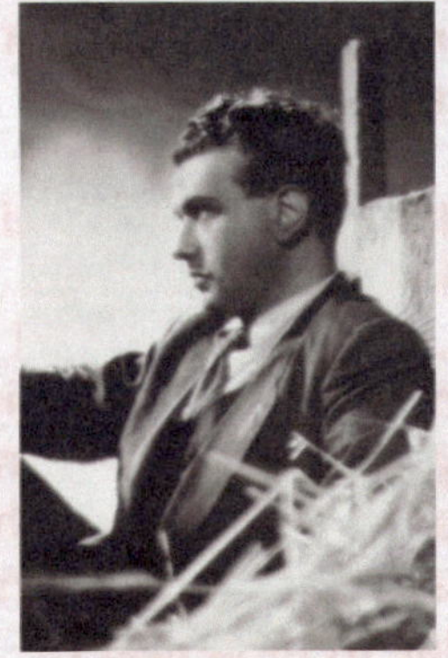

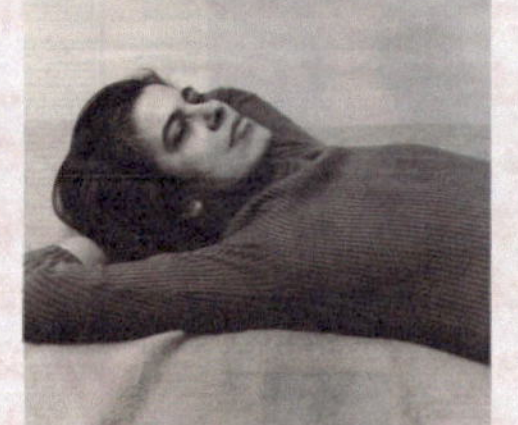

Just take a break from everything!

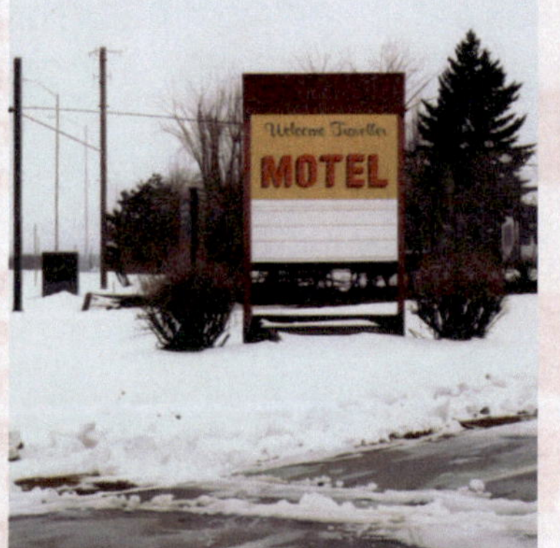

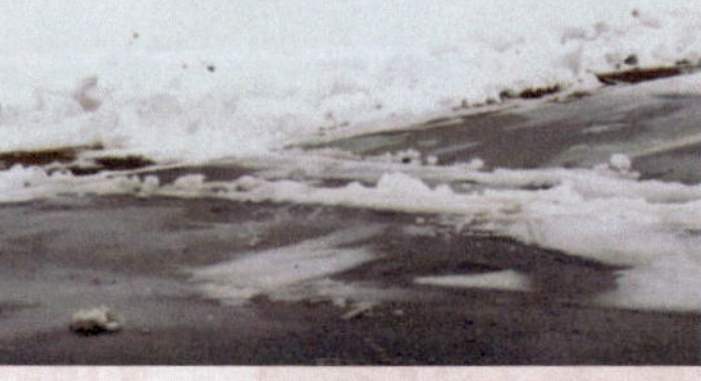

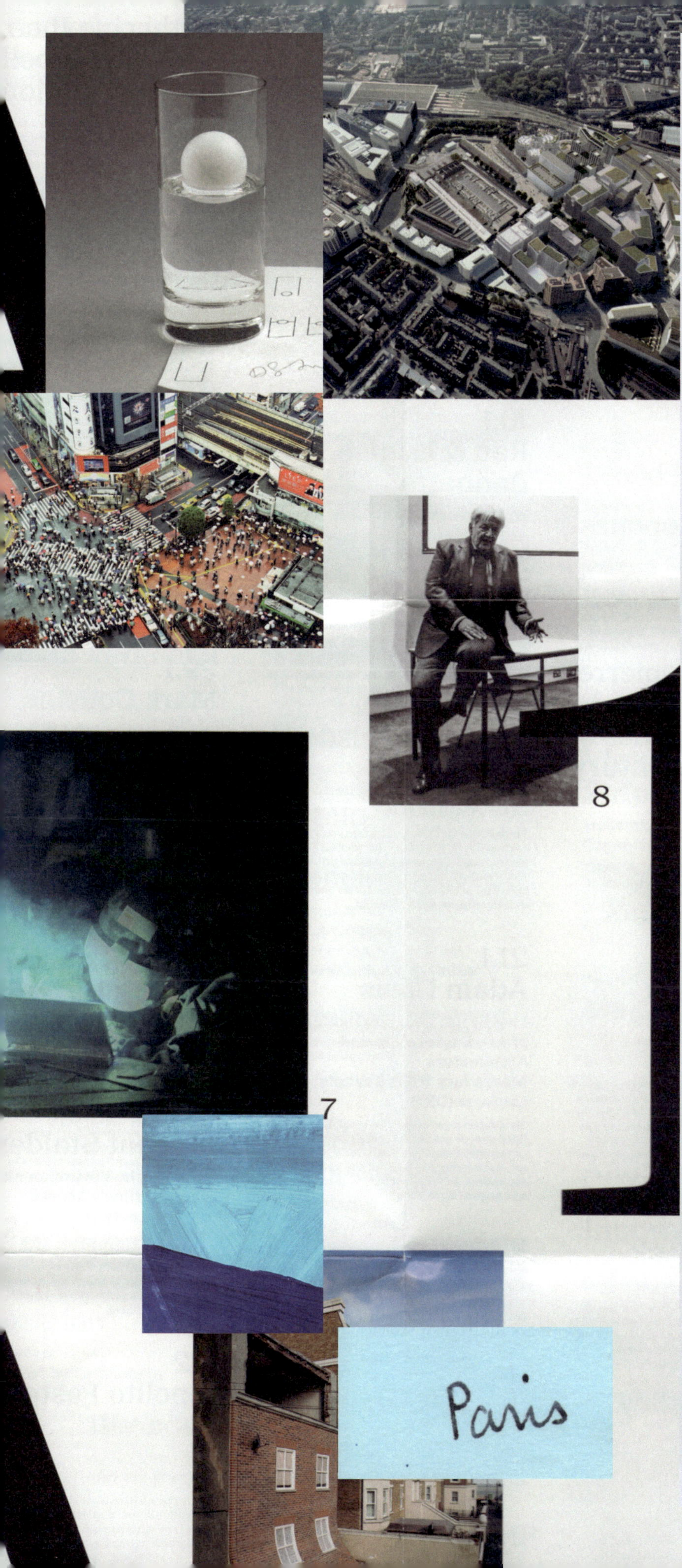

Situations

Starting on April 10, 2015

In April 2015 Fotomuseum Winterthur is launching a new exhibition format titled Situations, which will allow us to react more quickly to developments within photographic culture. The role of Situations is to define Fotomuseum Winterthur's vision of what photography is becoming, at the same time offering an innovative integration of physical exhibition space and virtual forum. Using tags and clusters as a mode of curatorial classification the aim is to integrate the real and the virtual in relation to exhibition in a new way. Numbered consecutively, a Situation may last a few hours, or two months, and might be photographic imagery, a film, a text, an on-line interview, a screenshot, a photo-book presentation, a projection, a Skype lecture, a performance etc. It might take place in Winterthur or perhaps in São Paulo or Berlin and be streamed on our website. The idea is to construct a constantly growing archive of Situations, reframing the idea of exhibition in relation to new technologies and both our local and global audiences.

The Situations programme will be organised around key clusters: *Relations* (the changing social ontology of photography in relation to digital culture); *Seeing Machines* (the power of the digital algorithm as a technology of seeing); and *Formats* (especially the exploration of lost or changing visual formats). Each cluster can then be searched and even reordered by visitors in the Situations on-line archive using a system of tags. Over time, new clusters and combinations – and new virtual exhibitions – will emerge.

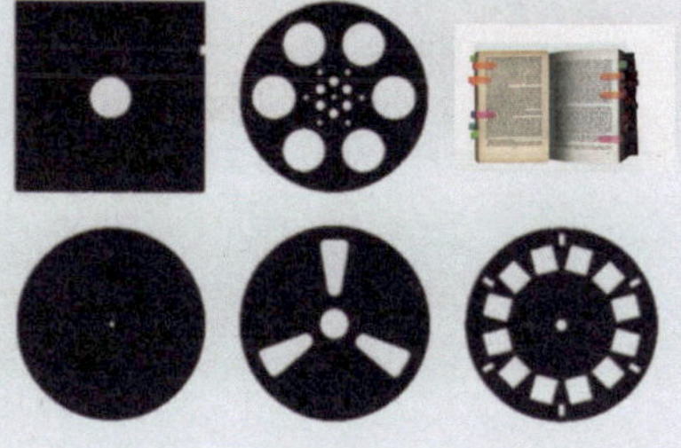

Experimental Jetset, from *Lost Format*, since 2000

8

7

Paris

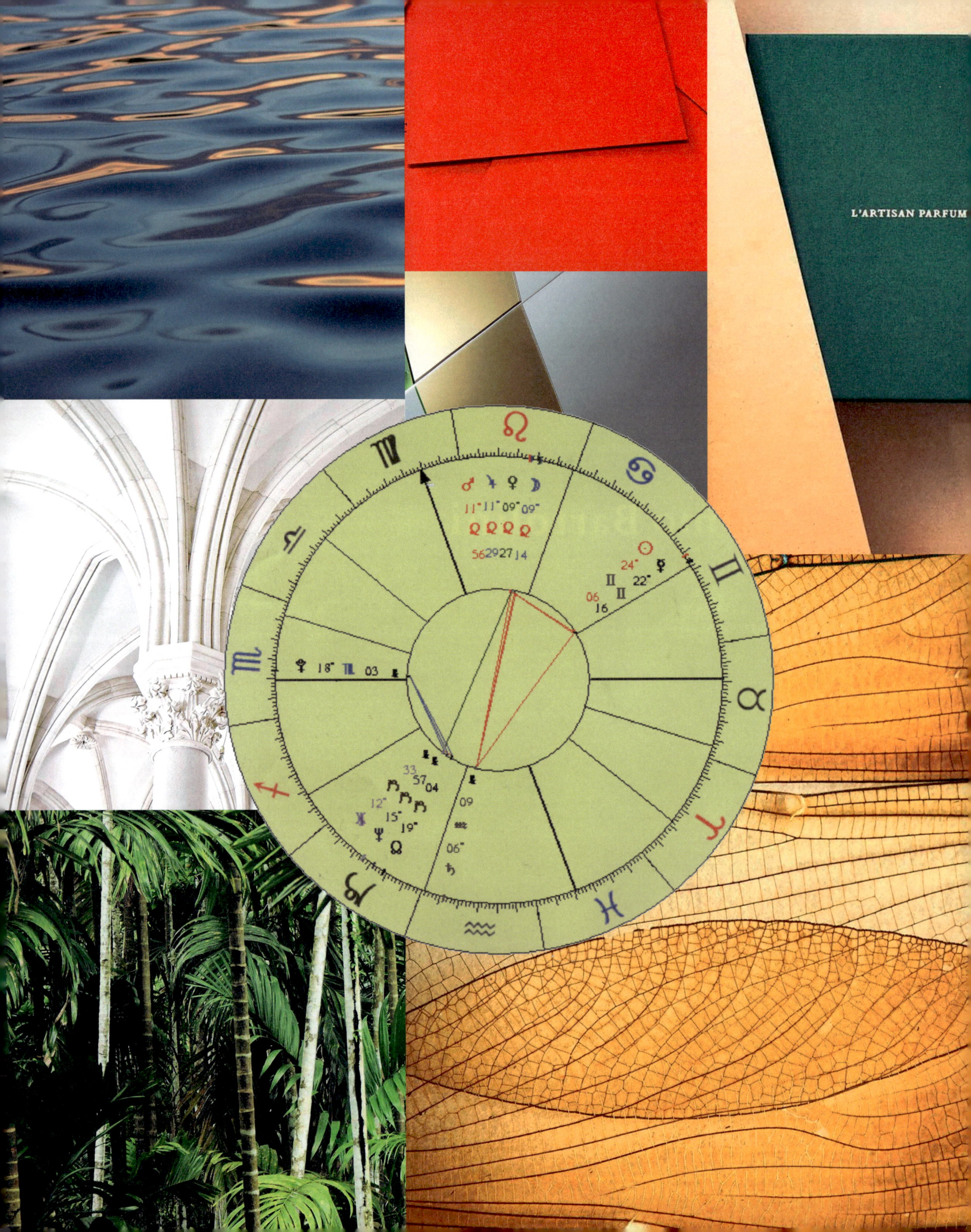
L'ARTISAN PARFUM

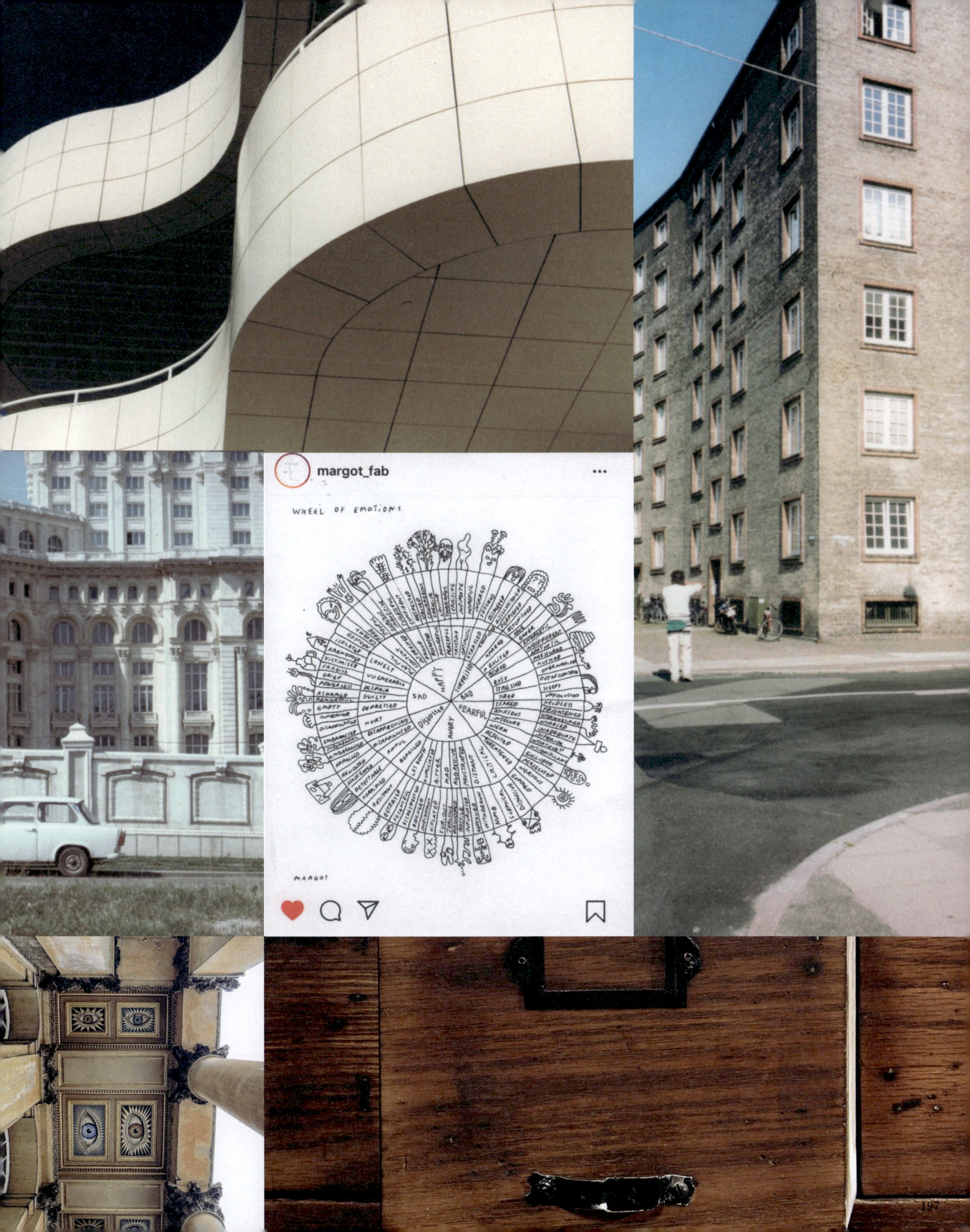
margot_fab
WHEEL OF EMOTIONS
SAD
HAPPY
BAD
FEARFUL
ANGRY
DISGUSTED
MARGOT

FLAMBOYANCY ISN'T A SIN

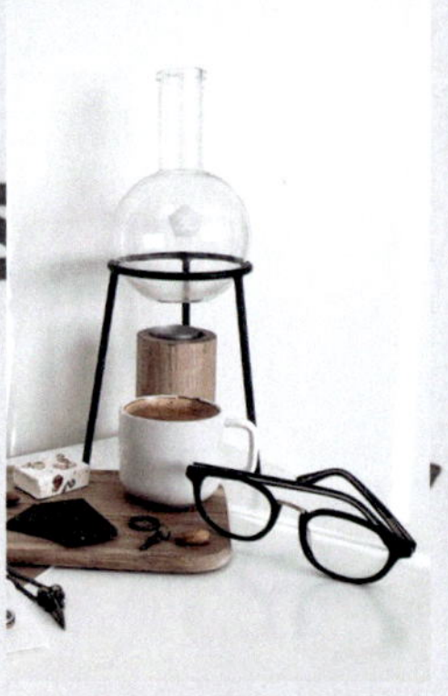

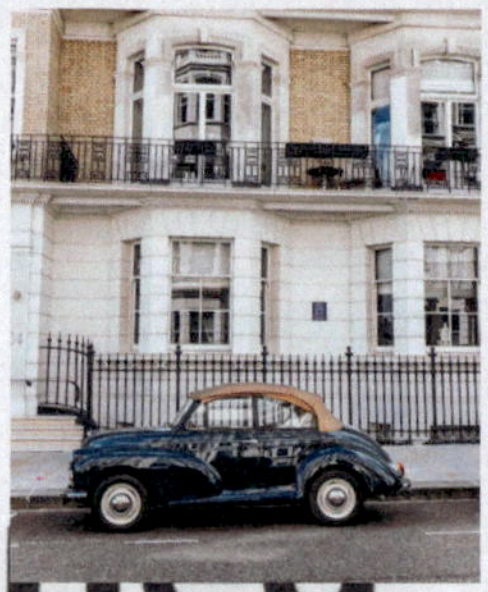

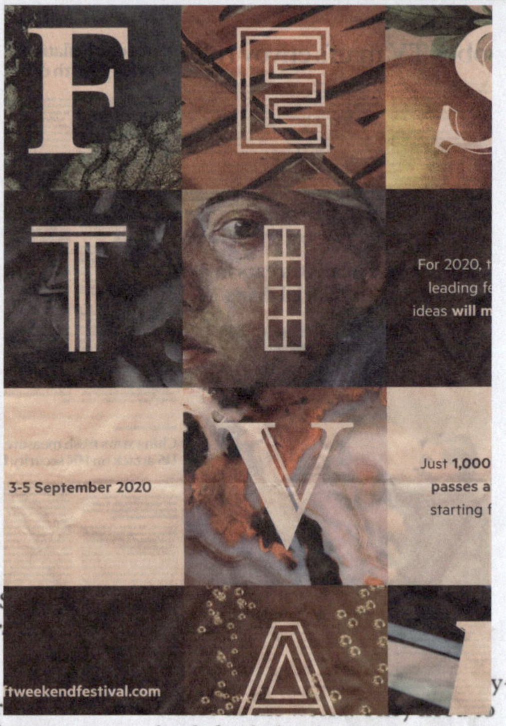

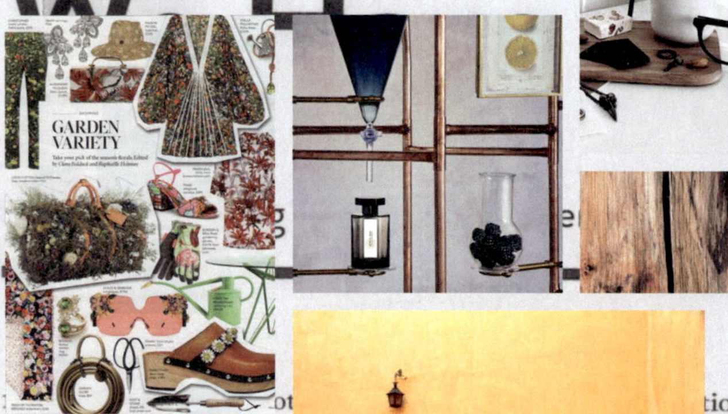

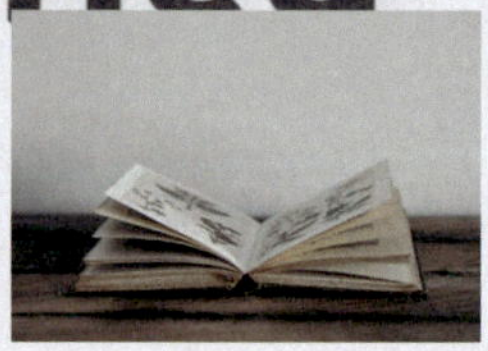

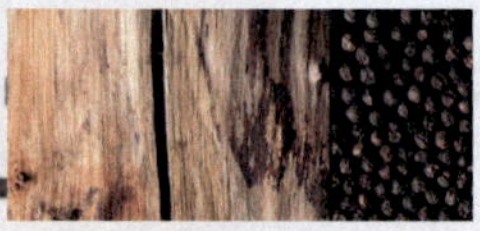

without alcohol, absurdity

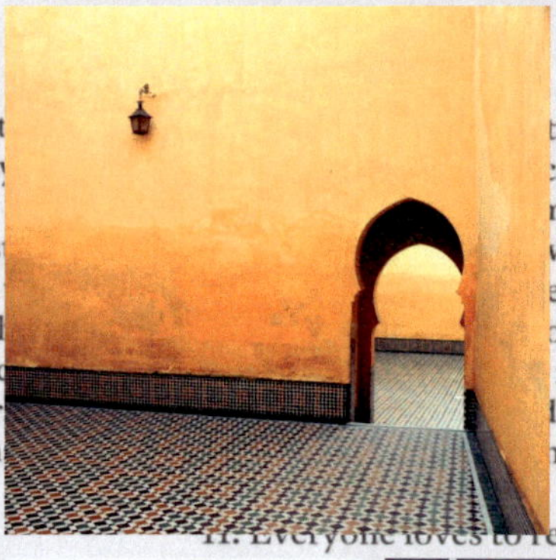

tion
ceive are
make us
wince or
elete', but
om the
represent
l faith that
nd show art.

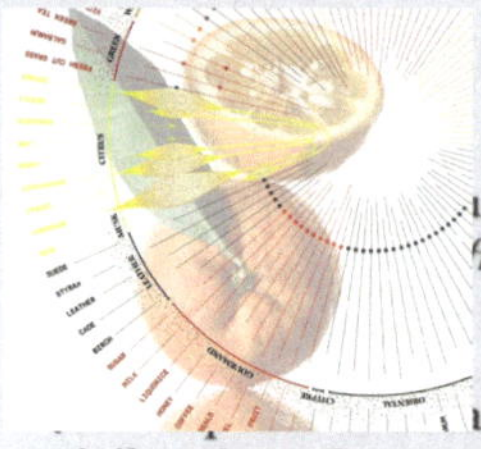

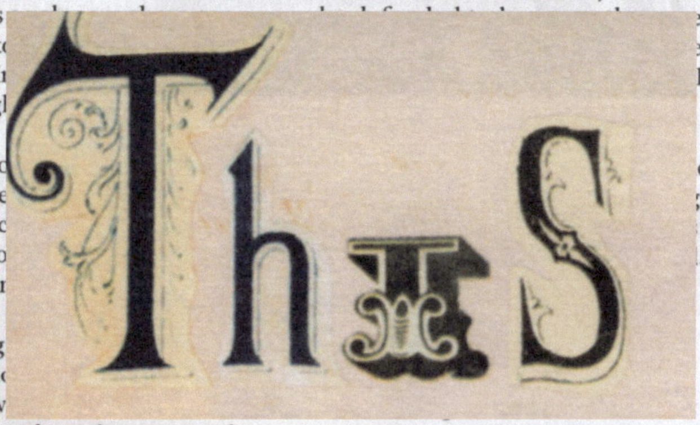

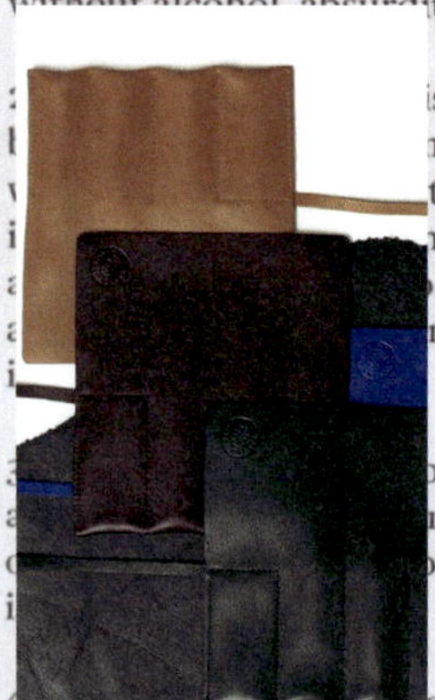

11. Everyone loves to read

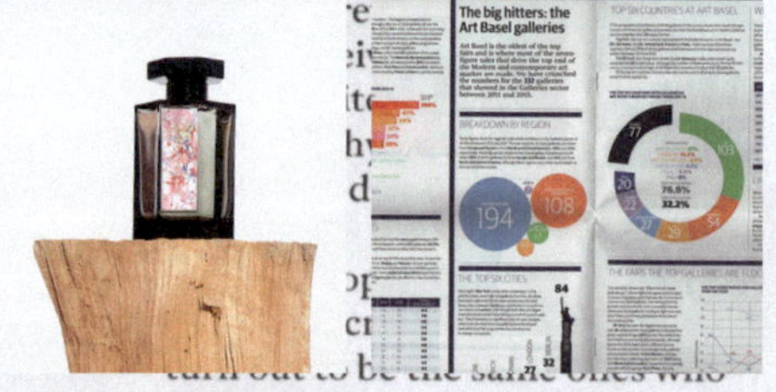

turn out to be the same ones who
to read much.

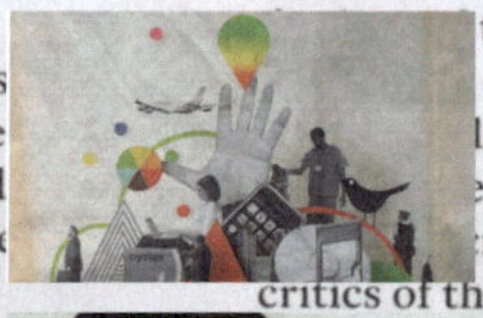

laim that 'the curatorial
e early 2000s caused
riticism by divesting
critics of their power. However,

seemingly infinite new wa

Faithful

responses to the magazine
when accompanied by int
enthusiastic responses – a
you're doing something ri

7. For example, putting si
Bryan Ferry on the cover
as we did in 2004, delight
some and left others splut
with dismay.

8. In writing, even the most
complicated ideas can usually

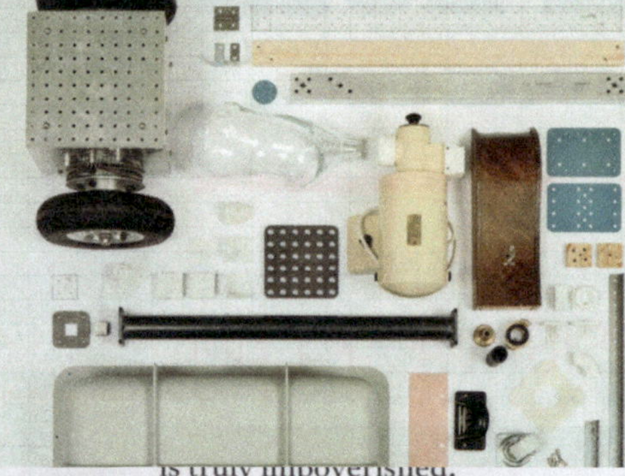

is truly impoverished.

15. Good art writing is as inventive and as interesting as the art that is being written about.

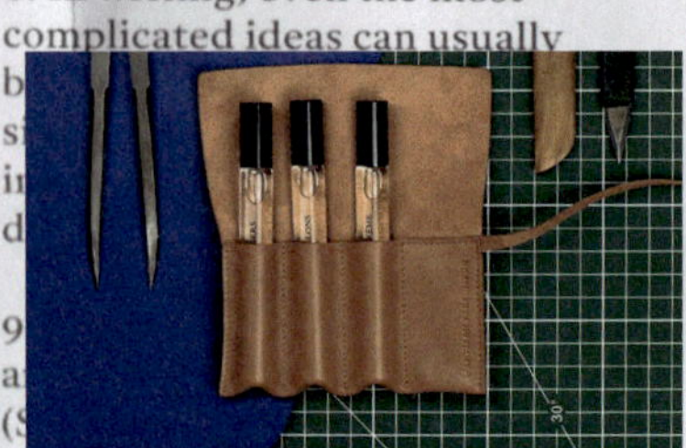

3-5 September 2020

For 2020, t
leading fe
ideas will m

Just 1,000
passes a
starting f

ftweekendfestival.com

privilege is
team. So, t
about the i
and the rig

18. We also
music, cine
ture is cruc
to learn fro
the horizon

19. Editing
a long peri
become aw
art, books and music come and

or a writer is to live in hope.

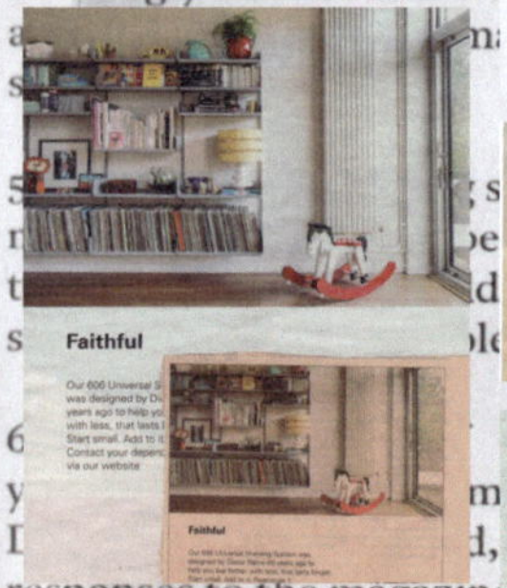

istory is a work
ss; criticism is the daily

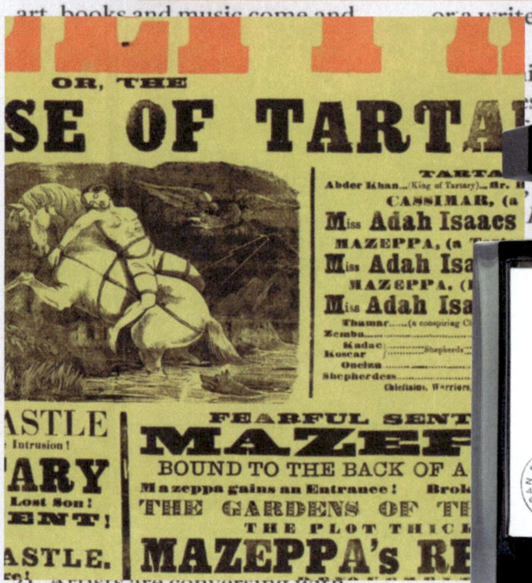

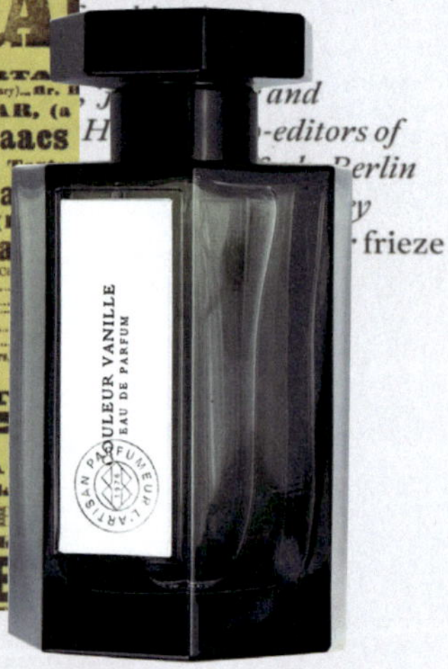

OR, THE
SE OF TARTA
Miss Adah Isaacs
MAZEPPA
BOUND TO THE BACK OF A
THE GARDENS OF TH
MAZEPPA's RE

and
-editors of
Berlin
frieze

ARTISAN PARFUMEUR L'ARTISAN
COULEUR VANILLE
EAU DE PARFUM

21. Artists are conversing with
the past as much as they are with
the future.

22. Sometimes, issues we had
put together thinking they were
merely a collection of articles
on unrelated topics turned out
to have a clear underlying theme.
This reiterates our fallibility
to ourselves.

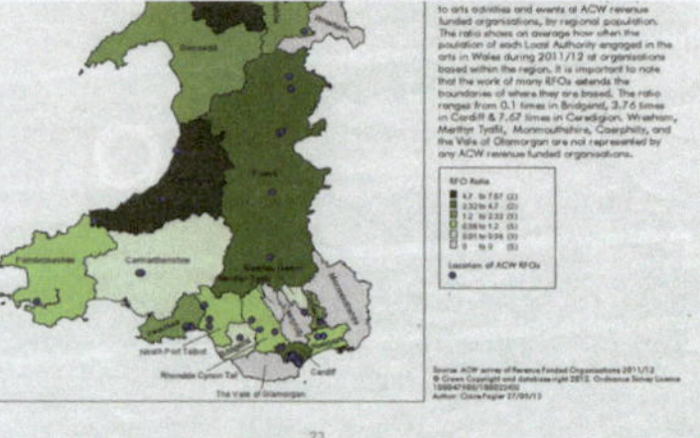

Oh, I want so much to do a political piece of art

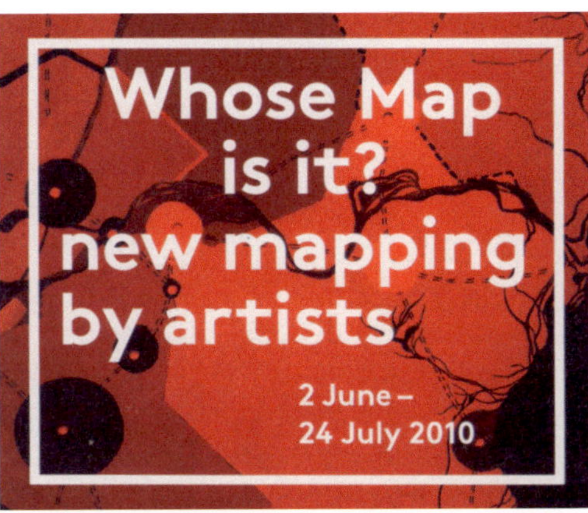

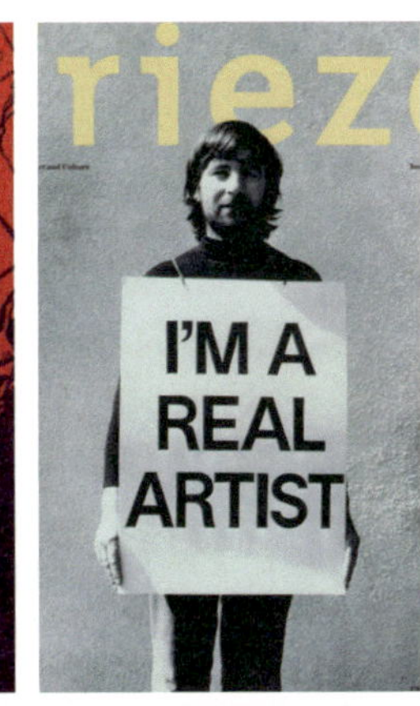

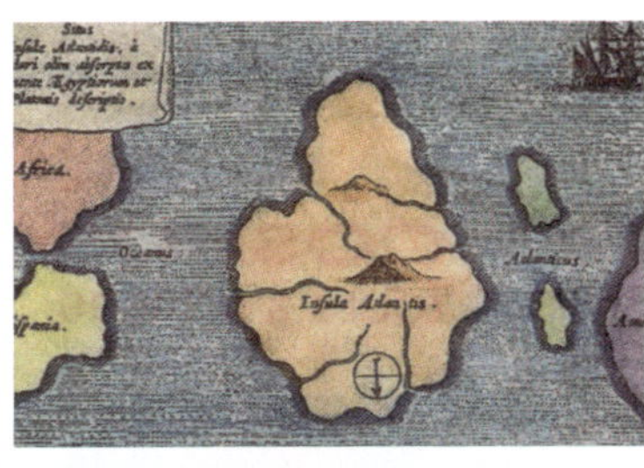

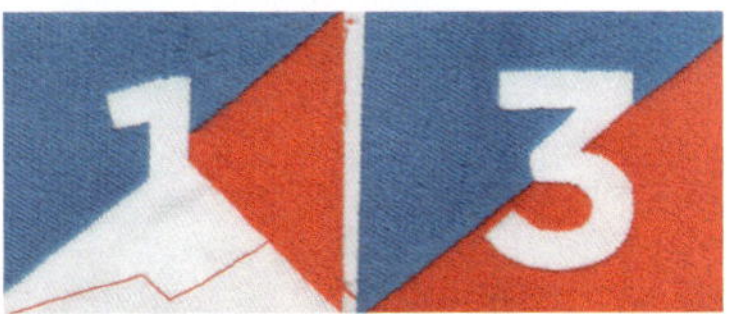

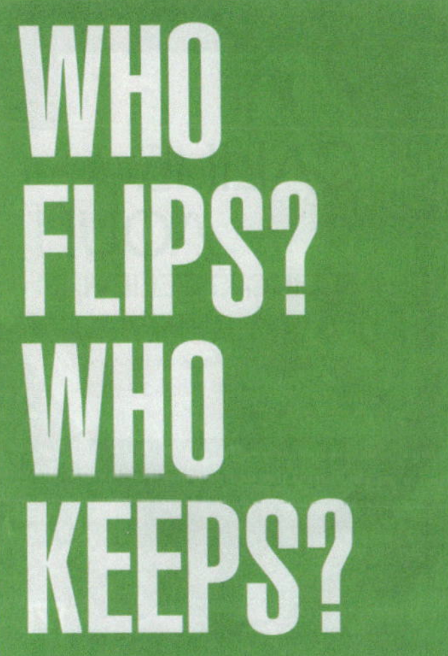

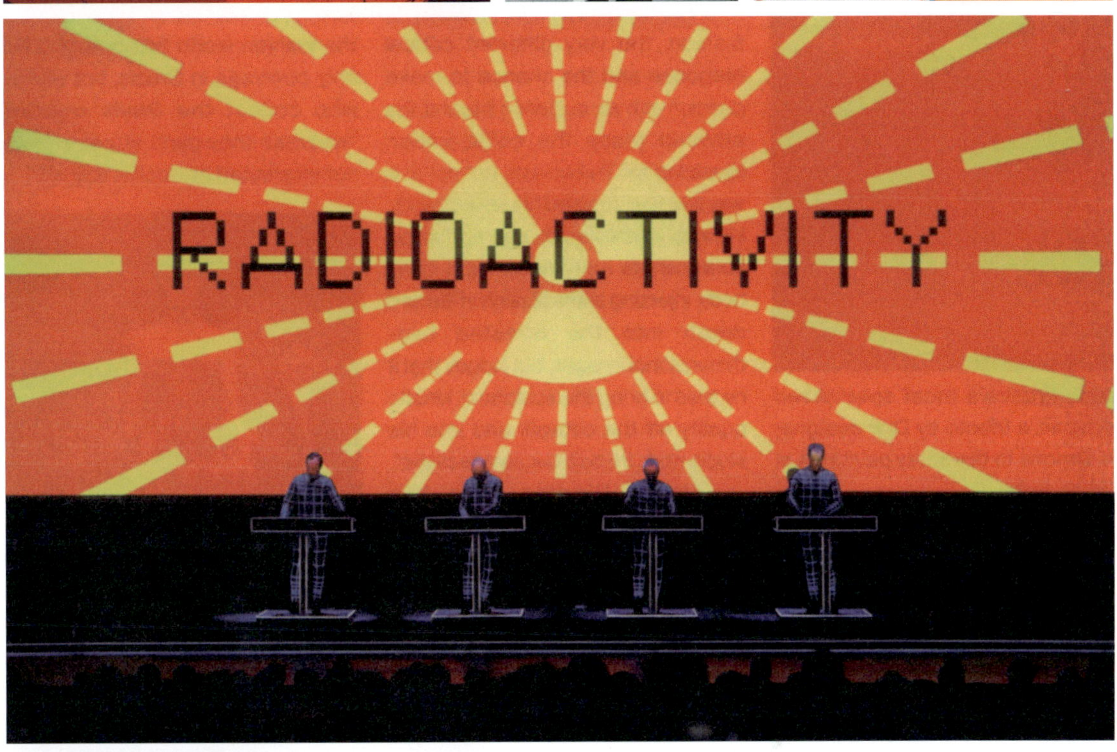

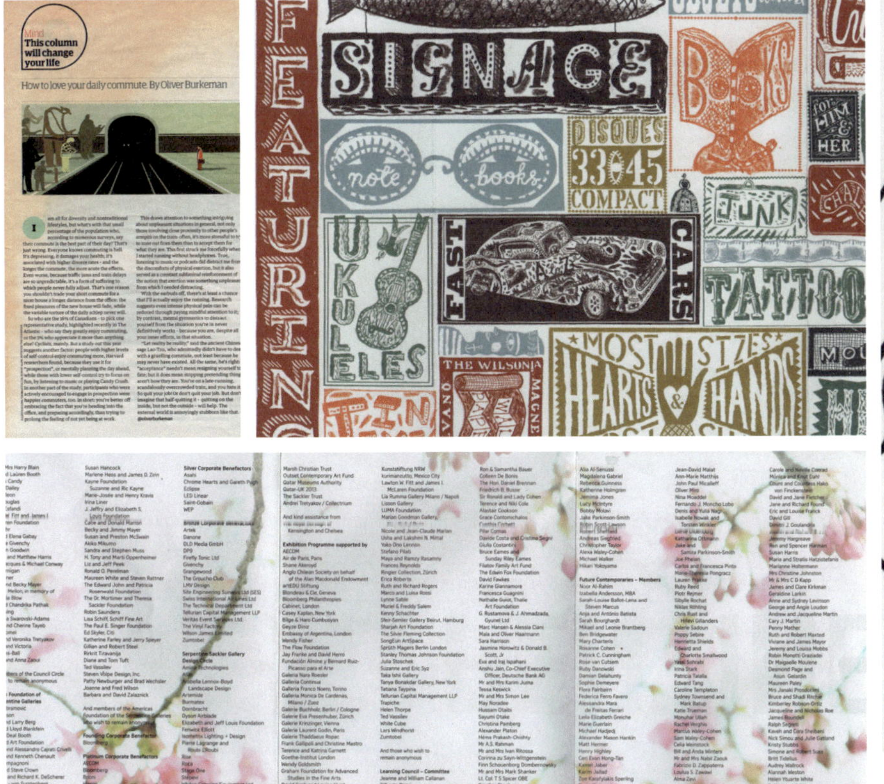

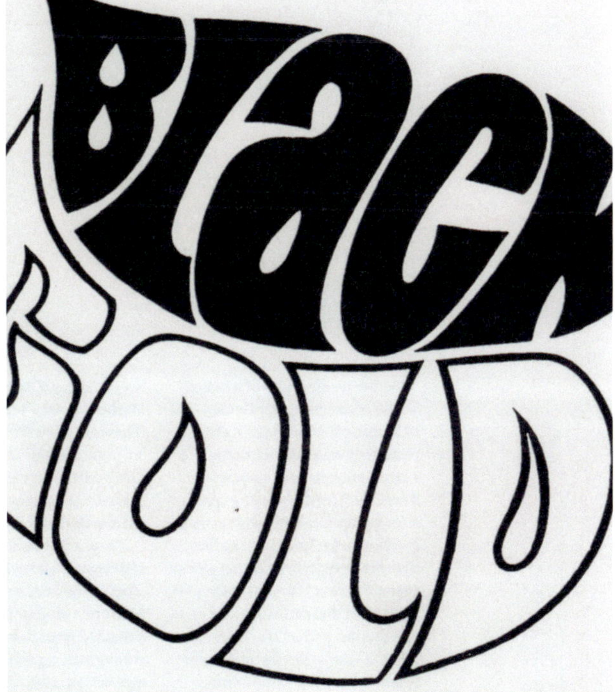

Mechanisms (Zarouhie Abdalian, Terry Atkinson, Lutz Bacher, Eva Barto, Neïl Beloufa, Patricia L. Boyd, Jay DeFeo, Trisha Donnelly, Harun Farocki, Richard Hamilton, Aaron Flint Jamison, Jacob Kassay, Garry Neill Kennedy, Louise Lawler, Park McArthur, Jean-Luc Moulène, Pope.L, Charlotte Posenenske, Cameron Rowland, and Danh Vo) *is on view*,

and Steh Pirce *is on our mind.*

WWW.WATTIS.ORG OCTOBER 12, 2017 – FEBRUARY 24, 2018 CCA, SAN FRANCISCO

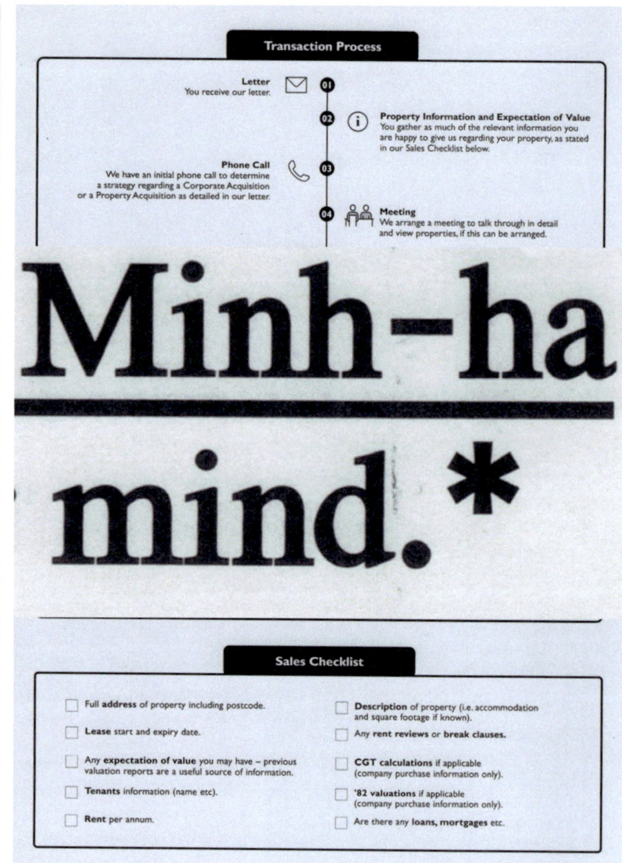

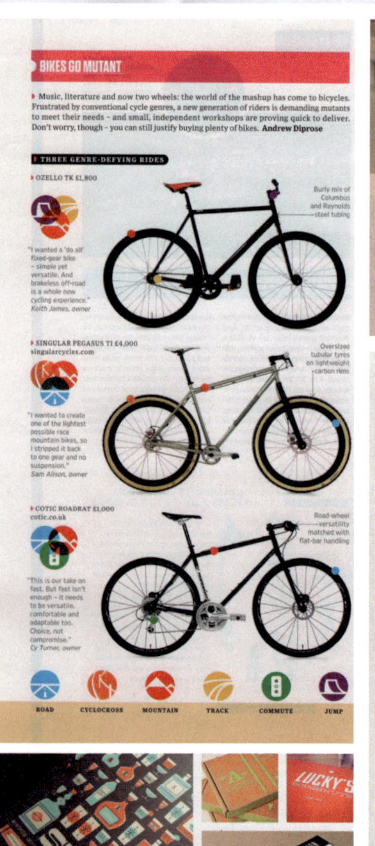

Screwed

Our cabinets are screwed together with standard screws. You can unscrew them to replace a part or to swap a damaged top panel with a bottom panel. Good design makes a product understandable.

vitsoe.com VITSŒ

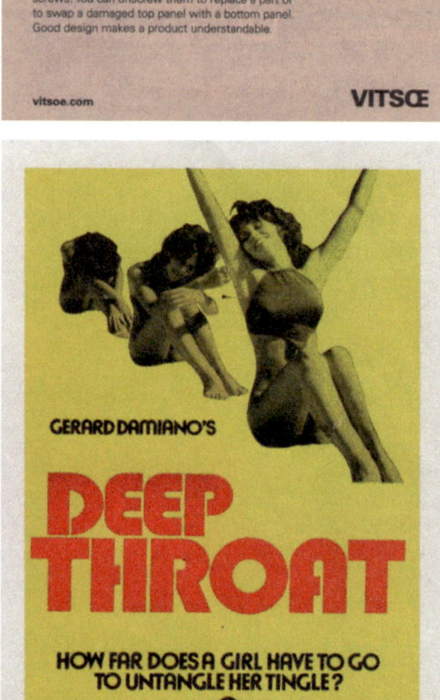

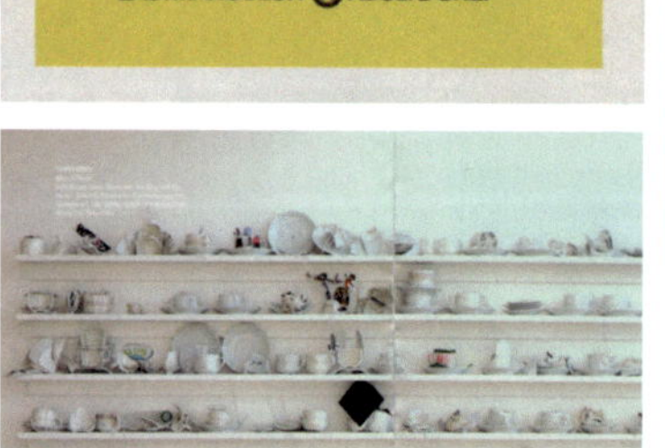

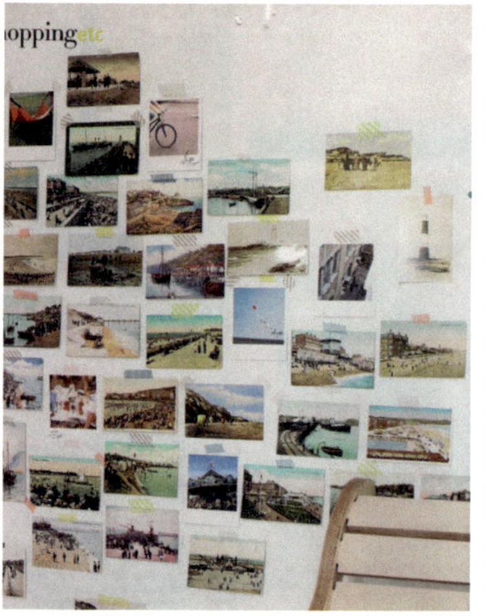

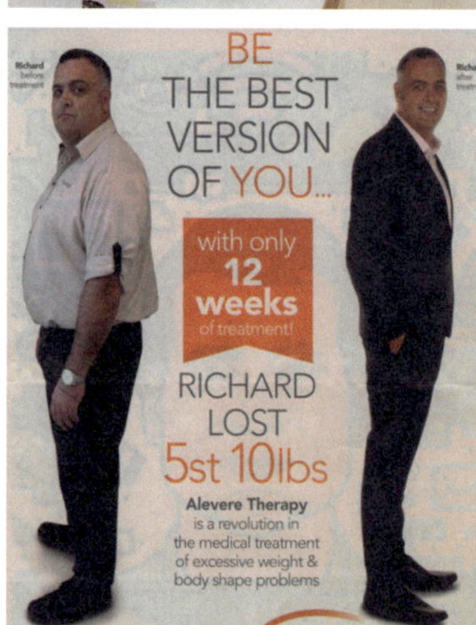

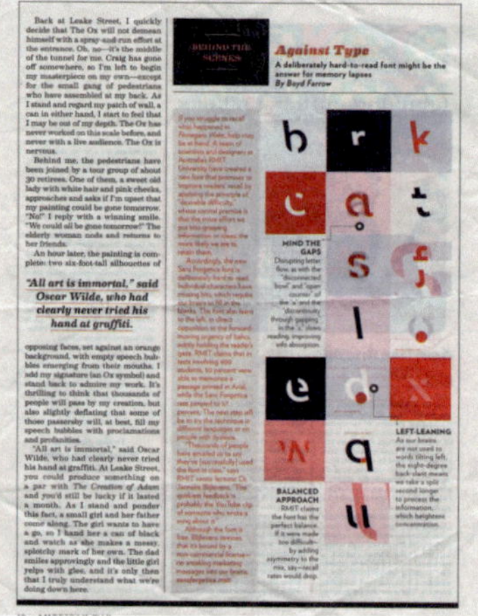

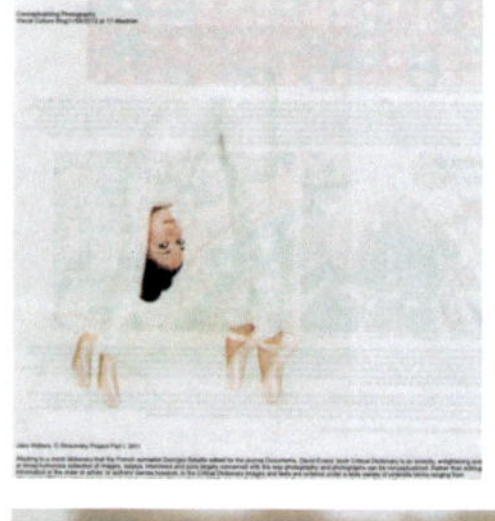

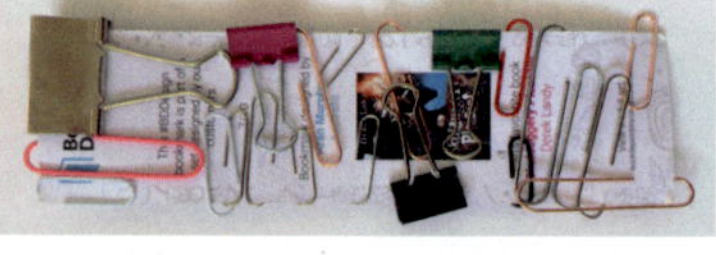

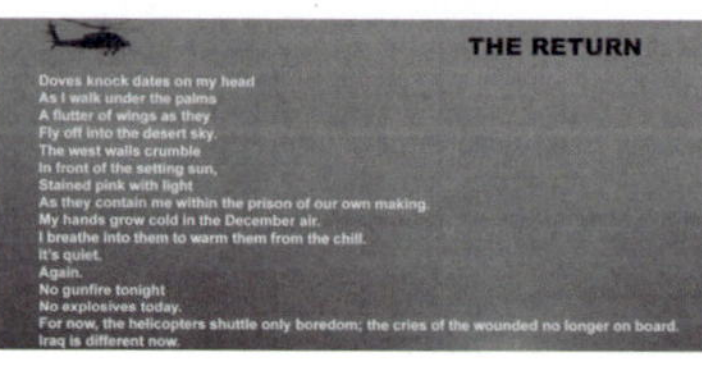

Gentle Wave

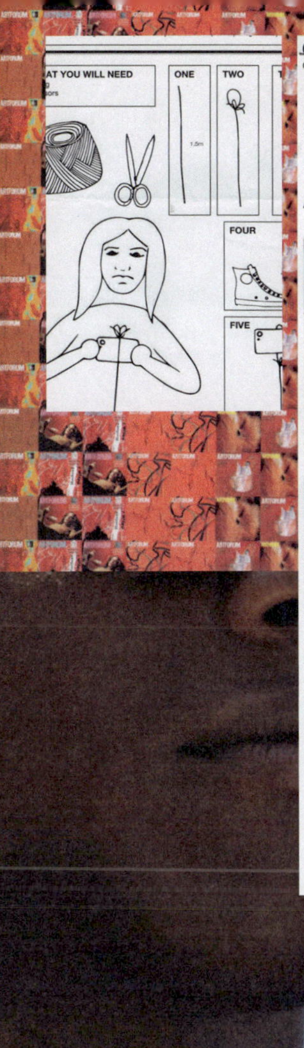

Off-Space Travels
OLIVER BASCIANO

NO 5: OR-BITS.COM

An ongoing series of journeys along art roads less travelled – this month a website

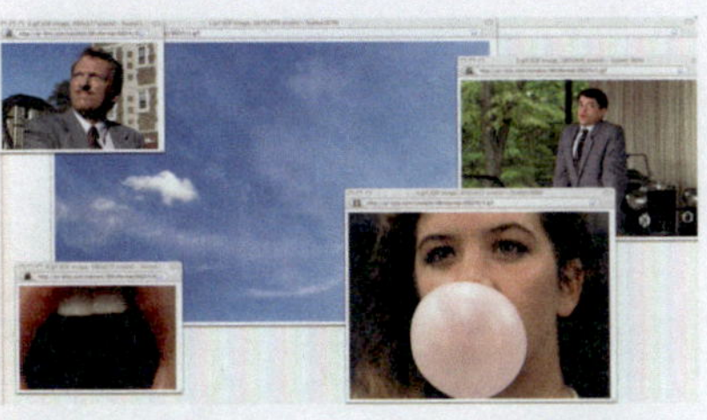

I'm looking at exhibition images on the website of an artist-run space in the east of England – and considering it a stop on this route around the UK. The work looks good, but it's hard to be sure from the small jpegs that document it. I start to think about that oft-quoted line from Buckminster Fuller – 'The most important part about tomorrow is not the technology or the automation, but that man is going to come into entirely new relationships with his fellow men' – in relation to this website and my use of it. I realise I'm taking it out of context, but I begin to think that Bucky might not be 100 percent correct in his assertion: perhaps the mechanisms that lie behind these new relationships *are* important after all, and perhaps using as advanced a tool as a website for mere documentary and directory purposes (which the media proves not much cop at) is doing the technology a disservice. The breakdown in the lines of communication between the offline and online realms (that is to say, the works and their digital documentation) that I'm experiencing has stemmed precisely from a lack of consideration of the technology. So instead, for this month's stop on the roadtrip, I'll put away the car keys and stick with the laptop (you can, if you wish, envisage me using the complimentary Wi-Fi at a roadside inn).

Marialaura Ghidini is a Newcastle-based curator and academic who, in 2009, set up or-bits.com after experiencing frustrations similar to those detailed above. The website, acting as a curatorial platform, has so far staged six online exhibitions, commissioning artists to produce new work specifically for the web. "There was a lack of curatorial endeavours on the web," Ghidini explains. "Yet the web browser is directly concerned with methods of arranging and displaying different media in the same space. It is an inherently curatorial medium." Her exhibitions are an antithesis of the indexes of

above:
Richard Healy
Leisure Rules 2010. Courtesy the artist and or-bits.com

below:
Ed Atkins
Dun-Coloured Veil (Reel 10) 2009. Courtesy the artist and or-bits.com

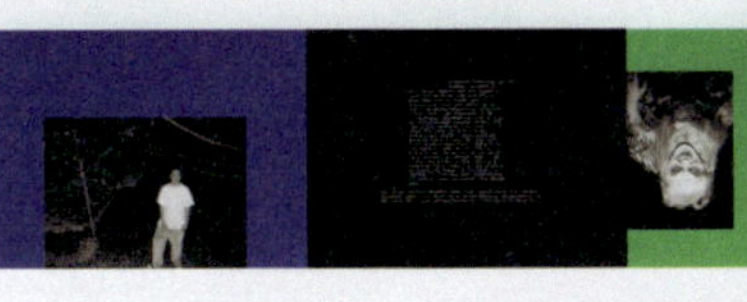

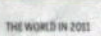

The World in 2036

Design takes over, says **Paola Antonelli**

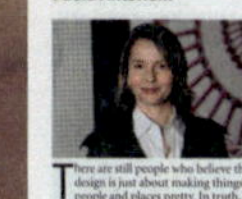

Doug Smith expects the weather forecast to improve

Nassim Taleb looks at what will break, and what won't

Schumpeter | Ideas reinvenTED

TED has revolutionised the ideas industry, in part by putting old wine in new bottles

SANDRA MUJINGA
selected by Kiki Mazzucchelli

Mujinga's work addresses how self-representation is performed in DIGITAL MEDIA – but it also points to what is LOST when the subject is reduced to a CONSTRUCTED IMAGE

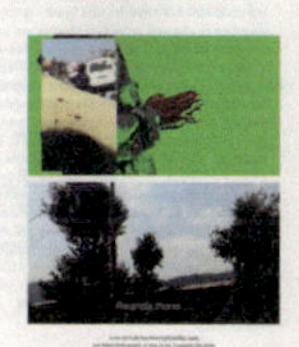

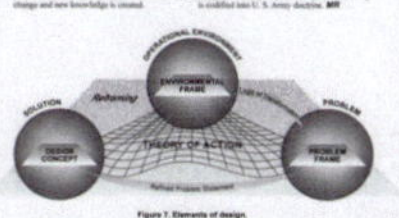

Figure 1. Elements of design.

THE ART OF DESIGN
A Design Methodology

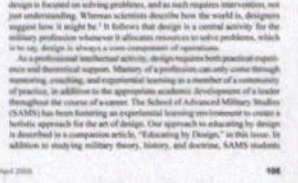

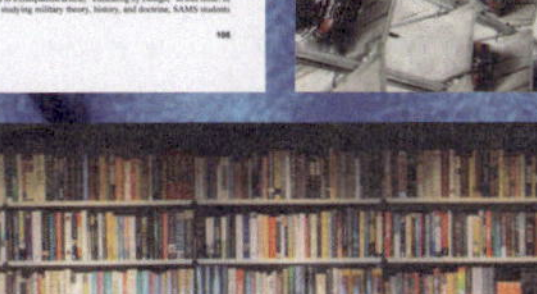

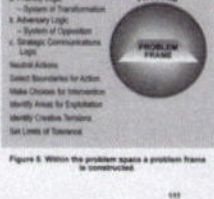

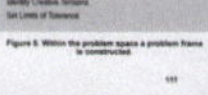

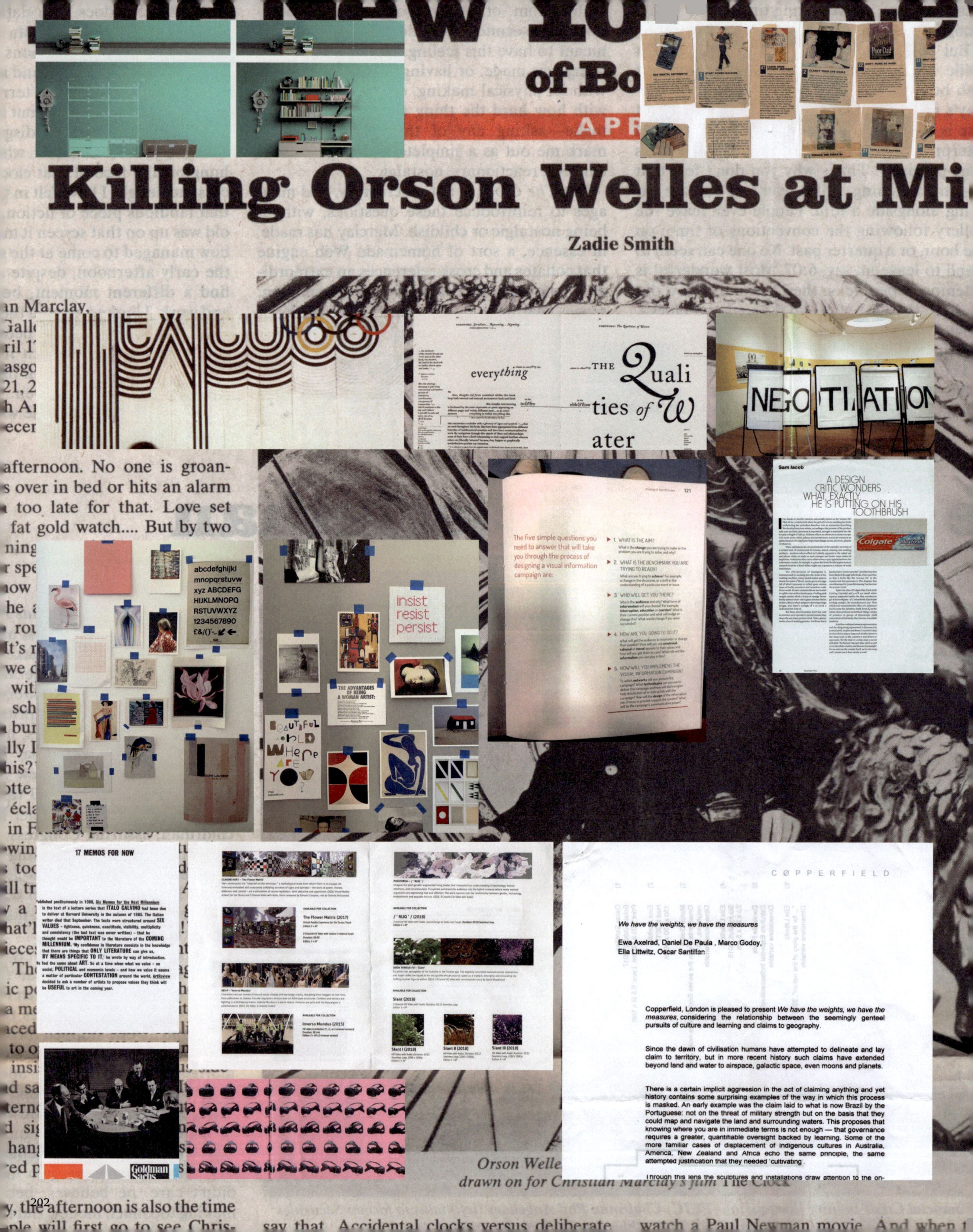

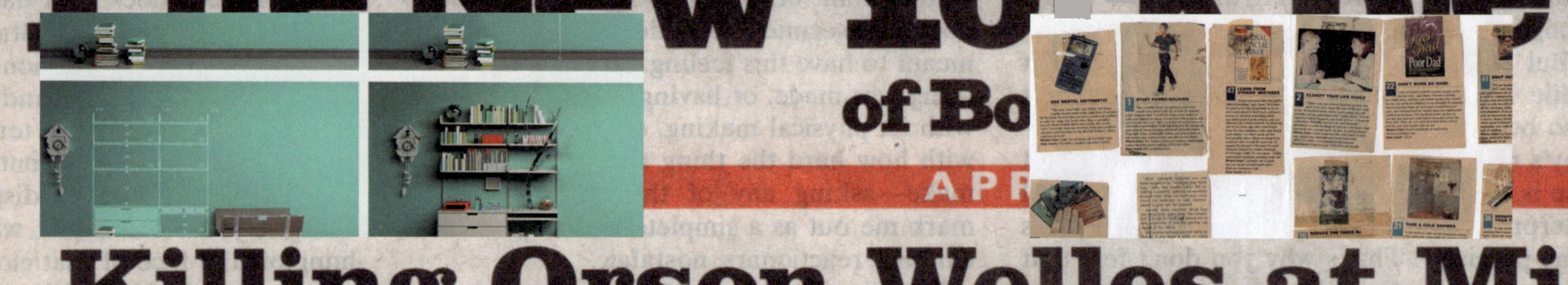

Killing Orson Welles at Mi

Zadie Smith

afternoon. No one is groan-
s over in bed or hits an alarm
too late for that. Love set
fat gold watch.... But by two

everything

THE Qualities of Water

NEGOTIATION

The five simple questions you need to answer that will take you through the process of designing a visual information campaign are:

1. WHAT IS THE AIM?
2. WHAT IS THE BENCHMARK YOU ARE TRYING TO REACH?
3. WHO WILL GET YOU THERE?
4. HOW ARE YOU GOING TO DO IT?
5. HOW WILL YOU IMPLEMENT THE VISUAL INFORMATION CAMPAIGN?

Sam Jacob

A DESIGN CRITIC WONDERS WHAT, EXACTLY, HE IS PUTTING ON HIS TOOTHBRUSH

abcdefghijkl
mnopqrstuvw
xyz ABCDEFG
HIJKLMNOPQ
RSTUVWXYZ
1234567890

insist
resist
persist

THE ADVANTAGES OF BEING A WOMAN ARTIST:

BEAUTIFUL WORLD WHERE ARE YOU?

17 MEMOS FOR NOW

Published posthumously in 1988, Six Memos for the Next Millennium is the text of a lecture series that ITALO CALVINO had been due to deliver at Harvard University in the autumn of 1985. The Italian writer died that September. The texts were structured around SIX VALUES – lightness, quickness, exactitude, visibility, multiplicity and consistency (the last text was never written) – that he thought would be IMPORTANT to the literature of the COMING MILLENNIUM. 'My confidence in literature consists in the knowledge that there are things that ONLY LITERATURE can give us, BY MEANS SPECIFIC TO IT,' he wrote by way of introduction. We feel the same about ART. So at a time when what we value – on social, POLITICAL and economic levels – and how we value it seems a matter of particular CONTESTATION around the world, ArtReview decided to ask a number of artists to propose values they think will be USEFUL to art in the coming year.

The Flower Matrix (2017)

Inverso Mundus (2015)

Slant (2018)

Goldman Sachs

C Ø P P E R F I E L D

We have the weights, we have the measures

Ewa Axelrad, Daniel De Paula , Marco Godoy,
Ella Littwitz, Oscar Santillan

Copperfield, London is pleased to present *We have the weights, we have the measures*, considering the relationship between the seemingly genteel pursuits of culture and learning and claims to geography.

Since the dawn of civilisation humans have attempted to delineate and lay claim to territory, but in more recent history such claims have extended beyond land and water to airspace, galactic space, even moons and planets.

There is a certain implicit aggression in the act of claiming anything and yet history contains some surprising examples of the way in which this process is masked. An early example was the claim laid to what is now Brazil by the Portuguese: not on the threat of military strength but on the basis that they could map and navigate the land and surrounding waters. This proposes that knowing where you are in immediate terms is not enough — that governance requires a greater, quantifiable oversight backed by learning. Some of the more familiar cases of displacement of indigenous cultures in Australia, America, New Zealand and Africa echo the same principle, the same attempted justification that they needed 'cultivating'.

Through this lens the sculptures and installations draw attention to the on-

Orson Welle... drawn on for Christian Marclay's film The Clock

y, the afternoon is also the time ... say that. Accidental clocks versus deliberate ... watch a Paul Newman movie. And when t

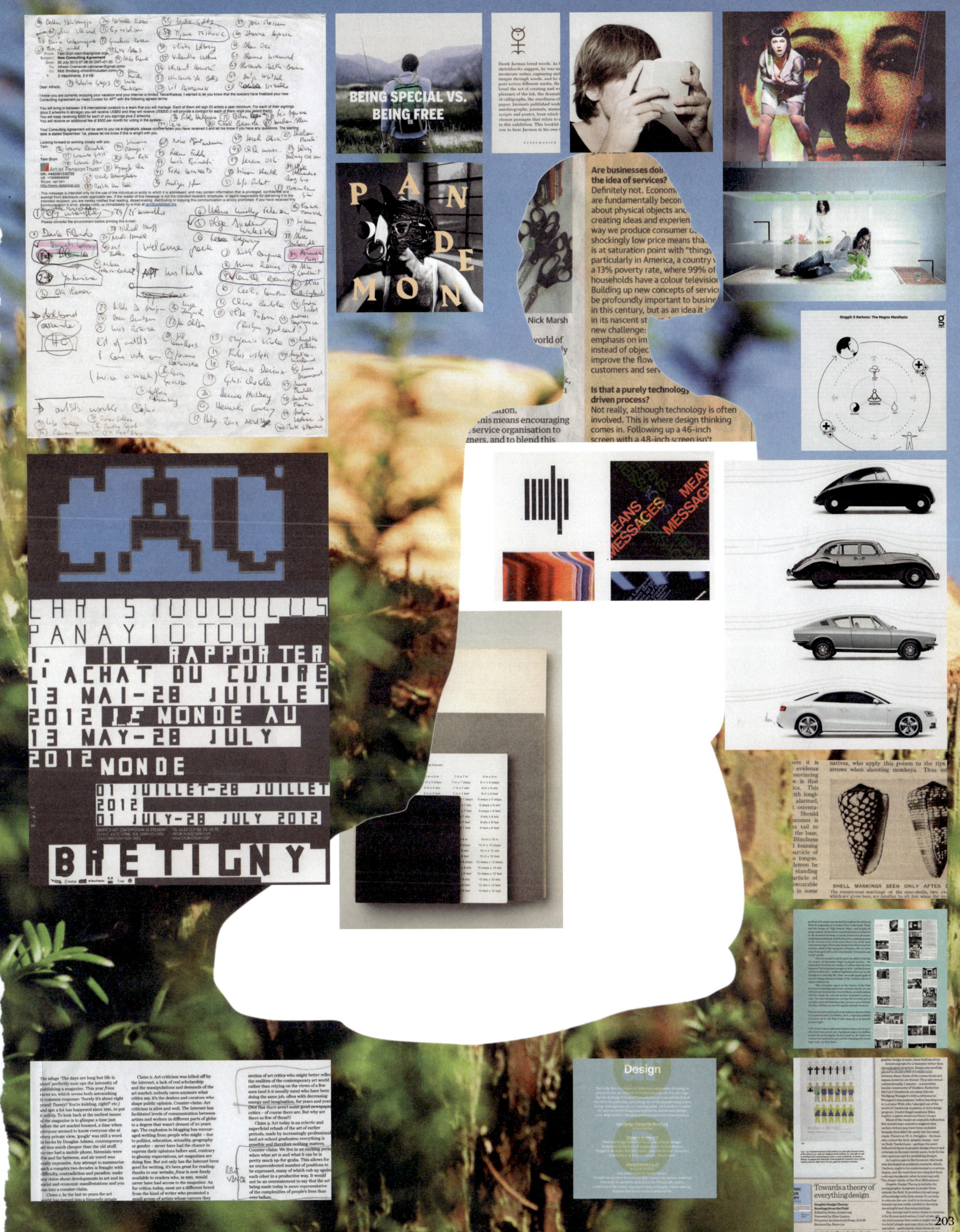
BEING SPECIAL VS.
BEING FREE
P A N D E M O N
Are businesses doi
the idea of services?
Nick Marsh
Is that a purely technolog
driven process?
Not really, although technology is often
involved. This is where design thinking
comes in.
Singgih S Kartono: The Magno Manifesto
MEANS MESSAGES
CHRISTODOULOS
PANAYIOTOU
I. II. RAPPORTER
L'ACHAT DU CUIRE
13 MAI-28 JUILLET
2012 LE MONDE AU
13 MAY-28 JULY
2012 MONDE
01 JUILLET-28 JUILLET
2012
01 JULY-28 JULY 2012
BRETIGNY
SHELL MARKINGS SEEN ONLY AFTER
Design
Towards a theory of
everything design

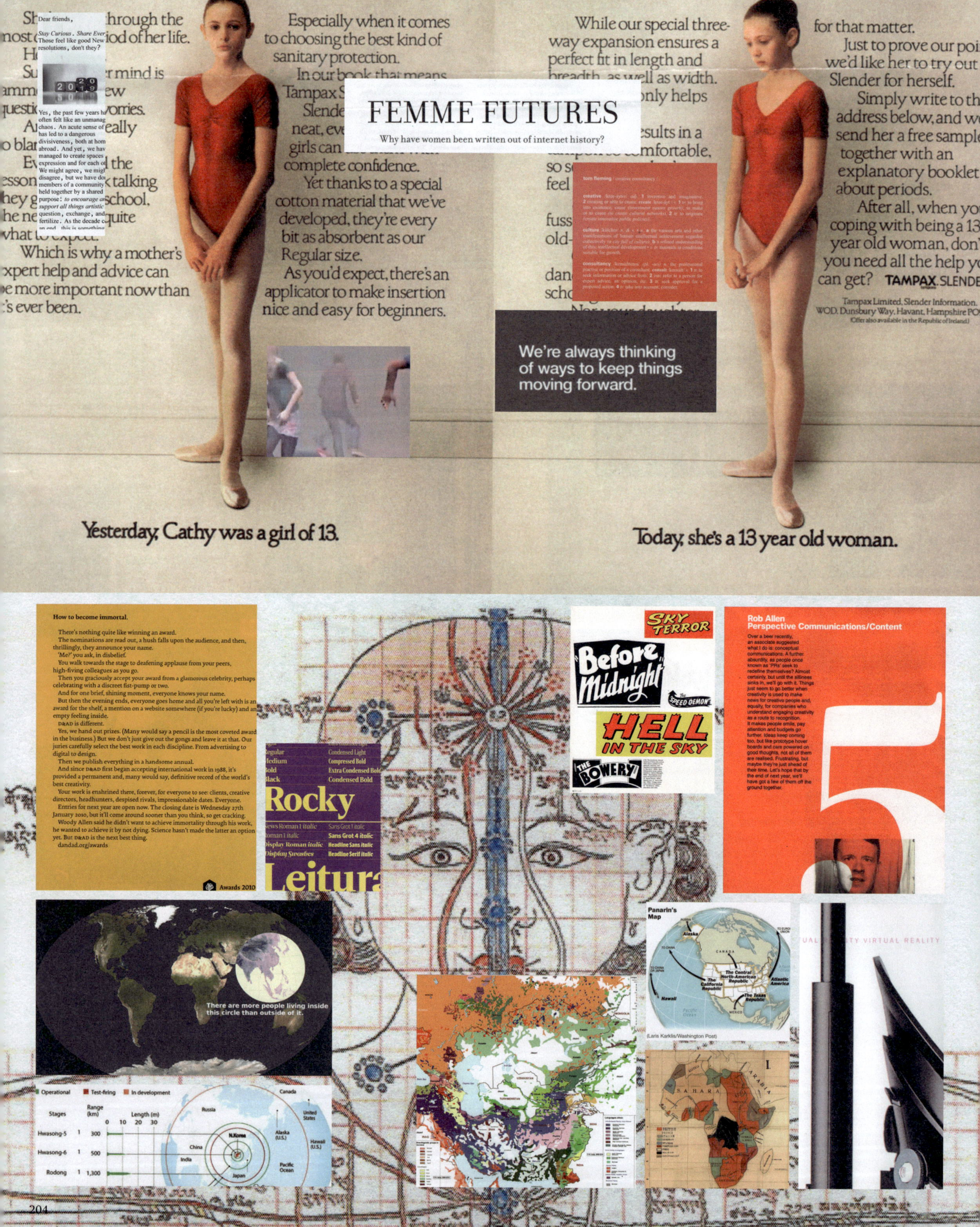
FEMME FUTURES
Why have women been written out of internet history?
Especially when it comes to choosing the best kind of sanitary protection.
Yet thanks to a special cotton material that we've developed, they're every bit as absorbent as our Regular size.
As you'd expect, there's an applicator to make insertion nice and easy for beginners.
Which is why a mother's expert help and advice can be more important now than it's ever been.
While our special three-way expansion ensures a perfect fit in length and breadth, as well as width.
for that matter.
Just to prove our point we'd like her to try out Slender for herself.
Simply write to the address below, and we'll send her a free sample together with an explanatory booklet about periods.
After all, when you're coping with being a 13 year old woman, don't you need all the help you can get?
TAMPAX SLENDER
Tampax Limited, Slender Information, WOD. Dunsbury Way, Havant, Hampshire
We're always thinking of ways to keep things moving forward.
Yesterday, Cathy was a girl of 13.
Today, she's a 13 year old woman.
How to become immortal.
There's nothing quite like winning an award.
The nominations are read out, a hush falls upon the audience, and then, thrillingly, they announce your name.
'Me?' you ask, in disbelief.
You walk towards the stage to deafening applause from your peers, high-fiving colleagues as you go.
Then you graciously accept your award from a glamorous celebrity, perhaps celebrating with a discreet fist-pump or two.
And for one brief, shining moment, everyone knows your name.
But then the evening ends, everyone goes home and all you're left with is an award for the shelf, a mention on a website somewhere (if you're lucky) and an empty feeling inside.
D&AD is different.
Yes, we hand out prizes. (Many would say a pencil is the most coveted award in the business.) But we don't just give out the gongs and leave it at that. Our juries carefully select the best work in each discipline. From advertising to digital to design.
Then we publish everything in a handsome annual.
And since D&AD first began accepting international work in 1988, it's provided a permanent and, many would say, definitive record of the world's best creativity.
Your work is enshrined there, forever, for everyone to see: clients, creative directors, headhunters, despised rivals, impressionable dates. Everyone.
Entries for next year are open now. The closing date is Wednesday 27th January 2010, but it'll come around sooner than you think, so get cracking.
Woody Allen said he didn't want to achieve immortality through his work, he wanted to achieve it by not dying. Science hasn't made the latter an option yet. But D&AD is the next best thing.
dandad.org/awards
Awards 2010
Rocky
Leitura
SKY TERROR
Before Midnight
The SPEED DEMON
HELL IN THE SKY
THE BOWERY
Rob Allen
Perspective Communications/Content
Over a beer recently, an associate suggested what I do is: conceptual communications. A further absurdity, as people once known as 'PRs' seek to redefine themselves? Almost certainly, but until the silliness sinks in, we'll go with it. Things just seem to go better when creativity is used to make news for creative people and, equally, for companies who understand engaging creativity as a route to recognition. It makes people smile, pay attention and budgets go further. Ideas keep coming too, but like prototype hover boards and cars powered on good thoughts, not all of them are realised. Frustrating, but maybe they're just ahead of their time. Let's hope that by the end of next year, we'll have got a few of them off the ground together.
5
There are more people living inside this circle than outside of it.
Panarin's Map
(Laris Karklis/Washington Post)
Operational
Test-firing
In development
Stages
Range (km)
Length (m)
Hwasong-5
Hwasong-6
Rodong
Russia
China
India
N.Korea
Japan
Canada
Alaska (U.S.)
Hawaii (U.S.)
Pacific Ocean
SAHARA
ARABIA

The Guardian | Saturday 15 December 2012

Herzog's climbing record was respectable but not spectacular, and making him leader was a risk. Devies clearly had doubts about whether the guides in particular would toe the line for the greater glory of France. Two days before departing, he made them all swear an oath of allegiance to their leader.

Herzog and his team performed one of the great feats of exploratory mountaineering, trekking up the Kali Gandaki valley to examine Dhaulagiri from the east and north. The mountain was judged, in Terray's phrase, "fiendishly difficult" and so the expedition turned its attention to Annapurna, so far unseen. Just getting a view would prove surprisingly elusive.

By mid-May, the team still hadn't made progress so Herzog called a council of war at their base camp in the village of Tukucha, and with time running out before the monsoon, committed his forces to the Miristi Khola, hoping to get lucky and find a practicable route to the top. Working at extraordinary speed, and after coming to a dead end on the peak's north-west spur, the team rapidly pushed a route and a series of camps up the north face. Terray and Herzog had proved the strongest and best acclimatised, but when the supply chain stalled, Terray gave up his chance for the summit to push supplies to a high camp. Lachenal took his place at camp IV.

Wearing leather boots that offered insufficient insulation, Lachenal was anxious about his feet, not least because losing toes could threaten his livelihood. What would Herzog do, he asked, if he turned around? "My whole being revolted against the idea," he wrote in Annapurna. "I should go on by myself," he told Lachenal. "Then I'll follow you," Lachenal replied.

They reached the summit at 2pm on 3 June, and while some historians question the validity of the summit photograph, they were close enough. Herzog was in a blithe mood – his spiritual mus-

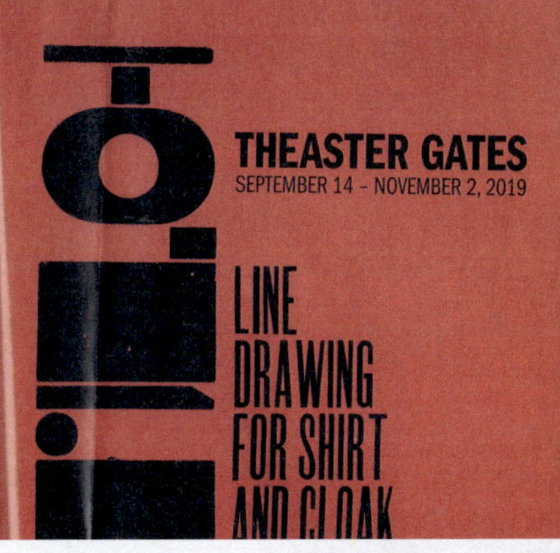

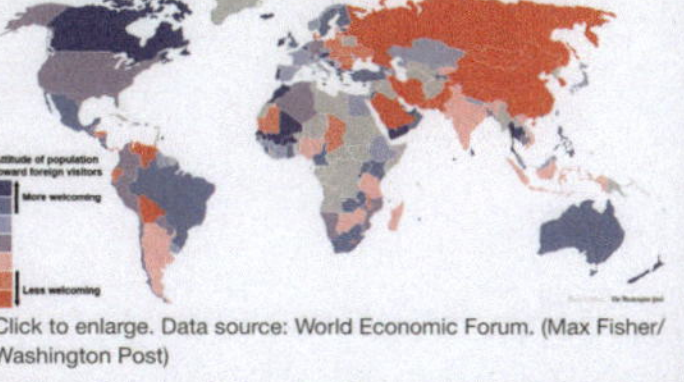

Click to enlarge. Data source: World Economic Forum. (Max Fisher/ Washington Post)

This might be useful in planning your next vacation, although there are some big surprises in the results.

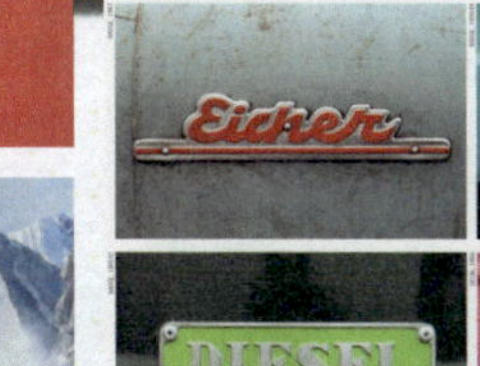

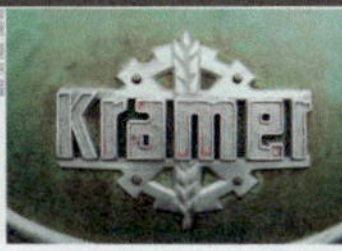

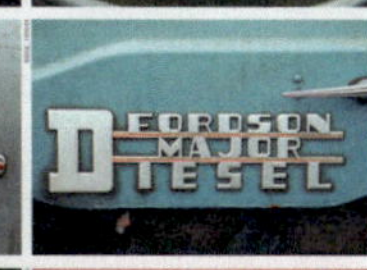

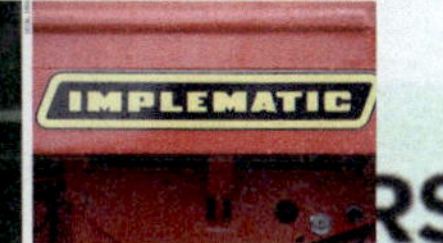

FARMALL

Heavy metal

These tractor badges survive as relics of a more heroic age: for them, the earth still moves

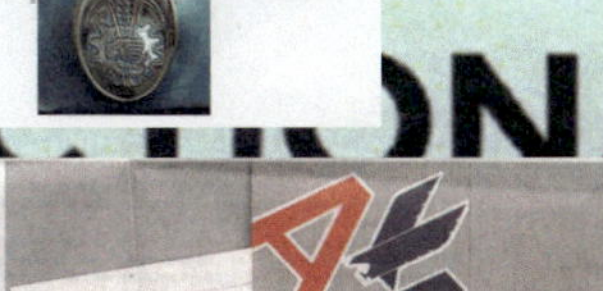

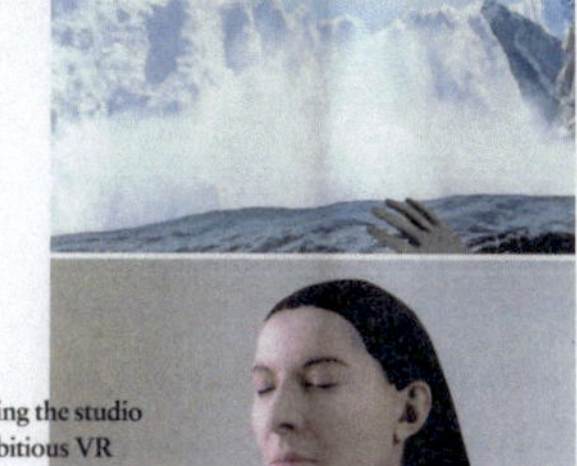

"My initial reaction after leaving the studio where I first encountered ambitious VR artworks was: *We are fucked.*"
—Daniel Birnbaum

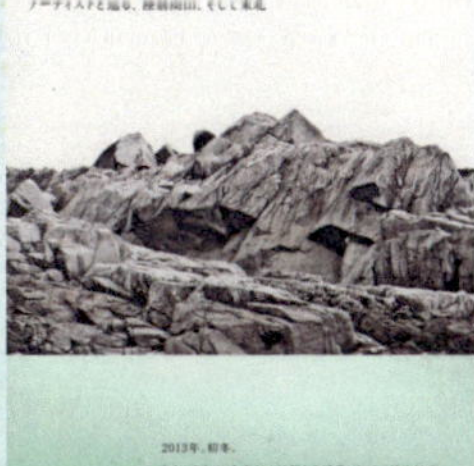

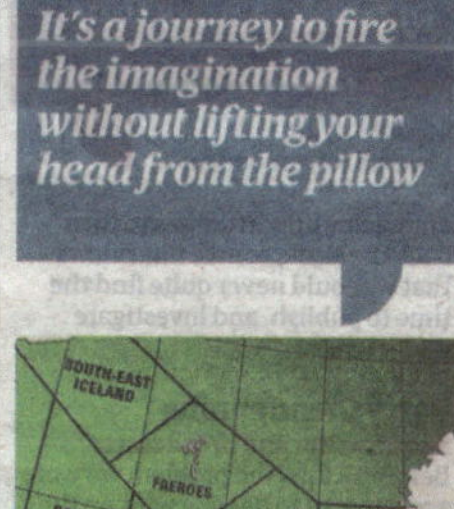

barbicanshop

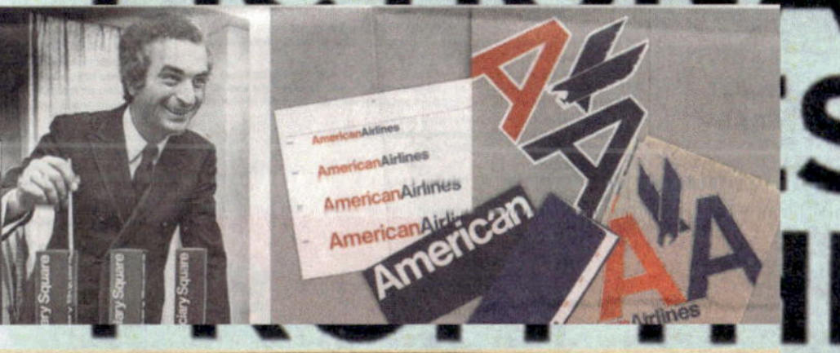

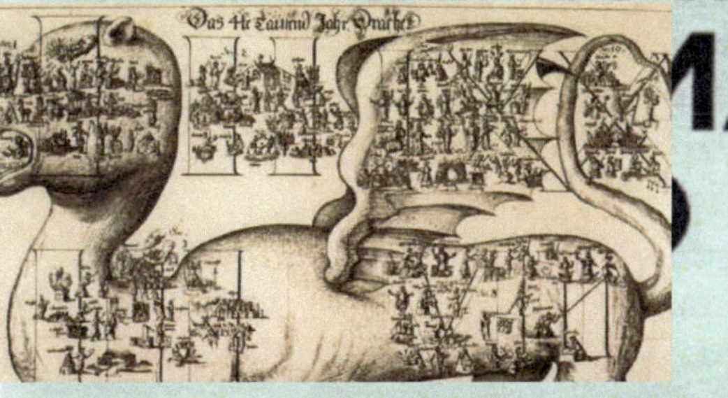

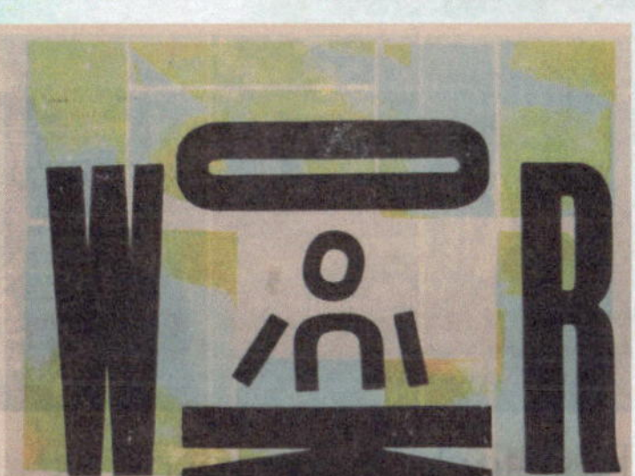

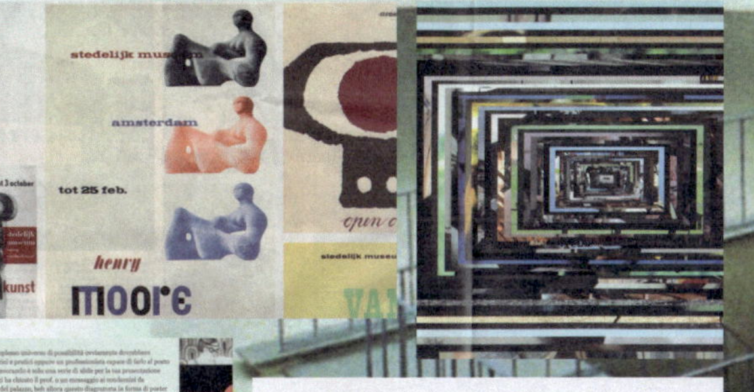

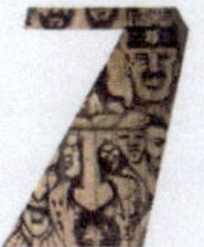

MAPS OF THE IMAGINATION

On a most fundamental level, maps are visual storytelling about the world — about what exists in it, what matters in it, and where we belong relative to it. In ***Maps of the Imagination: The Writer as Cartographer***, Peter Turchi explores how some of greatest storytellers in literary history employed maps as narrative devices, revealing some remarkable similarities between mapmaking, traditionally perceived as an analytical science, and the art of writing fiction. From Melville to Nabokov to Stevenson to the Marx Brothers, the book features hundreds of extraordinary illustrations from and about iconic works of literature.

Click to LOOK INSIDE

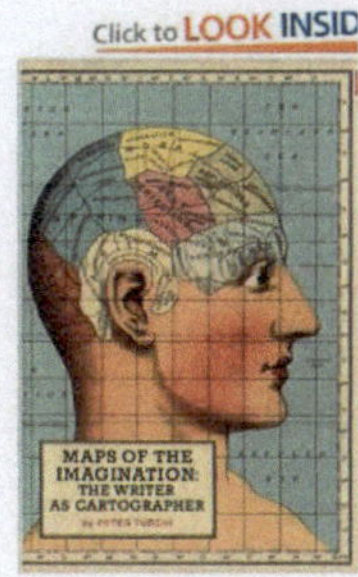

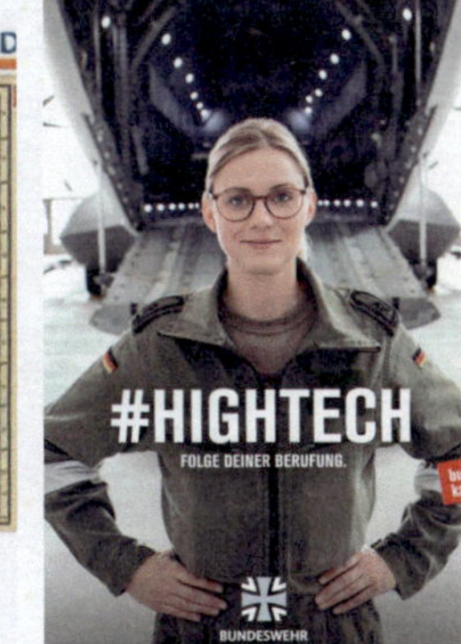

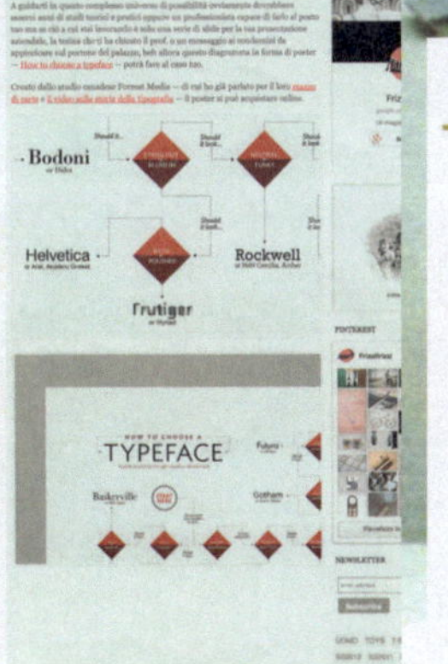

explore

activism advertising animation art books children's books collaboration creativity culture data visualization design diaries documentary education film food

In the curatorial text for this book, I referenced Warburg's *Mnemosyne Atlas* as the source of inspiration for the use of images in conversation with other images (the dialectical use of images). Walter Benjamin called this type of act an attempt to "develop to the highest degree the art of citing without quotation marks."

But if curation and juxtaposition are basic artistic gestures, then supporting and making them a reality are creative actions in themselves. Bringing images that belong to one kind of "flow" into another – making them juxtapose or integrate or oppose their visual cognates, requires not only the original spark by the author but also the vision of the producer. Rethinking an image to give it new life is a shared endeavour not a lonesome journey.

The travel companions of *Curating the Image: Notebook for a Visual Journey* are a selected group of individuals and organizations that believed in the journey without knowing the destination – true explorers of a visual approach to life, without whom the book couldn't have been realized:

The Ampersand Foundation
L'Artisan Parfumeur
Maria and Theodore Fatsis
Penhaligon's
Adam Prideaux
Carolin Scharpff-Striebich

Concept & Text
Alfredo Cramerotti

Copy Editing
Sandra Wynne

Production Management
Charlotte Riggert,
DISTANZ Verlag

Design
Laura Catania

Printing and Binding
optimal media GmbH,
Röbel/Müritz

Distribution
Edel Germany GmbH
www.edel.com
international-books@edel.com

ISBN 978-3-95476-352-8
Printed in Germany

Published by
DISTANZ Verlag
www.distanz.de